'This highly practical book is relevant to today's dynamic work   nt, leadership, and the entrepreneurial role of managers are core themes   e examples
alongside the findings from research make this text a perfect fi   ourse!'
                                        —**Florentin**   etherlands

'As the world becomes more complex, management becomes i   le value of
effective management. In this easily readable and eminently j   he necessary tools, knowledge, and skills to succeed in the work environment of the 21st century.
                                        —**Allan J. Sim**, *University of Aberdeen, UK*

'Sternad gets it right with his comprehensive overview and effective structure – one can literally see the line of
thought and follow it. The appendix on the history of management alone is worth buying this book! Moreover, the
emphasis on the need for self-management as well as the key role of leadership for managing others is
commendable.

While management has come a long way, it is baffling why so many mistakes are still made. Sternad's book can
hopefully fill a gap by stressing the need for consistent excellence in management to achieve organizational goals.'
                                        —**Roland Berberich**, *Xi'an Jiaotong-Liverpool University, China*

'This is an *extremely* valuable text for undergraduate, postgraduate and executive development courses in management. It demonstrates the realities of managerial work through real-life challenges and case studies.'
                                        —**Jennifer Nzonzo**, *Monash University, South Africa*

'Sternad has created a most valuable learner-centered resource. It provides well-selected, state-of-the-art examples
from around the globe focusing on effective managerial practice and people-oriented leadership. Discussing topics
such as appreciating diversity, intercultural collaboration, and virtual teamwork, Sternad emphasizes the opportunities and challenges that emerge in our digitalized and globalized environment. In doing so, he illustrates the
importance of values-based and ethical behavior for an organization to be sustainably successful. Based on seminal
and current research, this textbook offers the latest insights into practical management that students will appreciate
and benefit from.'
                                        —**Alain Neher**, *Charles Sturt University, Australia*

'*Effective Management* helps readers to develop key skills for the workplace. I would definitely recommend this
book to my students!'
                                        —**Scott Tuppen**, *Swansea University, UK*

'An ambitious and brave undertaking - I am particularly impressed by the emphasis on developing learners'
management skills and career readiness. This approach injects life into management study, making it an exciting
contribution to the discipline which I applaud enthusiastically.'
                                        —**Henry Shi**, *University of Adelaide, Australia*

'*Effective Management* is a well-researched text that provides thoughtful consideration of the application of
management theory in practice. Key themes of relevance to managers today are presented in an interesting and
accessible manner. The book provides a useful resource for both students on academic programs and practitioners
across all sectors.'
                                        —**Dorothy McKee**, *Ulster University, UK and Dorothy McKee Consulting*

EFFECTIVE MANAGEMENT

Developing Yourself, Others and Organizations

Dietmar Sternad

First published 2020 by
RED GLOBE PRESS

Red Globe Press in the UK is an imprint of Springer Nature Limited, registered in England, company number 785998, of 4 Crinan Street, London, N1 9XW.

Red Globe Press® is a registered trademark in the United States, the United Kingdom, Europe and other countries.

ISBN 978–1–352–00729–9 paperback

This book is printed on paper suitable for recycling and made from fully managed and sustained forest sources. Logging, pulping and manufacturing processes are expected to conform to the environmental regulations of the country of origin.

A catalogue record for this book is available from the British Library.

A catalog record for this book is available from the Library of Congress.

SHORT CONTENTS

CONTENTS

LIST OF FIGURES

LIST OF TABLES

PREFACE

There are those special moments in life when you really feel inspired. I experienced such a moment when I was studying in an executive MBA program at a small, innovative business school in Central Europe. I was the managing director of a media company at the time, and I was looking for an opportunity to upgrade my managerial skills. Of course, this is what you would expect from any MBA program, but what I got in this particular program went far beyond my initial expectations. I met people who changed my life. Some of the faculty members were extremely passionate about their role as management educators. They did not "teach" in a traditional way driven by academic theory, but confronted their students with **the realities of managerial work**. With the help of **case studies** and **real-life managerial challenges**, they encouraged their students to find their own solutions for the problems and issues that managers typically face. I was amazed at how much more effective this way of learning was for me than the "traditional" highly theory-based management education that I had received before. I actually enjoyed this new learning experience so much that I decided to change my career and become a management teacher.

One of the first courses that I taught in my new role was an introductory course in management at master's level. Wishing to emulate the exceptional experience of my own executive MBA studies, I wanted my course to be as **interactive, engaging, learner-centric**, and **experiential** as possible. I was convinced that **challenge-based and practice-oriented learning** could also be successfully applied in undergraduate and graduate management courses as well as in executive education. Moreover, I planned to cover all the **skills that managers need in the globalized and technologized business environment of the 21st century**, including, for example, intercultural competence, leading virtual teams, dealing with ethical issues, finding creative ways to solve complex problems, and harnessing new technologies to become more effective in the managerial role.

While designing the new course, I began, as many fellow teachers do, by searching for a textbook, ideally one that would:

- Be **highly practice-oriented**, cover the main managerial challenges, and provide methods and tools for mastering these challenges;
- Provide **insights into the realities of managerial work in the 21st century** (including new managerial trends such as using big data and artificial intelligence for making decisions or managing diverse teams across borders);
- Include **engaging case studies from all world regions**, featuring managers of organizations of different sizes;
- Take an integrated rather than the typical functional perspective on management with a strong focus on the **manager's role as a leader**;
- Be **very accessible** in style while still being based on the findings of academic research; and
- Be clearly focused on **helping students to build their skills in managing and developing themselves, others, and organizations**.

Maybe I was just a bit too demanding with my expectations, but however much I tried, I could not find a textbook that fulfilled all of my criteria. So I decided to create one myself, initially by preparing learning materials for my students on my own, and subsequently refining them through use in the classroom. The result of this work (which took me more than half a decade to complete) is the book that you are now holding in your hands!

Why is a new approach to management (and to learning about management) needed?

Three trends have strongly influenced the nature of managerial work in recent decades: **digitalization**, **globalization**, and **acceleration**. Digital technologies revolutionize the way in which we communicate and work. They disrupt existing business models, provide new insights and predictions based on processing vast amounts of data, and enable the close collaboration of geographically dispersed groups of people. Just as co-workers and partners can come from the other side of the globe, so can competitors. Isolation is not an option in a globalized world. Managers need to work across borders and cooperate with people from many different cultures. Both digitalization and globalization have fueled social and economic acceleration. Today's managers operate in a fast-changing, complex, and often ambiguous environment. They are frequently confronted with challenges and problems that have not been encountered before.

In such a **dynamic environment**, it is no longer enough for managers to master the "classic" managerial functions such as planning, organizing, or controlling. While managers are busy making plans or trying to make sure that everyone sticks to them, the world continues to rotate. Plans quickly become obsolete, and old formulas for success are rendered ineffective as circumstances change. This does not mean that managers should abandon planning, organizing, and controlling altogether. People in organizations still need to know which direction to follow, how best to cooperate with each other, and where they are on the path to achieving their organization's goals. But in a fast-changing environment, managers need to develop **a set of new skills** including:

- identifying what is most important in an endless stream of data and information;
- making decisions under conditions of ambiguity or pressure;
- being able to adapt to a changing environment;
- effectively working with teams of people from a variety of different backgrounds;
- finding creative and innovative solutions to complex problems.

As environmental conditions change, effective managers above all need to be **good leaders**. They must be able to motivate and influence others to follow new directions, but also empower them to find their own ways to contribute to the organization's goals. The term "management" actually stems from the Latin *manus* ("hand") and, hence, the Italian *maneggiare* ("to handle or deal with something"). **Management** as the process of "handling" organizations—of coordinating activities in order to achieve certain goals—cannot be separated from the **leadership** role in which managers need to deal with people and influence them to put their efforts toward achieving the organization's goals. There have been many attempts to distinguish management from leadership, usually along the lines of associating management with more "bureaucratic" tasks such as planning, building structures, systems, and processes, controlling, and optimizing the status quo while relating leadership to inspiring people, casting a vision, and initiating and implementing change. In this context, it has also become fashionable to criticize "managers" and celebrate "leaders." Just as it will be difficult for a leader to effectively lead an organization without setting up structures and processes, a manager who is unable to motivate and inspire others, who does not set a clear direction, and cannot initiate and handle change, will be unable to move an organization forward. Instead of laboriously searching for a clear distinction between management and leadership (which, despite many attempts, still remains very blurred anyway), we actually need "leader-managers" who are able to effectively combine the more "technical" and the more people-oriented aspects of the managerial role.

As the nature of managerial work changes, we also need to change the way in which we learn about management. Instead of following the old functional approach, in which planning, organizing, leading, and controlling are considered separately (as in many traditional management textbooks), we need **a more integrated approach** that enables (future) managers to meet the complex challenges of a dynamically changing world. We need to make sure that future managers are competent to manage themselves, lead other people, and with an entrepreneurial spirit, create, change, and shape organizations that are well adapted to a dynamic global business environment. Instead of ethnocentric managers who are convinced that there is only "one best" approach to management (which can stem from the management culture in which they are engaged), we need open-minded managers who are able to **appreciate and manage diversity** and are familiar with different **management practices around the world**. Finally, in a digitalized world, we also need managers who are familiar with the opportunities that **new technology** offers, without forgetting that management is still fundamentally about **achieving something together with other people**—about helping them to accomplish something that they would not be able to accomplish on their own.

What makes this book stand out?

During the development process of *Effective Management*, I always tried to keep the learner in mind. The basic idea was to create a learner-centric and skills-based textbook with a **clear focus on the challenges and needs of managers in our globalized, technologized, and fast-paced contemporary business environment**. The book is specifically geared to help (future) managers to acquire or enhance their abilities in leading and developing themselves, others, and organizations. Though being grounded in the findings of both classical and recent management and leadership research, it tries to avoid being too theory loaded. Instead of discussing leadership theories in all their detail, for example, it focuses on what you can do to effectively manage yourself, motivate and influence other people, build and lead high-performance teams across cultures, and create thriving organizations.

Rather than extensively (and exhaustively) describing everything that has been said and written about management, this book also has **a core theme**—**managerial effectiveness**, the ability to set and achieve the right goals, both on a personal as well as on an organizational level. The book can help you to explore how managers succeed in their work and aims to prepare you for succeeding in your current or future managerial role. In addition, **case studies** and **good practice examples** from all around the world enable you to **experience effective management first hand**.

Effective Management focuses on providing a realistic overview of the nature of a manager's job and making students familiar with methods and tools that enable them to perform well in a (future) managerial role. What is special about this book is that:

- It is **learner-centric** rather than theory-centric. That does not mean that theoretical models do not play a role, but the focus is clearly on their applicability for managerial practice rather than on theory as an end in itself.
- It covers the **main managerial challenges** and presents concepts and tools for mastering these challenges. Thus, this book can also be seen as a **"toolbox" for (future) managers**.
- It aims to support readers in enhancing their own **self-management, leadership, and management skills** (for example, the whole of Chapter 2 is devoted to managing and developing yourself).
- It includes a diversity of **case insights** and **illustrative examples** of successful managers in terms of both the range of industries explored and their geographical reach. The book showcases examples from both small and medium-sized enterprises and large multinational corporations, showing how the management concepts and tools are used in the real world. These examples are drawn from more than 20 countries on five continents, giving the book a **global perspective** and shining light on the **intercultural aspects** of management and leadership.

- It includes **state-of-the-art findings from management research**, but presents research results in a very **accessible format**—always with an eye on what it all means for managerial practice.
- It takes an integrated rather than a functional perspective and puts a strong emphasis on both the **leadership role** and the **entrepreneurial role** of the manager. While leadership-related topics like motivating and developing others, managing conflicts, leading virtual teams, or exerting influence on others can be found primarily in Chapters 3, 4, 5, and 8, insights into how managers can successfully pursue entrepreneurial opportunities are provided in Chapter 10.
- It covers issues that are particularly important for 21st century managers, including, for example, **digital strategy**, using **artificial intelligence**, **data analytics** and **decision-support systems**, managing **global virtual teams**, **diversity management**, or dealing with **different ethical standards** in a globalized business environment.
- It emphasizes the need to balance current performance against creating the potential for future performance, and has a clear emphasis on providing insights into what it takes to become **sustainably effective in the managerial role.**

Who is this book for?

This book can be used as a **concise textbook** for both **introductory courses in management** and **more advanced courses which are focused on enhancing management and leadership skills**. Most other (mainly theory-based) management textbooks are targeted primarily at readers discovering management-related topics for the first time. Instead, the skills- and challenge-based approach can be used as a basis for management courses at **graduate (Masters) and executive education level** (especially but not exclusively for students without prior business management-related knowledge) as well as in **more practice-oriented undergraduate courses** with the aim of preparing students for future management and leadership-related challenges.

The book is designed to allow students to explore the role and responsibilities of a manager on a personal, interpersonal, organizational, and societal level, and provides them with concepts and tools that can help them improve their effectiveness in a managerial role.

How is the book organized?

The book consists of ten chapters that are organized into four parts:

Part I (Enhancing personal effectiveness) provides a compact overview of the nature and the challenges of the managerial job and explores different strategies for effective self-management and self-development:

○ Chapter 1: The manager's role and responsibility
○ Chapter 2: Managing and developing yourself

Part II (Enhancing interpersonal effectiveness) focuses on how managers can influence the performance of other people, either in one-to-one relationships or in a team setting:

○ Chapter 3: Leading and developing others
○ Chapter 4: Working in teams
○ Chapter 5: Managing diversity across cultures

Part III (Enhancing organizational effectiveness) explores how managers can increase their effectiveness on an organizational level through making the right decisions, developing strategies for their organizations (including digital strategies), and implementing the necessary activities to successfully fulfill these strategies:

○ Chapter 6: Effective decision making
○ Chapter 7: Managing strategy
○ Chapter 8: The execution challenge

Part IV (Enhancing organizational success) discusses what managers can do to enhance the performance of their organizations in different results categories (including profitability, cash flow, and financial and non-financial value creation), set up new entrepreneurial ventures, or rejuvenate existing organizations:

○ Chapter 9: Achieving results
○ Chapter 10: The entrepreneurial manager

Each chapter includes four sections in which the core concepts of effective management are presented in an easily digestible format. Each section, in turn, begins with a short summary of the main concepts (**In brief**).

The chapters begin with:

- A **chapter outline** that provides the reader with a quick overview of the contents.
- **Learning objectives** (in the **This chapter will enable you to** feature) that clarify what readers can expect to learn from the chapter.
- An **introduction** that includes a short vignette that illustrates a managerial situation as well as information about how the chapter contents relate to the overarching theme of managerial effectiveness.

Each chapter also contains a suite of pedagogical features designed to:

- Explore real-world applications (see pp. xxv–xxviii for an overview of the companies and individuals profiled):

  ○ **Case studies** that relate the chapter contents to real-world managerial situations. The case studies provide context-rich narratives of managerial challenges, and can be used for reflecting on how managerial approaches and concepts can be applied in practice, as well as for exploring different ways of handling managerial challenges individually, in groups, or in the classroom.
  ○ The **CEO best practice** boxes feature short biographical accounts of the activities of well-known CEOs, highlighting specific behaviors that lead to long-term managerial effectiveness. All of the featured managers have appeared on the *Harvard Business Review* list of the "World's 100 best-performing CEOs."

- Promote individual skills development (see pp. xxix–xxxiv for an overview of the management and leadership tools covered):

  ○ **What would you do?** boxes that invite readers to think about how they would address a particular managerial challenge.
  ○ **Zooming in on...** boxes in which the application of managerial methods and tools is explained in a simple, step-by-step way.

- Invite the reader to take different perspectives on the managerial role:

  ○ **From a different angle** boxes that present new, sometimes surprising perspectives on management issues.
  ○ **Around the globe** boxes that offer a comparative perspective on different management practices across different countries and world regions.

At the end of each chapter:

- **Review questions** provide students with the opportunity to revise the key concepts.
- **Critical reflection questions** invite readers to revisit the contents of the chapter from a more critical perspective.
- **Managerial implications** include key takeaways that management students can build into their own management toolkit and skills repertoire.

As a special feature in the appendix to Chapter 2, there are five exercises that can be used by readers to **improve their personal effectiveness**.

The book's **Appendix, A very brief history of effective management,** offers a compact overview of the evolution of management study from its inception to the 21st century. Unlike in many theory-oriented textbooks, management history is not a core chapter in this book, as *Effective Management* has a clear focus on helping the reader to understand and master the management challenges of today and the future. Yet, for those who cover the history of management in their course, or for anyone who is interested in how the perception of effective management has changed over time, this Appendix has been included as an additional resource.

The book also includes a **glossary** with all the key terms additionally provided in the margins of the chapters. A **full list of references** allows the reader to track source materials and obtain further information about the topics that are discussed in the book.

Pathways through the book

There are different ways in which this book can be used in both undergraduate and more advanced courses on the principles of (effective) management. The four-part structure that takes you on a progressive journey through the personal (Part I), interpersonal (Part II), and organizational (Parts III and IV) aspects of the managerial role is just one suggestion.

Each chapter and even the four sections within each chapter are self-contained, so it is possible to use the chapters (or chapter sections) individually according to your personal teaching, learning, or professional interests. This allows you to create your own path through the managerial topics that are covered in this book.

For example, lecturers who decide to follow the "planning–organizing–leading–controlling" structure but would still like to emphasize skills development in their course could allocate the chapters in the following way:

- **Planning**: Chapter 6 (*Effective decision making*); Chapter 7 (*Managing strategy*);
- **Organizing**: Sections 8.1 (*The implementation path*) and 8.2 (*Designing the organization*); Chapter 10 (*The entrepreneurial manager*);
- **Leading:** Chapter 3 (*Leading and developing others*); Chapter 4 (*Working in teams*); Chapter 5 (*Managing diversity across cultures*); Sections 8.3 (*Exerting influence*) and 8.4 (*Making change happen*);
- **Controlling:** Chapter 9 (*Achieving results*); parts of Section 8.2 where control systems are discussed.

If your course also includes an introductory topic on the role of the manager and the history of management, you could cover Chapter 1 (*The manager's role and responsibility*) and the Appendix (*A very brief history of effective management*) at the beginning of the course. And even if self-management and self-development are not part of the official curriculum, Chapter 2 (*Managing and developing yourself*) might serve as interesting optional reading for course participants.

The lecturer manual on the companion website for this book (**macmillanihe.com/ sternad-management**) includes further suggestions for adapting the book to the requirements of different types of courses.

Whatever path you take to explore the contents of this book, I very much hope that it will be an exciting learning journey for you—a journey that provides you with new insights about managerial effectiveness and maybe also helps you to take a step further on your personal development path to becoming a (more) effective manager.

AUTHOR'S ACKNOWLEDGMENTS

Every textbook builds on the work of others. Numerous researchers have contributed to enhancing our knowledge of managerial effectiveness. Hundreds of them are cited in this book. As representative examples, I would like to mention two highly renowned management educators, Peter Drucker and Henry Mintzberg. Drucker (1909–2005) was an Austrian-American author, management consultant, and management professor who is widely considered as one of the most influential management thinkers of the 20th and early 21st century. His book *The Effective Executive*, first published in 1967, has become a timeless classic. Mintzberg, a Canadian management professor, is the author of countless seminal contributions about the manager's role and responsibility. All through their professional lives, these educators have both made invaluable contributions to throwing light on what managers do (or should do) in order to make themselves and their organizations more effective. As pioneers of studying managerial effectiveness, they also had a strong influence on my own understanding of what it means to become an effective manager. You will therefore find references to their work throughout this book.

I am also greatly indebted to all the other people who I have had the privilege to learn from, including first and foremost my parents Edith and Peter Sternad, my sister Gerlinde Sternad, my English and Latin teacher Wolf Dieter Wagner, all my former colleagues at Styria Media Group AG, the Styria book publishing group and Žurnal media, my co-authors and friends Katri Kerem, James J. Kennelly and Finbarr Bradley, the supervisors of my doctoral thesis, Werner Mussnig and Gernot Mödritscher, our Dean Dietmar Brodel and all my colleagues at Carinthia University of Applied Sciences (Fachhochschule Kärnten), Danica Purg and everyone at IEDC Bled School of Management, Olga Veligurska, Arshad Ahmad, Jim Ellert, J. B. Kassarjian and the whole team of CEEMAN and its International Management Teachers' Academy (IMTA), Harvard Business School Professor Rohit Deshpandé and all members of the Harvard GloColl faculty, Saša Praprotnik (who was the first reader of parts of this book), Iris Straßer, Robert Ukowitz, Francesca Visintin, Daniel Pittino, my colleagues at the International Seminars at IAE Aix-Marseille Graduate School of Management, and all my students who are a constant source of inspiration for me.

I would also like to thank the fabulous publishing team at Macmillan International Higher Education/Red Globe Press, including my editor Ursula Gavin, my development editors Nikini Arulanandam, Isabel Berwick, and Sophiya Ali for all your invaluable guidance and advice, production editor Aine Flaherty, copy editor Ann Edmondson, cover designer Toby Way, the book design team at Integra, marketing manager Philip Rees, and everyone in the sales and marketing team for all their efforts to make this book available to a wide audience. I also owe thanks to all the highly committed anonymous reviewers from around the world who both challenged and encouraged me, and provided me with an incredible number of excellent suggestions that I used to improve the book manuscript.

On a personal note, I would like to thank my wife Katja and our children Jakob and Elisabeth for their love and support, especially during the countless evenings in which their husband and father was working on the manuscript for this book.

Finally, I owe utmost gratitude to Horst Pirker, who taught me how to manage, as well as to Krzysztof Obłój and Joe Pons, who taught me how to teach.

PUBLISHER'S ACKNOWLEDGMENTS

We are grateful to the following organizations for granting us permission to use their material:

Academy of Management, for permission to reproduce Figure 4.1 The relationship between task interdependence and team performance. Adapted from Figure 2, p. 143 in Stewart, G. L. and Barrick, M. R. (2000) 'Team structure and performance: Assessing the mediating role of intrateam process and the moderating role of task type', *Academy of Management Journal*, 43(2): 135-148; permission conveyed through Copyright Clearance Center, Inc.

Berrett-Koehler Publishers, Inc., for permission to reproduce Figure 5.4 The communication process between people from different cultures. Adapted from Figure 5.1, p. 88 in *Cultural Intelligence: Living and Working Globally*, 2nd edition, copyright © 2009 by David C. Thomas and Kerr Inkson, Berrett-Koehler Publishers, Inc., San Francisco, CA. All rights reserved. www.bkconnection.com.

Boston Consulting Group (BCG), for permission to reproduce Figure 7.6 An example of a BCG portfolio. Based on ideas from Hedley, B. (1970) 'The product portfolio', https://www.bcg.com/publications/1970/strategy-the-product-portfolio.aspx, published 1 January 1970.

Committee of Sponsoring Organizations of the Treadway Commission (COSO), for permission to reproduce Figure 9.8 An example of a risk assessment map. Adapted from Exhibit 7: Illustrative Heat Map, p.16 in Curtis, P. and Carey, M. (2012) *Thought Leadership in ERM: Risk Assessment in Practice* (Durham, NC: COSO), available at https://www.coso.org/Documents/COSO-ERM-Risk-Assessment-in-Practice-Thought-Paper-October-2012.pdf. Copyright © 2012 COSO.

Christina Staubmann, for permission to reproduce Figure 7.7 Reasons for following a cooperative strategy. From Sternad, D., Knappitsch, E. and Mundschütz, C. (2012) Cross-Border Cooperation: European Institutional Framework and Strategies of SMEs (Stuttgart: Franz Steiner Verlag), p. 41.

Harvard Business Review, for permission to reproduce:

- Figure 1.5 Mintzberg's ten managerial roles. Adapted from 'The Manager's Roles' in 'The Manager's Job: Folklore and Fact' by Henry Mintzberg, March-April 1990. Copyright ©1990 by Harvard Business Publishing; all rights reserved.
- Figure 10.3 Key components of creativity. Adapted from 'The Three Components of Creativity' in 'How To Kill Creativity' by Teresa M. Amabile, September-October 1998. Copyright ©1998 by Harvard Business Publishing; all rights reserved.
- Table 3.1 Job requirements. Adapted from 'Summary', p. 7 in 'Note on the Hiring and Selection Process' by Michael J. Roberts, February 3, 1993. Copyright ©1993 by Harvard Business Publishing; all rights reserved.

Professor R. Edward Freeman, for permission to reproduce Figure 1.3 Stakeholder groups. Adapted from Figure 1.1, p. 7 in Freeman, R. E., Harrison, J. S. and Wicks, A. C. (2007) *Managing for Stakeholders: Survival, Reputation, and Success* (New Haven, CT: Yale University Press).

Robert Ukowitz (www.robert-ukowitz.com), for permission to reproduce Figure 3.9 The "F-R-E-P" model for structuring a termination meeting. Adapted from an extended version of his original Facts-Empathy-Perspective model.

SBS Swiss Business School, for permission to reproduce Figure 3.2 A framework of external factors influencing work motivation. Adapted from 'Towards an eclectic framework of external factors influencing work motivation' by D. Sternad, 2013, *Journal of Applied Business Research*, 2, p. 8. Copyright by SBS Swiss Business School.

South-Western, a part of Cengage, Inc., for permission to reproduce Figure 4.5 Communication tools according to their channel richness. Based on Daft, *Management*, 12E, p. 594, ISBN: 9781285861982. © 2016 South-Western, a part of Cengage, Inc. www.cengage.com/permissions

Taylor & Francis Ltd, www.tandfonline.com, for permission to reproduce Figure 2.6 The (self-) development cycle. Adapted from Figure 1, p. 246 in Sternad, D. (2015) 'A Challenge-Feedback Learning Approach to Teaching International Business', *Journal of Teaching in International Business*, 26(4): 241-257, DOI: 10.1080/08975930.2015.1124355.

University of Primorska, Faculty of Management Koper, for permission to reproduce Figure 1.4 The managerial responsibility grid. Adapted from Figure 1, p. 96 in Sternad, D. (2013) 'Managerial Long-Term Responsibility in Family-Controlled Firms', *Management*, 8(2): 93-107.

We are also grateful to all the photographers and illustrators who have provided images. Please see individual credit lines for details.

ABOUT THE AUTHOR

Dietmar Sternad is Professor of International Management and Program Director of the International Business Management master's program at Carinthia University of Applied Sciences/Fachhochschule Kärnten (Austria). He teaches several management and leadership-related subjects in undergraduate, graduate, and executive education programs. He has also given lectures and guest lectures at universities and business schools in Belgium, Finland, France, Ireland, Italy, Poland, and Slovenia, is an alumnus of the IMTA (CEEMAN) and GloColl (Harvard Business School) management teachers' programs and has received several national and international awards for creating case-based teaching materials and for teaching excellence. He is the first management professor to receive the *Austrian State Prize for Teaching Excellence "Ars docendi."*

Dietmar holds degrees from the Open University (Bachelor of Science), the University of Graz (Magister rer.soc.oec.), IEDC Bled School of Management (MBA) and the University of Klagenfurt (Doctorate in Social and Economic Sciences). In his prior managerial career, he was the Managing Director of one of Austria's leading trade book publishing groups and the CEO of Slovenia's highest-circulation daily newspaper. He also contributed to the founding of a market-leading cooking website, developed and led several in-house executive leadership education programs for multinational enterprises, and works as a strategy consultant.

Dietmar has (co-)authored and (co-)edited several books, among them *Strategic Adaptation* (Springer, 2011), *Handbook of Doing Business in South East Europe* (Palgrave Macmillan, 2011), *Grundlagen Export und Internationalisierung* (in German; Springer, 2013), *Digging Deeper: How Purpose-Driven Enterprises Create Real Value* (Greenleaf Publishing, 2016), and *Qualitatives Wachstum* (in German; Springer, 2018). His research has been published in a range of different scientific journals. His current research interests center on responsible and long-term-oriented management and leadership practices, the qualitative growth strategies of companies, and internationalization strategies for small and medium-sized enterprises.

GUIDED TOUR OF THE BOOK

Outline of chapter

Introduction

1.1 The challenges of a managerial role
    Managerial challenge 1: Performing through others
    Managerial challenge 2: The complexity of organizations

Outline of chapter provides an overview of the chapter contents.

This chapter will enable you to

- Recognize key managerial challenges.
- Identify managers' central responsibilities in an organization.
- Gain an insight into the day-to-day realities of management.
- Describe the primary roles that managers

This chapter will enable you to describes the main learning outcomes.

In brief

- The core of a manager's job is working through others to achieve an organization's goals. These "others," however, are not impassive robots but people with their own ideas, interests, and emotions. Managers therefore need to address the whole person when they want others to perform.

- Additionally, managers need to recognize that an organization is also a "whole"—a complex system of interdependent structures, processes, routines, and relationships. Interventions in one part of the system can lead to multiple repercussions in other parts.

- Organizations are open systems that are exposed to changes in the surrounding environment. Effective managers therefore need to understand all three factors that impact their role—people, the organization, and the environment—as well as the interrelations between them.

In brief boxes succinctly summarize the core concepts of each chapter section.

Case studies show how managerial challenges are addressed in practice. They provide opportunities to apply the concepts that are discussed in the chapter.

Performance with purpose: Indra K. Nooyi at PepsiCo

Indra K. Nooyi grew up in the Indian city of Madras (now Chennai). In a dinner table ritual initiated by her mother, she and her older sister had to make speeches about what they would do if they were powerful politicians. "So she gave us confidence to be whatever we wanted to be,"[18] strategy, reducing the company's environmental footprint was the second, and creating a positive and inclusive work environment for employees was the third. Nooyi did not see responsible behavior as an add-on that you do "after hours," but as a fundamental basis for business success.

CEO BEST PRACTICE

"There are many ways to climb Mt. Fuji"

Fujio Mitarai, the long-time president of Japanese camera and electronic equipment manufacturer Canon, has been steering his ship well during his tenure. The nephew of one

In addition to taking care of employees, Canon has invested heavily in the company's future under Mitarai's leadership, spending significantly more on research and

CEO best practice boxes include short accounts of the activities of well-known CEOs who have proven to be highly effective in the long term.

Zooming in on... boxes explain managerial tools and concepts in a simple step-by-step format.

Zooming in on ▶ STAKEHOLDER MANAGEMENT

Not only do organizations as a whole have stakeholders, but also departments and even individual projects. The next time you are in charge of running a team project (perhaps as part of your studies, for a club or society, or at work) work through the following steps to analyze and manage the most important stakeholder groups for that project:

1 *Identify all stakeholders*: Which people or groups are affected by the project? Who do you depend on to achieve the project's goals?

Imagine that you are the manager of a business hotel in the capital city of your country. What factors are likely to have the greatest influence on the performance of your hotel? Consider people (your team), the organization, and the micro and macro environments. How would you ensure that you would always be able to "see the whole picture" and remain aware of the current state and development of all these factors?

What would you do? boxes encourage you to think about how you would address specific managerial challenges.

AROUND THE GLOBE

Cross-cultural differences in networking

When attending a networking event, would you approach a representative from a company with which you are interested in working in the following way: "Hello, I see you are working for Company X. I am highly interested in your company, may I tell you a bit more about me?" Whereas in the US, this would be a perfectly fine start to a conversation, people from other cultures may find this approach much too direct or even assertive. They might think, like this Indian management consultant who was cited on the

In strongly relationship-oriented cultures, exchanges are primarily mediated. If you want to approach a person in Russia or China, for example, it usually works better when you are introduced by someone who is already well connected with the "target person" than to approach that person directly. Networks in these countries are characterized by mutual obligations and an expectation of exchanging favors—also in the sense of helping the friends of friends. As the rules of networking differ from culture to culture,

FROM A DIFFERENT ANGLE

Learning about long-term responsibility from family firms

On average, companies die sooner than human beings. Even Fortune 500 corporations have an average life expectancy of no more than 40 to 50 years.[13] There are some businesses, however, that have been in existence for hundreds of years, and are still thriving. The majority of these long-lived companies are family owned.

So what makes family businesses more resilient and

generations, identify strongly with the firm, have the desire to leave a legacy, and know whose money they are working with—their own.[14] Consequently, they often act more conservatively (i.e. they try to avoid unnecessary risks), strive to keep their businesses independent, and take special care to build and nourish good long-term relationships with their employees, customers, and the wider community. In short, they

Around the globe boxes explain how certain approaches to management can vary across cultures.

From a different angle boxes present less common, but potentially eye-opening perspectives on managerial issues.

Review questions and **critical reflection questions** at the end of each chapter can help you to revise and critically reflect on what you have learned.

✓ Review questions

1 What is challenging about the manager's job?
2 What levels of complexity does a manager need to deal with?
3 What are the main responsibilities of managers in an organizational context?

? Critical reflection questions

1 Why do managers (especially in top management positions) often receive exceptionally high salaries? Based on what you have learned in this chapter about the nature of the managerial job, do you think that these high salaries are appropriate?
2 Do you agree more strongly with the Friedmanite perspective or the social contract perspective on managerial responsibility? Provide arguments to support your choice.

Managerial implications

- Managers are responsible for ensuring that their organizations or organizational units serve their purpose (or create value) and, at the same time, for building the potential for future performance. Effective managers therefore strive to establish a balance between current performance and potential building.
- Managers perform through other people and work within complex social systems (organizations) that are, in turn, embedded in wider social systems (the micro and macro

Managerial implications summarize key takeaways that can help you to become more effective in your (future) managerial role.

Key terms are defined in the margins and listed in a **glossary**.

Cause and effect web:
Multiple causal relations (and interrelations) between different factors and elements in a complex system.

Let us assume, for example, that a manager aims to increase the revenues of a low-performing department. Thinking in a purely reductionist cause-and-effect way, the manager might undertake one intervention, such as introducing a new reward system for the sales team. It is possible that this action will have a positive effect if the former reward system was not very motivating. Acknowledging the complexity of **cause and effect webs** within an organization, however, the manager might instead initiate multiple changes, attacking the problem concurrently at different levels. Changing the structure of the sales team, providing training, creating new offers for customers, incentivizing referrals from satisfied consumers, adopting tighter day-to-day sales management, rethinking the pricing structure, or planning a new marketing strategy are further actions that could be used to complement the introduction of the new reward system. Combining several initiatives that

✎ Endnotes

[1]spiegel.de (2012).
[2]Hill and Lineback (2011), p. xi.
[3]Similar definitions of management have been put forward by Hales (1986) and Mintzberg (2011).
[4]Hill and Lineback (2011), p. 15.
[5]Pascal (2007), p. 408.

[44]Business Week (2002).
[45]Business Week (2002).
[46]ForbesCustom (2018).
[47]Rowley et al. (2005), p. 49.
[48]Maak and Pless (2006); Werhane (1999).
[49]Burton and Goldsby (2005).
[50]Confucius (2007), p. 37.

[51]Riegel (1935).
[52]Kolbjørnsrud et al. (2016).
[53]Kolbjørnsrud et al. (2016), p. 11; Pistrui and Dimov (2018).
[54]Rosa (2013).
[55]Roux (2017).
[56]Magpili and Pazos (2018); Renkema et al.

A **full list of references** allows you to obtain further information about the topics that are discussed in the book.

DIGITAL RESOURCES

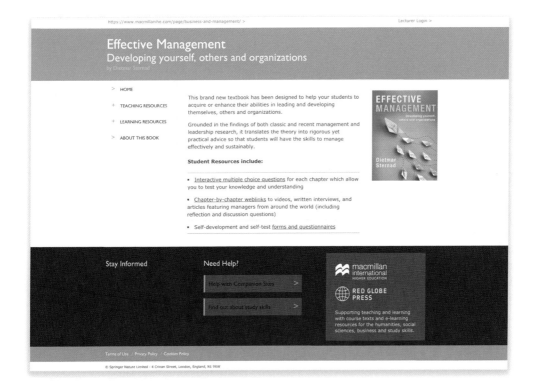

The companion website (**macmillanihe.com/sternad-management**) contains a range of different additional resources for both learners and lecturers.

Teaching resources
- A lecturer manual, including suggestions for adapting the book to the requirements of your specific course.
- A set of Microsoft® PowerPoint slides for each chapter as well as for the appendix on the history of management thought (including video links).
- Detailed teaching notes for each chapter including slide-by-slide teaching instructions, additional questions for class discussions, and case study debriefs.
- A test bank with 30 multiple choice questions for each chapter and the appendix.

Learning resources
- Interactive multiple choice questions for learners.
- Chapter-by-chapter weblinks to videos featuring managers from around the world (including reflection and discussion questions).
- Chapter-by-chapter weblinks to interviews with and articles about managers from around the world (including reflection and discussion questions).
- Self-development and self-test forms and questionnaires.
- Interactive flashcards of key terms.

LEARNING FROM REAL LIFE: CASE STUDY AND CEO BEST PRACTICE GRID

Each chapter contains numerous examples of existing businesses, as well as more detailed case studies and CEO best practice boxes which explore the specific actions taken by individuals or companies across the world.

Part I: Enhancing personal effectiveness

Chapter	Organization	Manager	Type of box	Industry	Location of the organization's headquarters	Main topics	Page
1 The manager's role and responsibility	Canon	Fujio Mitarai	CEO best practice	Manufacturing of imaging and optical products	Japan	Managerial responsibility; investing in the future; balance between exploration and exploitation (ambidexterity)	16
	PepsiCo	Indra Nooyi	Case study	Food and beverages	USA	Managerial challenges; managing in a dynamic environment; managerial responsibility; balance between performance and potential	17
	SABMiller	Graham Mackay	CEO best practice	Brewing and beverages	UK/South Africa	Agenda setting and implementation; sensemaking	26
	Envato	Collis Ta'eed	Case study	Online marketplace	Australia	Changing responsibilities of a manager in growing organizations; managerial effectiveness; organizational culture and values	30
2 Managing and developing yourself	Disney	Robert Iger	CEO best practice	Entertainment	USA	Knowing your strengths and weaknesses; learning orientation; self-development	41
	Jet.com	Liza Landsman	Case study	E-commerce	USA	Effective self-management; setting goals and priorities; work–life balance; managerial values	48
	Uniqlo/Fast Retailing	Tadashi Yanai	CEO best practice	Retail	Japan	Self-reflection; learning from failure; self-development	57
	Jugnoo	Samar Singla	Case study	Transportation network provider	India	Challenges for start-up managers; resilience; coping with setbacks; self-development	58

Part II: Enhancing interpersonal effectiveness

Chapter	Organization	Manager	Type of box	Industry	Location of the organization's headquarters	Main topics	Page
3 Leading and developing others	TJX	Carol Meyrowitz	CEO best practice	Retail	USA	People development; coaching; training	84
	Semco	Ricardo Semler	Case study	Multi-business enterprise	Brazil	Influencing the performance and developing the performance potential of others; democratic leadership	86
	Delta Air Lines	Richard Anderson	CEO best practice	Airline	USA	Hiring the right people; selection criteria; job interview	96
	ACL Services	Laurie Schultz	Case study	IT/Software	Canada	Recruiting; developing talent; organizational culture	99
4 Working in teams	Continental AG	Elmar Degenhart	CEO best practice	Automotive supplier	Germany	Team culture; values-based team leadership	115
	the7stars	Jenny Biggam	Case study	Media planning	UK	Developing a high-performance team; workplace culture; the role of rules versus flexible working arrangements	118
	Microsoft	Satya Nadella	CEO best practice	Software	USA	Fostering conflict as a way to bring about change in organizations	128
	Hachette Book Group	Michael Pietsch	Case study	Book publishing	France/USA	Conflict management; negotiation strategies; distributive versus integrative negotiations	131
5 Managing diversity across cultures	Gildan Activewear	Glenn J. Chamandy	CEO best practice	Apparel manufacturing	Canada	Diversity management; inclusion; corporate social responsibility	142
	Haier Group	Du Jingguo	Case study	Household appliances	China	Leading across cultures; cultural challenges; post-merger cultural integration	152
	Lockheed Martin	Marillyn Hewson	CEO best practice	Defense, aerospace, and advanced technologies	USA	Global business ethics; code of conduct; anti-corruption strategies; values	168
	IKEA	Marianne Barner	Case study	Furniture retail	Sweden/The Netherlands	Cross-cultural differences in ethical standards; preventing child labor; managing ethical issues across organizational boundaries	169

Part III: Enhancing organizational effectiveness

Chapter	Organization	Manager	Type of box	Industry	Location of the organization's headquarters	Main topics	Page
6 Effective decision making	Google	Eric Schmidt	CEO best practice	Internet services	USA	Risk preferences in decision making; managing risks	186
	Zara	Pablo Isla	Case study	Fashion retail	Spain	Operations decisions; decision support systems; big data analytics	197
	Amazon.com	Jeff Bezos	CEO best practice	Online retail	USA	Decision making; framing decision problems	203
	Royal Bank of Scotland	Fred Goodwin	Case study	Banking	UK	Decision failures; failure of governance	209
7 Managing strategy	Red Bull	Dietrich Mateschitz	Case study	Beverages	Austria	Industry analysis; competitive strategy; strategic choices	230
	Umicore	Marc Grynberg	CEO best practice	Materials technology	Belgium	Strategic alliance; exploiting new strategic opportunities	234
	Wolters Kluwer	Nancy McKinstry	CEO best practice	Publishing/ Information services	The Netherlands	Digital transformation; maintaining a sustainable strategic position	240
	Westfield	Steven Lowy	Case study	Retail/ Shopping centers	Australia	Portfolio strategy; digital strategy; dealing with the threat of online substitution	248
8 The execution challenge	Aon plc.	Gregory ("Greg") Case	CEO best practice	Insurance brokerage/Risk consulting	UK	Strategy execution; communication as a key task for managers during the implementation path	260
	Studio Moderna	Sandi Češko	Case study	Multi-channel retail	Slovenia	Organizational design; organizational structure; control systems	271
	L Brands	Leslie Wexner	CEO best practice	Fashion	USA	Change management; agile organization	280
	Comair	Erik Venter	Case study	Airline	South Africa	Change management; transition; introduction of an integrated IT system	285

Part IV: Enhancing organizational success

Chapter	Organization	Manager	Type of box	Industry	Location of the organization's headquarters	Main topics	Page
9 Achieving results	Starbucks	Howard Schultz	CEO best practice	Coffee company and coffeehouse chain	USA	Improving profitability; responsible cost cutting	299
	ALDI	Karl and Theo Albrecht	Case study	Discount retail	Germany	Cash management; cost leadership; price-based strategy	307
	Novo Nordisk	Lars R. Sørensen	CEO best practice	Pharmaceuticals	Denmark	Triple bottom line approach; social responsibility of a business; organizational purpose	316
	Brunello Cucinelli	Brunello Cucinelli	Case study	Luxury fashion	Italy	Drivers of business value; financial value versus societal value/"real value"	318
10 The entrepreneurial manager	Air Liquide	Benoît Potier	CEO best practice	Industrial gases and services	France	Corporate entrepreneurship; entrepreneurial spirit; innovation	328
	AmorePacific	Suh Kyung-bae	CEO best practice	Cosmetics	South Korea	Innovation as a source of competitive advantage; open innovation	333
	SoGal Ventures	Pocket (Yiqing) Sun	Case study	Venture capital investment	Singapore	Entrepreneurial mind-set; assessing business opportunities	338
	Yemeksepeti	Nevzat Aydın	Case study	Online food ordering marketplace	Turkey	Business model; recognizing entrepreneurial opportunities; approaches to entrepreneurship	350

DEVELOPING SKILLS: THE MANAGER'S TOOLBOX

In order to meet the challenges of real-life business, managers need to assemble a portfolio of tools and resources. These are discussed throughout the book, either in the main text, or illustrated in figures and tables, or described in more detail in Zooming in on... boxes.

Part I: Enhancing personal effectiveness

Chapter	Tool	Skills area	Application	Page
1 The manager's role and responsibility	Stakeholder management	Stakeholder management	Analyzing and managing the most important stakeholder groups of an organization or a project	13
	Agenda setting tool	Priorities management	Setting managerial priorities in the short, medium, and long term	25
	A model of managerial effectiveness	Priorities management	Focusing on the main building blocks of managerial effectiveness	26
	ABCDE monitoring chart	Monitoring	Maintaining an overview of ten factors (within and outside the organization) that managers should constantly watch	27
	Building and maintaining a supportive network	Networking	Building and maintaining a network of potential supporters	30
2 Managing and developing yourself	Feedback analysis	Self-awareness	Identifying your strengths and weaknesses; assessing your judgment	40
	Drucker's questions on how you perform best	Self-awareness	Identifying your strengths; matching tasks and strengths	40
	Criteria for determining priorities	Priorities management	Setting priorities	44
	Personal productivity management system	Personal productivity management	Finding a structured way of dealing with the many issues with which a manager is confronted	45
	Rules for creating a schedule	Personal productivity management	Effectively creating a schedule	46
	The monkey metaphor (avoiding reverse delegation)	Priorities management; leadership	Avoiding taking on subordinates' tasks; developing subordinates	48
	Strategies to sustain and regain energy	Personal energy management	Identifying strategies for positively influencing your energy level	51
	Work-related energy management strategies	Personal energy management	Increasing your energy level at work	51
	The ABC model of Rational Emotive Behavioral Theory	Resilience	Coping with difficult situations	53
	The development cycle	Self-development	Setting challenges and taking action to develop yourself	55
	Questions to yourself	Self-development	Reflecting on your self-development	57

Chapter	Tool	Skills area	Application	Page
	Setting your life goals	Self-awareness; priorities management	Setting overarching goals for your life	62
	From life goals to concrete next steps	Priorities management	Breaking down overarching life goals into more specific yearly goals and actionable next steps	63
	Drucker's questions on how you perform best	Self-awareness	Identifying your strengths; matching tasks and strengths	64
	Discover your strengths	Self-awareness	Identifying your strengths	64
	Reflect on your values	Self-awareness	Reflecting on your core values	66
	Identify your sources and drains of energy	Personal energy management	Identifying your sources and drains of energy as a basis for personal energy management	67

Part II: Enhancing interpersonal effectiveness

Chapter	Tool	Skills area	Application	Page
3 Leading and developing others	The performance equation	Performance management	Identifying the causes of employees' performance problems and finding the right strategy for dealing with performance problems	74
	Checklist for identifying the right motivational actions	Motivation	Identifying leverage points for positively influencing employee motivation	79
	Giving feedback	Performance management	Giving feedback to another person with the purpose of influencing this person's performance	82
	The people development process	People development	Determining the right steps to develop members of your team	83
	Coaching questions	Performance management	Coaching others through asking the right questions before and after they face a challenge	85
	The delegation process	Delegation	Structuring the delegation process	88
	The assignment meeting	Delegation	Assigning tasks to other people	89
	Structure of a performance review	Performance management	Structuring a performance review meeting	90
	Dealing with poor performance flow chart	Performance management	Deciding on the right tactics to deal with low-performing employees	92
	The hiring process	Recruitment	Taking a structured approach to hiring the right people	94
	Job requirements list	Recruitment	Making sure that no important qualifications, skills, or attitudes are forgotten in the hiring process	94
	Questioning techniques for job interviews	Recruitment	Asking the right questions to assess whether a candidate is suitable for a particular job	95
	"F-R-E-P" model	Managing layoffs	Structuring a termination meeting; conveying bad news	99
4 Working in teams	Mandating a team	Team building	Clarifying the framework conditions for ensuring effective teamwork	108
	Belbin's team roles	Team building	Combining complementary skills for creating well-functioning teams	108–9
	Six essential issues for newly formed teams	Team leadership	Taking the first steps as a team leader in building a high-performance team	109–10
	The theme-centered interaction (TCI) triangle	Team leadership	Finding the right balance between individual team members' needs, team cohesion, and focusing the team on the task	113
	Dealing with "ineffective" team members	Team leadership	Identifying the right strategy for dealing with team members who are impeding the team's effectiveness	117
	Dealing with social loafing	Team leadership	Dealing with group members who put in less effort at the expense of others	117
	Reflecting on the team process	Team leadership	Periodic appraisal of the adequacy of established team routines	118
	Communication tools according to their channel richness	Communication	Choosing the right communication channel	120
	Delivering a compelling business presentation	Presentation	Holding effective managerial presentations	121

Chapter	Tool	Skills area	Application	Page
	The effective meeting process	Meeting management	Preparing, conducting, and following up a meeting	123
	Conflict handling styles	Conflict management	Determining the best strategy for dealing with a conflict	127
	Tactics for claiming value in distributive negotiations	Negotiation	Enhancing the chances for a successful outcome in "zero-sum" negotiation situations	128–9
	Principles of integrative negotiations	Negotiation	Finding an agreement which is beneficial for all sides in a negotiation situation	129
	Being well prepared for your next negotiation	Negotiation	Preparing for negotiations	130
5 Managing diversity across cultures	Diversity climate checklist	Diversity management	Assessing the current status of diversity in the organization; identifying indicators of inclusivity	141
	Seven steps toward a more diversity- and inclusion-oriented organization	Diversity management	Developing an inclusive organization with a positive diversity culture	143
	Diversity practices	Diversity management	Managing diversity in an organizational context	143–4
	Diversity training	Diversity management	Enhancing the diversity awareness and diversity skills of the members of an organization	144
	Framework for analyzing cultural differences	Intercultural management	Understanding cultural differences	149–50
	Six leadership practices of effective leaders of virtual teams	Leading global virtual teams	Setting up and leading a well-functioning global virtual team	157
	Team norms for global virtual teams	Leading global virtual teams	Making sure that members of a global virtual team can collaborate effectively with each other	158
	LEARN model	Intercultural management/ leading global virtual teams	Ensuring effective communication in global (virtual) teams	159
	Four steps to ethical behavior	Ethical reasoning	Finding possible answers to the question of what is ethically right or wrong in a particular situation	162
	Dealing with an ethical dilemma	Ethical reasoning	Finding out what to do when ethical standards collide in a cross-cultural context	164–5
	Ethics quick test	Ethical reasoning	Making the right decision in a case of moral dilemma	168

Part III: Enhancing organizational effectiveness

Chapter	Tool	Skills area	Application	Page
6 Effective decision making	The rational decision-making process	Decision making	Structuring a rational-analytic decision-making process	179
	Checklist for defining the real decision problem	Decision making	Finding out whether the decision problem is framed in the right way	179–80
	Decision tree	Decision making	Providing a structured overview of a decision problem and its different possible outcomes	183–4
	Objectives comparison matrix	Decision making	Ranking multiple objectives that need to be considered when making a decision	187
	Weighted scoring model	Decision making	Resolving trade-off situations in complex decision problems	188
	Actively open-minded thinking	Decision making	Lowering the potential negative impact of decision-making pitfalls	202
	The path to effective group decisions	Group decision making	Improving the quality of group decision-making processes	207
	The team decision quality control checklist	Group decision making	Assessing the quality of group decision-making processes	208
7 Managing strategy	Five main questions for a strategist	Strategic analysis	Setting the agenda for a strategy process	216
	The strategic planning process	Strategic analysis	Overview of the main steps when formulating a strategy	218–9
	PESTEL analysis	Strategic analysis	Assessing trends and developments in the general (macro) environment	221–22
	Industry definition questions	Strategic analysis	Defining the industry (or industries) in which an organization competes	223
	Porter's five forces	Strategic analysis	Analyzing the attractiveness of an industry	224
	Strategic group map	Strategic analysis	Identifying competitors that are following similar strategies	224–5
	Industry life cycle	Strategic analysis	Assessing the life cycle stage of an industry	225
	Value curve	Strategic analysis	Identifying the main factors on which an industry competes	226
	VRIO analysis	Strategic analysis	Identifying resources and capabilities that can form the basis for competitive advantage	228
	SWOT analysis	Strategic analysis	Integrating internal and external strategic analyses	228
	I-O/O-I analysis	Strategic analysis	Matching organizational resources/capabilities and opportunities	229
	Tests for adding additional businesses	Strategic analysis	Analyzing whether adding an additional business unit makes sense for a corporation	232
	BCG portfolio	Strategic analysis	Displaying a portfolio of businesses	233
	Growth strategies analysis checklist	Strategic analysis	Analyzing the suitability and viability of growth strategies	236
	Integrated strategic positioning	Strategic positioning	Finding the right strategic positioning for an organization	240
	McKinsey 7-S Framework	Strategic positioning	Finding congruence between "hard" and "soft" factors of a business	242

Chapter	Tool	Skills area	Application	Page
	Aligned "hard" and "soft" factors of a business	Strategic positioning	Aligning "hard" and "soft" factors of a business	242
	Tactics to react to the entry of a low-cost competitor	Strategic positioning	Identifying options for reacting to the entry of low-cost competitors in your market	243
	House of digital strategy	Strategic positioning	Identifying the main spheres of activity for a digital business strategy	245
8 The execution challenge	The implementation path	Strategy implementation	Transforming a strategy into concrete organizational performance	257
	Basic organizational structuring principles	Organizational design	Identifying the right organizational structure for the organization	264
	Process flow chart	Organizational design	Graphically representing a process and all its individual steps as a basis for process optimization	268
	Overview of control systems	Organizational design	Finding the right form of control	270
	Playing the power game	Influencing	Gaining more power and influence in an organization	274
	Four elements of effective persuasion	Influencing	Persuading others to adopt certain ideas	274–5
	PCAN model	Influencing	Presenting a convincing proposal	275–6
	The influence map	Influencing	Mapping influence relationships in an organization	277
	Approaches to shaping organizational culture	Influencing	Influencing and shaping the culture of an organization	278
	Six key questions that people have about change	Change management	Preparing people for change processes	281
	Kotter's change management model	Change management	Instigating and implementing a change initiative	282
	Strategies for dealing with resistance to change	Change management	Addressing resistance to change	283–4

Part IV: Enhancing organizational success

Chapter	Tool	Skills area	Application	Page
	Driving and restraining forces of creativity and innovativeness in organizations	Innovation management	Creating conditions under which creativity and innovativeness can thrive in organizations	336
	Strategies for actively searching for opportunities	Recognizing business opportunities	Recognizing new business opportunities	341
	Value innovation	Innovation management	Identifying new, unique configurations of product and service offers	343–4
	The opportunity assessment process	Assessing business opportunities	Evaluating the potential of business opportunities	345
	Typical structure of a business plan	Business planning	Making a detailed description of a business opportunity	347–8
	Nine elements of the business model canvas	Business planning	Describing the main business decisions and economic logic of an entrepreneurial venture or a business development project	349–50

PART

ENHANCING PERSONAL EFFECTIVENESS

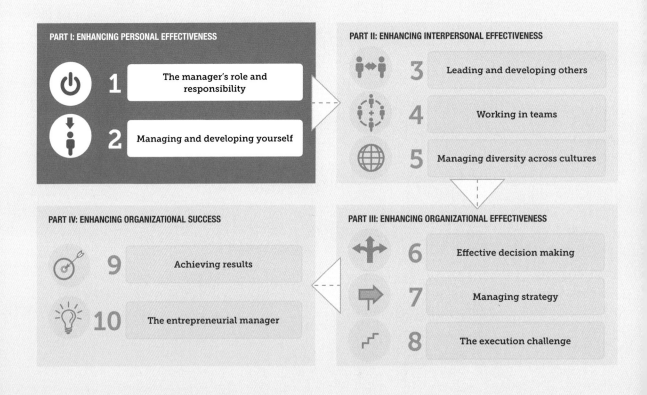

PART I: ENHANCING PERSONAL EFFECTIVENESS

1 The manager's role and responsibility

2 Managing and developing yourself

PART II: ENHANCING INTERPERSONAL EFFECTIVENESS

3 Leading and developing others

4 Working in teams

5 Managing diversity across cultures

PART IV: ENHANCING ORGANIZATIONAL SUCCESS

9 Achieving results

10 The entrepreneurial manager

PART III: ENHANCING ORGANIZATIONAL EFFECTIVENESS

6 Effective decision making

7 Managing strategy

8 The execution challenge

As a precondition for effectively managing and developing other people and organizations, managers must first be able to effectively manage and develop themselves in their job. Part I is devoted to gaining a better understanding of the nature and demands of the managerial job and exploring different strategies for effective self-management and self-development.

In **Chapter 1,** *The manager's role and responsibility,* we will try to find out what it means to be a manager. After getting an overview of the main challenges that are associated with trying to achieve something together with others in an uncertain and dynamic environment, we will take a closer look at the responsibilities that managers need to meet. We will also gain a clearer picture of how managers spend their working days and what they can do to satisfy the various role expectations they face. In the last part of Chapter 1 we will focus on recognizing what effectiveness—the core theme of this book—means in a managerial context. To come straight to the point: Effective managers set the right goals and achieve them. A model of managerial effectiveness explains how this can be accomplished with the help of other people.

Chapter 2, *Managing and developing yourself,* addresses what managers can do to ensure they are effective in their job. We will discuss several approaches to understanding and matching personal goals, strengths, and values as a first important step. Personal effectiveness also means being able to identify and focus on the really important issues and tasks. Therefore, we will investigate how managers can set priorities and enhance their personal productivity. Acknowledging that the fast-paced nature of managerial work can lead to high stress levels, we will discuss different strategies for coping with stress and setbacks, becoming resilient, and keeping personal energy levels high. In the final part of Chapter 2, we will look at what managers can do to further develop their competencies and skills, thus coming closer to reaching their full potential.

IDEAS
MANAGEMENT
PROCESS
EFFECTIVE
COMPETENCE
PROGRESS
TEAMWORK

iStock.com/cnythzl

THE MANAGER'S ROLE AND RESPONSIBILITY

Outline of chapter

This chapter will enable you to

- Recognize key managerial challenges.
- Identify managers' central responsibilities in an organization.
- Gain an insight into the day-to-day realities of management.
- Describe the primary roles that managers perform in organizations.
- Define effective management and explore how managers can become more effective.
- Examine your approach to two critical managerial tasks—networking and monitoring developments both within and outside the organization.

Introduction

In July 2012, newspapers around the world reported that a football (soccer) coach had been fired. Normally, firing the coach of a team ranked eighth out of twelve in the league of the Gulf Emirate of Dubai wouldn't make international news. However, in this case the coach of Al Wasl was no less than Argentine football legend Diego Armando Maradona, one of the best players in the history of the game. It was not for financial reasons that the club had decided to dismiss the former "Player of the Century," but because it was "in need of a better coach."[1] Sadly, this scenario was already a familiar one for Maradona. Two years earlier, he had to leave his post as Argentina's national coach after Germany knocked his team out of the World Cup in a clear 4-0 victory.

Many people become **managers** because of their exceptional performance in specialist, non-managerial functions. They get promoted and are suddenly responsible not only for their own work, but also for how other people perform. This is not an easy transition because they need a whole new set of skills and attitudes to become effective managers. The best player will not necessarily become the best coach.

> **Manager:**
> A person who is responsible for the performance and development of a group, an organizational unit, or an organization as a whole.

It can come as a surprise to many people who enter into a managerial role for the first time that their new role not only differs considerably from their prior role as experts, but also from what they expected about what it means to be a manager. Many people believe that a manager is a person "in control," someone who devises a grand plan, tells others what to do, sets up organizational structures and processes, and then checks whether the planned outcomes have been achieved. In reality, managers are often much less in control of their work than people in the role of expert. Indeed, they are exposed to a whole range of uncontrollable external influences and are strongly dependent on others for getting things done.

On their own, managers are worthless. After all, if there was no one and nothing to manage, the role would be superfluous. Managers are needed, however, in all types of organizations, whenever people are working together in an institutionalized environment in order to pursue a shared purpose. They add value when their managerial skills can help a group of people to become more effective in achieving a collective goal.

In this first chapter, we will take a closer look at what it means to be a manager and what it takes to be successful in this role:

- We will explore the **challenges of the managerial role**. Managers need to work with complex organisms (human beings) that are acting within other complex organisms (organizations), which are embedded in yet more complex organisms (markets and industry ecosystems) (*Section 1.1*).
- Being a manager first and foremost means **being responsible**. We will examine the different facets of managerial responsibility, in the short and long term, and in relation to both economic results and the impact of managerial decisions and actions on society (*Section 1.2*).
- Looking more closely at **what managers actually do** will reveal a fast-paced role centered on personal interaction and information exchange. We will therefore consider the multitude of role expectations which managers need to balance (*Section 1.3*).
- How do managers succeed in such a challenging role? How can they **be effective** in their endeavors? We will highlight the importance of having a clear awareness of what is important and what is not, and the need to understand the key factors that affect a manager's and an organization's performance (*Section 1.4*).

Managers, as we will see in this chapter, often work under great pressure, and are frequently caught in a maelstrom of day-to-day activities. It is precisely under such conditions that taking a step back and reflecting on *what* you are doing and especially *why* you are doing it can prove highly beneficial. Taking a closer look at the nature and purpose of the managerial role will help us understand how managers can become more effective.

1.1 The challenges of a managerial role

Getty Images/Aurora Open/Jared Alden 2009

In brief

- The core of a manager's job is working through others to achieve an organization's goals. These "others," however, are not impassive robots but people with their own ideas, interests, and emotions. Managers therefore need to address the whole person when they want others to perform.

- Additionally, managers need to recognize that an organization is also a "whole"—a complex system of interdependent structures, processes, routines, and relationships. Interventions in one part of the system can lead to multiple repercussions in other parts.

- Organizations are open systems that are exposed to changes in the surrounding environment. Effective managers therefore need to understand all three factors that impact their role—people, the organization, and the environment—as well as the interrelations between them.

"One thing is crystal clear: management is hard and is getting harder,"[2] wrote Harvard Business School Professor Linda Hill and her co-author Kent Lineback in their book *Being the Boss*. Being a manager is definitely a challenging job. Managers carry **overall responsibility for the performance and development of an organization or part of an organization**.[3] Because an organization is a group of people who together try to achieve collective goals in a structured way, managers need to rely on others to fulfill their own responsibility.

In doing so, managers have to deal with **three levels of complexity**:

1   Managers work with a variety of **people** who all bring their own thoughts, feelings, and often conflicting interests to work. People do not just follow managerial directives—they autonomously decide what to do and what not to do.

2   Managers need to create and develop **organizations**, which are complex webs of relationships, structures, systems, routines, and cultures. A change to any element in this interrelated system will have repercussions elsewhere in the system. Simple, isolated cause–effect relations rarely exist.

3   Managers must align their organizations to the wider world around them. They need to take care of customers' needs, react to competitors' moves, and adapt to significant changes in the nearer (micro) and wider (macro) **environments**.

Environment:
The sum of the external factors and forces that can influence the performance and development of an organization.

We will take a closer look at these different levels of complexity, which are also summarized in Figure 1.1.

Managerial challenge 1: Performing through others

Managers cannot do everything on their own—they **perform through others**. In other words, they need to persuade people to perform activities and accomplish tasks that contribute to implementing their agenda.

Managers must acknowledge, however, that people are not abstract resources that can be deployed, but are also human beings. As such, there are limits to their rationality, capability, and capacity to work. They bring their own interests, passions, and feelings to the workplace. They aspire, hope, and dream, but also carry fears, anxieties, jealousies, and frustrations. Their lives consist of more than just work, and their focus may not always be on their job. This is part of the managerial challenge: getting others to do something that is often not

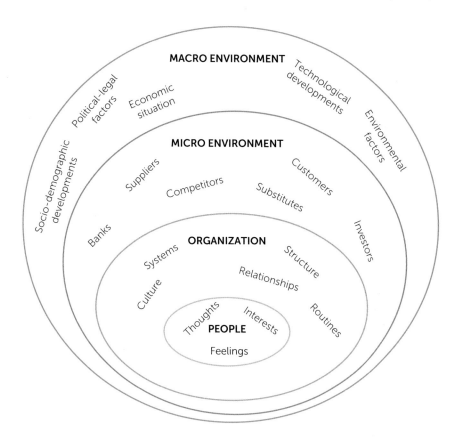

Figure 1.1 Levels of complexity that must be addressed by a manager

Influence:
Having an effect on the opinion, beliefs, or behavior of other people.

their natural first priority. Managers therefore need to learn how to **influence people** and give them reasons to follow the organization's interests rather than solely their own. This applies to team members over whom a manager has formal authority (not to be mistaken with real influence—see Chapter 8) as well as to other people within and outside the organization. As Hill and Lineback noted, managers try to exert influence "mostly by asking, requesting, kidding, cajoling, nudging, persuading, and coercing—almost anything but issuing direct orders, which they do rarely."[4]

People are **rational, emotional, and political beings**. They need clear, logical arguments for why they should do something—a task that is easier to state in principle than to deliver in reality, as miscommunication abounds in human interaction. In many cases, however, rational arguments—even if they are well understood—are not enough to convince a person, because, as philosopher Blaise Pascal wrote in his 17th-century work *The Art of Persuasion*, "it is necessary to have regard to the person whom we wish to persuade, of whom we must know the mind and the heart, what principles he acknowledges, what things he loves."[5] In other words, managers need to take people's thoughts, feelings, and interests into account in order to influence or change their attitudes and behaviors. However, we also need to go one step further. As recent research from the field of social neuroscience suggests, it is important to achieve a certain degree of synchronization—for example, in the thinking patterns, behaviors, or the language that we use—in order to be able to influence others.[6] Put simply, managers should try to understand how the world looks and feels to others and then get "in tune" with them.

Conflict:
A serious disagreement based on diverging interests, different points of view, or other incompatibilities.

In organizational settings, quite naturally, people's individual or group perspectives and interests can collide—sometimes with those of the organization (e.g. in salary negotiations) and sometimes between themselves (e.g. when several departments compete for limited resources). **Reconciling these different interests** and **managing conflict** is therefore another key issue that managers have to deal with in their day-to-day work (see Chapter 4).

Managerial challenge 2: The complexity of organizations

The decisions and actions of individuals or groups affect each other, and can have multiple repercussions throughout the organization. From their interactions, new structures, systems, relationships, routines, or ideas emerge, creating a "whole" which is more than its individual parts, while being in constant flux and development. This has an important effect on the nature of a manager's work, as former Wharton Professor Russell Ackoff noted: "Managers are not confronted with problems that are independent of each other, but with dynamic situations that consist of complex systems of changing problems that interact with each other. I call such situations messes … Managers do not solve problems; they manage messes."[7]

Fortunately, there is a way to deal with these messes (otherwise no functioning organizations would exist). It is true that complexity can complicate managerial work, as any decision or action can lead to **multiple consequences**, some of which are unintended. On the other hand, complexity can also be deliberately used by managers. They can combine **multiple, mutually reinforcing actions** at different points in the organizational system: these combined actions can get them closer to achieving their goals. This interaction of consequences and actions could be described by the term **"double multiplicity" of management** (see Figure 1.2).

"Double multiplicity" of management:
The phenomenon that in organizations that are complex open systems with many interrelated elements, one decision can lead to multiple consequences and multiple actions are often needed to reach one goal.

Multiple consequences   **Multiple actions**

One decision   **One goal**

Figure 1.2 The "double multiplicity" of management

Let us assume, for example, that a manager aims to increase the revenues of a low-performing department. Thinking in a purely reductionist cause-and-effect way, the manager might undertake one intervention, such as introducing a new reward system for the sales team. It is possible that this action will have a positive effect if the former reward system was not very motivating. Acknowledging the complexity of **cause and effect webs** within an organization, however, the manager might instead initiate multiple changes, attacking the problem concurrently at different levels. Changing the structure of the sales team, providing training, creating new offers for customers, incentivizing referrals from satisfied consumers, adopting tighter day-to-day sales management, rethinking the pricing structure, or planning a new marketing strategy are further actions that could be used to complement the introduction of the new reward system. Combining several initiatives that are all geared toward reaching a common goal can have a cumulative effect, and eventually start a virtuous cycle. Sadly, the same is also true for multiple actions that together lead in a negative direction. In this case, their interconnectedness and interdependence could trigger a vicious cycle.

Cause and effect web:
Multiple causal relations (and interrelations) between different factors and elements in a complex system.

The important point here is to see an organization as a complex and **dynamic system** with many interrelations, rather than as a simple structure that "implements" whatever a manager wants. Thus, it is the manager's job to choose the right **coordinated interventions** to steer the system in the right direction.

Managerial challenge 3: The changing external environment

Organizations are not closed, self-contained entities, but rather **complex open systems**. They are characterized by connectedness, interdependence, emergence, and **co-evolution with their environment**.[8] The very reason for their existence lies outside organizational boundaries. An organization can only survive when customers recognize that the organization's product or service creates value for them—and their way of showing that is usually their willingness to pay. The means of producing value for customers are also obtained externally, whether in the form of materials and services from suppliers or capital from banks and investors. Finally, a whole range of opportunities (e.g. new, untapped market segments) and threats (e.g. unexpected moves by competitors) also exist in the wider environment.

The sheer number of actors and factors within the environment, whose interrelations are rarely fully understood, adds to the complexity of the managerial role. Moreover, the **environment is constantly changing**. The business cycle oscillates between boom and recession, new technologies are rendering current working practices obsolete (see the discussion on digital strategies in Chapter 7), legal and institutional changes are altering the ways of doing business, societal trends are affecting customer attitudes and habits, and competitors are relentlessly developing new strategies to win more market share. Social acceleration—fueled by technological innovation, frequent social changes, and a quicker "pace of life"—is a constituting element of modern societies, and has a profound impact on organizations, too.[9]

To ensure long-term survival under such constantly changing environmental conditions, organizations must **adapt**.[10] A crucial part of the manager's job is to recognize and interpret relevant external developments, and to set the right interventions to align their organization with its environment. Take the case of Yell, the company behind the Yellow Pages telephone directory in the UK. After more than 50 successful years on the market, it decided to stop printing its directory from January 2019.[11] The environment has changed considerably for Yell. People have started to look for service providers online, and there were increasing concerns about the negative environmental impact of the millions of printed directory copies, including a nationwide *Say No to Phonebooks* campaign. Yell's management understood the sign of the times and adapted the company to the changing conditions. They decided to open a range of new income-generating digital services to make up for the lost revenue, turning the company's main website into the UK's leading online business directory.

Those who fail to respond to new environmental challenges in a timely manner, however, risk being dragged into a downward spiral with a predictable and highly undesirable outcome: bankruptcy.[12]

Seeing the whole picture

These managerial challenges—people with different emotions and interests, complex organizational systems, and a constantly evolving environment—all pose potential problems for a manager. The ultimate challenge, however, is to **make sense** of all the signals and pieces of information that a manager receives from individuals, the organization, and the environment, in order to create a coherent picture of how individual phenomena are interrelated. Seeing the whole picture—or "making something sensible,"[13] as the American organizational theorist Karl Weick put it—is a necessary precondition for effective managerial decision making—for figuring out what needs to be done and how it should be done. Mary Parker Follett, a pioneer in studying organizational behavior, explained this challenge in the following way: "Of the greatest importance is the ability to grasp a total situation ... This includes facts, present and potential, aims and purposes and men [sic!]. Out of a welter of facts, experience, desires, aims, the leader must find a unifying thread ... not a mere kaleidoscope of pieces."[14]

Making sense of and seeing "the evolving, the developing situation,"[15] as Parker Follett called it, requires **reduction**. It is about filtering out the essence of a situation, identifying the most important elements, and building theories about their interconnections. In even the most complex problems, we can often find some conceptual, structural simplicity.

Helicopter view:
The ability to see a problem in its overall context, while still being able to attend to details if necessary.

Trade-off:
In a trade-off situation, we need to give up something that we value in order to get something else that we value.

Identifying the underlying principles and being able to see the wood for the trees requires managers to take a "**helicopter view**." This term was introduced in the 1960s in the Royal Dutch/Shell Corporation to describe the ability to see a problem within its overall context, while still being able to attend to details if necessary.[16]

When taking a helicopter view, managers will recognize that there are **trade-offs** involved in many situations (see Chapter 6). Often, there are no absolutely correct answers to managerial problems. This also means that it is almost impossible for managers to please everyone. Decisions that are good for the organization as a whole are not necessarily good for all people affected by them. When a company needs to be restructured to ensure survival, layoffs are often unavoidable (see Chapter 3). Managers, therefore, "must sometimes do harm in order to do a greater good."[17] This notion is not easy to digest, but it is part of the managerial reality.

Imagine that you are the manager of a business hotel in the capital city of your country. What factors are likely to have the greatest influence on the performance of your hotel? Consider people (your team), the organization, and the micro and macro environments. How would you ensure that you would always be able to "see the whole picture" and remain aware of the current state and development of all these factors?

1.2   What managers are responsible for

iStock.com/gustavofrazao

In brief

- Managers are not only responsible for the performance of an organization or organizational unit, but also for building the potential for future performance.
- In fulfilling an important social function, managers need to be aware of the immediate and long-term impacts of their actions on different stakeholder groups.
- Responsible managers balance exploration—the search for new opportunities, renewal, and innovation—with exploiting their organization's existing resources and competencies.
- Responsible managers recognize that their role also involves an ethical responsibility to society and the environment.

Management, first and foremost, means **being responsible for an organization or organizational unit**. The word "responsible" has its roots in the Latin *respondere*, meaning "to answer." Managers are accountable for what they do. They need to provide answers—to their superiors and to the owners (or shareholders) of the organization, but also to other stakeholders and, not least, to themselves—about whether they are making the right decisions and carrying out the right actions for the organization or organizational unit for which they are responsible.[18]

Governance structures:
Systems and processes by which organizations are directed and controlled in a way that ensures accountability.

Outward responsibility, or accountability toward others, is often enforced through **governance structures**. Frequently, managers do not own what they are responsible for. They are entrusted with resources by investors (and creditors) and have the responsibility to use these resources in an effective and efficient way to accomplish the organization's purpose. This is a key issue in **agency theory**, an approach from economic theory that explains how to best organize the relationship between one person or entity (the "agent")

Agency theory:
An approach from economic theory that explains how to best organize the relationship between one person or entity (the "agent") who makes decisions and does work on behalf of another person or entity (the "principal").

Agency dilemma:
In agency theory, the agency dilemma (also known as the "principal-agent problem") describes a situation in which the "agent" (who makes decisions and works on behalf of the "principal") is motivated to follow their own best interest which might come into conflict with the principal's best interest.

Stewardship theory:
A theory that suggests that managers are intrinsically motivated to act in the best interest of the entity for which they are responsible.

who makes decisions and does work on behalf of another person or entity (the "principal").[19] The main challenge in agency theory is the **agency dilemma**: an agent (the manager) is hired by a principal (the owner) to pursue the principal's interests. Agents, however, also follow their own interests, while principals have incomplete information about what agents are really doing. It can be costly or sometimes even impossible for a principal to constantly oversee an agent's behavior. Principals therefore try to use contracts, incentive structures, reporting systems, or other governance structures (such as the board of directors in the US or supervisory boards in many European countries) to make sure that managers (as agents) act in a responsible way.

In addition to this extrinsic dimension, responsibility also has an intrinsic dimension. Managers can see themselves as **stewards**, as "servants" of their organization and its purpose. **Stewardship theory** suggests that managers are not necessarily always maximizing their own self-interest. They can also be intrinsically motivated to act in the best interests of their organization and its stakeholders, based on their need for personal growth, achievement, and self-actualization.[20]

Regardless of whether managerial responsibility is extrinsically or intrinsically motivated, it can manifest itself in different forms, which are described in more detail below.

Categories of managerial responsibility

Managers can see their responsibility as a purely economic one. The American economist Milton Friedman argued that a business's sole responsibility is making and increasing profits ("within the rules of the game," as he called it)—because the main benefits of profitable businesses should be the creation of wealth for their shareholders and the provision of employment opportunities.[21] If the shareholders then decide to distribute the wealth that the company has created for them, for example through donating to social causes, *they* should do so, rather than the company or its managers. Supporters of this view often put forward the argument that businesses are not properly equipped to tackle social problems, and that **corporate social responsibility (CSR)** initiatives can dilute a company's primary purpose.[22] Thus, from a **Friedmanite perspective**, managerial effectiveness can only be measured in terms of economic success (under the condition of staying within the boundaries of the law).

If you were a director of a publicly listed corporation, would you agree to release toxic substances that are potentially harmful for people's health into the environment if this were legal and would considerably increase your corporation's profits? Why or why not?

Corporate social responsibility (CSR):
A management concept that orients businesses toward making positive impacts on society and the natural environment.

Shareholder value:
The total monetary value that shareholders (also called "stockholders") obtain from their investment in a company (including dividend payments, gains from share price increases, or any other payouts).

When directors of US Fortune 200 corporations were confronted with the question in the *What would you do?* box, more than 85 percent said that they would vote for releasing the toxic substances into the environment if this action was legal and improved their corporation's profitability, mainly because they saw it as their legal duty to always act in the best interests of their shareholders.[23] Lynn Stout, a professor at Cornell Law School, disagrees with this perspective. She calls the view that directors and executives of public companies are shareholders' agents a "misleading claim." Shareholders do not "own" the company, just shares, which give them limited legal rights.[24] Therefore, she continues, "shareholders stand on equal footing with the corporation's bondholders, suppliers, and employees, all of whom also enter contracts with the firm that give them limited legal rights."[25]

Many others agree that business should not only be about maximizing **shareholder value**. For example, for former Stanford Professor James March, "[s]uch a monolithic conception is demeaning to business, to the society that sustains business, and to the human spirit. It inhibits an awareness of a manager's responsibility for the esthetics of life."[26] As society is providing the institutional framework that enables companies to conduct their

Social contract perspective:
The idea that there is an implicit "contract" in which both society and businesses have certain obligations toward each other (e.g. society providing businesses with a functioning legal system, the right to own resources, infrastructure, an educated workforce, and businesses providing jobs, taking care of workers' interests, or doing no harm to the environment).

Stakeholders:
All the parties that have an interest in an organization or are affected by the actions of an organization.

business (for example, transport infrastructure, a functioning judicial system, or an education system that provides a qualified workforce), it is also legitimate to demand that companies and their managers give something back to society. Under the **social contract perspective**, businesses, in addition to their economic responsibilities, also have **ethical responsibilities** (acting in line with societal expectations and ethical norms) as well as wider **social responsibilities** (contributing to the well-being of the community and of society).[27] Following this view, socially responsible businesses have a moral obligation to be "good corporate citizens," but they can also reap additional benefits through responsible behavior:[28]

a They contribute to the creation of a healthy social climate in which a company can sustain its business in the long term.
b They help to avoid potentially detrimental legislation.
c Their responsible behavior can have a positive effect on the company's image and therefore also on its potential to attract customers and employees.

In most cases, it is less costly to avoid social problems in the first place than to solve them.[29] In an age of **deregulation** (the reduction of government influence on certain industries in order to create a higher degree of competition) and **privatization** (the transfer of ownership of organizations from the public sector to the private sector)—as the state carries fewer and fewer responsibilities—it is becoming all the more relevant that businesses engage in CSR activities. The societal responsibility of managers is manifested in taking care of the interests of all parties affected by the organization—also known under the term **stakeholders** (see Figure 1.3).

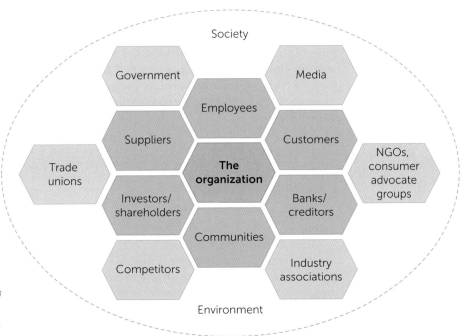

Figure 1.3 Stakeholder groups
(Primary stakeholders in green, secondary stakeholders in blue).

Source: Adapted with permission from Figure 1.1, p. 7 in Freeman, R. E., Harrison, J. S. and Wicks, A. C. (2007) *Managing for Stakeholders: Survival, Reputation, and Success* (New Haven, CT: Yale University Press).

Primary stakeholders:
Stakeholder groups that are in frequent direct contact with an organization and that are crucial for its continuing existence (e.g. customers, suppliers, employees, or shareholders).

Primary stakeholders are those groups with which businesses are in frequent contact, and without whose continuing support they would cease to exist. They usually include *shareholders* and other types of *investors* (who expect a return on their investment), *employees* (who demand a safe working environment, adequate pay, consideration of work–life balance, and good social relations at work), *customers* (who value ethical and harm-free products, quality, and good service), *suppliers* (who want to be treated in a fair and trustful way), *banks* and other *creditors* (who want their money back, usually including interest), and the *communities* in which an organization is operating (who are interested in the support of local initiatives, care for the local environment, and the creation and protection of jobs, for example).[30]

Secondary stakeholder groups are less often in direct contact, but can also either affect or be affected by the actions of the organization.[31] They might include the *government* and *public administration authorities*, the *media* (including Internet platforms), *non-governmental organizations (NGOs)* (e.g. consumer advocacy or environmental protection groups), *industry associations*, *trade unions* and, not least, *competitors*. In a wider sense, *society* at large and the *environment* can also be seen as "stakeholders." Although they are not distinctly identifiable groups of people, they are still affected by an organization's actions.

Secondary stakeholders:
Stakeholder groups who are not very often in direct contact with an organization, but still have an interest in or are affected by its actions.

Zooming in on ▶ STAKEHOLDER MANAGEMENT

Not only do organizations as a whole have stakeholders, but also departments and even individual projects. The next time you are in charge of running a team project (perhaps as part of your studies, for a club or society, or at work) work through the following steps to analyze and manage the most important stakeholder groups for that project:

1 *Identify all stakeholders*: Which people or groups are affected by the project? Who do you depend on to achieve the project's goals?
2 *Identify key stakeholders*: Out of all the stakeholders, which people are most affected by the project or most relevant for achieving the project's goals? Which people or groups have the highest potential influence on the success of the project?
3 *Analyze stakeholder needs*: What are the needs and interests of the individual stakeholder groups regarding the project?
4 *Manage stakeholder expectations*: Get in touch with key stakeholders and try to align their expectations with what can realistically be delivered.
5 *Keep key stakeholders informed*: Which information needs to be shared with stakeholders? When and how should they receive the information?
6 *Include key stakeholders in decision processes*: Are there decisions in which key stakeholders need to be included? How will they be involved in these decisions?
7 *Stakeholder review*: Has the situation changed over the course of the project? Do you need to consider new stakeholders or changing stakeholder interests?

Both economic and societal managerial responsibility can be either short-term or long-term oriented, resulting in the four categories of the **managerial responsibility grid** (see Figure 1.4).[32]

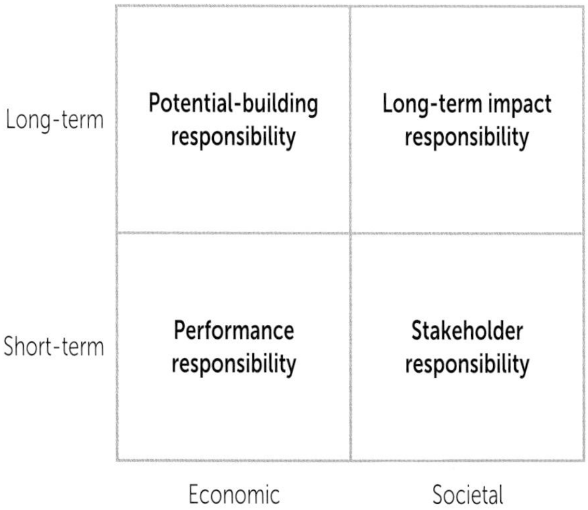

	Economic	Societal
Long-term	Potential-building responsibility	Long-term impact responsibility
Short-term	Performance responsibility	Stakeholder responsibility

Figure 1.4 The managerial responsibility grid

Source: Adapted from Figure 1, p. 96 in Sternad, D. (2013) 'Managerial long-term responsibility in family-controlled firms', *Management*, 8(2): 93–107.

FROM A DIFFERENT ANGLE

Learning about long-term responsibility from family firms

On average, companies die sooner than human beings. Even Fortune 500 corporations have an average life expectancy of no more than 40 to 50 years.[33] There are some businesses, however, that have been in existence for hundreds of years, and are still thriving. The majority of these long-lived companies are family owned.

So what makes family businesses more resilient and able to survive in the long term? Family executives usually care about more than just immediate business results. They have a natural concern for future generations, identify strongly with the firm, have the desire to leave a legacy, and know whose money they are working with—their own.[34] Consequently, they often act more conservatively (i.e. they try to avoid unnecessary risks), strive to keep their businesses independent, and take special care to build and nourish good long-term relationships with their employees, customers, and the wider community. In short, they take their long-term responsibility seriously, thus laying the foundations for the sustainable success of their companies.

Source: Sternad, D. (2013) 'Managerial long-term responsibility in family-controlled firms', Management, 8(2): 93–107.

In the short term, managers have a responsibility to achieve a certain level of economic performance, which can be measured, for example, in terms of profit, revenue growth, market share, or other financial or non-financial indicators that determine the extent to which an organizational unit serves its economic purpose (**performance responsibility**). Narrowly focusing on the short term, however, can harm the future prospects of the organization. Therefore, managers also need to take a long-term perspective, which includes a responsibility for building potential and ensuring sustainable performance, ideally beyond their own tenure (**potential-building responsibility**). The focus of the potential-building responsibility is on creating value that lasts, on ensuring that today's actions (e.g. building a team with the right skills, research and development, or investing in new machinery) also lay the ground for tomorrow's economic success.

In a similar way, when fulfilling their societal responsibility, managers can think and act either in the short term, taking the immediate effects of their decisions on the different stakeholder groups into account (**stakeholder responsibility**), or in the long term, keeping potential societal and environmental impacts and consequences in mind (**long-term impact responsibility**) (see *Learning about long-term responsibility from family firms*). Responsible managers think about all four quadrants in Figure 1.4 when they make decisions for their organizations and consider the potential short- and long-term economic and societal effects of their actions on others, both within and outside the organization.

Balancing performance and potential

Tomorrow's results are based on today's actions. One of the basic principles of business is that **building performance potential** is a precondition for performance. In the words of the ancient Greek philosopher, Aristotle, "of all the things that come to us by nature we first acquire the potentiality and later exhibit the activity."[35]

Human beings, however, are often inclined to focus on short-term results. In the 1970s, Stanford psychologist Walter Mischel conducted his famous **marshmallow experiment** on delayed gratification (the ability to resist the impulse of getting something right away in exchange for obtaining something of more value in the future).[36] In Mischel's experiment, children aged between four and six were offered one marshmallow or pretzel (dependent on their taste). They were promised that they would get two marshmallows or pretzels instead of one if they refrained from eating the first one within a certain timespan. Only one-third of the test group of children were able to defer gratification and resist the temptation to eat the first sweet. Years later, follow-up studies were conducted with some of the participants of the original test group. Interestingly, those children who had been able to delay gratification in their pre-school years were, on average, performing significantly better in terms of their cognitive and academic competencies, and their frustration and stress tolerance, when they became young adults.[37] The findings from these psychological studies have two implications in a managerial context. First, we need to be aware that human beings (including managers) show a **tendency toward preferring short-term gains**. Second, that those who are able to refrain from short-term temptation and make investments can potentially reap more profits and achieve superior performance in the future. Whether managers are more short-term or long-term oriented does not only depend on individual temporal predispositions, however. The temporal orientation of managers can also be influenced by institutional factors (e.g. the level of pressure from capital markets or the bonus system for managers) as well as by cultural factors (e.g. the degree of long-term orientation in the national and organizational cultures).[38]

Managers have responsibility not only for the current performance of an organization, but also to ensure **sustainable performance**. **Sustainability** has been defined on a global scale as fulfilling "the needs of the present without compromising the ability of future generations to meet their needs."[39] In a business context, this means investing enough today—into people, technology, products, relationships, or market development—to be able to perform well in the future. Most corporations, however, still reward their managers solely on the basis of their short-term performance, much to the dismay of Henry Mintzberg, who is convinced that "[e]xecutive impact has to be assessed in the long run, and we don't know how to measure performance in the long run, at least as attributable to specific managers. So executive bonuses should be eliminated. Period."[40]

The long-term survival of a company, according to Levinthal and March, is contingent on the ability to "engage in enough exploitation to ensure the organization's current viability and engage in enough exploration to ensure its future viability."[41] The ability to balance **exploration**—searching for new opportunities, investing, taking risks, or innovating—and **exploitation**, getting the most out of what already exists or what an organization already possesses, is also called **ambidexterity**.[42] An example of a manager who emphasizes both exploration and exploitation is provided in the *CEO best practice* box, *There are many ways to climb Mt. Fuji.*

Ethical responsibility

Anyone who assumes a responsible role within society—and managers are definitely in such a role—also has an ethical responsibility to develop an understanding of what is morally right or wrong, and when in doubt to opt for the former when making decisions. A range of corporate scandals triggered by unethical managerial behavior, which have had disastrous consequences for the organizations involved, highlight the necessity for managers to live up to moral standards. Just look at the Volkswagen emissions scandal as one salient example. In 2015 the German carmaker was accused of using emission control software for diesel engines only during testing, thus intentionally misrepresenting the real level of pollution emitted by its diesel vehicles. This led not only to severe damage to the company's reputation but also to criminal charges and an avalanche of claims for compensation. The scandal cost the company billions of euros and the CEO his job.

In order to develop **ethical intelligence**, a manager needs adequate skills in:

a   **Moral awareness** (recognizing and distinguishing your own and others' values, norms, and interests);
b   **Moral reflection** (taking the interests of others into consideration); and
c   **Moral imagination** (understanding a context from different perspectives and imagining the effect of your decisions and actions on others).[48]

Sustainability:
The ability to meet current needs while at the same time retaining the capacity for meeting future needs.

Exploration:
Organizational activities that are oriented toward ensuring the future viability of an organization (e.g. through exploring new opportunities, building new competencies, learning, or innovating).

Exploitation:
Organizational activities that are oriented toward efficiently exploiting existing competencies.

Ambidexterity:
An organization's ability to balance exploration (preparing for future opportunities and challenges) and exploitation (efficiently managing its current activities).

Ethical intelligence:
The intellectual ability to make decisions based on principles of morality.

CEO BEST PRACTICE

"There are many ways to climb Mt. Fuji"

Fujio Mitarai, the long-time president of Japanese camera and electronic equipment manufacturer Canon, has been steering his ship well during his tenure. The nephew of one of Canon's original founders, Mitarai propelled the firm to become an innovator and global market leader in digital photography, and developed Canon into one of Japan's most profitable manufacturers. Although he was trained in the US and is very much efficiency-, profit- and cash-flow-oriented in his thinking, he also adheres to the Japanese definition of managerial responsibility, which places a high emphasis on providing lifetime employment to workers. In Mitarai's words: "In exchange for providing job security, companies gain the loyalty of their staff."[43] When he needed to close an unprofitable division, Fujio Mitarai tried to move its staff to a profitable one. When asked in an interview what he would say to analysts who criticized his no-layoff policy, Mitarai responded: "Companies should be judged on the basis of their value."[44] He pointed out that Canon has a different approach to increasing corporate value than the typical short term-oriented US business system: "There are many ways to climb Mt. Fuji ... You have to go with what works in the society where you are based."[45]

In addition to taking care of employees, Canon has invested heavily in the company's future under Mitarai's leadership, spending significantly more on research and development than its rivals. In the decade between 1995 and 2005, Canon filed over 17,000 US patents—more than any other company except IBM. In 2018, when he was already over 80 years old, Mitarai continued to fully focus Canon on the challenges of the future: "For Canon, it is a life-or-death issue," he said. "We must keep innovating if we want to grow."[46]

Responsibility for the long-term sustainability of his company lies at the core of Mitarai's thinking. In his own words: "We have to plant the seeds for the next decade and beyond."[47]

→ Key takeaway

Effective managers consider the long-term sustainability of their organizations. Retaining a loyal workforce and investments in research and development play a key role in this context.

Sources: Based on information in Business Week (2002); ForbesCustom (2018); Rowley et al. (2005).

Even with the best skills in moral reasoning, it is often very hard to determine what is "right" or "wrong", especially when a decision is beneficial to one stakeholder group and harms another. There is one ethical maxim, however, which has almost universal value, even in the most diverse cultures around the world. It is known as the **"Golden Rule"**: *Treat others as you would like to be treated yourself.*

The Golden Rule has been formulated in different ways in many different religious and philosophical traditions (examples are known from Islam, Judaism, Christianity, Hinduism, Buddhism, and classic Greek philosophy, amongst others).[49] It has been formulated in both a positive way, as in the famous version from the New Testament ("Do to others as you would have them do to you" [Luke 6:31]) and as a prohibition, as in the words of Confucius: "What I don't want others to do to me, I want to avoid doing to others."[50] The Golden Rule has also received criticism, for example that we cannot assume that everyone has the same desires and preferences.[51] However, applying the Golden Rule in combination with moral awareness, moral reflection, and moral imagination—thinking from the perspective of those who are affected by our decisions and considering how we would like to be treated in their position—can be a powerful approach to acting and managing in a responsible way.[52]

Further approaches to ethical reasoning, and in particular dealing with cross-cultural contexts, are discussed in Chapter 5.

Performance with purpose: Indra K. Nooyi at PepsiCo

ndra K. Nooyi grew up in the Indian city of Madras (now Chennai). In a dinner table ritual initiated by her mother, she and her older sister had to make speeches about what they would do if they were powerful politicians. "So she gave us confidence to be whatever we wanted to be,"[53] said Nooyi, whose career steps had included positions at a global consulting firm and other multinational corporations, before joining PepsiCo in 1994. Nooyi was PepsiCo's first female CEO, leading one of the world's largest food and beverages companies from 2006 to 2018. In an interview with *Fast Company,* she noted that her previous years as a consultant had been very useful for her senior management role. They taught her "how to think of the problem in micro terms but also to zoom out and put the problem in the context of its broader environment and then zoom back in to solve the problem."[54]

Nooyi needed to put this lesson into practice when she was faced with changing environmental conditions after her first few years as CEO. PepsiCo was facing regulatory pressures in different countries, as well as consumers who were becoming increasingly health conscious. The core market in North America had slowed down, competition was fierce, and as a publicly listed company, PepsiCo continuously faced high growth and short-term profitability demands from investors. Nooyi refrained from relying on simple short-term cost cutting alone, acknowledging that this "wouldn't have yielded long-term success."[55] Instead, she tried to strike a balance between initiatives that reap benefits in the short term and those with a long-term impact. In addition to "slimming down" the company, she focused on building new capabilities (for example, in fields like design or the biology and chemistry of taste), investment in marketing, and transforming the product portfolio to include healthier ("good for you") products, as well as reducing ingredients such as salt, sugar, and fat in the core, "fun for you" product line.

Nooyi summarized this new direction with the slogan "performance with purpose." This signaled that the company needed to focus on having a positive impact on both society and the environment in order to ensure its sustainable business performance. Building a healthier product portfolio was the primary pillar of PepsiCo's new

strategy, reducing the company's environmental footprint was the second, and creating a positive and inclusive work environment for employees was the third. Nooyi did not see responsible behavior as an add-on that you do "after hours," but as a fundamental basis for business success. For example, she pointed out that, when plastic costs go up, fuel costs are volatile, and recycling and water-use rules become stricter, environmental performance is closely linked to financial performance.

Nooyi believes that the market environment is becoming more dynamic and that cycles are getting shorter. "The rule used to be that you'd reinvent yourself every seven to 10 years. Now it's every two to three years," she commented in an interview with *Harvard Business Review.* "There's constant reinvention: how you do business, how you deal with the customer."[56] This means that as CEO, Nooyi constantly needs to stay up to date. She sees herself as a lifelong student and a "voracious reader," saying that she has "a couple of bags of mail"[57] that she spends three hours reading every evening, first prioritizing the information which is worth reading in detail and that which just needs to be skimmed through. Overall, she considered being a CEO as a 24-7 job as there are always issues to resolve in a globally active corporation.

In an interesting dialogue with jazz legend Wynton Marsalis, Nooyi said that organizations reminded her less of symphony orchestras than of improvisational jazz groups in which "players take their cues from each other" and where there "is freedom to give and take, to be creative and spontaneous."[58] This does not mean, however, that everyone should play solos all of the time. She is convinced that it is necessary for people in organizations to "operate within a framework," but that within that framework, "people also need the creative freedom to give their best."[59] As a leader, she sees her role as looking at the business with a long-term perspective, "connecting the dots, and trying to make out pictures and shapes where other people see only point estimates, ... convincing the organization of the need to change direction, ... [and] to constantly communicate how the change is going to make things better."[60]

Sources: Burnison (2011); Feloni (2015); Friedersdorf (2014); Ignatius (2015); Marsalis and Nooyi (2014); Safian (2014); Snyder (2016).

💬 Discussion questions

- What are Indra Nooyi's main challenges as the CEO of a large corporation?
- What are a senior manager's main tasks in a dynamic environment that demands, as Nooyi notes, "constant reinvention" of organizations?
- How would you characterize Nooyi's general attitude toward her responsibility as manager?
- How did Nooyi deal with the conflicting demands between short-term needs and building the potential for sustainable long-term performance?

1.3   What managers really do

iStock.com/maselko099

In brief

- When taking a closer look at the habits of practicing managers, we can see that many of them spend a lot of time communicating with others inside and outside the organization. They are constantly receiving and disseminating (often informal) information and are strongly driven by events as they occur. When problems arise, managers frequently need to act as troubleshooters.

- Delving further, we will find out that the fluid and fragmented nature of managerial work is a function of the multiple role expectations that managers need to meet.

- Setting clear priorities (deciding what to do and what not to do) and turning obligations into opportunities are two strategies that managers can use to effectively perform in their multiple roles.

In 1916, an Istanbul-born French mining engineer, Henri Fayol, published *Administration industrielle et générale*, in which he proposed that a manager fulfills five main functions: planning (or forecasting), organizing, commanding, coordinating, and controlling.[61] Fayol's ideas have proven to be enduring. More than a century later, there is still a widespread belief that this is what managers do in their day-to-day work, despite overwhelming counterevidence. From the 1950s on, researchers have studied how managers spend their time and what their job really entails.[62] A seminal work in this field was Henry Mintzberg's *The Nature of Managerial Work*, published in 1973. It revealed that managers did not spend their days focusing on Fayol's classic managerial functions. In fact, Mintzberg called the image of management as a highly systematic and carefully controlled job "folklore." Instead, as Rosemary Stewart vividly summarized, studies of what managers really do suggest that they live in "a whirl of activity, in which attention must be switched every few minutes from one subject, problem, and person to another." Managers work in an uncertain and dynamic environment, in which useful sources of information can include "gossip and speculation," and where developing "a network of people who can fill one in on what is going on and what is likely to happen" is important.[63] Since managers are dependent on others for getting things done, they must "learn how to trade, bargain, and compromise." Stewart also notes that managers live "in a political world," so they need to "learn how to influence people other than subordinates, how to manœuvre, and how to enlist support for what they want to do."[64]

How can managers achieve results in such a fluid context? H. Edward Wrapp suggested that they need to learn to "muddle with a purpose," setting themselves clear goals and seeing in every new piece of information, in every event, and in every encounter an opportunity to get closer to achieving their goals.[65]

The day-to-day activities of managers

Let us take a closer look at the **typical day-to-day activities of managers**. There are some common denominators that we can identify in their behavior:

- **Managers "work at an unrelenting pace."**[66] They jump from one task to another, are frequently interrupted, and often need to change their focus. Thus, their day can become very fragmented. While checking financial figures, a manager can receive a phone call from an important customer who complains about unacceptable service. When the problem with the customer is resolved, the next meeting is already ten minutes overdue. Meanwhile, five new requests from members of the manager's team have arrived via e-mail. Different studies observed that the average time that a manager spends on one activity lies between eight and 31 minutes.[67] Rarely is any issue explored in real depth.[68] As Mintzberg noted, "[t]o be superficial is an occupational hazard of managerial work."[69]

- **Managers work long hours.** Spending sixty to eighty hours per week on work-related issues is not uncommon for senior managers.[70] Modern communication technology has also enabled managers to be online and reachable 24 hours a day, seven days a week—which has brought more work home and to other places outside the office. In addition, time spent on travelling has considerably increased over recent decades.[71] Managers in global companies, in particular, frequently travel abroad.

- **Managers constantly receive, review, and disseminate information.** These three activities account for approximately 60 percent of managers' total working time, according to a study conducted among Swedish CEOs.[72] A lot of information is informal and "soft" in character, including hearsay, gossip, and speculation, as "today's gossip may be tomorrow's fact."[73] Mintzberg gave the example that finding out that a company's biggest customer is playing golf with its main competitor could have an important influence on the company's future sales.[74]

- **Managers spend most of their time in face-to-face communication with other people.** A considerable share of their working time is devoted to verbal communication because "[m]uch managerial activity consists of asking or persuading others to do things."[75] The most frequent activity is holding meetings, whether scheduled or unscheduled. Meetings often account for more than half of a manager's day (see Chapter 4 for how to manage meetings effectively). In the 1970s, it was observed that managers spent an average of 28 hours per week on meeting other people, while a more recent study counted an average of more than 45 hours for CEOs of companies that were listed on the Stockholm stock exchange.[76] In 2018, Porter and Nohria published the results of a study that revealed that CEOs of large companies took part in an average of 37 meetings per week, together taking up more than 70 percent of their total working time.[77] In many instances, managers also talk about issues that are not directly related to work.[78]

- **Managers have become e-mail slaves.** This is, of course, quite a provocative statement. Modern means of communication such as cell phones, videoconferences, and e-mails have added to managers' flexibility and productivity. On the other hand, there is a substantial amount of evidence that e-mail, in particular, is related to high stress levels because managers often feel overwhelmed by the sheer mass of incoming information and requests.[79] Whether e-mail can really reduce knowledge workers' mental sharpness—even more than marijuana consumption, as claimed in some news media reports[80]—has not yet been scientifically confirmed. E-mail overload, has, however, clearly developed into a severe challenge for many managers in the 21st century.

- **Managers are event-driven rather than intention-driven.** They are often unable to predict what challenges they will face during their working day. Managers therefore need to react opportunistically to new situations, and tend to act immediately as they receive important information.[81] Responding to requests and "troubleshooting" as problems arise is more common than following a clearly structured agenda. Recent research also confirms an overall tendency of managers to adjust to new circumstances with temporary solutions, rather than systematically following clear plans.[82]

- **Managers often experience conflicts.** These come in two categories. On the one hand, managers are frequently confronted with ambiguous information, conflicting pressures, and contradictory goals that need to be reconciled and dealt with. On the other hand, there are also conflicts of interest and personal conflicts between different people or groups of people that managers need to address, either because they are involved as a party in the conflict themselves or because the conflict potentially affects the achievement of their organization's goals (see the section on managing conflicts in Chapter 4). As a consequence of having to deal with so many conflicts, the managerial job is also emotionally intense: "Managers, like everyone else, sometimes make choices influenced by complex and often irrational emotions,"[83] writes Stefan Tengblad, who has conducted extensive research into the nature of managerial work.

Which aspect of the day-to-day work of a manager (as outlined on the previous pages) would you personally see as the most challenging? What would make it challenging for you? What could you do to overcome these difficulties?

Although these characteristics of managerial work have remained quite stable across organizational types, sectors, and cultures over time (with the exception of the increasing influence of information and communication technology in recent years),[84] they are not necessarily universal. It has been observed, for example, that executives in smaller firms spend a lower proportion of their time in formal, scheduled meetings than their counterparts in large organizations.[85] In addition, there are cultural differences. For example, one study revealed that general managers in Japan and South Korea tend to work in a less fragmented way than their American colleagues (more information about cultural differences in management is provided in Chapter 5).[86]

It is also not imperative that managers *must* work in the way that has been outlined. Managers have some degree of **choice of what to do and what not to do**. And even in cases where they do not have a choice because they just need to fulfill important obligations, they can at least **turn obligations into opportunities**.[87] A routine meeting can be a chance to evaluate and develop team members, for example; or an otherwise boring evening event could become an opportunity to extend your network. As Hill and Lineback put it, "effective managers bend each interruption and problem to achieve a managerial end. They find in every activity thrust on them a seed of progress."[88]

Managerial roles

Why is it that managers constantly switch from one task to another? Why do they have such a restless job? Part of the answer lies in the fact that managers need to satisfy many different role expectations. Mintzberg clustered these expectations into three basic categories: **interpersonal**, **informational**, and **decisional roles** (see Figure 1.5).

The manager's roles

INTERPERSONAL ROLES	INFORMATIONAL ROLES	DECISIONAL ROLES
Figurehead	**Monitor**	**Entrepreneur**
Performing ceremonial duties, e.g. receiving important customers	Identifying relevant information from inside and outside of the firm	Actively adapting an organizational unit to changing circumstances
Leader	**Disseminator**	**Disturbance Handler**
Selecting and developing staff and influencing their performance	Passing on important information, particularly to subordinates	Responding to pressures, solving (immediate) problems
Liaison	**Spokesperson**	**Resource Allocator**
Making and maintaining contacts outside the manager's own unit	Informing (and satisfying) stakeholders outside the organization	Deciding who gets which resources (including the manager's time)
		Negotiator
		Trying to achieve the best possible outcome when interests collide

Figure 1.5 Mintzberg's ten managerial roles

Interpersonal roles. The lion's share of a manager's time is used for interaction with other people. Spending over 80 percent of their time interacting with others—mostly in meetings—is not unusual for CEOs.[89] Three out of Mintzberg's ten managerial roles are concerned with relationships:

- fulfilling ceremonial duties as a **figurehead**, representing and personifying the organization at events or welcoming important visitors;
- interacting with team members in the **leader** role to positively influence their performance (see also Chapter 3);
- acting as a **liaison**—a link to the outside—connecting the organization to key stakeholders such as customers, suppliers, competitors, investors, banks, or the government.

Informational roles. Managers act as information hubs in their organizations:

- playing the role of **monitor** and keeping track of the main events and developments that can affect the organization by obtaining the latest facts and gossip through internal and external networks (see Section 1.4);
- acting as a **disseminator** by spreading information in a targeted way; of the plethora of information they receive, managers need to select those pieces that are relevant for other people—in particular the members of their team—in terms of reaching their goals;
- acting as a **spokesperson** when the information is shared with stakeholders outside the company (e.g. a CEO speaking at an official annual shareholder meeting).

Overall, as Mintzberg noted, "the job of managing is significantly one of information processing, especially through a great deal of listening, seeing, and feeling, as well as a good deal of talking."[90] To perform their informational roles, managers need to be well connected, so building an effective network of internal and external information sources is essential (see Section 1.4).

Decisional roles. Information is the crucial input for managerial decisions. Managers must:

- decide who gets which resources (in the **resource allocator** role);
- decide how to handle urgent problems (in the **disturbance handler** role);
- decide what to give and what to demand in negotiations with other parties inside or outside the organization (in the **negotiator** role);
- in their **entrepreneurial role**, constantly advance their organizational units, adapting them to changes in the environment in innovative ways (see Chapter 10, which is fully devoted to the manager's entrepreneurial role).

Different groups of people hold various **expectations** about what a manager should or should not do within these ten managerial roles. These expectations can be conflicting, for example, when employees expect high salaries while shareholders demand higher returns, or when the public expects information that could potentially hurt the business if it was released. The manager's job can therefore also be seen as a constant balancing act, and involves making compromises as well as finding creative solutions to reconcile different interests.

The changing nature of managerial work

Many aspects of the social function that managers fulfill have remained relatively stable over time (see *Has management fundamentally changed over the last century?*). There have been some developments in the last few years and decades, however, that are changing the nature of managerial work.

Digital technologies have had a profound impact on how managers communicate and make decisions. For example, videoconferencing tools and live messaging tools enable managers to lead geographically dispersed teams (see also the section on leading global virtual teams in Chapter 5). Information technology that enables the combination and

Has management fundamentally changed over the last century?

Managers are, among other tasks, required to:

- understand the operations for which they are responsible;
- coordinate and maintain balance between specialized activities (according to their relative importance and urgency);
- delegate tasks and responsibilities to their subordinates;
- induce (and motivate) subordinates to follow the organization's goals;
- inform superiors about the developments in the unit for which they are responsible;
- cooperate with other managers within the organization (and understand their work);
- pool ideas;
- visualize, detect, and develop business opportunities;
- integrate different opinions bearing in mind the overall goals of the organization;
- "give and take" (trying to find mutually acceptable solutions);
- negotiate with customers, suppliers, employees, and investors;
- bargain on an ethical level;
- set up clear and mutually advantageous contracts;
- judge the advantages, disadvantages, and monetary values of goods, services, or rights;
- handle controversies;
- work with customers and competitors to improve industry practices;
- represent the organization in public relations;
- appraise and manage risks (which are inherent in business activities under dynamic conditions);
- divide effort and expenditure wisely between different projects and opportunities (also keeping risks in mind);
- develop their subordinates; and
- engage in long-range (strategic) planning.[91]

Many of today's managers would probably agree that this list quite accurately describes the main elements of their job. It might come as a surprise, though, that it was compiled in 1935 by John W. Riegel, who was, at the time, a professor at the University of Michigan. This indicates that the set of expectations regarding the behavior and obligations of the social function that a manager fulfills have actually remained quite stable over time.

Source: Based on information in Riegel (1935).

analysis of huge amounts of data supports managers in prediction and decision-making tasks (see Chapter 6). There are also claims that artificial intelligence (AI), IT systems, and machines that are able to learn from experience and improve the ability to recognize patterns in data, will relieve managers of most administrative work such as scheduling and controlling tasks, answering routine employee questions, or preparing reports.[92] This means that the manager's job will probably be more oriented toward what management consultants have called "judgment work," including, for example, interpreting data, creating ideas together with others, learning to develop new practices through experimentation, and developing strategies for their organizations.[93] Although we can assume that intelligent systems will not replace managers altogether in the foreseeable future, managers will have to learn how to combine and integrate the data processing and analysis capabilities of these systems with the creative and social skills of human beings.

The emergence of digital information and communication technologies is also a major driver of **globalization**, the expansion of the number and frequency of interactions between people and organizations across national boundaries. As a consequence of globalization, managers need to understand the global contexts in which their organizations operate and develop intercultural skills to effectively work with customers, employees, and partners from all parts of the world. They also need to be able to work with remote teams that include people from very diverse backgrounds (see Chapter 5).

Both digital technologies and globalization are contributing to **social and economic acceleration**.[94] In a constantly changing environment, where companies "are no longer seen as static, but as dynamic, fluctuating entities in constant motion,"[95] the entrepreneurial role of the manager is becoming increasingly critical. Managers need to think innovatively and explore and exploit the opportunities that a dynamic environment presents (see Chapter 10). When organizations are required to flexibly adapt to a fast-changing environment, self-managing teams are often seen as a more suitable approach to organizing work than traditional top-down authoritarian structures with their long decision-making processes.[96] Therefore, as "contemporary managers are shifting from traditional command and control models to more inclusive group-oriented management styles," team-oriented roles (such as being a team builder, team leader, and team player) are becoming more and more important in addition to Mintzberg's traditional roles (see Chapter 4).[97]

1.4 Managerial effectiveness

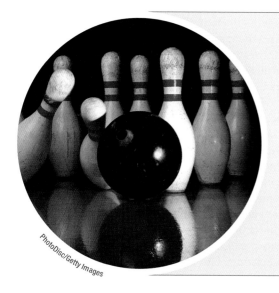

PhotoDisc/Getty Images

In brief

● Effective managers set the right goals and achieve them.

● To become effective, managers need to constantly monitor and make sense of what is going on in and around their organizations; draw the right conclusions; set an agenda with a coherent set of both short-term and long-term goals and initiatives; identify, recruit, and develop the best people; build and maintain a network of supporters; and influence their team members and activate their network to help them realize their agenda.

● A structured monitoring process should enable managers to keep an eye on five important factors that can strongly influence the sustainable performance of their organizations: results, potential building, environmental trends and developments, value creation for customers, and competitors' actions.

Efficiency:
The state of doing something in the most economical way.

Efficacy:
The power or capacity to produce a certain effect.

Effectiveness:
The degree to which desired results or effects are reached.

First-level effectiveness:
The state of achieving a certain goal or desired outcome.

"Organizations as well as executives need to work systematically on effectiveness and need to acquire the habit of effectiveness," wrote Peter Drucker in his widely read book *The Effective Executive*. "They need to work on making strengths productive. They need to concentrate and to set priorities instead of trying to do a little bit of everything."[98] Effectiveness is often confused with efficiency and efficacy, although these are distinct concepts:

– **Efficiency** means doing something in the most economical way (i.e. achieving set goals with a minimum use of resources or yielding the highest possible output from a given resource base).

– **Efficacy** refers to the capacity to produce a certain effect. When psychologists, for example, speak of self-efficacy, they refer to people's beliefs that they are capable of accomplishing something.[99]

– Finally, **effectiveness** is about actually achieving the desired results or effect, or, as Peter Drucker famously said, "getting the right things done."[100]

Thus, **effective managers** are those who get their job done—who set the right goals and achieve them. There are two levels of effectiveness: (a) **first-level effectiveness**, achieving a

Second-level effectiveness:
The ability to set the right goals.

certain goal or desired outcome, and (b) **second-level effectiveness**, which is about setting the right goals in the first place. How do we assess whether managers are effective? We can do that mainly through looking at whether the units for which they are responsible serve their purpose well, whether they achieve the results that are expected from them, and whether they are developing well over time.[101]

What makes managers effective in their work?

How managers spend their time can have an impact on the performance of their organizations.[102] In his seminal study on managerial effectiveness, Fred Luthans found evidence that *successful* managers (whom he defines as those who get promoted quicker than others) tend to set different priorities than those who he calls *effective* managers (whose units show a high performance and whose direct reports voice a high level of satisfaction).[103] He observed that the most successful managers spend considerably more time in networking activities, such as socializing, building and maintaining relationships outside of the organization, and politicking. Effective managers, on the other hand, emphasize information exchange and human resource management activities (e.g. staffing, developing and motivating people, or managing conflict). Relatively few managers in Luthans' study (under 10 percent!) made it into the top one-third in both categories: success in terms of career advancement and effectiveness. For those that did, the patterns of their activities did not fit neatly into either category. Rather, these exceptional managers tried to strike a balance between communicating, networking, human resource management, and the traditional management activities of planning, decision making, and controlling.

The results of Luthans' research raise the question of why it often seems that managers are not promoted on the basis of their effectiveness. They also highlight the importance of taking care of both **the performance and the development of employees** and **building a network** that can support managers in reaching their organizations' goals. These results are supported by a more recent study conducted by Michael Porter and Nitin Nohria of Harvard Business School. They observed that the CEOs of large companies spent an average of 25 percent of their time developing people and relationships, and 30 percent of their time in interactions with outsiders (including, among others, customers, suppliers, investors, consultants, PR firms, representatives of media, the government, and industry associations, but also community relationships and philanthropic activities).[104] Porter and Nohria concluded that "[t]he time CEOs spend building social capital through a network of personal relationships has many benefits and is time well spent."[105]

Agenda setting:
The activity of defining priority issues for the organization.

The key role of networking was also confirmed in another study by John Kotter, who additionally highlights the importance of **agenda setting** for managerial effectiveness. "Effective executives develop agendas that are made up of loosely connected goals and plans that address their long-, medium-, and short-term responsibilities," he writes. "The agendas usually address a broad range of financial, product, market, and organizational issues. They include both vague and specific items."[106] Kotter points out that a managerial agenda does not necessarily need to be formally written down, and is usually developed and adjusted continuously, and often unconsciously, in a largely internal process.[107] Nevertheless, managers can also approach this task in a more systematic way with the help of an **agenda setting tool** (see Figure 1.6). This tool can help managers to structure their main goals in four key areas of managerial responsibility: organizational results (both financial and non-financial – see Chapter 9), organizational development (organizational structures, processes, systems, and culture – Chapter 8), people development (Chapter 3), and personal development (Chapter 2). After defining their long-term goals in these four areas, managers can derive the appropriate short-term goals which are conducive to achieving them. Making both long-term and short-term agenda items explicit can foster the development of a coherent set of goals.

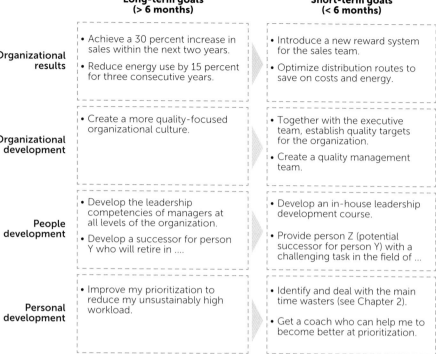

	Long-term goals (> 6 months)	Short-term goals (< 6 months)
Organizational results	• Achieve a 30 percent increase in sales within the next two years. • Reduce energy use by 15 percent for three consecutive years.	• Introduce a new reward system for the sales team. • Optimize distribution routes to save on costs and energy.
Organizational development	• Create a more quality-focused organizational culture.	• Together with the executive team, establish quality targets for the organization. • Create a quality management team.
People development	• Develop the leadership competencies of managers at all levels of the organization. • Develop a successor for person Y who will retire in	• Develop an in-house leadership development course. • Provide person Z (potential successor for person Y) with a challenging task in the field of ...
Personal development	• Improve my prioritization to reduce my unsustainably high workload.	• Identify and deal with the main time wasters (see Chapter 2). • Get a coach who can help me to become better at prioritization.

Figure 1.6 Agenda setting tool (with an example of a managerial agenda)

Having a clear agenda helps managers to **channel their energy** and allows them, as Kotter suggested, "to react in an opportunistic (and highly efficient) way to the flow of events around them, yet knowing that they are doing so within a broader and more relational framework."[108] Thus, the agenda can be used in every meeting or every conversation— including informal ones—as a "focusing tool" to spot opportunities for advancing the manager's goals. Moreover, a manager's agenda can have a strong influence on other people in the organization or organizational unit because "whatever gets in the agenda is taken as a signal of what matters in the unit."[109]

A model of managerial effectiveness

Figure 1.7 presents an **integrated model of managerial effectiveness**. Following John Kotter, managers need to set the **right agenda** (i.e. they need to achieve second-level effectiveness), both in terms of long-term strategy and short-term initiatives. For that purpose, managers need to **monitor and make sense** of the events and developments within and around their organizations. As pointed out earlier in this chapter, it is thereby crucial to see the whole picture and how the individual dots are connected.

The right agenda alone does not make a manager effective and successful, though. The agenda also needs to be implemented with the help of others, who can be either members of the manager's team or other people from the manager's network. Emphasizing both **finding and developing the best people** and **building and maintaining a good network** is in line with Luthans' research results on what makes a manager both successful and effective. Finally, managers need to **influence their team members** and **activate their network** in order to actually realize their agenda.

We will discuss the individual building blocks from the model of managerial effectiveness in the different chapters of this book. Part II (*Enhancing interpersonal effectiveness*) is focused on developing team members and influencing their performance. Staffing is addressed in Chapter 3. Agenda setting is closely connected to decision making (Chapter 6) and creating a strategy for the organization (Chapter 7). Finally, agenda implementation is the main topic of Chapter 8. The other key activities in the model, **monitoring** and

Network:
A group of people with whom managers connect for the purpose of exchanging information and services.

Monitoring:
The activity of identifying and obtaining relevant information to understand what is going on both within and outside the organization.

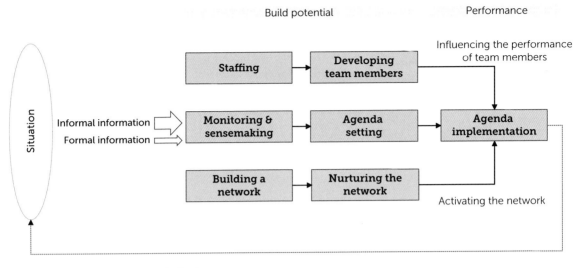

Figure 1.7 A model of managerial effectiveness

Sensemaking:
The process of giving meaning to and trying to understand the potential impact of the events and develop-ments that are going on both within and outside the organization.

sensemaking, on the one hand, and building and nurturing a network, on the other, are discussed in the remainder of this chapter.

Monitoring and sensemaking

To be able to set the right agenda, managers need to constantly make sense of what is going on within and outside their organization (see also the example in the *CEO best practice* box *Beer is high on the agenda*).

CEO BEST PRACTICE

Beer is high on the agenda

As the former CEO of SABMiller, Graham Mackay elevated the brewing company from its South African roots to become a major global player. With a relocation of the headquarters from Johannesburg to London and acquisitions all over Africa, Europe (e.g. Pilsner Urquell), the Americas, Russia, India, China, and Australia (e.g. Foster's), SABMiller developed into one of the world's leading brewers, second only in beer volume to Anheuser-Busch InBev, the company that acquired SABMiller in 2016.

Alan Clark, a member of SABMiller's management team who succeeded Mackay as CEO, described Mackay's management style in an interview with *Management Today*: "I cannot recall ever being given an instruction by Graham,"[110] Clark commented, pointing out that nevertheless he always knew what needed to be done to align his efforts with Mackay's strategy. He characterized Mackay as someone who "has a way of arranging the steps—thinking about the stage and how the industry will

unfold. Then he selects and sets up the dancers in the piece he has designed."[111] He noted that when Mackay started something off he had a clear vision of the result, but after that, he allowed others to work toward it.

Mackay, in turn, considered himself as "pretty much a low-key manager" who tried "to provide a vision for the company, a coherent view of the world, a making sense of things."[112] Closely monitoring and recognizing what is going on in the industry, setting a clear agenda, and making sure the team understands it are three habits of effective management that contributed to Graham Mackay's success as leader of SABMiller.

→ Key takeaway

Effective managers set a clear agenda based on a keen understanding of what is going on in the environment, and entrust the right people to implement it.

Source: Based on information in Management Today (2006).

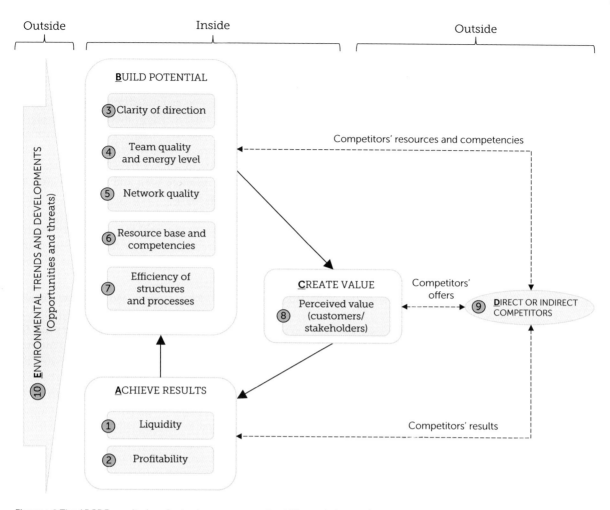

Figure 1.8 The ABCDE monitoring chart: where managers should focus their attention

ABCDE monitoring chart:
A tool that allows managers to get an overview of key factors that can influence the sustainable performance of an organization.

Liquidity:
The ability of an organization to meet all immediate and short-term payment obligations.

Given the amount of information that managers receive on a day-to-day basis, they must make choices about where to direct their attention. Figure 1.8 presents the **ABCDE monitoring chart** as a tool for gaining an overview of ten key factors that a manager should ideally monitor constantly.

Categories A, B and C of the ABCDE monitoring chart are focused on information about the organization itself:

A **Achieve results: which (financial) results does the organization achieve?**
Positive financial results keep an organization alive. A close monitoring of the **liquidity situation** (including forecasts) is essential for ensuring that the organization will be able to meet all its payment obligations and avoid insolvency (❶ on the ABCDE chart). Equally, maintaining adequate **profitability levels** (❷)—yielding enough revenue while keeping expenses under control—is a must for the long-term survival of a business. Profits are needed so that the organization is able to reinvest into activities that build its future performance potential. More information about what managers can do to monitor and influence the liquidity and profitability levels of their organizations is provided in Chapter 9.

B **Build potential: does the organization build sufficient potential for future performance?**
As discussed earlier in this chapter, building potential is a precondition for future performance. Effective managers set a **clear direction** for their organization (❸ on the ABCDE chart) because it is hard to achieve anything if you do not know where to go. It is

important to ensure that all members of the organization understand the strategy (see also Chapter 7). In addition, managers need to ask themselves whether they have **the right people** in their team (④) to be able to reach their organization's goals (Do members have the right skill sets? Do their skills complement each other? Are members functioning well as a team? Are they developing in the right direction?). Having the right team is not enough, though. The team members must also be motivated to reach their goals. Constantly sensing the **energy level** within the team is therefore another key managerial monitoring task. As well as their team, managers use their **networks** (⑤) to implement their agenda. Ideally, they will periodically review whether they have the necessary connections and relationships of sufficient quality to achieve their goals. Another key question is whether the organization's current **resource base and competencies** (⑥) adequately prepare the organization for future challenges. If this is not the case, managers need to find ways to either acquire the necessary resources or competencies, or to look for a new direction that is more feasible. Finally, managers need to question whether the way in which their organization is producing value (including structures, processes, and routines) is really **efficient** (⑦), i.e. whether (and where) there is still potential to improve the **productivity** of the organization's **operations**.

Productivity:
A measure of efficiency commonly defined as the ratio of outputs to inputs.

C   **Create value: does the organization create value for customers and other stakeholder groups?**
A business's *raison d'être*—the fundamental reason why it exists—lies in creating **value for customers** (⑧). This is equally true for organizational units that create value for **internal customers** within the organization. Making sure that customers see value in what the organization creates is a key obligation for managers. For that reason, they need to be up to date with customer needs, customer satisfaction levels, and customer perceptions of the organization and its products or services. Obtaining market research results is often insufficient for this purpose. The best way to stay tuned to what customers really think is to maintain frequent direct personal contact. But businesses can also create (or sometimes destroy) value for other stakeholders (e.g. employees or local communities), which can have repercussions for the organization's financial results. Managers should therefore keep track of the impact their organization has on other stakeholder groups and the environment.

Operations:
An organization's activities that are oriented toward transforming inputs (resources and competencies) into outputs (goods and services that create value for customers).

Organizations do not live in a vacuum. As open systems, they are highly dependent on the external environment. Therefore, in addition to monitoring and making sense of the situation within the organization, managers also need to look externally. In addition to maintaining customer contact, this especially means asking the following two questions:

Internal customer:
A person or organizational unit that uses goods or services supplied by another person or unit within the same organization as inputs to their work.

D   **Direct or indirect competitors: what are others who create similar value doing?** (⑨)
Competitors' moves can have a tremendous impact on the fate of an organization. Its very existence can be called into question when customers start perceiving the offerings of other suppliers to be superior. This is equally valid for products and services—even from outside the core industry—that can act as **substitutes** to the organization's offerings. Therefore, managers must keep themselves informed about what competitors and potential competitors offer or plan to offer, and how this relates to their own organization's products or services. Likewise, they should try to find out about competing organizations' *competencies* and *results* relative to their own. Both can affect the rivals' future potential to upgrade their offerings.

Substitutes:
Goods or services that can satisfy the same customer needs as other goods or services.

E   **Environmental trends and developments: which of them pose a threat or create an opportunity for the organization?** (⑩)
As mentioned earlier in this chapter, all kinds of external factors, from political decisions to technological developments, and from economic cycles to changing lifestyles, can alter the parameters of doing business for an organization. Therefore, managers need to monitor what is going on both in their industry and in the macro environment to ensure that they are able to adapt their organization to changing circumstances in a timely manner (see also Chapter 7).

A little caveat needs to be added here. The ABCDE monitoring chart does not imply that the ten factors are the only ones that need to be monitored. Rather, the tool can help managers who are caught in their day-to-day activities to return to the bigger picture and not to lose sight of some of the major influences on their organization's short-term viability as well as its long-term development and sustainability.

Building and nurturing a network

No single manager and no organizational unit can succeed without the help of others who provide information and resources, back them up in power struggles, or support them in exploiting opportunities. For that purpose, managers need to build a **network**, which is defined as "a set of ongoing, enduring relationships with those you depend on and who depend on you, based on a real understanding of each other's needs and mutual dependencies."[113]

AROUND THE GLOBE

Cross-cultural differences in networking

When attending a networking event, would you approach a representative from a company with which you are interested in working in the following way: "Hello, I see you are working for Company X. I am highly interested in your company, may I tell you a bit more about me?" Whereas in the US, this would be a perfectly fine start to a conversation, people from other cultures may find this approach much too direct or even assertive. They might think, like this Indian management consultant who was cited on the website of *Harvard Business Review*, that trying "to sell myself, bragging about my abilities to a stranger ... feels so weird and selfish."[114]

In cultures where people generally accept that there are clearly defined hierarchies, like India, it is uncommon to informally and directly approach higher-ranked persons in the same way as in the US.

In strongly relationship-oriented cultures, exchanges are primarily mediated. If you want to approach a person in Russia or China, for example, it usually works better when you are introduced by someone who is already well connected with the "target person" than to approach that person directly. Networks in these countries are characterized by mutual obligations and an expectation of exchanging favors— also in the sense of helping the friends of friends. As the rules of networking differ from culture to culture, it is important to understand the cultural logic first. Learning from what others do and finding out more about which behaviors work (or do not work) can help you to become a more effective cross-cultural networker.

Sources: Based on information in Michailova and Worm (2003) and Molinsky (2012).

There are three key elements in this definition of a network:

a   **Mutual dependency**: Strong relationships are built on reciprocity; you give something and you get something. This can work in both positive and negative ways, and it has not changed since the times of the Greek philosopher Aristotle (384–322 BC): "Men seek to return either evil for evil ... or good for good—and if they cannot do so there is no exchange, but it is by exchange that they hold together."[115]

b   **Understanding each other's needs**: Managers can only provide something of value to others if they know what others value. Therefore, managers must be good listeners and try to put themselves into other people's shoes to find out what could be beneficial to them. This is a precondition for managers to be able to add new fruitful reciprocal relationships to their network.

c   **Ongoing, enduring relationships**: Relationships require continuous investment. Top managers have pointed out the importance of doing things together and sharing experiences for maintaining good relationships.[116] It is too late to try to build relationships only at the point when they are needed. In networking, investment needs to be made long before the benefits are sought.

Zooming in on ▶ BUILDING AND MAINTAINING A SUPPORTIVE NETWORK

How can you actually build and maintain a supportive network? The following practical advice can help you to "weave your own web of influence":[117]

1 *Think about your own goals*. What do you (or your organizational unit) need to succeed? What are the critical success factors? Who is dependent on you and who do you depend on?

2 *Identify your target network*. Write down the names of people who you depend on (and who depend on you) now and especially in the future (both inside and outside the organization). Assess the importance of each contact and the current state of the relationship.

3 *Assess who the influential people are within your organization or within the domain that you are interested in*. Who are the formal and informal leaders? Who is listened to? Who is close to whom? Who could be most important for your future career?

4 *Actively work on improving your network*. Find ways to contact the most important people on your list—even those who have been in conflict with you. Think about how you could help or support them, and try to establish a personal relationship. Use existing contacts as a bridge to establish new relationships.

5 *Attend networking events*. Professional conferences, career fairs, or events organized by chamber of commerce groups, associations, and clubs can open opportunities for getting in touch with interesting people, often just through casual conversations.

6 *Use the possibilities that social media networks offer*. Professional social media networks such as LinkedIn offer a range of possibilities for networking. You can search for people with specific competencies, join groups and communities, and present yourself in a way that makes you a potentially attractive networking partner for others.

7 *Nourish your network*. Share information that others in your network need; help your contacts to connect with each other; keep personal communication alive (e.g. send congratulations messages on birthdays or job changes).

Building and maintaining a supportive network takes time and effort (see *Zooming in on building and supporting a supportive network*). It is, however, an essential part of the effective manager's job, not least because political struggle is a normal feature of organizational life (see Chapter 8). When different individuals or groups that depend on each other differ in their needs and interests and compete for limited resources, disagreements are a natural consequence.[118] Without a powerful network, it is difficult for managers to achieve their agenda. For important agenda items, managers can use their entire network, calling on "peers, corporate staff people, subordinates reporting three or four levels below, bosses reporting two or three levels above them, suppliers and customers, and even competitors to help them get something done,"[119] as John Kotter vividly described. In other words: effective managers need to be effective networkers.

From web designer to top manager: Collis Ta'eed at Envato

Collis Ta'eed grew up in Papua New Guinea and later moved to Australia. He was working as a freelance web designer when he decided to start an online business with his wife Cyan and his best friend Jun Rung in 2006. The three entrepreneurs launched an online marketplace for graphics and animations that were produced with Adobe Flash (the dominant software platform for producing online multimedia content at that time), and later expanded the business to include further marketplaces for digital assets (for example, WordPress themes, audio files, videos, or online tutorials) and website creation tools for small businesses and consumers. Over the following ten years, Ta'eed's company, Envato, developed into a highly successful 300-person organization. Two-thirds of the employees were based at the Melbourne headquarters, while the rest were spread around the world.

The founders had used their savings and credit cards to fund the launch of the business, and had put in a lot of unpaid hours. Ta'eed remembered that after the first revenues came in, the team "knew that they were on to *something*."[120] As his next step, he focused the company's efforts on product improvements, marketing, and what he calls "grassroots community building" (e.g. through forums or networking with people). He was always eager to try out new approaches and constantly kept pushing when something worked out well: "It's like when you start a fire,"[121] commented Ta'eed. Their fire was soon flaring and, as the company was growing fast, the focus shifted to finding the right people to keep it going. One principle that Collis and Cyan Ta'eed followed was to ensure that they were always hiring for future needs: "You've got your one year runway, your two year runway and your five year runway,"[122] noted Cyan Ta'eed, pointing out the need to look far ahead.

As the company evolved, CEO Collis Ta'eed had to adjust his management style. He went from being the hands-on co-founder of a start-up that operated out of a basement at his parents-in-law's, to using a more structure- and process-oriented approach as required by a growing multi-business company. "These days I spend a lot more time with spreadsheets and people in suits,"[123] he revealed, reflecting on how his managerial duties had changed over time. When asked for a role description during an interview for a *Management Disrupted* blog, Ta'eed explained that "thinking about the big picture" and "being a bit of a culture and values custodian for the company" would probably be the most important aspects of his role. Half-jokingly, he added that he sometimes feels like a "chief email officer" and that "[w]hatever is not done by everybody else, I guess that's me."[124] At times Ta'eed felt that he was still too involved in day-to-day issues, such as website designs. However, he also acknowledged that it might be wrong to just look at the big picture without

taking care of the details. Thus, he tries to establish a balance between looking at more strategic issues (which he prefers to do in the morning, free of interruptions) and operative work.

Ta'eed places a strong emphasis on preparing plans and strategies for the future, and then making sure that everyone in the organization understands Envato's goals and their own contribution to achieving these. Ta'eed believes that expressing the company's strategy through stories can be helpful in this context, but he also realizes that as a company leaves the start-up phase and grows, it needs a more systematic approach, including a clear organizational structure and key performance indicators. This means—in Ta'eed's words—that everyone "should know what part of the organisation they live in, what that part of the organisation is working towards, how that works towards the broader strategy, and what part they play in that part of the organisation."[125] Within this framework, Ta'eed allows Envato's employees a lot of autonomy in how they reach the desired outcomes.

Once a week, Ta'eed holds one-to-one meetings with the people who directly report to him (for example, the general managers of different business units and the directors of head office functions such as legal, finance, or HR), checking on their progress, discussing future plans and strategies, as well as important operative issues. Every two weeks, he also holds an "All Hands" meeting in which, for example, new employees are introduced and announcements or short presentations are made (including by remote staff via videoconferencing). In a company that relies on a geographically dispersed workforce, effective communication is a key success factor. When asked what he knows after ten years in business that he wished he had known at the start, Ta'eed responded: "I think I wish I understood, especially around managing, how important it is to be clear with people. Clear about goals, clear about feedback and clear about expectations."[126]

Sources: Dias (2016); Janssen (2013); Pell (2016); Ta'eed (2015, 2016).

💬 Discussion questions

- Referring to Collis Ta'eed's story, how does a manager's role change when a company develops from a small start-up into a medium-sized or larger organization?
- Envato has a high proportion of remote workers in its team. What effects could that have on the role of a manager?
- Where does Ta'eed's focus lie as he strives to be an effective manager?
- How would you interpret Ta'eed's statement that "being a bit of a culture and values custodian for the company" is one of the most important aspects of his managerial role? How are culture and values linked to managerial effectiveness?

Conclusion

As we have seen in this chapter, management can be a challenging job. Managers are responsible for the performance of systems that they cannot fully control. They need to work through other people with different capabilities, interests, and motivations, in an environment where they are exposed to various unforeseen events. Moreover, managers are subject to a multitude of role expectations, and they constantly need to balance conflicting interests when they try to meet their responsibilities for the performance of the organization, for building potential for future performance, for addressing stakeholder needs, and for the short- and long-term societal and environmental impacts of their decisions.

Nevertheless, when conducted in an effective way, management can also be a very rewarding job. Managers can make a difference. They can create value for others—customers, employees, and the community alike—and see individuals and organizations grow and develop as a result of their actions.

This chapter began with an example of one of the world's best football (soccer) players and the difficulties that he faced in trying to succeed as a team manager. A quite contrary example is Sir Alex Ferguson, who is considered to be the most successful manager in British (and maybe also the world's) history of the game. During his exceptional 26 years as the manager of Manchester United, his team won 13 Premier League titles, five FA Cup titles and two UEFA Champions League titles (besides a range of other trophies).[127] Sir Alex did what other effective managers do. First of all, he was always trying to *see the big picture* (i.e. being able to make sense of what is important within the team, the organization, and the constantly changing environment). "I came to see observation as a critical part of my management skills," he said. "The ability to see things is key."[128] He obviously also knew how to set and implement the right agenda for his team, and he was well aware that in order to perform through other people, you first need to develop them. In his own words, "[t]he job of a manager, like that of a teacher, is to inspire people to be better."[129]

A manager's impact is not only seen in the short- and long-term business results and societal effects, but also in what managers do on a day-to-day basis, in how they behave toward others, and in the kind of teams and organizations they build. It makes a difference whether managers treat employees as "resources" only, constantly pressuring them to perform, or if they try to create organizations that are "communities of engagement," which are characterized by a strong level of commitment to both the common purpose and the well-being of all group members.[130] Managers who really want to make a difference can follow Manfred Kets de Vries' advice and "create the kinds of organization that bring out the best in people, that help them become more human ... In these kinds of organizations, people find meaning in their work; they enjoy the people they work with; they take pride in what they are doing; and they trust the people they work for and with."[131] In other words, it is not only *what* managers do that shows their real quality, but also *how* they do it. This is how every single manager can make a difference and get the feeling, as described by the famous French aviator and writer Antoine de Saint Exupéry, that "when setting one's stone, ... one is contributing to the building of the world."[132]

✓ Review questions

1   What is challenging about the manager's job?
2   What levels of complexity does a manager need to deal with?
3   What are the main responsibilities of managers in an organizational context?
4   What is the difference between intrinsic and extrinsic responsibility?
5   How does the Friedmanite perspective on managerial responsibility differ from a social contract perspective?
6   Who are the main stakeholders of an organization and what are their primary interests?
7   What is ambidexterity and how is this concept linked to the responsibilities of managers?

8   How can the "Golden Rule" help managers in meeting their ethical responsibility?

9   How would you describe a manager's typical working day?

10   What are the ten managerial roles that Henry Mintzberg identified?

11   What is the difference between efficiency, efficacy, and effectiveness?

12   What does it mean for a manager to be effective?

13   Which tasks do managers need to perform in order to become effective in their job?

14   How can the ABCDE monitoring chart help managers to keep an overview of the key factors that can influence the sustainable performance of their organizations?

15   Why is network building an important task for managers and what can managers do to build and maintain a supportive network?

⑦ Critical reflection questions

1   Why do managers (especially in top management positions) often receive exceptionally high salaries? Based on what you have learned in this chapter about the nature of the managerial job, do you think that these high salaries are appropriate?

2   Do you agree more strongly with the Friedmanite perspective or the social contract perspective on managerial responsibility? Provide arguments to support your choice.

3   The interests of different stakeholder groups can collide. How could you deal with such a situation as a manager?

4   Why should managers who are evaluated and compensated on the basis of the short-term performance of their organizations care about building potential for the future?

5   Is it really realistic for a manager to fulfill all the expectations that are associated with the managerial role? If not, which aspects of the managerial role would you focus on if you had to prioritize them?

☞ Managerial implications

- Managers are responsible for ensuring that their organizations or organizational units serve their purpose (or create value) and, at the same time, for building the potential for future performance. Effective managers therefore strive to establish a balance between current performance and potential building.

- Managers perform through other people and work within complex social systems (organizations) that are, in turn, embedded in wider social systems (the micro and macro environments of an organization). It is the manager's task to make sense of all the information received from these systems, to "see the whole picture." Managers need to recognize the key factors that influence the performance and potential of their organizations, including the interrelations and trade-offs between them, and to set the right coordinated interventions to move their organizations forward.

- Managers are faced with multiple role expectations and a whole range of different tasks that usually need to be accomplished within a short timeframe. To become effective in their managerial role (i.e. to reach their organization's goals and achieve its purpose in a sustainable manner) they must set the right priorities (by means of an agenda) and influence others to support them in their efforts to implement them.

- As a precondition for obtaining the support of others, managers need to create and develop a team with the requisite competencies and motivation, and build and nurture a network of potential supporters within and outside the organization.

- Managers fulfill an important social function. How they think, decide, and act can have a strong impact on other people. They can create or destroy value for their organization and its stakeholder groups. Therefore, it is important for managers to develop a good understanding of their role and responsibility in order to be able to live up to them.

/ Endnotes

[1] spiegel.de (2012).
[2] Hill and Lineback (2011), p. xi.
[3] Similar definitions of management have been put forward by Hales (1986) and Mintzberg (2011).
[4] Hill and Lineback (2011), p. 15.
[5] Pascal (2007), p. 408.
[6] Falk and Scholz (2018).
[7] Ackoff (1979), pp. 99–100.
[8] Mitleton-Kelly (2003).
[9] Rosa (2013); Wajcman & Dodd (2016).
[10] Sternad (2011).
[11] Greenfield (2017).
[12] Hambrick and D'Aveni (1988).
[13] Weick (1995), p. 16.
[14] Graham (2003), pp. 168–169.
[15] Graham (2003), pp. 168–169.
[16] Mahieu (2001).
[17] Hill and Lineback (2011), p. 19.
[18] For the contents of this and the following paragraphs cf. Sternad (2013a).
[19] For an overview of agency theory see Eisenhardt (1989).
[20] Davis et al. (1997).
[21] Friedman (1962), p. 133.
[22] Carroll and Shabana (2010).
[23] Rose (2007).
[24] Stout (2013).
[25] Stout (2013).
[26] Interview with James March in Podolny (2011), p. 504.
[27] Carroll (1991; 1999); Donaldson (1982).
[28] Carroll and Shabana (2010).
[29] Carroll and Shabana (2010).
[30] Freeman et al. (2010).
[31] Freeman et al. (2010).
[32] Sternad (2013a).
[33] De Geus (1997).
[34] Sternad (2013a).
[35] Aristotle (2009), p. 23.
[36] Mischel et al. (1972).
[37] Shoda et al. (1990); Eigsti et al. (2006).
[38] Sternad and Kennelly (2017).
[39] Brundtland (1987), p. 8.
[40] Mintzberg (2011), p. 225.
[41] Levinthal and March (1993), p. 105.
[42] March (1994).
[43] Business Week (2002).
[44] Business Week (2002).
[45] Business Week (2002).
[46] ForbesCustom (2018).
[47] Rowley et al. (2005), p. 49.
[48] Maak and Pless (2006); Werhane (1999).
[49] Burton and Goldsby (2005).
[50] Confucius (2007), p. 37.
[51] Burton and Goldsby (2005).
[52] Bruton (2004).
[53] Feloni (2015).
[54] Burnison (2011).
[55] Ignatius (2015), p. 85.
[56] Ignatius (2015), p. 84.
[57] Safian (2014).
[58] Marsalis and Nooyi (2014).
[59] Marsalis and Nooyi (2014).
[60] Marsalis and Nooyi (2014).
[61] Fayol (1917).
[62] For instance, Burns (1957) or Stewart (1967).
[63] Stewart (1983), pp. 96–97.
[64] Stewart (1983), pp. 96–97.
[65] Wrapp (1967), p. 95.
[66] Mintzberg (1975), p. 50.
[67] Mintzberg (1973); Noel (1989); O´Gorman et al. (2005); Tengblad (2006).
[68] Hill and Lineback (2011), p. 15.
[69] Mintzberg (2011), p. 23.
[70] Tengblad (2006).
[71] Tengblad (2006).
[72] Tengblad (2006).
[73] Mintzberg (1975), p. 52.
[74] Mintzberg (1975), p. 52.
[75] Hales (1986), p. 104.
[76] Mintzberg (1973); Tengblad (2006).
[77] Porter and Nohria (2018).
[78] Kotter (1982).
[79] Barley et al. (2011).
[80] BBC News (2005).
[81] O'Gorman et al. (2005).
[82] Holmberg and Tyrstrup (2010).
[83] Tengblad (2017), p. 339.
[84] Johnson and Dobni (2016).
[85] O'Gorman et al. (2005).
[86] Doktor (1990).
[87] Mintzberg (1975).
[88] Hill and Lineback (2011), p. 26.
[89] Bandiera et al. (2011).
[90] Mintzberg (2011), p. 56.
[91] Riegel (1935).
[92] Kolbjørnsrud et al. (2016).
[93] Kolbjørnsrud et al. (2016), p. 11; Pistrui and Dimov (2018).
[94] Rosa (2013).
[95] Roux (2017).
[96] Magpili and Pazos (2018); Renkema et al. (2018).
[97] Laud et al. (2016), p. 491.
[98] Drucker (1999a), p. 142.
[99] Maddux (2009).
[100] Drucker (1999a), p. 132.
[101] Mintzberg (2011).
[102] Bandiera et al. (2017).
[103] For the results described in this paragraph see Luthans (1987).
[104] Porter and Nohria (2018).
[105] Porter and Nohria (2018), p. 48.
[106] Kotter (1982), p. 160.
[107] Kotter (1982), p. 161.
[108] Kotter (1982), p. 166.
[109] Mintzberg (2011), p. 51.
[110] *Management Today* (2006).
[111] *Management Today* (2006).
[112] *Management Today* (2006).
[113] Hill and Lineback (2011), p. 97.
[114] Molinsky (2012).
[115] Aristotle (2009), p. 88.
[116] Kets de Vries (2009).
[117] The quote is from Hill and Lineback (2011), p. 95; some of the following points are inspired by Hill and Lineback (2011), pp. 102–109.
[118] Hill and Lineback (2011).
[119] Kotter (1982), p. 163.
[120] Ta'eed (2016).
[121] Ta'eed (2016).
[122] Dias (2016).
[123] Janssen (2013).
[124] Pell (2016).
[125] Pell (2016).
[126] Pell (2016).
[127] premierleague.com (2019).
[128] Elberse (2013), p. 124.
[129] Elberse (2013), p. 118.
[130] Mintzberg (2011), pp. 233–234.
[131] Kets de Vries (2011), pp. 7 and 10.
[132] de Saint-Exupéry (1968), p. 60.

 Visit the companion website at macmillanihe.com/sternad-management to access multiple choice questions, useful weblinks and additional materials.

iStock.com/AndreyPopov

MANAGING AND DEVELOPING YOURSELF

Outline of chapter

This chapter will enable you to

- Recognize how self-management forms the basis for effectively managing people and organizations.
- Examine how managers can identify their goals, strengths, and values, and how this is linked to effectiveness in the managerial role.
- Reflect on how to set priorities and enhance your personal productivity.
- Develop strategies for dealing with major obstacles to effective priority management.
- Explain what managers can do to cope with high stress levels, setbacks, and frustrations.
- Identify what managers can do to (further) develop the abilities and skills that they need to perform well.

Introduction

Akzo Nobel, the world's largest paints and coatings company by sales volume, lost 5.5 percent of its share value only one day after announcing that its new CEO, Ton Büchner, had been granted special leave due to a diagnosis of "temporary fatigue."[1] High hopes had been placed on Büchner, who had previously managed Sulzer AG, a large Swiss industrial company, very successfully. On that day in September 2012, however, Akzo Nobel had to admit, using a Dutch saying, that "he took a bit too much hay on his pitchfork," adding that "CEOs are also human beings."[2]

Ton Büchner is not alone. There are more and more reports of exhausted managers who pay their dues by working under ever-increasing demands and at an unrelenting pace. "Long hours are the real killer," notes Cary Cooper of Lancaster University in the *Financial Times*, pointing out that, along with the incessant pressure, they can lead to a detachment "from natural social support systems like your family."[3] Performance anxieties and fears of not living up to expectations can further increase managerial stress levels.[4]

How can managers be effective in such an environment, without compromising their emotional well-being, health, and family lives? First of all, they need to **take control**. One of the main reasons for perceived high stress levels is that managers are overwhelmed by other people's demands, expectations, and problems. Their subordinates, bosses, and peers, as well as customers, suppliers, the media, and many other stakeholders all require their attention, time, and energy. Taking control means not just blindly following demands, but instead setting the right goals for yourself and your organization, and then developing the right skills and reserving enough time to perform the actions that are necessary to reach these goals.

To effectively manage other people and organizations, managers first and foremost need to become **effective self-managers** who know how to:

- best spend their time and **set the right priorities** (*Section 2.2*);
- keep their **energy levels** high and replenish their energy stores when they are at risk of becoming drained (*Section 2.3*);
- become **resilient** and cope with setbacks (*Section 2.3*); and
- **develop the requisite abilities and skills** which they need to reach their goals (*Section 2.4*).

A major precondition for succeeding at self-management is being able to **understand yourself**, and in particular your goals, main strengths, and values (*Section 2.1*).

2.1 "Know thyself"

Pixabay/Walkerssk

In brief

- Self-management and self-development both begin with understanding yourself. Having clear goals is as important in this context as knowing your strengths.

- Matching goals and strengths is a key requirement for superior performance. Personal strengths can be identified, for example, with the help of feedback analysis (comparing the outcomes of your actions to your prior expectations) or through reflecting on the reasons for successful performance in the past.

- Understanding your personal values (defined as stable beliefs and ideals) is another step towards doing the right things—and therefore becoming an effective manager.

In ancient Greece, whoever approached the Temple of Apollo to consult the famous Oracle of Delphi, the Pythia, first needed to pass through a forecourt. There, the advice-seeking visitor was greeted—and warned—by an inscription with the words "Know thyself."[5] **Knowing and understanding yourself**—in particular, your strengths and weaknesses, goals, desires, values, habits, potential, limitations, and sources and drains of energy—is not only useful when consulting a prophetic priestess such as the Pythia, but also for managing an organization.

As we have discussed in Chapter 1, effective managers are those who reach their goals and achieve the desired outcomes for their organizations. To be able to do so, they have to first identify what these goals and organizational objectives are, and then **match them to their strengths**.

Top performers know why they are able to succeed, and deliberately work on nurturing the sources of their performance. Research has shown that low performers frequently make erroneous judgments about their abilities, often dramatically overestimating them.[6] In other words, incompetence often goes hand in hand with a lack of self-insight.[7] Without knowing your strengths and capabilities, it is difficult to develop them further—thus, in turn, limiting your potential to develop other people and organizations.

In this section, we will take a closer look at how managers can identify their goals and strengths, before discussing the important role that values can play as a guiding "compass" for managerial work. Taken together, knowing your goals, strengths, and values can show the path to effective self-management (see Figure 2.1).

Know your goals

Let us start with the most encompassing goal—*what do you want to achieve in life?* The answer to this question is anything but straightforward, not least as we tend to change our goals during the course of our lives. Nevertheless, being aware of our **long-term goals** obviously increases our chances of reaching them because we can then take deliberate steps to bring us closer to these goals and achieve something substantial. When you know that you would like to become a manager, you can prepare yourself with management education (or with reading a book like this one), for example. We can set ourselves goals not only for our **work and career**, but also for other areas of life, such as our **family and social life**, for contributing to the **community** or a broader cause, and—not least—for **developing ourselves**.[8]

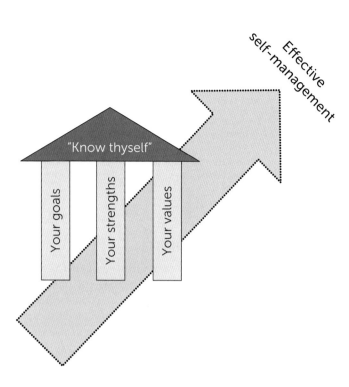

Figure 2.1 Knowing yourself: the basis for effective self-management

It is important for managers to understand not only their work goals, but also their goals for other realms of life, because sometimes the various goals can come into conflict. Therefore, it is necessary to prioritize them, thinking about what really matters in life. One way of doing this is trying to define what "success" actually means to you. A study of top executives and other successful professionals came to the conclusion that these people only felt really successful in their lives when they had reached an adequate level in four different spheres:[9]

1 **Happiness**: a feeling of well-being and being content with your life.
2 **Achievement**: accomplishing something that both you and others value, and which compares favorably to similar goals that others are pursuing.
3 **Significance**: making a difference in other people's lives.
4 **Legacy**: supporting others (especially the next generation) in their own success.

Reaching an adequate level does not mean "as much as possible," but rather "just enough."[10] Everyone needs to determine what "just enough" means in their particular case. Nevertheless, it makes sense to carefully probe your own definition of success, for example with the following questions:

● What really makes me happy? What has given me lasting satisfaction in life?
● Why do I want to achieve something? What do I expect from reaching a certain goal?
● For whom do I want to make a difference? What is the difference that I want to make?
● What do I want to leave behind? What would I like to be remembered for?

Once you have a better understanding of your overall life goals, you can start to break these broader goals down into smaller, more specific ones. (In a similar vein, it is also possible to break down more encompassing long-term organizational goals into smaller, more proximate goals.) What needs to be done this year, this week, or even today to bring you closer to reaching your life goals? To become effective in achieving your long-term goals, you need to maintain focus, always determining and implementing the **next step** (concrete action) that will bring you closer to reaching them (see the box *Zooming in on setting and reaching your life goals*). Every step that you take in the right direction can give you a positive feeling of progress.

Zooming in on ▶ SETTING AND REACHING YOUR LIFE GOALS

In the appendix to this chapter, you will find some tools that can help you in your endeavor to improve your personal effectiveness. Exercises 1 and 2 are devoted to better understanding your life goals and breaking them down into more concrete next steps. Turn to these two exercises now:

1 Keeping in mind the questions listed on the previous page, complete Exercise 1 to identify your life goals in four key areas: work and career, family, self-development, and contribution to the community.
2 Work through Exercise 2 to establish concrete goals and action plans for the next year which bring you closer to achieving your life goals.

Know your strengths

"We know very well that errors are better recognized in the works of others than in our own," wrote Leonardo da Vinci.[11] On the other side of the same coin, management expert Peter Drucker noticed that "[m]ost people think they know what they are good at. They are usually wrong."[12] It is often more difficult to accurately assess ourselves than to assess others. Nevertheless, as we discussed before, knowing your strengths (and weaknesses) is a key precondition for becoming effective in the managerial role. But how can you find out more about your own strengths? One option is trying to get honest and specific **feedback** from the people you work with (e.g. "Do I give others the feeling that their opinions count?").[13] You need to be sure, however, that these people are really telling the (sometimes hard) truth. Another approach to better understanding your strengths is to think back to situations in which you performed exceptionally well and then try to examine which of your strengths and capabilities contributed to your exceptional performance. Drucker suggested two further **methods to reveal your real strengths** and find out how you work best:[14]

- **Feedback analysis**: Whenever you have to make an important decision or take an action with potentially wide-ranging consequences, write down what you think will be the outcome of your decision or action. Nine to twelve months later, compare the actual outcome with your prior expectations. This method will reveal which of your endeavors are working well, and where you are failing. Reflecting on the results can provide you with a better understanding of your strengths, as well as your judgment.
- **Find out how you perform best** by answering the following questions:[15]

    1 Do I work best with other people or alone?
    2 How do I learn best—through reading or listening?
    3 Am I better at advising others or at making decisions myself?
    4 Do I perform better under stress or in a predictable environment?
    5 Do I prefer to work in smaller or larger organizations?

Staff function: Organizational functions that support line managers (e.g. with analysis, advice, or other forms of assistance) in performing effectively in their role, but do not directly work on the main purpose of the organization.

Line management: Management functions with subordinates who are directly involved in the core business activities of an organization.

Zooming in on ▶ YOUR STRENGTHS

Return to the appendix at the end of this chapter. Complete Exercise 3 to find out more about your strengths. What have you learnt as a result of this process?

Your answers to Drucker's questions in part 2 of Exercise 3 can help you to identify goals and activities which match your strengths. For example, if you are better at advising others than at making decisions yourself, you might consider consulting or **staff function** roles rather than **line management**.

One of the secrets of top performers is that they tackle and complete work in which they can make use of their strengths. In particular, they are able to excel at the **critical tasks** that their jobs encompass.[16] If the critical tasks for a salesperson are building good relationships with customers and being able to close deals, for example, people with highly developed interpersonal, negotiation, and sales closing skills will probably be the best match for the job. Robert Kaplan, a former Harvard Business School Professor of Leadership Development, suggested that managers should identify the three to four main activities that are essential for their success in a certain role or endeavor, and then deliberately work on developing the skills for achieving excellent performance in these activities.[17]

CEO BEST PRACTICE

A CEO who does his homework every night

Robert Iger became CEO of the Walt Disney Company at a time of turmoil after severe conflicts within the company's top management team. Iger steered the Disney boat back into calm waters, acquired Pixar, Marvel, and Lucasfilm, including their rich content assets and creative potential, and led the company to new all-time highs in innovation (ranking among the 10 most innovative companies in the world) and financial results.[18] At the beginning, however, Iger's career was not smooth sailing. At the age of 23, he was told by his boss at the US television network ABC that he was not promotable. Nevertheless, he continued to believe in his capabilities, proving his former boss wrong. Understanding his own strengths and weaknesses was a crucial factor in driving his career in the right direction. When he was young, he actually wanted to become a newscaster and started off as a weatherman. "I learned very quickly I wasn't very good at it," he commented in an interview with the *New York Times*. "I'd say the first lesson I learned is, if you're not good at one thing, try something else."[19] So he changed jobs, learned—as he said—"to listen better" and

"be more patient," convinced that it would be a mistake to make career decisions out of impatience.[20] Iger believes that "[n]othing beats hard work"[21] and is strongly focused on lifelong learning: "I believe in the need to be a great student," he disclosed in an interview with *Harvard Business Review*. "I remind my 12-year-old son of this all the time when he complains about homework: 'But you see Dad doing homework every night.'"[22] Knowing himself, listening carefully to others, and having a strong learning orientation, together with a combination of relentless optimism and a clear focus on innovation, international expansion, and creativity enabled Iger to lead Disney to become a widely admired and sustainably successful company again.

→ Key takeaway

Knowing your own strengths and weaknesses and showing a constant willingness and desire to learn are key ingredients for achieving personal effectiveness.

Sources: Based on information in Bryant (2009b), goldmansachs.com (2018), and Ignatius (2011).

Values:
Lasting beliefs of a person or group about what is right or wrong, good or bad, or desirable or undesirable.

Socialization:
The process of acquiring attitudes, behaviors, and values by means of learning from what others do or deem acceptable in a certain group or society.

Know your values

In addition to knowing their goals and strengths, managers also need to be clear about their **values**, which can be defined as enduring beliefs that act as criteria "to select and justify actions and to evaluate people (including the self) and events."[23] In simpler terms, values are our beliefs about what is important in life and how we think we and others should behave. Our values determine what we find desirable and what we reject. They influence how we feel about situations and subsequently our behavior—and they also form the basis for acting in an ethically correct way.[24] Not least, leaders' values can influence the culture of their organizations.[25]

We acquire our values through a process of **socialization**, which means that values can significantly differ between cultures (see also Chapter 5).

Social psychologist Milton Rokeach identified two general categories of values:[26]

a   **Terminal values**: desired end states, such as freedom, happiness, equality, family security, pleasure, social recognition, or a sense of accomplishment. These values represent the higher goals that individuals want to achieve in their lives.

b   **Instrumental values**: desirable modes of behavior in the attempt to achieve your goals. Examples include being ambitious, honest, responsible, helpful, forgiving, polite, broad-minded, capable, or courageous. The latter three were ranked as the most important managerial values in a cross-national study of managers from 12 different nations.[27]

In another study that included both managers and production workers, the following four values were found to be particularly important as behavioral standards in an organizational context: **achievement**, **concern for others**, **honesty**, and **fairness**.[28] These four values also form the basis for effective collaboration in work settings.[29] Harvard Business School Professor Christensen further emphasizes **humility** as a key value that managers should hold. He argues that the most humble people—those who treat others with respect and who show a high degree of modesty—generally also have a high degree of self-esteem, know their place in life and are very comfortable with it, and usually have the attitude that they can learn something from everybody—which they consequently also do, thus becoming more effective in their jobs.[30]

Zooming in on ▶ YOUR VALUES

Turn to the appendix at the end of this chapter again. Use Exercise 4 to reflect on your values. How could these values influence the way in which you (would) work in a managerial role?

Trade-off:
A situation in which it is not possible to attain all objectives at the same time. In a trade-off situation, we need to give up something that we value in order to get something else that we value.

Many managerial decisions include a **trade-off of values**.[31] When a manager needs to decide whether to lay off an underperforming team member, for example, performance-orientation could clash with social responsibility toward the employee. In other situations, loyalty might conflict with fairness. For instance, should you remain loyal to a long-standing supplier or give another supplier with a better offer a chance to prove themselves? It is important that managers clearly understand their values and make them explicit. In particular, managers need to know whether their values are congruent (a) with the demands of their roles, (b) with their strengths, and (c) with the values of the organization they are working for.[32] If there is a mismatch, for example between the values of their organization and their personal values, managerial effectiveness can suffer. In some cases, a clash of values can also lead to ethical issues that need to be considered, such as a company demanding something from a manager that goes against his or her personal values (see the box *What would you do?*). For a detailed discussion on dealing with trade-offs in decision situations, see Chapter 6.

Let us assume that you are taking on the job of an assistant manager at a well-known global Internet company. Your manager asks you to make up some numbers to support a proposal for a new web service. You feel that the manager's request goes against your core values of honesty and integrity. You confront your boss with your concerns, but receive the reply: "Just do it. That's the way we do things around here and we need to meet our targets." What would you do in this situation?[33]

2.2 Managing priorities

Getty Images/Brand X/Thinkstock

In brief

● Being able to concentrate on the really important future- and opportunity-oriented issues is one of the main qualities of effective managers.

● Doing "first things first" also implies deliberately deciding against doing other things.

● Personal productivity can be enhanced through a systematic way of organizing projects and the steps that need to be taken to successfully complete them, and by using an intelligent scheduling system that puts priority tasks first, consolidates similar tasks, and leaves enough time for unanticipated events.

● Recognizing and developing strategies for dealing with the three main "enemies" of priorities management—overloading, time wasters, and reverse delegation—can further help managers to focus their energy on those issues and actions with the highest impact for the organization.

Time management: The systematic process of allocating time to different activities.

Many management books point out the pivotal role that **time management** plays for managerial effectiveness. As we discussed in Chapter 1, managers need to satisfy many different role expectations, and performing well in each role takes time.

Top managers, especially, often see managing time as one of their biggest challenges.[34] But can time really be managed? There is no doubt that time is a scarce good for managers. When we consult the dictionary, we find a definition of **time** as "the indefinite continued progress of existence and events in the past, present, and future regarded as a whole."[35] As such, time does not really lend itself well to being managed. What can be managed instead are **priorities**—what to do and what not to do.

Priorities management: The systematic process of first classifying issues and tasks into more or less important ones and then allocating more time to the important ones.

Priorities management includes the classification of issues and tasks into more or less important ones (setting priorities), devoting your time to doing the important things (personal productivity), and overcoming obstacles that can distract you from dealing with the important issues (the "enemies of priorities management"). In the following paragraphs, we will take a closer look at all of these three aspects.

Setting priorities

Effective managers know where to **focus their energy**. They identify a limited number of significant issues that are essential for the further development of their organizations, and then give these issues their full attention. As Peter Drucker noticed, effective managers "concentrate—their own time and energy as well as that of their organization—on doing one thing at a time, and on doing first things first."[36] Setting priorities is about identifying the most important task at a certain moment, and then fully focusing on this one task. This requires judgment as well as discipline, given the external pressures of all kinds that are exerted on a manager. Setting priorities is as much about which tasks not to do now (the posteriorities) as it is a decision on which tasks to do.

Managers can use the following question to determine what the "first things" they need to do are: *What is the single most important issue for the future of our organization?* This question is also reflected in the first of four rules that can be used for **determining priorities** (see also Figure 2.2):[37]

1 The future has precedence over the past.
2 Opportunities are more important than problems.

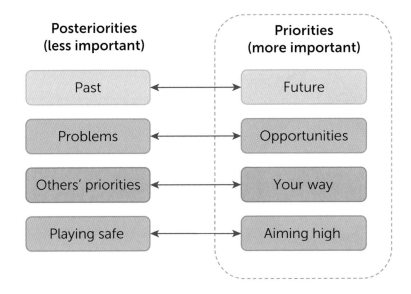

Figure 2.2 Criteria for identifying priorities

Source: Inspired by concepts in Drucker (1999a).

3   Follow your own way, rather than just doing what others say or do.

4   Aim high and make a difference, rather than playing safe.

Focusing on the future rather than on the past also means devoting enough time to **building the potential for future performance** amidst the requirements of day-to-day management (see Chapter 1), following the French proverb "Sharpening your tools is not a waste of time."[38]

Knowing your priorities is half the battle—only one half, however. The second half is **self-discipline**—being able to resist all the distractions and seemingly "urgent matters" (another term for other people's priorities) that continuously appear during a manager's day, and stick to the one, most important task. "First things first" also means "second things not at all."[39] This "secret" of effective management was even used by the Roman Emperor Marcus Aurelius (121–180 AD), who regarded setting priorities as a key part of his role as the "manager" of the Roman Empire. As he wrote in his famous *Meditations*: "At every step, therefore, a man should ask himself: 'Is this one of the things that are superfluous?' … [in order to] never become unduly absorbed in things that are not your first importance."[40]

Overcoming the "urgency addiction" is definitely not easy, but learning not to do certain things at all is at least as important as knowing what your priorities are.[41] One way of probing whether something is really necessary is to ask yourself the following question when you are about to make a decision or take action: *What effect will this have on customers or other important stakeholders?*[42] If it does not have an effect on customers or other important stakeholders, it is probably not that important after all.

Personal productivity:
A measurement for the ratio between the output that a person achieves and the efforts (e.g. in terms of working time) that are needed to achieve this output.

Enhancing personal productivity

Productivity can be defined as the ratio between an output and the input required to produce it. Managers with all their different tasks and roles (see Chapter 1) need to think about their **personal productivity**—about how they can obtain results (output) without drowning in their work (input). But how can this be achieved?

Suppose that you feel that you are already working at considerably more than 100 percent of your capacity. You have many unfinished tasks and projects, and dozens of new e-mails that demand your attention landed in your inbox this morning. To top it all, your boss has just told you that there is another big project that you need to work on with a deadline at the end of next week. What would you do to organize your work in a way that ensures that you will be able to complete all the *important* tasks (without having to work long hours every day)?

David Allen, a personal productivity consultant and author of the bestselling book *Getting Things Done,* emphasizes the **value of "clear space,"**[43] of getting things out of your head (or "externalizing" them) through making lists of everything that needs to be done. Allen's specific suggestions are presented in the box *Zooming in on a personal productivity management system.*

Zooming in on ▶ A PERSONAL PRODUCTIVITY MANAGEMENT SYSTEM

David Allen's personal productivity management system can very briefly be summarized as follows (see also Figure 2.3):[44]

1 *Write down whatever you need to do to "get things done"* because if you do not write it down, it will not get done. First, evaluate new incoming issues on whether they are important and actionable. If they are, document them either in your calendar (if they have time constraints) or on a "next actions" list. If more than one action needs to be taken to resolve an issue, record the issue on a "projects list." If the issue requires someone else to take the next step, delegate the task and make a note in a "waiting for others" file.

2 *Cut bigger projects into smaller pieces.* Go through the "projects list" and determine the next step for each—the one specific action that needs to be taken next in order to get ahead with the project. Focusing on smaller steps is less daunting than a big project that is piling up in front of you.

3 *Pool similar "next steps" in context-specific lists*, for example, a phone list, an e-mail list, other computer-based tasks, and things that need to be done next time you visit the city center. Grouping similar tasks allows you to work on them one after the other without changing location or the work medium.

4 Finally, *review the lists* on a daily and weekly basis and *work on one specific next action at a time* until it is finished.

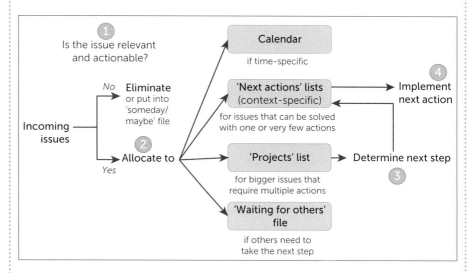

Figure 2.3 A simplified version of David Allen's personal productivity system

Source: Inspired by concepts in Allen (2001) and Allen and Schwartz (2011).

Try implementing David Allen's system for all the things you need to "get done." Did it help you to become more productive? What aspects of the system were most helpful to you personally? Why? Did you find anything particularly challenging? Why do you think this was?

Such a comprehensive and structured system for dealing with the many issues that a manager encounters on a day-to-day basis will be seen as too inflated or bureaucratic by many people (including the author of this book). Nevertheless, we can still acknowledge that it has certain advantages. First, by writing things down, we can be sure that nothing important will be forgotten. Second, by concentrating on next steps which are easily manageable, bigger projects no longer look too daunting. And third, the system allows us to focus on **one task at a time,** instead of being bombarded with a plethora of thoughts and issues. Thus, even if we think that Allen's personal productivity management model does not fit our personal style as a whole, we can still learn something from it.

There are also a range of **personal task management** software tools available for managers to support them in coping with an ever-increasing number of tasks (for example, Todoist, Wunderlist, Google Tasks, or Microsoft To-Do). These tools can, for example, be used to organize projects, tasks, and ideas; prioritize; check off completed tasks; attach documents or links; set reminders; or assign work to other team members. There are very different approaches to using these systems, however. While some managers adopt standard software or use a personalized version of electronic tools, others still prefer to use simple resources such as paper, Word documents or calendars.[45]

As well as deciding what to do, another important aspect of achieving personal productivity is deciding **when to do it**. There are different strategies for approaching this. Some people prefer to start the day with "**quick wins**," resolving smaller issues first, thus feeling that they have made progress. Recent research findings, however, suggest that an overreliance on this strategy (also known as "task completion bias") tends to improve performance in the short term, but can backfire and hurt performance in the long run.[46] A different strategy is to start the day with the most important task, or a sub-component thereof, even before checking e-mails or voicemail. The idea behind this approach is that finishing your most important work in the morning means you are not spending large chunks of time worrying over when you will have time to do it. Starting off with the most important task has one precondition, though: you first need to know what your most important task is. Some managers use the evening before to think about their priorities and most important tasks for the following day; others prefer to organize their daily priorities in the morning.

Decisions on timing and scheduling will also depend on the individual manager's circadian rhythm. Some people are most energetic in the morning, others in the afternoon or evening. Scheduling the most important tasks for high-energy periods and routine tasks for low-energy periods can contribute to enhancing personal productivity.[47]

A key tool for managing priorities is the **calendar**. Using a calendar wisely can have a strong effect on productivity. Here are a few suggestions on **how to create a schedule**:[48]

1 Add the top-priority tasks to your calendar first.
2 Leave enough time for unanticipated developments.
3 Combine similar tasks whenever possible.
4 Be realistic about what can be done in one day.

The last point is especially important. Stress often results from overloading yourself. It is always easier and less time-consuming to have ideas and make plans for projects than to actually carry them out. For that reason, knowing how much you are really able to do within a certain timeframe is—in addition to knowing your goals, strengths, and values—an essential component of knowing yourself.

Quick wins:
Visible improvements that can be achieved quite quickly and easily.

AROUND THE GLOBE

Different perceptions of time

In some cultures, time is perceived as linear. Under this perspective, time is relentlessly moving forward and is seen as a resource that is in limited supply. "Time is money," Americans often say, and to their mind, time that remains "unused" for making decisions and taking actions is "wasted" or "lost." In cultures with a linear perception of time like the US, Great Britain, Scandinavia, Germany, Switzerland, or the Netherlands, it is important to work according to detailed schedules,

be punctual, and keep to deadlines. "Saving time" whenever possible is considered a virtue.

In other cultures, time is perceived in a completely different way. For people from India, Italy, the Middle East, or South America, for example, it is usually a lot more important to complete a conversation than to begin or end a meeting on time. The relationship has precedence over finishing a task within a certain timeframe. In such cultures, time is related to events or personal encounters, and can be "manipulated, molded, stretched, or dispensed with, irrespective of what the clock says."[49] In some cultures, notably in Asia, time is also seen as a cyclical rather than a linear phenomenon. This means that time is not "racing away," but is moving in circles, just like the alternation of day and night and the seasons during a year. Under this perspective, it is not necessary to do everything as fast as possible, as opportunities will arise again—maybe even at a time that is more appropriate. Thus, it might be perfectly fine to allow yourself a further period of reflection and postpone a task to a later, more suitable point in time.

As the perception of time differs in different cultures, so does priority setting. Whereas in cultures with a linear perception of time, it is very important to meet deadlines, there are often quite different priorities in relationship-oriented cultures or cultures with a cyclical perception of time (where the notion of having a "line" after which something should be "dead" does not make sense at all). In such cultures, the focus lies more on reserving enough time for personal interactions and doing things at the "right time" rather than finishing tasks at a particular scheduled hour or day.

Source: Based on information in Lewis (2006) and Pant (2016).

Enemies of priorities management

Managers need to be aware of anything that might distract them from their true priorities. A particularly ubiquitous example is **e-mail**, which, over the past few decades, has turned into a major interruption. Many people behave like Pavlov's dog when they receive an e-mail. In his experiments, the Russian physiologist Ivan Pavlov (1849–1936) found out that dogs salivate not only when they actually get food, but also when they hear a sound that they often heard at the same time as they were presented with food. Seeing the notification of a new incoming message, some people react in a similar way. They drop whatever they are working on at that moment to check the news, fearing that they might miss out on some crucial information. But many e-mails are neither important nor urgent (if there is an urgent issue to resolve, people can always make a phone call), and they can distract our focus from the really important things, thus reducing our productivity and effectiveness. One way of dealing with e-mail overload is to switch off notifications of incoming messages and instead open the mailbox once a day, or at least very few times per day, and then work on processing and responding to a whole batch of e-mails one after the other. Corporations are also beginning to recognize the problem and have started to develop their own strategies for dealing with e-mail overload (see the box *Fighting e-mail overload*).

Fighting e-mail overload

E-mails ought to increase personal productivity. Instead, in many organizations, employees drown in a flood of "carbon copy" (cc) e-mails that constantly interrupt work, intrude into the private space (mainly through mobile devices), increase stress levels, instill a sense of being overwhelmed and an anxiety of falling behind, and have a negative effect on concentration.[50] Slowly, companies have begun to view e-mail overload as a problem and have developed some solutions. Leading German car manufacturer Daimler, for example, provides employees with the option to automatically delete all e-mails that they receive during their holidays.

"This new e-mail absence rule is a significant measure to enable our staff to relax during recovery phases,"[51] highlighted Daimler board member Wilfried Porth. In an even more radical approach, Thierry Breton, former French finance minister and CEO of global information technology service firm Atos, announced that he wanted to ban intra-organizational e-mailing altogether. "It is not normal that some of our fellow employees spend hours in the evening dealing with their e-mails," he argued, claiming that less than 10 percent of the messages employees received were of any use.[52]

When used incorrectly, e-mails are a prime example of time wasting, one of the "enemies" that managers can face in their endeavor to focus on their priorities. The other key enemies are overloading yourself with work and reverse delegation.[53] Here are some potential strategies to deal with these obstacles:[54]

- **Time wasters** come in many forms. In addition to e-mails, they might include unnecessary travel, disorganized or pointless meetings, excessive paperwork, interruptions by visitors—especially those who come unannounced and without any specific purpose—and browsing through social media or other websites, to name just a few. Time wasters keep managers from focusing on what really counts for implementing their agenda. How can we deal with time wasters, then? The first step lies in identifying them, for example, through thinking about how much time we spend on particular tasks. Step two is to question whether the tasks really create additional value. If not, we can develop a strategy for avoiding them. If you spend a lot of time travelling to meetings that do not add much value, for example, you could suggest a different way of keeping each other up to date (e.g. a short telephone conference).

- **Overloading**—putting more things in your schedule than you can possibly work on to a sufficient level—can be avoided through (a) clearly identifying and focusing on your key responsibilities, tasks, and priorities, (b) effective delegation (see Chapter 4), (c) not doing the work of others, (d) not assuming that everything you are confronted with is equally important, and (e) learning to say no. In addition to setting priorities, managing the demands and expectations of others (including your boss or peers) can also help to avoid work overload in the first place.

Reverse delegation:
A situation in which subordinates delegate tasks to their managers.

- **Reverse delegation**—taking over tasks that are actually your subordinates' responsibility—can be discouraged by using an "anti-monkey strategy." In a *Harvard Business Review* article called "Management time: Who's got the monkey?" Oncken and Wass suggested that managers should picture approaching subordinates as having a monkey on their shoulders.[55] The monkey is a metaphor, representing the next step that needs to be taken to resolve a certain issue or problem. As soon as the manager agrees to take care of the problem, the (virtual) monkey jumps onto the manager's back. Over time, the result is a "zoo" full of monkeys in the manager's office, or, in other words, a whole lot of additional work. Oncken and Wass's advice is clear: make sure that the monkey leaves the office on the subordinate's shoulders. By no means does this imply that managers should ignore their subordinates when they ask for help, though. They could, for example, offer advice, quickly help out with one step (e.g. a telephone call) while the subordinate is still in the office, or agree a strategy for solving the problem and a date by which the subordinate should report back. Managers should, however, avoid taking over the whole job if it does not lie in their domain, and ensure that taking the next step remains the subordinate's responsibility.[56]

Effective managers will be able to defeat these "enemies" of priorities management and focus on the tasks that really make a difference. Instead of just following an *"activity maximization"* strategy, in which they try to squeeze as many activities into a certain period of time as possible, they pursue an *"outcome maximization"* strategy with the aim of *"making each activity count* and achieving the desired outcomes."[57]

Liza Landsman: Setting the right priorities at Jet.com

In 2017, Liza Landsman, who describes herself as "a big math geek and lover of data,"[58] was named president of Jet.com. The company is a fast-growing e-commerce venture that had been acquired by Walmart, the world's largest retailer, the year before her appointment. Before joining Jet.com, initially as chief customer officer (with responsibility for marketing, advertising, and creating a compelling customer experience based on data analytics), she had held several other management positions in companies such as E*TRADE Financial, BlackRock, Citigroup, and IBM. She also serves on the board of directors of the GO project, a non-profit organization devoted to supporting school children in need.

In a keynote speech to an executive women's network, Landsman recalled an incident from her high school years when she competed to be the high school yearbook editor. Her mother asked her whether she wanted the job for the position's sake or in order to create a great yearbook. That incident taught her that "we can accomplish just about anything we want in this world as long as we don't care who gets the credit."[59] A further foundation for her leadership career was laid when she worked as a waitress during her college years, an experience that made her realize "the value of great customer service, kindness to others and a very intense work ethic,"[60] as she noted in an interview with the *Huffington Post*.

Landsman highlights the importance of setting clear goals, both for her company (where she sees "delivering a great user experience"[61] and "evolving our strong culture"[62] as priorities) as well as for herself. "Know what you want and then ask for it,"[63] is one of her credos. She points out that actively asking for advice, help, roles, resources—or whatever else is needed to achieve her goals—has helped her tremendously during her career. At the same time, as a "believer in the karmic boomerang,"[64] she acknowledges that asking for support also needs to go hand in hand with supporting others when they need it.

Setting the right goals and knowing what you want means making "hard choices about what matters most,"[65] as Landsman put it. She emphasizes the value of simplicity in a complex and dynamic environment, of distilling the essence and getting rid "of all the distracting and excess stuff around it."[66] When an issue

needs to be resolved at Jet.com, she and her team try to break it down into smaller tasks that can be solved more quickly by a small group of people. In what she calls a "squad-based organizational structure,"[67] dedicated teams work on very specific issues, for example optimizing the checkout of Jet.com's e-commerce portal.

Landsman is convinced that managers need to make choices between their private and professional lives, and considers work–life balance to be a myth. Because you cannot do everything at once, there are some times when work has to take precedence and other times when your private life takes higher priority. Jet.com's president, who is also a mother, is of the opinion that we must make a conscious choice as to when to focus on each, admitting that it is a hard decision in which we sometimes need to disregard other people's expectations.

Landsman was characterized by a colleague as decisive, a "truth teller," and someone who considers the overall picture, but also as "incredibly funny and kind and lovely to work for."[68] She often travels between different geographic locations, but also makes time to see colleagues in Jet.com's open plan office in the company's headquarters in Hoboken, New Jersey. She uses a built-in app on her smartphone to manage her to-do list.

Self-development ranks high in Landsman's priorities. She notes that several mentors have supported her during her career, especially in encouraging her to step out of her comfort zone, challenging her thinking, and helping her to find out when she needed to learn new things. Thus, she became more accustomed to taking risks, which she claimed that she would have been unlikely to do if she had just listened to her "internal pragmatist," as she put it.[69]

Sources: *Birkner (2016); Douglas (2017); Dunn (2017); Molloy (2017); Souza (2017).*

💬 Discussion questions

● How does Liza Landsman approach setting her priorities and "getting things done"?
● What roles do values play in Landsman's professional career?
● Referring to what Landsman said, how can the notion of simplicity help managers to perform in a dynamic and complex environment?
● What else can we learn from Landsman about effective self-management?

2.3 Energy level and resilience

Getty Images/BraunS

In brief

- The nature of management often leads to perceived work overload and psychological strain. It is therefore important for managers to be able to replenish their energy stores.

- Managers can gain energy either through the job itself (e.g. when they are experiencing progress on meaningful tasks or have positive encounters at work) or through high-quality time-out in the evenings, on weekends, or during holidays.

- As managers are frequently confronted with setbacks, they also need to learn how to cope with frustrations. Finding meaning even in hard times, maintaining strong relationships, rejecting or disputing unproductive and negative thoughts, and being able to refocus on new goals when current ones cannot be achieved are all strategies that can help managers to strengthen their resilience.

Stress:
Physical and mental tension resulting from excessive pressure or other demanding circumstances.

Long work hours, highly interdependent jobs that require significant coordination with others, constant availability on e-mail and phone, and job insecurity are forces that drain energy from today's knowledge workers, resulting in fatigue, high stress levels, and in some cases even burnout.[70] Key **sources of stress** for managers include:

- work overload;
- the feeling of lacking control;
- conflicts in interpersonal interactions;
- unfavorable working conditions (e.g. frequent interruptions or a noisy workplace);
- rapid change;
- expectations of unpleasant events; and
- anxiety and fear.[71]

Many managers resort to working long hours and to multitasking as ways to cope with the constant pressures they are facing. Neither of these strategies is likely to succeed in the long term, however. On the contrary, multitasking slows down our brain, hampers creativity, and can make us even more anxious.[72]

One of your colleagues looks a bit worried. You ask him how he feels, and he tells you that he is overwhelmed by the amount of work, and that he does not have enough energy to cope with all the demands. What advice would you give to your colleague to help him "recharge his batteries" and return to a higher energy level again?

Personal energy management

Everyone's energy becomes depleted, and consequently—following a widely used analogy with batteries—needs to be regularly recharged. Several strategies can help managers to **sustain and regain their energy** (see Figure 2.4).

Off-work   Work-related

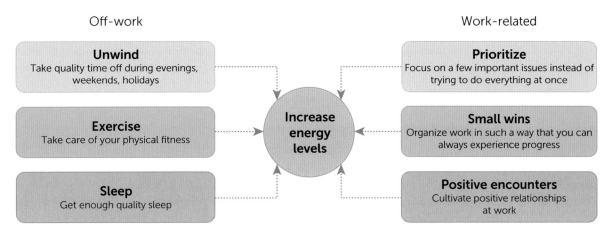

Figure 2.4 Strategies to sustain and regain energy

Just as top athletes need to alternate times of strain with phases of planned rest, personal performance expert Tony Schwartz encourages managers to take a recovery break after every 90 minutes of work.[73] Quality **time-out** from work during evenings, weekends, and holidays, ideally filled with relaxation and positive mastery experiences (successfully performing enjoyably challenging tasks, e.g. in sports), can help to reduce fatigue, as does healthy nutrition, an adequate amount of sleep, and regular physical exercise.[74] The only problem with the latter is that "[w]ith exercise, the key is actually doing it."[75] It only works if it becomes a habit—and habits can only be formed by making something (e.g. exercise) a priority, actively taking the first step, and then having the self-discipline to continue.

Results from a study of knowledge workers in a US software company reveal that in addition to taking time off to recharge, **work-related energy management strategies** can also have a positive effect on vitality levels (ranked in order of magnitude below):[76]

1 Learning something new.
2 Focusing on what gives you joy in your work.
3 Setting yourself a new goal.
4 Doing something that will make a colleague happy.
5 Showing gratitude to someone you work with.
6 Seeking feedback.
7 Reflecting on how you make a difference at work.
8 Reflecting on the meaning of your work.

In their research on creative work in a business context, Teresa Amabile and Steven Kramer examined why people consider a working day to be particularly good or bad in terms of their motivation levels, emotions, and general mood. [77] The results of their study reveal that the most important determinant of a "positive work day" is the experience of **making progress in meaningful work**—even if it's relatively minor—whereas the worst workdays are usually characterized by setbacks. Every step forward in tackling your main priorities can be felt as progress. But Amabile and Kramer also suggest deliberately including "**small wins**," moderately important tasks that can be completed within a short timeframe, in your workdays in order to keep your energy levels high.[78]

In addition, it has been found that **positive relationships at work** have an energizing effect, whereas negative experiences with bosses, colleagues, or customers can have a distinct negative impact on a person's energy levels.[79] Taking your time to attentively listen to what others have to say, providing positive feedback, saying a few encouraging or praising words, or helping others to succeed in their role through sharing resources and information are a few ways of building and nurturing positive relationships at work.

Effective managers know what energizes them and what drains their energy. They are able to **manage their energy levels** through first clearly identifying activities and relationships that have either a positive or a negative impact on them, and then by increasing those activities and encounters which have an energizing effect and reducing those that drain their energy, respectively. You can also use Exercise 5 in the appendix to this chapter to explore your own sources and drains of energy.

Coping with setbacks

Some people are able to cope perfectly well with stress and quickly recover from hardships or misfortune. This quality of being able to positively deal with frustrations and bounce back from setbacks is called **resilience**. It is defined as "patterns of positive adaptation during or following significant adversity or risk."[80] Being faced with problems and stressful situations is a natural feature of the manager's job, so resilience is a key virtue of effective managers. Herbert Stepic, the former CEO of Raiffeisen International, one of the leading banks in Central and Eastern Europe, sees "**frustration tolerance** as the essential quality of a manager," adding: "You are tumbling from time to time, but you must pull yourself out of the mud again."[81]

So what do people who are able to "pull themselves out of the mud again" and **overcome adversity** have in common? Research results suggest that:[82]

1   They have a **clear sense of reality** and are able to understand and accept a situation as it is (without pretending that it is better than it actually is, but also without over-catastrophizing it).

2   They **find meaning even during the hardest times**—just as the Austrian neurologist and psychiatrist Viktor Frankl did when, amidst the terror of a Nazi concentration camp, still found purpose in his fate as he contemplated giving a lecture on the psychology of these camps to outsiders once he was released.[83] Resilient people do not abandon hope even under the worst circumstances, but are still able to find some meaning in their situation.

3   They have a **bricolage attitude**; in other words, they are adaptive and ingenious when it comes to finding tools and strategies to deal with a particular problem they face. Improvisation and problem-solving skills are particularly important in unknown and difficult situations.

4   They have **positive relationships** that provide them with a "safety net" and the possibility to share and come to terms with their problems.

Resilience is primarily a **cognitive challenge**. It is closely linked to how we think about negative experiences. When we face adversity, we actually have a choice of which attitude we take toward it. American psychologist Albert Ellis developed the **Rational Emotive Behavior Theory** (or REBT, in short) as a psychotherapeutic approach to handling difficult situations and disturbances in life. REBT was inspired by the works of philosophers such as Epictetus, who wrote that people "are disturbed, not by things, but by the principles and notions which they form concerning things."[84] As a key concept of REBT, Ellis proposed the **ABC model** to explain the interactions between thoughts and emotions when we experience difficult situations.[85] The model (see Figure 2.5) suggests that it is very often not the adversity (A) itself that causes negative psychological consequences (C), but the beliefs (B) that we hold about the adversity. Thus, it is not the disturbance itself but our attitude toward this disturbance that counts. As human beings are sometimes inclined to think irrationally (for example, through catastrophizing or "all-or-nothing" thinking), the beliefs that we form about adversity are often a lot worse than the objective situation. If we successfully challenge (or dispute) these beliefs, we can avoid the negative emotional consequences of the event or development that was perceived as an adversity (see also the example in the *Zooming in on the ABC model* box).

We can put things into perspective by asking questions such as "What would happen in the worst-case scenario—and why shouldn't I be able to cope with the outcome?" or "How

Resilience:
The ability to adapt to or bounce back from adverse situations.

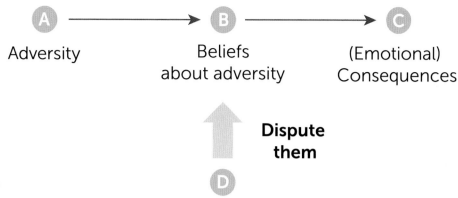

Figure 2.5 The ABC model of Rational Emotive Behavioral Theory

Source: Inspired by concepts in Ellis (1994).

Zooming in on ▶ THE ABC MODEL

How does Albert Ellis's ABC model (see Figure 2.5) work in practice? Let us take the following example:

1 Imagine that the CEO of one of your company's key customers tells you that she wants to cancel their supply contract because her team has been dissatisfied with the service levels (this is our adversity, A).
2 You might start to worry that by losing this customer, you will not reach your budget targets, and could even lose your job (these are your beliefs about the adversity, B).
3 This might lead to negative emotional consequences (C), for example anxiety and heightened stress levels.
4 Alternatively, you also have the option of rejecting or disputing (D) your beliefs by identifying and challenging irrational negative thoughts. Instead of worrying about all the bad things that could happen if your company lost the customer, you might think about strategies that could help to convince them to stay or—if there really is no chance of retaining the customer—examine how this incident could help your company to improve its service levels. Thus, through taking a different perspective, the difficult situation that you have encountered could be seen as a trigger for developing more positive customer relations in the future.

When faced with a problem in the future, try challenging any negative beliefs. Then reflect on whether using the model helped you.

---

important will this problem seem a month/a year/five years from now?" What seems to be an immense problem right now often turns out to be a rather minor issue from a distance. The process of identifying and changing negative and irrational thoughts has also been termed **cognitive restructuring**, and has been identified as a critical skill for coping effectively with adverse situations.[86]

Cognitive restructuring:
The process of identifying and disputing negative and irrational thoughts and beliefs.

Another cognitive technique that is linked to becoming more resilient is **adaptive self-regulation of unattainable goals**.[87] People usually experience psychological distress when they do not reach the goals that they have set for themselves. If something does not turn out as expected, we can either lament our fate, or take the stance of the dean of a renowned Swiss business school who said "Failure is not a category for me. Outcomes, whether positive or negative ones, just create new situations. In every new situation, I again have the chance to decide, and to choose what seems best at that point."[88] Research has confirmed that the ability to disengage from a prior, unattainable goal and to reengage with new goals is clearly linked to well-being.[89] Being able to adjust your expectations and set new goals as the situation demands is therefore another building block for becoming a resilient manager.

2.4 Developing yourself

iStock.com/mihailomilovanovic

In brief

- It is a natural aspiration for all people—including managers—to grow. Personal growth starts with identifying the key skills and strengths that are needed to achieve personal and organizational goals.
- People develop by following a cycle of:
  - (a) setting concrete, challenging, but achievable development goals;
  - (b) deliberately undertaking those activities which are necessary for achieving these goals;
  - (c) seeking feedback about their performance; and
  - (d) persevering (in the case of success) or adapting (in the case of unfulfilled expectations).
- Building relationships with people who you can learn from, asking honest questions about your self-development, and working on your attitudes are further strategies for tapping into your full managerial potential.

Potential:
Latent abilities that a person could be capable of developing in the future.

Developing yourself is about striving to reach your **potential**, growing, and finding fulfillment in your work. Two preconditions for effective personal development have already been discussed in this chapter: knowing your personal as well as your organization's goals, and knowing your main strengths. Development is about strengthening strengths. The importance of focusing on strengths was empirically confirmed by a leadership research project conducted by the Gallup market research institute. Based on interviews with more than 20,000 leaders and more than 10,000 people who reported on why they followed the person they considered as the most important leader in their life, the Gallup researchers concluded that investing in strengths is one of the most important habits of effective leaders.[90] That is not to say that weaknesses are entirely unimportant—but **success always comes from harnessing strengths**, so this is where the main focus of development should lie. As Roman statesman and writer Cicero advised, we should "work hardest at the things for which we are best suited."[91]

Which kind of strengths do managers need to develop? Several studies have been conducted to identify the **key skills for effective managers**. Whetten and Cameron, for example, found that skills in the following four categories were particularly important:[92]

- **Self-management skills** (self-awareness, managing time and stress);
- **Communication skills** (verbal communication, listening);
- **Leadership skills** (motivating and influencing others, delegating, team building, managing conflict);
- **Following the right priorities** (decision making, problem recognition and problem solving, goal setting, creating a vision).

Managers need to develop these skills (which are all discussed in this textbook) over time. They can do so by going through a development cycle.

Development cycle:
A four-step process (Challenge—Act—Feedback—Reflect and correct) that describes how people can effectively develop skills and competencies.

The development cycle

Comparing personal (or organizational) goals with current strengths and skills will reveal your development needs. Once these needs are clearly defined, the four-step **development cycle** can start (see Figure 2.6):[93]

1 **Challenge:** Set yourself a concrete goal linked to your development need—strive to master something that you have not been able to do before. Development goals should be

challenging, but not unachievable. The aim is to get one small step closer to your ultimate ambition and stretch your abilities. Let us assume, for example, that you would like to improve your presentation skills. For that purpose, you could set yourself the challenge of holding an effective presentation for the management board.

2 **Act:** Take deliberate action toward achieving your goal. Research has found that **deliberate practice** is crucial for achieving excellence in a certain domain.[94] To know exactly which action to take, you can either imitate a successful role model or use a trial-and-error approach.[95] In our example, you could watch online videos of successful presentations and then deliberately focus on a certain aspect of the presentation (e.g. connecting with your audience through eye contact) when you deliver your own.

3 **Feedback:** Learning only takes place when we understand why some of our actions either succeeded or failed. Feedback, either from the task itself (e.g. whether or not we have progressed) or from other people (e.g. our boss, co-workers, or customers), can support us in critically evaluating our own performance. In our example, you could ask members of the management board for critical feedback on your presentation.

4 **Reflect and correct:** Reflection on feedback that you have received is the basis for taking corrective action in case the outcome was not as expected. If the original actions were successful, they can be replicated. Otherwise, they need to be adapted. Depending on what you noticed during the presentation and the feedback that you received, you could think about what to improve in future presentations.

Deliberate practice: A learning process in which the learners try to enhance their performance through repeating activities with a conscious focus on improving certain aspects of these activities and reflecting on feedback that they receive on how they performed the activities.

Once the development cycle is complete, it can start again with a new goal, preferably one that takes you beyond your prior achievement level.

The development cycle (shown in Figure 2.6) is not only suitable for developing yourself, but can also be used as a basis for setting the right initiatives and actions for developing others in your team (see Chapter 3).

Think about one skill or competency that you would like to develop further. Which challenge could you set yourself for improving this skill? Who could give you honest critical feedback on how you performed on this challenge? What else could you do to develop the skill or competency?

Figure 2.6 The (self-) development cycle

Source: Adapted from Figure 1, p. 246 in Sternad, D. (2015) 'A Challenge-Feedback Learning Approach to Teaching International Business', *Journal of Teaching in International Business*, 26(4): 241–257, DOI: 10.1080/08975930.2015.1124355. Reprinted by permission of the publisher Taylor & Francis Ltd: www.tandfonline.com.

In essence, self-development is about **setting yourself the right goals and learning from the results of the actions** that you are taking in your endeavor to reach these goals. It is an ongoing process, and it quite naturally includes setbacks. After all, as the mountaineer and adventurer Reinhold Messner (the first man who climbed all of the world's 14 summits over 8,000 meters) said, "we learn almost exclusively through failure."[96] He is convinced that "human beings are predisposed to just learn when we have a setback," pointing out that we cannot improve through our successes if we do not really know why we succeeded.[97] This is in line with writer and novelist William Faulkner's advice not to bother so much with being better than others but rather to "[t]ry to be better than yourself" and "[t]each yourself by your own mistakes."[98]

Although self-development is everyone's personal responsibility (see the box *Benjamin Franklin's virtuous self-management* for one example of how to exercise this responsibility), it is not necessarily a lonely task, but can also be supported by other people. Top athletes cannot excel without a coach. Likewise, it makes sense for managers to have someone around to whom they can turn for feedback on their performance and development (see Chapter 3 for more detailed information on the coaching process). Thus, **building good relationships with people who you can learn from** is as crucial for personal growth as setting the right development goals and choosing the right challenges. This was also noticed by philosopher Michel de Montaigne more than 400 years ago when he wrote that "our mind is strengthened by contact with [other] vigorous and well-ordered minds."[99]

FROM A DIFFERENT ANGLE

Benjamin Franklin's virtuous self-management

Benjamin Franklin (1706–1790) was a successful businessman, author, scientist, inventor, postmaster, and a leading politician and diplomat of his time. His achievements range from the invention of the lightning rod to being one of the Committee of Five who drafted the Declaration of Independence in 1776, thus becoming one of the Founding Fathers of the United States of America.

How can one man be effective in so many domains at the same time? Benjamin Franklin provided some insight into his self-management principles in his autobiography:[100]

1 *Franklin was values-driven*. He set up "Thirteen Virtues" that he wanted to achieve for himself: temperance, silence, order, resolution, frugality, industry, sincerity, justice, moderation, cleanliness, tranquility, chastity, and humility. Each of these virtues was accompanied by simple precepts (e.g. for silence, "Speak not but what may benefit others or yourself; avoid trifling conversation"[101], or for frugality, "Make no expense but do good to others or yourself; i.e. waste nothing"[102]).

2 *Franklin devised a system to give feedback to himself*. To transform his virtues into habits, he tried to concentrate on each of them, one after the other, over thirteen weeks. For that purpose, he kept a little book with tables in which he would note down every day whether he had achieved the virtue that was the consideration for that particular week, thereby providing himself with visible feedback on his progress.

3 *Franklin tried to bring order into his days*. His little book contained a page with a 24-hour schedule which he aimed to follow. The ideal day would start with the question in the morning: "What good shall I do this day?"[103], would include four hours of work in both the morning and afternoon (quite a low amount compared to the long hours that today's managers often work), provide enough time for music, conversation, and other entertainment, and end with an examination of the day and the question: "What good have I done this day?"[104] Franklin admitted that he found it extremely difficult to follow his own schedule, and frequently failed to do so altogether. Yet he felt that he was "by the endeavor, a better and happier man than ... [if he] had not attempted it."[105]

Source: Based on information in Franklin (2008).

Asking yourself questions

In addition to continuously going through the self-development cycle and learning from others, self-development also means regularly reflecting on your actions by asking yourself questions, and in particular tough ones such as:

- Do I really attend to the most important issues or do I let myself be distracted?
- What is my dominant response pattern under pressure and stress?
- Do I put the interests of my organization ahead of my own?
- Am I adequately taking care of the needs of people around me?
- Am I really listening to others?
- Do I blame others or circumstances for my own low performance?
- Have I developed detrimental habits that I would like to get rid of?
- Am I making progress on my development goals?
- Do I stay true to myself and to my values or do I wear a mask in my job?
- Am I really happy with my career choice?

For Whetten and Cameron, "developing management skills—that is, the skills needed to manage one's own life as well as relationships with others—is a ceaseless endeavor."[106] It is an endeavor that starts with self-awareness and self-examination. Once you stop questioning what you are doing, you also stop learning. We often try to avoid the difficult questions in order to avoid having to confront ourselves with the truth. In order to develop yourself, a realistic assessment of your competencies, strengths, weaknesses, and habits is a necessary precondition.

CEO BEST PRACTICE

Learning from failure at Uniqlo

The Japanese businessman Tadashi Yanai opened his first Unique Clothing Warehouse in Hiroshima in 1984. It became an instant success, so he expanded the business with hundreds of additional stores under the Uniqlo brand in suburban roadside locations all across Japan. In 2001, in an effort to replicate Uniqlo's success abroad, he decided to enter the British market. Out of the 21 stores that were opened over two-and-a-half years in what Yanai later called "a devastating debut,"[107] 16 had to close because the local management was unable to get the business off the ground. Yanai, however, was convinced that in every failure, there is also a "seed of the next success."[108] He established a set of management principles for himself and his company in which he highlighted the value of setting yourself challenges and taking action ("Be proactive and challenge yourself"), reflecting on which of your actions were right or wrong ("Be your own toughest critic"), and learning lessons from both successes and failures in order to "improve and renew yourself."[109] Yanai learned his lessons well. He changed the strategy for the international expansion of his retail chain, focusing on attention-attracting stores in prime locations instead of suburban stores. In 2018, Fast Retailing, the holding company that Yanai built to manage Uniqlo and other associated brands, ran more than 2,100 stores with over 50,000 employees in Asia, Australia, North America, and Europe. With his willingness to learn and develop himself, Yanai, whose autobiography carries the revealing title *One Win, Nine Losses*, made it to the top of the rich list in Japan.

→ Key takeaway

For managers, both successes and failures can provide great learning opportunities if they carefully reflect on why they succeeded or failed. If you challenge yourself and take action you may fail, but you will definitely take one step forward on your development path.

Sources: Based on information in businesstimes.com.sg (2016); fastretailing.com (2019); Takeuchi (2012).

Self-development does not only mean working on your skills—it also involves working on **attitudes**. How we see a problem (or whether we see a problem as a problem at all, or rather as an opportunity), for example, very much depends on our own interpretation of what we experience. Manfred Kets de Vries, Professor of Leadership Development at INSEAD, refers to an African tale about a hyena and an eagle. A grandfather was telling his grandson about a war between them, in which the hyena stood for "anger, hatred, revenge, spite, vindictiveness, sadness, and despair" and all other "emotions that may destroy our soul," while the eagle stood for "hope, joy, faith, generosity, optimism, growth, resilience, laughter, and love," all feelings and values that are good for our soul.[110] As the little boy asked his grandfather who would win the war, the grandfather said: "The one we feed."[111] So who do you feed, your hyena or your eagle?

Samar Singla: Hailing the auto-rickshaw to success

Together with a colleague, Samar Singla developed the idea of a mobile phone app for booking auto-rickshaws (three-wheeled carts used for carrying passengers and goods in many Asian cities). The Jugnoo app, which was launched in the north Indian city of Chandigarh in 2014, allows drivers (who pay a 10 percent commission to Jugnoo) to connect with potential customers. Singla had estimated that the five million auto-rickshaws in India were only active 30 percent of the time, mainly due to the inefficient conventional ("analogue") hailing process. Jugnoo was able to provide a more effective way to match customers and drivers, thus reducing drivers' waiting times between the rides. By maximizing capacity, the auto-rickshaw driver could generate a higher income.

The concept of offering an online auto-rickshaw "hailing" system with a standardized pricing model soon gained a considerable following. Three years after Jugnoo had been founded, it claimed to have five million active users, 12,000 auto-rickshaws (also known as tuk-tuks) actively operating in its network, and around 40,000 transactions per day. During the same period, the company received US$16 million in funding from several investment rounds.

Following a "cockroach approach," Jugnoo aims for growth in India's tier-two and tier-three cities which the two large transportation providers Uber and Ola Cabs have not seen as priority targets. In an effort to further benefit from the transportation capacity that Jugnoo has aggregated, Singla also complements the passenger transport service with what he calls "hyperlocal commerce": local delivery services for meals, groceries, and other goods based on its existing network of auto-rickshaws. An additional revenue-generating opportunity has been created by offering the Jugnoo software to other companies in more than 100 countries worldwide.

During the first few years in business, however, Singla was faced with several challenges:

- At the beginning, drivers were reluctant to use the new technology and comply with standard fares. "Changing behavior is always difficult,"[112] commented Singla, but he and his team were able to convince the drivers, one by one, of the benefits of using the Jugnoo system.
- Jugnoo faced a challenging competitive environment. In 2015, the major player Uber entered into the auto-rickshaw business. According to Singla, Jugnoo's larger competitors were "willing to burn money on taxis, which creates artificial pricing pressure on us, so our margins aren't as decent as we'd like."[113]
- A competitor was accused of "unethical practices"[114] in which it set up fake Jugnoo accounts allegedly in order to make several thousand cancellations, leading to a considerable loss of revenue for both Jugnoo and the auto-rickshaw drivers.
- In what have been called "major hiccups in the otherwise seamless journey,"[115] Jugnoo had to temporarily roll back its meal and fresh produce delivery services due to a lack of demand, but only to relaunch them later.

Singla, who claims to have adopted a "focused approach" in which he tried to "solve one problem at a time,"[116] has quite a pragmatic view when it comes to dealing with challenges and setbacks. He considers every failure to be a learning experience, one step forward in the journey of success: "Nobody remembers your failures, once you succeed,"[117] he said in an interview with *Daily Indian*. He sees entrepreneurship as a "continuous marathon" in which the value of learning "cannot be emphasized enough."[118] If he starts something new, his attitude is: "if it works, it works. If [it] does not, we move on."[119]

In a fast-moving and challenging environment, Singla sometimes needs to recharge, either through 15-minute power naps or by spending quality time with his daughter. But he is also careful not to waste energy on "activities that suck your time without yielding any worthy results."[120]

Learning and developing himself and others rank high on Singla's agenda. In an interview with the personal productivity advice website *Lifehacker India*, he gave the advice not to give up easily but to leave your comfort zone, and "keep trying despite failures … the more you try, the more you learn and grow."[121] At the same time, he emphasized the need to learn from mistakes, highlighting the importance of quickly understanding "what is working for us and what is not."[122]

A strong development orientation also lies at the basis of Singla's leadership philosophy. He aims to empower his team members through encouraging them to take ownership of their work and giving them "the freedom and space to make mistakes and take responsibility of fixing them when they happen."[123] Providing others with the possibility to participate and share their ideas, refraining from micro-management, and giving timely and constructive feedback are further activities that the founder of Jugnoo sees as key characteristics of "good leaders."

Sources: Bhargava (2016); Blaggan (2017); dailyindian.com (2016); Overby (2017); startuptalky.com (2018); Thomas and Bhattacharya (2016).

 Discussion questions

- What challenges do managers of start-up companies like Jugnoo typically face?
- How does Samar Singla try to cope with challenges and setbacks?
- How would you describe Singla's approach to learning and self-development?
- What are the potential advantages and disadvantages of this approach?

Conclusion

At the start of this chapter, we looked at the case of Ton Büchner, the CEO of the Dutch paints and chemicals group Akzo Nobel, who took almost three months leave due to fatigue, resulting in a drop in the company's share value. However, on returning to work, Büchner announced the completion of a deal in which his company sold part of its coatings business for more than one billion US dollars. This led to an immediate 7.6 percent rise in Akzo Nobel's share price, overshadowing the earlier drop. A *Wall Street Journal* article called the story "a fine advertisement for the restorative powers of time off."[124]

Although investors reacted negatively to his withdrawal in the short term, Büchner's time out did not do any harm to the company. The loss in share price following the announcement of his temporary leave was soon recovered. For those who take a long-term view, Büchner's courageous move made perfect sense. As well as knowing his strengths, the CEO also seemed to understand his weaknesses, and acted accordingly. He recharged his batteries, and returned strengthened and with a lot more energy. By coping with the setback and taking control again, he also showed resilience, and conveyed the impression that if he is able to manage himself during difficult times, he would probably also be able to do the same for his organization. Büchner went on to lead Akzo Nobel successfully until he resigned in 2017.[125]

As the example of Ton Büchner shows, we have to acknowledge that managers are human beings, not machines. As such, they are on a constant development path which requires skills in self-awareness, self-reflection, and self-management.

The self-development process for managers is also highly relevant to the development of the organizations for which they work. "The intrapsychic themes of the CEO often dictate the structure of priorities of the organization,"[126] writes Kets de Vries in his book *The Leader on The Couch*. "Because organizational neurosis is rooted in personal neurosis, organizational change is predicated on personal change."[127] Thus, effective self-management is one of the main pillars of the effective management of organizations.

✓ Review questions

1 What should managers know about themselves as a precondition for becoming effective in their self-development?
2 What can you do to better understand your strengths?
3 What role do values play in managerial effectiveness?
4 What is meant by "priorities management"?
5 How can managers identify priorities?
6 What can managers do to enhance their personal productivity?
7 What are the advantages and potential disadvantages of using a structured personal productivity system?
8 What are the main "enemies" of effective priorities management and how can managers deal with them?
9 Why do managers often experience high stress levels?
10 What can managers do to reduce their stress levels and increase their energy levels?
11 What is meant by the term "resilience" and why is it important in a managerial context?
12 What can managers generally do to cope with the setbacks and frustrations that they encounter?
13 How can Albert Ellis's ABC model help managers in coping with difficult situations?
14 What can managers do to develop their skills and competencies?
15 Which questions could you ask yourself in order to reflect on your own self-development process?

⑦ Critical reflection questions

1 Managers are sometimes faced with situations in which their own values collide (e.g. achievement and concern for others). Do you think that it is necessary for managers to have a personal hierarchy of values? Which values would you put at the top of your own personal hierarchy?
2 In your opinion, what are the advantages and disadvantages of using a structured personal productivity system to manage your priorities?
3 Managers often seem to be stressed in their work. Do you see stress as an unavoidable side-effect of managerial work or could you also imagine stress-free management?
4 Reflecting on your strategies and actions is a key element of the self-development cycle. How often do you systematically reflect on your self-development? What could you (and managers) do to increase the level of reflection?
5 Is it really necessary for managers to put so much emphasis on self-management and self-development? Wouldn't it be better for managers to focus their energy fully on managing and developing their organizations instead?

☞ Managerial implications

- Effective management begins with effective self-management, and the basis for effective self-management lies in matching your goals with your strengths. As a precondition, you first need to understand your goals and strengths well.
- Values and attitudes matter in the management role. Values can help managers to follow the right goals and do the right things, and positive attitudes can help them to see opportunities and overcome challenges.
- Effective managers know how to set priorities and then focus their energy on these priority issues. Setting priorities also means not overloading yourself with things that might, at first sight, look "important," but which do not actually contribute to significantly advancing the organization.

- Managers can only be effective if they have enough energy to carry out their priorities. It is therefore important to actively monitor your personal energy levels, know your sources and drains of energy, and deliberately invest in recharging your batteries.
- Due to the nature of the managerial role, managers often face frustrations and setbacks. For this reason, it is imperative for managers to become resilient, which is mainly a matter of attitude toward challenging situations.
- Effective managers are focused on both the development of their organizations and the development of their own skills and competencies. Setting challenging goals for yourself, deliberate practice, seeking feedback about your performance, and reflecting on why something worked well or not so well are crucial steps in the self-development process.

Endnotes

[1] ft.com (2012); independent.co.uk (2012).
[2] ft.com (2012).
[3] ft.com (2012).
[4] Kets de Vries (2006), p. 164.
[5] Pausanias (1918), 10.24.1.
[6] Ehrlinger et al. (2008).
[7] Ehrlinger et al. (2008).
[8] Nash and Stevenson (2004).
[9] Nash and Stevenson (2004).
[10] Nash and Stevenson (2004).
[11] da Vinci (2008), p. 208.
[12] Drucker (1999b), p. 66.
[13] Kaplan (2007; 2008).
[14] Drucker (1999b), pp. 66–69.
[15] Drucker (1999b).
[16] Kaplan (2008).
[17] Kaplan (2008).
[18] Ignatius (2011).
[19] Bryant (2009b).
[20] Bryant (2009b).
[21] goldmansachs.com (2018).
[22] Ignatius (2011), p. 114.
[23] Schwartz (1992), p. 1.
[24] Rokeach (1973).
[25] Gao (2017).
[26] Rokeach (1973; 1979).
[27] Bigoness and Blakely (1996).
[28] Ravlin and Meglino (1989).
[29] Williams (2011).
[30] Christensen (2010).
[31] Urbany et al. (2008).
[32] Drucker (1999b).
[33] This situation is inspired by a real situation reported on by Badaracco Jr. and Webb (1995).
[34] Porter and Nohria (2018).
[35] Oxford Dictionaries (2017).
[36] Drucker (1999a), p. 87.
[37] Drucker (1999a), p. 93.
[38] The French original is "on ne perd pas de temps quand on aiguise ses outils" (Möller 2012, p. 78).
[39] Drucker (1967), p. 24.
[40] Marcus Aurelius (2004), pp. 35–37.
[41] Drucker (1999a), p. 92.
[42] Yeomans (1998).
[43] Allen and Schwartz (2011), p. 84.
[44] Allen (2001); Allen and Schwartz (2011).

[45] Haraty et al. (2016).
[46] KC et al. (2017).
[47] Luecke (2004).
[48] The suggestions are taken from Luecke (2004).
[49] Lewis (2006), p. 57.
[50] Barley et al. (2011).
[51] spiegel.de (2012).
[52] telegraph.co.uk (2011b).
[53] Luecke (2004).
[54] Some of the following suggestions are based on Luecke (2004).
[55] Oncken and Wass (1974).
[56] Oncken and Wass (1974).
[57] Malkoc and Tonietto (2019), p. 49.
[58] Birkner (2016).
[59] Souza (2017).
[60] Dunn (2017).
[61] Molloy (2017).
[62] Dunn (2017).
[63] Souza (2017).
[64] Dunn (2017).
[65] Molloy (2017).
[66] Molloy (2017).
[67] Molloy (2017).
[68] Birkner (2016).
[69] Dunn (2017).
[70] Fritz et al. (2011), p. 29.
[71] Whetten and Cameron (2011), p. 139.
[72] Dean and Webb (2011).
[73] Allen and Schwartz (2011).
[74] Fritz et al. (2011), p. 30.
[75] Pozen (2011), p. 130.
[76] Fritz et al. (2011), p. 34.
[77] Amabile and Kramer (2011).
[78] Amabile and Kramer (2011).
[79] Dutton (2003).
[80] Masten et al. (2009), p. 118.
[81] trend (2005); translated from German by the author; emphasis in bold by the author.
[82] Coutu (2002); Masten et al. (2009).
[83] Frankl (2006).
[84] Epictetus (2019).
[85] Ellis (1994).
[86] Arnkoff (1986).
[87] Wrosch et al. (2003).
[88] The quote is taken from an oral statement that Katrin Muff, Dean of BSL Business School

Lausanne, gave at a class discussion at IMTA International Management Teachers' Academy in Bled, Slovenia, 10 June 2010; the quote was confirmed by Katrin Muff in an e-mail to the author on 4 November 2017.
[89] Wrosch et al. (2003).
[90] Rath and Conchie (2008).
[91] Cicero (2001), pp. 39–40.
[92] Whetten and Cameron (2009), p. 31.
[93] Sternad (2015).
[94] Ericsson (2018).
[95] March (2010), pp. 19–20.
[96] sueddeutsche.de (2010b), translated by the author.
[97] sueddeutsche.de (2010b), translated by the author.
[98] Faulkner and Stein (1956).
[99] de Montaigne (2004), p. 32.
[100] Franklin (2008).
[101] Franklin (2008), p. 101.
[102] Franklin (2008), p. 101.
[103] Franklin (2008), p. 107.
[104] Franklin (2008), p. 107.
[105] Franklin (2008), p. 109.
[106] Whetten and Cameron (2011), p. 27.
[107] businesstimes.com.sg (2016).
[108] Takeuchi (2012), p. 11.
[109] Takeuchi (2012), p. 27.
[110] Kets de Vries (2009), pp. 17–18.
[111] Kets de Vries (2009), pp. 17–18.
[112] Overby (2017).
[113] Overby (2017).
[114] Bhargava (2016).
[115] startuptalky.com (2017).
[116] Blaggan (2017).
[117] dailyindian.com (2016).
[118] Thomas and Bhattacharya (2016).
[119] Thomas and Bhattacharya (2016).
[120] dailyindian.com (2016).
[121] Blaggan (2017).
[122] Blaggan (2017).
[123] dailyindian.com (2016).
[124] wsj.com (2012).
[125] Dean (2017).
[126] Kets de Vries (2006), p. xv.
[127] Kets de Vries (2006), p. 327.

Visit the companion website at macmillanihe.com/sternad-management **to access multiple choice questions, useful weblinks and additional materials.**

Appendix: Exercises for improving your personal effectiveness

Exercise 1: Setting your life goals

This exercise can help you to reflect on your most important goals.

Think about the overarching goals that you would like to achieve in life in what Nash and Stevenson (2004) called the four main "realms of life." Write down a minimum of one goal per area.

1 **Work and career:** *What would you like to achieve in your career? What would you want to be remembered for at the end of your career?*

_____
_____
_____
_____
_____
_____
_____

2 **Family:** *What are your main goals for your family life?*

_____
_____
_____
_____
_____
_____

3 **Self-development:** *What are your main self-development goals (e.g. related to which knowledge and skills you would like to acquire, which attitudes or habits you would like to develop, or which dreams you would like to realize)?*

_____
_____
_____
_____
_____
_____

4 **Contribution to the community:** *What contribution would you like to make to other people's lives/to the community?*

_____
_____
_____
_____
_____
_____

Exercise 2: From life goals to concrete next steps

This exercise can help you to break down your life goals into more specific yearly goals and actionable next steps.

1   Take **one** of the life goals that you identified in Exercise 1, and think of a specific goal that you could set yourself **over the next year** in order to make progress toward your life goal.

2   Determine concrete and actionable **next step(s)** that will help you to achieve this goal.

3   Repeat the exercise for the other life goals from Exercise 1.

Write down your **life goal:**

_____
_____
_____
_____
_____
_____
_____
_____
_____

▼

Which specific goal can you set yourself for **one year from now** *which brings you closer to achieving your life goal?*

_____
_____
_____
_____
_____
_____
_____
_____
_____

▼

Determine the **next step(s)** *that you need to take to achieve your yearly goal:*

_____
_____
_____
_____
_____
_____
_____
_____
_____

Exercise 3: Discover your strengths

In this exercise, you will try out three approaches to identifying your strengths.

1   *In the list below, draw a circle around the five terms that best describe your personal strengths. You can also add additional terms if what you consider to be your most important personal strengths are not covered in the list.*

Ability to concentrate	Discipline	Persuasiveness
Ability to delegate	Eagerness to learn	Positivity
Ability to take criticism	Enthusiasm	Prudence
Accuracy	Flexibility	Reliability
Adaptability	Good listener	Resilience
Analytical thinking	Good networker	Responsibility
Articulateness	Good presenter	Risk taking
Assertiveness	Humor	Self-confidence
Commitment	Initiative	Self-control
Communication skills	Innovativeness	Self-initiative
Creativity	Kindness	Self-motivation
Critical thinking	Leadership ability	Social intelligence
Curiosity	Mental balance	Spontaneity
Dependability	Open-mindedness	Tactfulness
Detail orientation	Organizational skills	Team player
Determination	Patience	Trustworthiness
Diligence	Perseverance	Willingness to learn
_____	_____	_____
_____	_____	_____

2   *Rate yourself against each of the following attributes by placing an "X" in the positions which best represent you.*

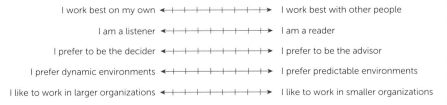

Source: *Inspired by concepts in Drucker (1999b).*

3 *Describe one event in your life (e.g. during your education, at work, or in sports) where you performed exceptionally well.*

_____
_____
_____
_____
_____
_____
_____
_____
_____
_____
_____
_____
_____
_____
_____
_____
_____
_____
_____
_____
_____
_____
_____
_____
_____
_____
_____
_____
_____
_____
_____

Which of your strengths contributed to achieving this exceptional performance level?

Strength 1: _____
_____

Strength 2: _____
_____

Strength 3: _____
_____

Exercise 4: Reflect on your values

This exercise will help you to reflect on your core values.

1   *Take a look at the list of values below. Draw a circle around the five values which you consider to be most important for you personally. You can also add additional values on the lines below the list.*

Achievement	Cooperation	Improvement	Recognition
Advancement	Courage	Independence	Responsibility
Authenticity	Empathy	Individuality	Service orientation
Autonomy	Equality	Influence	Status
Balance	Excellence	Innovation	Success
Care for others	Fairness	Integrity	Sustainability
Community	Flexibility	Optimism	Transparency
Compassion	Harmony	Power	Wealth
Competence	Honesty	Professionalism	Winning
Credibility	Humility	Quality orientation	Wisdom
_____	_____	_____	_____
_____	_____	_____	_____

2   *Take the five values that you selected from the list above. Try to rank them according to how important these values are for you, starting with the most important.*

Value no. 1:   _____

Value no. 2:   _____

Value no. 3:   _____

Value no. 4:   _____

Value no. 5:   _____

Exercise 5: Identify your sources and drains of energy

This exercise can help you to get a better overview of what gives you energy and what drains your energy.

(a) Identify your sources of energy

Which work-related activities give you energy?

_____
_____
_____
_____
_____
_____
_____

Which non-work activities give you energy?

_____
_____
_____
_____
_____
_____
_____

Which relationships give you energy?

_____
_____
_____
_____
_____
_____

Which food gives you energy?

_____
_____
_____
_____
_____
_____

Which other energy sources do you have?

_____
_____
_____
_____
_____
_____

(b) Identify your drains of energy

Which work-related activities drain your energy?

_____

_____

_____

_____

_____

_____

Which non-work activities drain your energy?

_____

_____

_____

_____

_____

_____

Which relationships drain your energy?

_____

_____

_____

_____

_____

_____

Which food drains your energy?

_____

_____

_____

_____

_____

_____

What else drains your energy?

_____

_____

_____

_____

_____

_____

(c)   Take action to increase your energy levels

→ Think of activities that you could initiate next week in order to increase your energy level (either through deliberately tapping into a source of energy or avoiding an energy drain).

→ For one of the activities that you identified above, focus on changing your habits by doing this for one week (note down at the end of every day if you have achieved your aim).

→ Reflect on the results. Do you want to continue with the new habit?

_____
_____
_____
_____
_____
_____
_____
_____
_____
_____
_____
_____
_____
_____
_____
_____
_____
_____
_____
_____
_____
_____
_____
_____
_____
_____
_____
_____
_____
_____
_____
_____
_____
_____
_____
_____
_____
_____
_____
_____
_____

Source: *Partly inspired by ideas in Clawson (2012).*

II

ENHANCING INTERPERSONAL EFFECTIVENESS

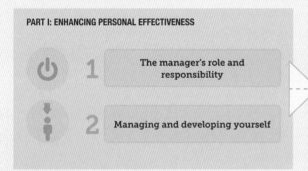

PART I: ENHANCING PERSONAL EFFECTIVENESS

1   The manager's role and responsibility

2   Managing and developing yourself

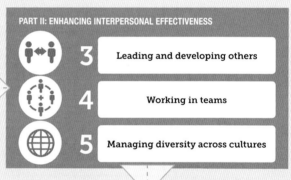

PART II: ENHANCING INTERPERSONAL EFFECTIVENESS

3   Leading and developing others

4   Working in teams

5   Managing diversity across cultures

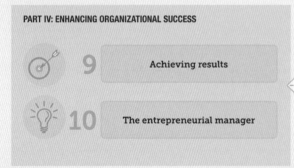

PART IV: ENHANCING ORGANIZATIONAL SUCCESS

9   Achieving results

10   The entrepreneurial manager

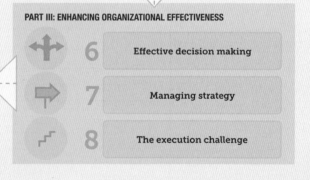

PART III: ENHANCING ORGANIZATIONAL EFFECTIVENESS

6   Effective decision making

7   Managing strategy

8   The execution challenge

Managers achieve their goals together with other people. In Part II, we focus on how managers can influence the performance and develop the performance potential of others, both on an individual level and on a team level. We will also become acquainted with the principles of well-functioning teamwork and analyze how managers can effectively work with diverse teams and in an intercultural context.

In **Chapter 3,** *Leading and developing others,* we will explore what contributes to the performance of people in an organizational context. Specifically, we will take a look at key factors that can have an impact on employee motivation and reflect upon what managers can do to influence the motivation of others. We will also discuss the processes and tools that managers can use for developing the performance potential of their team members as well as for dealing with poor performance. These include, for example, effective delegation, performance reviews, and coaching. The last part of the chapter provides information about how managers can recruit the right people, and how they can deal with one of the most challenging aspects of the managerial job—managing layoffs.

Chapter 4, *Working in teams,* is devoted to finding out how managers can build and lead high-performance teams. Team composition, team dynamics, and the tasks and responsibilities of the team leader are some of the main topics that we will analyze in this context. One of the key factors that contributes to effective teamwork is communication. Choosing the right communication channel, presenting ideas in an effective way, and making meetings productive are key issues that we will discuss in this chapter. Finally, we also need to acknowledge that when different people want to achieve something together, it is possible that interests collide. The chapter therefore also includes strategies and tactics for dealing with conflict situations, as well as for preparing and conducting negotiations.

Chapter 5, *Managing diversity across cultures,* acknowledges that managers are often faced with situations in which they have to interact with people from very different backgrounds. It analyzes the advantages and disadvantages of diversity in a work context and presents different diversity management strategies and practices that managers can use to create more inclusive organizations. Cultural differences are a particularly salient diversity dimension in organizations that are internationally active. We explore what managers can do to better understand cultural peculiarities and communicate more effectively in an intercultural environment. In a globalized world, geographically dispersed virtual teams are becoming a common phenomenon. We therefore also examine the pros and cons of global virtual teams, as well as strategies for making them work. Finally, we discuss how managers can address ethical issues that can arise when they work across cultures and with people who have different interests, values, and worldviews.

LEADING AND DEVELOPING OTHERS

Outline of chapter

This chapter will enable you to

- Explain what contributes to the performance of people in an organizational context and how managers can support others to improve their performance.

- Assess how managers can influence employee motivation.

- Devise strategies to support people who are not performing to their full potential.

- Explain how managers can use coaching, delegation, and performance reviews as tools for influencing the performance of others.

- Describe the main steps of a systematic hiring process and the main issues that managers need to consider during this process.

- Identify the main challenges of managing layoffs.

Introduction

Because managers perform through other people, the key challenge of management is to **influence other people in their performance**—to make sure that they act in a way that is conducive to reaching organizational goals. The process in which one person is influencing other people to accomplish certain tasks or achieve certain goals is also called **leadership**.

The discourse on the nature of managerial work has substantially changed over recent decades. From the 1980s on, we can observe a major shift from a focus on analytical tools, optimizing structures and processes, as well as planning, forecasting, and controlling to what organizational scientist Alan Bryman termed "**the new leadership approach**."[1] Under this approach, managers were no longer viewed as administrators of bureaucratic organizations, but as "leaders that are able to achieve extraordinary levels of follower motivation, admiration, commitment, respect, trust, dedication, loyalty, and performance."[2]

Many authors followed this new way of thinking, claiming that we need **leaders** instead of **managers**. Henry Mintzberg, however, called into question whether the distinction between a manager and a leader has any practical meaning in everyday organizational life: "How would you like to be managed by someone who doesn't lead?", he asks. "This can be awfully dispiriting. Well, then, why would you want to be led by someone who doesn't manage? That can be terribly disengaging."[3] If managers spend most of their time interacting with and working through other people, it does not really make sense to separate management from the leadership role. Hence, we will take a pragmatic and integrated approach and expect that managers generally also assume a leadership responsibility.

Countless articles, books, and seminars have fueled what Harvard Kennedy School lecturer Barbara Kellerman called the "leadership industry" in her bestselling book *The End of Leadership*. For Kellerman, this "industry" has led people to believe that leadership can be learned quickly and easily, rather than as a long and ongoing process that requires accumulated experience and reflection over time.[4] Against this background, this chapter is not designed to offer a recipe for how to become a "great leader in changing times." Instead it provides an overview of how managers can positively influence individual team members' performance and so become more effective in achieving their organizations' goals through others. Leadership is a core element of the managerial role. Yet—as many examples of managers who are not thought of as good leaders by the members of their team show—it is not always easy to master.

In this chapter, we will:

- explore what managers can do to **influence employee motivation** as one of the key factors that determine the performance of individuals (*Section 3.1*);
- discuss how managers can contribute to **developing the** performance potential of others to meet the future needs of the organization (*Section 3.2*);
- find out how **delegation**, **performance reviews**, and **coaching** are important ways in which managers can help to improve the performance of both themselves and their team members (*Section 3.3*).
- discuss managers' need to understand how to **hire the right people** and how to approach the rather difficult, yet sometimes necessary, aspect of the managerial role of **managing layoffs** (*Section 3.4*).

In some of the processes that we will discuss in this chapter, managers often work in close collaboration with the **human resource management** (HRM) function of their organization. HRM specialists can provide guidance and professional support on these matters, but the ultimate responsibility for the performance of the team members in their organizational unit always remains with the manager.

Influence:
Having an effect on the opinion, beliefs, or behavior of other people.

Leadership:
A process of social influence in which one person is able to convince other individuals or groups of people to accomplish certain tasks or achieve certain goals.

Leader:
A person who is able to convince others to follow them (in thought and action) in order to achieve certain goals.

Manager:
A person who is responsible for the performance and development of a group, an organizational unit, or an organization as a whole.

Performance potential:
The capacity to perform in the future.

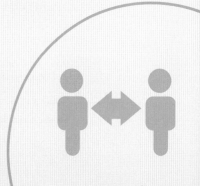

3.1 Motivating others

Getty Images/Hero Images

In brief

● Three basic elements determine people's performance at work: (1) Do they have the right abilities and skills for the job? (2) Are they motivated to put in enough effort? (3) Do they have the right opportunities in terms of tasks that match their personal strengths?

● Although motivation is an internal process that takes place inside our brain, managers can also influence some of the factors that can have a positive or negative effect on the motivation of employees. These factors are related to the work task, the work process, and the outcome of the work for the employee.

● A motivation framework that is based on the findings of several widely acknowledged theories of human motivation can help managers to identify the right motivational action for a particular person in a particular situation.

Managers perform through other people. This is the essence of management. The sum of the performance of individuals will determine the overall organizational performance, and therefore also managerial effectiveness. People who perform well also tend to feel better, meaning good performance not only has a positive effect on the organization, but also on the well-being and satisfaction of the individual employee.

How can managers influence other people's performance? To answer this question, we first need to take a look at what job performance is all about. **Performance**, defined in general terms, is "what the organization hires one to do, and to do well."[5] A major precondition to good performance is the requisite **ability**—having the necessary knowledge and skills to carry out a certain task. Second, sustained performance is not possible without a minimum degree of **motivation**, an inner drive to follow certain goals. The two key factors of job performance, ability and motivation, are also strongly interconnected.[6] Someone who has all the necessary knowledge and skills but is unwilling to tackle a task will be as unsuccessful as someone who is fully devoted to a goal but lacks the ability to achieve it.

Motivation:
The inner drive to do something and to follow certain goals.

Ability and motivation, while necessary, are not sufficient for job performance. They only come into effect when people have the **opportunity** to perform in a job that fits their skills and motivations.[7] Matching the right individuals with the right tasks is therefore a central challenge for managers. Combining the three factors, we can set the **performance equation** in Figure 3.1.[8]

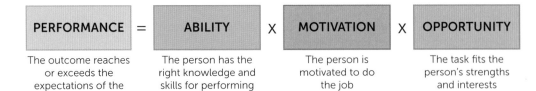

PERFORMANCE	=	ABILITY	X	MOTIVATION	X	OPPORTUNITY
The outcome reaches or exceeds the expectations of the organization		The person has the right knowledge and skills for performing well in the task		The person is motivated to do the job		The task fits the person's strengths and interests

Figure 3.1 The performance equation

Source: Inspired by concepts in Maier (1955) and Anderson (1974).

When managers sense a problem with an employee's performance, they need to first identify the underlying cause:

- Does the person have the right knowledge and skills to accomplish the task? (**Ability**)
- Is the person motivated to do the job? (**Motivation**)
- Do the tasks and job characteristics match with the person's strengths and interests? (**Opportunity**)

The underlying cause for poor performance is not always easy to identify. If an employee seems to be very committed and hardworking, but is still unable to produce adequate work results, that might be a sign of a lack of ability. Absenteeism, a decrease in work productivity in tasks the employee used to perform well, or negative feedback from colleagues about the attitude of a co-worker could be warning signs for motivational problems. If an employee repeatedly tells others about the ambition to take on a different role, that could be a hint that the individual's strengths are not well used in their current position. When managers first sense a performance problem, the best way to find out about the underlying reasons is, of course, to discuss the issue directly with the employee.

Depending on the outcome of this analysis of the underlying causes of poor performance, managers can decide on specific interventions:

- In the case of a lack of ability, **training**, **coaching** or other **development measures** (see Section 3.2);
- In the case of a lack of motivation, trying to **influence the state of motivation** of the employee;
- In the case of a lack of opportunity, **reallocating tasks** to better fit the strengths of the individual employee (see also Section 3.3).

The keys to employee motivation

One constituting element of the performance equation is **motivation**, a psychological process that directs an individual's attention, effort, and persistence toward performing a certain task or achieving a certain goal.[9] Motivated people have

a   a clear **intent** to do something ("I want");
b   confidence that they are able to reach a certain goal (**self-efficacy**) ("I can");[10] and
c   a strong personal commitment to an intention (**volition**) ("I will").[11]

Because motivation refers to an internal process, it can be hard to "motivate" others. Strictly speaking, people can only motivate themselves. There are, however, external factors that can influence the state of motivation. These factors, in turn, can be influenced by managerial actions.

Figure 3.2 presents an "eclectic" framework, informed by different sources, of **external factors influencing work motivation**.[12] In this particular case, the framework is based on a comprehensive review of the findings of several widely acknowledged motivation theories (including, for example, goal-setting theory, social cognitive theory, self-regulation theories, expectancy theory, organizational support theory, or organizational justice theories).[13] The framework categorizes external motivational factors (i.e., those factors that can potentially be influenced by managers) into three dimensions of work:

1   **Work task**, the kind of work that needs to be carried out;
2   **Work process**, the way in which work is actually performed; and
3   **Work outcome**, what a person gets as a result of the work performed.

The impact of these three external factors can be analyzed on two different levels, that of the individual employee and that of their relationship with others within a specific reference group (e.g. a team or the organization as a whole).

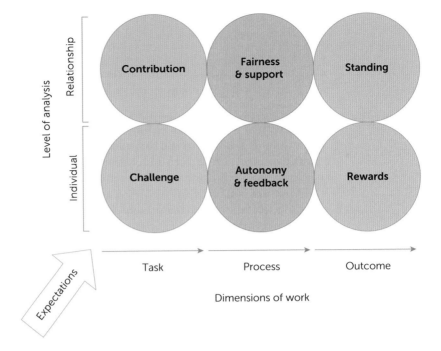

Figure 3.2 A framework of external factors influencing work motivation

Source: Adapted from 'Towards an eclectic framework of external factors influencing work motivation' by D. Sternad, 2013, *Journal of Applied Business Research*, 2, p. 8. Copyright by SBS Swiss Business School. Adapted with permission.

In the following section, we will take a closer look at each of the motivational factors in the Figure 3.2 motivation framework.

The nature of the task as a motivational factor

Goal-setting theory: A theory of human motivation that suggests that people are motivated when they (a) have specific, challenging, and accepted goals; and (b) regularly receive feedback on whether they are getting closer to reaching these goals.

One of the most widely acknowledged modern motivation theories, **goal-setting theory**, sees people's performance as contingent on having specific, challenging, and accepted goals.[14] Goals consciously and subconsciously guide efforts in a certain direction.[15] We soon lose interest in repetitive, boring tasks that do not engage our minds. A certain amount of **challenge** is necessary to get and keep people going. In the context of goal-setting theory, "challenging" means somewhat difficult, with an opportunity for the individual to grow. If goals are set too high, so that they seem impossible to reach from the outset, they can have a demotivating effect. To have a motivational effect, goals need to have a certain degree of difficulty while still being seen as achievable.

In addition to having challenging tasks, people also need to see meaning in their work. Meaning comes from having the feeling that your work is significant to others, or—in other words—that you make a **contribution** to the overall performance of a group or an organization. **Perceived social impact**, that is, the positive impact that work has on other people's well-being, also plays a key role in this context.[16] Research results have shown that commitment levels tend to be higher when employees are in direct contact with the beneficiaries of their work, and directly experience its positive effects on them (e.g. when a teacher sees the learning progress of a student).[17]

Motivating factors in the work process

If people have **autonomy** (i.e. a certain degree of discretion about how to perform their work), they usually feel more in control and also more responsible for work outcomes, which in turn can lead to higher motivation levels.[18] A lack of autonomy, especially in jobs which are psychologically demanding, can lead to high levels of job strain, which, according to research findings, can even result in a higher risk of cardiovascular disease.[19] At the same time, too much autonomy can also be detrimental if people feel that they do not get enough direction or orientation from management. Managers therefore need to make sure that employees in their unit have an amount of

Feedback:
Information that is given to an individual or a group of people about their prior behavior with the aim to either adjust or reinforce the behavior.

Organizational justice:
Employees' perceptions of how fairly they are treated within an organization.

Distributive justice:
Perceived fairness in the distribution of goods, benefits, and duties.

Procedural justice:
Perceived fairness in the process of reaching and implementing a decision.

Informational justice:
Perceived fairness in receiving adequate information about organizational decisions and processes.

Interactional justice:
Perceived fairness and respect in the way that people treat one another in an organization.

control over their own work processes that is in line with their individual autonomy needs.

In the words of Amabile and Kramer, "of all events that can deeply encourage people in their jobs, the single most important is to make progress in meaningful work."[20] When people follow challenging and worthwhile goals, they also want to know where they stand in relation to these goals. **Feedback** is therefore a crucial tool to keep people motivated in order to maintain their efforts toward a goal. Feedback can be inherent in the task itself; for example, when artists directly see or feel the progress of an artwork that they are working on. The other form of feedback is social feedback—others' reactions to a person's work. Regardless of whether the feedback is positive, indicating that someone is doing well, or negative, pointing out current deficiencies, it is one of a manager's main motivational tools if presented in an open, respectful, and non-threatening way (see also *Zooming in on giving feedback* box on page 82).

On the level of the relationship between the individual employee and other organizational members, two further factors have motivational relevance: fairness and perceived supervisor support.

The importance of **fairness** in the workplace was emphasized by behavioral psychologist John Stacey Adams. In his equity theory, Adams proposed that people compare their work-related inputs (e.g. effort, commitment, and skills) and outcomes (e.g. salary, benefits, and recognition) to those of others. They become demotivated if they perceive a mismatch in this input–outcome relationship.[21] Equity theory is considered a predecessor of the **organizational justice** theories. These provide further detail on the different ways that people can become demotivated when they feel unfairly treated. They include:

- **distributive justice** ("Do I get a fair share of rewards or acknowledgement compared to my peers?");
- **procedural justice** ("Is the process of reaching a decision fair? Am I adequately included in the process?");
- **informational justice** ("Am I adequately informed about the decisions and procedures in our organization?"); and
- **interactional justice** ("Am I treated by others with dignity and respect?").[22]

Research has shown that unfair treatment can become a major tipping point for employee burnout. If people who already show early-warning signals such as exhaustion or cynicism experience unfairness in the workplace, burnout is more likely to develop.[23]

Perceived supervisor support, the extent to which employees feel that their manager cares about their needs and well-being and creates a friendly and supportive work environment, also plays a major role in the motivational state of employees.[24] As employees infer **perceived organizational support** (beliefs about how the organization as a whole cares for them) from perceived supervisor support, the way in which managers treat their subordinates is critical to establishing a committed team across an organization.[25]

AROUND THE GLOBE

Cultural influences on motivation

One important factor for the motivation of employees is perceived supervisor support—the degree to which team members feel that their manager cares about their needs and well-being. But what do people mean when they refer to a "supportive manager"? The answer to this question will depend on the culture that both the manager and the team members have been

socialized in. In Japan, for example, relationships between managers and employees are often influenced by the cultural value of *amae* (which could be described as the dependent kind of love seen in a parent–child relationship). Therefore, it is quite common for Japanese managers to take great interest in the personal lives of their employees, and for employees to ask their managers' opinions on personal matters. In contrast, we would usually observe much more formal interactions between French managers and workers, and a greater social distance between them, because French management style is influenced by a strong societal emphasis on bureaucratic, hierarchical structures.

There are also potential cultural differences in the degree of autonomy that people would see as motivating. Managers who have been socialized in the US, for example, will often see delegation and empowerment of their employees as key pillars of good and effective leadership. In other parts of the

world, however, subordinates could feel overwhelmed with too much autonomy. A manager who led a business in China, for example, was cited in *Harvard Business Review* as saying: "You can't be a hands-off manager in China. You can—but you won't last long."[26] These examples show that when managing diverse teams (for example, in multinational corporations), it is important to take cultural preferences regarding the factors in the motivation framework into account.

Sources: Based on information in Paine (2010); Thomas and Inkson (2009).

Work outcomes as motivational factors

Expectancy theory:
A theory of human motivation that suggests that people are motivated to put in more effort when they expect that their effort leads to higher performance that, in turn, can lead to positive outcomes that they value.

Following Vroom's classic **expectancy theory**, managers often think that **rewards** (either monetary or non-monetary) are the primary means of motivating their team members. According to this theory, people will be motivated and committed to putting more effort into reaching the organization's goals when they expect their efforts to lead to a certain performance (*expectancy*) and that performance will be instrumental in getting rewards (*instrumentality*) which are of value to them (*valence*).[27] If as a student, for example, you believe that your efforts to learn more about effective management will lead to a degree, and that the degree, in turn, will give you a better chance of securing a job in management, expectancy theory predicts that you will be motivated to invest more in your studies.

It is quite obvious that minimum standards of reward for a person's work (e.g. a certain minimum level of salary) are necessary to avoid demotivation. However, research results show that **rewards can be a double-edged sword** because they can (a) induce people to put in substantial effort only when they feel that they will get something in return (thus potentially undermining **intrinsic motivation**—doing something because it feels personally satisfying), (b) induce employees to set lower goals in order to make it easier to gain rewards, (c) instill feelings of being unfairly treated if others receive higher rewards, or (d) discourage them altogether when they do not see any possibility of reaching the desired performance levels that would make them eligible for rewards.[28] Therefore, reward systems need to be carefully designed and implemented, always keeping their potential negative side-effects in mind.

Intrinsic motivation:
The drive to do something because performing the activity is in itself rewarding for an individual (including in the absence of any external rewards or control).

Finally, people want to be recognized for their work contributions. They have a need for a certain level of **standing** within their social reference group. For most people, this is also an important outcome of their achievements at work. Thus, motivation levels can be considerably influenced by the desire to be an accepted and respected member of a team (or, in other words, by the need to belong).[29]

Applying the motivation framework

The key question of how a manager can influence the motivation of other people is easier to answer when we understand the different external factors that potentially influence work motivation. Specifically, the motivation framework presented in Figure 3.2 can be used to diagnose which of the factors might have a positive or negative effect on an employee's motivation. But it is also vital to bear in mind that individual employees have their own **expectations** regarding the different factors. Someone who is new to a job, for example, might need more guidance and feedback from the manager, whereas more experienced employees would probably expect a much higher degree of autonomy without constantly being reminded of what the manager thinks about their performance. Every person is different and so are the optimal strategies to enhance their motivation level.

The framework in Figure 3.2 can be used as a **checklist for identifying the right motivational actions** for a specific person in a particular situation:

1   Does the task have the right degree of **challenge** for this person?
2   Does the person clearly see and understand the **contribution** of their work to the common goal of the organization and the well-being of the beneficiaries of the work?
3   Does the person have the requisite **autonomy** in performing the work tasks?
4   Does the person get enough **feedback** on how their work is progressing, either from the task itself or from management?
5   Does the person feel that they are **treated fairly** by the manager and the organization?
6   Does the person perceive that they are receiving all the necessary **managerial support** to perform at work?
7   Does the person feel that successful work outcomes are adequately **rewarded**?
8   Does the person feel that they gain adequate **respect** and **recognition** from management and other team members?

As discussed, influencing employee motivation requires a deep understanding of other individuals and their expectations, as well as the ability to identify and implement suitable interventions in different dimensions of work. Influencing people's motivation levels is a complex endeavor. However, if managers can master the art, they will be able—in the words of Henry Mintzberg—"to bring out the energy that exists naturally within people."[30]

Managers should direct just as much attention to avoiding **demotivation** as to enhancing motivation. "It's not insults that cause the greatest harm, but rather callousness about people's time," says Harvard Business School Professor Rosabeth Moss Kanter. "Horrible bosses want control. They expect subordinates to be on call 24/7 and to hit unrealistic deadlines with limited resources. When the work product is delivered, horrible bosses may ignore it for long intervals, making it clear that the deadline was artificial and the stress unnecessary."[31] Further guidance on how to avoid the demotivation of team members can be found in the box *How to kill employee commitment*.

FROM A DIFFERENT ANGLE

How to kill employee commitment

By analyzing 12,000 daily electronic diaries from professionals working on innovation projects in seven North American firms, Teresa Amabile and Steven Kramer observed four traps for senior executives which almost certainly lead to employee disengagement:[32]

1   *The mediocrity trap*: Telling your employees that your organization aspires to greatness, but doing the opposite (e. g. just focusing on cutting costs). Thus, people will get the feeling that they are working for a mediocre organization.

2   *The "strategic attention deficit disorder"*: Quickly changing from one strategic direction to another without explaining the rationale behind the changes to employees. When managers constantly start new strategic initiatives, it is more difficult for employees to see a clear purpose in their own and their organization's work.

3   *The coordination trap*: Only concentrating on the big vision and not paying attention to coordinating everyday work. Thus, employees may be able to see "the big picture," but do not know what they should actually be doing and how they can contribute.

4   *"Too big to be true"*: Making grandiose statements about goals that have nothing to do with the realities of the workforce (e.g. "Next year, we want 50 percent more revenue and a 35 percent return on equity.") Such abstract goals do not energize employees, who more often think in terms of providing quality to their customers. In addition, if these goals are unrealistic, they will create cynicism.

Source: *Based on information in Amabile and Kramer (2012).*

Matching tasks and strengths

As we saw in the performance equation in Figure 3.1, in addition to the ability and motivation to perform well, people need the right **opportunity**—the chance to perform tasks that suit their strengths. Peter Drucker observed that all too often, rather than appointing people who will excel in the role, managers fill jobs with people who are the "least misfit," those with the fewest serious weaknesses who are able to "adequately" fulfill job responsibilities.[33] According to Drucker, this is a strategy that usually only reaps mediocrity.[34] Achieving excellent results requires a different perspective: **staffing from strengths**. This means thinking about what individuals can do exceptionally well and assigning tasks that match their greatest strengths, regardless of any weaknesses in other areas.[35] As Peter Drucker says,

> First-class people must always be allocated to major opportunities, to the areas of greatest possible return for each unit of effort. And first-class opportunities must always be staffed with people of superior ability and performance.[36]

Let us take Drucker's own example of an opera house. As the artistic director, would you prefer to work with a famous prima donna with an irresistible voice (but also some difficult personal idiosyncrasies) in the title role, or with a mediocre singer without any major weaknesses or wishes for special treatment? The mediocre singer will probably be easier to work with, but to achieve the main goal—in this case, high ticket sales to the performance—you will need to work with the prima donna because of her unique strengths and despite her apparent weaknesses.

Staffing from strengths does not imply that weaknesses should be ignored altogether. If there is a weakness with a potentially strong negative impact on the performance of the individual or on others in the team (for example, the tendency of some team members to dominate every discussion and impose their view on others), it needs to be considered and addressed. (See also the discussion on developing the performance potential of others in Section 3.2.) It is a question of where the focus lies, however. When assigning a task, ideally managers should first think about who has exceptional strengths that could be the best fit for an outstanding performance in this task.

Staffing from strengths not only ensures that the most capable people are working on the most important tasks. Offering challenging tasks that match people's strengths can also raise their motivation and enthusiasm for the job, and provide opportunities to further build their strengths, i.e. for developing people.

3.2 Developing the performance potential of others

MACMILLAN

In brief

- To ensure the sustained success of their organizations, managers need to make sure that they develop the performance potential of the members of their team.

- People development is an ongoing process in which the current skill level of employees is assessed, development goals are agreed upon, adequate challenges are identified, and feedback on progress toward the development goals is provided.

- Coaching—talking another person through a challenge before it is tackled or providing possibilities to reflect on the learning from a particular challenge—is a powerful tool to support other people in developing their performance potential.

It is one thing to influence other people's performance, but another to build their performance potential in the first place. "Your job [as a leader] is to walk around with a can of water in one hand and a can of fertilizer in the other hand. Think of your team as seeds and try to build a garden,"[37] said Jack Welch, the legendary former CEO of General Electric. Managers need to make sure that their team members have the potential to successfully meet the organization's future challenges. Developing others is therefore a key managerial responsibility. But how can a manager "develop" another individual? According to Henry Mintzberg, "the job of development is perhaps best seen as managers helping people to develop themselves."[38]

The Swedish psychologist K. Anders Ericsson extensively studied how expert performers in different domains such as sports, music, or chess achieved excellence in their field.[39] He observed that a necessary precondition to high levels of professional achievement lies in extensive experience in the relevant discipline. Experience, however, is not sufficient. There are thousands of regular golf-players. However, not all of them become a Jack Nicklaus or Tiger Woods. So what makes the difference? How do people develop themselves from average performers into the top class of their domain?

First of all, high performers **strive for high performance**. This may sound trivial. However, as Ericsson noted, many people tend to just maintain their standard once they reach an acceptable level of performance. In Herbert Simon's terms, they *satisfice*—they continue to develop until a point where they think they are "good enough"—rather than *optimize* or *maximize*, trying to reach their full potential.[40] Outstanding performance starts with a deliberate decision to strive for excellence. This decision also means a dedication to frequent and continuous practice.

In this section, we will first take a look at how managers can support the development of their team members through providing them with opportunities for what Ericsson called **deliberate practice**. We will then see how the two main elements of the process of deliberate practice—assigning challenging tasks and providing feedback—can be integrated into a more encompassing model for developing the performance potential of others, the **people development process**. Finally, we will discuss how managers can use **coaching** to help their team members to grow with their challenges.

Deliberate practice

In many domains, for example in sports, arts, or science, high performance is the result of more than ten years of deliberate practice.[41] Deliberate practice means sequentially mastering new tasks that are somewhat outside of the individual's current abilities, and then gradually repeating these tasks, supported by feedback from a teacher or a coach.[42] High jumpers will first repeatedly practice at lower heights before putting the bar to increasingly higher levels. Violinists will first try to master easier works and then continuously progress to more difficult musical pieces. And young managers will probably first develop and practice their skills in a smaller project before taking over the responsibility for larger organizational units. Deliberate practice is more than just trying to tackle new, more challenging tasks, however. It requires a clear focus on the task, willingness and intent to learn and improve from feedback, and, of course, a **coach** who understands both the current level of expertise and the level of challenge that could potentially be mastered by team members if they stretched their performance (see also the later discussion on coaching).

Learning from the findings of the research on expert performers, managers can develop people by carefully providing them with opportunities to tackle challenges and, as a consequence, achieve more than they themselves thought possible. In short: managers should provide their team members with **opportunities to grow**, while making sure that they also receive honest and encouraging **feedback** that enables them to reflect on their progress (see also the box *Zooming in on giving feedback*).

Deliberate practice:
A learning process in which the learners try to enhance their performance through repeating activities with a conscious focus on improving certain aspects of these activities and reflecting on feedback that they receive on how they performed the activities.

Coach:
A person who helps another person to reach their potential, usually through discussing work-related issues and providing guidance and advice.

Zooming in on ▶ GIVING FEEDBACK

If you convey it in the right way, feedback can help another person to perform better in the future, and it can also have positive motivational effects. Next time you give feedback to another person with the purpose of influencing their performance, consider the following suggestions about what is considered to be effective feedback:

1 *Keep the prime intention of feedback in mind.* Your feedback should focus on helping the other person and attaining the goals of the organization.

2 *Be specific.* Provide concrete examples about what exactly worked well or did not work well. Limit your feedback to one or only a few points because too much feedback can also potentially lead to confusion or a lack of focus.

3 *Give feedback right away.* Feedback is usually more effective when it is provided as close to the action to which it refers as possible. Make sure, however, that you give feedback only at a point in time when the other person is also ready to receive it.

4 *Offer relevant advice.* Include specific information that the recipient can use to improve performance (discuss with the person what exactly they could do differently) and be realistic about what you can really expect to be changed.

5 *Strive for clarity.* Make sure that the feedback is understood by the other person. Observe the recipient's behavior for any signs of confusion or misunderstanding, and maybe also ask them to restate the main points in their own words.

6 *Do not consider feedback to be a one-way street.* To become effective, feedback needs to be a dialogue. Instead of being evaluative, try to describe what you observe, but also ask questions to get a better common understanding of the situation and of what could be improved in the future.

Sources: Based on information in Luthans (2011); Mone and London (2018); Phoel (2009).

What is considered to be appropriate feedback can be contingent on culture. In order to ensure that constructive feedback has the desired positive effects on developing people, managers need to take cultural differences on a societal level into account. In Asian, South American and Middle Eastern societies, for example, negative feedback is usually communicated in a more indirect way because directly pointing out what is wrong is often seen as offensive.[43] For example, instead of telling someone else that their idea is flawed, people from these cultures might just choose to remain silent (and the lack of enthusiasm would itself be a form of feedback).[44] But there are also variations within Western countries: the American way of "sandwiching" negative feedback between two positive messages could be seen as "false" in some European countries like the Netherlands, where frank feedback—saying exactly what you mean—is usually highly welcome.[45]

Managers need to ensure that giving and receiving feedback becomes a natural part of the organizational culture. "This means," says Kets de Vries, "teaching, by word and example, that criticism is an opportunity for new learning and not a total, unrecoverable catastrophe."[46] Constructive feedback is also a key element of the people development process, a model which managers can use to systematically help their team members to develop the skills required for achieving the organization's goals.

The people development process

Effective managers start by setting the right development goals for their team members, and then select and apply the right development measures to help them reach these higher performance levels. The **people development process** (see Figure 3.3) explains how managers can achieve this in a structured way.

A challenge- and feedback-oriented people development process consists of the following six steps:

1 **Understand the future challenges for the team** (or the organization) and the skills that are required to successfully master these challenges.

Figure 3.3 The people development process

2 **Assess the current skills level of individual team members** in relation to the future skills needed by the organization.

3 **Agree on development goals** with each team member. Research has found that high performers usually have a stronger focus on long-term development goals.[47]

4 **Assign challenging tasks** that help each team member to try out, test, and develop the relevant skills.

5 **Support each team member in performing the challenging tasks**, if necessary, through coaching or additional formal training. In any case, give constructive feedback that provides the team member with information on their progress both in terms of reaching the goals and in skills development.

6 If the skills of the team members have improved, the cycle starts again, this time with an **even more challenging task** that can bring each team member another step further in the development process.

The development process follows the logic of the development cycle presented in Chapter 2: a clear, challenging goal is set (in this case together with the employee), opportunities for deliberate practice are provided, and feedback can be used to correct and adapt action—in other words, to learn.

Further concrete **actions that managers can take to develop their employees** are:

- discussing **individual development plans** (at least once per year as part of a structured performance review, which we will discuss further later in this chapter);
- seeing **every interaction as an opportunity to assess a team member's progress** and provide feedback and motivating encouragement;
- **coaching**—talking the team member through an activity either before or after it is performed with the aim of improving their ability to competently execute this activity (see later in this section);
- **discouraging reverse delegation**—letting team members tackle their own challenges—supporting them, but not taking over *their* work (remember the monkey in Chapter 2).[48]

Reverse delegation: A situation in which subordinates delegate tasks to their managers.

Another important factor to consider in the people development process is **identity**, an individual's self-definition, for example, as a skilled craftsperson, a capable sales manager, or an effective leader. A strong identity can motivate people to learn more and seek out new challenges and developmental opportunities.[49] Identity usually develops over a longer time span. For example, a person who consistently gets praise from others for the quality of their presentations is more likely to form a strong identity as being "a good presenter." Managers can support the identity development of their team members through giving them feedback on their strengths, providing them with developmental opportunities that allow them to further enhance these strengths and follow their interests, and by encouraging employees to reflect on the purpose and meaning of their professional role.[50]

Assume that a young graduate from a local university has just joined the team that you are managing. The graduate seems to be competent in his field of expertise, but is usually quite reluctant to speak in front of others. He does not want to give presentations, and is also very quiet in team meetings. You believe that if he could overcome his reservations about speaking in public, he would be able to contribute a lot more to the success of the team. What would you do to help the team member to develop his public speaking skills over the next few months?

Coaching

Coaching:
A development process in which one person helps another person to reach their potential, usually through discussing work-related issues and providing guidance and advice (often through asking questions that help the other person to thoroughly reflect on an issue).

"Everyone needs a coach," said Bill Gates, the founder of Microsoft in a TED talk. "We all need people who give us feedback—that's how we improve."[51] Every world-class athlete has a coach, and so do many top executives. The purpose of **coaching** in a business context is to help improve the personal effectiveness of an employee. External consultants are increasingly used as executive coaches.[52] Coaching is, however, also a tool that can be used by managers to develop other people (see also the box *Teachable moments at TJX*). Coaching can help to build new skills and competencies, enhance existing strengths, improve the quality of interactions and relationships at work, or prepare employees for a new task.[53] It can also have positive motivational effects. A recent scientific meta-study (a statistical analysis of the results of different studies on the issue) has shown that workplace coaching by internal coaches can have very positive effects on employee learning and development, and particularly also on their performance.[54]

CEO BEST PRACTICE

Teachable moments at TJX

Carol Meyrowitz was the CEO of the retailing group TJX (the parent company of T.J. Maxx, HomeGoods, and Marshalls) between 2007 and 2016, having served the group in other positions for over two decades. TJX was particularly active in the off-price retailing segment, providing quality goods at cheap prices. Meyrowitz was ranked among the most powerful women in business by both *CNN* and *Forbes* magazine. Every single year of her tenure—even during the economic crisis of 2008–09—TJX continued to increase sales, with profits nearly tripling during the whole period.

The business model of the TJX stores strongly relied on its 700 buyers, who purchased from thousands of global suppliers (including well-known brands) at a minimum price in order to provide consumers with bargains that they could then find in a "treasure hunt" shopping experience in the TJX stores.[55] Developing the buyers was always high on Meyrowitz's agenda. TJX offers extensive formalized training through its own corporate university (a centralized organizational unit that bundles training and learning activities in order to support a corporation's strategic

intents). However, Meyrowitz also saw coaching (or, as she called it, "teaching") people as her personal responsibility. "My role as a teacher goes beyond our buyer training program—it's part of everything I do," she wrote in an article for *Harvard Business Review*. "Whenever I walk into a meeting in any area of our company, I'm thinking, *What can I teach during this meeting?*"[56] Rather than imparting her opinion on a topic, she would use a typical coaching approach, asking questions like: "Do you see the similarities between this and that? If we decide this way, what will be the ramifications five or 10 years from now?"[57] She noted that she was constantly looking for "teachable moments," seeing it as a priority for leaders in the organization to "create an environment in which our associates can grow and learn every day."[58]

→ Key takeaway

Coaching is a powerful tool that can be used by managers at all levels (including top managers) to develop their team members.

Sources: Based on information in Meyrowitz (2014); O'Donnell (2011).

In essence, coaching means discussing work-related issues with the employee, either before a challenge that the employee is facing (to identify the best way to proceed) or to jointly evaluate the learning from either a successfully completed or a failed challenge. The main tools of coaches are questions that enable employees to dig deeper and think through a problem for themselves.

Here are some examples of **coaching questions** that can be asked **before a challenge**:

- What is your biggest work-related challenge at the moment?
- How do you think other people see this challenge?
- Have you already experienced a similar challenge? How did you approach it? What worked? What did not work?
- What is the goal that you want to achieve?
- Why is this goal important?
- What are the actions that you intend to take?
- Which positive or negative consequences do you expect when taking these actions?
- Could you do something to mitigate potential negative consequences?
- Do you have any other options?
- What are the main constraints?
- Is there a way to overcome these constraints?
- Do you need any support to get it done?
- What is the most important next step?

The following questions can be used to **reflect on a completed challenge**:

- What have you learned from this challenge?
- What was the most difficult aspect for you? Why?
- What went fairly easily? Why?
- What does your performance in this challenge tell you about your personal strengths and weaknesses?
- What can you learn from this challenge about your development needs?
- Would you do something differently if you faced a similar challenge in the future?

One of your best friends has committed to taking over the role of team leader in a student project. It is a market research project for a local company that plans to internationalize its business to a neighboring country. There are five students in the project team, and your friend has told you that two of them already have somewhat of a reputation for their lack of effort and relatively poor performance in student projects. Now let us assume that you are a coach. Which questions would you ask if you—as a coach—were to help your friend, the newly appointed project leader, in successfully mastering this kind of leadership challenge?

Depending on the specific need, managers can support their employees as coaches in the following ways:[59]

- **Being available as a discussion partner (or a "sounding board").** Asking questions that help the employee to develop a better understanding of the situation; questioning conclusions; letting them think through the issue as an attentive listener.
- **Scrutinizing proposed actions.** Asking critical questions to help the team member assess whether their hypotheses are right; discussing potential consequences; making sure they understand the possible implications and repercussions of their proposed actions.
- **Providing additional input to expand the frame of reference.** Sharing experiences from comparable prior situations; helping team members to see the issue in a wider context.
- **Providing guidance.** Suggesting alternative approaches to tackle a particular issue; high-lighting and examining possible steps that could be taken to manage a difficult situation.
- **Generating ideas.** Developing new options in a joint brainstorming effort.

Coaching is not necessarily a formal process. Every interaction can be seen as an opportunity to help another person to take a step forward. Through "talking someone through an activity, either before or after they do it, in order to improve their performance,"[60] as Hill and Lineback characterize coaching, managers can continually develop the members of their team.

The Semco way of achieving high performance levels

Ricardo Semler was just 21 years old when he took over the leadership of Semco (a Brazilian manufacturer of hydraulic pumps for ships) from his father in 1980. Aware of the severe challenges that the industry faced at the time, he wanted to steer the company in a different direction—much to the dismay of some of Semco's top managers, 60 percent of whom he fired on his first day in office. Step by step, mainly through acquisitions and license agreements, he reduced the company's dependence on the shipping industry and transformed Semco into a diversified multi-business enterprise, growing the company from US$4 million in annual revenue and less than 100 employees in 1980 to more than US$200 million and almost 3,000 employees in 2003.[61] Semco remained unscathed as Brazil suffered severe political and economic crisis times, and had a remarkably low employee turnover rate of only 2 percent (compared to an industry average of 18 percent) under Semler's leadership.

Semler became widely known for his democratic leadership style at Semco. He based his leadership philosophy on the notion of treating employees "like responsible adults"[62] and on running the business in a "simpler" and "more natural way."[63] Semco did not have an official organizational chart, mission statement, human resource department, long-term business plan and budget, rulebooks or guidelines. Semler was of the opinion that most regulations and norms were actually "poppycock."[64] Consequently, he replaced them with the ground rule of using common sense and a short, comic-book style "Survival Manual" that introduced new employees to the "Semco way."

Rather than a typical hierarchical organization, Semco was organized in concentric circles. The inner circle consisted of five people (called "counselors") who integrated the activities of the whole company. A second circle was formed by the divisional heads (called "partners") who were responsible for the performance of their division. The third circle included all other employees (called "associates"), some of whom temporarily or permanently took over coordinative roles. Even when Semco went through a period of high growth, there were never more than three management layers. The company

also tried to keep individual units small so that people could collaborate well, be more involved, and see their personal contribution to the final results. "Our people have a lot of instruments at their disposal to change directions very quickly, to close things and open new things,"[65] is how Semler described the benefits of Semco's flexible and adaptive structural setup.

Democracy was a core value in the organization. The associates could choose their own managers, and subsequently also evaluated them twice a year. Decisions were generally made democratically, on important issues even by a company-wide vote. Employees could decide what time they wanted to start and finish work (the coordination went smoothly among themselves). Everyone could choose their own job titles and even determine their own salaries, aided by an analyst who collected benchmark salary levels from other companies. The salaries could, however, also be discussed (after the first year) with the employees if they did not match with the employee's performance and contribution.

Two other elements of the Semco leadership philosophy were full transparency and profit sharing. Everyone's salaries were published (a practice that provided peer pressure regarding the issue of choosing an individual's own pay level), and each worker was fully informed about the financial results of their division (all Semco employees also attended financial literacy classes). Part of the profits was shared among the employees in each division in a way that the majority voted for (usually, it would result in equal distribution).

But Semco was actually very rigorous in other aspects. Financial controls were strict, with all numbers being ready on the fourth day of the month. Every half-year, each unit would determine how many people were needed for the next period and employees were anonymously assessed by peers in order to be reinstated in their jobs.[66] "To survive here you have to get on someone's list of people they need for the next six months,"[67] said Semler, pointing out that the democratic system of Semco also included a free market element. People were deliberately encouraged to move around the organization and work in different jobs and departments.

Semler considered this practice, that helped employees to follow their interests and develop new skills at the same time, to be "another avenue for them to dip into their reservoir of talent."[68]

Semler disseminated his unique leadership style in bestselling books, as a guest lecturer at Harvard and MIT, and through the Semco Style Institute, a training company designed to help other organizations implement Semco management practices. As he turned his attention to other ventures, Semco Group was transformed into a partnership structure. The successor firm Semco Partners became specialized in forming joint ventures with global companies in the Brazilian market.

Sources: Based on information in Caulkin (2003); Fisher (2005); Semco Partners (2017); Semler (1989; 2004; 2018); semcostyle.org (2018).

Discussion questions

- What are the main elements of Ricardo Semler's approach to influencing the performance of Semco's employees?
- How would you judge the motivating effect on employees of the individual elements of the "Semco way"?
- In Semco's democratic leadership system, how can management influence the performance of employees?
- What effects could Semler's unique approach to organizing his company have on the development of the performance potential of the people who are working within the organization?

3.3 Delegation and performance management

In brief

- Effective delegation starts with analyzing the task and identifying the right person to accomplish the task. Clear communication in the assignment meeting is as important as a thorough follow-up for making sure that the delegated task will be performed in the right way.
- The performance review provides an opportunity to evaluate the performance and potential of employees in a structured way. Seen as a dialogue, it can also contribute to improving the manager–employee relationship.
- Sometimes, managers also need to deal with poor performance. As a precondition, they must first clearly understand the underlying reason for the performance problem.

Managers need to make sure that employees are motivated to follow the organization's goals and develop the capabilities to excel in their organizational roles. This requires emotional intelligence, building trust and productive working relationships, and the ability to provide others with a purpose. But managers also need to give people the chance to perform certain tasks in the first place. In other words, they must be able to **delegate** effectively. Another important managerial responsibility is to ensure that team members are performing well on an ongoing basis. The **performance review** is a key instrument for assessing and influencing the performance of others. If applied in the right way, delegation and performance reviews can both help to achieve employee motivation and an enhancement of employees' abilities. When used in combination, their effectiveness is further amplified. For example, a performance review can be used to evaluate a person's performance in their allocated tasks, but also to identify which tasks could be delegated next in order to help the employee to further develop their skills.

It is, however, dangerous to reduce leadership to following checklists or formulas. Holding a performance review once a year does not exempt managers from staying in touch with their employees in between, from sensing their moods and feelings, and from supporting them whenever they may be struggling. Leadership is not technical perfection in using specific tools (as helpful as they may be), but an ongoing dialogue with the aim of positively influencing the performance of other individuals.

Effective delegation

Delegation:
The transfer of both responsibility and authority for completing a task to another person.

Delegation—the act of assigning a task and transferring responsibility to another person—is at the heart of what management is about. In essence, performing through others means performing through delegation. Managers who are new in their job often hesitate to delegate tasks, especially if they think that they can perform more effectively and to a higher quality themselves. However, this is short-sighted, as they end up doing operative tasks at the expense of their primary task—*managing*.

Through effective delegation, managers can focus on their core tasks—monitoring and making sense of all relevant developments within and around the organization, setting the agenda, making sure that the right people are in the right jobs, developing people, building a network, and setting the right initiatives to implement their agenda with the support of their subordinates and network (see also Figure 1.7, the model of managerial effectiveness in Chapter 1). But employees can benefit from delegation, too. Every delegated task is an opportunity for them to learn and grow. It can also help managers to assess the capabilities of their team members, and is therefore a key tool for people development.

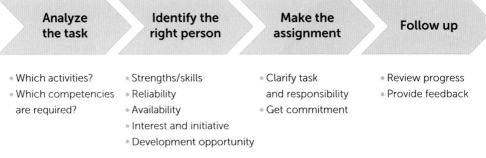

Analyze the task	Identify the right person	Make the assignment	Follow up
• Which activities? • Which competencies are required?	• Strengths/skills • Reliability • Availability • Interest and initiative • Development opportunity	• Clarify task and responsibility • Get commitment	• Review progress • Provide feedback

Figure 3.4 The delegation process

Source: Inspired by concepts in Harvard Business School Publishing (2005).

An **effective delegation process** usually follows four steps (see Figure 3.4):[69]

1   **Analyze the task**: Which kind of activities need to be performed, and which competencies are required for this assignment?

2   **Identify the right person**: Who has the necessary strengths and skills to accomplish the task? Who is reliable and conscientious in accomplishing delegated tasks? Who has shown interest and initiative for this kind of work? Who is available and has spare capacity? For whom could this task be a development opportunity?

3   **Make the assignment**: Discuss the task or project with the chosen team member, transfer responsibility, and obtain their commitment.

4   **Follow up**: When something is delegated, it is not yet accomplished. Therefore, managers need to stay in touch with the employee after the assignment, review the progress, and provide feedback if necessary.

The core of the delegation process is making the assignment, a meeting (ideally face to face) in which the task is delegated by the manager and accepted by the employee (see also the box *Zooming in on the assignment meeting*).

Zooming in on ▶ THE ASSIGNMENT MEETING

The effectiveness of a delegation process greatly depends on the effectiveness of the assignment meeting. All parties involved should clearly understand what the expectations are. Try it out for yourself: think about one task that you would like to delegate to someone you know and then conduct an assignment meeting.

During the meeting, make sure to address the following points:[70]

1 Clearly describe the task that needs to be accomplished.
2 Provide information about the purpose of the task (especially also about the importance of the task in an overall organizational context).
3 Define the scope of responsibilities.
4 Discuss the **accountability** for accomplishing the task within a specified timeframe.
5 Define a performance standard. (How will you measure success in accomplishing the task?)
6 Clarify the availability of resources and support for accomplishing the task.
7 Discuss who else is involved (or needs to be involved) and who plays which role.
8 Agree on a follow-up process. (How and when will you monitor progress?)
9 Get a clear commitment from the other person that they will take responsibility for the task.

Ideally, the assignment meeting is not a monologue but a dialogue in which two people gain a common understanding of what needs to be done and why.

Accountability:
The obligation to take responsibility for your actions and give defendable reasons for them.

Delegation can also have an **impact on employee motivation**. People can see an assignment as either a positive challenge or a nuisance. As we have discussed, they can be demotivated if they consider the distribution of work and tasks to be unfair. Loading too many tasks on one person can lead to feelings of being exploited or to accusations of playing favorites. Therefore, managers should keep in mind that delegation also has a social dimension and can play a role in determining group dynamics (see also Chapter 4).

The performance review

Performance review (or appraisal interview):
A formal discussion (usually conducted annually) between a manager and an employee about their performance and development.

The **performance review** (sometimes also known as **appraisal interview**) is a face-to-face discussion between an employee and their manager to evaluate the employee's past performance and future development possibilities. The instrument has received a lot of criticism; for example, for being based on a rather pessimistic mind-set that generally assumes that "[c]lose surveillance is required to eliminate the risk of shirking or other deviant behaviours."[71] An article in the *New Yorker* magazine pointed out that formal performance reviews can reinforce rigid hierarchies, cause psychic strain, or hurt relationships between managers and subordinates—especially if they are not well conducted.[72] Much of this criticism is linked with a rather outdated view of the performance review as a top-down "grading" of the employee's performance by the manager. Ideally, however, the performance review is not a one-way appraisal, but a joint review based on a dialogue—a review that fosters mutual understanding of expectations, goals, strengths, and weaknesses with the aim of positively influencing an employee's capacity to contribute to the performance of the organization.

Many organizations require their managers to conduct at least one formal performance review per year, usually following a semi-structured discussion guideline. For the rest of the year, the process of monitoring performance is usually more informal, for example, in the form of progress reports in weekly *jour fixe* meetings or feedback meetings when a project is finished.

If effectively implemented, performance reviews can have several **beneficial outcomes**, for example:

- increasing employee motivation and commitment;
- increasing trust between the manager and the employee;

- providing an opportunity to address problems in the organizational unit (for example, unclear distribution of responsibilities or conflicts within the team);
- providing recognition for the employee's work;
- identifying the employee's strengths and weaknesses and devising strategies to enhance the former and eliminate the latter;
- providing an opportunity to monitor employee performance over time;
- recognizing training and development needs and reaching joint agreement on development goals.

For many employees, the performance review is also seen as an opportunity to focus a manager's undivided attention on their personal concerns—which is very rare in today's fast-paced business world. It is therefore also highly advisable that managers do not postpone or reschedule a performance review at short notice because this can give employees the feeling that they and their concerns are not a priority issue for the manager and the organization. This could potentially damage perceived supervisor support and perceived organizational support (see Section 3.1). If badly conducted, performance reviews can also have a negative effect. Employees can be demotivated, for example, if they receive undifferentiated negative feedback. Some employees might also consider the formal atmosphere of the performance review uncomfortable and stressful.

An effective performance review starts with **effective preparation** from both the manager's and the employee's side. The manager can make notes about observations on the employee's strengths, performance, and development needs, as well as on goals that they would like to agree upon with the team member. The employee can summarize achievements during the last year, perceived strengths, the degree to which goals were met (and reasons for struggling with or not meeting some goals), job-related challenges, and potential development opportunities.

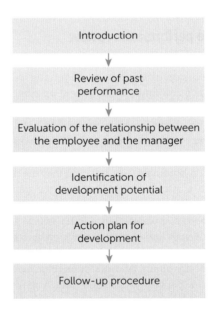

Figure 3.5 Typical structure of a performance review

The **performance review** itself will usually consist of five parts (see Figure 3.5):

1 The **introduction**, in which the manager tries to create a positive atmosphere and clarifies the purpose of the meeting.
2 The **review of the employee's performance** from both perspectives, starting with a self-evaluation by the employee, followed by the assessment of the manager and a dialogue to reach a common understanding of the expected and achieved performance level.

3   The **relationship between the employee and the manager** (and the organization): Where does the employee see the manager's strengths and weaknesses? Does the employee receive all the support they need to perform well?

4   Discussion of **potential for development**: how the employee's strengths could be further developed, and what both the organization and the employee could do to maintain or, if necessary, to increase the employee's performance levels.

5   Agreeing on an **action plan**, with clear goals and specific measures for developing the employee in the following period (usually the following year).

In many organizations, the main results of the performance review are also documented in written form. Some organizations also use performance review software that can help employees to obtain "360 degree" feedback from managers, peers, people who report to them (if they are managers themselves), or even customers. Standardized electronic question-naires can be used to quickly provide feedback on a more regular basis.

Regardless of whether a performance review is conducted in the traditional face-to-face form or in a software-assisted version, it is always important to focus constructive feedback and the resulting action plan on a few major points, and to agree on an adequate **follow-up procedure**.

As we can see in the structure described in Figure 3.5 (especially in the evaluation of the relationship between the employee and the manager), a performance review is not neces-sarily a "one-way street." It can also be used as an opportunity for managers to receive feed-back on their own performance and development potential in their management role. A simple and non-threatening way to obtain feedback is to ask employees to prepare answers to two questions that are then discussed during the performance review:

a   What are the three things that your manager is doing particularly well in the role of a leader?

b   What are the three things that your manager could improve in the role of a leader?

The aggregated answers to these two questions from all subordinates can provide managers with a good overview of their own strengths and development needs in their role.

Dealing with poor performance

When a team member's continual poor performance becomes apparent, either through a structured performance review or simply from observing performance problems in their day-to-day work, managers need to address the issue with the employee. Following the discussion on the individual elements of the performance equation at the beginning of this chapter, Figure 3.6 presents a process model that can help a manager develop a general strategy for dealing with poor performers in a team.

In dealing with a low-performing employee, the main task for a manager is to find out the **underlying reason for the performance problem.** This might be (a) a lack of resources provided by the organization to fulfill the task, (b) a lack of ability, (c) a lack of motivation, (d) a lack of congruence between the job requirements and the person's strengths, or (e) a non-work-related problem.

If both training and development measures (in the case of ability problems) and interven-tions regarding the external factors affecting employee motivation (in the case of motiva-tional problems) do not lead to better performance, a manager should evaluate whether there are alternative tasks which could be better suited to harnessing the specific strengths of that team member. If none of these strategies work, termination of the employment contract needs to be considered as a last resort; however, with all the necessary care (see also Section 3.4 for details on how to manage layoffs).

If the reason for poor performance is not directly linked to the work environment, it is also possible that **non-work-related challenges** such as health issues or private problems are playing a role. In this case, it is certainly not the manager's task to resolve the problem. Managers can, however, offer support in terms of temporarily adjusting the tasks and

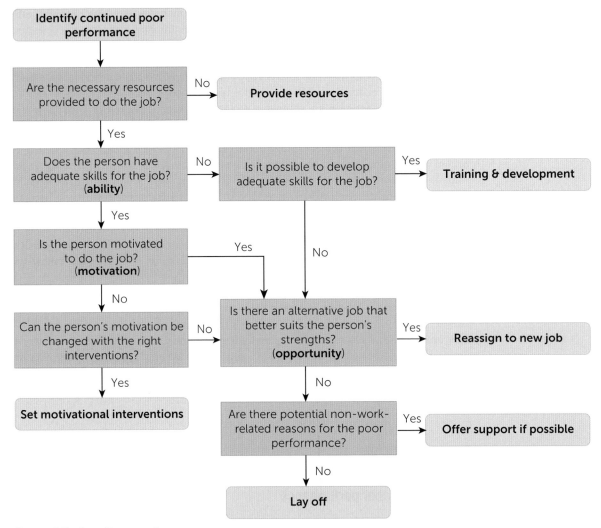

Figure 3.6 Dealing with poor performance

responsibilities of the employee (keeping in mind that this should not be seen as unfair 'special treatment' by other team members) or referring the employee to professional help (for example, an occupational health doctor or professional counselor).

In any case, it is advisable for a manager to engage in a **dialogue** with the team member to find out the real cause for poor performance. Finally, managers should also reflect on whether the root cause of poor performance really lies with the team member, or in their own behavior. "One of the most common blockages occurs when employees feel that their bosses don't really care about them,"[73] says Nigel Nicholson, pointing to the key role that managers all too often play in demotivating others.

Assume that you are leading a project team. There is one team member who used to be one of the top contributors in team meetings. She delivered all her tasks on time and to the required quality until about three months ago. Since then, her performance level has dropped significantly. She constantly misses deadlines, which is delaying the whole project, and she also stays very quiet during team meetings. What would you do to address and resolve this performance problem?

3.4 The right person in the right place

Getty Images/BraunS

In brief

- Having the right people with the right qualities working at the right place is a cornerstone of managerial effectiveness.

- Following a structured hiring process can help to identify the right person for a particular job. The process starts with a clear definition of the job requirements, and is then designed to attract and select suitable candidates who meet these requirements.

- On the other side of the coin, layoffs are another part of the managerial reality. When they are deemed unavoidable, having assessed all alternatives, the way in which they are conducted can make a big difference to both the performance and the reputation of the organization.

- Thorough preparation, a clear communication strategy (toward those who must leave, but also toward those who remain in the organization), and taking a socially responsible approach are preconditions for handling layoff situations effectively.

- Understanding how people typically react when they are confronted with bad news can help managers to cope with such emotionally laden situations.

Unsurprisingly, an extensive Gallup leadership survey revealed that the most effective leaders "surround themselves with the right people."[74] A well-designed hiring process is therefore one of the most important requirements for effective managers. There are, however, also situations in which people must leave the team, either for business reasons (e.g. a lack of orders in an economic crisis) or employee-related reasons (e.g. an ongoing lack of individual performance). In such cases, the way that layoffs are managed can also have an impact on the performance of both the individuals and the organization.

The hiring process

Getting the right people on board is not an easy task. Even experienced managers can make hiring mistakes, which can become very costly, not only due to additional recruiting expenses, but also because the job is not adequately filled in the meantime. Following a well-structured hiring process, in which the job requirements are clearly defined and against which candidates are assessed, can increase the chances of hiring the right person. A typical hiring process follows six steps (see Figure 3.7).

Although these steps are generally sequential, it is sometimes necessary to repeat steps or loop back to earlier steps. If there are not enough suitable **résumés/CVs**, for example, or if no candidate seems to be a good fit after the interview stage, managers can decide to go back and try to source more candidates. It is also worth noting that in some organizations, the reference check is used as a final control, following a conditional job offer to a candidate.

Résumé (or curriculum vitae (CV)):
A written summary of a person's education, work experience, and skills.

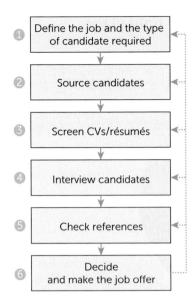

Figure 3.7 The hiring process

Let us now take a closer look at the main tools and techniques that are used during the six steps of the hiring process:

1 **Define the job and the type of candidate required**. Before managers start recruiting, they need to define the role they are hiring for by compiling a clear **job profile**, including the role's main responsibilities and tasks, and then, derived from that profile, a list of requirements the potential job holder should fulfill. If the new recruit will work with a number of different people in the organization, it makes sense to discuss these key requirements with the main internal stakeholders. Requirements can be categorized into background characteristics and personal characteristics (see Table 3.1 for a list of factors that are usually taken into account).

Job profile:
A description of the tasks, responsibilities, and required qualifications and skills for a particular position in an organization.

Table 3.1 Job requirements

Category	Subcategory	Examples
Background characteristics	Education	Educational level Qualifications
	Relevant experience	Industry experience Functional experience (relating to a specific task) Managerial experience
Personal characteristics	Intellectual ability	Analytical skills Creativity Problem-solving skills Decision-making style
	Personality	Formality (inclination to fully adhere to rules and guidelines) Patience Extraversion Presence and influence Conscientiousness
	Interpersonal skills	Empathy Communication skills Listening skills Negotiation skills Teamwork skills
	Motivation	Clear goals Interests Energy level

Source: Reprinted by permission of *Harvard Business Review.* Adapted from 'Summary', p. 7 in 'Note on the Hiring and Selection Process' by Michael J. Roberts, February 3, 1993. Copyright ©1993 by Harvard Business Publishing; all rights reserved.

2   **Source candidates.** Once the job requirements have been clearly defined, the next task is to attract a number of qualified candidates. There are several options when recruiting, including considering internal candidates, posting job ads in general newspapers and professional periodicals, Internet-based recruiting platforms, professional social media websites such as LinkedIn, recruiting agencies, university campus job fairs, or personal referrals. Referrals from existing employees or trusted sources can be particularly effective because people are unlikely to risk their own reputation by recommending an unqualified candidate.

3   **Screen CVs/résumés.** The aim of the screening process is to find out which candidates best match the key requirements set out in the job profile. In addition to assessing CVs/résumés against a checklist of basic requirements, hiring managers can also look for signs of past accomplishments, gaps in employment history, and patterns of job progression. A series of rapid job changes is often a sign that they should be cautious. It is not usually advisable to rule out candidates who seem to be "overqualified" at this stage—maybe they have a good reason for changing their career path. Organizations are also increasingly using technological solutions for supporting managers and human resource specialists to pre-select suitable candidates; for example, with automated keyword matching in CVs/résumés based on artificial intelligence algorithms or with online psychometric assessments.

4   **Interview candidates.** The purpose of the interview is to get the best possible impression of how a candidate matches the job requirements. One of the most important steps for an effective interview is good preparation, particularly referring back to the list of key requirements and making notes of any questions that emerge from reading the CV/résumé. The interview itself might be conducted either individually or by a team, and either face to face or in a videoconference. It usually begins with the interviewer(s) introducing themselves and explaining the structure of the interview. Then, the core part of the interview consists of the interviewer(s) asking questions to elicit information about the suitability of the candidate for the role. Job interviews are especially useful for assessing personal characteristics, which cannot be easily determined or verified from a CV/résumé. Some questioning techniques to use in job interviews are presented in Table 3.2. It is also good practice to take notes during the interview to remind yourself of the key points during the subsequent decision-making process. The last part of the interview is used for answering any additional questions that the candidate might have and for outlining the next steps in the process (e.g. any additional assessments or interviews and when the candidate is likely to hear back).

Table 3.2 Questioning techniques for job interviews

Questioning technique	Examples
Detailed direct questions about past experiences	• Could you give us an example of how you positively influenced a team member's motivation? • Could you please describe a situation where you had to work under extreme time pressure? Did you manage to meet the deadline? Why? Why not? • Your CV/résumé mentions that you increased the profitability of your department by 30 percent. What specific actions did you take to achieve this?
Self-appraisal questions	• Can you explain which of your personal characteristics helped you to successfully complete project X? • Is there anything that you would do differently in project X if you were to undertake it again today?
Scenario- or situation-based questions	• How would you deal with a member of your project team who constantly puts in less effort than the others? • Suppose you have two very valuable team members who seem to have a personal conflict with each other, and that has a detrimental effect on the group's spirit. How would you try to resolve this conflict?
Comparison questions	• Do you usually perform better when you work alone or in collaboration with others? Could you give us an example? • Do you perform better under pressure or in a calm environment? • Would you see yourself as patient or as assertive?

Source: Questioning technique categories partly based on Kennedy (1987).

5 **Check references**. References from previous employers or acquaintances can provide valuable background information about a candidate (provided that they are honest accounts). Using the telephone rather than e-mail, spending time building a positive rapport with the referee, and asking specific questions can help to elicit more valuable information. Examples for questions to a referee include:[75]

- What type of tasks did Susan perform particularly well? Which tasks are maybe less suited for her?
- What did her team like the most/the least about her?
- Are there any tasks that could be difficult for her?
- In what kind of working environment does she perform best?

An interesting way of checking references was proposed by Pierre Mornell in his book *45 Effective Ways for Hiring Smart!* He suggested leaving a message for the referees, asking them to please call back "if the candidate was outstanding."[76] In this case, silence can be an informative answer. The situation is more tricky if the candidate is currently employed by the referee. On the one hand, candidates often do not want their current employers to know that they applied for another job, and on the other hand, current employers might not want to lose them if they are outstanding. This is why some organizations refrain from asking for references from the current employer altogether, while others ask the current employer in consultation with the candidate as a final check before they sign the employment contract.

6 **Decide and make the job offer**. A decision can be made once there is enough information to assess the candidate's suitability against the key requirements of the role. Asking key stakeholders for their assessment of the top candidates can also help in ensuring organizational support.[77] The ultimate yardstick should always be: *Which candidate will be able to contribute the most to the organization?*

CEO BEST PRACTICE

Hiring the right people for Delta Air Lines

Richard Anderson was highly successful as the CEO of Delta Air Lines for almost a decade between 2007 and 2016, before he switched roles and became executive chairman of Delta's board.

During his tenure as CEO, Delta was ranked by *Fortune* magazine among the 50 most admired companies in the world. Anderson became widely known for challenging traditional behavioral patterns in the airline industry (for example, he decided to enter the oil refineries business in order to achieve better fuel prices) and for creating a values-based culture with a strong focus on employee engagement and outstanding customer service.[78] "You've got to be thankful to the people who get the work done, and you've got to be thankful to your customers," he once said in an interview with the *New York Times*, adding that he sends about half a dozen handwritten notes per day to both employees and customers.[79]

In the same interview, he also explained how important it is for him to get the right people on board and what he looks for in job candidates. The ability to communicate well in both written and oral form, adaptability in the face of changing circumstances, a strong work ethic, and what he calls the "human intangibles" are of particular importance to him in this respect. Aiming to understand what kind of people the job candidates really are, he asks them, for example, about the books they read and qualities they like about themselves. He also wants to know more about their families, upbringing, and values. Emotional intelligence—the ability to recognize, understand and manage your own emotions as well as the emotions of other people—is another important criterion for new recruits, he says, because people need "to understand what's right culturally," both within and outside the organization.[80]

→ Key takeaway

Try to understand the full person, and do not only look at professional qualifications, when you want to hire the right people for your organization.

Sources: Based on information in Bryant (2009a); delta.com (2016).

Recruiting traps

Managers should be aware of potential **psychological traps** during the selection process, such as:

- Unconscious bias—judging people by an immediate first impression (for example, based on their age, gender, ethnicity, race, or appearance), and then spending the rest of the interview just looking for confirming evidence, without undertaking a fuller assessment of their character.
- Mistaking introversion for a lack of motivation.
- Assuming that graduates of top-ranked schools/universities or former employees of well-known organizations are automatically better qualified.
- Letting one characteristic or experience of the candidate outshine all the others (a tendency known in psychology as the "halo effect").
- Deciding based on a feeling that the connection and "chemistry" seem right, rather than on reliable facts.
- Favoring candidates who remind them (maybe even unconsciously) of themselves.[81]

It is important for managers to remember that the aim of recruitment is not to find a "best friend," but the person who will most likely perform best in a particular job. This does not mean that **cultural fit**—"the likelihood that someone will reflect and/or be able to adapt to the core beliefs, attitudes, and behaviors that make up your organization"[82]—is not a valid selection criterion. Value congruence between employees and the organization can indeed have positive effects on employee satisfaction and commitment (see also the box *Hiring the right people for Delta Air Lines*).[83] To avoid any misunderstanding, this does not mean losing the benefits of a diverse workforce (see Chapter 5), since common work-related values or attitudes can also be shared by a very diverse set of people.

Another aspect that should be given due consideration in the recruitment process is the phrasing of job advertisements and questions to avoid any unintentional bias toward people from a particular social or cultural background. Managers also need to consider local **anti-discrimination laws**, including any questions which might be prohibited (e.g. which religion an applicant practices or whether an applicant plans to have children). However, inclusivity and appropriate questioning are not only important for legal reasons, but also because the quality of the recruitment process affects the organization's reputation. After all, there are many more candidates who do not get a job than those who eventually join—and those who do not succeed should not leave the process with a negative impression of the organization.

Managing layoffs

Layoff:
A term that was originally used for temporary suspension of employment, but is now more often used for the termination of an employment contract by the employer.

Bringing in the right people in a well-managed hiring process is an important managerial task. Likewise, managers also need to be able to deal with existing employees who are not right for the job, either because of their ongoing poor performance or because changes in the company structure make certain jobs redundant. **Layoffs** are among the most difficult tasks for a manager because they usually create highly emotional situations with a strong (and often negative) impact on other people's lives (see the box *Phases of grief as a reaction to layoffs*). Nevertheless, they are part of the managerial reality, and may become necessary in certain situations so that managers can fulfill their responsibility of ensuring their organization's continued survival and success.

Phases of grief as a reaction to layoffs

It can be helpful for managers to understand the range of different reactions they can expect from those they are letting go. Reactions can range from silence to rage, and from seemingly composed acknowledgment to complete incomprehension. Whatever the reaction, managers should not take it personally. When faced with a decisive negative turning point in their lives (whether it is the loss of a close relative, a divorce, or a job loss), people express their grief in different ways like denial, anger, bargaining, or depression. These responses might not necessarily follow a predetermined order, as Swiss-American psychiatrist Elisabeth Kübler-Ross proposed in her "five stages of grief" model (see Figure 3.8). Most people do need to pass through at least some of those stages, however, in order to be able to accept the loss and start thinking positively about the future again.

First shock	Denial	Anger	Bargaining	Depression	Acceptance
	Denies that the situation is really true; seems to be "under shock"	Outward-focused negative emotions; often aimed at others	Tries to negotiate for a different outcome	Shows signs of despair; appears sullen	Regains emotional stability; able to look ahead again

Figure 3.8 The five stages of grief

Source: Inspired by concepts in Kübler-Ross (2014).

In a layoff process, no matter whether one or many employees are affected, five steps are usually indispensable:

1 **Assess alternatives.** Before deciding on layoffs, managers should check whether there are other options available (e.g. **natural employee turnover**, **short-time work**, or reallocating jobs and tasks).

Natural employee turnover:
The "normal" percentage of employees who leave an organization without being forced to leave within a certain timeframe.

2 **Prepare thoroughly.** Managers need to consider legal issues; for example, whether the employee may have a claim to receive severance or redundancy payments. There may also be a set deadline to be observed. Preparing a detailed schedule and a checklist of what to say, what to do, and what not to forget in the process can help a manager to keep track even through difficult, emotional situations.

3 **Communicate clearly.** Uncertainty can paralyze people. To avoid uncertainty, managers should inform employees about their situation in a timely manner. Providing comprehensible reasons for the layoff is equally important as clear information about the further steps.

Short-time work:
An agreement between the organization and its employees that everyone works less hours for less pay in order to avoid layoffs.

4 **Act responsibly.** Layoffs can deeply affect people's lives. Social fairness, respectful personal communication, and offering support for their next steps (e.g. in the search for a new job) are important behaviors of responsible managers.

5 **Do not forget the others in the team.** Layoffs can also have an effect on the remaining team members. They might need to take on additional tasks to cover the dismissed employee or fear that they could be the next one to be dismissed. Clear communication with the remaining team members—including providing them with information about the reasons for the layoffs, implications for them, and an outlook for the future—is therefore highly important to avoid uncertainty in the team.

If you were in a situation in which layoffs seem to be inevitable to ensure the survival of the organization, to whom would you give notice first? Those who joined the organization most recently? Those who showed the lowest performance during the last year? Those who would have the best employability prospects with another company? Or would you take completely different criteria into account?

Although managers can harness the support of other professionals (e.g. lawyers or human resource management specialists) in layoff processes, the **termination meeting** itself is a non-delegable task of managers. The **"F-R-E-P" model** can help to structure the meeting (see Figure 3.9).[84]

Figure 3.9 The "F-R-E-P" model for structuring a termination meeting

Source: Based on an unpublished idea by Robert Ukowitz (www.robert-ukowitz.com) who kindly permitted the author to use an extended version of his original Facts-Empathy-Perspective model in this book.

"F-R-E-P" model: A model for structuring a termination meeting in four phases: facts (coming straight to the point), reasons (inform the person about the reasons for terminating the employment contract), empathy (accept and understand emotional reactions), and perspective (provide information about future steps).

The four "F-R-E-P" steps for structuring the termination meeting are:

- **Facts.** Small talk is inappropriate for termination meetings. Coming straight to the point is important. Employees need to be informed about the layoff decision in a clear, unequivocal way.

- **Reasons.** People will naturally want to know why they are being let go. It is therefore a matter of fairness to clearly explain the reasons for the layoff. Managers need to be careful, however, to avoid (a) giving reasons that could have detrimental legal consequences (it is important that the manager understands the local legal regulations about non-permissible reasons for layoffs); and (b) turning the meeting into a debate about the validity of these reasons (reasons should be given as information, not as justification).

- **Empathy.** Because a layoff is an exceptional situation, managers should expect and accept emotional reactions, for example anger or tears (see the *Phases of grief as a reaction to layoffs* box). Sometimes, people need some time to digest the information. In this case, it is better to give people the time they need rather than rushing to complete the termination meeting.

- **Perspective.** People whose employment contract is being terminated have many questions, including how long they will still stay in the organization, whether they will be eligible to severance pay, whether they can continue using their office, or whether they will get support in finding a new job, to name just a few issues. Managers should use the last part of the meeting for providing information about the next steps. It is also good practice to thank the person for their contributions to the organization. After all, everyone—even those who are dismissed for reasons of poor performance—has usually contributed at least something.

Hiring and developing talent at ACL Services

Laurie Schultz joined ACL Services, a Vancouver-based software company, as chief operating officer in 2011, and in the same year also took over the CEO role from Harald Will, who had co-founded the company with his father in the 1980s. The company, with offices in Canada, the UK, and Singapore employs around 300 people and sells software solutions to several thousand customers in 140 countries. ACL's audit analytics solutions help to detect and eliminate fraud or operational waste in organizations through analyzing massive volumes of data.

Schultz led the company on a rejuvenation path, creating a start-up-like atmosphere and following the strategic aims of mobilizing talent, disrupting the industry, and achieving double-digit growth. She strongly invested in technology and converted the business model from software sales to a subscription-based software-as-a-service model. Above all, however, she focused on developing talent.

"What my DNA is about is to discover people that are amazing and create an environment where they can practice developing [their] skills,"[85] she was quoted in *Business Vancouver*. From the beginning, she has been highly committed to identifying people who could really make a difference. For that purpose, she started to hold town hall meetings with groups of around 15 employees without their managers, engaging them in open conversations about what works well and what could be improved in ACL, and about what they would change. These meetings not only provided her with good ideas for moving the company forward, but also with an opportunity to judge the quality of ideas suggested by employees as well as their ability to prioritize and to influence and convince others. With the help of these town hall meetings, she identified "change agents," as she called them. "Find your change agents. Next, challenge them by putting them in charge of new ideas," she wrote in the *Globe and Mail*. "Push them into leadership positions, maybe even before they are ready."[86] As a result, around 90 percent of ACL's employees are in roles that they did not have five years ago.

In addition to spotting talent within the company, Schultz also hired a lot of new people to keep up with the high growth pace of the company. When she hires, she looks for people with a high degree of curiosity, energy, emotion and "spirit"—people who have the potential to inspire others. She tries to find that out, for example, through a question about the candidate's proudest career moment, and she values good stories as an answer to that question more than just sales or profits figures. She also asks people a thought-provoking question about what they would want to be when they "grow up." The aim of this rather untypical job interview question is to probe the ability of the candidate to define a future and think strategically. For her, the combination of being able to define a future and inspire people is a good precondition for being successful in a future leadership role.

When the right people are on board, Schultz is convinced that top managers need to take genuine interest in their career goals and advancement, acknowledging that helping people to advance in their career plays a key role for employee motivation. Her advice for managers is to take their time to "dig in deep" and communicate a lot with employees; for example, through discussing their career path in lunch meetings or formulating 90-day learning goals.[87] For people who are especially able and motivated to "champion the vision and mission of the company,"[88] as she calls it, she also tries to provide direct career support from herself and other members of the top management team in addition to opening opportunities to participate in special projects.

To symbolize an organizational culture in which "everyone's opinion matters,"[89] all ACL employees (including the CEO) moved to an open space office that is complemented by lots of casual spaces, small meeting places, and café areas. A symbol that can be found everywhere around the office is the moose. Borrowing from the phrase "the elephant in the room," Schultz wants everyone at ACL to "put the moose on the table,"[90] meaning that people should be open to talk honestly about everything—especially also uncomfortable issues. Twice a year, ACL uses an electronic survey in which employees rate the effectiveness of their managers and their satisfaction with the work environment, talent management, and career development. There are publicly announced target levels for the survey, and the ACL's management is committed to take action wherever there are still gaps between the goals and the current status as seen from the employees' perspective. For Schultz, it is clearly the task of every manager to understand how employees would like to develop themselves and, as she wrote in an article for the *Globe and Mail*, to "ensure that they receive the job they want instead of finding it somewhere else."[91]

Sources: *biv.com (2014; 2016); Bryant (2013); Schultz (2016; 2018); Stone (2016); Woods (2017).*

 ## Discussion questions

- How do Schultz's approaches to hiring and developing talent support the strategic goals of the company?
- What role does the cultural fit of people play in ACL's hiring and people development processes?
- Could the town hall meetings and the lunch meetings in which career paths and learning goals are discussed be seen as alternatives to a traditional performance review? What advantages and disadvantages do these approaches have in comparison to traditional performance reviews?
- Are the approaches to recruiting and people development specifically suitable for a smaller organization with a "start-up atmosphere"? Or could they also be successfully implemented in larger organizations?

Conclusion

Are we really experiencing the "end of leadership" as Barbara Kellerman claims in her book of the same name? That would imply that managers are no longer able to influence others to follow common, worthwhile goals—and this is certainly not the case. What is changing is the way we look at leadership in organizations. It is no longer about emulating the great leaders of world history or the outstanding business leaders of our times. It is not about the difference between "mundane" managers and heroic leader figures who, by virtue of their charisma, inspire followers to work toward a brighter future. Leadership in today's organizational contexts is much more down to earth—it is simply a function that managers need to fulfill in order to make sure that other people perform well and enable the organization to achieve its goals.

In this chapter, we discussed a key component for managers to become effective in their role as leaders: making sure that people have all the necessary abilities to accomplish their tasks, the right kinds of tasks to fit their strengths, and that they are kept motivated by providing meaningful challenges and the requisite autonomy to master them, feedback on progress, fair and respectful treatment, recognition and support, and the feeling that the outcome of their work is meaningful and valued. The other key leadership role is setting a clear direction for the organization, which will be covered in Chapter 7.

The leadership function involves the long-term responsibility of developing people, providing them with opportunities to grow, both personally as well as in their contributions to the organization, and the task of combining different competencies and personalities in well-functioning teams (see Chapter 4).

To be able to perform effectively in the leadership role, managers above all need to understand and match the needs of the organization and the skills and needs of each individual team member, remembering that they are performing through people. In Manfred Kets de Vries' words, "without feelings there are no actions. Without feelings there is no passion. Everything important to human beings is affect-ridden."[92] People have moods, hopes, desires, anxieties, and fears that make leadership a deeply "emotion-laden process."[93] To influence other people's performance, managers therefore need to understand and address their **emotional needs**. People need positive relationships just as much as they need challenges at work. There is truth in the old saying that "People go to work for a company but quit a boss."[94] If managers do not treat others well, they will not be able to perform through them.

✓ Review questions

1   What are the main factors of the "performance equation" and how are they interrelated?
2   What can managers do to influence the motivation of other people?
3   Which strategies can managers use to develop the performance potential of other people?
4   What should managers be aware of to avoid the demotivation of employees?
5   What does it mean to "staff from strengths"?
6   How should managers ideally give feedback?
7   What are the main steps of the people development process?
8   What is coaching and how can managers use coaching to improve other people's performance?
9   What does an effective delegation process look like?
10   What are the potential benefits of a performance review (appraisal interview)?
11   How is a performance review typically structured?
12   How can managers deal with poor performance?
13   What are the main steps of a systematic hiring process and what should a manager consider in each of these steps?
14   Which traps should be avoided during a recruiting process?
15   How can managers responsibly handle a layoff process?

Critical reflection questions

1   Many people complain that the behavior of their managers demotivates them. To your mind, what are the main reasons behind that?

2   Human resource managers sometimes point out that a new generation of young employees tends to put more emphasis on their social life than on job-related performance. Do you think that such alleged changes in priorities require new forms of leadership and performance management?

3   Are there tasks that you would see as absolutely non-delegable for a manager?

4   Annual performance reviews have come under criticism; for example, for their subjectivity, for reinforcing rigid hierarchies, for being too fixated on the past, or for being too bureaucratic to administer. What is your opinion about the value and potential drawbacks of performance reviews?

5   Some people voice doubts about whether the performance of a candidate in a job interview is really a good indicator of future performance in the job. What is your opinion about the usefulness and potential disadvantages of job interviews?

☞ Managerial implications

- Managers can only perform effectively through other people if they adequately fulfill their leadership task, i.e. succeed in influencing others to achieve a common goal.

- In order to influence the performance of other people, managers first need to understand the three main factors that enable performance: ability, motivation, and opportunity. Thus, they can also create the right environment to improve performance: helping people develop their abilities, keeping them motivated, and providing opportunities to grow and perform in the form of challenges and tasks that match individual strengths.

- Delegation lies at the heart of what effective management is all about. A thorough analysis of the task and the competencies required for accomplishing the task, a good match between tasks and people, a clear assignment that ensures commitment, and an appropriate follow-up and review process are major factors that can influence the success of a delegation process.

- Through the use of instruments such as coaching and performance reviews, managers can help their team members to develop themselves and perform well in their organizational roles.

- Managers can only be effective if they work with the right people with the right qualities in the right places. Managers can identify the right people through following a systematic hiring process in which asking the right questions plays a key role.

- Managing layoffs is a difficult, yet in some situations unavoidable, part of the reality of the managerial job. Responsible managers, however, will always ask whether there are alternatives. If there are no alternatives, they can at least make a difference by responsible handling of the layoff process.

✎ Endnotes

[1]Barley and Kunda (1992); Bryman (1992).
[2]Den Hartog and Koopman (2001), p. 173.
[3]Mintzberg (2011), p. 8.
[4]Kellerman (2012).
[5]Campbell et al. (1993), p. 40.
[6]Maier (1955).
[7]Blumberg and Pringle (1982).
[8]Anderson (1974).
[9]Ployhart (2008).
[10]Bandura (1977).
[11]Ghoshal and Bruch (2003).

[12]The following description of the eclectic framework and its individual factors is based on Sternad (2013b).
[13]A detailed overview of the underlying theories is provided in Sternad (2013b).
[14]Locke and Latham (1990).
[15]Bandura and Locke (2003); Latham (2018).
[16]Grant (2008); Van Loon et al. (2018).
[17]Grant (2012).
[18]Spector (1986).
[19]Theorell and Karasek (1996).
[20]Amabile and Kramer (2012), p. 124.

[21]Adams (1965).
[22]Colquitt et al. (2001); Furnham and Treglown (2018); Karam et al. (2019).
[23]Maslach and Leiter (2008).
[24]House (1996).
[25]Eisenberger et al. (2002); Kurtessis et al. (2017).
[26]Paine (2010), p. 106.
[27]Vroom (1964).
[28]Sternad (2013b).
[29]Deckers (2018).
[30]Mintzberg (2011), p. 66.
[31]Kanter (2011), p. 42.

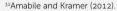

[32]Amabile and Kramer (2012).
[33]Drucker (1999a), p. 64.
[34]Drucker (1999a), p. 64.
[35]Drucker (1999a).
[36]Drucker (1993), p. 149.
[37]Stanford University (2007).
[38]Mintzberg (2011), p. 67.
[39]Ericsson (2018).
[40]Simon (1957).
[41]Ericsson et al. (1993).
[42]Ericsson (2018).
[43]Maurer and Meyer (2015).
[44]theconversation.com (2017).
[45]Maurer and Meyer (2015).
[46]Kets de Vries (2006), p. 178.
[47]Sonnentag and Frese (2001).
[48]Hill and Lineback (2011), pp. 201–205.
[49]Miscenko et al. (2017).
[50]Clapp-Smith et al. (2018).
[51]Gates (2013).
[52]Feldman and Lankau (2005).
[53]Athanasopoulou and Dopson (2018).
[54]Jones et al. (2016).
[55]O'Donnell (2011).

[56]Meyrowitz (2014), p. 48.
[57]Meyrowitz (2014), p. 48.
[58]Meyrowitz (2014), p. 48.
[59]Garvin and Margolis (2015), p. 69.
[60]Hill and Lineback (2011), p. 203.
[61]Semler (2004).
[62]Semler (1989).
[63]Fisher (2005).
[64]Fisher (2005).
[65]Fisher (2005).
[66]Semler (2018).
[67]Caulkin (2003).
[68]Semler (2004).
[69]Harvard Business School Publishing (2005).
[70]Harvard Business School Publishing (2005).
[71]Evans and Tourish (2017), p. 271.
[72]Vauhini (2015).
[73]Nicholson (2003), p. 60.
[74]gallup.com (2016).
[75]Harvard Business School Publishing (2002); Roberts (1993).
[76]Mornell (2003), p. 179.
[77]Fernández-Aráoz et al. (2009).
[78]delta.com (2016).

[79]Bryant (2009a).
[80]Bryant (2009a).
[81]Harvard Business School Publishing (2002); Roberts (1993).
[82]Bouton (2015).
[83]Amos and Wheatington (2008); Byza et al. (2017).
[84]The model is based on an unpublished idea by Robert Ukowitz (www.robert-ukowitz.com) who kindly permitted the author to use an extended version of his original facts-empathy-perspective model in this book.
[85]biv.com (2014).
[86]Schultz (2016).
[87]Schultz (2018).
[88]Schultz (2018).
[89]Woods (2016).
[90]Stone (2017).
[91]Schultz (2018).
[92]Kets de Vries (2006), p. xxii.
[93]George (2000), p. 1046.
[94]Hill and Lineback (2011), p. 25.

Visit the companion website at macmillanihe.com/sternad-management **to access multiple choice questions, useful weblinks and additional materials.**

Getty Images/Yuri_Arcurs

WORKING IN TEAMS

Outline of chapter

This chapter will enable you to

- Explain what managers need to consider in building a high-performance team.
- Identify the main building blocks of effective teamwork.
- Assess the quality of team processes and suggest actions to improve the effectiveness of teams.
- Choose the right communication tools and conduct productive meetings.
- Describe different strategies for managing conflicts.
- Distinguish between distributive and integrative negotiations and develop strategies for conducting both.

Introduction

In July 2015, the board of British bank, Barclays, decided to sack its CEO. In a BBC News article, John McFarlane, the chairman of the 325-year-old globally active financial institution, explained the reasons for this move. He said that the bank was not efficient and profitable enough, and that "cultural change was urgently required."[1] More specifically, McFarlane pointed out that Barclays needed to become "leaner and more agile."[2]

"**Agile**" (often written with a capital "A") has become an almost ubiquitous buzzword in the business world of the 21st century. It describes an organizational approach that is no longer based on strict hierarchies, but on self-managing multi-functional teams that are fully focused on creating value for customers. Instead of following detailed plans and schedules, these teams are supposed to work in short iterative cycles with frequent interactions with the customers or users of the team's output.[3] The Agile movement started in software development in 2001 with agile methods such as "scrum" (in which small cross-functional teams try to reach certain goals in short "sprints" of no longer than a month and track their progress in 15-minute daily stand-up meetings). These were seen as better suited to coping flexibly with changing customer demands and other unpredictable challenges. The idea has since spread from managing software development teams to transforming organizations as a whole, because becoming more agile has been seen as an effective way to cope with the fast-changing, complex environment with which many of today's organizations are faced. In a *Forbes Insights* survey conducted among over 1,000 executives around the world in 2018, 81 percent of all respondents said that agility was "the most important characteristic of a successful organization."[4]

> **Agile:**
> An approach to organizing work that is based on using self-managed multi-disciplinary teams to tackle tasks in short iterative cycles and in close interaction with customers.

At the heart of the Agile movement lies **effective teamwork**, the ability of a small group of people to synchronize their efforts and achieve a common goal. Even if the teams are self-managing (i.e. without being under the constant supervision of a formally appointed manager), as is the case in the idealized agile organization, the processes of building and running a team still need to be managed by someone. In this chapter, we will explore how this can be done effectively, regardless of whether there is a formally appointed manager or collective responsibility for managing the team.

- In *Section 4.1*, we will explore what managers need to consider in **setting up a well-functioning team**.
- We will then turn our attention to the role and responsibilities of the **team leader** as a driving force for achieving high performance levels in a team (*Section 4.2*).
- *Section 4.3* is devoted to one of the most essential skills for managers who are leading teams—**effective communication**. Choosing the right communication channel is as important in this context as the message itself and the manager's behavior during the communication, whether it is a presentation, a meeting, or a one-to-one dialogue.
- Even the most effective teams are not immune to conflicts. In *Section 4.4*, we will look at how managers can handle situations when diverging interests collide and need to be reconciled. We will analyze different approaches to **managing conflicts,** as well as strategies and tactics for preparing and conducting **negotiations**.

4.1 Building teams

Pixabay/rawpixel

In brief

● Teams are the right choice for working on complex tasks that require the close interaction of people with different skills and experience. When relatively little interaction is required, loosely connected, co-acting groups can be more efficient than highly interconnected teams.

● To increase the team's effectiveness, managers who are setting up teams need to formulate clear team goals, clarify resource availability and reporting structures, and select the right mix of team members with complementary skills.

● Team leaders need to be aware of the crucial importance of the launch phase of the team. During this phase, it is essential to clarify who the team members are, what skills and strengths they bring, what the purpose and goals of the team are, who the stakeholders are that the team is dependent on, and which resources it has access to. Agreeing on behavioral norms for the teamwork is also an important task for leaders of newly formed teams.

Managers not only perform through other individuals, they also need to be able to build a team and mandate it with accomplishing a certain mission or task. A **team** is a (usually small) group of people who work together for a **common purpose**.[5] To really function as a team, its members should contribute complementary skills and feel responsible and committed toward joint goals and take a coordinated approach to reaching these goals. **Common commitment** and **mutual accountability** are key factors that distinguish a team from other types of groups.[6]

What does it mean for a team to be effective? Effectiveness, as discussed in Chapter 1, is about achieving a desired outcome. In a team context, this first and foremost means that the team **accomplishes the task or mission** for which it was set up. Consistently successful organizations keep building long-term performance potential as well as short-term performance in mind. Therefore the evaluation of a team's effectiveness is not complete without looking at how the team experience supports individual team members in their professional development, and enhances their ability to work together productively in the future.[7]

These different **facets of team effectiveness**—(a) accomplishing the task, (b) supporting individual team members in their development, and (c) enhancing the ability of the team members to collaborate with each other—are intertwined. Common wisdom holds that teams in which people are satisfied will perform well. In reality, in most cases, it is exactly the other way around: people feel satisfied when they experience productive teamwork that leads to valuable outcomes, even if certain steps during the process were not entirely satisfying for all team members.[8]

We will now take a closer look at how managers can set up an effective team.

Setting up a high-performance team

There is one essential question that every manager should ask before building a team: **Is a team really the right choice for this particular task?** Teams are not a panacea for all organizational endeavors. Managers need to carefully evaluate when to use a team, and when to opt for another method of organizing the work. One of the world's foremost authorities on the effective management of teams, J. Richard Hackman, refers to a Finnish saying, "*Joukossa tyhmyys tiivistyy*" ("In a group, stupidity condenses"), when explaining that many teams do not perform according to expectations.[9] It is not only that individuals might sometimes act unwisely under the influence of group pressure as the Finnish proverb suggests. Teamwork often also entails friction, for example, in the form of motivational problems, **social loafing**, or interpersonal conflict, and requires additional coordination costs. Individuals often complete specific tasks much quicker than a team because they do not need to engage in lengthy discussions with others before taking action. In many cases, individuals—especially if they are distinguished specialists in their fields—are able to achieve higher quality and ingenuity in their work than teams (just think about composer Ludwig van Beethoven's performance in composing symphonies or physicist Albert Einstein, who single-handedly developed theories that revolutionized the way in which we see our world).

Social loafing:
The tendency of certain group members to "free ride"—to put in less effort in a group situation (because they expect others to do the work).

Working through teams does make sense:

- for **complex tasks** which can only be fulfilled by combining a variety of different, interdependent skills and perspectives; and
- when **more resources and flexibility in deploying resources are needed** to accomplish a particular task than one individual is able to contribute, and if it is not possible to split the task into smaller portions that could be independently completed by individuals.[10]

Some tasks can be divided into separate components so that individuals can work on them independently and in parallel. The outcomes of these sub-tasks can later be combined to achieve an overall outcome. In such cases, **co-acting groups** with relatively little interaction between individuals are often more efficient than "real" teams with high levels of interconnection and interdependence.[11]

Co-acting group:
A group that is working toward achieving a common goal without much personal communication and interaction.

Research has shown that for **conceptual tasks** (e.g. planning, decision making, or negotiating), both co-acting groups and highly interdependent teams can perform well. In co-acting group arrangements, conflict levels are usually low and individual contributions are clearly visible, while in integrated teams, open communication and a clear understanding of the other team members' strengths and weaknesses facilitate effectiveness. Performance problems can occur in semi-integrated groups in which members are mutually dependent but have not (yet) developed the ability to communicate openly with each other.[12] For **executing tasks** (e.g. manufacturing on the shop floor), this relationship was found to be inverse, with a medium level of integration leading to higher performance levels than very low or very high levels of interaction (see also Figure 4.1).[13] Teams executing tasks need some degree of interaction to be able to work in a coordinated way, but too much interaction can distract them from their actual task and "getting things done."

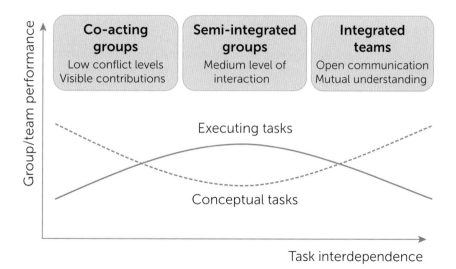

Figure 4.1 The relationship between task interdependence and team performance

Source: Adapted with permission of Academy of Management, from Figure 2, p. 143 in Stewart, G. L. and Barrick, M. R. (2000) 'Team structure and performance: Assessing the mediating role of intrateam process and the moderating role of task type', *Academy of Management Journal*, 43(2): 135–148; permission conveyed through Copyright Clearance Center, Inc.

After deciding that a task requires **mandating a team**, a manager needs to take a few more preparatory steps, including:

1 **formulating clear goals** for the team;
2 defining the **right team size** (dependent on the task and skills needed);
3 selecting the **right team members**;
4 defining **formal roles and responsibilities** (especially assigning a formal team leader);
5 clarifying which **resources** the team has access to;
6 defining a **reporting process** on the progress of the teamwork;
7 deciding on an **incentive system** for the team (if necessary).

One particularly important resource for teamwork is **team members' time**. To ensure effective teamwork, a manager who sets up a team needs to clarify (a) how much of their time individual team members can and should contribute to the team, and (b) how the demands of the team and of the team members' regular jobs should be reconciled.

Combining complementary skills

One of the main reasons for building a team is to combine different skills which are required to reach a certain objective.

On the one hand, teams can strongly benefit from a **diversity** of skills, experience, cultural backgrounds, and perspectives. A team that needs to develop a new technical product for a global market, for example, would ideally include both engineers and marketing specialists, as well as colleagues from different world regions who understand the specific needs of the local target markets. On the other hand, diversity can also lead to conflicts and require integration of diverging positions in arduous discussions. Engineers might have different ideas about the "perfect product" than marketers (and each group might have difficulties understanding the jargon of the other group), and communication is usually also more difficult between people from different cultures who speak different languages. It is often easier for more homogeneous teams to build trust and a good communication climate among their members. Because there are both advantages and disadvantages, **diversity and similarity need to carefully balanced** when building a team. This does not necessarily mean convergence toward a middle point on both dimensions. Dependent on the specific task and context, a more homogeneous or a more diverse team might be appropriate.[14] If the task is to specify the functions of a new product for the global market, for example, a diverse team that includes both marketing experts and engineers will probably be more suitable than a team that only consists of either engineers or marketers. During the technical implementation phase, however, a homogeneous team that only consists of engineers would most likely be the more efficient choice.

Often, team members will be selected for their functional expertise and their cognitive or specialist skills. However, this type of selection process does not guarantee high team performance. Adequate interpersonal skills, such as listening, recognizing the contributions of others, and providing constructive feedback are also important to ensure that a team can work together effectively. Well-functioning teams need **team roles** (i.e. certain sets of behavior that people usually show in a team setting) to be fulfilled.

Team role:
A certain set of behaviors that a person usually shows in a team setting.

A seminal contribution to the discussion on team roles was made by J. Meredith Belbin, who identified nine roles that can usually be found within well-functioning teams (also known as the **Belbin team roles**):

- **Coordinator**, who delegates work and integrates different team members' activities;
- **Shaper**, who drives the team forward and keeps everyone focused on the task;
- **Plant**, who contributes new ideas and creative solutions to team problems;
- **Monitor Evaluator**, who analyzes, weighs, and judges different ideas and alternatives;
- **Resource Investigator**, who establishes and uses contacts outside of the team to acquire new information and resources;
- **Implementer**, who turns ideas into concrete, operative actions and carries them out;

- **Completer Finisher**, who controls the quality of the work of the team, finds final errors, and makes sure that everything is completed on time and according to the appropriate standards;
- **Teamworker**, who cares for the well-being of individual team members and for the cohesion of the team as a whole;
- **Specialist**, who contributes specific expertise or skills which are necessary to complete the team's tasks. [15]

In Belbin's view, effective teams need to strike a **balance** between these nine team roles. If there are only Plants in one team, for example, many ideas will be put forward but hardly any implemented. Without a Plant, on the other hand, the team might lack the creative ideas that it needs to move forward. Similarly, no representatives—or too many—of any of the other team roles can also be detrimental for team performance. It is therefore the responsibility of a manager who is setting up a team to evaluate prospective team members, not only on the basis of their functional expertise, but especially also on their suitability to take on certain team roles. Belbin's team roles concept has received both support and criticism in follow-up studies. In a more recent summary of research results, the model was accredited an adequate level of validity.[16]

Although having the right mix of skills and roles is important for team success, it is not necessary, and often not feasible, for team members to possess all the required skills at the outset. Managers can also select people on the basis of their **skills potential**, with the added value that employees can develop themselves (and therefore also their value for the organization) during the team assignment.[17] This may be one of the main reasons why certain people are selected for a particular team challenge.

Newly formed teams

Hackman described a conversation that he had with the internationally renowned British conductor Christopher Hogwood. He asked the conductor about the importance of the first rehearsal with an orchestra: "What do you mean, the first *rehearsal*," Hogwood replied, "All I have is the first few minutes."[18]

The **first meeting** is a critical stage. People tend to form judgments of other people very quickly. First impressions count, and first encounters set the tone for the interactions that follow. Team norms and team culture—the way team members interact with each other—are established very early. It is therefore worth paying special attention to thorough preparation of the first team interactions.

In the process of constituting themselves, **newly formed teams** need to clarify six essential issues:

1 **Who is part of our team?** The answer to this question is less obvious than it sounds. In a study conducted by Harvard scholars, less than 10 percent of senior managers completely agreed about who was on their senior management team.[19] Clarifying where the boundary lies, who is part of the team and who is not, is therefore a crucial step in generating mutual accountability.
2 **What is our purpose and what are our specific goals?** Although defining the mission for a team is also the commissioning manager's responsibility, often the assignment remains rather vague. Therefore, team members together with their leaders should put considerable efforts into clarifying the team's overall purpose on the one hand, and setting clear, specific performance goals on the other hand. Research shows that teams that fail to do so will usually achieve considerably weaker results.[20]
3 **Which resources do we have access to?** This is not only about material resources or funds that the team can use to achieve its purpose. A team must also understand how much of the individual team members' time is available for the team project. It needs to be clarified among the team members whether the combined resources are sufficient to achieve the team's goals.

4   **What are our team members' skills and strengths?** As a manager who mandates a team should think about assembling people with the right mix of skills, team leaders and all other team members need to understand their co-workers' strengths in order to be able to deploy them in an effective alignment of tasks and skills. Making strengths and styles explicit, for example through discussing experiences, team role preferences, or personality types, can help to gain a better understanding of how each individual can contribute to the success of the whole team.

5   **Who are we dependent on?** Some relationships with external stakeholders are essential to obtain the resources and support necessary to achieve a team's goals. Identifying the key players who can provide the necessary resources, developing a strategy for building and maintaining good relationships with major stakeholders, and assigning networking responsibilities to team members are therefore essential tasks for a leader of a newly formed team.

6   **How are we going to work together?** Productive teams have a clear and (at least implicitly) commonly agreed approach on how to interact with each other and get their job done. That includes certain behavioral norms, how to make decisions and deal with conflicts, a clear understanding of who will take care of particular tasks, of what is expected of the individual team members, and how they will be held accountable.[21] Agreeing on clear rules of behavior up front is good practice and can considerably ease the process of working together (see Table 4.1).

Table 4.1 Exemplary rules of behavior for teams

Rules related to	Examples
Attendance	No cell phone calls during team meetings.
Discussion	Everyone will have a voice.
Confidentiality	Contents of team discussions will remain confidential unless we agree upon making specific information public.
Analytical approach	We first consider alternatives before we jump to conclusions.
Constructive confrontation	Don't get personal.
Contribution	Every team member fulfills the assigned task by the agreed date.

Source: Inspired by concepts in Katzenbach and Smith (1993), p. 118.

Assume that you have just been appointed as the leader of a project team that consists of seven people (including yourself). The only person you already know is a long-term colleague of yours. You will meet five of the team members for the first time in the initial team meeting scheduled for next week. How would you approach the first meeting? What would you do in order to make sure that the team will be able to successfully work together during the project?

Quick wins:
Visible improvements that can be achieved quite quickly and easily.

Once the team has been set up and has clarified the main constitutional issues, it should ideally also have a few challenging goals that can be achieved within a relatively short timeframe.[22] Such **quick wins** will give the team members a feeling of progress, and the feedback that they are well on their way to accomplishing their task. For example, a product development team could set itself the intermediate goal of presenting a first prototype with basic functionality within eight weeks instead of just having the long-term goal of developing a marketable product within the next two years. In another example, a team that is in charge of the introduction of a new IT system could first set the goal of implementing the system in one small department before rolling it out throughout the whole organization. Early visible success can strongly contribute to the morale and the cohesiveness of a team.

4.2 Effective teamwork

Getty Images/iStockphoto/Sportstock

In brief

- Teams are dynamic social systems that typically progress through a couple of development stages before they become fully productive. During these stages, team members get accustomed to each other's strengths and weaknesses and adopt certain standards of working together.

- Team leaders are responsible for striking a balance between attending to the task, taking care of individual team members' needs, improving the teamwork process, and taking stakeholder interests and influences into account.

- Team leaders also need to deal with "ineffective" team players, for example free riders who rely on others to do the work.

- Teams can make use of a range of digital tools to increase their productivity.

Understanding team dynamics

Before teams become fully productive, they usually progress through a series of development phases. Bruce Tuckman identified **four stages of group development** (see Figure 4.2) which he called **forming, storming, norming,** and **performing**.[23] Understanding Tuckman's stages model can help team leaders to reach higher performance and productivity levels in newly formed teams more quickly.

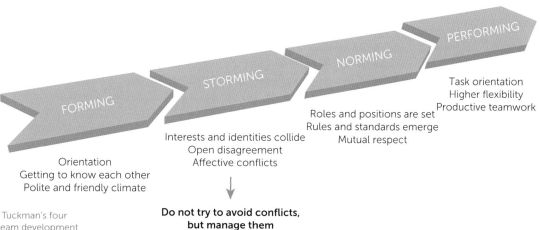

FORMING

Orientation
Getting to know each other
Polite and friendly climate

STORMING

Interests and identities collide
Open disagreement
Affective conflicts

↓

**Do not try to avoid conflicts,
but manage them**

NORMING

Roles and positions are set
Rules and standards emerge
Mutual respect

PERFORMING

Task orientation
Higher flexibility
Productive teamwork

Figure 4.2 Tuckman's four phases of team development

Source: Inspired by concepts in Tuckman (1965).

The four phases of team development are:[24]

1. **Forming**: When a new group is established, the group members go through an orientation phase ("forming"), in which they try to find out more about the others while still often being a bit insecure in how to approach them. Team members try to make an impression on others but also test their fellow group members, thus finding their own identity within the group. The tone is usually polite and friendly, and people tend to attend to the task.

2. **Storming:** The atmosphere often changes in groups when identities and interests start to collide. In the "storming" phase, interpersonal issues come to light, sometimes leading to conflicts. This is not necessarily a negative development. When group members openly disagree with each other, they also learn about their counterparts' intentions and

personalities. Understanding each other's perspectives as well as the strengths and weaknesses of the individual group members is a major precondition for being able to collaborate in a productive way. The way in which conflicts are managed in this phase can have a strong influence on the further performance of a team (see also the discussion on conflict management in Section 4.4). A cooperative rather than a competitive approach to conflict management is usually more effective.[25]

3   **Norming:** As the group members begin to find their roles and their place within the group, in the "norming" stage they adopt (implicit) standards of working together. Everyone gets a feel for what is and is not acceptable, how to deal with each other's idiosyncrasies, and how to harness the strengths of each individual to reach common goals. **Group norms** develop, for example, about who has influence and power in a team, how team members communicate with each other, what topics should or should not be discussed, or how conflicts are managed.[26]

4   **Performing:** When the first three phases have successfully passed, the group can enter the "performing" stage. When the relationships between the group members are well defined and functioning processes of working together are in place, all the energy can be devoted to achieving the task. Usually, group members become a bit more flexible regarding their roles, as they do not see the actions of other team members as a potential threat to their own identity. Clearly defined roles and tasks remain a key success factor for productive teamwork in the performing stage, however.[27]

Group norms:
Standards for what is considered "normal" or "correct" behavior in a certain group.

Tuckman's model was later complemented by a fifth stage, **adjourning**.[28] This phase is only relevant for teams that are disbanded, either because they have accomplished their purpose or are no longer deemed necessary. The role of the team leader in this stage is to ensure a positive closure of the teamwork (e.g. through celebrating success, reflecting on what everyone learned from the team process, and suggesting ways of staying in contact with other team members after the team project is finished). Research results suggest that teams with a **stable membership** are more likely to perform well than those with a constant exchange of members. Stability avoids the need to repeatedly put energy into mutual adaptation of new and existing team members because the arrival of new members can trigger new rounds of progression through Tuckman's four phases.[29]

Some researchers argue that Tuckman's model has become dated. It is, however, still considered "the most famous lifecycle model" of team dynamics and is also widely used in managerial practice.[30] Managers should not assume that all groups will always follow the Tuckman stages, but the model can at least help us to better understand some of the social processes that take place within a team. When team membership changes more frequently, especially in geographically dispersed virtual teams (see Chapter 5), Tuckman's model with its successive stages might become more difficult to apply. For these more volatile teams, cyclical and punctuated equilibrium models often more adequately describe team dynamics. **Cyclical models** propose that groups can cycle between different stages (e.g. return to a former stage when a new team member joins the team). **Punctuated equilibrium models** suggest that groups alternate between relatively stable periods and times when there are significant shifts in the interpersonal setup.[31]

A potential threat to the effectiveness of teams is the formation of rival **subgroups**. This can be poison for both the climate within a team and its ability to accomplish its tasks. When polarization starts to emerge, team leaders need to address this early on, for example, by openly discussing any underlying subgroup interests or emphasizing the common purpose of the whole team.

Communication plays a key role in the development processes of teams. Frequent interactions between team members and regular team meetings are cornerstones of team effectiveness. Research findings reveal that in successful teams, everyone talks and listens roughly equally, "short and sweet" contributions are the norm, members connect directly with each other (and not only with the leader) in positive, energetic discussions, and also constantly use outside connections to gain new valuable insights and perspectives that can help the team accomplish its tasks.[32]

The role of the team leader

The **team leader** plays a crucial role in facilitating team performance. In order to manage a team in an effective way, a leader needs to attend to four main factors:

a   Accomplishing the **task**;
b   Taking care of **individual team members' needs and development**;
c   Enhancing the ability of the whole team to **work together productively**;
d   Taking **stakeholders' interests and influences** into account.

Based on psychoanalytic theories and group-therapeutic experience, psychotherapist Ruth Cohn developed a method called **theme-centered interaction (TCI)** and suggested a model which includes the four factors outlined above (see Figure 4.3).[33] She saw the first three factors—"I" (the individual), "WE" (the group), and "IT" (the task or "theme")—as three corner points that are present in each group interaction. The resulting triangle is embedded in a "GLOBE" which represents the context for the teamwork, i.e. all the external constraints as well as influences and demands on the group. Cohn suggested that team leaders should strive to keep the individual, the task, and group cohesion in a dynamic balance, while also taking stakeholder demands into account.

All too often, teams drift too far in one direction:

- team relations suffer when there is an exclusive focus on the task;
- if the attention is just on the needs of individuals, the group can fall apart as it fails to create a "We-feeling";
- a constant focus on cohesion and integration of a group can lead to the phenomenon of **groupthink** (forced conformity and the suppression of diverging opinions in groups based on compliance pressure)[34] with all its potentially detrimental consequences such as flawed group decision making (see Section 6.4).

It is therefore the team leader's responsibility to gauge whether one of the three factors is dominating—that is, too much "I", "WE", or "IT" in a certain situation—and to take appropriate action to bring the triangle back into balance. Examples of such interventions are focusing the group back on the task (intervention toward "IT"), actively involving team members who were not getting enough voice in the discussion (intervention toward "I"), or addressing latent or overt conflicts among team members (intervention toward "WE").

Theme-centered interaction (TCI):
A method for working in groups developed by the psychotherapist Ruth Cohn. Part of TCI is the four factor model in which team leaders should keep the needs of individuals ("I"), the needs of the group as a whole ("WE"), the focus on the task ("IT"), and the consideration of outside influences and requirements ("GLOBE") in a dynamic balance.

Groupthink:
A term introduced by social psychologist Irving Janis to explain the phenomenon of forced conformity and consent in groups in which diverging opinions are suppressed.

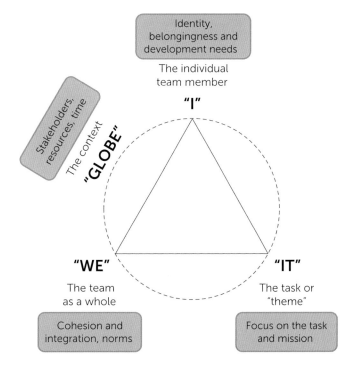

Figure 4.3 The theme-centered interaction triangle

Source: Based on Cohn (1975), pp. 113–114 and Spielmann (2017), p. 15. For more information, visit the Ruth Cohn Institute for TCI – international, https://www.ruth-cohn-institute.org/home.html.

Managing a team means much more than just setting the direction and coordinating tasks. Agenda setting, making sure that the team attends to the output that it has to deliver, aligning tasks and team member strengths, and coordinating the work of team members are important facets of the team leader's job. However, as Ruth Cohn's TCI model clearly visualizes, team leaders also have a responsibility for:

a   **coaching and developing** individual team members (using the tools and techniques we discussed in Chapter 3), making sure that they are able to fulfill their roles, and providing them with feedback on their performance;

b   increasing the **productive capacity of the team** as a whole through optimizing team processes, shaping team norms and culture, and managing conflicts between team members; and

c   making sure that the **environment** is adequately attended to (to recognize any developments that could have a potential impact on team effectiveness), that all the necessary resources are obtained, and that those **external relationships** which are crucial for the success of the team are well managed.

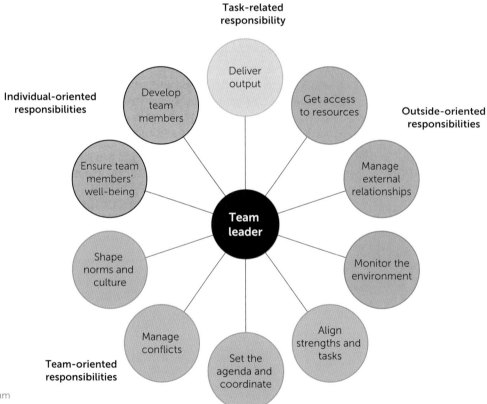

Figure 4.4 Main responsibilities of a team leader

A summary of the **main responsibilities of a team leader** is provided in Figure 4.4. It includes tasks that are oriented toward all four elements of TCI: "IT"—task-oriented responsibility, "I"—individual-oriented responsibilities, "WE"—team-oriented responsibilities, and "GLOBE"—outside-oriented responsibilities.

A particularly important responsibility of a team leader is to **shape team norms and team culture** (see also Chapter 8). Creating a positive atmosphere in which people sense a "WE" feeling or "team spirit" can make a significant contribution to the development of a high-performance team (see also the box *The CEO as a values-based team leader at Continental*).

The CEO as a values-based team leader at Continental

Elmar Degenhart is CEO of Continental AG, a leading German car parts supplier with over 200,000 employees. When he took over as CEO in summer 2009, the company faced multiple challenges, from high debt levels and problems with the integration of acquired companies to major customers who were threatening to change supplier.[35] Degenhart successfully tackled all these challenges, leading to a more-than-tenfold share price increase between June 2009 and June 2018.[36] He did not resolve all these problems on his own, however, and is quick to highlight the achievements of the whole team. When he was asked about his share in the success story, he answered that it was all "a team performance," and that leaders should not claim credit for themselves.[37] "He is our guide," said one of the managers in his team. "He gives us the direction, and then lets us do our job."[38] His colleagues in the management team also praised the new team spirit

at Continental. Degenhart is convinced that good team leadership is essential for organizational performance: "Leadership competence is necessary to reach effectiveness in an organization. Effectiveness, in turn, is the precondition for creating value."[39] He is a values-based team leader, focusing on creating a certain type of culture in which trust, a passion to win, freedom to act, and working "for one another" prevail.[40] A "Values Day" held at the corporate headquarters in Hanover had the tagline "Values Create Value," succinctly summarizing Degenhart's approach.

→ Key takeaway

Team leaders can influence the performance of their team through creating a strong values-based team culture.

Sources: Continental (2015); Lamparter (2013); manager-magazin.com (2016); Spinnarke (2015).

Self-managing teams:
Teams that are operating autonomously without being under the constant supervision of a formally appointed manager.

With the rise of the **Agile** movement (see the Introduction to this chapter), many organizations also use **self-managing teams** (sometimes called self-managed or self-directed teams or autonomous work teams). Unlike other ("normal") teams, they do not have a formal supervisor. Instead, the team members are jointly responsible for organizing the team processes and producing the desired outcomes. A self-managing team more or less autonomously decides how the work is performed, and leadership responsibilities are typically rotated between team members. Hierarchical control is replaced by peer-based control.[41] One of the ideas behind the use of self-managing teams is that people in such teams feel more responsible for their own work and for meeting the team goals, and that this higher degree of ownership will also lead to a higher degree of commitment. Self-managing teams are also often seen as more flexible in reacting to changing circumstances than hierarchically managed teams. As in any other team, however, the performance of a self-managing team also depends on effective coordination.[42] Even when there is shared leadership, all the main responsibilities of a team leader need to be covered by someone. And distributing and coordinating all these responsibilities among all team members can in many cases also take more time and effort than having a clearly responsible team leader in the first place.

Digital tools for supporting effective teamwork

Collaborative software:
Digital tools that are specifically designed to help teams accomplish their common tasks.

A range of different digital tools can be used to support the members of a team in working together effectively. Digital tools that are specifically designed to help teams accomplish their common tasks are known under the term **collaborative software**. Examples of collaborative software solutions that support teams in communicating, managing data, and organizing and coordinating tasks include:

- **Messaging tools:** enable the team to send, archive, and search messages on a single platform. In an open messaging area, all team members have access to the team conversations without having to send e-mails to each other all of the time. It is also possible to have private conversations in which only a limited number of team members can participate.

- **File sharing systems:** allow team members to store and share documents as well as video and audio files in one place. These systems can be seen as a team's knowledge repository and help to organize data that is created and used by a team.
- **Collaborative document creation systems:** enable real-time collaborative editing of documents by several team members.
- **Audio and videoconferencing systems:** enable geographically dispersed team members to interact directly with each other, either individually or in a group call (see also the section on global virtual teams in Chapter 5).
- **Project management systems** and **task management systems:** help team leaders and team members to organize and keep track of what needs to be done by whom and by which deadlines. These systems can be used, for example, for project planning, breaking down complex projects into individual tasks, assigning and prioritizing tasks, creating timelines for project activities, allocating resources, and controlling which stage the work is at, and whether tasks are accomplished on time and within budget.
- **Electronic calendar and scheduling systems:** support teams in coordinating meetings.
- **Meeting management systems:** include tools for improving the efficiency of meetings; for example, for invitation management, agenda setting (including document sharing), real-time collaborative note taking, brainstorming, polls, or minutes management.
- **Time tracking tools:** allow team members to record and track working hours. This is especially useful for teams billing their working hours to customers.

There are stand-alone software solutions for all categories of tools, and also some integrated "all-in-one" collaborative software solutions that include a wide variety of different functions. Many tools are cloud-based (meaning that they can be accessed over the Internet from different devices) and also available as apps for smartphones and tablets. The main reason for using these tools is enhancing the productivity of the team. Using such tools can, however, potentially also decrease productivity. First, there is usually a form of associated financial cost. In addition, the use of cloud-based tools also entails security and data protection issues. What is more, it is also possible that people just see them as an additional hassle that undermines their autonomy or creates unnecessary additional work. Chances are high that just telling team members to use a new software tool instead of the good old e-mail client could lead to demotivation rather than productivity gains. It is therefore important to carefully select the right tools and make sure that team members are really convinced that the tools help them to facilitate their joint endeavor to achieve the team goals.

Dealing with "ineffective" team players

A major issue in managing teams is dealing with team members who are negatively influencing the performance of a team, or, as Glenn Parker called them, **"ineffective" team players**.[43] They either distract or dominate the team, discourage the thorough analysis of different viewpoints, or do not contribute at all. Table 4.2 provides a typology of ineffective team players and different strategies that team leaders can use to keep the team on track.

If direct interventions during team discussions do not have the desired effect, alternative strategies include meeting with the person in private to discuss the problem, clearly emphasizing team norms at the beginning of team meetings, positively reinforcing acceptable behavior in team meetings, or as a very last resort, thinking about removing a person from the team, assigning them other tasks instead.[44]

The last category of "ineffective" team player covered in Table 4.2 is the **free rider**, team members who just rely on others to do the work. The box *Zooming in on how to deal with social loafing* provides more information about how team leaders can address this issue in particular.

Table 4.2 Dealing with "ineffective" team players

Type	Characterization	Main problem	Tactics: How to react as a team leader?
Doubter	Does not voice an opinion, lets others decide	Does not contribute	• Encourage person to voice opinion • Recognize contributions
Distracted	Often talks about things that are not relevant to the main issue that the team needs to discuss, thereby distracting the others	Hampers efficiency of discussion and the decision-making process	• Guide discussion back to the main issue • Postpone sideline discussions to breaks
Diplomat	Always strives for consensus and wants to avoid arguments	Impedes beneficial constructive conflicts	• Encourage constructive conflict • Ask the diplomat for a clear opinion (maybe in a break)
Dominator	Does not listen and constantly tries to impose their views on others	Constrains the team's ability to objectively analyze several alternatives	• Ask all team members for their opinions • Ask the dominator to listen
Defeatist	Constantly criticizes all suggestions from other team members	Creates a negative climate, discourages the exploration of alternatives	• Ask for solution-based rather than problem-based contributions
Free rider	Relies on others to do the work, does not adequately contribute to teamwork	Puts in less effort at the expense of other group members (social loafing)	• Make individual contributions clearly visible • Directly discuss the problem with the person • Assign tasks according to individual strengths • Let the team agree on the consequences of social loafing before teamwork starts

Source: Inspired by concepts in Cardona and Miller (2000), pp. 12–13.

Zooming in on ▶ HOW TO DEAL WITH SOCIAL LOAFING

Social loafing—where a group member puts in less effort at the expense of others—is a phenomenon that many people in teams at work and on student projects complain about. As a team leader, what can you do to make sure that everyone adequately contributes to the teamwork? Here are some suggestions about how to curb free riding in teams:

1 *Take preventive action.* At the beginning of your teamwork, let the whole team jointly set expectations and rules, as well as sanctions for rule breakers. It is more difficult for team members to challenge rules and sanctions later when they took part in setting them up in the first place.

2 *Make individual contributions clearly visible.* Create some form of individual performance measurement system so that everyone is informed about the contributions of each team member (to increase peer pressure). Hold people accountable for their individual work.

3 *Invest time and effort in team building.* Social loafing is less common in more cohesive groups.[45] When team members have stronger relationships with each other, the chances are lower that they will feel comfortable with leaving others to do their work.

4 *Assign tasks according to individual strengths.* As we saw in Chapter 3, people tend to put in more effort and perform better when they can work on challenging tasks that match their strengths and interests. Splitting up a task equally between everyone is more often than not a waste of resources rather than a sign of fairness. Instead, invest time in finding out who is best suited to specific tasks.

5 *Make sure that everyone works on relevant tasks.* Everyone needs to understand that their contributions really matter for achieving the team's goals. This is also related to group size. Make sure that the group is only as big as it needs to be, so that everyone can work on relevant tasks and no one can hide behind other team members.

Reflecting on the team process

One final important task of the team leader is to regularly reflect on the **quality of the team process**. This can also be done with the whole team, either by asking for feedback on positive and negative aspects of the process of working together at the end of team meetings, or through a more formal periodic appraisal of the adequacy of established team routines, including questions such as:

- Are we clearly **focusing on our main purpose and goals** in our interactions?
- Are the team processes **perceived as fair**?
- **Does everyone adequately contribute** to the common effort?
- Are there any **dysfunctional team norms**?
- Is the team vulnerable to **groupthink**? (see also Section 6.4)
- Does the team have **efficient routines** for working together?

Teams are dynamic social systems. As such, they develop over time. In order to keep the team productive, team leaders need to constantly keep an eye on whether the way in which the team is working together is still conducive to achieving the common goals. If teams are well composed and well led, they can be very powerful. US basketball superstar Michael Jordan once said that he would prefer to have five less-talented players who are willing to work together as a team than five star players who do not want to sacrifice themselves for another. Jordan concluded that "[t]alent wins games, but teamwork and intelligence win championships."[46]

Developing a high-performance team at the7stars

In 2005, Jenny Biggam and Mark Javis founded a media planning and buying agency that turned into the UK's largest independent media agency with more than 200 employees and a billing volume of over £300 million.[47] They called their company *the7stars* in reference to one of their favorite pubs, and followed the vision of building a "modern, open, transparent, honest media agency."[48]

One of the factors that distinguished the company from the typical big agency networks and enabled its rapid growth was a unique workplace culture based on flat structures and teamwork. Biggam summarized it as "having fewer rules and focusing instead on creating a great place to work."[49] Bureaucracy and unnecessary paperwork were banned, and everyone at the7stars was allowed to have flexible hours and take as much holiday as they liked, as long as the work got done.[50] Company financials were fully transparent to everyone in the agency, and profit bonuses were shared on an equal basis. There were also no job titles in the agency to discourage internal hierarchical competition and to enable people to be more flexible in taking up new tasks and to shape their own career path.

Biggam is also a strong believer in delegation. "To hire the best people and then trust them to care as much about the business as you do"[51] was a key leadership principle that she followed, though she also acknowledged

that delegating was not always easy. Generally, the agency's management followed a strongly team-oriented approach. For example, when the company moved to a new office space, project teams with members from all across the organization decided on details such as the decoration and hot-desking, a flexible work arrangement in which people use different desks. In the company's weekly Wednesday meetings, people were encouraged to come up with the "idea of the week," which won £10. This was just one of the measures that the management took in order to make people feel that they could make a difference to the business.

The agency's top management put a strong emphasis on building the best possible team. For Biggam, that meant attracting the best people, putting a lot of effort into training people, and making sure that people were motivated in their jobs. Many of the agency's staff were hired directly as graduates and then trained in house, following Biggam's argument that if "you are going to clients and saying we are better than the competition, so surely we should be training our own people."[52] Every new recruit went through group interviews in which four or five people tried to find out whether the candidates were bright, creative, able to get along with other people and, as Biggam said, "on our wavelength."[53] For her, it was important that the candidates not only talked about themselves, but also provided good reasons for why they wanted to become part of the the7stars team.

Once people were on board, the company provided them with gym membership. There was also a "well-being week" with yoga and other health offers. Everyone in the agency participated in a job-swap week. For example, Biggam spent a week in reception, learning, in her words, "just how tough and overlooked that role is."[54] Another important ingredient of the7stars' corporate culture cocktail was humor. The company had a "prank week," for example, which Biggam explained as "a week dedicated to maximizing mucking about."[55] She saw good personal connections and a good sense of humor as major ways of defusing tensions at the workplace. As a consequence of the strong emphasis on good teamwork, the agency repeatedly appeared on the *Sunday Times* list of the UK's "100 best small companies to work for," which helped the7stars a lot in attracting talented people.

The company's business model based on full transparency and high-class service delivered by a highly committed team was in such high demand that the founders decided to launch a second media agency with a strong focus on digital media. Again, they borrowed a pub's name and called the new agency *Bountiful Cow*. The main reason for setting up a separate company was to protect the unique team-oriented culture, which they did not want to jeopardize by oversizing the7stars.

Sources: Bassett (2016); coachmag.co.uk (2016); Cockburn (2015); Hine (2014); Melchers (2014); the7stars.co.uk (2017).

💬 Discussion questions

● How did Biggam try to develop a high-performance team?

● In what ways can workplace culture influence the performance of a team?

● What did Biggam do to create a positive workplace culture in the agency?

● What is the role of rules versus flexible working arrangements in supporting or hindering effective teamwork?

4.3 Effective communication

iStock.com/monkeybusinessimages

In brief

● Effective communication includes both formulating the message in a way that the receiver can understand and choosing the right channel to get the message across.

● The choice of communication channel depends on several factors, for example whether direct feedback, personal interaction, or permanent record are required.

● Managers often need to present their ideas to others, and should therefore know how to make effective presentations.

● For some issues, it is preferable to engage in a dialogue that can lead to the joint development and implementation of new ideas. Meetings are often used for this purpose.

● For meetings to be effective, the preparation and follow-up stages are as important as managing the core meeting itself.

To effectively perform through others, managers must first be able to communicate in an effective way. Exchanging information within a team, across teams, and with stakeholders outside of the organization is a key managerial task. **Communication**—the process of sharing ideas with others—is the main tool for managers to coordinate activities in teams and organizations. Effective communication is also an essential precondition for organizational learning and development, and therefore plays an important role in both ensuring team performance and building performance potential for the future.

Choosing the right communication tool

Leaders consider communication as one of the main factors that can lead to the success or failure of a project.[56] Communication always involves two parties, the sender and the receiver. Both sides are equally important because a sender's message that is not correctly interpreted by the receiver is worthless. One way to improve communication is to obtain **feedback** from the receiver that allows the sender to assess whether the message was correctly understood.

Managers can choose from a range of different **communication tools** that can generally be clustered in three different categories: simultaneous and personal, simultaneous over distance, and asynchronous (see Table 4.3).

Table 4.3 A categorization of communication tools

Type of communication	Examples
Simultaneous and personal	Face-to-face meetings, oral presentations, informal talks
Simultaneous over distance	Telephony or video telephony — both one to one or in the form of a conference with several participants
Asynchronous	Usually in written form, e.g. reports, e-mails, letters, minutes, bulletin board, newsletters, social media; but also voice and video messages

Source: Inspired by concepts in Katzenbach and Smith (1993), p. 118.

The **choice of the right communication tool** depends on what a manager wants to achieve as well as the required channel richness (see Figure 4.5). For example, issues that require fast feedback and are potentially emotionally charged are likely best discussed in person. When it is necessary to record a message for future reference, written communication will be preferred. It is also possible to combine different communication tools. For example, the main points of a telephone conversation can be summarized in a follow-up e-mail, or minutes can be distributed after a meeting. The choice of communication channel not only depends on the type, number, and geographical location of the recipients, but also on the nature of the message—whether it is complex, urgent, important, confidential, or personal (following the philosopher and media theorist Marshall McLuhan's dictum: "The medium is the message."[57]) It can also depend on the cultural background of the people who are involved in the communication process. Research results have shown that in cross-cultural and multi-lingual settings, for example, a combination of synchronous communication channels (such as face-to-face meetings or telephone calls) and asynchronous media (such as e-mail or messenger services) is often more effective than the use of only one medium.[58] On the one hand, using e-mail gives non-native speakers more time to formulate their message or process contents. On the other hand, in direct personal communication, it is possible to ask for clarification if something has not been well understood. Repeating a message through combining different media can also foster mutual understanding.[59] Generally, for effective communication, choosing the right form of communication is as important as the contents.

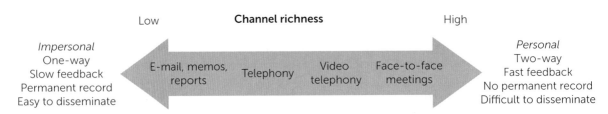

Figure 4.5 Communication tools according to their channel richness

Source: Based on Daft, *Management*, 12E, p. 594, ISBN: 9781285861982.

Before beginning any communication, managers should ask themselves the following questions:

- What is the desired effect of the communication?
- What kind of action do I want the other person(s) to take?

Managerial communication is purpose-directed communication.[60] Let us take **written messages** as an example. It is not enough for managers to know *what* they would like to say. It is equally important to think about *how* to say something. The message should be structured and formulated in a way that is most likely to trigger a certain desired action by the recipient.[61] It is also good practice to revise written messages for clarity of expression, the right tone, brevity and completeness of contents before they are sent.

Which communication channels and strategies would you use in the following managerial situations:

a   You want to congratulate one of your team members on an exceptional performance.
b   You need to inform the employees in your organization that due to a lack of customer orders, there will be a large-scale layoff in which 20 percent of the staff will lose their jobs.
c   You want to make sure that everyone in your organization understands the core organizational values.

From presentations to dialogue

Business presentations can be a powerful tool for managers to communicate their ideas—and also to present themselves because the audience very often remembers the presentation style and quality more than the contents. See the box *Zooming in on delivering a compelling business presentation* for more details on how to deliver an effective presentation.

Zooming in on ▶ DELIVERING A COMPELLING BUSINESS PRESENTATION

An effective presentation is, in essence, a clear and compelling story that a manager tells to a group of people. Here is some advice on how to create a presentation that catches the attention of your audience:

1   *Know your audience*: Who are they? What are their expectations?
2   *Consider the context*: Is it formal or informal? What is the layout and size of the room? What technical equipment is available?
3   *Be clear about your goal*: What is the message that you want to get across? What should the audience think or do after your presentation? What are the main points that you want to make? Can you summarize the story that you want to tell in 60 to 90 seconds?
4   *Have a clear structure for your presentation*: Include an *introduction* outlining the purpose of the presentation, its importance, and a preview of the main points; the *body* of the presentation with the main points and supporting arguments; and a *conclusion*—a summary of the key messages and a call for action to the audience.
5   *Connect with your audience*: Use eye contact or moments of silence to let your message "sink in."
6   *Think about the appropriateness of the terminology that you intend to use for the audience*: How do you avoid unnecessary jargon? Will your ideas be clearly understandable for the audience?
7   *Practice before you present*: Learn the first and last few sentences of your presentation by heart (because the first and last impressions are usually the strongest ones).
8   *Use notes if you need them, but do not read full sentences (except quotes)*: A speech should be spoken, not read.
9   *Use appropriate visual aids*: Less is usually more in terms of the amount of content.
10 *Think about how you would deal with difficult situations* (e.g. technical problems) before you start presenting.

To have an effect on the behavior of others, one-way presentations are often not enough. As Edgar Schein points out, organizational transformation requires a **dialogue**.[62] By definition, a dialogue goes beyond just sending a message. But it also goes beyond a discussion. Whereas discussion (from Latin *discutere* = dissipate, plead case, strike down) is associated with advocacy and a competition of ideas and interests, dialogue (from Latin *dialogus* = [philosophical] conversation) is more about understanding the other side and trying to build a common ground.[63] The ability to build such common ground is a key factor for effective communication (see the box *The neuroscience of managerial communication*). Engaging in a dialogue means trying to thoroughly understand the perspective of another person. This requires active listening and paying full and undivided attention to what is said, both verbally and with non-verbal signals. A real dialogue is also about being open to questioning one's own assumptions. It is therefore a precondition for higher-level learning. Constructive dialogue can be a powerful tool for managers because it can lead to the development of other people, and of the organization. Theories of dialogical leadership even suggest that through dialogue and reflection, leaders can become more aware of their own self and their role as a leader, which in turn enables them to lead in a more authentic way.[64]

FROM A DIFFERENT ANGLE

The neuroscience of managerial communication

Findings from the field of neuroscience can help us understand why some communication strategies work better than others. To begin with, human beings do not transmit thoughts directly from brain to brain, but use symbolic codes to communicate with each other. Examples of symbolic codes are language, pictures, music, gestures, or facial expressions. In order to be able to fully understand what the sender wants to convey, the receiver needs to understand the code and be able to correctly interpret the message. This means that if the sender and receiver do not share a code, they will not be able to understand each other.[65] Thus, managers need to make sure that their communication partners also "speak the same language" (i.e. understand jargon or use the same cultural codes).

Studies in neuroscience have also shown that during a face-to-face dialogue, the neural activities of the communication partners are much more synchronized than in a face-to-face monologue or in situations where people cannot see each other.[66] This is one of the reasons why face-to-face communication is usually more appropriate when managers need to discuss more complex or difficult issues.

Finally, scientific findings also suggest that "under conditions where the deployment of attentional resources is limited ... emotional information is prioritized and receives privileged access to attention and awareness."[67] This means that a manager who wants to make sure that a message really "gets across" should try to get beyond facts and also integrate emotional appeals in their communication approach.

Making meetings work

A communication setting that is particularly widespread in teams and organizations is the **meeting**, despite the fact that meetings can also be a real nuisance. When people come together in a more or less formal setting to exchange information or decide on different issues, these gatherings are often inefficient, unfocused, and time-consuming. Frequently, people get stuck in endless discussions without any viable outcomes, wasting time and distracting them from their "real" work. Despite these commonly voiced—and in many cases certainly valid—reservations against meetings, they can also make a crucial contribution to a team's and an organization's performance, provided that they are well managed. Productive meetings can lead to better communication and better decisions.

Productive meetings do not start when people enter the meeting room, but well in advance, during the preparation phase. Likewise, they do not end when people leave the room, but with a thorough follow-up and implementation of what was agreed in the meeting. Figure 4.6 presents the main steps necessary for holding an effective meeting over three phases: preparing, conducting, and following up.

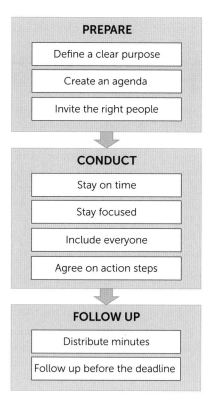

PREPARE
Define a clear purpose
Create an agenda
Invite the right people

CONDUCT
Stay on time
Stay focused
Include everyone
Agree on action steps

FOLLOW UP
Distribute minutes
Follow up before the deadline

Figure 4.6 The effective meeting process

The **preparation** stage includes the following tasks:

- **Define a clear purpose.** Before setting up a meeting, managers should always ask themselves why the meeting is needed and, even more importantly, if it is really necessary at all. Whenever a problem can be solved without a meeting, it is better not to waste everyone's precious time. Meetings with more than two participants can be very useful when input from different people is needed; for example, to make a well-informed decision on a complex issue. They are not useful for discussing tasks or issues that could be more efficiently solved in a one-to-one setting between two persons.
- **Create an agenda.** People who are invited to a meeting should know well in advance what is on the agenda to be able to prepare adequately. Estimating the time that will be spent on each agenda item can help to keep the meeting within the set time limits. It is also good practice to define objectives for the individual agenda items (e.g. information, generating and evaluating ideas, gaining commitment, or making a decision).
- **Invite the right people.** Who is invited will mainly depend on the objectives of the meeting. To identify the right participants, managers can ask: Who could make valuable contributions to the key issues that are going to be discussed? Who has a stake in the outcomes of the meeting? Who has the power to approve decisions and ensure that the necessary action is taken? Who could be crucial for implementing the decisions?

With a clear purpose, a focused agenda, and the right people invited, the chances for holding a productive meeting are already high. The effectiveness of the meeting, however, also strongly depends on how it is **conducted**, considering the following four points:

- **Stay on time.** Managers should respect the time of others. Thus, starting a meeting on time is as important as ending on time. At the beginning, the purpose and objectives of the meeting must be clarified. If managers realize that they are falling behind schedule, they can either suggest prioritizing the remaining issues together with the participants or postpone some agenda items to the next meeting.[68] Generally, it also makes sense to discuss the most important agenda items early in the meeting.

- **Stay focused.** Off-topic discussions are the main enemy of efficient meetings. Keeping digressions in check is therefore a key task of the person running the meeting. This can, for example, be achieved by putting ideas that are off-topic in a "parking lot," i.e. on a flip-chart, whiteboard, or list of ideas that will not be further discussed in the current meeting, but could be addressed in another context.[69] Instead of discussing for discussion's sake, productive meetings are action focused.
- **Include everyone.** Considering and integrating different points of view can improve the quality of decisions. This is one of the reasons why meetings are needed in the first place. It does not make sense to invite people to a meeting if they do not have anything to contribute to the main points on the agenda. Therefore, managers should avoid any one individual dominating a meeting, and instead try to give a voice to everyone. The feeling of having been heard can also raise the level of perceived fairness, and thus improve the commitment to the decisions taken in a meeting.[70]
- **Agree on action steps.** Meetings should not conclude without an agreement on an action plan that includes the answers to the following questions: (1) Which steps need to be taken next? (2) Who is responsible for which action step? (3) By when are the tasks to be completed?

For meetings to become really effective, managers need to ensure that the decisions made during the meeting are also **implemented**. Two steps are crucial in this respect:

- **Distribute minutes.** Every participant from the meeting and everyone else who is affected by the decisions made in the meeting should be properly informed (note that there are cultural differences to consider here—see the *Around the globe* box *To write it down, or not to write it down, that is the question...*). A detailed account of who said what is usually not necessary. Instead, effective minutes succinctly summarize key points, the decisions that were made, and the action steps with responsibilities and deadlines.[71]

AROUND THE GLOBE

To write it down, or not to write it down, that is the question...

It is commonly seen as good practice for managers from Northern Europe or North America to take minutes at meetings or negotiations and share them with all the participants. In other cultural contexts, this practice could potentially backfire. In parts of Africa or Asia, for example, summarizing the main points of a discussion in writing could be regarded as a signal of distrust. After all, if something has been verbally agreed, why would you need a written confirmation if the negotiation partners fully trust each other? This is a particularly sensitive issue when there are also legally binding written agreements involved. INSEAD Professor Erin Meyer, for example, cited one Nigerian manager who said that "the moment ... you pull out a contract and hand me a pen, I start to worry. Do you think I won't follow through? Are you trying to trap me?"[72]

In countries with a well-functioning judicial system like the US, people tend to rely on detailed written contracts. They know that there is always a judge to turn to if the contract partner does not conform with the agreement. In world regions with weaker legal systems, however, it could be significantly more difficult to enforce contracts. In such regions, written contracts often play a very different role. In Nigeria or Indonesia, for example, contracts might be considered as a "first commitment" to a business relationship rather than a document that is fully binding in all details. As circumstances change, negotiation partners from these countries might also want to change what has been agreed on paper.

Source: Based on information in Meyer (2015).

- **Follow up before the deadline.** Managers need to make sure that those who are responsible for certain action steps actually implement them. There is nothing worse than items that continuously reemerge on the agenda, just because someone is not adequately executing them. In order to avoid this, managers need to check the progress that the responsible persons make on agreed action steps well in advance of the deadline.

Virtual meeting:
A meeting in which people do not meet in person, but remain in different physical locations and connect with each other with the help of technological means (e.g. videoconferencing software).

Managers who respect their team members' time will avoid scheduling meetings outside normal office hours. This is not always possible, however, in **virtual meetings** that include participants from different time zones by means of teleconference or videoconference. In this case, teams can agree to rotate starting times so that the meetings are not always scheduled at a time that is inconvenient for participants from one particular part of the world. For virtual meetings to be productive, it is also important to set some ground rules; for example, refraining from multitasking (doing other things on the computer while the meeting takes place) or "checking out" of the meeting from time to time.[73]

In any case, whether face to face or virtual, meetings must be well prepared and well managed, and be complemented by appropriate follow-up measures, or they risk fulfilling the prophecy of American economist and author John Kenneth Galbraith who wrote that "[m]eetings are a great trap ... they are indispensable when you don't want to do anything."[74] Effective managers avoid this trap. They understand that meetings are just one of a range of different communication tools. They are able to choose the right communication tool based on what they are trying to achieve as well as on the required channel richness. They know how to present their ideas in a convincing way, and they recognize the power that lies in entering into real dialogue with other people. In short, effective managers are effective communicators.

4.4 Managing conflicts and negotiations

Blend/JGI/Jamie Grill

In brief

- Both conflicts and negotiations are situations in which different parties need to reconcile their seemingly incompatible interests. While affective interpersonal conflict usually has a negative influence on team performance, constructive task-related conflict can also be beneficial—at least up to a certain level.

- The main strategies for managing conflict are dominating, avoiding, obliging, compromising, and integrating. The effectiveness of these approaches strongly depends on the particular situation.

- There are different strategies for dealing with distributive negotiations (in which several parties claim their share of a "fixed pie") and integrative negotiations (in which the involved parties try to create value together before they negotiate on how to split this value between them).

- In any case, obtaining as much information as possible to better understand the interests, preferences, and options of all parties involved is key to both successful negotiation and conflict resolution.

When different people want to achieve different personal and organizational goals, it is natural that interests collide. This is especially valid also in teams, where the "storming" phase is a typical stage in the team development process (see Section 4.2). Managers

Conflict:
A serious disagreement based on diverging interests, different points of view, or other incompatibilities.

Negotiation:
A process in which two or more parties try to reach a mutually acceptable solution for an issue in which they have diverging interests or goals.

Interpersonal conflict:
A conflict that arises from personal differences (e.g. in values, attitudes, or personality) between two or more individuals.

Conflict management:
The practice of finding solutions that maximize positive outcomes and minimize negative outcomes in conflict situations.

Affective conflict:
A conflict that arises from incompatibilities in interpersonal relationships.

Substantive conflict:
A conflict that arises from task- or content-related disagreements.

need to be able to deal productively with these clashes of interests, whether they appear in the form of conflicts or in negotiation situations. **Conflicts** and **negotiations** are very similar in their nature. In both cases, there are disagreements and incompatible goals—at least at the beginning. When conflicts and negotiations are well managed, however, it is possible to reach integrative solutions that create value for all sides. As social interactions, both conflicts and negotiations are also contingent on cultural influences (see Section 5.2).

Strategies for managing conflict situations

Conflicts are an inevitable part of the organizational reality. As people with different interests and personalities come together, conflicts can arise between individuals (**interpersonal conflict**), within a group (**intragroup conflict**), or between groups (**intergroup conflict**). Unmanaged conflicts can lead to a number of detrimental consequences, including a loss of motivation, emotional distress, wasted time and energy, and a loss of productivity. Conflicts in themselves are, however, not necessarily all "bad." They can potentially also lead to positive outcomes such as finding creative solutions, increasing positive competition, helping to clarify and overcome persistent organizational problems, or enhancing the problem-solving abilities of the parties involved.[75] Conflicts can even improve the effectiveness of a team, as long as they remain constructive and are properly managed.[76]

Rahim suggests three pillars of an **effective conflict management** strategy:[77]

1 **Minimize affective conflict.** Affective conflicts arise from incompatibilities in interpersonal relationships. They are usually emotionally laden and can have a strong negative impact on both the well-being and performance of individuals and groups. Managers should therefore strive to recognize potential affective conflicts early and try to resolve them as soon as possible.

2 **Ensure a moderate level of substantive conflict.** Substantive conflicts arise when there are task- or content-related disagreements. As this type of conflict can help people to recognize and integrate different perspectives, it can have positive effects on organizational performance. Too high levels of substantive conflict, however, can also trigger affective conflict, and are thus potentially dangerous for the functioning of the organization.

3 **Apply the appropriate conflict management strategy.** There are a range of strategies for dealing with conflicts. None of them is inherently better than the others. Effective managers have a repertoire of conflict management styles, and are able choose the most appropriate one in a particular situation.

Building on previous thinking, Rahim developed a general model of conflict handling styles based on the level to which the parties that are involved in a conflict care for themselves and for the other party (see Table 4.4). **Dominating** involves having a win–lose orientation, trying to push one's interest through to the detriment of others; **avoiding** basically means withdrawing from the conflict; and **obliging** means playing down the differences and accommodating others through trying to satisfy their concerns. **Compromising** is about finding a solution that is acceptable for all sides, with everyone giving up on something. Finally, **integrating** involves an open search for the best alternative in order to reach a solution that creates benefits for all sides.[78] The effectiveness of different conflict handling styles varies with the situation (see Table 4.4).

Imagine that you have two team members who are constantly in conflict with each other even over very minor issues. You suppose that there is an underlying interpersonal problem between the two. Their constant conflicts are detrimental to the effectiveness of the team. As a team leader, what would you do to address this problem?

Table 4.4 Conflict handling styles

Conflict handling style	Concern for self	Concern for others	Effective in the following situations
Dominating	High	Low	Unpopular action needs to be implemented; very fast decision is necessary
Avoiding	Low	Low	Potential negative outcomes for both sides without many benefits when the conflict is resolved; cooling-off period is needed
Obliging	Low	High	Own position is weak or maybe wrong
Compromising	Medium	Medium	Power balance between the parties; difficult to find an integrative solution
Integrating	High	High	Possibility of finding a solution with benefits for all sides

Source: Inspired by concepts in Rahim (2002) and Rahim and Magner (1995).

Interpersonal conflict—especially when it becomes affective—is particularly hard to manage. Trying to find a compromise or even integrating is possible if there is an underlying substantive issue that could potentially be solved. If this is not the case, confrontation mediated by a third party is another possible strategy. Ideally, the conflicting parties would at least listen to one another and try to understand both the interests and the feelings of the other party. This could form the basis for jointly creating alternatives for a potential "win–win" solution.[79] If this also turns out to be impossible and the conflict seems to be difficult to resolve, at least for the moment, there are several **options for keeping an interpersonal conflict under control**:[80]

- Preventing or reducing interaction between the conflicting parties (e.g. separating them physically or reallocating tasks so as to minimize overlaps).
- Clearly specifying the rules of interaction (e.g. which discussion topics are allowed and which not; imposing specific reporting formats).
- Changing the conditions that foster the conflict (e.g. eliminating a position for which two people were competing).
- Offering personal counseling opportunities (e.g. trying to help the individuals who are involved in a conflict to look at the situation in another way and develop new strategies for problem solving or coping with emotional stress).

Conflict management strategies are not an end in themselves. Whatever works best to ensure that people can refocus their energy on organizational goals is a good strategy. In all their efforts to mitigate conflict, however, managers should not forget that "[c]onflict is simply the active expression of difference, and an essential part of human development," as American sociologist Philip E. Slater aptly expressed, adding that "[w]ithout conflict change would be impossible"[81] (see also the box *Shaking up corporate culture at Microsoft*).

Effective negotiations

As already pointed out, negotiations are similar to conflicts, in that they are also social interactions in which different interests collide. In negotiations, however, all sides see a potential benefit in reaching an agreement—that's why they negotiate in the first place.

The optimal approach that managers can take toward negotiations depends on the **type of negotiation**:[86]

Distributive negotiation: A competitive negotiation in which all parties try to gain the larger share of a fixed amount of resources.

- **Distributive negotiations** are "zero-sum games" in which the involved parties negotiate about how to split a "fixed pie" between them. Only one party can "win" to the detriment of the other in such a negotiation situation. Claiming as much value as possible for yourself is the main objective in this type of negotiation. For example, when a salesperson and

Shaking up corporate culture at Microsoft

In 2014, Satya Nadella, born in Hyderabad (India), started his tenure as the third CEO in the history of technology giant Microsoft, following founder Bill Gates and his successor Steve Balmer. In an effort to transform Microsoft from a company that was mainly focused on selling software licenses for personal computers to offering a wide range of cloud-based services, Nadella wanted to create a new organizational culture which "allows people to do their best work,"[82] as he said in an interview with *USA Today*. Every year, Microsoft's top executives would meet in an exclusive mountain retreat to discuss strategic issues. In a decision that was allegedly not very popular among the exclusive circle of the corporation's most senior executives, Nadella decided to extend invitations to young founders of start-ups that Microsoft had acquired, although they were not officially qualified to attend the retreat. "They asked questions,"[83] wrote Nadella in his book *Hit Refresh*—and most probably, there were also tough questions. But Microsoft's new CEO was convinced that "[t]hey pushed us for the better."[84] He also urged the members of the senior management team to get into vans and visit clients during the retreat, and then assigned discussion tables with remixed groups after their return. Nadella did not shun conflict with his senior management team when he decided to design the retreat experience in such an unusual way. We can assume, however, that the senior managers were confronted with completely new perspectives on Microsoft's strategy and their own work, and that the clash of different perspectives may also have sparked some substantive conflicts. As a result, the cross-functional, cross-business, and cross-hierarchical teams engaged in long discussions, and Nadella concluded: "The [cultural] change was coming from within."[85]

→ Key takeaway

Deliberately fostering some degree of substantive conflict through confronting people with new perspectives can help in bringing about change in organizations.

Sources: Della Cava (2017); Nadella et al. (2017); Weinberger (2017).

Integrative negotiation:
A joint problem-solving approach in which the negotiation partners try to find a "win–win" solution that creates value for all parties.

a buyer negotiate about nothing other than the purchasing price of the product, every cent that one of the two parties wins will be lost to the other party.

- **Integrative negotiations**, also known as "principled" negotiations or "interest-based bargaining," are about finding an agreement in which both sides can preserve their interests. In integrative negotiations, the negotiation partners first try to jointly create additional value before claiming a part of the value for themselves. For example, a salesperson and a buyer could first discuss what their interests are before entering into price negotiations. They might find out that the buyer is highly concerned about high after-sales service quality while the salesperson would like the buyer to try out a new product line. The salesperson could then try to convince colleagues in the after-sales service department to guarantee a high service level, for which the buyer would then be willing to pay a slightly higher price. The buyer, in turn, would also agree to try out a new product line, but at a very special introductory price. Ideally, this would lead to a win–win situation for both sides.

Distributive negotiations

Tactics that managers can use to **claim value in distributive negotiations** include:[87]

- Having a clear **understanding of one's own alternatives and objectives** (including a distinction between primary and secondary objectives, and the point at which it would be better abandon the negotiation).
- Trying to **obtain as much information as possible** about the other side's interests, preferences, options, decision-making processes, and constraints while disclosing as little information as possible about oneself. Asking questions and listening are better strategies

than talking in this respect. Crucial information about the negotiation partner can either come from third parties who know something about the counterpart or by asking direct questions and interpreting both answers and non-answers.

- Setting a **psychological anchor point** with a first offer that is high but still realistic (if there is enough information available to make an estimate of the position of the negotiation partner). In cases where there is high information asymmetry between the negotiation partners, however, it can be better not to make the first offer.[88]

- Thinking about **proposals that could be made to the negotiation partner** (including arguments that support these proposals), counterarguments to possible proposals of the negotiation partner, and answers to tough questions that the counterpart could potentially ask.

- Investing in the development of **alternative courses of action.**

Referring to the last point, the key to successful negotiations actually often lies outside of the negotiation situation itself. In every negotiation, it is crucial to understand one's own and the other party's **BATNA**, the "best alternative to a negotiated agreement."[89] It is the alternative action that a negotiator would choose in the case that no agreement can be reached. The BATNA defines the point where a negotiator can walk away from the negotiation table without losing anything. Negotiating parties with a strong BATNA have a clear advantage over their counterparts with a weak BATNA. Developing promising alternative courses of action without the negotiation partner can strengthen one's BATNA, and therefore also the relative position in the negotiation.

Integrative negotiations

A strategy for conducting **integrative negotiations** was proposed by Roger Fisher, William J. Ury, and Bruce Patton in their widely cited book *Getting to Yes*. Their approach can be summarized with the following three principles:[90]

- **Focus on interests rather than on positions.** The key to successful integrative negotiations is to not just discuss *what* the parties want (the positions) but find out *why* they want something (the basic interests behind the positions).[91] While positions often collide, there is a higher chance that interests are compatible. Trying to map the underlying interests of all involved parties is therefore a first crucial step for a successful integrative negotiation.

- **Create options from which both sides can profit.** If more options are on the table, it is no longer an "either-your-way-or-my-way" situation. The joint work on developing options that could benefit all sides can also contribute to building trust between the negotiation partners. For example, they can think about how one party could help to mitigate the constraints of another (e.g. party A has financial resource constraints that make a deal seem impossible; party B suggests providing credit that enables party A to deliver what party B needs). The main task is finding out what each party can do for the other without high costs for themselves.

- **Use objective criteria for selecting between the options and make an agreement.** When the negotiation parties agree on a set of objective criteria for making a selection between the options, the process—and therefore also the outcome—will more likely be perceived as fair, thereby increasing the chances of finding a solution to which all sides can agree.

Integrative negotiations are not easy. Managers often face the **"negotiator's dilemma"** described by David Lax and James Sebenius. They can disclose information to create more value together with the other parties, but the disclosure can also potentially lead to a worse position in the game for claiming value.[92] It is therefore not sufficient for one party to follow the *Getting to Yes* approach. It only works well when the others cooperate, too. The situation is very similar to the famous **prisoner's dilemma** in game theory. The prisoner's dilemma is a situation where two individuals who are acting rationally (with the aim of maximizing their self-interest) would prefer not to cooperate despite the fact that collaboration from both sides

---

BATNA:
An acronym for "best alternative to a negotiated agreement"—the most favorable alternative option for a particular negotiation party in case agreement cannot be reached in a negotiation.

Negotiator's dilemma:
The problem that disclosing information to a negotiation partner could help to maximize gains for all sides, but at the same time also put the party who discloses the information in a worse position for claiming value.

could lead to a better overall outcome. The classic example is of two prisoners who cannot communicate with each other and who could avoid prison by betraying the other, who would then get a long sentence. If they cooperated, they would both get only a short sentence in prison. The prisoner's dilemma can be overcome if the parties have full trust in each other, and especially if they know that there is a high chance that they will face a similar situation with each other again in the future. Similarly, the negotiator's dilemma can be overcome if all parties understand that they will probably see each other again and that their negotiation strategy will have an effect on their reputation and therefore also on their chances of getting a favorable outcome in future negotiation situations. It is all about **building trust**—and to build trust, someone has to start sharing information to encourage reciprocity. Having trust also means expecting honest behavior from the negotiation partner from the outset. Research results suggest that negotiators who have a low opinion about the ethical behavior of their negotiation partner tend to be more willing to use deceptive negotiation tactics themselves, thus starting a vicious cycle that obstructs constructive integrative negotiations.[93]

The negotiation situation changes when **multiple parties** are involved. In this case, **forming coalitions** is an important strategy to achieve the negotiation goals. A common piece of advice for all types of negotiation, whether distributive or integrative, two-party or multiple party, is to **be well prepared** (see also the box *Zooming in on being well prepared for your next negotiation*). Preparation is not a distinct phase, however, that takes place only before the "real" negotiation starts. In fact, gathering and analyzing information as well as planning ahead should be ongoing activities that are conducted throughout the negotiation process until an agreement can be reached.[94]

Zooming in on ▶ BEING WELL PREPARED FOR YOUR NEXT NEGOTIATION

The better prepared you are for a negotiation, the higher the chances that you will succeed in achieving a favorable outcome for both yourself and the other parties involved. Here are some questions that you should always consider before entering into a negotiation:

1 What are your negotiation goals? What would you see as the ideal outcome for yourself or your organization? What is the minimum outcome that would still be acceptable for you?

2 What are your alternatives to a negotiated agreement—and which alternative is the best one (BATNA)?

3 What are the likely interests and preferences of the other parties involved? What are their options and what would you consider as their best alternatives?

4 Where do your own interests overlap with the interests of the other parties? Where do they potentially collide?

5 Which options could be mutually beneficial (i.e. preserve the interests of all parties)?

6 What is the preferred negotiation style of the other parties? Which moves and suggestions will they probably make? How would you respond to these moves and suggestions?

7 Which additional background information could help you in being better positioned for the negotiation? Where could you obtain the necessary information?

8 Which questions would you like to ask the other parties during the negotiation (to gather more information about their interests and to steer the discussion in the right direction)?

With all the tactical advice provided here, it is easy to forget that "winning the deal" is very often not the ultimate purpose. Deals are not ends in themselves, but means to accomplish something—and this usually requires cooperation. As Danny Ertel and Mark Gordon, both partners in a consultancy firm that specializes in helping companies to negotiate, point out, "the way you deal with each other during the negotiation will impact how you work together during implementation."[95] A fair negotiation process can lead to a fair deal, and a fair deal, in turn, is the key to successful implementation.

Hachette's dispute with Amazon

In April 2014, one year after Michael Pietsch had taken over the CEO role at Hachette Book Group (the US subsidiary of the French book publishing group Hachette Livre), he faced a considerable challenge. Hachette's contract with Amazon had just expired, and the online retail giant demanded pricing control rights over e-books as a key condition for a new contract. This would give Amazon the opportunity to considerably lower most e-book prices to a standard price of US$9.99. Amazon felt that publishers were getting too high a share of the e-book price, arguing that e-books did not carry the high production, warehousing, and shipping costs of their printed counterparts.

Hachette refused to comply with Amazon's demands, however, fearing that lower margins from e-books could potentially threaten the production of serious literature, and the print business model. As a consequence of Hachette's negative reaction, Amazon provisionally prolonged the contract under the old terms and engaged in what observers called "aggressive"[96] or even "bullying"[97] negotiation tactics. All of a sudden, delivery times to customers began running into several weeks (rather than the usual one week or just a few days). Some titles allegedly did not appear in search results as they would usually do, and it was no longer possible to pre-order upcoming Hachette titles. These measures seemed to have a very negative impact on Hachette's sales (Hachette Book Group reported an 18.5 percent decrease in US sales in the third quarter of 2014 compared to the year before), as Amazon accounted for more than 40 percent of the overall new book sales market in the US at the time.

Hachette was just one of 70,000 suppliers for Amazon. But Hachette also had a sort of "monopoly" on the books that it published (while, of course, consumers could also choose similar books from other publishers as substitutes).

Hachette's authors, amongst whom there were some of the most widely known names in the literature business, also felt the negative effects of the stalemate between their publisher and Amazon. Almost a thousand of them formed a coalition called Authors United and started to publicly denounce Amazon's tactics of impeding Hachette's book sales. They even urged the US Department of Justice to investigate whether Amazon had misused its monopoly status. There were also media reports about some people who were "walking away from Amazon as a retailer because of its dispute with Hachette."[98]

On the other hand, some authors, for example from the self-publishing scene, sided with Amazon, and the online retailer actively tried to get authors on its side with a letter that suggested that until the parties solved their conflict, 100 percent of e-book profits should go to the authors (which would mean that both parties would lose a lot of money). The proposal was rejected by Hachette. The negotiations continued, as did public pressure, especially on Amazon, who was "cast as a bully in publications across the ideological spectrum,"[99] as the New York Times reported. But there was also public criticism of book publishers' high-price policy for e-books, as e-book margins were considerably higher than margins on traditional books.

In November 2014, the media reported a breakthrough in the negotiations. Amazon and Hachette reached a multi-year deal in which the publisher retained control over setting the prices for its e-book, but would get financial incentives from Amazon to lower prices. Michael Pietsch was relieved, stating that the new agreement (which also included the renewal of normal trading relations and promotional agreements) would give Hachette "enormous marketing capability with one of our most important bookselling partners."[100]

The deal was warmly welcomed by the authors, as it came just in time for the Christmas season, in which more books are sold than at any other time of the year. Observers were wary about whether the dispute between the publishers and the dominating book retailer would be resolved once and for all. "If anyone thinks this is over, they are deluding themselves,"[101] said Douglas Preston, who initiated the formation of Authors United, in the New York Times, while the Economist's website wrote about a "frozen conflict that could easily heat up again."[102]

Sources: Bertrand (2014); economist.com (2014); Ellis-Petersen (2014); Kellogg (2014); Streitfeld (2014); Worstall (2014).

💬 Discussion questions

- Why did the conflict between Hachette and Amazon start?
- Which strategies and tactics did both Hachette and Amazon use to manage the conflict and their negotiations to resolve the conflict?
- What is the difference between approaching this conflict situation with a distributive or an integrative negotiation mind-set?
- How did the way in which the two conflict parties communicated the situation with other stakeholders and the general public influence the outcome of the negotiations?

Conclusion

At the beginning of this chapter, we learned that in 2015, Barclays decided to change its CEO in an effort to become more efficient and more agile. Transforming the very traditional financial institution with over 100,000 employees into a more agile, team-centered organization was strongly in the focus of the bank's new leadership. Agile training and coaching programs were introduced, and after only two years, more than 15,000 people were applying the Agile principles in over 1,000 teams across the whole organization. They were working in small cross-functional teams, in short iterations of work, and with fast feedback from customers and end users.[103] Teams were empowered to experiment and to find out what worked best in their particular context—all within a general framework that was still needed in the strongly regulated financial industry.[104] As a result, Barclays became faster in offering new products to customers, and could also report improvements in quality and employee engagement.[105] **Effective teamwork** was key to achieving better organizational outcomes.

The change to a new way of working did not come without **conflicts**, however. Many long-tenured managers who were used to hierarchical structures and to telling people what they had to do were reluctant to accept the idea of self-managing teams. The shift from a command-and-control mind-set to an Agile mind-set was all but easy to achieve. Jonathan Smart, who led the Agile initiative at Barclays, even said that the "A-word" became a "toxic word" in the organization, especially for people who were more reluctant to change.[106]

What was required in this situation was a change in **communication**. Instead of talking about Agile, Smart started to talk about "better ways of working."[107] The communication also shifted from "what" (the methodology) to "why" (the outcomes that the organization wanted to achieve with the Agile transformation)—in Barclays' case to creating better products and value for customers faster, safer, and also in a way that made people happier.[108] "My advice is [to] focus on the outcomes, on what you are trying to achieve," said Smart in an interview with London Business School Professor Julian Birkinshaw, "and then empower the teams to work [it] out for themselves and support them with capability building."[109]

As we can see in the case of Barclays, organizations that are able to use the power of effective teamwork can become more productive and more flexible at the same time. In order to reap these benefits, however, managers who lead organizations and teams within these organizations also need to cope competently with conflicts, and to be able to communicate well with the team members and all other stakeholders. With a combination of team building and teamwork skills, conflict management skills, and communication skills, managers are better equipped to tackle the challenges of a fast-changing business environment.

✓ Review questions

1   Under what conditions are teams the best choice for dealing with a particular task?
2   How can Belbin's team roles concept help managers to build more effective teams?
3   What are the main issues that newly formed teams should discuss and clarify when they are constituted?
4   What usually happens in the four stages of group development?
5   What are the main tasks of a team leader?
6   How can team leaders deal with different types of "ineffective" team players?
7   Which digital tools can be used to improve a team's productivity?
8   Which questions would you ask in order to assess the quality of a team process?
9   What are the main criteria for choosing between different communication tools?
10   What are the "secrets" of effective presentations?
11   What does an effective team meeting look like?
12   Which conflict management strategies are appropriate in which kind of situations?
13   What is the difference between distributive and integrative negotiations?
14   What are the main tactics to claim value in distributive negotiations?
15   How can managers conduct integrative negotiations?

⑦ Critical reflection questions

1   Better students sometimes have a dislike for teamwork because they do not want to work with people who are in their view less committed or less capable than they are. Critically reflect on this attitude.

2   There is a broad range of digital tools that supposedly increase the productivity of teams. Why are many teams not making use of these tools?

3   Many organizations try to become more agile through fostering self-managing teams. In your opinion, what are the main advantages and disadvantages of self-managing teams? Under which circumstances would you see a self-managing team as the right choice for organizing work?

4   Many people in organizations hate meetings and see them as a waste of time that keeps them away from their real work. Do you agree with this critical stance toward meetings?

5   Would you say that it is better to avoid conflict wherever possible (to foster harmonious relationships within the organization) or to consciously maintain a certain level of conflict (so that conflicting interests are clearly visible and can always be openly discussed)?

☞ Managerial implications

- Managers can accomplish bigger tasks by creating high-performance teams. Team success starts with selecting the team members with complementary functional, interpersonal, and problem-solving skills as well as with complementary aptitudes in terms of types of team roles.

- In order for teamwork to become effective, team leaders must strive to maintain a good balance between attending to the task, caring for the individual needs of team members, creating team cohesion, and taking external stakeholders' interests and influences into account.

- The manager's most important tool for getting things done is communication. A careful choice of communication channels and approaches can increase the chances of reaching a mutual understanding of what is important and what needs to be done.

- Meetings are often (maybe even too often) used as communication setting in teams and organizations. Sticking to some basic rules can help to make meetings more productive. The preparation and follow-up stages are of particular importance in this context.

- In teams and more generally in the organizational world, it is natural that interests collide. Effective managers have a repertoire of different strategies to deal with conflict and manage negotiation situations. Ideally, they try to find integrative solutions with benefits for all sides, although this is not always possible.

✎ Endnotes

[1] bbc.com (2015).
[2] bbc.com (2015).
[3] Denning (2018); Forbes Insights (2018).
[4] Forbes Insights (2018), p. 9.
[5] Katzenbach and Smith (1993).
[6] Katzenbach and Smith (1993).
[7] Hill (1994); O'Neill and Salas (2018).
[8] Coutu (2009).
[9] Coutu (2009); Hackman (2011).
[10] Hackman (2011).
[11] Hackman (2011).
[12] Stewart and Barrick (2000).
[13] Stewart and Barrick (2000).
[14] Hill (1994).
[15] Belbin (1993; 2004).

[16] Aritzeta et al. (2007).
[17] Katzenbach and Smith (1993).
[18] Coutu (2009), p. 103.
[19] Coutu (2009).
[20] Katzenbach and Smith (1993).
[21] Katzenbach and Smith (1993).
[22] Katzenbach and Smith (1993).
[23] Tuckman (1965).
[24] Tuckman (1965).
[25] Maltarich et al. (2018).
[26] Hill (1994).
[27] Gratton and Erickson (2007).
[28] Tuckman and Jensen (1977).
[29] Hackman (2011).
[30] Humphrey (2014).

[31] Forsyth (2019).
[32] Pentland (2012).
[33] The ideas presented here and in the following paragraphs were first described by Cohn (1975).
[34] Henningsen et al. (2017); Janis (1971).
[35] Lamparter (2013).
[36] Continental share price on 15 June 2009: EUR 20.81; share price on 15 June 2018: EUR 225.20 (according to www.continental-corporation.com/en/investors/shares/share-price-chart, accessed on 12 December 2018).
[37] Lamparter (2013).
[38] Lamparter (2013).

[39] Spinnarke (2015).
[40] Continental (2015).
[41] Stewart et al. (2012).
[42] Stephens and Lyddy (2016).
[43] Parker (1990).
[44] Parker (1990).
[45] Wech et al. (1998).
[46] Jordan (1994), pp. 20-24.
[47] ipa.co.uk (2018).
[48] Hine (2014).
[49] Cockburn (2015).
[50] Bassett (2016).
[51] Cockburn (2015).
[52] Hine (2014).
[53] Hine (2014).
[54] Bassett (2016).
[55] coachmag.co.uk (2016).
[56] Roither (2014).
[57] McLuhan (1964), p. 23.
[58] Tenzer and Pudelko (2016).
[59] Tenzer and Pudelko (2016).
[60] Daft (2016).
[61] Malik (2004).
[62] Schein (1993).

[63] Schein (1993).
[64] van Loon and van Dijk (2015).
[65] Berezin (2013).
[66] Jiang et al. (2012).
[67] Vuilleumier (2005).
[68] Craumer (2001).
[69] Krattenmaker (2008).
[70] Thibaut and Walker (1975).
[71] Craumer (2001).
[72] Meyer (2015), p. 80.
[73] Ferrazzi (2015).
[74] Galbraith (1969), p. 84.
[75] Ware and Barnes (1985).
[76] O'Neill et al. (2018).
[77] Rahim (2002).
[78] Rahim and Magner (1995).
[79] Ware and Barnes (1985).
[80] Thiel et al. (2018); Ware and Barnes (1985).
[81] Slater (1992), p. 29.
[82] della Cava (2017).
[83] Nadella et al. (2017), p. 83.
[84] Nadella et al. (2017), p. 83.
[85] Nadella et al. (2017).
[86] Harvard Business School Publishing (2003).

[87] Harvard Business School Publishing (2003); Malhotra (2010).
[88] Maaravi and Levy (2017).
[89] Fisher et al. (2011).
[90] Fisher et al. (2011).
[91] Malhotra and Bazerman (2007).
[92] Lax and Sebenius (1986).
[93] Mason et al. (2018).
[94] Watkins and Rosen (2001).
[95] Ertel and Gordon (2008).
[96] Ellis-Petersen (2014).
[97] Kellogg (2014).
[98] Kellogg (2014).
[99] Streitfeld (2014).
[100] Ellis-Petersen (2014).
[101] Streitfeld (2014).
[102] economist.com (2014).
[103] Denning (2018).
[104] Linders (2016).
[105] Basar (2017); Linders (2016).
[106] London Business School (2018).
[107] London Business School (2018).
[108] London Business School (2018).
[109] London Business School (2018).

Visit the companion website at macmillanihe.com/sternad-management to access multiple choice questions, useful weblinks and additional materials.

Pixabay/Gerd Altmann

MANAGING DIVERSITY ACROSS CULTURES

Outline of chapter

This chapter will enable you to

- Explain the benefits of diversity as well as the challenges of managing a diverse group of people.
- Describe what managers can do to create more diverse and inclusive organizations.
- Determine cultural differences and devise strategies for effectively communicating in cross-cultural settings.
- Identify the specific challenges and tasks that leaders of global virtual teams are facing.
- Appreciate the importance of ethical behavior in an organizational context.
- Analyze moral or ethical issues that arise in organizations with the help of basic ethical principles.

Introduction

Leena Nair, a young engineer, joined Hindustan Unilever (HUL), the Indian subsidiary of the global consumer goods company Unilever, as a management trainee in 1992. Only around 2 percent of HUL's employees were female at the time, a fact that directly impacted on Leena's experience. For example, Leena became the first woman to volunteer to work in one of HUL's manufacturing plants, but found that there were no female toilet facilities there. "I've experienced what it's like to be undermined or seen as 'different'—and the visibility and stereotyping that goes with it,"[1] she later said.

From the beginning of her career, Nair has challenged stereotypes. When everyone told her that women had never been on a night shift, she just said: "What if I am the first? Let me set the pace."[2] She soon became known for this. She was the first woman to take up a sales job at HUL, the first female member of HUL's management committee, and was appointed Unilever's first female, first Asian, and youngest ever chief human resources officer in 2016. In this job, she leads the global people agenda of the corporation with a workforce of more than 160,000 employees. In her top management role, she sees building "an inclusive environment where all members of our diverse society can contribute and succeed in equal measure"[3] as one of her most important goals. Championing diversity ranks high on Nair's agenda not only because of her personal experience as a member of a minority group within the company, but also because it makes business sense. "We need to look at bringing in the best of diverse talent," she says, "so that we have a workforce that is equipped with the qualities that are needed to run a successful business."[4]

Globally active businesses in particular (Unilever is present in more than 100 countries around the world) face a wide variety of different customer needs, work habits, communication styles, and culture-specific values. Only a diverse team will be able to deal with such diverse demands. It is therefore important for managers to embrace diversity and become effective in leading teams with members from diverse backgrounds.

In this chapter, we will examine how managers can competently meet the challenges that they can encounter in **diverse and cross-cultural environments**. More specifically, we will focus on:

- understanding the advantages and potential pitfalls of working with a diverse group of people and examining the basics of **managing diversity** (*Section 5.1*);
- exploring how managers can analyze **cultural differences** and find ways to effectively communicate with people from other cultures (*Section 5.2*);
- assessing the benefits and challenges of **global virtual teams** and identifying practices for effectively leading such culturally diverse and geographically dispersed teams with the help of modern communication technologies (*Section 5.3*);
- discussing how managers can address **moral dilemmas** and deal with **different ethical standards** as they collaborate with people from different cultural backgrounds (*Section 5.4*).

In an open and increasingly globalized world, effective managers must be able to work with—and through—people from different cultures. They must appreciate the power that lies in diversity and view differences as an opportunity for learning and growth, while also being able to acknowledge and manage the challenges that diverse teams can entail.

Diversity:
Variation among people in visible and invisible characteristics (including, for example, age, gender, ethnicity, social class, religion, sexual orientation, values, personality, or physical ability).

Global virtual teams:
Geographically dispersed teams composed of team members from different countries who are interacting primarily with the help of modern communication technology.

Moral dilemma:
A decision situation in which moral principles come into conflict.

Ethical standards:
Principles of what is considered morally right behavior in a certain group or culture.

5.1 Understanding and embracing diversity

Pixabay/rawpixel

In brief

- Effective managers are able to work with people from diverse backgrounds and with a range of different characteristics.

- Organizations can benefit from diversity through achieving higher decision quality, creating better connections with a range of different customer groups, attracting and retaining talent, increasing flexibility and responsiveness, and boosting their innovativeness.

- Diversity can also lead to challenges—especially in terms of higher communication costs and potentially lower group cohesion.

- To reap the benefits of diversity without succumbing to its potential disadvantages, managers can follow a diversity management strategy. In addition to introducing diversity policies and practices, they can also try to shape the diversity climate and influence diversity-related attitudes in their organization.

Every person is unique. People differ in visible dimensions (e.g. gender, race, or age), invisible dimensions (e.g. educational background, marital and parental status, or income), values (e.g. based on their religion or cultural socialization), and personality (see Figure 5.1).[5] In an organizational context—in particular, but not exclusively, in organizations that operate across borders—managers need to work with groups of people from very different backgrounds. This is getting ever more important in societies that are becoming increasingly multicultural (for example, in the US, over 20 percent of the population aged over five years speak a language other than English at home).[6] The term **diversity** is used to describe "all the ways that human beings are both similar and different."[7] In diverse organizations, people with very different characteristics interact, and those differences can have an impact on how well people collaborate and perform.

VISIBLE CHARACTERISTICS
Age   Gender   Race   Appearance   Physical ability   . . .
INVISIBLE CHARACTERISTICS
Work experience   Social class   Marital and parental status   Sexual orientation   . . .
VALUES
Religion   Cultural values   Lifestyle   Attitudes   Beliefs   . . .
PERSONALITY
Extraversion   Emotional stability   Agreeableness   Conscientiousness   Openness   . . .

Figure 5.1 Layers of workforce diversity

Human beings actually tend to think in differences, particularly when they judge others (see also the section on thinking in categories in Chapter 6). Whereas thinking in differences (or dichotomies) can help us make sense of the world, we need to be careful not to fall victim to oversimplification, stereotyping, and limiting observations to *"binary* oppositions."[8] An anti-categorical approach to diversity recognizes that putting people into categories can also contribute to the perpetuation of stereotypes.[9] Rather than seeing oneself "in opposition to" someone else, we should acknowledge that differences exist, and that, as management professor and author Mary Gentile noticed, "we all have multiple identities, one or another of which we may identify with more strongly at different moments in our lives and in different contexts."[10]

Similarities attract, and people usually like to work with others who hold similar identities, especially those with whom they share values, beliefs, and attitudes.[11] Organizations that become too homogeneous and exclude people who are seen as "different" can run into severe difficulties. They can, for example, lose their innovation capacity or fall victim to groupthink (see Chapter 6). One example is the case of Swissair, a once-thriving airline that was even called "the Flying Bank" because of its financial stability—before it went bankrupt as a result of a failed expansion strategy in 2001. Scholars who analyzed the collapse of Swissair concluded that groupthink (e.g. in the form of an illusion of invulnerability and a lack of critical voices within the group) contributed to bad management decisions, and that this could have been caused by the composition of the board, which included managers with quite similar backgrounds and values.[12] As Frost and Kalman note, "sameness is very seductive"[13] because we are naturally attracted to "people like us." In organizations that operate in complex and dynamic environments, however, "diversity trumps individual ability." It increases resilience and can help to improve decision-making processes.[14] Effective managers therefore actively strive to avoid the homogeneity pitfall, and are able to understand, appreciate, and manage diversity.

The pros and cons of diversity

Diversity is a double-edged sword. On the one hand, it can be the source of multiple benefits, but on the other hand, it can also lead to challenges. Before we discuss the concept of diversity management, we first need to understand both aspects.

Research results suggest that workforce diversity can become a **source of competitive advantage** or an "invisible asset,"[15] mainly for the following reasons:[16]

1 **Higher decision quality**: Diverse teams have more access to information, which can be particularly useful for solving complex problems. When people with different backgrounds and expertise interact, they will usually see problems from different perspectives, which can result in a broader consideration of difficult issues and, in turn, lead to better decisions.

2 **Connection with customer groups**: If the members of an organization and its different customer target groups share certain characteristics, it can help the organization to better understand customer preferences and ease communication with customers. A more diverse organization raises the chance to connect more closely with a range of different customer groups.

3 **Source of creativity and innovation**: Innovation usually occurs at interfaces, where different experiences, functions, ideas, or cultures meet. People with different backgrounds and attitudes are also often more inclined to question the status quo and put forward new ideas that can lead to innovative solutions which can move the organization forward.

4 **Attracting and retaining talent**: If organizations succeed in attracting people from diverse backgrounds, they have access to a wider talent pool. Avoiding discrimination, unfair treatment, and biases in promotion decisions can help in retaining and making the best use of talented employees.

5 **Reputation as a responsible organization**: Open, welcoming organizations in which everyone is valued regardless of their backgrounds are usually also well respected by different stakeholder groups.

6 **Increasing flexibility and responsiveness**: In a dynamic global market environment, having team members with diverse experiences and different problem-solving capabilities can help in finding the right answers to new challenges and reacting flexibly to formerly unknown situations.

The main **challenges of diversity** relate to higher communication costs:

Inclusion:
The act of creating an environment in which differences are valued and no one feels marginalized or excluded.

1 It is usually easier for people in a more homogeneous group to interact with each other as they share a common language and similar worldviews.[17]
2 In more diverse groups, it is often more difficult to create group cohesiveness and group attachments.[18]
3 Higher levels of diversity can also lead to lower employee commitment and higher levels of conflict within a group.[19]
4 It might also become more difficult to find the performance management and motivation systems that are suitable for the whole team if the team members hold very different work-related values.[20]

Diversity policies:
A system of goals and principles that are used as a guideline for fostering diversity in an organization.

The two sides of diversity—its benefits and challenges—have led to inconsistent research conclusions about its relationship with organizational performance. Some studies have found strong positive correlations between diversity and performance, whereas others have found negative correlations.[21] One reason for these inconclusive results could be that there is indeed high potential in workforce diversity—but this potential can only be transformed into actual higher performance when diversity is well managed.

Suppose that you have a vacant managerial position in your organization. There are three candidates: Candidate A, a member of a majority identity group in your organization; Candidate B, a member of a minority group that is already well represented in the organization; and Candidate C, a member of a minority group that is clearly underrepresented in the organization. All three candidates meet all the basic criteria that were set up for the position. A scoring system was introduced to make the selection processes as objective as possible (based on criteria that was set up for the assessment of the CV/résumé and the interviewers' assessment of the candidate's performance in the job interviews). Candidate A scored 94 points (out of 100), Candidate B 93 points, and Candidate C 90 points. Who do you choose for the job and why?

Diversity practices:
A set of practices that are used to foster diversity in an organization.

Diversity management

In order to reap the benefits of diversity and avoid the problems that are associated with it, managers need to familiarize themselves with the concept of diversity management. The term **diversity management** refers to the practice of deliberately and voluntarily promoting diversity, fostering **inclusion** (creating an environment that actively values differences and reduces marginalization and exclusion), and supporting respectful and productive working relationships within a diverse group of people in an organizational context. Diversity management goes beyond legal requirements in the fields of **equal employment opportunities** (policies that protect employees from discrimination in all fields of employment, for example recruitment, promotion, pay, or layoffs) and **affirmative action** (policies that favor members of groups that have been disadvantaged or discriminated against in the past, e.g. hiring quotas for minorities).[22]

Diversity climate:
The extent to which members of an organization share the opinion that fostering diversity and inclusion should be valued and supported in the organization.

There are different **fields of action for diversity management** in organizations (see Figure 5.2). Managers can focus on visible "above the line" **diversity policies** (e.g. setting diversity-related goals or establishing diversity guidelines) and **diversity practices** (e.g. bias-free job descriptions or diversity training), but they can also try to influence the more unconscious, "below the line" stance to diversity issues. Fostering a positive **diversity climate**—a common understanding that diversity matters and that it should be valued and

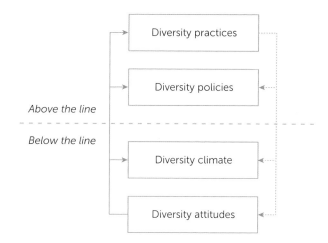

Figure 5.2 Fields of action for diversity management in an organizational context

supported by the organization through its practices and policies—can lead to higher levels of job satisfaction, employee involvement, feelings of empowerment, and better performance.[23] It can also help to mitigate the potential negative effects of higher in-group diversity such as higher levels of conflict or lower commitment.[24] Table 5.1 provides a checklist with questions that can help managers to assess whether their organization has a positive diversity climate which shows **indicators of inclusivity**.[25]

Inclusivity:
The practice of including people from all diversity-related backgrounds without marginalizing or discriminating against any group of people.

The diversity climate and the "above the line" activities are influenced by the **attitudes** that managers and other powerful group members hold about diversity. Human resource management researcher Carol Kulik notes, for example, that "there are 'diversity champion' and 'bad apple' line managers who make or break their organization's diversity programs."[26] Deep-rooted fears of being treated unfairly if members of other (underrepresented) groups are promoted could underlie unwillingness by some to participate in an organization's diversity program, while others simply feel uncomfortable at the idea of being told what to think and do.[27] The *Los Angeles Times* reported on one example of a software engineer at Google who disagreed with the recommendations of the company's diversity training and was angry about being told what he was not supposed to say and do at work. He wrote a long memo against what he called an "ideological echo chamber" at Google and was subsequently fired "for perpetuating gender stereotypes."[28] Diversity champions like Leena Nair, whose story we heard in the Introduction to this chapter, however, believe that more diversity will be beneficial for their organization, especially in terms of attracting and retaining talent and

Table 5.1 Diversity climate checklist

Diversity climate checklist (indicators of inclusivity)

- Do people feel accepted in the organization regardless of their diversity-related differences?
- Are the key diversity characteristics adequately represented in the senior management team?
- Are ideas from all groups welcome at all levels of the organization?
- Are discriminatory jokes (e.g. about race, ethnicity, or with sexual overtones) unwelcome?
- Is subgroup building and cliquishness avoided?
- Are a variety of dressing styles accepted?
- Are there positive, collegial relationships between members of the organization from different backgrounds?
- Does the organization show adequate sensitivity for different cultural or religious customs?
- Do food offerings in the work environment cater for the needs of different groups of employees?
- Is the organization flexible enough to allow employees to balance work and non-work responsibilities?

Source: Inspired by concepts in Gardenswartz and Rowe (2010), p. 233.

being able to combine a greater diversity of thought for solving complex challenges in fast-changing business environments.[29] The diversity-related attitudes of the senior management team are particularly relevant for shaping a positive diversity climate, establishing diversity policies, and fostering diversity practices (see the box *Diversity and inclusion as strategic goals at Gildan Activewear*).

CEO BEST PRACTICE

Diversity and inclusion as strategic goals at Gildan Activewear

Glenn J. Chamandy is one of the founders as well as the president and CEO of Gildan Activewear Inc., a Montréal-based apparel and socks manufacturing company. Gildan distinguishes itself from other clothing manufacturers because it generates almost 90 percent of its US$2.75 billion revenues (2017) from products that are manufactured in house. Having control over the whole production process allows the company to follow its corporate social responsibility strategy of having a positive impact on people, the environment, local communities, and product quality across the value chain. Gildan has around 50,000 employees in North America, Central America (where it operates its largest production facilities), Asia, and Europe. The company is strongly committed to ensuring healthy, safe, and fair working conditions that are considerably above industry standards, and provides free medication and subsidized meals for its employees. Chamandy firmly believes that Gildan's "strength comes from always fostering a culture of diversity and inclusion while leveraging our collective strengths."[30] In order to create such an inclusive culture, the company launched the Gildan Diversity and Inclusion Policy in 2016. It was designed to ensure that there are no systematic barriers for any employee group and includes the clear commitment of the senior management team to create and maintain an

environment in which differences are valued and embraced and in which all employees are treated with respect and dignity. The policy is also supported by concrete strategic diversity management initiatives in the fields of talent acquisition (e.g. increasing efforts to attract a diverse pool of candidates), employee development (e.g. diversity and inclusion awareness training and initiatives to develop female talent across the company), and community involvement (e.g. a women's empowerment program and investments in supporting the socio-economic development of the communities in which the company operates). A monitoring system helps to track the company's development on diversity-related performance indicators. Chamandy is convinced that through the various programs and initiatives, the company will be able "to better support a culture that encourages the development of each individual, enabling them to recognize and reach their full potential."[31]

→ Key takeaway

Policies and actions that foster diversity and inclusion can help both individuals and organizations to reach their full potential.

Sources: Based on information in Gildan (2016); genuinegildan.com (2017a; 2017b); gildancorp.com (2017; 2019).

Many managers are not aware of their biases. They might consider themselves as tolerant and open, yet unconsciously they still prefer to work with people who think and act in similar ways, promote those in whom they see themselves (the "clone effect"[32]), easily jump to conclusions without hearing different views on a story, already have a picture in mind of the person who would best fit into the team before they hire someone, hold false assumptions about people based on assuming that all members of a particular group share certain common characteristics, or prefer not to openly challenge discriminatory jokes or remarks.[33] Managers who want to have a positive influence on the diversity attitudes and climate of their organizations need to start with an honest **self-assessment** of their own diversity-related assumptions and behavior, for example, with reflective questions like:

- What are my first thoughts and feelings when I meet a person from a minority group (e.g. a transgendered person, a person with different religious beliefs, or a person with a different skin color)?

- When I think about the five to seven people with whom I most closely collaborate at work—how do they differ from myself in terms of diversity-related dimensions? Am I aware of the differences in values and work-related attitudes and behaviors that could be caused by these diversity-related differences?
- Is diversity management an important item on my managerial agenda?

Just as "below the line" thinking modes can influence "above the line" activities, it is also possible that there are repercussion effects, in which diversity policies and practices send a strong message to the employees about the general stance of the management (and of the organization as a whole) toward diversity.[34] Thus, diversity practices and policies can help to shape the diversity climate and influence the diversity attitudes in an organization. A combination of different diversity initiatives is usually more effective in this respect than individual measures.[35] Figure 5.3 outlines a seven-step model of how organizations can become more diversity and inclusion oriented.

Figure 5.3 Seven steps toward a more diversity- and inclusion-oriented organization

Source: Inspired by concepts in Gardenswartz and Rowe (2010), p. 308.

1. Ensure top management commitment
2. Diagnose and assess the diversity status in the organization
3. Install diversity- and inclusion-promoting roles (diversity manager, council, or task force)
4. Launch diversity training initiatives
5. Establish diversity-related norms, policies, and systems
6. Measure and evaluate progress (using diversity-related performance indicators)
7. Integrate diversity thinking in all areas of organizational decision making and behavior

Diversity practices

The following **diversity practices** are often used in organizations in which diversity management is seen as a key success factor:[36]

- Including diversity signals in recruitment materials;
- Recruitment activities that are targeted specifically toward groups which are currently underrepresented in the organization;
- Offering internships for underrepresented groups;
- Establishing affiliations with minority organizations;
- Using objective criteria and tests for job applicants to reduce subjective judgment and fight bias in recruitment processes;
- Offering diversity training for managers and other members of the organization;
- Offering **mentoring** and career development programs for members of disadvantaged groups;
- Supporting people with special needs (e.g. offering flexible working hours, ensuring accessibility, or providing meals for different dietary requirements in the canteen);

Mentoring:
A relationship in which a more experienced person (the mentor) offers personal and career guidance to a less experienced person (the mentee).

Diversity manager:
A person who has the task of developing and implementing policies and practices that foster diversity and inclusion in an organization.

- Setting up distinct diversity-related organizational functions and roles for championing diversity issues within the organization (e.g. **diversity managers**, diversity councils or task forces with members from different departments, and employee networking groups that consist of members from certain identity groups to focus on their particular concerns);
- Linking managers' bonus programs to diversity-related performance indicators;
- Introducing a grievance system for dealing with cases of discrimination or harassment.

A recent study among US firms found that, despite good intentions, tests for job applicants, grievance systems, and mandatory diversity training did not have the desired effects on promoting diversity.[37] Some managers used tests only selectively or ignored their results altogether, people often refrained from officially reporting discriminatory behavior, and mandatory training was sometimes seen as "force-feeding."[38] Other diversity practices such as targeted college recruitment, mentoring programs, diversity managers, task forces, and voluntary training were found to have a more positive impact, since they exposed managers to people from different backgrounds and encouraged them to actively participate in the creation of a more diverse organization.[39]

Diversity training activities can be offered in the form of (a) **diversity awareness training** (in which people are familiarized with the value of diversity and inclusion, identify their own assumptions, biases, and stereotypes, and try to develop a higher degree of sensitivity and openness toward people with different backgrounds and characteristics); and (b) **diversity skills training** (which is oriented toward improving the ability to constructively communicate and collaborate with people who are different than oneself).[40] The box *Zooming in on diversity training* has two activities that can help you to enhance your diversity awareness and diversity skills.

Zooming in on ▶ DIVERSITY TRAINING

If you want to work on your own diversity awareness and diversity skills, here are two examples of diversity training activities that received empirical support in terms of having positive pro-diversity attitudinal and behavioral outcomes:

- *Diversity training activity 1—Perspective taking:*
  1 Imagine that you are a member of a certain minority group.
  2 Write down a few sentences about the challenges that you would probably face as part of that particular minority group.
- *Diversity training activity 2—Goal setting:*
  1 Set yourself one or two specific goals related to the promotion of diversity in your organization (e.g. the goal of challenging inappropriate comments about minority groups in the future).
  2 Write down the goals.
  3 Revisit your diversity promotion goals regularly to assess whether you are achieving them.

Source: *Based on information in Lindsey et al. (2017)*

Diversity initiatives sometimes also span the boundaries of the organization. They can be oriented toward developing a more **diverse portfolio of suppliers** that includes, for example, businesses owned by women or ethnic minorities. Reasons for trying to increase diversity in the supply chain range from creating market opportunities through social responsibility to reputational considerations and sustaining legitimacy in the eyes of different stakeholder groups.[41]

Whether within an organization or along the supply chain, managing diversity is not an easy endeavor. Stereotyping, thinking in differences and "us-versus-them" categories, or unconscious discrimination cannot just be abolished by the stroke of a pen. Managers must also expect a lack of understanding or even resistance when they introduce new diversity- and inclusion-related policies and practices in their organization; for example, when some people feel that diversity-related rules threaten their autonomy or affirmative action seemingly unfairly favors colleagues from underrepresented groups (e.g. in promotion decisions).[42]

Although it is not always easy to achieve, managers can make a difference. Through recognizing the benefits of diversity, setting an example by including diversity-related considerations in their own decision-making processes, and—in addition to introducing diversity- and inclusion-promoting policies and initiatives—also trying to make sure that the members of their team understand *why* these measures are useful and necessary, they can bring about positive change. Thus, they can help to create a place where diversity thrives and is seen as a valuable asset. To reap the full benefits of diversity and to turn it into a unique strength and advantage for their organization, however, managers also need courage and persistence.

5.2 Developing intercultural competence

Getty Images/Blend Images/KidStock

In brief

- As more and more organizations work across national and cultural boundaries, they need culturally intelligent managers who are able to understand cultural differences and communicate effectively with people from different backgrounds.

- Cultures vary across a range of different dimensions, and these differences can have a strong impact on how people interact with each other. Knowledge about cultural differences across various dimensions can help managers to better assess cross-cultural communication situations and adapt their behavior accordingly.

- Culturally intelligent managers are also careful to avoid stereotyping because not every individual necessarily behaves according to what the central tendencies of a certain culture would suggest.

- Cultural differences can also play an important role in negotiation and conflict situations. Managers who are able to bridge the cultural gap will be able to deal more effectively with the challenges that these situations involve.

Organizations are by definition entities that perform through collaborative activity. To orchestrate this collaborative activity, managers need to communicate well. That means that they must be able to interchange messages with others in a way that the intended meanings are mutually understood. Communication generally works through **codes** (e.g. graphical signs, spoken language, mimic expressions and gestures, or digital data) and **conventions**, norms about which codes are generally used in which context to convey certain ideas.[43] Codes and conventions, in turn, are strongly influenced by culture.[44] As managers become more immersed in multi-cultural work environments, they also need to become competent in intercultural communication.

The word **culture** refers to basic assumptions, values, beliefs, norms, and tendencies in behavioral patterns that are shared among the members of a certain group or community.[45] Geert Hofstede famously defined it as "the collective programming of the mind which distinguishes the members of one human group from another."[46] "Programming" also means that

Culture:
Basic assumptions, values, beliefs, norms, and tendencies in behavioral patterns that are shared among the members of a certain group or community.

Cultural intelligence:
The ability to interact effectively with people from different cultural backgrounds.

Low-context culture:
A culture in which the information that is transmitted in oral or written form usually does not carry implicit meanings (i.e. people mean exactly what they say).

High-context culture:
A culture in which the context of how a message is delivered (e.g. body language, the tone of voice, facial expressions, or what is not said) provides important additional clues about what the sender really wants to convey.

Cultural dimensions:
A generalized framework of relatively enduring sets of values and norms that are used to describe differences and commonalities between different cultures.

culture is a learned behavior. It is not innate but instead transmitted through social interactions. People who are part of a specific culture share certain communication patterns (both in terms of codes and conventions) and usually have a similar way of making sense of what is going on in their environment and what other people's behavior means. Culture can serve as "a kind of glue—a social adhesive—that binds a group of people together and gives them a distinct identity as a community,"[47] but it can also raise barriers for communication between people from different cultures.

The ability to interact effectively with people from different cultural backgrounds is also known as **cultural intelligence**. Culturally intelligent managers are aware of cultural differences, are able to judge whether certain aspects of a communication situation are influenced by these differences, and can adapt their verbal and non-verbal behavior accordingly.[48] Being culturally intelligent also means being able to distinguish between behavior that is characteristic of a certain group and behavior that is peculiar only to a certain person, for example due to that person's personality traits.[49]

Cultural dimensions

Several researchers have tried to identify general cultural dimensions that can be used as a framework for assessing cultural differences. One of the most frequently used concepts is the anthropologist Edward T. Hall's distinction between **low-context** and **high-context cultures**.[50] This can be used to better understand cross-cultural differences in how people communicate with each other.

In a low-context culture (e.g. Germany or other Western countries), the information that people want to convey lies primarily in the message itself. This means that people are usually explicit about what they want to convey. In high-context cultures (e.g. China, Japan, other Asian countries, and many Latin American or Middle Eastern countries), the message itself carries less information. There is a stronger emphasis on non-verbal signals, on how something is said, or on what remains unsaid. A person from a low-context culture who does not like your proposal would probably answer: "Sorry, but I don't think this is a good idea." Someone from a high-context country would rather avoid confronting you directly and could respond with "I will think about it" or not respond at all (in both cases this means "No"). In low-context cultures, behavioral norms are usually made explicit; for example, in the form of written instructions or signs, whereas high-context cultures tend to rely much more on social control in the form of correction by another person if a social norm is broken.[51] While detailed contracts are often used (and enforced in sophisticated juridical structures) in low-context cultures, high-context cultures rely more strongly on reciprocal personal relationships in doing business.[52]

Another frequently used concept to categorize cultures is **Geert Hofstede's cultural dimension model** which the Dutch social psychologist derived from a study of work-related values of IBM employees in dozens of different countries in the 1970s. You can use this model to understand how people from different cultural backgrounds typically prefer to interact with others.

According to Hofstede, cultures differ in four dimensions:

- **individualism** (the tendency to prefer a society in which individuals care mainly for themselves and their immediate family) versus **collectivism** (the tendency to emphasize group interests as well as identification with and loyalty to the group);
- **masculinity** (a cultural preference for values that are often stereotypically attributed to the male gender, e.g. assertiveness, achievement orientation, or competitiveness) versus **femininity** (a preference for values that are often attributed to the female gender, e.g. cooperation, modesty, seeking harmony, and caring for quality of life);
- high versus low **uncertainty avoidance** (the degree to which people in a certain culture want to avoid ambiguity and unknown situations); and
- high versus low **power distance** (the extent to which inequalities and an unequal distribution of power are accepted in a society).[53]

As a result of his cooperation with Michael Bond, Hofstede later added a fifth dimension, **long-term orientation** (a strong focus on the future and the feeling that perseverance will help to change things) versus **short-term orientation** (a stronger focus on traditions, the present, and stability).[54]

Further examples of widely cited research on cross-cultural differences include:

- The work of the social psychologist **Shalom H. Schwartz**, who distinguishes between **seven basic value types** (harmony, egalitarianism, intellectual autonomy, affective autonomy, mastery, hierarchy, and conservatism) and observes that national cultures differ on the relative importance of these value types.[55] Schwartz also sees a relationship between these basic value types and work-related norms. For example, the pursuit of power is generally more acceptable in cultures where mastery and hierarchy values are more important (e.g. in China or the US) than in cultures in which harmony and egalitarianism are held in high esteem (e.g. in Scandinavian countries).[56]
- **Trompenaars and Hampden-Turner's model of cultural differences**, which, among other dimensions of cultural differences, also distinguishes between "neutral" cultures in which people are more reserved in terms of showing their emotions (e.g. in the UK or Japan) and "emotional" cultures in which emotions are more openly expressed (e.g. in Italy or Mexico).[57]
- The **GLOBE project** (based on the survey response data of 17,000 middle managers from 62 cultures and over 5,000 senior executives from 24 different countries), which showed that societal culture can have a strong influence on the expectations that people hold regarding the leadership behavior of managers.[58]
- The **World Values Survey**, a periodic survey on societal values and attitudes that is conducted in almost 100 different countries by a global network of researchers.[59] The results of this survey suggest that "attitudes among the population are also highly correlated with the philosophical, political and religious ideas that have been dominating in the country."[60]

The common insight of all this research work is not surprising: cultures differ on a range of different dimensions, and these differences can also become highly relevant in a managerial context.

Of course, we need to be careful not to fall victim to stereotyping. Cultural dimensions might describe a "central tendency"[61] within a group, but they do not necessarily reveal the actual values and behavioral tendencies of individuals. A Thai person who has been educated in the US and has worked in Europe for more than a decade might, for example, hold very different cultural values than the central tendencies for Thailand would suggest. And although national cultures are the salient unit of analysis, they are neither the only cultural influence on individuals (who can, at the same time, also be influenced by the organizational, professional, age-related, or other cultures in which they have been immersed), nor does the focus on national cultures recognize that in many countries, cultures can vary considerably on a sub-national level (there are more than 60 ethnicities in China, for example).[62]

If you were appointed to manage a team in another country (with a culture that is significantly different from your own), what would you do to prepare yourself for the intercultural challenges that you could be facing?

Understanding cultural differences

Understanding central tendencies in cultural values is important for managers who want to become interculturally competent. But values are not the only category on which people in different cultures differ from each other. Attitudes, customs, and behavioral patterns that are seen as appropriate (or not) can vary as well (see the box on *The role of business etiquette*).

FROM A DIFFERENT ANGLE

The role of business etiquette

In business relationships, there are certain expectations about how to behave appropriately, also known as "business etiquette." Some important issues in the field of business etiquette are:

- punctuality—how important is it to be on time?;
- greeting customs—e.g. the importance of handshakes and who reaches out for the hand first;
- how to introduce others—e.g. introducing the lower-ranked person to the higher-ranked person;
- what to wear in a business context—e.g. whether to wear a suit versus being more casually dressed;
- how to behave during a business meal—e.g. table manners, how to deal with undesirable food, and which topics should or should not be addressed during a dinner conversation;
- how to address others in the workplace and in business relationships—e.g. when to use first names;
- how to address conflicts—openly or in a more subtle way;
- when and how to ask questions in meetings—at any time or only if you are directly encouraged;
- acceptance of gifts—seeing it as a courtesy or an attempt to bribe;
- when and how to use mobile phones or computers—e.g. sending text messages or checking e-mails during a meeting.

The rites and manners that are either expected or not appropriate in the business community can vary from culture to culture. In South Korea, for example, being introduced by the "right person" is important for establishing a relationship, as are the exchange of business cards with two hands, holding several personal meetings before starting a business relationship, or giving (inexpensive but good quality) gifts. Comparatively, in Australia, informal interactions are more common in business (for example, people are addressed by their first names and casual clothing habits are quite common), people like some small talk but then soon come to the point in meetings, and exchanging gifts is not a common practice. Learning the etiquette of the cultures with which they interact can help managers to avoid social blunders that can potentially harm business relationships.

Sources: Based on information in Lee (2012) and Martin and Chaney (2012).

Harris and Moran suggest the following **taxonomy of cultural differences** that can have an impact on the attitudes and especially also on the behavior of people:[63]

1. **Sense of self and space**: Members of different groups can differ in their self-identity (e.g. humility versus assertive, macho-like behavior) and in the degree of closeness to others that they feel comfortable with (both in terms of physical space as well as regarding the formality in relationships).

2. **Communication and language**: Basic language differences between cultures are obvious, but there are also more subtle differences, for example in jargon that is used in different professions or social strata, or in the use of non-verbal communication signals and how they are interpreted.

3. **Dress and appearance**: Different cultures have different dress codes. This does not only apply to national cultures, but also to different age groups or different professional cultures (e.g. medical doctors versus factory workers).

4. **Food and feeding habits**: What people eat and how they eat (e.g. with chopsticks, knife and fork, or by hand) can strongly differ between cultures. In many cultures, there are also food restrictions (e.g. devout Muslims are not permitted to eat pork and drink alcohol).

5. **Time and time consciousness**: People in different cultures have different senses of time. In some cultures (e.g. in Switzerland), people often follow precise, scheduled timing, while in others (e.g. in Latin America or the Middle East), time is more "elastic," and things are not necessarily done at a certain hour and minute, but rather when the time "feels right."

6 **Relationships**: How people relate to each other, in families as well as in workplaces and in public, varies from culture to culture. In China, for example, personal connections between people (*guānxi*) play a pivotal role in business life. Some cultures also put a higher emphasis on hierarchy and status than others.

7 **Values and norms**: Different cultures develop different standards of what is right or wrong, and how people should behave in relation to each other. Whereas the US is generally seen as a highly individualistic and competitive society, in which the rights of the individual rank among the highest goods, there are other cultures (e.g. in Asia) in which the well-being and cooperation of the group are generally seen as more important than the interests of the individual.

8 **Beliefs and attitudes**: Religious differences can have a powerful influence on what people believe and on how they see themselves and the world around them. General attitudes can also differ; for example, regarding the role of women and minorities in society, protecting the environment, or the preferred social order.

9 **Mental processes and learning**: In the same way as teaching and learning habits differ across cultures (e.g. in both national and professional cultures), so can the preferred use of problem-solving approaches (e.g. very methodical versus more unsystematic).

10 **Work habits and practices**: What is the role of work in life? What kind of work is more valued than others? How should work be organized? How important is self-initiative in the working environment? These are just some of the questions that will receive different answers across cultures because the way in which people see and conduct work can vary between different communities.

These ten general categories of cultural differences can help to examine how certain cultures differ from each other (see Table 5.2). Table 5.2 can also be used on a more individual level to analyze differences between a manager and an employee with a different cultural background, thus identifying areas that could cause misunderstandings or conflicts in the working relationship.[64]

Table 5.2 A framework for analyzing cultural differences

Aspects of culture	Possible questions	Own culture	Different culture
Sense of self and space	<ul><li>How do people see themselves and their role in society?</li><li>How formal is the culture?</li><li>What is the preferred level of closeness versus distance to others?</li></ul>		
Communication and language	<ul><li>Do people prefer direct or indirect communication?</li><li>What is the main language that is spoken in the culture?</li><li>What are common non-verbal communication signals?</li></ul>		
Dress and appearance	<ul><li>What is the typical dress code in this culture (business, leisure)?</li><li>What else is important in terms of appearance?</li></ul>		
Food and drinking habits	<ul><li>Are there any restrictions regarding food and drinks in this culture (e.g. religious rules)?</li><li>What are the preferred food and drinks?</li><li>How important is eating as a social experience?</li><li>How/when do people eat?</li></ul>		
Time and time consciousness	<ul><li>Is time seen as an "exact" or "elastic" concept?</li><li>How important are prompt replies in this culture?</li><li>How important is it to be on time?</li></ul>		
Relationships	<ul><li>What is the role of families in this society?</li><li>How important are relationships in business?</li><li>What is the role of hierarchy?</li></ul>		

Aspects of culture	Possible questions	Own culture	Different culture
Values and norms	• Does the emphasis lie on individuals (and independence) or on groups (and conformity)? • How are conflicts usually resolved (confrontation versus seeking harmony)? • Are rules or relationships more important? • What is taboo in this culture?		
Beliefs and attitudes	• What is the general attitude toward authority in this culture? • Which religious beliefs can have an impact on business relationships? • What is the general attitude toward gender equality?		
Mental processes and learning style	• What is the preferred problem-solving style in this culture (e.g. analytic versus bricolage)? • How do people prefer to learn?		
Work habits and practices	• What is the general role of work in life (work as a necessity versus intrinsic value of work)? • What is the status of certain types of work? • How are people usually rewarded in the working environment? • How important is self-initiative?		

Sources: Inspired by concepts in Gardenswartz and Rowe (2010); Harris and Moran (1991); Moran et al. (2011).

How can managers **learn more about other cultures**? Of course, they can attend formal cross-cultural training programs where they may examine cultural awareness case studies or participate in role plays to help explore how differences in the way that people communicate both verbally and non-ve.rbally can cause cross-cultural misunderstandings. Another way to learn about another culture is to create an open conversation around it and ask people (e.g. employees) from that particular culture to explain the cultural norms, especially trying to understand why these different norms exist. As well as speaking to colleagues who have already been immersed in the culture for a long time, managers may consult books about the nuances of the respective culture. Spending time in other cultures, and non-judgmental observations of how people with different cultural backgrounds behave and communicate can be valuable sources of information.[65] Research has shown that deep immersion experiences in other cultures, especially longer periods of working and studying abroad, can have a particularly strong effect on developing a person's cultural intelligence.[66] But managers can also try to include intercultural experiences in the day-to-day business. For example, a manager could pick a variety of different authentic ethnic restaurants to dine at if there are special team events. This would give team members the opportunity to immerse themselves in different cultures through cuisine and behavior and maybe also to explore different areas of a city which might be dominated by other ethnicities.

Intercultural communication

Understanding cultural differences is a first step to developing cultural intelligence. Culturally intelligent people can then build on their knowledge, and use it for judging specific situations, so that they are able to adapt their communicative behavior according to the needs of the situation.

For **cross-cultural communication** to succeed, the sender and receiver of a message must share a common code and use the same conventions of communicating (see Figure 5.4).[67]

The most important **code** in human communication is **language**. In a cross-cultural setting, people with different first languages interact with each other. Sometimes, they do

Figure 5.4 The communication process between people from different cultures

Source: Reprinted with permission of the publisher. Adapted from Figure 5.1, p. 88 in *Cultural Intelligence: Living and Working Globally*, 2nd edition, copyright © 2009 by David C. Thomas and Kerr Inkson, Berrett-Koehler Publishers, Inc., San Francisco, CA. All rights reserved. www.bkconnection.com. Original figure based on Schramm (1954).

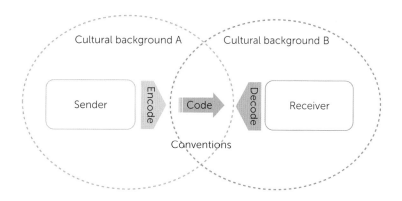

not share a language code at all (in this case, they will have to resort to translators or interpreters). Often, however, people with different first languages use English as a *lingua franca* (a sort of "bridge language"). Although this actually provides a basic common code—especially for business settings—it poses new challenges. Even if the same language is used, the words can carry different meanings (e.g. in Hong Kong, students who have an appointment with their professors say that they are "dating" them).[68] Difficulties can also arise when people who have a different level of command of the English language (for example a native speaker and a person who speaks English only at a very basic level) interact with each other. People with a better command of English can automatically assume a higher power position, which can impede the free exchange of information.[69] Techniques that managers can use to communicate more effectively with people with a limited command of the English language include using visual aids, talking slowly and with a clear pronunciation, avoiding colloquial expressions and jargon, showing the other person what they mean (e.g. demonstrating how to perform a certain task in a work situation), watching for non-verbal signs of understanding or confusion, and repeating important points.[70]

Communication conventions are particular patterns of how codes are typically used and interpreted in communication situations.[71] As previously mentioned, communication styles can vary between highly explicit in low-context cultures and implicit (with a much higher importance of the communication context) in high-context cultures. In the latter, the listener usually has to put a lot more effort into interpreting not only *what* is said but also *how* something is said. Whereas people with a low-context cultural background would probably directly say "no" to a proposal that they do not want to accept, people from high-context backgrounds would send the message in a different way; for example, through silence, a reply that does not directly answer the question, a counter question, or a statement like "I will think about it." Even in the case that the proposal is actually getting a "yes," it does not necessarily really mean consent, but could also just mean "Yes, I am listening to you."[72] The role and acceptance of silence can vary across cultures, too, as can the use and meaning of certain gestures and facial expressions, the importance of eye contact, and the acceptance of touching and certain postures during a conversation.[73] Experimental research results suggest, for example, that people from an East Asian culture (in which eye contact is less common) tend to perceive another person's face as more unpleasant when making eye contact than people from a Western European culture (in which eye contact is more common).[74]

Different conventions can also play a role in **intercultural negotiations**. Not only can different parties misinterpret words or non-verbal signals, but there are also different negotiation styles (see Chapter 4). In some cultures (e.g. the US), the aim of negotiating is to reach a contractual agreement, while in others (e.g. some Asian countries), it is often not the signed contract but rather the established relationship that counts.[75] Cultures can also differ in terms of having a zero-sum versus a win–win attitude to negotiations (i.e. in their preference for either competition or harmony), in the desired degree of formality of negotiations, in sensitivity to time, in the preferred sequence of discussing issues (sequential versus simultaneous), in the preference for rational arguments versus emotional appeals, or in the preferred form of agreement (rather general or very specific and detailed).[76] Authority and hierarchical structures within a negotiation team can also vary, especially between cultures with higher and lower power distance. It is therefore important to understand the decision making and power structures of the different negotiation parties. Knowing who can make binding commitments can be important for reaching an agreement.

The way that people perceive **conflict situations** can also be culture bound. Conflicts can be seen as a disruption of harmony or as a risk of **"losing face,"** which people in certain cultures (especially in Asian and Middle Eastern countries) would usually prefer to avoid at all costs.[77] Managers should try to avoid all potential embarrassment for others (especially in front of others) in cultures that put a strong emphasis on "saving face."

In order to **communicate and negotiate effectively across cultural boundaries**, managers can follow a few simple rules:[78]

1   Try to learn about and understand the other culture.
2   Do not assume that everyone who is associated with a culture is thinking and behaving in the same way (i.e. avoid stereotyping).
3   Try to bridge the cultural gap, either through carefully adopting some elements of the other person's culture, making cultural differences explicit to foster a common understanding of these differences, or trying to create a distinct cooperation culture that integrates elements of different cultures.

Building bridges between different cultures is a key task for 21st-century managers who want to become effective in a globalized business world.

Haier: How a Chinese company overcame cross-cultural challenges in Japan

In 1984, Zhang Ruimin took control of the loss-making Qingdao General Refrigerator Factory in Qingdao, China (later renamed to Haier). Zhang quickly steered the company on a qualitative growth path. According to a story that is still often told in Haier, Zhang had 76 defective refrigerators sledgehammered to "hammer home" the importance of quality to his staff. A joint venture with the German appliance maker Liebherr helped the company to acquire the necessary technology to develop and produce quality refrigerators. Riding the waves of China's rapid economic expansion, Haier soon established itself as the market leader in China.

With the opening of the Chinese economy following China's accession into the World Trade Organization in 2001, Haier followed a deliberate internationalization strategy with the aim of developing a global brand. The basic idea was to start with more difficult and

developed markets in order to learn how to compete with the world's most advanced household appliance manufacturers. Haier tried to adapt to local needs (e.g. through the investment into local R&D and design centers) and often relied on experienced local staff to run its foreign operations.

In 2002, Haier entered the Japanese market through an alliance with the established local player Sanyo Electric Co. The alliance was later formalized as a joint venture. The two companies reciprocally opened their sales and distribution channels for each other in China and Japan. The alliance helped Haier to establish its brand name on the Japanese market, but the market share remained very low compared to the big Japanese brands. In general, Japan was seen as a market that was very difficult to penetrate, as Japanese consumers traditionally showed a strong preference for local brands and had very high demands regarding product quality. In 2012, in what was later called a "milestone event" in its corporate history, Haier fully acquired Sanyo's washing machine and consumer-use refrigerator business in Japan, along with subsidiaries in Indonesia, Malaysia, the Philippines, and Vietnam.

The manager who was put in charge of the integration of Sanyo into Haier group was Du Jingguo, vice president of Haier Group. Du, a Chinese native who had lived in Japan for several years, was married to a Japanese woman and had also been responsible for the Haier–Sanyo joint venture. In the press release that announced the takeover which transferred 3,100 employees from Sanyo to Haier, Du saw "the integration of cultures and management philosophies"[79] as the key success factor for the acquisition and pointed out Haier's determination to respect local cultures. The integration seemed likely to become a challenging task because there were fears that Haier would just want to snatch away Sanyo's technology, and because this was a meeting of two very different cultures.

Sanyo was a typical Japanese company in which lifelong employment and promotion based on seniority and length of service were the norm. In contrast, Haier had a strong merits-based culture that encouraged and rewarded individual performance. "Complete obedience to leaders" had to be replaced by "complete obedience to customers,"[80] as Haier's management system was based on an "inverted triangle." In this approach, the team members who were directly in touch with customers (in the fields of manufacturing, marketing, and R&D) were regarded as "their own CEOs,"[81] who were assisted by a number of support functions and a top management team that was in charge of identifying and developing new strategic opportunities.

Du also met resistance when he wanted to introduce incentives for individual performance, as Sanyo's managers and employees emphasized values like equality and team spirit, based on Japan's collectivist culture. One employee also said he was afraid that the new system "may create a division between those who enjoy the system more, especially younger people, and those who have worked too many years under the Sanyo system."[82]

Du was fully aware of these cultural challenges. When he assumed the responsibility for Haier's Japanese operations, he divided the workers into smaller teams and would go out drinking with one of these teams every few nights (in Japan, it is usual practice that managers take a deep interest in their subordinates' personal situations).[83] One result of these nightly efforts was that Du developed a gastric ulcer. More importantly, however, he gained a deep understanding of the employees' attitudes and concerns, which helped him to take the company on a smooth transition path. For example, he gave senior people honorary titles along with new responsibilities when he promoted younger employees based on their higher performance. Du did not force people into Haier's individualized compensation system, but tried to convince them in long discussions that sometimes took several months. When he wanted his Japanese team to set and achieve higher sales targets, Du refrained from imposing them. Instead, he asked his people what constraints they saw and their suggestions about how to best deal with these constraints. In a joint effort, the team found several ideas to overcome existing obstacles, leading to significant increases in both sales targets and actual revenues. "As a manager, I can issue an order," Du was cited in the *Financial Times*, "but if people don't agree in their hearts, the order will be meaningless."[84]

Haier managed to turn around the loss-making Japanese business within one year. The lessons from the Sanyo acquisition formed the basis for Haier's further successful international expansion. Haier Group's acquisition of GE Appliances in the US in 2016 further strengthened its position as the global market leader in household appliances with sales in over 100 different countries.

Sources: Clegg (2017); haier.net (2011; 2017); iese.com (2013); Sánchez-Runde et al. (2012; 2013).

💬 Discussion questions

- What were the main cultural challenges and intercultural conflicts that Haier faced during the integration of Sanyo?
- How did Du try to tackle these challenges? How would you assess the effectiveness of his approach?
- Would the way in which Haier managed the Sanyo integration also work in other cultures (e.g. for the GE Appliance integration in the US)?
- Should Haier try to enforce its management culture across all countries, or would you suggest a stronger adaptation that better reflects the diversity of local cultural traditions?

5.3 Managing global virtual teams

Getty Images/Image Source

In brief

- As global virtual teams with team members from different nationalities based in various locations around the world are becoming a common means of collaborating in organizations that operate across borders, managers need to familiarize themselves with the benefits and challenges of such teams.

- In addition to the tasks that leaders of all teams face, leaders of global virtual teams also need to manage diversity, use electronic communication technology effectively, and put special emphasis on making individual and team contributions visible in the organization.

- Clear team norms regarding communication, expected contributions, and the use of communication technology form the basis of a well-functioning global virtual team.

As companies extend their geographical reach and as communication technologies become more and more sophisticated, global virtual teams proliferate. Recent surveys among knowledge workers report that at least three-quarters of the respondents say that they have experience with working in virtual teams.[85] These teams can be a means of bridging space and time. They open new possibilities for organizations—from combining talents in different parts of the world to increased productivity through saving office and travel costs—as they remove restrictions imposed by the constraint of one physical location. It is quite challenging to manage such diverse and geographically dispersed teams, though. One study that was conducted among 70 global teams, for example, revealed that 82 percent of the teams did not reach their intended goals and one-third were even considered as being largely unsuccessful.[86] It is therefore important for managers to familiarize themselves with the specifics of global virtual teams if they want to use and lead them effectively.

A **global virtual team** can be defined as "a temporary, culturally diverse, geographically dispersed, electronically communicating work group"[87] with a shared purpose. It differs from a traditional co-located team along the following five dimensions (see Figure 5.5):

- **Communication channel**: A global virtual team relies mainly on electronic communication tools such as e-mail, chat rooms, social media, cloud-based file- and application-sharing platforms, group calendar and group decision support systems, and teleconferencing or videoconferencing. In these teams, face-to-face meetings are rare or non-existent.
- **Location**: A global virtual team is not bound to a certain place, but brings together people who are spread over different countries and continents.
- **Culture**: With team members from around the world, a global virtual team usually has a high degree of cultural diversity. Intercultural communication skills (see Section 5.2) are therefore particularly important for leaders and members of global virtual teams.
- **Language**: Along with cultural differences, members of global virtual teams usually have different first languages and a different degree of proficiency in the team's working language.
- **Time**: Time zone differences and the use of asynchronous media (e.g. e-mail or group discussion forums) make non-simultaneous communication more common in global virtual teams.

As in any other team, the members of a global virtual team need to effectively communicate and collaborate in order to accomplish certain organizational tasks. Members of a global virtual team must also be able to handle the technological complexity, high levels of diversity, and challenges that distance (in all dimensions) brings along.

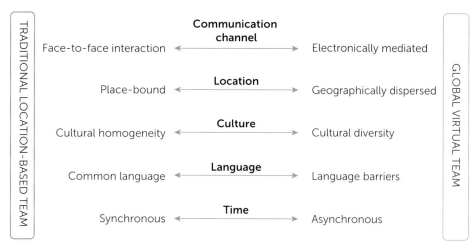

Figure 5.5 Differences between traditional location-based and global virtual teams

Benefits and challenges of global virtual teams

There are a range of **advantages of global virtual teams** over traditional, location-based teams:[88]

- Teams can be formed independently of the location of the individual team members.
- They can bring exceptional talent with complementary competencies together from all over the world and allow organizations to recruit the best people regardless of their physical location.
- They help to save on the travel and real estate costs of having a single office location.
- Through reducing travel, they can also contribute to a reduction in the organization's ecological footprint.
- They enable faster project completion and a reduction of the time-to-market cycle by means of "following the sun" in a 24-hour relay workflow (e.g. team members in the Asia-Pacific region pass the work on to their colleagues in Europe or Africa after they finish their working day, with the American colleagues taking over until they hand the baton across the Pacific).
- They can take advantage of all the benefits of a diverse team such as bringing a range of different perspectives, expertise, and knowledge together, thereby avoiding groupthink, having higher creativity and innovation potential, or having access to a wider range of networks and information sources (see also Section 5.1).
- They can make use of all the possibilities that modern information and communication technology offers (e.g. having instant access to all desktop, intra-organizational, and Internet resources at a fingertip).
- They can create motivation and job satisfaction, especially for people who like to work with greater autonomy.
- They can provide additional opportunities for the inclusion of people with special needs (e.g. physical disadvantages) into teams.
- They make it easier for people to contribute to several teams.

Channel richness: The extent to which a communication channel or technology allows the transmission of verbal and non-verbal information.

Despite the many advantages of global virtual teams, there are also some drawbacks. The main **challenges** that can be faced with such boundary-spanning collaboration structures are:[89]

- Electronic communication channels lack the media **channel richness** of face-to-face encounters, thus making it harder for the team to transfer tacit knowledge and to use and interpret non-verbal communication signals.

- Time zone differences can slow down communication and require higher coordination efforts, especially regarding finding the right time for synchronous (video) conference calls (in consideration of the needs of all team members and their families in different time zones).
- Language differences can create further communication barriers—this might also become a problem when team members with a lower level of language proficiency are not able to fully contribute their expertise.
- Cultural differences can lead to misunderstandings and biases, which, in turn, can have negative effects on group dynamics.
- It can be more difficult to build relationships and trust over a physical distance because there is less opportunity for socializing, which is generally seen as an important factor in building a well-functioning team (there is no "virtual watercooler").
- Social cohesion forces can be weaker in geographically dispersed virtual teams, which can result in lower commitment to the team and in social loafing (see Chapter 4).
- Differences in the institutional environment (e.g. different rules, different performance appraisal systems, or the different expectations of the local management) can pose further difficulties because team members may lack insight and understanding of their colleagues' local contexts.
- Local priorities might override the team priorities (the "out of sight, out of mind" effect), especially if reward systems are not aligned so that team members' contributions to the success of the virtual teamwork are not adequately included.
- Virtual teams are dependent on a well-functioning technological infrastructure on the sites of all team members, and setting up and maintaining such infrastructure can be costly. Additional training is often needed in order to ensure that the technology can be used effectively.
- Not everyone is suited to working in global virtual teams. Communication skills, emotional intelligence, a certain degree of openness, cultural sensitivity, and the ability to work independently are preconditions for becoming a valuable member of a global virtual team.

Some of the disadvantages of virtual teams can also become more pronounced in specific cultural settings. In high-context cultures, for example, the absence of non-verbal clues in electronic communication channels could pose higher challenges than in low-context cultures.[90] For representatives of cultures with a higher level of power distance, it might also be difficult to interact in an environment where there are fewer social cues about the social status of individual team members.

If you were to lead a global virtual team, could you formulate five rules for yourself that could help you to effectively address the challenges that such a geographically dispersed team arrangement entails? Write down the rules that you would use by following this template: *As a team leader, I will...* and *As a team leader, I will not...*

Leadership tasks in a global virtual team

Despite their idiosyncrasies, virtual teams remain—above all—teams. Therefore, leaders of global virtual teams generally face all the tasks and challenges that team leaders of co-located teams face. For example, they have to ensure that the team develops a unified sense of purpose, formulate clear goals and set the agenda, align tasks and strengths, make sure that everyone finds their specific role in the team, develop and support individual group members, build trust among team members, manage conflicts if they arise, shape the norms and culture of their team, and keep in touch with project sponsors in senior management ranks to ensure that there are adequate resources and support to be able to fulfill the team's purpose (see Chapter 4 for more details on effective team leadership). Some leadership tasks are more difficult to accomplish in global virtual teams due to the specific challenges that arise from geographical distance, technology-bound communication, and cultural differences.

Based on a combination of survey data and an in-depth analysis of several dozen virtual teams, Arvind Malhotra and his colleagues have identified **six leadership practices of effective leaders of virtual teams**:[91]

1 **Establishing trust between team members** through setting and repeatedly emphasizing clear team norms; for example, requiring team members to regularly upload their work outputs so that everyone can see the progress, and rotating teleconference times in order to equally distribute the "suffering" from "unsuitable" work times across time zones. (See Table 5.3 for an overview of norms that members of a global virtual team might agree upon.) Regular meetings that are devoted to discussing the quality of the team process help in reexamining norms and reminding everyone of the shared purpose of the team. If possible, holding at least a few face-to-face meetings can also help to build trust among team members.

2 **Ensuring that everyone understands and embraces diversity.** Expertise directories (with team members' knowledge and experience profiles) or a **skills matrix** that is easily accessible on the **team's repository** can help everyone to appreciate the specific competencies of their fellow team members and understand why they are included in the team. Leaders can also put small sub-teams (each consisting of two team members from very different backgrounds) in charge of certain tasks on a rotating basis. Thus, team members have the chance to get to know each other more closely.

3 **Ensuring that virtual meetings are well managed.** Effective leaders put strong emphasis on preparing the meeting (including summarizing the status of the main tasks, sending out an agenda to all team members, and making sure that everyone reports their progress on the team's repository prior to the meeting), give team members the opportunity to "reconnect" personally with a bit of small talk at the beginning of the meeting, involve all team members during the conference call (e.g. through using online voting tools or asking questions that can be answered by everyone using an instant messaging tool), and document and distribute the results (decisions and to-do lists) immediately after the meeting.

4 **Using technology to monitor team progress.** When they notice that individual team members are not adequately contributing on the team platform according to what was agreed, effective virtual team leaders are quick to follow up, investigate, and discuss problems with the "underperformers." It has also been suggested that managers should always try to make sure that all team members have multiple tasks so that they can turn to another task when they are held up on their priority task (in case one team member does not deliver the agreed output on time).[92]

5 **Ensuring the external visibility of the team.** Effective leaders try to understand the expectations that the local managers of their team members hold and establish a systematic "report out" routine to keep all sponsoring managers informed about the progress of the team.

6 **Ensuring that all team members see the benefits of being part of the team**, for example, through praise, public recognition, virtual celebrations of individual and group accomplishments, rewards for successes, informing local managers about the positive contributions of team members from their units, and making sure that team activities themselves are both interesting and an opportunity for individual team members to grow.

When managers introduce a reward system for members of a global virtual team, they also need to take cultural differences into account. People from an individualistic culture often prefer to be rewarded for their individual contribution, while in more collectivistic societies, an equal distribution of rewards for the team success might be considered as more

Skills matrix:
An overview of the knowledge, skills, and competencies of all members of a team.

Team's repository:
A virtual (computer-based) central place in which all the important documents that a team needs for effective collaboration are stored and to which all team members have access.

Table 5.3 Team norms for global virtual teams

Category of team norms	Examples
Rules for conducting teleconferences and videoconferences	• Clarifying the tasks of the moderator of a virtual meeting • Saying one's name before making a contribution • Distributing an agenda before the meeting • Assigning a person who is responsible for taking and distributing minutes
Clear timeframes	• How promptly should e-mails, telephone calls, and other messages be answered?
Attendance rules for meetings	• General obligation to attend team meetings • Full attendance during the meeting instead of engaging in multitasking
Meeting scheduling procedures	• How often are synchronous meetings held? • Which group-scheduling system is used? • Agreement on a rotation of meeting times to cater for the needs of team members in different time zones
Standards for task completion	• Clear definition of what is meant by "successful completion" of assigned tasks • Everyone holds to deadlines • Inform everyone in plenty of time when a deadline cannot be met
Standards for the use of electronic tools	• Which tools are used for what communication purposes (e.g. use one-to-one video calls instead of e-mails for discussing sensitive interpersonal issues)? • How to deal with software updates in order to avoid incompatibilities • Rules for e-mail messages (e.g. whom to include as recipients, when to flag them as "urgent")
Communication rules	• Offering suggestions instead of criticizing others • Trying to keep a friendly and positive tone • Highlighting action items in e-mail communication
Documentation and reporting rules	• Who reports what to whom at what frequency? • Guidelines about the use of (electronic) documentation and reporting systems

Sources: Inspired by concepts in Berry (2011; 2014); Duarte and Snyder (2006); Hill and Bartol (2018).

Synchronous media:
Means of conveying messages in real time (i.e. the sender and receiver of the message are present at the same time).

Asynchronous media:
Means of conveying messages in a way that does not require the sender and the receiver to be present at the same time.

adequate.[93] In general, rewards for group success are more conducive to creating a cooperative rather than a competitive spirit in the team.

A particularly important task for leaders of virtual teams is to find the right **balance between the use of** synchronous and asynchronous media. Teleconferences or videoconferences are often seen as the "lifeblood" of virtual teams because they provide an opportunity to keep team members engaged and aligned toward achieving a common purpose.[94] Synchronous interactions in channels with higher media richness can help to add the personal touch that it takes to build trust and good working relationships within the team. Asynchronous media (e.g. e-mail and discussion forums) can have advantages for non-native English speakers, as they have more time to express their thoughts and decode the messages of other team members. Thus, for example, using e-mails can reduce miscommunication in cross-cultural virtual teams.[95] It is not a good idea, however, to try to resolve interpersonal issues over e-mail or chat rooms—richer media are more appropriate in this case.[96]

In between the virtual meetings, team members can use electronic discussion forums or shared documents to develop and refine ideas.[97] It has also been suggested that team leaders should use a technique called **"weaving"** to summarize the discussion thread and try to distill the lessons and potential next steps.[98] This means to give all team members a regular summary update (e.g. in the form of an e-mail or discussion group posting) of what has happened so far, where the team stands now, and where it could—and should—go from here.

A whole range of **digital tools** are now available to foster smooth communication and collaboration within a virtual team. Examples include document sharing and document management tools (such as Dropbox, Microsoft Sharepoint, or Google Drive), instant messaging tools (such as Slack or Google Hangouts Chat), task management tools (such as Trello, Asana, or Basecamp), meeting tools (such as GoToMeeting, Zoom, or Adobe Connect), and intra-organizational social network and intranet software (such as Yammer or Jive).

Whatever specific software tools are used, managers of virtual team leaders need to ensure that **communication lines are kept open** between them and their team members as well as among team members. Uneven distribution of information can have negative effects on the motivation of team members—it is therefore important to "keep everyone in the loop."[99] This can be achieved either by establishing a regular timetable for virtual meetings in which all team members participate or by setting up virtual one-to-one meetings with team members who have fewer opportunities to connect informally with the team leader.

Succinctly expressing one's thoughts in carefully composed and unambiguous messages is a precondition for **establishing a good communication flow** in multicultural teams.[100] It is also important to avoid joking, judgmental comments, or taking an ironic tone that could either be misinterpreted due to a lack of non-verbal contextual clues or perceived as a loss of "face" by team members with a different cultural background.[101] The box *Zooming in on effective communication strategies for cross-cultural teams* provides further advice on how to overcome cultural challenges in global virtual teams.

Zooming in on ▶ EFFECTIVE COMMUNICATION STRATEGIES FOR CROSS-CULTURAL TEAMS

In order to overcome cultural challenges in global virtual teams, Yael Zofi suggests five cross-cultural communication strategies that she succinctly summarized under the acronym *LEARN*:[102]

1 *Listen carefully* and ask questions to really understand what the other person wants to say.
2 *Effectively communicate* by offering balanced feedback, using positive and reinforcing messages, building on ideas, and carefully weighing words in order to avoid exacerbating conflict situations.
3 *Avoid ambiguity*, for example through sharing information about team members' cultural backgrounds or including feedback loops to ensure that a message is well understood.
4 *Respect differences*, be open to seeing things differently and avoid overgeneralizations, stereotyping, and the "be like me"[103] demand.
5 *No (premature) judgment*, but try to describe and interpret the situation and then carefully and objectively make an evaluation rather than rushing to a conclusion.

Imagine yourself as a leader or a member of a global virtual team. What can you do to ensure effective collaboration between all team members?

The team leader must also ensure that every team member has access to the required hardware and software and that everyone is **adequately trained** on using the technology to be able to participate fully. Further training on the basics of effective communication in both virtual and intercultural settings might also be needed.

Skills for managing global virtual teams

In order to lead a global virtual team effectively, managers require a specific set of skills. In addition to **intercultural communication skills** (which we discussed in Section 5.2), managers of virtual teams need to develop:

- **Virtual communication skills**. These include the ability to match the technology to the task[104] as well as proficiency in using the LEARN framework as described in the box *Zooming in on effective communication strategies for cross-cultural teams*. Communication is the "glue" of every team. A major precondition for the glue to stick, however, is that all team members also understand the messages that their colleagues want to get across to them. With a lack of the non-verbal information that lies in facial expression and body language, managers of virtual teams must be able to communicate very clearly and in a simple and understandable language in both verbal and written form. Research results show that making your intentions "crystal clear" is very important for effective collaboration in virtual teams.[105] Therefore, managers also need to encourage everyone to ask direct and specific questions instead of making assumptions about what other people want.[106] Needless to say, managers also need good listening skills when there are fewer facial and gestural clues available, as well as the ability to refrain from making premature assumptions about others.

- **Virtual socialization skills**. Leaders of virtual teams must ensure that new team members are included in the team as quickly as possible so that they can contribute to the team's success. New team members should receive all important information when they join; for example, about the team's purpose and goals, the main stakeholders, the distribution of tasks between team members, the timeline of a project, the communication channels that are usually used, and the core values of the team. At the same time, it is important not to overload the onboarding team members with too much information. Newcomers usually go through a socialization process in which they learn to adapt to the values and norms of the team. Learning the "technical" norms such as meeting schedule or reporting procedures is relatively straightforward, as they are quite easy to communicate. It is more challenging, however, to understand the social norms of the group (like work-related values and expectations that team members hold) because it is difficult to convey this type of information through electronic media and in the absence of non-verbal clues.[107] This is another reason why managers of virtual teams need to develop the ability to substitute the information that is tacitly conveyed (usually through the silent observation of others) in co-located group settings with a more explicit form of communication (for example, through establishing clear behavioral guidelines or providing answers to frequently asked questions regarding team norms).[108] Another way of ensuring that newcomers understand the social norms of the team is to partner them with experienced team members.[109]

- **Virtual collaboration skills**. When all team members are on board, managers need to motivate and facilitate effective collaboration within the team. First and foremost, this means establishing trust between team members. In virtual teams, trust building can be fostered, for example, by open communication in a positive tone, knowledge sharing, timely responses to other team members' requests, and giving positive feedback.[110] Being able to create a positive social atmosphere is as important for building a good collaborative environment as making sure that everyone understands the focal team task, their own contribution toward completing this task, and the progress that is made on the team's goals.[111] Some team leaders deliberately schedule social events such as "virtual coffee chats" or make sure that team members have the opportunity to chat informally before an official conference call in order to cultivate positive social interactions.[112] This is also important because some team members might hesitate to contribute if they fear being criticized by others.[113] As in traditional co-located teams, it is important for managers of virtual teams to have team leadership skills—not only in terms of supporting the team on its way to achieving the task but also in ensuring team cohesion and taking care of the needs of individual team members (see Chapter 4). This also means not forgetting to recognize the individual efforts of remote team members.

Global virtual teams only become fully productive if they use the full potential of all of their team members. Intercultural and virtual communication skills, virtual socialization skills, and virtual collaboration skills are the basis for enabling managers to create the open and inclusive atmosphere in which everyone in the team has the feeling that their voice counts and their contribution matters.

5.4 Business and management ethics across cultures

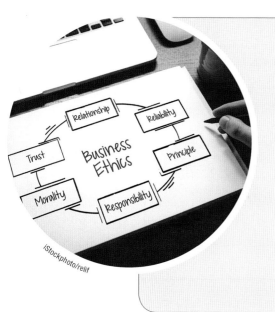

iStockphoto/relif

In brief

● When they work across cultures and in an environment where interests collide, managers can face situations in which they have to decide what is the right (or ethical) course of action.

● Managers can resort to basic ethical principles when they try to find answers to moral dilemmas. Examples of basic ethical principles are "Maximize the overall good" (utilitarianism), "Respect others' rights" (rights approach), "Ensure a fair distribution of benefits and burdens" (justice approach), "Exhibit care for others—especially those who are dependent on you" (ethics of care), or "Find solutions in a fair discourse" (discourse ethics).

● As moral standards can vary across cultures, managers can use human rights as the ultimate yardstick. They can also establish codes of conduct for their organizations and use other instruments for guiding their team's ethical behavior.

Various scandals and reports on corporate misconduct (e.g. concerning accounting fraud, exploiting child labor, inhumane working conditions, bribery and other corrupt practices, environmental pollution, discrimination in the workplace, or deceiving customers) highlight the importance of ethics in an organizational context. A study based on an analysis of news reports revealed that 40 percent of Fortune 100 companies have been associated with

Unethical behavior:
Behavior that violates general principles of what is deemed as morally right or proper behavior.

unethical behavior.[114] And that is only the tip of the iceberg, the instances that made it into the news. Besides the newsworthy scandals, managers face countless ethical issues in their day-to-day work because they need to consider the potentially harmful consequences of their everyday decisions and actions. When their organizations are active across borders, they can also be confronted with different employment and environmental protection standards, corrupt practices, disrespect for human rights, or—more generally—different moral standards and ethical traditions.

Before we discuss basic ethical principles and how to deal with different ethical standards in a cross-cultural context, we first need to define two key terms:

Moral standards:
Norms and beliefs that individuals or groups hold about what kind of actions are deemed right or wrong.

● **Moral standards** are norms and beliefs that individuals or groups hold about what kind of actions are deemed right or wrong.

● **Ethics** is the process of conscious deliberation about moral issues (i.e. about what is right or wrong, "good" or "evil," or a virtue or a vice) and is concerned with finding and applying principles that help to determine and defend what the right action is beyond an individual's moral intuition.[115]

Ethics:
The process of conscious deliberation about what is morally right or wrong.

Typically, there are four steps that lead to **ethical action** (see Figure 5.6):[116]

1 **Awareness**: A situation first needs to be recognized as an ethical situation. Usually, this means that we understand that the outcomes of a decision or an intended course of action could have harmful effects on others.

2 **Judgment**: Once we have recognized that we face an ethical issue, we can try to build our judgment on what is the right course of action based on moral standards and ethical principles. It is important to keep in mind that our judgment is also based on the information that we have about the situation, and that the information base could also be incomplete, biased, or distorted. In this context, it also matters how decision problems are framed (see also the *From a different angle* box).

3 **Decision**: It is not enough to know what the right course of action could be. We also need to take the decision to actually do what is right. This decision can be influenced by the social situation (e.g. the "ethics climate" in the organization) and other situational constraints.

4 **Implementation**: Finally, to act in an ethically correct way, good intentions need to be translated into real action. We need to overcome social pressures and maybe also internal drives and emotions to do the right thing, even if it might not be the easiest option or maybe even leads to personal costs.

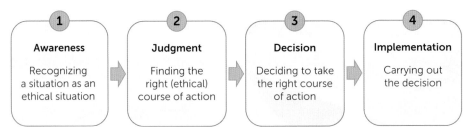

Figure 5.6 Four steps to ethical behavior

Source: Inspired by concepts in Velasquez (2014), pp. 49–56.

| FROM A DIFFERENT ANGLE |

How ethical decision problems are framed matters

The two famous psychologists Amos Tversky and Daniel Kahneman conducted an interesting experiment in which they presented a moral dilemma to two groups of people. For the first group, they framed the problem in the following way: You can decide between two programs that aim to save people from a highly contagious disease which is expected to kill 600 people: Program A will save 200 people. With Program B, there is a 1/3 possibility that everyone will be saved and a 2/3 probability that no one will be saved. The second group was told a slightly different story. They could also decide between two programs that would potentially save people from a highly contagious disease which is expected to kill 600 people. With the adoption of Program C, 400 people would die. With Program D, there is a 1/3 possibility that no one will die and a 2/3 probability that everyone will die. All of the programs lead to the same expected outcome. Nevertheless, 72 percent of the respondents decided for Program A and 28 percent for Program B in the first group, while only 22 percent voted for Program C and 78 percent for Program D in the second group. Exactly the same moral dilemma—just presented in a different way—was judged completely differently by the two test groups. From this example, we can see that it matters how ethical decision problems are communicated or framed.

Source: Based on information in Tversky and Kahneman (1981).

We will now review basic principles that can guide managers' judgments and decisions when they are faced with ethical issues.

Basic ethical principles

It is not always easy to determine what is right or wrong in a particular situation. There are, however, several basic ethical principles that can help managers to reflect on moral dilemmas (see Figure 5.7 for an overview). Each of these principles is based on a distinct tradition of moral philosophy.

Utilitarianism refers to the idea that any actions, policies, or decisions should be focused on maximizing "utility" (i.e. benefits over burdens) for society as a whole. According to Jeremy Bentham (1748–1832), who together with John Stuart Mill (1806–1873) is considered the main proponent of utilitarianism, we should strive to create "the greatest happiness for the greatest number."[117] Managers who follow a utilitarian approach will try to find out what

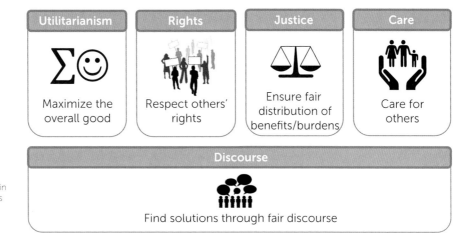

Figure 5.7 Basic ethical principles

Sources: Inspired by concepts in Velasquez (2014), p. 131. Images by OpenClipart-Vectors and Clker-Free-Vector-Images (Justice image) from Pixabay.

the choices are in a particular situation, assess the benefits and costs for everyone affected, and decide on the option with the highest net utility (the result of subtracting the sum of the costs from the sum of the benefits). Although the general principle sounds simple in theory, it is not easy to use in practice. Certain values, benefits, and costs are difficult if not impossible to measure (values like health, love, equality, or life are salient examples).[118] Moreover, solutions that are found through thinking in terms of maximizing net utility can potentially violate the rights of individuals or lead to unfair treatment, because some individuals could get a bigger share of benefits or burdens than others.[119]

A different tradition of ethical reasoning builds on the idea that every individual has certain **moral or human rights**. This approach focuses on the legitimate interests of individuals rather than on aggregated utility at a group or societal level. The philosopher Immanuel Kant (1724–1804) succinctly summarized rights-based thinking in his famous **categorical imperative**: "Act so that the maxim of thy will can always at the same time hold good as a principle of universal legislation."[120] In other words, think about what would happen if everyone acted like you want to act. Kant also reminds us never to treat humanity merely as a means but to always see it as an end in itself.[121] Thus, he points out the inherent value and worth of human beings (also known as **human dignity**) that goes hand in hand with the right of every human being to be treated with respect and equal to everyone else. Respecting the rights of others is not only an ethical maxim, however. It also has a practical effect on the performance of teams and organizations. In their study of 238 professionals from 26 project teams, Teresa Amabile and Steven Kramer observed that treating team members decently as human beings was one of the two basic managerial behaviors that had the most positive influence on people's work performance (the other one was enabling them to move forward in their work).[122] Kant's precepts are not without limitations, however. People with different cultural backgrounds might have divergent opinions about which behavior could qualify as a universal law. The imperative to always respect the rights of all other people might also lead to an impasse when different equally valuable rights collide (e.g. the rights of different stakeholder groups).

A third basic principle of ethical reasoning is **justice** or **fairness**. We can distinguish between **distributive justice** (perceived fairness in distributing benefits and burdens within a certain group or society) and **procedural justice** (the perceived fairness of the procedures that lead to certain outcomes).[123] The principles of justice and fairness are actually based on the acknowledgment of individual moral rights. If we agree that every individual has the right to be treated as a free and equal person, we will also try to make sure that there is an equal distribution of benefits and burdens.[124] As we discussed in Chapter 3, the perception of fairness can also have a strong effect on the motivation (and especially the demotivation) of people. Therefore, it is important for managers to ensure that their decisions and actions are perceived as fair by the members of their team. Managers also need to consider that there are

Human dignity:
The idea that every single person has an inherent value and the right to be treated with respect and equal to everyone else.

Distributive justice:
Perceived fairness in distributing benefits and burdens within a certain group or society.

Procedural justice:
Perceived fairness of the procedures that a group of people use to achieve certain outcomes.

cross-cultural differences in justice perception. For example, a study has shown that distributive justice was more strongly related to overall fairness perception for Chinese and Koreans than for Americans and Japanese, and that it is also more likely for Americans than for Chinese and Koreans to quit their jobs when they feel unfairly treated.[125] Managers cannot assume that everyone will perceive the fairness of certain actions and policies in the same way. If they are aware of the cultural differences, however, they can adjust their behavior accordingly (e.g. making sure that rewards are more equally distributed in the form of a team bonus rather than using highly diverging individual bonuses when they work with predominantly Chinese or Korean teams).

In her work on women's moral reasoning, Carol Gilligan highlights the importance of the concepts of **responsibility** and **care**. She describes another moral imperative that is based on "an injunction to care, a responsibility to discern and alleviate the 'real and recognizable trouble' of this world."[126] Following an **"ethics of care"** means caring for the well-being and avoiding the harm of people who are close and important to us, especially those who depend on us.[127] For managers this could mean, for example, feeling responsible for the well-being of the members of their team or standing behind them if they are attacked by others. On the downside, this approach can lead to favoring people who are closer to ourselves over those who are more distant, which often happens in organizations but can come into conflict with Kant's categorical imperative and fairness demands.

Depending on the basis of our ethical reasoning—whether it is utilitarianism, the rights approach, striving for justice, or ethics of care—we can come to different conclusions when we face ethical dilemmas. This problem can be aggravated in an intercultural context, for example, when different rights or fairness perceptions collide. The German philosopher Jürgen Habermas proposed the principle of **discourse ethics** that can be of help in such situations. According to Habermas, only those moral norms on which all the affected parties can agree can be considered valid. Such an agreement should be reached through a process of "practical discourse."[128] He emphasizes the importance of a rational process of argumentation in which people can put forward their viewpoints free of constraints and coercion.[129] In an organizational context, managers can, for example, encourage team members to express their views freely and put all arguments on the table, perhaps through giving every team member a voice and acknowledging their contributions even if they differ from the manager's own opinion on a certain issue. Although applying discourse ethics can lead to conclusions even in cases where different ethical principles collide, the concept also has its limitations. It is based on the assumption of full rationality (i.e. that people always put forward logical arguments), equality and objectivity, and on the premise that the viewpoints of all affected parties are considered and equally valued. These assumptions will hardly pass the reality test in an organizational context where bounded rationality, personal interests, and power games often prevail.

Despite their limitations, the approaches to ethical reasoning that were briefly discussed here can help managers in making moral judgments. A summary of the main questions that managers could ask themselves in difficult situations involving an ethical issue is provided in the box *Zooming in on dealing with an ethical dilemma*.

Zooming in on ▶ DEALING WITH AN ETHICAL DILEMMA

When you are facing a situation that you perceive as an ethical dilemma (a decision situation in which moral principles come into conflict with each other), you can try to collect as much factual information as possible about the situation and then ask yourself the following questions:[130]

1 Who is affected by the decision and what are the consequences for the individual stakeholder groups? Which action could maximize the benefits and minimize the burdens for all stakeholder groups? (*Utilitarianism*)

2 Does the action that I am considering respect the rights of those who are affected? (*Rights*)

3 Does the action ensure that benefits and burdens are distributed in a fair way? (*Justice*)

4 Is the action in line with my responsibility to care for the well-being of people who are in a close relationship with us or dependent on us? (*Ethics of care*)

5 Did we come up with the solution to the ethical dilemma in an open discourse in which the viewpoints of all affected parties have been adequately considered? (*Discourse ethics*)

Dealing with different ethical standards

Because values differ in different cultures, so do ethical standards. What is perceived as right in one culture might well be seen as wrong in another. When managers work across cultures, with business partners or team members from other countries, they can be confronted with different attitudes on moral issues. Environmental protection or labor standards can, for example, vary significantly between developing and developed countries. Different levels of tolerance of corrupt practices (e.g. bribery) are another salient example. The reasons for the differences in ethical standards could either lie in conflicts of relative economic development (e.g. low wage levels in developing countries) or in conflicting cultural traditions (e.g. a different view on women's rights in Europe and some Islamic countries).[131] This raises the question of how managers can approach ethical dilemmas that arise from such conflicting standards in a cross-cultural context.

Your mechanical engineering company is competing to supply machines to a customer in a country with much lower labor safety standards than your own. These standards apply to the assembly workers who are assembling the machines (which can be quite a dangerous process) that you are hoping to sell. You always try to uphold your home country's standards when you do business abroad, although this is not legally required. In this particular case, however, you fear that you would lose a rare opportunity to establish your company in a potentially very lucrative market if you make an offer that completely complies with your home country's labor safety standards for assembly workers. What would you do—make a high-priced offer for the assembled machines that upholds your high home country safety standards for local workers (with the high risk of losing the business) or a lower-priced offer that only complies with the low local safety standards (with a much higher probability of getting the business)?

Ethical ethnocentrism:
The general belief that the ethical standards and values of one's own group or society are the "right" ones.

There are three basic approaches to dealing with different ethical standards away from home: ethical ethnocentrism, ethical relativism, and ethical universalism.

Ethical ethnocentrism is the belief that one's own values and standards are always the "right" ones, and that these standards should be maintained when doing business in another country with different standards. So, for example, a European company with very strict rules regarding gift giving would also impose the same standards when doing business in Japan, although exchanging gifts between business partners is a much more common practice there (see the box *Around the globe: What exactly constitutes corruption?*).

The opposite of the "my-truth-is-the-only-truth" stance is **ethical relativism**, the belief that ethical standards in different cultures are not necessarily better or worse, but just different. This would mean that what is "right" or "wrong" depends on the context and on the belief system of a certain group of people (e.g. a certain national culture or religion), and that we can—and maybe even should—adjust our behavior to the norms of the culture that we are interacting with ("When in Rome, do as the Romans do" is an often-cited saying in this context). But does that mean that it is ethically correct for companies from countries with high environmental, labor law, and anti-corruption standards to dump toxic waste, accept child labor, and bribery in countries where such practices are more common? Many people will feel morally uncomfortable with this thought.

Ethical relativism:
The general belief that the ethical standards and values of one society are just different, but not necessarily better or worse than those of another society.

AROUND THE GLOBE

What exactly constitutes corruption?

For managers who strive to behave ethically, special attention must be paid to avoiding instances of corruption. Every year, the global civil society organization Transparency International publishes the *Corruption Perception Index* (CPI), which ranks countries around the globe according to their perceived levels of corruption on a scale of zero (highly corrupt) to 100 (very clean). The 2018 CPI saw Denmark and New Zealand at the top of the scale as the least corrupt countries in the world (with scores of 88 and 87, respectively). At the bottom of the scale, sub-Saharan Africa (with an average score of 32) and Eastern Europe and Central Asia (both with an average score of 35) were considered as the regions with the highest level of corruption. Does this mean that people in certain regions of the world are more ethical than others? People in different societies hold different assumptions about what they see as corrupt in the sense of undermining their cultural system. For example, Westerners will usually see bribery and nepotism as corrupt practices because they undermine the rule-based system on which society is built. However, in the more relationship-oriented cultures of Africa, Eastern Europe, or Central Asia, a bribe might help you to

"buy a relationship" in an environment which is characterized by "a fine line between legitimate relationships and quid-pro-quo bribery, which makes it easier to slip from one to the other."[132] Gifts and reciprocal favors are usually more acceptable as a way of building and maintaining good relationships in relationship-oriented cultures than in more rule-based societies. Likewise, "facilitating payments," which is seen as highly corrupt behavior in many Western countries, might be regarded as necessary in India, because they help to increase the meager salaries of officials and are a way to overcome the inefficiencies of the official system. Conversely, people from more relationship-oriented societies often see the Western practice of filing lawsuits against business partners who are accused of a breach of contract as unacceptable behavior that "corrupts" a trust- and relationship-based system. The examples of regional differences in the perception of corruption show that what is considered as "ethical" or "unethical" managerial behavior is difficult to judge without taking local cultural norms and values into account.

Sources: Based on information in Hooker (2009) and Transparency International (2019).

Ethical universalism: The general belief that there are moral values and a universal ethic that apply to everyone in the world, regardless of their cultural background or any other diversity-related characteristic.

A third basic approach to dealing with different ethical standards is **ethical universalism** (also known under the term "moral universalism"), the idea that there are moral values and a universal ethic that apply to everyone in the world, regardless of their cultural background or any other diversity-related characteristic. There have been attempts to discern and codify universal standards that are shared by all human beings, most notably in the **Universal Declaration of Human Rights** that was proclaimed by the United Nations General Assembly in 1948. Following the general guideline that "[a]ll human beings are born free and equal in dignity and rights,"[133] it declares that everyone is entitled to basic rights that range from the right to life, liberty, and security of person through the right of not being subjected to slavery or inhuman treatment, the right to a standard of living adequate for the health and well-being of oneself and one's family, the right to equal pay for equal work, the freedom of peaceful assembly and association, to the right to rest and leisure (including a reasonable limitation on working hours and periodic holidays with pay), to name just a few.[134] The United Nations also put forward the **UN Guiding Principles on Business and Human Rights** that set clear standards on what businesses should do in order to respect human rights and prevent or mitigate potential adverse human rights impacts that are either linked to their own actions or the actions of their business partners.[135]

The **UN Global Compact** is another United Nations policy initiative that suggests ten basic principles for doing business in an ethically correct way in the areas of:

Collective bargaining:
A negotiation of terms of employment (e.g. salaries or work hours) between an employer and union members who are negotiating on behalf of a group of employees.

- human rights (respecting human rights; avoiding complicity in human rights abuses);
- labor (respecting the freedom of association and the right to **collective bargaining**; eliminating all forms of forced and compulsory labor; abolishing child labor; and non-discrimination);
- environment (taking a precautionary approach to environmental challenges; promoting environmental responsibility; and being engaged in developing and diffusing environmentally friendly technologies);
- anti-corruption (working against all forms of corruption).[136]

Businesses can apply to become part of the UN Global Compact and submit annual reports on their progress in the areas that it covers, thus expressing their commitment to the ten principles.

How to ensure ethical behavior

So what can managers who work across cultures do in **concrete situations in which different ethical standards collide**? The following principles could help managers to find the right answer to this question:[137]

1 Respect universal human rights.
2 Do not treat others as "tools" or as a means to an end, but respect human dignity (following Kant's categorical imperative).
3 Have respect for local traditions and recognize that context matters when deciding what is "right" or "wrong."

Code of conduct:
A set of general rules of behavior for a certain group of people (e.g. for all members of an organization).

4 Have a **code of conduct**, but leave room for individual judgments in culturally sensitive situations.
5 If you are working in a business environment with lower ethical standards, set a good example in your own decision making—and then talk about it.

On an **organizational level**, managers can use several instruments for setting ethical standards and guiding employees' ethical behavior (see also the box *Setting ethical standards at Lockheed Martin*), including, for example, codes of conduct for employees and partners along the value chain, ethics awareness training, appointing ethics officers or ethics committees, certification and audits, confidential whistle-blowing processes (anonymous helplines), or transparency measures (e.g. reports and audits on social and environmental impacts).[138]

In addition to these more "technical" instruments, managers can also contribute to the creation of a good **ethical climate**, in which ethical behavior is encouraged and unethical behavior discouraged. This is closely related to defining and upholding **organizational values**, those commonly agreed core principles that guide the behavior of members in the organization. According to Deal and Kennedy, "values are the bedrock of any corporate culture."[139] It is not sufficient just to write a value statement, however. In order to effectively implement values in an organization, managers need to reinforce them in all communications, recognize and reward behavior that is consistent with these values, take action when values are violated, and—perhaps most importantly—lead by example and strictly live and abide by these values themselves.[140]

A strong managerial commitment to ethical behavior is not only an end in itself—it can also contribute to enhancing organizational performance. For example, a recent study observed a positive connection between customers' perceptions of the ethicality of an organization and its brand image.[141] A study of the 500 largest publicly held corporations in the US showed a statistically significant link between the commitment of management to ensuring compliance with ethical standards and the financial performance of the organization.[142] Thus, ethical behavior can also be good for business.

CEO best practice: Setting ethical standards at Lockheed Martin

Marillyn A. Hewson became president and CEO of Lockheed Martin in 2013, taking over from an executive who had to resign after violating the company's ethics code through his relationship with another employee. Hewson led the American aerospace, security, and defense technology company on a growth path, acquired the helicopter maker Sikorsky Aircraft and expanded its global business, especially in Asia. In an industry that has often been under public scrutiny and criticism regarding ethical concerns, Hewson put reinforcing integrity standards across the corporation high on her agenda. "We never allow our ethics or integrity to be compromised by our desire to succeed, regardless of the circumstances of our business,"[143] she writes at the beginning of Lockheed Martin's Code of Ethics and Business Conduct, which goes far beyond legal requirements. The code is complemented by a range of detailed policies that set standards of conduct for all members of the corporation including, for example, very strict anti-corruption rules. Employees are regularly informed about these standards through business conduct compliance training and ethics awareness training. Hewson personally trains her staff on a yearly basis, and all other leaders across the corporation are expected to do the same. Video scenarios based on actual cases are used in the training, and everyone is familiarized with the corporation's five "Voicing our Values" techniques, (1) asking questions, (2) obtaining data, (3) talking to others, (4) reframing the issue (taking a different perspective), and (5) reporting violations. Lockheed Martin also reaches beyond its own organization through providing ethical resources for suppliers, for example, a supplier code of conduct, detailed rules about gifts, hospitality, and business courtesies, ethics webinars for suppliers, and one-to-one support in an ethics supplier mentoring program. Hewson is convinced that acting in an ethically correct way is a basic precondition for success in business when she says that "operating with integrity secures our customers' trust and enables us to win business around the world."[144]

→ Key takeaway

Especially (but by no means exclusively) in industries in which there are a lot of ethical issues, clear guidelines about what is considered as ethically correct behavior and ethics training activities can help managers and employees to make the right decisions.

Sources: Based on information in Drew (2012); Lockheed Martin (2015; 2016; 2017).

In addition to comprehensive corporate ethics policies and codes of conduct, organizations can also provide their employees with simple, "down-to-earth" guidelines of how to deal with ethical challenges. The US technology company Texas Instruments, for example, equips its employees with a business card-size "mini pamphlet" that carries an **"Ethics Quick Test"** which can help them to make the right decision if they are unsure how to handle a difficult situation. It includes the following questions:

- "Is the action legal?
- Does it comply with our values?
- If you do it, will you feel bad?
- How will it look in the newspaper?
- If you know it's wrong, don't do it!
- If you're not sure, ask.
- Keep asking until you get an answer."[145]

"Keep asking" is a particularly important piece of advice. Deciding to speak up—to make ethical issues an issue in the organization—is the first step to creating a culture of integrity and a climate in which people care for doing the right thing.

Although ethical policies and codes of conducts can be an important instrument for communicating expectations, they do not guarantee ethical behavior. Managers will still sometimes need to **deal with unethical behavior**, and in order to avoid accusations of unfair treatment, they should do so in a consistent way. If managers observe behavior that clearly violates the ethical policies of the organization, they can respond in several ways, dependent on the severity of the issue. Minor offenses will usually be handled with a reprimand in a face-to-face meeting or with an oral warning. In more serious cases, written warnings are issued, and in very severe cases, ethical misconduct can lead to dismissal. When the behavior is not only unethical but also illegal, managers need to consider taking legal action. In all cases, it is good practice to have the right for employees to make appeals against disciplinary actions or dismissals (for example, to an ethics appeal board). In any case, managers are not only responsible for setting up ethical guidelines, but also for ensuring compliance. Being a role model in behaving in an ethical way is as important in this context as rewarding ethical and punishing unethical behavior and creating an atmosphere where people do not have to fear any negative consequences when they speak up to report alleged ethical misconduct.[146]

Preventing child labor at IKEA

CASE STUDY

Poverty, illiteracy, and indebtedness of parents, a lack of understanding of the potential negative effects on the child, entrenched social norms, and a lack of quality education are some of the reasons why child labor is still a widespread phenomenon in India. More than ten million children between the ages of 5 and 14 were considered "economically active" in India's 2011 census.

Marianne Barner was first confronted with this issue in the 1990s when she was heading the carpet business area of IKEA, the world's largest furniture retailer. At that time, IKEA faced media allegations in several countries that some of its Indian suppliers of rugs were exploiting child labor.

IKEA's basic business concept—providing well-designed furniture at affordable prices—was created by the company's founder Ingvar Kamprad in Sweden after World War II. IKEA rapidly spread around the world from the 1970s on and, over time, expanded its product range from furniture to a full line of home furnishing products, including home textiles and rugs. IKEA uses all possible cost-cutting opportunities that do not affect the quality of its core products; for example, deliberately designing the products for easier transport in flat packages, "outsourcing" delivery and assembly to the customer, and sourcing in high quantities from suppliers based in low-wage countries.

When one of IKEA's Indian rug suppliers was accused of being an employer of child labor in a German TV program in 1995, IKEA immediately terminated its contract with the supplier. In this particular case, police investigations later revealed that the TV producer had fabricated the whole story. As a consequence, the supplier relationship was reinstated, and the settlement with the TV station was handed over to the supplier. This episode, along with other accusations about IKEA's suppliers and the concomitant negative publicity, convinced IKEA's management that the issue of child labor demanded stronger attention.

Barner agreed to take over the role of IKEA's children's ombudsman. An ombudsman (or ombudsperson) is officially in charge of representing the interests of a particular group and investigating individuals' complaints against an organization. Within this role, Barner also assumed responsibility for initiating activities to prevent child labor. She reported directly to the CEO. Barner soon found out that child labor was a very complex issue that could not be solved just by terminating supplier relationships when an incident of child labor was reported and confirmed. Among the potential unintended consequences of such a move were that numerous children could be thrown onto the streets, child labor could be shifted to more hazardous industries (quarrying, for example), or children were relocated to sub-suppliers which were much more difficult to control. The well-intended social initiatives of other companies had not really improved the situation. Barner said that when she was visiting India's "carpet belt" and saw "many empty schools everywhere, some of them bearing the names of international companies," she started to understand "that you had to delve deeper."[147] Acknowledging that it was not feasible to put every single hand loom in India under direct surveillance, IKEA declined to join Rugmark, an international label that claims to guarantee child labor-free rugs through making regular inspections of the looms and factories where carpets are made.

IKEA's own initiatives tried to target root causes and focused on adult illiteracy, poverty, and access to education. The company started to support UNICEF in its efforts to establish community development projects and provide educational possibilities for children in India's carpet belt. Alternative learning centers that acted as a sort of "bridge school" to bring children into the regular school system were set up in the region, followed by a healthcare initiative. IKEA also tried to address the issue of parents' indebtedness through supporting self-help groups in which women collectively saved money that allowed them to open group bank accounts, borrow from these accounts (instead of from moneylenders who tie credits to child labor), and become financially independent entrepreneurs. Barner was convinced that "if we empowered women, this would have the same effects on their children. We knew this had to be achieved through education."[148] As a result of these efforts, which were focused on several hundred villages in India, tens of thousands more children attended school.

IKEA also set up new minimum requirements for its suppliers regarding social and environmental standards based on international conventions and declarations, called the "IKEA Way in Purchasing Products, Materials and Services (IWAY)," as well as general principles on how to prevent child labor. These guidelines made it clear that although IKEA respects the different values and traditions of other cultures, the company does not accept child labor. IKEA also holds workshops for suppliers about how to handle child labor issues. According to the IWAY guidelines, all actions that are taken must be "in the best interest of the child."[149] IKEA reserves the right to make unannounced visits to all production sites of suppliers—

including their sub-suppliers—or assign third parties with inspection tasks. If instances of child labor are found, the supplier must deliver and implement a corrective action plan that includes "viable and sustainable alternatives for the child's development."[150] In case of repeated violations, IKEA will terminate the business relationship with the supplier.

Despite these efforts, child labor is still prevalent in India. An increased level of buyer awareness, legislative action, and international pressure have, according to UNICEF India, resulted in a relocation of child labor away from factories to less visible places such as business owners' homes. A 2014 study by the FXB Center for Health and Human Rights at Harvard University reported that "an astonishing level of outright slavery and child labor for carpet weaving appears to be all but the norm" in the northwestern part of the Indian region of Uttar Pradesh, which was termed the "New Carpet Belt." The study pointed out that many Western retailers are still sourcing from exporters and importers that are violating human and children's rights.[151]

Sources: *Bartlett et al. (2006); IKEA (2007; 2016); latimes.com (1997); Kara (2014); Luce (2004); McCorquodale (2009); UNICEF India (2017).*

 Discussion questions

- Which steps did IKEA take to ensure that their suppliers are not exploiting child labor?
- How would you evaluate the actions that IKEA has taken to combat child labor? Do you agree with all the practices or do you have any reservations about them?
- Was it a good idea for IKEA not to join a certified label that guarantees that the rugs that it sources from India are child labor-free?
- What could be the basic ethical principles that the management of IKEA used as a basis for taking the decisions on how to deal with the issue of child labor?

Conclusion

As humans, we are cultural beings. We are shaped in our thinking and behavior by the culture (or several cultures) in which we are socialized. We express ourselves, understand the world, and make our judgments about ethical issues based on the traditions, values, attitudes, and behaviors that we have learned over time. In their leadership role, managers need to acknowledge that culture matters. As with other dimensions of diversity, cultural diversity can open up new opportunities for integrating different perspectives and devising new solutions to organizational problems. But as we have seen in this chapter, it can also increase the level of complexity that managers need to deal with. Managers who develop intercultural communication skills (e.g. being aware of cultural differences and able to adapt their verbal and non-verbal communication accordingly), competencies in diversity management (e.g. to establish diversity-related norms, practices, and training activities), and a well-founded ethical approach to decision making in a cross-cultural context (following the four steps to ethical behavior in Section 5.4) are better equipped to navigate the rough seas of today's dynamic and uncertain global business environment.

Acquiring these skills is becoming all the more essential for managers who are leaders or members of virtual global teams. Because this is an increasingly common way of organizing work in a globalized world, managers must also be able to combine their intercultural and diversity management skills with virtual socialization, communication, and collaboration skills. In a world that never stands still, we need managers who never stop learning.

As for every learning endeavor, trying to become competent in managing diversity across cultures takes time—for individual managers as well as for organizations. While Leena Nair progressed in her successful career journey (from management trainee in the male-dominated environment of the Indian subsidiary of Unilever to the global consumer goods corporation's first Asian and female chief human resources officer), Unilever also proceeded on its own transformation path. Strategic initiatives to advance diversity and inclusion across the whole organization have included, for example, a campaign to fight stereotyping and unconscious bias, a code of conduct which guarantees fair and equal treatment for all employees regardless of their backgrounds, a special program for attracting and developing female talent, mentoring programs, clear diversity targets to improve the representation of underrepresented groups in the workforce, and an inclusion learning program with the aim of building—in the words of Leena Nair—"a shared awareness of a more connected, caring culture so everyone at Unilever feels uniquely valued and supported."[152]

Unilever has become a role model of a culturally diverse organization and has won several awards for its diversity-related initiatives. In 2017, Unilever reported that more than one-third of all managers at Hindustan Unilever and almost half of all managers globally were women.[153] The more diverse workforce has also helped Unilever to reach exceptional business results, with an increase in turnover from 2009 to 2017 of more than one-third and an increase in operating profits during the same period of almost 77 percent.[154] But even a good practice company like Unilever is not immune to falling into intercultural pitfalls. In 2017, Dove, one of Unilever's brands, was accused of racism because of a social media advertisement that showed a black woman turning into a white one after using a body lotion. The company apologized right away and acknowledged that it had "missed the mark" with the advert.[155]

Unilever is just one example that underlines how important it is for managers to embrace diversity and to be sensitive to diversity-related issues. Everyone is different. That is what makes us strong when we join forces. Effective managers dig deeper to better understand the differences in (cultural) values, personality, and other visible or invisible characteristics of people, reflect on why these differences exist, and find the right strategies to work out integrative solutions that are both ethical and beneficial for the development of the organization.

✓ Review questions

1   What are the main benefits and challenges of diversity in teams that are composed of people from diverse backgrounds?
2   What can managers do to foster diversity and inclusion in their organizations?
3   Which cultural dimensions can help to understand cultural differences?
4   What aspects of culture can have an impact on the attitudes and behaviors of people in an organizational context?
5   What are the main barriers for effective intercultural communication?
6   What can managers do in order to effectively communicate and negotiate across borders?
7   What distinguishes a global virtual team from a traditional location-based team?
8   What are the main advantages of global virtual teams?
9   Which challenges do leaders of global virtual teams usually face?
10   How can leaders of global virtual teams ensure effective teamwork?
11   Which media can be used for which purposes in virtual teams?
12   Why is it important for managers to pay attention to the ethical implications of their decisions and actions?
13   Which basic ethical principles can managers apply when they face moral dilemmas?
14   How can managers deal with different ethical standards when they work across cultures?
15   What can managers do to foster ethical behavior in their own organizations and in partner organizations along the value chain?

⑦ Critical reflection questions

1   *Fortune* magazine reported that in 2016, only 28 percent of the newly appointed board
    members in *Fortune 500* companies (a list of the 500 largest firms in the US) were women.[156]
    Why—despite all diversity management efforts—is there still a lack of diversity in the highest
    business ranks?

2   Do you think that the use of cultural dimension models could foster stereotyping?

3   What does it mean for individuals if they are working primarily in global virtual teams rather
    than in traditional location-based teams? What are the potential impacts, for example, on
    motivation, social relationships, or loyalty toward the organization?

4   Despite all the talk about the importance of business ethics, we still read a lot of reports
    about unethical managerial behavior in newspapers or news websites. In your opinion, are
    organizations doing enough to ensure that their (top) managers act in an ethically
    appropriate way?

5   Ethical standards differ across cultures, and we could often come to different conclusions on
    how to deal with a moral dilemma when we use the different ethical principles that were
    introduced in this chapter. With all of these differences, can we really judge whether a certain
    managerial action was morally right or wrong?

☞ Managerial implications

- Effective managers are able to harness the power that lies in diversity—in bringing together
  different perspectives, approaches, capabilities, and strengths—to advance their organizations
  with new ideas that emerge when people from very different backgrounds join forces.

- In order to become beneficial for organizations, diversity needs to be well managed. To
  influence the diversity practices in their organizations, managers can introduce and enhance
  "above the line" diversity policies. At least as important, however, are the "below the line"
  attitudes toward diversity and inclusion as well as the development of a positive diversity
  climate.

- To effectively lead teams and organizations in an environment where different cultures meet,
  managers must develop intercultural competence. Recognizing and appreciating cultural
  differences is a first step that must be complemented by the ability to bridge the cultural gap
  through consciously adapting one's communication strategies to the specific cross-cultural
  situation.

- Global virtual teams are a means to overcome geographic and time barriers. They have their
  own challenges, though, and leaders of these teams must be able to manage diversity, focus
  on building trust and visibility, set clear communication norms, and ensure that the right
  communication technology is used effectively.

- Managers are often confronted with moral dilemmas—situations in which they must decide
  what is the right or wrong thing to do. Being aware that ethical issues matter, the ability to
  apply some basic principles of ethical reasoning, understanding the tools for guiding
  employees' ethical behavior in organizations, and critically questioning one's own perspective
  and behavior can help managers to deal with difficult decision situations and choose the
  (ethically) right course of action.

∥ Endnotes

[1]Nair (2016).
[2]Kabir (2018).
[3]Nair (2019).
[4]Nair (2016).
[5]Jonsen et al., 2011.
[6]census.gov (2015).

[7]Gardenswartz and Rowe (2010), p. 24.
[8]Gentile (1995), p. 3.
[9]Mercer et al. (2015).
[10]Gentile (1995), p. 11.
[11]Stahl et al. (2009); Williams and O'Reilly (1998).
[12]Hermann and Rammal (2010).

[13]Frost and Kalman (2016), p. 21.
[14]Frost and Kalman (2016), p. 21.
[15]Itami and Roehl (1987).
[16]Aytemiz Seymen (2006); Gardenswartz and
    Rowe (2010); Robinson and Dechant (1997);
    Slater et al. (2008); Stahl et al. (2010).

[17]Richard et al. (2004).

[18]Slater et al. (2008).

[19]Jehn et al. (1999); Stahl et al. (2010); Tsui et al. (1992).

[20]Aytemiz Seymen (2006).

[21]Jonsen et al. (2011).

[22]Jonsen et al. (2011).

[23]Kulik (2014); McKay et al. (2008).

[24]Kulik (2014).

[25]Gardenswartz and Rowe (2010), p. 233.

[26]Kulik (2014), p. 133.

[27]Dobbin and Kalev (2016); Kidder et al. (2004).

[28]Pierson and Lien (2017).

[29]Johnson (2017).

[30]gildancorp.com (2017).

[31]genuinegildan.com (2017a).

[32]Gardenswartz and Rowe (2010), p. 393.

[33]Daft (2016); Graham (1997).

[34]Kulik (2014).

[35]Wentling (2004).

[36]Bartels et al. (2013); Daft (2016); Dobbin and Kalev (2016).

[37]Dobbin and Kalev (2016).

[38]Dobbin and Kalev (2016).

[39]Dobbin and Kalev (2016).

[40]Daft (2016).

[41]Worthington et al. (2008).

[42]Dobbin and Kalev (2016); Kidder et al. (2004).

[43]Thomas and Inkson (2009).

[44]Thomas and Inkson (2009).

[45]Salacuse (1999).

[46]Hofstede (1984), p. 21.

[47]Salacuse (1999), p. 218.

[48]Crowne (2008).

[49]Earley and Mosakowski (2004); Triandis (2006).

[50]Hall (1976).

[51]Hooker (2009).

[52]Hooker (2009).

[53]Hofstede (1984).

[54]Hofstede (2011); Hofstede and Bond (1988).

[55]Schwartz (1999).

[56]Schwartz (1999).

[57]Trompenaars and Hampden-Turner (2012).

[58]Globe Project (2019); House et al. (2004).

[59]worldvaluessurvey.org (2019a).

[60]worldvaluessurvey.org (2019b).

[61]Hofstede (1984), p. 51.

[62]Jonsen et al. (2011).

[63]Harris and Moran (1991); Moran et al. (2011).

[64]Gardenswartz and Rowe (2010).

[65]Gardenswartz and Rowe (2010).

[66]Crowne (2008).

[67]In this section, we follow a functional approach to communication, which is focused on how (effective) intercultural communication works. There are other approaches to understanding communication, for example, the meaning-centered approach, which is more focused on understanding how human interaction defines (organizational) reality (Shockley-Zalabak, 2015).

[68]Jonsen et al. (2011).

[69]Jonsen et al. (2011).

[70]Gardenswartz and Rowe (2010).

[71]Thomas and Inkson (2009).

[72]Brett et al. (2006).

[73]Thomas and Inkson (2009).

[74]Akechi et al. (2013).

[75]Salacuse (1999).

[76]Cai et al. (2000); Salacuse (1999).

[77]Gardenswartz and Rowe (2010).

[78]Salacuse (1999).

[79]haier.net (2011).

[80]haier.net (2017).

[81]Sánchez-Runde et al. (2012), p. 5.

[82]Sánchez-Runde et al. (2012), p. 13.

[83]Thomas and Inkson (2009).

[84]Clegg (2017).

[85]Ferrazzi (2014); RW³ (2016).

[86]Govindarajan and Gupta (2001).

[87]Jarvenpaa and Leidner (1999), p. 792.

[88]Bergiel et al. (2008); Berry (2011); Jimenez et al. (2017); Nydegger and Nydegger (2010).

[89]Bergiel et al. (2008); Berry (2011); Ferrazzi (2014); Jimenez et al. (2017).

[90]Nydegger and Nydegger (2010).

[91]Malhotra et al. (2007).

[92]Berry (2014).

[93]Thomas and Inkson (2009).

[94]Malhotra et al. (2007).

[95]Shachaf (2008).

[96]Hill and Bartol (2018).

[97]Malhotra et al. (2007).

[98]Nydegger and Nydegger (2010).

[99]Hill and Bartol (2018).

[100]Greenberg et al. (2007).

[101]Greenberg et al. (2007).

[102]Zofi (2012).

[103]Thomas and Inkson (2009), p. 117.

[104]Hill and Bartol (2018).

[105]Hill and Bartol (2018).

[106]Lepsinger (2018).

[107]Ahuja and Galvin (2003).

[108]Ahuja and Galvin (2003); Makarius and Larson (2017).

[109]Ahuja and Galvin (2003).

[110]Gilson et al. (2015).

[111]Gilson et al. (2015).

[112]Lepsinger (2018).

[113]Ardichvili et al. (2002).

[114]Clement (2006).

[115]Wicks (2009).

[116]Velasquez (2014).

[117]Bentham (1839), p. 138.

[118]Velasquez (2014).

[119]Velasquez (2014).

[120]Kant (1788).

[121]Sensen (2011).

[122]Amabile and Kramer (2007), p. 81.

[123]Tyler (1994).

[124]Velasquez (2014).

[125]Kim and Leung (2007).

[126]Gilligan (1977), p. 511.

[127]Velasquez (2014).

[128]Habermas (1999), p. 93.

[129]Habermas (1999).

[130]Velasquez (2014), p. 131.

[131]Donaldson (1996).

[132]Hooker (2009), p. 254.

[133]United Nations (1948).

[134]United Nations (1948).

[135]United Nations (2011).

[136]United Nations (2019).

[137]Donaldson (1996).

[138]Kusyk (2010).

[139]Deal and Kennedy (2000), p. 21.

[140]Levin (2017).

[141]Iglesias et al. (2019).

[142]Verschoor (1998).

[143]Lockheed Martin (2016), p. ii.

[144]Lockheed Martin (2015).

[145]Texas Instruments (2019).

[146]Trevino and Brown (2004).

[147]Luce (2004).

[148]McCorquodale (2009).

[149]IKEA (2016), p. 1.

[150]IKEA (2007), p. 2.

[151]Kara (2014), pp. 40; 48.

[152]Quote from Nair (2018); diversity-related measures at Unilever are also described in Unilever (2019).

[153]Unilever (2019); Hindustan Unilever (2019).

[154]Unilever (2018).

[155]Slawson (2017).

[156]Jones and Donnelly (2017).

Visit the companion website at macmillanihe.com/sternad-management **to access useful weblinks, multiple choice questions and additional materials.**

PART

III

ENHANCING ORGANIZATIONAL EFFECTIVENESS

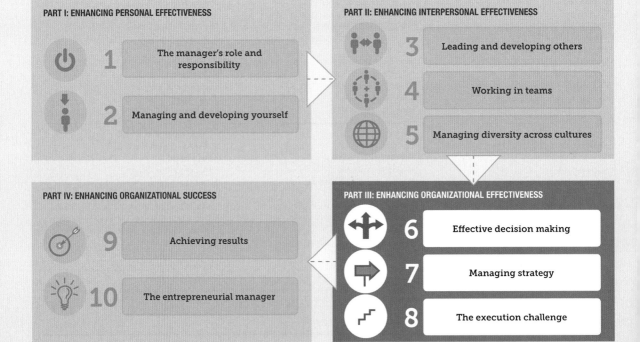

PART I: ENHANCING PERSONAL EFFECTIVENESS

1 The manager's role and responsibility

2 Managing and developing yourself

PART II: ENHANCING INTERPERSONAL EFFECTIVENESS

3 Leading and developing others

4 Working in teams

5 Managing diversity across cultures

PART IV: ENHANCING ORGANIZATIONAL SUCCESS

9 Achieving results

10 The entrepreneurial manager

PART III: ENHANCING ORGANIZATIONAL EFFECTIVENESS

6 Effective decision making

7 Managing strategy

8 The execution challenge

In Part III, we change our focus from the interpersonal and team level to the organizational level. In this part, we will explore how managers can shape their organizations through making the right decisions, developing strategies, and paving the way for an effective implementation of these strategies.

Chapter 6, *Effective decision making,* examines how managers can enhance their decision-making skills. We will first go through all the steps of a structured, rational-analytic decision process, but then acknowledge that managers also often use more unconscious and intuitive thinking modes to make decisions. After analyzing how to best apply the different thinking modes and how modern computer-based decision support systems can help managers in making the right decisions, we will familiarize ourselves with a range of potential decision-making pitfalls in order to be able to identify and avoid them. The last part of Chapter 6 is devoted to group decision processes. We will recognize common deficiencies in such processes and discuss what managers can do to improve decision making in group settings.

Chapter 7, *Managing strategy,* introduces the core concepts of strategic management. In this chapter, we will try to find out what it means to think and plan strategically in order to provide an organization or an organizational unit with a clear direction. After outlining the main steps of a strategic planning process, several tools for both internal and external strategic analyses are presented. We will also explore how managers can define strategic positions for their organization both on a corporate level and on the level of a single business unit, and assess different tactics for dealing with competitive threats. In the Internet age, managers also need to think about the digital strategy of their organization, so we will examine the role of digital technologies in a strategic context.

Chapter 8, *The execution challenge,* is about how managers can translate strategies into concrete organizational action. The implementation path includes five key steps: identifying critical tasks, matching tasks and people, coordinating the work, energizing the team, and controlling the direction. Managers can use structures, processes, and systems to organize, coordinate and control the work that needs to be done in order to execute a strategy; but they can also influence others by using "softer" means such as persuasion, forming strong relationships, or shaping the culture of their organizations. Most strategy implementation initiatives also trigger change processes in organizations. We will therefore also take a closer look at how organizational change can be managed in an effective way.

Photo by Victoriano Izquierdo on Unsplash

EFFECTIVE DECISION MAKING

Outline of chapter

This chapter will enable you to

- Identify the main building blocks of a rational-analytic decision-making process.
- Apply basic decision-making tools such as a decision tree, an objectives comparison model, and a scoring model.
- Distinguish between the different thinking modes that managers use when making decisions.
- Assess the role of decision support systems and data analytics in managerial decision making.
- Beware of common decision pitfalls and devise strategies for avoiding them.
- Recognize potential obstacles to effective group decision making and suggest improvements to group decision processes.

Introduction

In 1996, thirteen renowned publishers received a letter from London-based Christopher Little Literary Agency with a book proposal from a 31-year-old author. Evaluating the manuscript pages according to their guidelines and based on their extensive experience, twelve publishers decided that the text was not worth publishing. Finally, one publishing house, Bloomsbury, picked up the offer and forwarded an advance payment of £1,500—a very low sum in this business, indicating that they too doubted the book's potential. But to everyone's surprise, they made a profit. Indeed, the book, entitled *Harry Potter and the Philosopher's Stone*, would become a literary phenomenon and its author, Joanne K. Rowling, one of the richest women in England. Bloomsbury had discovered a goldmine.[1]

Out of thirteen publishers, twelve made a decision that probably still causes them headaches more than two decades later. These publishers were well versed and experienced in their profession and yet their decision was—at least judged in retrospect—at best somewhat flawed. The Harry Potter example illustrates that decision making is not always straightforward. Managers are often portrayed, quite misleadingly, as rational actors who make decisions based on detailed analysis and comparison in order to achieve specific goals. This perspective overlooks one crucial factor: managers are human. They have feelings and emotions, as well as limitations and flaws. They act in social environments, navigating relationships and power structures, and they also have a life outside their organization. It is the whole human being who makes decisions, not merely the rational managerial self.

In this chapter, we will use different viewpoints to investigate how we can make effective decisions that bring us closer to our goals, despite the numerous limitations that we all, as members of the species *Homo sapiens,* possess.

- First, we will employ a surgeon's approach, dissecting decisions into separate components, thus gaining a better understanding of the **anatomy of a decision** (*Section 6.1*).
- Recognizing that decision making is a cognitive task, we will look through a psychologist's lens to explore the **different thinking modes of managers** (and other people, too). Having this awareness of our thought process can improve our ability to make effective decisions (*Section 6.2*).
- Given that decision makers are mortal, we will then take a pathologist's view and delve into the depths of **decision failures**, which are frequently based on flawed thinking. We will learn strategies for avoiding or circumventing these potential pitfalls (*Section 6.3*).
- Finally, we will turn into social psychologists, acknowledging that decision making in organizations is not only a cognitive but also a social process. We will focus on **group decision-making processes** and how they can be improved (*Section 6.4*).

It is hard to imagine a manager who makes the "right" decisions at all times. First of all, what is "right" or "wrong" often lies in the eyes of the beholder, as people have different perceptions and diverging interests. In addition, it is possible in the continually changing business environment that decisions which originally seemed right can—as circumstances change—lead to detrimental outcomes. A successful CEO of a media corporation once said that you do not need to be 100 percent right in all your managerial decisions. In fact, thinking that you could ever be 100 percent right is a sure way to failure.[2] It is necessary, however, to get the large majority of your decisions right. That will enable you to propel the organization in the right direction.

In this chapter, we will take a closer look at the processes that allow us to become more effective in decision making.

6.1 The anatomy of a decision

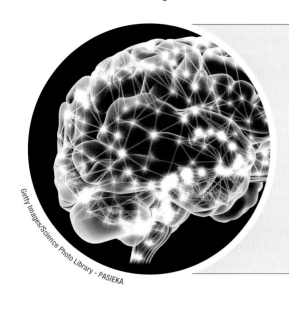

Getty Images/Science Photo Library - PASIEKA

In brief

- Many situations involve a high degree of complexity. A good understanding of the constituent components of a decision can help us to navigate through this confusion.
- Before considering and evaluating potential solutions, it is essential to clearly define the problem and the objectives to be achieved.
- It is important to identify and assess any uncertainties, together with the range of possible outcomes (and their probabilities) that might result from different decisions.
- Considering the main trade-offs can contribute to a more comprehensive evaluation of the situation, and thus improve decision making.

Before discussing what it means to make effective decisions, we will try to understand what a decision really is and what is typically involved. In other words, we need to explore the individual elements that, together, constitute what we call **"a decision."**

In a basic definition, a "decision is a choice of action—of what to do or not do."[3] This sounds quite simple, but becomes more complex once we recognize how many interlinking factors we need to take into account.

A manager who wants to make a **rational decision** should consider the following questions:[4]

- What is the **problem**?
- What **objectives** do I have when making this decision?
- What **options** do I have to address the problem?
- What are the **possible outcomes** of these options?
- What are the **uncertainties** surrounding the decision and the **probability** of each potential outcome?
- What is my willingness to take **risks**?
- How do the outcomes relate to my objectives and what **trade-offs** are involved?

The component parts of a decision are all connected. Therefore, in the same way that doctors study anatomy to understand complex human systems, it makes sense for managers to familiarize themselves with the complex anatomy of decisions. Figure 6.1 provides an overview of a rational decision-making process, including all the aforementioned decision elements, which will be described in more detail later.

Step 1: Define the problem

The first step in making an effective decision is to clearly and unambiguously **define the problem**. As highlighted by Peter Drucker, "decision-making is not a mechanical job ... The 'right answer' (which usually cannot be found anyway) is not central. Central is understanding of the problem."[5]

The way in which a problem is framed strongly influences the subsequent decision process. Simply adopting the first and most obvious definition of the problem can lead to an unnecessarily early narrowing of the possible solutions. If, for example, recession hits

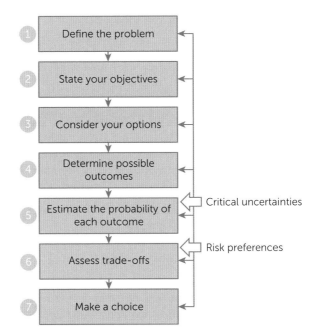

Figure 6.1 The rational decision-making process

Source: Inspired by concepts in Hammond et al. (1999).

a company and a manager defines the problem as "How can we cut costs to survive during the recession?", this manager could miss out on alternatives for dealing with an economic downturn, including, for example, the introduction of low-price product lines or exploring opportunities for selective investment in marketing to gain additional market share. A different **framing** of the problem, as "How could we strategically react to the recession?", might lead to another—in this case more comprehensive—set of potential choices.

Given the influence that the framing of a problem can have on the range of possible options considered, and subsequently on the outcome of a decision, it makes sense to think about the definition of your problem in depth. Why is the decision being made? Is the decision really addressing the **underlying problem** or merely a **derived** one? A manager might, for example, try to solve a team member's underperformance through closer supervision, when the problem was actually due to work overload. In this case, the underperformance is just a derived problem. The real issue is allocating too many tasks to one person.

Like a good doctor, a good manager should always make a thorough **diagnosis**, striving to detect the disease rather than only the symptom. With complex systems, it is advisable to observe their behavior for some time, trying to recognize patterns of relationships and **co-variations** between different factors.[6] Returning to the previous example, the manager could try to establish whether the underperformance coincided with any other changes, thus concluding that performance always decreases whenever there is a high workload and increased pressure.

The main diagnostic tool available to decision makers is **interrogation**: asking questions that lead to a more in-depth understanding of the issue and the different factors involved. Here are some questions that can help to **define the real problem**:[7]

- **Who first identified the problem?** Is your perspective biased because the issue was raised by a particular group of people (perhaps following their own interests rather than the organization's)?
- **Is the problem too narrowly defined?** Are there any constraints when setting out the problem? Does the framing of the problem automatically exclude certain options for dealing with the issue?

Framing:
Setting a problem within a particular context that can determine the set of potential options to address the problem.

Co-variation:
Two or more variables are changing at the same time (in correlation with each other).

- **Is the problem too widely defined?** Does its definition enable a focused search for solutions?
- **How would outsiders see the problem?** Would experts or friends view it differently?
- **Are there follow-up decisions dependent on this choice?** Does the decision limit the range of future opportunities? Should related decisions be considered concurrently?

The last question is particularly important, as decision makers often think about immediate options and their possible outcomes, failing to take into account that their decision could lead to further choices that again bear opportunities and risks. For example, a manager might consider laying off an underperforming team member, but this decision could result in further issues that need to be resolved:

- Is it possible to find an adequately qualified replacement?
- How might the employee's tasks be split up among the remaining team members?
- Would these other team members be willing to take on the additional tasks given their own high workloads?

Failing to take these follow-up decisions into account can lead to negative consequences (e.g. dissatisfaction among the other team members). Kahneman and Lovallo call this phenomenon "narrow framing," suggesting that "people tend to make decisions one at a time, and in particular that they are prone to neglect the relevance of future decision opportunities."[8]

In any case, it can be helpful, especially for important issues, to **write the problem down**. It is easier to question a statement that is on paper than something that is in your mind. The same is also true for the objectives that managers would like to achieve with their decisions.

Step 2: State your objectives

Objectives are the measure by which the options for solving a problem are later evaluated. Many managers do not spend enough time thinking about what they want to achieve. They quickly jump from a (sometimes only very narrowly defined) problem to the first available solution, thereby missing out a crucial step: the outlining of their objectives. As decision criteria, objectives strongly influence the final choice. Focusing on too few objectives can lead to unbalanced decisions in which the outcomes do not reflect the variety of the decision maker's underlying motives.[9] Deciding between different candidates for an open job position solely on the basis of their work experience, for example, might neglect other objectives of the organization, such as promoting diversity, developing potential for the future, or creating a team with a shared value base.

To **clarify their objectives**, decision makers can do the following:

1 **Write down all the important points** that they wish to address with a particular decision, followed by a statement that converts these points into **concrete objectives**, best represented by the combination of a verb and an object, such as "Increase the diversity of the team," "Develop management potential for our organization," or "Ensure qualification of our team members at least on the following level: ...".

2 Take one step back and identify the real **ends behind the means**, inquiring (usually with several "Why?" questions) whether the set objectives really address the fundamental underlying concerns (e.g. "Why do I want to increase the diversity of the team? Do I want to foster the creativity and decision-making quality in our team through including different perspectives, or do I want our team to be better able to connect with different customer groups?").

3 Clarify whether an objective is **defined clearly enough**: instead of using "Maximize qualification levels" (which is somewhat vague), it would make more sense to explore

what qualification actually means in a particular situation (e.g. "Ensure that the candidate holds at least a business degree and has at least two years of experience in our industry").

Quantification trap:
Focusing on quantifiable objectives and neglecting qualitative factors that are not easy to capture in numbers.

4   Avoid the **quantification trap** of giving preference to quantifiable objectives, because some of the most important things in life (and in business) cannot be expressed in numerical terms.[10] It is almost impossible to quantitatively measure attitudes or values, for example. Yet, finding people with the right attitudes and values can be an important objective in a hiring decision.

Although objectives ideally remain stable during the decision-making process, decision makers should remain open to including new objectives if circumstances change considerably.[11]

Step 3: Consider your options

A decision can only be as good as the options that are considered. Focusing on too few options is one of the major obstacles to making effective decisions. If the best options are never even raised, how can the decision process lead to an optimal outcome?

Many decision makers do not spend enough time on the search for alternatives because they simply concentrate on the two or three most obvious options. The main problem here is straightforward: **lack of thought**, which, according to Hammond et al., can come in many forms:

- **Business as usual**: relying merely on habit instead of actively searching for alternative options;
- **Incrementalizing**: simply making small changes to previous solutions instead of thinking afresh;
- **Choosing the first possible solution** instead of actively looking for innovative ways of dealing with a situation;
- **Choosing between alternatives presented by others** instead of thinking of your own options;
- **Being stuck with what's left**: waiting until the best solutions are no longer available instead of deciding as soon as you have sufficient information.[12]

Identifying and comparing a range of feasible alternatives can improve the quality of our decisions. **Widening the options space** should therefore be one of the main concerns of diligent managers who are facing important decisions. But how can this be achieved?

- Decision makers can **challenge constraints**.[13] If it is the manager's task to find an exclusive distribution partner for selling smoothies in a foreign market, for example, would it really be necessary to find a distributor who is also able to take over all marketing and public relations? Would it perhaps be possible to split these functions—distribution, marketing, and public relations—between different specialists? Very often, constraints are not even made explicit but exist in our mind. Writing them down is the first step to overcoming them.
- By keeping the problem in mind and relating it to everything that we experience (especially outside our immediate work environment), we can generate **analogies** that lead to new solutions. If we want to improve the performance of one of our team members, for example, we could think back to a technique that worked well when a sports coach or music teacher supported us. Realizing how our different experiences relate to the problem can be a way to come up with new, innovative responses.
- We can also **learn from others**. How are global industry leaders tackling this particular problem? Are there organizations in other industries that have resolved a similar issue? Learn from the best in the world by researching, contacting, or visiting them! In a classic example, Southwest Airlines reportedly learned from the pit stop

crews of Formula 1 racing teams how to reduce airplane turnaround times to the absolute minimum.[14] For many problems, it does not make sense to reinvent the wheel.

- **Involving colleagues and outsiders** can provide a fresh perspective. People with different experiences inevitably have different approaches to solving problems. For example, researchers from the medical division of industry conglomerate 3M were able to develop a solution for infection control during surgery after learning how to prevent facial skin infections from a theatrical-makeup specialist.[15] People from different backgrounds can generate a wealth of new ideas which one person alone could never have conceived. Letting people come up with their own solutions before revealing yours can help to avoid bias. When a wider group of people with different perspectives is included in a decision, it also becomes more likely that potential ethical issues will be raised and considered.
- **Separate the formation and evaluation of ideas**. Many options are prematurely abandoned because they are criticized too early on. Phrases like "This never worked!" or "Yes, but..." are popular killers. It is advisable to look for more ideas before judging those you have. This opens the space for new and unusual solutions.
- **Not doing anything** is an option. This alternative is actually often overlooked. Some (but definitely not all!) problems subside even when we decide not to do anything about them. For example, the washing powder "Persil Power" was introduced by Unilever in the 1990s. It contained a new special ingredient, called "the accelerator," which was advertised as providing an improved cleaning performance. Competitors who decided not to react and enhance their own washing powders with "the accelerator" were probably very relieved when they heard that the new formula was actually too powerful and harmed the clothes, so that Unilever was forced to withdraw the product from the market.[16]

Steps 4 and 5: Determine possible outcomes and their probabilities in the face of uncertainty

Once the options have been outlined, you need a clear understanding of the possible consequences when deciding between them. What will happen if a particular decision is chosen? What outcomes can be expected? What external factors might influence these outcomes? For example, let us consider whether or not to order a marquee for an outdoor promotional event. The success of such events can vary significantly depending, among other factors, on the weather conditions. The weather is an **uncertainty**, an external event beyond the decision maker's influence. Dependent on our decision and the external uncertainties (in this case, the weather and the number of people who would attend the event if it were raining), there are a range of possible outcomes (see the **decision tree** in Figure 6.2). Note that we have assumed full attendance in the case of no rain and partial attendance, at two different potential levels, in the case of rain.

Decision tree:
A tool for visualizing the options, critical uncertainties and their probabilities, and potential outcomes of decisions.

Almost any major decision in an organization involves factors that are subject to at least some degree of uncertainty regarding the outcomes. For instance, will customers accept our new product? How will competitors react? Will the regulatory environment change? There are numerous external influences that can potentially affect the outcomes of managerial decisions (see also Chapter 1). The existence of uncertainty is also the reason why even the best decisions do not always lead to the desired consequences.

Assigning probabilities is a way of dealing with uncertainty. A **probability** is a numerical measure of how strongly we believe in a certain proposition.[17] Let us take the following proposition as an example: "Our industry will show a strong growth rate of over 5 percent next year." If we assign a probability of 0.8 to this proposition, this will indicate that we are 80 percent certain that the proposition will hold and that the industry will in fact grow by more than 5 percent during the next year. A probability of 0.1, on the other hand, would imply that we do not strongly believe in the proposition, and that we see a 90 percent chance that the

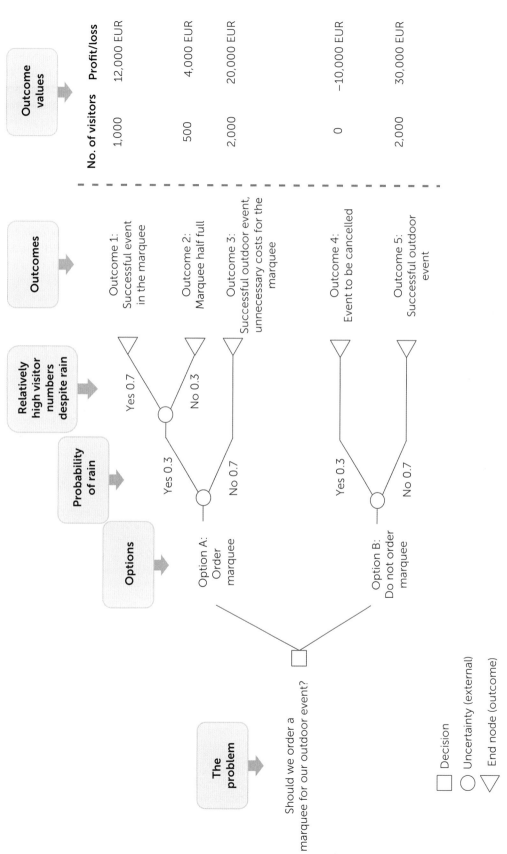

Figure 6.2 An example of a decision tree

industry will not grow at a rate of more than 5 percent. A probability of 0.5 is actually another way of expressing "I have no idea what will happen," as we then believe that there is an equal chance of the proposition being verified or falsified. The important point here is that probabilities represent **beliefs**. As everyone knows, believing is not knowing. Although the numerical expression conveys accuracy, probabilities are just estimates about the future. They are opinions, not facts (although the opinions can be formed on the basis of facts). Assigning probabilities is not an easy task and might require searching for a considerable amount of information including, for example, consulting experts (such as a weather forecaster in the case of planning an outdoor event).

Critical uncertainties:
Those external events beyond the decision maker's influence that have the highest possible impact on the variation of the outcome of decisions.

At this stage, managers can also think about how to **reduce the critical uncertainties**. For example, an organizer of an open-air event could order a marquee as a backup, thereby reducing the negative consequences in the case of rain. This example shows that decision makers can influence the potential outcomes, although sometimes (as in the case of the marquee) at a cost.

A **decision tree** (see Figure 6.2, and the detailed description in the box *Zooming in on the decision tree*) is a useful tool for visualizing the uncertainties involved in a decision. This tree-like graphic depicts the various options, the probability of external non-controllable influences, and the possible outcomes of different choices together with (monetary) outcome values. A decision tree alone is usually not sufficient to make a decision. It can, however, help managers to improve their understanding of a situation, and is also used in other professions in which high-stakes decisions are taken (for example by doctors).[18]

Zooming in on ▶ THE DECISION TREE

Think of a decision you need to make, either in your personal life, your academic life or your work life. Draw your own decision tree by following these seven steps:

1 Define the problem in a simple and unambiguous way (e.g. "Should we order a marquee for our outdoor event?" in the example in Figure 6.2).

2 Identify the various options that you have to address the problem (e.g. Option A: "Order marquee", Option B: "Do not order marquee").

3 Think about the critical uncertainties that could have a considerable effect on the outcome of the decision (e.g. rain versus no rain; a higher versus a lower number of visitors in the case of rain).

4 Assign probabilities to these critical uncertainties (e.g. 0.3 for a 30 percent chance of rain).

5 Determine the outcomes for each option under different scenarios (e.g. for Option B "Do not order marquee," there are two possible outcomes: either the event needs to be cancelled if it starts raining, or there will be a successful outdoor event if there is no rain).

6 Assign (monetary) values to the outcomes (e.g. How much money will we lose if the event needs to be cancelled?)

Expected value:
In probability analysis, the expected value is computed by multiplying the value of each possible outcome with the probability that this particular outcome will occur, and then adding together all the resulting values.

7 Calculate the **expected value** for each option. In the case of the decision in Figure 6.2, the expected value for Option A: "Order marquee" is (**0.3** *the probability of rain* × **0.7** *the probability of a relatively high number of visitors* × **12,000** *the profit made with this number of visitors and a marquee*) + (**0.3** *the probability of rain* × **0.3** *the probability of a low number of visitors* × **4,000** *the profit made with this number of visitors and a marquee*) + (**0.7** *the probability of no rain* × **20,000** *the profit made with full attendance and a marquee*) = **16,880 EUR**. The expected value for Option B: "Do not order marquee" is (**0.3** *the probability of rain* × **−10,000** *the loss made if the event is cancelled*) + (**0.7** *the probability of no rain* × **30,000** *the profit made with full attendance and no marquee*) = **18,000 EUR**.

8 Interpret the results of the expected value calculation. In our case, Option B ("Do not order marquee") has an expected value that is statistically slightly more likely to lead to a higher outcome value than Option A ("Order marquee"), at least in the long run (i.e. if the decision were repeated many times). Because it is a one-time decision, however, the higher expected value does not necessarily mean that Option B is the "better" option, because expected value calculations fail to consider the risk preferences of the decision maker.

Consider the decision tree in Figure 6.2. If you had to make this decision, how would you decide? Would you choose the option with the higher expected value? Why would you decide in this way? What role does your willingness to take risks play in your decision?

Key consideration: Understand risk preferences

Risk:
In a managerial context, risk is mostly seen as the potential of losing something that is of value. Sometimes, the term risk is used in a wider sense that can include the potential of gaining something.

As defined in classical economic decision theory, **risk** reflects the **variability of possible outcomes**, regardless of whether these outcomes are positive or negative. Most managers, however, do not regard the possibility of positive outcomes as a "risk," but rather focus on the negative side: they see risk as the potential that choosing a certain option will lead to detrimental outcomes. In an organizational context, managers can, for example, face demand risks (customers who do not want to buy your products), supply risks (suppliers who are unable to deliver the materials and services that the organization needs), credit risks (customers who don't pay), competitive risks (competitors' moves that have negative effects on your business), technological risks (e.g. cyber attacks), regulatory risks (potentially detrimental new laws), or the risk of losing key members of the team—to name just a few.

Although most managers are generally averse to loss, they vary in their propensity to engage in risky activities. Some are more risk averse, favoring choices with a low likelihood of failure, while others are more willing to take risks in exchange for a high upside potential.

Risk preferences:
The tendency to either be willing to take risks or to try to avoid risks.

Risk preferences are partly embedded in personality—some people are just more risk averse than others—but can also be influenced by cultural factors, mood and emotions (people tend to be more risk seeking when they are angry, less so when they are fearful),[19] the way in which problems are framed, or the context of the decision.[20] Managers might have different risk preferences, for example, dependent on whether they are dealing with their organization's money or their own.

Loewenstein et al. conceptualize **risk as feelings**, including both the emotions that decision makers attach to the potential outcomes and the emotions they have during the decision process, such as fear or anxiety.[21] If you are anxious that something bad might happen as a result of your decision, you will probably consider the risk to be higher. As March points out, there are two "guesses" involved even in seemingly rational decision processes: "The first guess is a guess about future states of the world, conditional on the choice. The second guess is a guess about how the decision maker will feel about the future world when it is experienced."[22]

Dual focal value theory (see Figure 6.3) posits that decision makers have two reference points regarding their risk preferences: the target level of performance and the minimum level for survival. March and Shapira suggest that: (1) above target level (e.g. when the organization has met all its financial goals), people tend to be more risk averse as they want to avoid failure; (2) below target level (e.g. when their goals haven't been met), more risks are accepted as they want to achieve their aims; and (3) close to the survival point—facing the possibility of losing everything (e.g. if failure could potentially lead to a job loss for the manager)—an awareness of risks and potential dangers comes to the forefront again.[23]

Risk intelligence:
The ability to assess risks based on experience.

For managers, it is important to understand both their general risk preference and their own estimation of risk in a particular situation. David Apgar argues that managers can acquire a competency he calls **risk intelligence**.[24] Rather than having to succumb to the perception that all risks are random, he asserts that some risks are learnable. If we spend time and effort in discovering more about them, we can reduce the uncertainty in these risks. If we carefully study our main competitor's moves over time, for example, we can raise our chances of correctly guessing this competitor's reaction to the new strategy that we plan to implement.

Figure 6.3 Risk preferences according to the dual focal value theory

Source: Inspired by concepts in March and Shapira (1987).

Apgar advises managers to assess their level of experience with different risks, and then allocate more resources to projects where they better understand the risks involved, or where they are able to learn about them more quickly. This will also enable managers to take **calculated risks**, as in the example of former Google CEO Eric Schmidt (see the box *Taking calculated risks at Google*).

CEO BEST PRACTICE

Taking calculated risks at Google

Serving as the CEO of Google Inc. from 2001 to 2011, Eric E. Schmidt was a leading contributor to the rise of the start-up from search engine enterprise to global corporation dominating the Internet.

Constant innovation, one of the pillars of Google's success, does not, however, come without risks. Schmidt therefore put a high emphasis on managing these risks: "You cannot eliminate all risk, but you can certainly put yourself into situations where the failures are not horrific," he said in an interview. It is better to "fail early," he explained, than to wait until the project has become much bigger. At the start, failure might cost you "a couple million dollars" and a few people's time. If you have already invested a lot in a project, however, failure becomes much more expensive. As Schmidt said, a space shuttle blowing up would cost you "a trillion dollars."[25]

Taking Schmidt's example, it is also worth considering that any major disaster would not only lead to large financial losses in the short term, but could also cause long-lasting harm due to negative publicity. Perhaps we should all welcome the learning opportunities that early failure can provide.

→ Key takeaway

Managers sometimes need to take risks to keep their organizations innovative. It is advisable, however, to take risks primarily in those situations where failure does not lead to serious consequences.

Source: Based on information in Schmidt and Larson (2010).

Steps 6 and 7: Assess trade-offs and make a choice

Trade-off:
A situation in which it is not possible to attain all objectives at the same time. In a trade-off situation, we need to give up something that we value in order to get something else that we value.

In many situations, one option will bring us closer to one objective, while an alternative will produce more favorable results for a different objective. If a manager needs to decide between three different data analysis and decision support software solutions to invest in, for example, there might be a conflict between the lowest cost of the first solution, the best functionality of the second solution, and the easiest integration with an existing database of the third solution. If this is the case, we are experiencing a typical **trade-off situation**. It is necessary to give up something from one objective in order to achieve another one.

An important step in addressing the trade-off problem is to think about the **relative importance of objectives**. In many cases, there are **required objectives** that definitely need to be achieved and **desired objectives** that reap advantages without being an absolute must.

Options that do not fulfill the criteria of a required objective do not need to be considered further. If a new software system absolutely needs to work with an existing database, for example, a manager deciding on which software system to invest in will no longer consider any systems that are unable to provide a compatible interface for that database. Likewise, those options that are clearly worse than at least one alternative choice for all of your objectives can be eliminated. The main problem, however, is how to rank the remaining (desired) objectives.

A first step is a crude classification into **primary desired objectives** (which are very important for the decision maker, albeit not in a "meet or die" sense as for the required objectives) and **secondary desired objectives** (that decision makers would ideally want to achieve, but do not rank among the most important ones). In our decision support software example, a few good references from within the same industry will probably rank higher than a number of references from other industries if it is important for the manager to get some proof that it is possible to analyze industry-specific data with the new software. Industry-specific references could therefore be seen as a primary desired objective, and references from other industries as a secondary desired objective.

The ranking of objectives is an important exercise because it forces decision makers to think about their real priorities. At least for the primary desired objectives, individual direct comparisons are advisable. An **objectives comparison matrix** (see Table 6.1) is a useful tool for ranking multiple objectives.

Table **6.1** An example of an objectives comparison matrix for different software systems

		(a)	(b)	(c)	(d)	(e)	Votes	Weighted score
(a)	Easy to upgrade		b	a	d	e	1	2.5
(b)	Industry references			c	d	b	2	5.0
(c)	Support (help desk)				d	e	1	2.5
(d)	Price (total costs)					d	4	10.0
(e)	Easy to use						2	5.0

Zooming in on ▶ THE OBJECTIVES COMPARISON MATRIX

The objectives comparison matrix can help to identify those key objectives that are more important to you. Think of a decision you need to make, either in your personal life, your academic life or your work life. (You could, for example, be in the position of trying to decide between different potential job offers.) Take the following steps to create your own matrix, referring back to the example in Table 6.1.

1 Identify all the objectives that you would like to achieve as a result of this decision.
2 Create a table, listing the objectives both horizontally at the top of the table and vertically down the left side.
3 Compare the objectives one by one. For example, where objectives (a) and (b) meet, decide which of them is more important to you. If you decide that (b) is more important than (a), type "b" into the cell.
4 Once you have compared all the objectives, count how many times you decided in favor of each one (this is the "Votes" column).
5 Assign the objective that received the highest number of votes a weighting of 10.
6 Divide 10 by the number of votes that the highest ranking objective received to get the base weighting for each vote (e.g. 10/4 votes = 2.5 points per vote).
7 Multiply the votes for each objective by the base weighting to obtain the overall score for each objective (e.g. the score for (b) "Industry references" is: 2 votes × 2.5 = 5.0 points).
8 This will give you a weighted score for each objective on a scale of 0 (unimportant) to 10 (high importance).

Table 6.2 An example of a weighted scoring model for comparing different software systems

Objective	Weight	Software A score	Software B score	Software C score	Software A weighted score	Software B weighted score	Software C weighted score
(a) Easy to upgrade	2.5	9	6	3	22.5	15.0	7.5
(b) Industry references	5.0	3	10	5	15.0	50.0	25.0
(c) Support (help desk)	2.5	7	3	5	17.5	7.5	12.5
(d) Price (total costs)	10.0	1	7	6	10.0	70.0	60.0
(e) Ease of use	5.0	5	6	10	25.0	30.0	50.0
Sum of weighted scores					90.0	172.5	155.0
Rank					*3.*	*1.*	*2.*

Weighted scoring model:
A tool that allows decision makers to choose between different options by means of evaluating their relative perfor-mance on meeting the weighted objectives that the decision makers want to achieve in a decision situation.

Even with a clear ranking of objectives, there are still situations in which some options score more favorably for some primary desired objectives and less so for others. When this is the case in complex decision problems, managers can resort to a systematic approach to **resolving the trade-off situation**. One widely used method is the **weighted scoring model** (see Table 6.2 and the *Zooming in on the weighted scoring model* box for an example).

Zooming in on ▶ THE WEIGHTED SCORING MODEL

The weighted scoring model is a tool for prioritizing different options according to the extent to which they help us reach our most important objectives when making a decision. Refer to Table 6.2 for an example of how it works:

1 Write down your objectives and assign a weight to each of them. You can use the weighted score from your objectives comparison matrix as the weights.
2 For each option (in our example, Software A, Software B, and Software C), evaluate the extent to which they meet each objective (on a scale of 0 = "does not meet the objective at all" to 10 = "fully meets the objective").
3 Calculate the weighted scores. To do this, multiply the evaluation scores for each option from step 2 with the weight of the respective objective (e.g. in Table 6.2, Software A received a score of 9 on the objective "Easy to upgrade" which has a weight of 2.5. The calculation for the weighted score is therefore 9 × 2.5 = 22.5).
4 For each option, sum the weighted scores for all objectives (e.g. for Software A, 22.5 + 15.0 + 17.5 + 10.0 + 25.0 = 90.0).
5 Rank the objectives by the sum of the weighted scores. In our example, Software B is the top-ranked option. That means that it best meets the weighted objectives.

Return to the decision you used for the activity in *Zooming in on the objectives comparison matrix*. Follow the steps explained above to help you to make your decision.

Alternative approaches to resolving trade-off situations include:[26]

- **Elimination by aspects**: First, a threshold value is set for the most important objective. All options that fall below this value are eliminated. For example, if price (total costs) is your most important objective when deciding between different software solutions, you could set a maximum price as a threshold value and then eliminate all options that do not meet this threshold. Continue the process with your second most important objective, followed by the third most important and so on, until there is only one option left.

- **Frequency of good and bad aspects**: Again, as in elimination by aspects, positive or negative threshold values (or criteria) are set for different objectives (e.g. a maximum price for the software, a minimum number of industry references, a maximum reaction time for the support help desk, a vendor guarantee about the next upgrades, and positive feedback about the usability of the software system in a small-scale focus group test). Each option is then evaluated on the basis of whether it meets these threshold criteria. The option that meets the most criteria will be chosen.
- **Majority of confirming dimensions**: One pair of options is compared across all objectives, and the option which wins across the greatest number of objectives is retained. For example, you might start by comparing Option X and Option Y. If Option X beats Option Y in five out of seven criteria, X will be retained and Y will be eliminated. In the next step, Option X will be compared against the next option. Again, the option which meets the highest number of criteria wins. This procedure is repeated until one option has beaten all the others in the pairwise comparisons.

Sensitivity analysis:
A test of the robustness of a decision through calculating different scenarios of what would happen if the probabilities of critical uncertainties or the outcome values of different options change.

The different strategies for dealing with trade-offs can also be used in combination. If all of them come to the same conclusion, the decision will be more robust. Once a decision has been made and one option has been selected, two tests can further improve the outcome of the decision-making process.

The first test is **sensitivity analysis**. Probabilities and outcome values are often opinions and estimates rather than clear-cut facts. As Bazerman and Moore note, "people play a crucial role in models. People decide which variables to put into the model and how to weight them."[27] Thus, it makes sense to test the stability of the decision when different (but still reasonable) probabilities and outcome values are assigned. Returning to the marquee example from the decision tree in Figure 6.2, we could test what would happen with a 10 percent or a 50 percent chance of rain rather than the 30 percent chance assumed in the base scenario. Would that change our decision?

"No regrets" test:
As a final stage in a decision-making process, the outcome of the decision is assessed for potential negative consequences together with a judgment by the decision makers of whether they would be willing to cope with these consequences.

Second is the **"No regrets" test**. Harvard Business School Professor David E. Bell argues that decision makers usually desire to avoid any negative outcomes of their decisions that they will later regret.[28] Therefore, the chosen solution should be tested for potential negative consequences. Is there anything that could go wrong with this choice? Could there be obstacles to its successful implementation? Potentially adverse consequences should be made explicit, together with their probability and the seriousness of their impact. After making a final judgment and deciding in favor of one option, an action plan for addressing the potential adverse consequences of this choice can be developed. "One should always look for a possible alternative, and provide against it," says the fictional detective, Sherlock Holmes, in *The Adventure of Black Peter*. "It is the first rule of criminal investigation"[29]—and also good advice for making decisions in a managerial context.

Find one article about a company from the business section of a newspaper or website. What kind of decisions might have led to the situation that made the news? If you were leading that company, how would you approach such a situation? What might be the biggest challenges involved in making subsequent decisions?

6.2 Thinking about decisions, decisions about thinking

© Royalty-Free/Corbis

In brief

- Decisions are preceded by thought processes. Managers do not always think in a rational-analytical way, but also employ two unconscious thinking modes: (1) categorical thinking, in which they put people, objects, or situations into "mental boxes" or categories (e.g. young/old), triggering certain associations related to that grouping; and (2) intuitive thinking, which is a more holistic pattern-recognition process based on experience.

- Modern computer-based data analytics and decision support systems can help managers to make more rational decisions.

- Instead of preferring one thinking mode over another, managers can also combine them. Intermodal thinking integrates a rational-analytic approach with intuition.

- Being aware of the different ways of thinking and their appropriate application can help decision makers to use their brains more effectively.

Bounded rationality:
The idea that decision makers work under certain constraints including, in particular, limited information, the limited information-processing capacity of the human brain, and the limited time that is available for decision making.

Thinking modes:
General ways in which our mind can approach the thinking task.

System 1 thinking:
A fast thinking mode in which our brain uses the automatic information-processing system.

System 2 thinking:
A slow thinking mode in which our brain uses the rational informa-tion-processing system.

To decide between various alternatives, managers inevitably need to think. The quality of thinking has an important influence on the quality of the outcome of the decision-making process. In the traditional literature on management, it is often assumed that organizations are full of rational decision makers, using sophisticated instruments like decision trees or evaluation models to determine the optimal solution for complex problems. The notion of the manager as a rational being prevails more than half a century after Herbert Simon made us aware that people—including managers—are constrained by **bounded rationality**, being more prone to **satisfice** than to optimize, with the tendency to jump to the first best solution instead of carefully analyzing and weighing up all the options for solving a problem.[30]

Does that mean that we need to completely abandon the notion of rational decision makers? Should we rather think about managers as constant oversimplifiers who never get to the bottom of things? Maybe the truth lies, as so often, in a synthesis of both points of view, acknowledging that we are neither analytic machines nor completely simplistic in our thinking.

Research in cognitive science has found that we can operate in **different thinking modes**. Psychologists generally distinguish between two human information-processing systems: the **automatic (or experiential) information-processing system** that is character-ized by an unconscious and seemingly effortless way of reaching conclusions on the one hand, and the **rational (or deliberate) system** that allows us to consciously follow a particular line of thought on the other hand.[31] One example of automatic information processing is deciding to delegate a task to a particular team member without giving it much thought, simply because in our experience this team member has always performed similar tasks well. If the same decision were made using a rational system, we would probably consider addi-tional aspects; for example, who in the team has the right skills, who has spare capacity, or for whom could this task be a good development opportunity? We would then make a delib-erate criteria-based decision on who is best suited to undertake this task.

The automatic, largely unconscious thinking mode has also been referred to as **System 1 thinking**, and the more intentional, effortful, conscious, and analytic way of thinking as **System 2 thinking**.[32] In most of our everyday life, we are using the former, nonconscious system, processing information without too much deliberate analysis. We know the outcomes of our thinking process, but we do not really know how we arrived at these outcomes. Particularly when we are busy and under stress, we are more inclined to use System 1 thinking.

Categorical thinking

It is essential for human beings to be able to adapt to new and surprising situations. This requires a fast (System 1) thinking mode that allows us to quickly capture the essence of a situation, so that we can react accordingly in due time. In this fast thinking mode, rather than thoroughly analyzing all the individual components of a complex system, we **categorize stimuli** in a mental process that is known as **categorical thinking**.

Categorical thinking:
A fast thinking mode (a sub-category of System 1 thinking) in which we quickly react to stimuli through the use of heuristics and simplified categorizations.

Faced with a new situation, it is a normal human reaction to compare what we are currently experiencing with similar situations that we have encountered before. Thus, we place the new situation in a category that is already known to us. Once we have this categorical representation, we are confronted with everything our brain associates with this particular category.[33] When a job candidate enters the room for an interview, for example, there are already multiple opportunities for categorization open to the hiring manager, such as male/female, young/old, professional/unprofessional appearance, energetic/lacking in energy, to name just a few. Each classification potentially triggers a whole chain of associations stored in our mind from previous experiences with other representatives of the respective category. These associations, in turn, will influence our actions—in this case which candidate gets the job. In short, "[c]ategorization of an object we encounter determines what we do with it."[34] When we think categorically, we **generalize from prior experiences** with similar objects or situations as we put the new stimuli into a "mental box"—a category.

A category can be present in our mind either as a combination of former cases or in condensed form as a **prototype**—a representative example of this category. So we could, for example, unconsciously combine different experiences that we have had with investment bankers, or have a "typical" investment banker (as a prototype) in mind as we decide on how to approach a forthcoming meeting at an investment bank.

Another way of thinking about categories is to consider the **boundaries** between them (e.g. a proposal is considered an "attractive investment" if it breaks even within three years; otherwise it's an "unattractive investment").[35] This example shows that categories and their boundaries are often subjective, situation-based, and highly dependent on a person's past experiences. What is considered "attractive" or "unattractive" can be totally different in different industries or business environments. The categories that we use depend on our current objectives, on our attention and interests, but especially on our prior experiences. Thus, we can assume that a birdwatcher will have a more fine-grained categorization system for birds than an average manager (not counting those with specific bird-related interests, of course).

Heuristics:
Simple rules or "mental shortcuts" by which decisions are made on the basis of learning from prior experience in similar situations.

Related to categorical thinking is the concept of **heuristics**: educated guesses or "rules of thumb" that we apply by categorizing a problem based on past experience and finding an approach which has already worked well. Bingham and Eisenhardt suggest that not only individuals but also firms as a collective learn through generating what they call a **portfolio of heuristics**: an easy-to-remember set of simple rules such as "Cut costs whenever a recession is approaching" or "Whenever a competitor is launching a new product, copy it."[36]

As useful as heuristics can be in everyday situations, they also bear the danger of bias and systematic error. For example, we may incorrectly presume that one instance in the past is also representative of all situations of that kind in the future. Take the case of Pets.com, a start-up that sold pet supplies directly to consumers in the early days of the Internet. It followed a widespread heuristic of the dot.com boom, a period of excessive speculative investments in Internet companies at the turn of the millennium: "raise brand awareness at any cost in order to get big fast." Spending millions of dollars on advertising campaigns, including a $1.2 million national Super Bowl TV ad, did not reap the intended sales benefits, however. (The Super Bowl commercial at the annual championship game of the National Football League would have generated extremely high viewership and a lot of attention all across the US and beyond.) "While they made the whole nation aware, people just weren't interested,"[37] wrote one commentator. What had worked for others did not work for Pets.com because the market was not yet ready for the home delivery of pet supplies. Instead, Pets.com survived for two years before ending up on a list of the "greatest dotcom disasters."[38]

We often employ categorical thinking and heuristics when we lack the motivation or time to think more deeply and more concisely about an issue, or when we do not have the cognitive capacity to do so, for instance because we are too preoccupied with other things.[39] Managers, however, are frequently faced with complex problems that cannot simply be put into a certain "box" or category. Nevertheless, they often make quick decisions without deeply analyzing an issue. If they are asked about the rationale behind their decision-making process, they state that they simply relied on their intuition, on gut feeling, or on their experience. Although it is also an unconscious mental process, intuitive thinking clearly differs from pure categorical thinking.

Intuitive thinking

While categorical thinking is reductionist in the sense that we only allocate stimuli to certain categories, intuition is a more **holistic pattern-recognition process** in which we subconsciously link "disparate elements of information"[40] by means of associations that enable us to see the whole picture (the "pattern") rather than only its individual parts.[41] In Aristotle's words, intuition is about "grasping the first principles."[42] We feel that we "know" without actually knowing why.[43]

Intuition:
A fast thinking mode (a sub-category of System 1 thinking) in which we quickly react to stimuli through the use of an experience-based holistic pattern-recognition process that leads to an emotional response.

Chess grandmasters, for example, are able to recognize 50,000 patterns or more, each of them with associated risks and opportunities.[44] When they play multiple games at the same time in simultaneous chess, they neither have the time nor the processing capacity to analyze all the possible options move by move. They need to make fast, intuitive decisions. This example also indicates that domain-specific intuition is not something we are born with. Have you ever seen a one-year-old playing simultaneous chess? **Intuition** comes with learning, practice, and experience (see the box *Learning intuition*). In order for intuition to work effectively, a decision maker needs **extensive domain-relevant experience** and a deep understanding of complex connections in the field in which an intuitive decision is made.[45] Intuition, thus, "does not come easy; it requires years of experience in problem-solving and is founded upon a solid and complete grasp of the details of the business."[46]

FROM A DIFFERENT ANGLE

Learning intuition

Can intuition be learned? The results of psychological studies on expert performance suggest that it is possible through a combination of three factors:[47]

- *Intense practice* (to gain relevant experience that the mind can combine and refer to when making intuitive judgments).

- *Critical self-appraisal* (to judge candidly whether decisions were correct or not, even playing devil's advocate in relation to your own judgments).
- *Sincere and open feedback* (obtaining concrete, constructive ideas to improve intuitive judgment).

Intuition is linked to **emotions**—intuitive judgments are usually affectively charged, or in other words, shaped by emotion.[48] In fact, neuroscientists have linked intuition with emotional stimuli connected to the activation of *basal ganglia* in the human brain.[49] This link between intuition and emotions is also epitomized in the term **gut feeling**. Managers often report that a certain decision simply "feels right," or, in turn, that they have "a bad feeling" about something, without being able to state exactly where this feeling comes from. Emotionally significant experiences in the past play an important role here, as they can influence our feelings about and reactions to novel situations.[50] For example, if a manager without further rational analysis suddenly has a bad feeling about investing in a new product, this could have been triggered unconsciously by a prior negative experience with a similar product that failed.

Intuition can be a bad as well as a good advisor, however. The experiences on which our intuitions are based can stem from different situations or domains that might not be comparable with the current situation. Decision makers should therefore strive to attain what psychology Professor Linda Pelzmann calls a **qualified intuition**.[51] She argues that people should only follow their intuition in their field of specialization, for which they have acquired the level of competence and domain-relevant experience necessary to distinguish relevant from irrelevant information. If a manager only has experience of working with people from the same cultural background, for example, they cannot assume that their intuition will help them when they encounter the cross-cultural challenges of leading a globally dispersed team for the first time (see also Chapter 5). Following our intuition based merely on a few very random incidents can lead to heavily biased conclusions, and thus to suboptimal decisions. Furthermore, Pelzmann reminds us that in dynamic environments, intuitive decisions can lead to fallacies if they assume constant conditions and are not adapted to the specifics of a particular situation.[52]

The rational approach to decision making

Consciously thinking more deeply about an issue is the domain of the rational, deliberate "System 2." A **rational-analytic approach** to decision making usually involves a stepwise process following a logical chain of reasoning, including several or all of the elements described in Section 6.1, *The anatomy of a decision*. A problem—a gap between a desired state and an existing state—is defined, and the objectives that the decision maker aims to achieve are then set out. Potential solutions are subsequently developed, and uncertainties, outcomes, and their probabilities are assessed. A systematic selection process then leads to the adoption of the best possible solution according to the decision maker's objectives and risk preferences.

There are, however, some assumptions underlying this model: first, problems are supposed to be clearly definable; second, the decision maker is expected to have complete information about all the options, the uncertainties involved, and the probabilities of different outcomes; third, it supposes that there are precise criteria for the evaluation of these options; and fourth, that the decision maker always acts completely rationally in an effort to maximize economic return for the organization.[53] In many decision situations, these assumptions do not hold.

The rational-analytic model is a **normative** one: it describes how decision makers should *ideally* take decisions.[54] Although it is quite straightforward and taught in many management programs, this is not the most common way in which managers actually approach problems. In an empirical study on managerial decisions, it was found that the decision process often "kept cycling back, interrupted by new events, diverted by opportunities and so on, going round and round until a final solution emerged."[55] In fact, the rational thinking approach to decision making can work well with clearly defined problems, reliable data, and a stable, structured context.[56] How often, however, are these conditions met in complex organizations that are operating in dynamic environments?

Think about how you came to the decision of applying for the course that you are currently studying. Did you use categorical thinking, intuitive thinking, or a rational-analytic approach during the decision process? Judging from what you have read so far in this chapter, would you say that you used the right thinking mode(s) for your decision? Is there anything that you would change regarding your decision process if you had to make the decision again?

Data analytics and decision support systems

Rapid developments in information and communication technology have provided new tools for supporting managers in making rational decisions. Computer systems can be used to monitor and analyze data, to optimize operations, make forecasts, or create scenarios. The application areas for computerized data-driven decision making are widespread, ranging from supply chain and manufacturing process optimization to improving product offerings, customer service, financial management and budgeting, or sales and distribution decisions. Although decision support systems, which use rule-based models to structure data in a way that provides managers with well-founded recommendations for various problems, have been in use for decades, recent technological advances have opened up many new possibilities.

Data warehouses (central repositories of data combined from different sources) and **OLAP** (online analytical processing: a tool that can be used to extract valuable information from large amounts of data) are key components of **business intelligence**, a strategic approach to collecting and analyzing business-related data. A new generation of decision support systems is based on "**big data**," a catchphrase that is widely used for the analysis of an extremely high volume of real-time (or nearly real-time) data that are integrated from different sources.[57] Modern analytics can discover complex relationships in vast amounts of data. **Correlations** and significant patterns that are found in the data can help us to draw conclusions about potential **causalities** on a more general level (keeping in mind, however, that false cause–effect attributions are always possible). They can also help to make predictions in individual cases (e.g. about actions that an individual customer is likely to take).[58] The systems can be designed in such a way that decisions are automated according to certain rules or as a support for human decision makers.

You can see data analytics in practice in many major businesses. If you have ever used Netflix or a similar video-on-demand platform, your viewing habits, together with data from the millions of other subscribers, will have been used to make decisions on which programs to create or buy. Similarly, telecommunications company T-Mobile USA combines social media and transaction data to predict customer defections, while British Airways customers receive targeted offerings through combining existing loyalty information with data about online behavior.[59] International package delivery company UPS has saved enormous amounts of fuel and miles through fleet optimization decisions made thanks to the analysis of delivery data and telematics (truck tracking systems).[60]

Investment in technology alone is, however, not sufficient for improving decision processes. It is also important (1) to base the system on **undistorted raw data** from reliable sources, (2) to find out where analytical efforts can potentially reap the biggest benefits (thus avoiding **"analysis paralysis"** and "drowning in data"[61]), and (3) to develop the necessary **data-handling and interpretation skills** as well as a certain mind-set in the managerial team. MIT scientists Andrew McAfee and Erik Brynjolfsson, for example, recommend that managers get into the habit of asking questions like "What do the data say?", "Where did the data come from?", "What kinds of analyses have been conducted?", or "How confident are we in the results?" when they are confronted with important decisions.[62] Moreover, managers should also be aware that what is measured can be subjective, and is therefore a decision in itself.

With all the excitement about the possibilities that big data applications are opening up for improving managerial decision making, it is important to point out that predictions can also fail if circumstances change, for example in the case of rare and non-computable "**black swan events**" that are new and surprising but can still have a major effect.[63] Inadequate sample sizes, coincidental correlation patterns, and systematic biases in data collection (e.g. when a sample that is meant to be representative of the whole population only includes students) are further potential pitfalls when relying on big data systems.[64] Another issue that needs to be taken into account is privacy. When personal information is collected and combined, adequate protection mechanisms must be in place to avoid the misuse of data. For example, in the European Union, the General Data Protection Regulation (GDPR) contains very strict rules regarding the processing of the personal data of individuals.

Data warehouse:
A large, central database that is used as a repository of data generated by all parts of an organization for analytical or reporting purposes.

OLAP:
Online analytical processing: Computer-based tools that allow an ad-hoc analysis of large amounts of multidimensional data.

Business intelligence:
A strategic approach that uses technology to collect, integrate, and analyze large amounts of data for the purpose of supporting decision making in organizations.

Big data:
Extremely large sets of both structured and unstructured real-time (or near real-time) data that are integrated from different sources in order to be analyzed with the help of computer technology.

Correlation:
A measure that indicates the extent to which two or more variables are statistically related to each other. When variables correlate, they occur or fluctuate together. This does not automatically imply that they are also causally connected.

Causality:
A cause–effect relationship between different variables.

Intermodal thinking

As we have discussed, managers operate either in a rational-analytic, categorical, or intuitive thinking mode when making decisions (see Figure 6.4 for a simplified overview). But should we prefer one thinking mode over the others? An understandable reaction would be to demand that managers are as rational as possible in making their decisions, and therefore ought to employ the rational-analytic thinking mode (ideally also supported by modern data analytics) as often as possible.

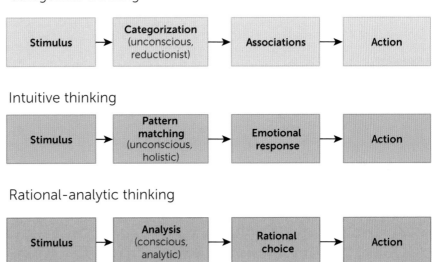

Figure 6.4 The three basic thinking modes

However, rational-analytic thinking is not necessarily superior to categorical and intuitive thinking, which both offer advantages in reaction time and in the efficient use of limited cognitive processing resources, or in other words your brain.[65] Rosch, for example, argues that "the task of a category system is to provide maximum information with the least cognitive effort."[66] Because categorical thinking needs less mental capacity, our brain can pay more attention to noticing and interpreting further clues that are potentially useful for the decision.[67] Of course, these advantages come with major drawbacks that are inherent in categorical thinking. Undifferentiated answers that are based solely on past experience and have not been reflected upon can also lead to fatal misperceptions and totally inadequate conclusions in novel, complex situations.

Holistic, intuitive thinking that enables us to recognize patterns and create multiple connections between different phenomena can be more appropriate in the face of environmental complexity.[68] "When making a decision of minor importance, I have always found it advantageous to consider all the pros and cons," said psychoanalyst, Sigmund Freud. "In vital matters, however, such as the choice of a mate or a profession, the decision should come from the unconscious, from somewhere within ourselves. In the important decisions of our personal life, we should be governed, I think, by the deep inner needs of our nature."[69] Research results show that intuitive decision making is positively linked with performance in complex and unstable environments.[70] Internet start-up companies, for example, are often faced with a rapidly evolving market environment, in which consumer behavior is difficult to predict, competitors can quickly enter their market niche, and investors can move their money from one project to another. In such a fast-changing environment in which many different factors play a role, the ability to synthesize disparate information is essential. In stable environments, however, gut feelings need to be used with care, as rational analysis can usually lead to more accurate results.[71] When decisions or tasks include definite objective criteria, a rational approach usually leads to superior outcomes.[72]

Table 6.3 Overview of thinking modes

Thinking mode	Categorical thinking	Intuitive thinking	Rational-analytic thinking
Type	Automatic/experiential information processing	Automatic/experiential information processing	Rational/deliberate information processing
Main application	Heuristics (learning from experience)	Synthesis	Analysis
Advantages	• Fast • Efficient use of cognitive resources • Less effort • Frees up attentional resources	• Fast • Holistic and integrative • Ability to synthesize information • Understanding of complex systems	• More accurate • Use of explicit decision rules • Objective • Possibility of finding the optimal solution to a well-defined problem
Disadvantages	• Simplistic • Lack of reflection • Undifferentiated • Based solely on past experiences • Inadequate for complex problems	• Does not work without sufficient practice and experience in a domain • Decisions can be seen as arbitrary by others	• Requires time • High effort • Does not make adequate use of the right side of the brain (the more creative side) • Lack of integration and synthesis
Adequate for	Simple decisions and problems without major potential for repercussions	Unstructured, complex decision problems	Structured, complex decision problems

If different thinking modes can be more efficient and/or more effective in different situations (see Table 6.3 for an overview), it is important that managers learn to use the whole repertoire. But can we actually deliberately choose between different thinking modes? Harvard Professor Daniel M. Wegner's theoretical model of self-control of mental states suggests that we can suppress unwanted thoughts, such as inappropriate heuristic conclusions, if we use two processes:

- a **monitoring process**, in which we actively scan whether we have used any unintended thought processes (i.e. consciously asking yourself "Am I thinking about this in the right way?"); and
- an **operating process**, in which we consciously try to use the appropriate thinking approach ("What would be the best approach to deal with this issue?").[73]

When aiming to switch our thinking mode, the monitoring process is especially important. Increased awareness and self-monitoring about how we think can help us to deliberately switch from categorical thinking to a rational-analytic mode if necessary.

Most managerial decision processes need both **analysis** (of different factors that influence the decision) and **synthesis** (bringing it all together again in choosing one particular way forward). As Herbert Simon notes, "intuition is not a process that operates independently of analysis; rather, the two processes are essential complementary components of effective decision-making systems."[74] Therefore—at least when decisions are really important and when there is sufficient time available—effective managers will use both modes, thus practicing **intermodal thinking**.

According to Hodgkinson and Sadler-Smith, "intuitive and analytic approaches to the processing of information are both required," as "the ultimate skill, ... in contemporary work organizations, must be the ability to adapt the ways in which information is processed, switching back and forth from 'habits of mind' to 'active thinking,' as appropriate to each particular situation."[75] One possibility for practicing intermodal thinking is first to write down one's gut feeling about an issue, subsequently to undertake a rational analysis of the situation, and finally to compare the outcome of this analysis with the original intuition before making a concluding judgment.

Intermodal thinking:
Using a combination of different thinking modes to come to a conclusion; for example, first listening to our intuition and then consciously using a rational-analytic approach to make a decision.

There is another very effective activity for managers who are facing tough and complex decisions: **having a good night's sleep**! Neuroscientists have discovered that sleep considerably enhances category learning,[76] as well as generally facilitating a process called "assimilation," in which new information is integrated into the network of related information already stored in the brain.[77] Sleep therefore helps our brain to process and link new information to existing knowledge, thus creating the neural connections necessary to improve our thinking—no matter whether it is categorical, analytic, or intuitive—as a precondition of effective decision making.

Data analytics as a decision-making tool at Zara

CASE STUDY

In 1963, Amancio Ortega Gaona, who later became one of the richest people in the world, opened a workshop for producing dresses and gowns in his Spanish hometown A Coruña. In 1975, he opened his first store under the Zara brand name, followed by more than 7,000 additional outlets (under various brands) all around the world over the following 40 years. Today, Zara is part of the holding company Inditex, a global market leader in the fashion industry led by CEO Pablo Isla since 2005. The company is active in 93 markets and employs more than 160,000 workers. Zara is known for inexpensive, trendy fashion products that are sold in stores with an upmarket feel in prime retail locations. It is seen as the role model for "fast fashion" retailers that offer new styles multiple times during the season, quickly following the latest fashion trends.

There are three main decisions that fashion retailers have to make, and Zara has revolutionized the fashion industry in all three:

1 *Sourcing decisions*: Fashion retailers need to decide on their suppliers and on order quantities. A typical large fashion retailer will place sizeable orders with suppliers in low-cost countries (often in Asia) on a seasonal basis to minimize purchasing costs. Following this strategy, retailers risk either running out of stock in the case of high demand or being left with unsold stock in the case of low demand. Zara takes a different approach, initially producing small quantities in nearby factories (mainly in Spain, Portugal, and North African countries) and then using the early data on consumer demand to forecast and produce the quantities that the market actually requires.

2 *Design decisions*: Traditional fashion retailers would choose their designs once per season following the trends of the catwalk and the advice of industry experts. Long cycle times from the first designs to the final distribution limit the capacity to adapt to changing demands. Zara tries out different designs in limited quantities first and then changes them many times per season in response to sales data and qualitative consumer feedback from all over the world. Thus, unlike the traditional model, consumers determine production.

3 *Distribution decisions*: Multi-store retailers must decide on the quantities they send to each store. They need to ensure that there are enough products available in each store according to consumer demand while avoiding high inventory costs. Usually, retailers would use centralized inventory management systems to accomplish this task. When stores are running out of stock, they would be replenished. Zara again chose a different model: if a product is no longer available in the most important sizes, it is moved to another store with complementary sizes. Stores are stocked twice a week, so that consumers can always find new offers. As a side-effect, Zara needs to sell fewer items at a discount.

A key enabler for the innovative decision-making approach at Zara is big data analytics. Zara runs a central data processing center in which it collects and analyzes quantitative (sales) data from all stores around the world in real time, with a separate team being devoted to analyzing qualitative consumer feedback. The data are shared with Zara's commercial team and over 300 designers who create new outfits on a daily basis, in line with global trends in consumer demand. It only takes the company about 20 days to design and deliver new garments to its international store network (compared to the industry standard of several months).

Inditex rarely invests in advertising, apart from social media marketing. According to information provided by an Inditex company spokesman to the *Strait Times*, around 80 percent of the company's investments flow into the stores, and the "remaining 20 percent into building up its technology capabilities."[78] Technology is also used for forecasting, price optimization, tracking apparel items, self-checkouts, or interactive fitting rooms. New technological solutions for tracking footfall in stores and virtual assistants that can optimize the shopping experience for customers are tested in Inditex's innovation unit.

Zara's unmatched flexibility is partly based on the company's technological capabilities, and partly on its optimized supply chain with factories, distribution hubs and store networks in relative proximity. With further expansion plans in Asia where local competitors like Uniqlo are trying to follow a similar "fast fashion" strategy, Zara is facing challenges in fully implementing its model overseas because the distribution costs and times are much higher than within the tightly knit network in Europe. The company is, however, already expanding its production capacities in Asia.

Sources: Caro and Martinez de Albéniz (2013); Dowsett (2018); Hansen (2012); Inditex (2015; 2017).

💬 Discussion questions

- How would you frame the main decision problems that Zara is facing?
- What are the critical uncertainties and trade-offs that Zara has to deal with in these decisions?
- What role does intuition, on the one hand, and a rational-analytic approach, on the other, play in the fashion industry in general and in Zara specifically?
- How do big data and decision support systems change the way in which the fashion industry works?

6.3 Potential pitfalls in decision making and how to avoid them

iStock.com/jockermax

In brief

- To err is human. When we as human beings make decisions, we are prone to mistakes due to the peculiarities of how our brains work.

- We draw analogies based on the first available examples that come to our mind, overestimate our abilities, ignore potentially conflicting evidence, obstinately cling to decisions we once made, and often follow our emotions rather than rational arguments.

- Most decision-making pitfalls can be avoided or at least mitigated using strategies such as treating our own beliefs as hypotheses rather than the truth, considering alternative solutions in a dialectic thinking approach, or involving trusted outsiders in the decision process.

In many situations, managers do not consider all the alternatives, do not acquire all the necessary information about possible consequences, do not calculate the probabilities of the consequences, or are even unsure about their preferences, having "incomplete and inconsistent goals, not all of which are considered at the same time."[79] In short, managers are inclined to **satisfice**, looking for the first solution that comes along or for an action that is just good enough for a certain level of aspiration rather than striving to achieve the optimal solution.[80] The reasons for this cognitive and behavioral tendency lie in the limitations of the human brain, specifically in its limited capabilities and capacity for attention, memory, comprehension, and communication.[81] Because "[d]ecisions will be affected by the way decision makers attend (or fail to attend) to particular preferences, alternatives, and consequences,"[82] it is necessary to take a closer look at the **cognitive limitations** that can impede effective decision making.

The top ten fallacies in decision making

Psychology Professor Jonathan Baron identified no fewer than 53 different forms of bias; that is, 53 possible ways of flawed thinking when we make decisions.[83] Keeping them all in mind for every single decision would probably be overkill. However, understanding some of the most salient fallacies can prevent managers from making the worst mistakes during the decision-making process. Here is an overview of ten quite common **decision-making pitfalls**:

1   **Relying on examples that are easily brought to mind**. This is one of the main mental shortcuts (or heuristics) described by Nobel laureate Daniel Kahneman and his colleague Amos Tversky. The **availability heuristic** works in the following way: the more easily certain similar instances come to mind, the higher the decision maker tends to judge the probability of their occurrence. Recency and vividness are important factors in making an event stick out. For example, you are more likely to believe that there will be a plane crash if two such events have been reported on the news recently.[84] Similarly, having a vivid picture of a subordinate's recent negative performance in mind can bias a manager's overall judgment of this person in a performance appraisal.[85]

2   **Being blinded by similarity**. We tend to judge the probability of an event by comparing it to a similar event from the past, thereby ignoring that there are different base rates, i.e. relative frequencies of occurrence of events. For example, if a hiring manager has already assessed three candidates who graduated from a business degree program, and all three of them are weak in statistics, this manager could infer from that knowledge that a new candidate, who is also a graduate from that particular school, would also be weak in statistics. Thus, the hiring manager would fall victim to the phenomenon known as the **representativeness heuristic**[86]—ignoring the fact that in every class there are some students who are better and others who are worse in a specific subject. It might be possible that the three students who the manager had assessed previously were among the 15 percent who were least skilled in handling and interpreting statistical data, while the new candidate is among the top 10 percent of their cohort. The effect is similar to stereotyping, and can also lead to ethical problems when managers generalize their experiences with one or a few individuals and start to judge people based on certain groupings (e.g. ethnicity or social class).

3   **Underestimating extremely unlikely events**.[87] The Fukushima nuclear power plant in Japan was designed to withstand earthquakes of a magnitude of 7.0 on the moment magnitude scale. On March 11, 2011, however, disaster struck in the form of the extremely unlikely event of a magnitude 9.0 earthquake with its epicenter near the island of Honshu, followed by more than 13-meter-high tsunami waves that hit the Fukushima power plant. The rest of the story is well known: the nuclear meltdown and release of radioactive radiation caused untold damage. Such an event was highly unlikely. However, it did happen, with all its tremendous consequences. There is a human tendency to overestimate the likelihood that events that we have already experienced can occur again, and to underestimate the probability of events that have not yet occurred.[88]

4   **Overestimating your role**. As James March points out, people tend to attribute success to their capabilities, and failure to circumstances or bad luck.[89] An overt "can-do" mentality, especially on the part of managers who were successful in the past, can lead to a systematic underestimation of risks. People are prone to overestimate not only their capabilities but also their judgments, which can be particularly detrimental when important decisions need to be taken.

5   **Belief conservation**. This term was used by James March to describe the phenomenon that decision makers tend to interpret new information in a way that is consistent with their existing beliefs.[90] However, the issue was actually recognized 400 years ago, when Sir Francis Bacon (1561–1626), the well-known English philosopher and statesman, wrote that "[t]he human understanding when it has once adopted an opinion ... draws all things else to support and agree with it."[91] We do not like to be confronted with the bitter truth that up to now we have been holding fallacious beliefs. Thus, we merely consider confirming evidence while ignoring potentially disruptive information—a tendency that is also known as **confirmation bias**.[92]

Availability heuristic:
A mental shortcut in which more salient and immediate examples more easily come to mind, thus potentially biasing our decision-making process.

Representativeness heuristic:
A mental shortcut in which we base our judgments of people or objects on their similarity to people or objects that we already know (viewing the examples that come to mind as "representative" of a certain population).

Confirmation bias:
The tendency of the mind to seek and favor information that confirms existing beliefs.

Hindsight bias:
The (false) perception that an event or development has been predictable, although this perception was only formed after the event.

6 **"I knew it all along."** Looking back after an event has occurred, people tend to argue that they could have easily predicted the event beforehand. This is a phenomenon known as **hindsight bias**. In retrospect, we always know better. For example, many people claim that they had long predicted the financial and economic crisis of 2007—although we did not really hear their voices before the crisis. This feeling that "we always knew" prevents us from learning, as we do not investigate why we misjudged the probability that a certain event would occur, thinking that in any case we predicted it correctly. In a wider context, March argues that "human interpretations of history consistently exaggerate the coherence and necessity of realized history, the role of human intention and action in history, and the comprehensibility of historical forces."[93]

Structural interruptions:
Unexpected shifts or changes in trends.

7 **Failing to reassess your success strategy in the wake of changed circumstances**. We often tend to see the future as a prolongation of the past, failing to acknowledge the possibility of **structural interruptions**. "What worked last time will also work this time" is a common thinking pattern among executives. Following success, managers often do not see a need to reconsider their strategies, even though changed environmental circumstances could render the old approaches ineffective. Thus, existing strategies can be what "blinders are to horses: they keep them going in a straight line but hardly encourage peripheral vision."[94] Decision makers fall into the **competency trap**, in which the prolongation of practices that were effective in the past leads to failure under changed circumstances.

Competency trap:
The (false) belief that the practices that were effective in the past will also continue to work in the future (despite changing environmental circumstances).

8 **Escalation of commitment**. Managers hate to admit that they failed. They also do not want to appear inconsistent in their decisions in the eyes of others. Therefore, they usually try to do everything possible to justify the decisions that they made, even if that means that they will have to "throw good money after bad." Like gamblers increasing their stakes without an increased chance of success, managers often do not stop projects even if their chances of success are objectively very low, just so that they do not have to admit to themselves and others that the initial investment decision was a mistake. Empirical research has shown that the tendency to invest more in uncertain projects is higher when the decision makers are provided with an external justification of failure.[95]

Focusing illusion:
A cognitive bias in which we attach too much weight to only one aspect of a particular situation or choice.

9 **Neglecting important facets of a decision due to a narrow focus**. The **focusing illusion** occurs when we make judgments about an entire object or category by focusing only on one salient subset of it.[96] For example, if we compare the quality of life in two different regions, one particular distinctive difference (e.g. the difference in climate) could be given relatively more weight than it would actually have in a rational analysis of all the important criteria for the decision (e.g. job options, cultural offers, safety, and educational opportunities). Schkade and Kahneman observed that counter to the stereotype that "Californians are happier in life because they have more sun," there were no differences in general life satisfaction between people living in California and those living in the Midwest of the United States when several factors relating to quality of life were rated in the two regions. This led them to conclude that: "Nothing that you focus on will make as much difference as you think."[97]

10 **Decision making by emotions (only)**. Our decisions can be influenced by emotions such as envy, anger, or anxiety. Although emotions play an important role in judging whether or not a decision "feels right" (i.e., in intuitive thinking, as was pointed out in Section 6.2), they can also lead to suboptimal decisions when we rely on them exclusively. Momentarily salient issues or current mood can equally instill bias, for example through an underestimation of our resilience in the face of negative events.[98] Likewise, decisions can also be influenced by positive emotions (see the box *Cultural differences in decision making*).

Have you made any bad decisions at university or at work? Or have you heard about a bad decision in the business news? Can you recognize in that decision any of the common decision-making fallacies discussed in this chapter? Can you spot any additional decision failures? What would you do to avoid the pitfall(s) that you have identified in your future decision-making processes?

In addition to thinking traps linked to cognitive limitations, managers can also face very negative consequences when they overlook **ethical issues** in their decision-making process. Making the "right" choice for the organization is often not enough if managers do not consider what is "right" or "wrong" in an ethical sense. (See Chapter 5 for more information on how to include ethical principles in decision making.)

FROM A DIFFERENT ANGLE

Cultural differences in decision making

How we make decisions is based on how we think. How we think, in turn, can be influenced by the culture in which we have been socialized. Studies have shown, for example, that for people with a Western cultural background, affective forecasts—specifically expectations of a feeling of enjoyment after making a certain decision—can play an important role in influencing their choice. For East Asians, however, expected enjoyment does not seem to matter to the same extent. One possible reason for this difference could lie in our understanding of the self, either as an independent individual (in Western cultures) or as

strongly interdependent with others as part of a collectivistic society (in Asian cultures). If people feel that they are part of a greater whole, they might place less emphasis on their own enjoyment and focus more on their obligation toward others when they make decisions. In addition to the ethical issues that arise here—are decision makers from some cultures acting more ethically because they place greater consideration on the well-being of others?—this could also mean that the "decision making by emotions (only)" thinking trap could be more or less salient in different cultures.

Source: Based on information in Falk et al. (2010).

How to avoid falling into thinking traps

Distilling the essence of the top ten decision-making pitfalls, we can conclude that decision makers rely too much on their (often limited) experience, which manifests itself in an over-reliance on conclusions drawn from similar events in the past. Thus, they limit their search for alternatives, fail to take all possible outcomes into account, and do not investigate in sufficient detail the probabilities of an outcome occurring. In short, they do not spend enough time and effort on finding additional—and sometimes also conflicting—evidence because they rely on their initial beliefs.

We are all human beings and therefore not immune to these thinking flaws. Being aware of them, however, is the first step toward reducing their potential negative impact. Other **strategies to counter decision-making pitfalls** include:

- **Thinking in hypotheses**: To avoid the trap of favoring the first beliefs that they develop, decision makers can benefit from a "scientific" approach to their thinking, treating their own beliefs not as the truth but rather as hypotheses. As Sir Karl Popper—one of the most renowned philosophers of science of the 20th century—noted, hypotheses should generally be treated as *falsifiable*, meaning that they are potentially subject to contradiction.[99] Thinking in hypotheses means (a) being open to the possibility that what we think about a certain object, situation, or person could be incorrect; and (b) objectively judging whether evidence supports or refutes our beliefs.[100] The hypothesis approach should particularly be applied to beliefs that are based on prior experience, following James March's advice: "Treat experience as a theory."[101]

- **Taking an experimental approach to management**: This advice from Harvard Professor Max Bazerman and his colleague Don Moore acknowledges that even the best decisions can lead to unforeseen and unwanted consequences. When commitments made in prior decisions no longer make sense, it is important to be open to revising them, to admit (to yourself and to others) that you chose the wrong path, and to embark on a different course of action when necessary.[102] In other words, in addition to treating your beliefs as hypotheses, your decisions should also be treated as falsifiable and revisable rather than being made once and forever.

Dialectic thinking:
The ability to see both sides of a situation, weigh arguments ("thesis") and counter-arguments ("antithesis") in order to find a solution that integrates both points of view ("synthesis").

- **Dialectic thinking** (see Figure 6.5): As discussed earlier, one of the main flaws in decision making is the failure to consider alternatives. An easy remedy here is simply to "consider the opposite."[103] The dialectic method, first practiced by the ancient Greeks, contrasts a thesis with its antithesis (the opposite), objectively weighing the contending arguments of both sides to create a synthesis, a "third way" that combines the best of both. This method can lead to superior results as it widely increases the number of possible options that are considered. This opens up new perspectives, which Henry Mintzberg and his colleagues see as "critical for effective management."[104]

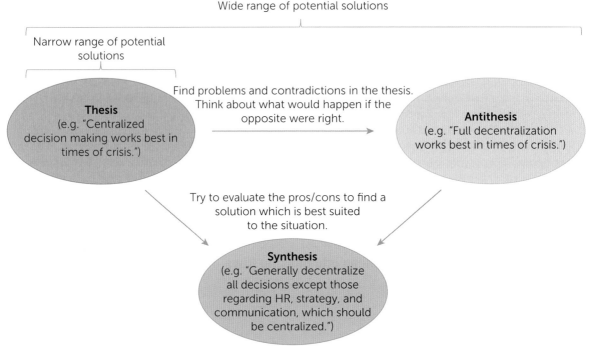

Figure 6.5 Dialectic thinking

- **Involving a trusted outsider**. When making decisions, we often adopt an insider's view, seeing problems only from our own perspective, relying on the most readily available data and opinions, and sometimes also being overoptimistic regarding the possible outcomes. Changing the perspective to an outsider's view, in which we see the situation not as unique but as an instance of a broader category, can improve our judgment.[105] As Bazerman and Moore note: "Interestingly, when a friend is building a house, we often predict that construction will cost more and take longer than expected. Our friend is the only one who doesn't know this!"[106] Asking trusted personal friends or a mentor for their opinion on an important decision can help to avoid this problem.

In addition to the strategies outlined here, managers can generally profit from a more critical approach toward their own thinking, recognizing that no one is completely immune to the decision pitfalls described in this chapter. University of Pennsylvania Professor Jonathan Baron, for example, suggests three principles of "**actively open-minded thinking**," by which decision makers can avoid biases:[107]

1 Consider the relative importance of the decision and ensure that you spend an adequate amount of time looking for solutions according to its significance.
2 Be as confident as appropriate given the amount and quality of thinking done.
3 Be fair to other possibilities, not just to the one initially favored.

According to Baron, "[t]he real danger is not in thinking too little, then, but rather in behaving as though we had great confidence in conclusions that were reached with little thought."[108] Questioning our own underlying assumptions as well as those of others, considering the available data in context instead of quickly assuming that everything will be identical to similar situations in the past, and genuinely considering an adequate number of options instead of jumping to the first best conclusion are some first important steps on the way to greater effectiveness in decision making.

Decision making at Amazon.com

In the fourth quarter of 2001, after seven years in business and more than a billion US dollars in accumulated losses, the market-leading online retailer Amazon.com reported a small profit for the first time. It had introduced its zShops business segment in September 1999, a marketplace in which everyone could offer the same items as Amazon itself—new and used—even at a lower price. The decision to introduce this new feature was controversial. Would Amazon be growing its own competition?

Jeff Bezos, founder and CEO of Amazon.com, remembered how he approached the decision. He noted that there was a lot of discussion, but "when the intellectual conversation gets too hard because of these potential cannibalization issues, we take a simpleminded approach."[109] He recalled a method attributed to Warren Buffet, who allegedly had three boxes on his desk: "in-box, out-box, and too hard."[110] When Bezos and his team were confronted with a problem that was "too hard", like the zShops decision, they tried "to convert it into a straightforward problem by saying, 'Well, what's better for the consumer?'"[111]

By focusing, in Bezos's words, on "making money when we help customers make purchase decisions"[112] rather than solely through selling things, Amazon.com surged ahead, going from $1.6 billion in turnover and $720 million of losses in 1999 to a $34 billion business with over $1 billion in net income in 2010. The profits from that year alone covered all seven years of start-up investment. In 2019, more than 50 percent of Amazon's total unit sales were attributable to its Marketplace, formerly known as zShops.

→ Key takeaway

When deciding on complex issues, it can sometimes help to focus on the most important organizational objective (e.g. "What is best for the customer?").

Sources: Based on information in Kirby and Stewart (2007); Amazon.com annual reports; amazon.com (2019b); Thomas and Reagan (2018).

6.4 The group decision process

Getty Images/Hero Images

In brief

- Like individuals, groups are not immune to decision fallacies. Some of the most common group decision-making deficiencies lie in adopting the first available solution that achieves enough support, the desire to please all group members (leading to premature consensus), failure to recognize the value of constructive conflict, and not taking advantage of diversity.

- Extreme forms of groupthink, in which any arguments and facts that go against the mainstream opinion are discounted, can lead to total decision-making failure.

- Following a few simple rules aimed at creating an open and honest discussion, in which several different options each receive adequate consideration, can help to avoid such issues and allow a group to reach high-quality decisions to which its individual members are then committed.

In an organization, decisions are not always made by individual executives alone. Whether in top management teams or in other management committees, many decisions are based on the interaction of a group of people (see the box *Who is the real decision maker?*). The main benefit of this is **diversity**. If managed well, group members' different experiences, knowledge and information bases, ideas, and problem-solving approaches can be combined to make better decisions (see also Chapter 5). In addition, some of the thinking traps for individuals that were presented in Section 6.3 can be avoided in an open discussion in which alternative options are evaluated from different points of view. Indeed, group decisions usually involve different personalities, conflicting opinions, and diverse and often diverging interests. The downside to this is that diversity can also be a source of potentially detrimental conflict and of political behavior that is more oriented toward personal gain than toward reaching the goals of the organization.

Subgroup:
A part of a larger group with common interests (that are not necessarily in congruence with the interests of the larger group) and a high degree of interaction between its members.

In this context, we need to be aware that "[i]n organizations, people operate in a world of subgroup norms, political ideologies, consensus building, and self-presentation."[113] Whenever an idea is put forward, advocated, or criticized in a managerial meeting, it could be (a) a genuine contribution to resolving the problem in the best interests of the organization; (b) a political move to promote one's own or a **subgroup**'s ideas; (c) an attempt to present oneself in the best light; or (d) an overt or hidden message on the interpersonal level. Sometimes, it is all four things at the same time.

Political behavior:
In an organizational context, political behavior refers to behavior that is oriented toward influencing the power relationships in an organization.

For a manager, it is therefore not an easy task to steer a group through a rational decision process. In each of its steps—defining the problem; stating objectives; considering options; discussing uncertainties, risks, and trade-offs; and finally deciding on a solution—**political behavior** can intrude. Individuals might try to set their own agenda, putting forward only objectives and solutions that support their personal goals, dismissing unwanted options, downplaying the risks of their preference, or influencing trade-off considerations in a particular direction.

Managers need to be careful, especially as they are often aiming to achieve two goals at the same time: reaching a **high-quality decision** for their organization and obtaining the **commitment of the group members**, with the latter being a prerequisite for the successful implementation of a decision.

FROM A DIFFERENT ANGLE

Who is the real decision maker?

When we ask employees who has a determining influence on important decisions in their firm, the answers do not always correspond to the formal top management team. There are always some people who have the ear of the CEO—unofficially, but with real influence. Such groups of unofficial advisors (sometimes also called "kitchen cabinets") also have their virtues. First, usually being small groups, they can be more efficient in reaching closure than large formal committees. Second, because these advisors are more discreet, proposals do not cause as much disruption as

in official meetings. Thus, such inside groups can be more creative in finding new solutions. Finally, because there is no fixed and named group, CEOs can be flexible about including those with the right expertise for a particular decision.[114] On the downside, ethical issues could arise with the use of kitchen cabinets, for example, in terms of fairness (Is it fair that some people bypass the formal hierarchy?) and transparency (What criteria does the CEO use when deciding on whom to include in the kitchen cabinet?).

Source: Based on information in Frisch (2011).

Common deficiencies in group decision making

We have seen in the previous section that individuals are far from perfect when it comes to decision making. In group settings, there are some additional potential pitfalls to consider:

- **Valence of solutions**. This term was used by Norman Maier to highlight the phenomenon that the first solution proposed which achieves a high number of positive comments tends to be adopted by the group, regardless of its quality.[115] This tendency is even more pronounced if powerful group members openly show their support for a particular option.

- **The "tyranny of consensus."** Many groups assume that it is necessary for a solution to please all members. Consequently, they strive to reach a consensus by all means, even if it results in compromising on the quality of the decision outcome (see also the box *"Big D" and "small d" decisions*). Compromises are often the lowest common denominator rather than the optimal solution. Managers aiming to achieve effectiveness should ask themselves "What is best for the organization?" rather than "What makes most people in this meeting happy?"
- **Failing to understand the value of constructive conflict.** Conflict in decision-making groups comes in two forms: in task conflicts, people have different opinions on the decision itself; in relationship conflicts, interpersonal issues that are not directly task related come to the fore.[116] While interpersonal conflicts usually have a negative impact on the quality of decisions and especially on the commitment to decisions, several studies have shown that constructive conflict can have positive effects, such as avoiding **groupthink** or taking a greater variety of perspectives into account.[117] Stanford Professor Kathleen Eisenhardt and her colleagues, for example, have observed that "the highest conflict top management teams led the highest performing firms."[118] Suppressing constructive conflict can lead to suboptimal decisions.
- **Some group members are more equal than others**. Not only in George Orwell's classic *Animal Farm* but also in organizational contexts, some people's suggestions are more attended to than others', regardless of their quality. Usually, the statements of more powerful group members carry more weight (also known as "**HiPPO**," which stands for "the highest paid person's opinion"). If powerful group members voice their opinions too early, other, especially lower-status, group members might refrain from contributing conflicting evidence because they do not want to challenge their superiors. In its extreme form, one influential person (or sometimes an influential subgroup) dominates the whole discussion. Thus, the group fails to take advantage of its diversity.
- **Failing to acknowledge the importance of emotions**. Group discussions are not usually completely rational exchanges of facts and opinions. Former Harvard psychology Professor David McClelland argues that, in addition to what they directly communicate, people have three implicit motives closely linked to emotion: achievement, affiliation, and power.[119] Individuals want to be recognized for their contributions, as they have a need to belong and the fear of not being accepted. If the decision process does not provide adequate consideration of group members' emotions, there is a risk of losing some people along the way, leading to passive resistance rather than commitment to the decision.
- **The "I understood it differently" trap**. Group decisions are sometimes made in such a way that they include quite a degree of ambiguity. As James March notes, "[i]t is easier to conceal or ignore disagreements if policies are written with provisions or terminology that can be interpreted differently by different people."[120] This strategy might ease the decision-making process, but it will frequently lead to conflicts and failure during the implementation phase, if the parties involved interpret the original decision in completely divergent ways.

The ultimate group decision-making trap

"How could we have been so stupid?"[123] With this quote, attributed to John F. Kennedy, Irving L. Janis started his famous article on the phenomenon of **groupthink**. Janis analyzed the group decision-making processes of US President Kennedy's team of advisors that led to the disastrous Bay of Pigs invasion of Cuba in 1961. He concluded that a combination of different factors led to a narrow-minded thinking pattern within a group that was too coherent, thus not allowing any criticism of the mainstream opinion. The most important **symptoms of groupthink** that Janis identified are:

- **The illusion of invulnerability**, leading to false risk assessments.
- **Discounting of warnings**, as the group collectively forms rationalizations of why negative feedback is irrelevant.
- **Feeling morally superior**, thus ignoring ethically questionable consequences of the group's decisions.
- **Stereotyping** about outsiders, as the group forms an "us versus them" stance.

Groupthink:
A term introduced by social psychologist Irving Janis to explain the phenomenon of forced conformity and consent in groups in which diverging opinions are suppressed.

HiPPO:
"The highest paid person's opinion"—the term is used to describe the tendency of a group to follow the opinion of its most powerful members.

Stereotyping:
Judging members of a group of people based on an oversimplified image about this group.

AROUND THE GLOBE

"Big D" and "small d" decisions

Although you might expect management styles in Russia, Saudi Arabia, and the US to be very different, they do have one thing in common: managers are used to making decisions on their own rather than taking long detours to try to reach a group consensus. For example, although American managers may ask for their team members' opinions, they are likely to follow this by quickly determining the way forward themselves, following the motto that "any decision is better than no decision."[121] This is in sharp contrast with the decision-making style that we can observe in many German, Swedish, or Japanese companies, where managers would typically try to involve key stakeholders when they want to make an important decision.

Negotiating with different groups of people and finding a consensus will usually take a lot more time than top-down decisions. But once a consensual decision is reached, there is also a strong commitment from all sides to implement the decision without any changes. Therefore, INSEAD Professor Erin Meyer calls such decisions "big D" decisions. In top-down decision-making cultures, "small d" decisions are more common. "Small d" means that decisions can more easily be revised, as they are often seen as "simply an agreement to continue discussion."[122] Using the distinction between "small d" and "big D" cultures can help managers who work across cultures to understand how to best approach or interpret decision-making situations in different cultural contexts.

Source: Based on information in Meyer (2017).

- Applying **pressure on deviators**, not accepting arguments that are outside the group norm.
- **Self-censorship** of members who keep silent, even if their opinion would be different to the group mainstream.
- The **illusion of unanimity**, as only supporting arguments are put forward.
- **"Mindguards,"** group members who are actively striving to "protect" the others from potentially disruptive information.[124]

Many universities offer opportunities to run team projects. For example, you might undertake a consulting project in which a team of students support a local company to achieve a specific goal. If you were to lead a team project as part of your studies, which rules would you set for your team to ensure that it will not fall into the group decision traps, including groupthink, outlined in this section?

When groupthink occurs, the quality of decision making rapidly deteriorates. The number of possible alternatives is usually limited, information search is restricted, and the group members fail to take the drawbacks and risks of their favored option into account. The outcome is predictable: the decisions taken will be biased and suboptimal.

How can groupthink be avoided?

Janis offers several suggestions, such as encouraging group members to become critical evaluators, with at least one playing the role of devil's advocate to openly challenge the majority position; inviting outsiders with different perspectives to team meetings; dividing the group into subgroups to discuss topics separately; or holding "second-chance meetings," in which everyone is encouraged to express their doubts about the chosen path. Team leaders should furthermore show impartiality toward different options, encouraging an open discussion including all group members before voicing their own opinion, which could strongly influence the others. Finally, when the issue involves relationships with other parties, Janis proposes that the situation should be seen through the eyes of those counterparts, charting and discussing all their options, too.

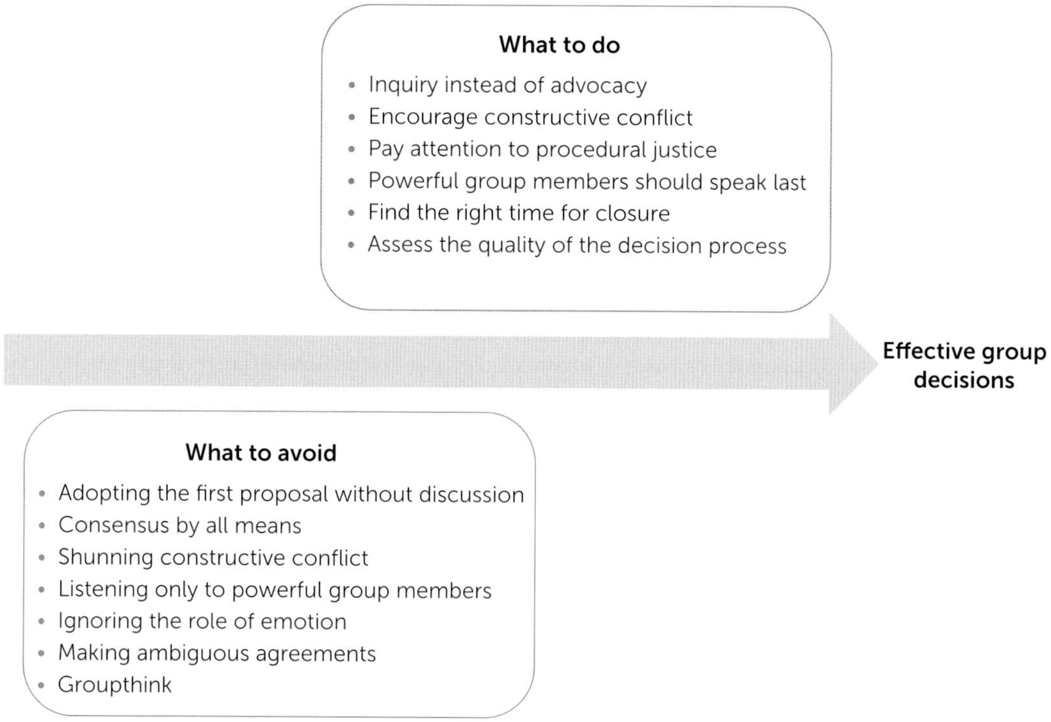

What to do

- Inquiry instead of advocacy
- Encourage constructive conflict
- Pay attention to procedural justice
- Powerful group members should speak last
- Find the right time for closure
- Assess the quality of the decision process

Effective group
decisions

What to avoid

- Adopting the first proposal without discussion
- Consensus by all means
- Shunning constructive conflict
- Listening only to powerful group members
- Ignoring the role of emotion
- Making ambiguous agreements
- Groupthink

Figure 6.6 The path to effective group decisions

Source: Inspired by ideas in Garvin and Roberto (2001).

How to make effective decisions in groups

A basic precondition for making effective group decisions is to understand that decision making is not a single event, but a process that unfolds over time: a process in which different people with their unique personalities and their own and their subgroups' agendas and interests meet.[125] The group decision process can be improved by following a few suggestions proposed by David A. Garvin and Michael A. Roberto (see Figure 6.6):[126]

- **Inquiry**, an open process in which different options are proposed and genuinely jointly evaluated, usually leads to higher-quality decisions than advocacy, in which the parties are entrenched in a "we-need-to-show-the-others-that-our-solution-is-the-right-one" mode. One of the key managerial tasks in facilitating a group decision process, therefore, lies in fostering open inquiry to investigate several alternatives. This can also be supported by separating the idea creation and evaluation phases, giving new approaches the chance of being carefully considered rather than being shot down by criticism just a second after they are voiced.
- Managers should **encourage constructive conflict** while curbing interpersonal or affective (emotional) conflict, following the advice of philosopher Michel de Montaigne: "So contradictory judgments neither offend me nor irritate me: they merely wake me up and provide me with exercise ... I move towards the man who contradicts me: he is instructing me. The cause of truth will be common to us."[127] Encouraging constructive conflict is not an easy task because critical feedback—even when it is meant in a constructive way—can often be taken personally. Therefore, we need to pay attention to the language used in discussions. Fostering open debate rather than suppressing critical voices can help in decreasing the risk of falling victim to groupthink.
- Managers should pay attention to **procedural justice**:[128] group members need to feel that they are given a "voice" in the decision process; in other words, that what they are saying is really considered. It has been found in academic research that people who felt that their opinions were taken seriously—regardless of the eventual outcome—evaluated the process as fairer

Procedural justice: The notion that the processes of making decisions, resolving conflicts, and allocating resources should be perceived as fair by all the parties involved.

and consequently showed more acceptance of the final decision.[129] Through active listening, giving group members the feeling that their contributions are heard and are important for reaching the final decision, managers can create greater commitment to the outcome.

- Leaders should **speak last**. Revealing preferences early can lead to premature consent. Some people might not dare to speak up against the opinion of the boss. It is better to encourage discussion, weigh the arguments carefully, and, when making a final choice, explain the rationale behind it as well as how the individual arguments helped in reaching it.
- **Find the right time for closure**. Closing a discussion without sufficient consideration of different views and alternatives, and with some people still showing through their body language that they strongly disagree with what has been said so far, would be too early. Endless discussions about one and the same topic with continually repeating arguments might be a sign, however, that—as Garvin and Roberto put it—it is time to "call the question."[130]
- Finally, managers can **assess the progress of the decision-making process** by checking (a) whether several meaningful options have been adequately considered; (b) whether "facts" are really facts or merely assumptions or assertions; (c) whether the team has clearly defined the problem and their objectives; (d) whether there has been enough open debate in which different points of view have been seriously taken into account; and (e) whether the opinions of individual members have been considered in a way that they perceive as fair.

Sunk costs:
Costs that cannot be recovered because they were incurred in the past.

A further tool to assess the effectiveness of group decision processes is the **team decision quality control checklist** presented in Table 6.4, based on an original proposal by Daniel Kahneman and colleagues.[131] It can be used as a means of quality control for decision makers judging team decisions of high importance. The questions address some of the most frequently occurring group decision biases.

Table 6.4 The team decision quality control checklist

	Questions that address some of the most frequently occurring decision biases
1	Is there a significant risk of errors driven by *team members' self-interest* (such as financial interest, power gain, or concern for reputation)?
2	Has the group "fallen in love" with their project and the solution? Are there *emotionally influenced decision flaws*?
3	Is the team a potential victim of *groupthink*? Did the team allow dissenting opinions and were these sufficiently addressed?
4	Could the decision be influenced by the team's memory of a past success (in the form of a *salient analogy*)?
5	Did the team consider enough *credible alternatives* (not merely pseudo alternatives that never had a chance of being chosen)?
6	Is there any *information missing* that would be particularly relevant to the decision (and could the data situation be more favorable if the decision were made at a later point in time)?
7	*Where do the numbers come from?* Are they facts or estimates? On what rationale were the estimates based? Did the team simply extrapolate from the past?
8	Is the team making *simple cause–effect attributions* (e.g. assuming that a certain person or approach that worked in one situation will also work in another)?
9	Are the proposals *influenced by past decisions*? Is the team likely to fall victim to escalation of commitment even though the outcomes of past decisions (e.g. **sunk costs**) do not affect the present situation?
10	Is the team *overly optimistic* in presenting its case (founded, for example, on overconfidence or ignoring potential competitor moves)?
11	Has the team *really considered the worst case* in its worst-case scenario? Have all possible negative external events and influences been examined, not only individually but also in combination?
12	Is the team *too cautious*? Are team members too conservative because they want to avoid losses?

Source: Inspired by ideas in Kahneman et al. (2011).

"Multiple poor decisions" at the Royal Bank of Scotland

Fred Goodwin, as the new CEO of the Royal Bank of Scotland (RBS), was celebrated for the bank's successful takeover of NatWest, another large UK bank, at the beginning of the new millennium. Through various measures, including cutting thousands of jobs, he delivered the synergies that had been promised in the deal.

In an attempt to replicate this success, RBS acquired the US bank Charter One in 2004. "The deal broke all the lessons learned from NatWest,"[132] the *Sunday Telegraph* later wrote about the takeover, referring to a lack of transparency as well as poor investigations and analyses of the bank prior to signing the contract. This time, the acquisition failed to reach its income targets.

Despite this setback, growth and market dominance by any means still seemed to remain at the core of RBS's strategy, very much in line with the general industry trend at the time. In 2007, an RBS-led consortium entered into a bidding war with its British rival Barclays over the acquisition of the Dutch bank ABN Amro. When the takeover—at the time the largest deal in the history of financial services—was completed, however, RBS had little to celebrate. Excessive speculation on housing prices in the US led to the collapse of several financial institutions, and the global financial industry slid into a severe crisis. The ABN Amro deal significantly expanded RBS's exposure to risky asset categories, which could—and did—lose a lot in value. With the market value of the bank's assets plummeting and with limited capital reserves and liquidity available (the bank was funded with high levels of debt), RBS had to turn to the British government (and taxpayers) for a multi-billion pound emergency bailout. Sir Fred Goodwin had to step down as CEO of the bank in 2008, and was stripped of his knighthood (an award given by the Queen for outstanding achievements) in the aftermath. The following year, RBS reported a loss of more than £24 billion, the largest ever in the UK's history.

The British Financial Services Authority (FSA) launched an investigation to shed light on the reasons for the bank's failure. The 452-page FSA report came to the conclusion that the RBS disaster was not attributable to dishonest practices, but rather to "multiple poor decisions"[133] that were made in the bank. For example, the ABN Amro acquisition was considered "an extremely risky deal,"[134] made on the basis of very limited data ("two lever arch folders and a CD"[135]). The investigation process before buying the bank was seen as inadequate because it did not reveal ABN Amro's real risk profile. RBS management—relying too heavily on their prior experience of the successful NatWest acquisition—had underestimated the challenge of integrating ABN Amro, as well as the risks associated with the takeover. Management's attitude toward the balance between risk and growth was firmly criticized.

The FSA report concluded that "the pattern of poor decisions which RBS made suggests that there are likely to have been underlying deficiencies in RBS's management, governance and culture which made it prone to making poor decisions."[136] Specifically, the following questions were raised about the decision-making culture of the bank:

- Did the board adequately question and challenge the CEO's ideas and strategies?
- Was the CEO's management style discouraging dissenting voices?
- Did the RBS board have enough information about the risks that were involved in certain strategic moves?
- Was the bank too focused on revenue, profit, and share price growth while neglecting capital, liquidity, and asset quality issues?
- Were there adequate risk management structures in place?

The British media also reported on potential deficiencies in the bank's decision-making processes, including "an internal culture that put the sale of questionable products ahead of concerns about the risks those products would create,"[137] deals that were "brimming with ego,"[138] or "the inability or fear of other directors to speak up."[139]

The FSA supervision process was also heavily criticized in the FSA report. For example, it was pointed out that there weren't adequate checks to ensure that the bank had a sufficiently large capital buffer to cope with unexpected risks; the authorities wrongly held the belief that financial markets and their regulatory regimes were stable; there was political pressure not to overburden British banks in order to keep them competitive in the global market; and assumptions by the bank's management were not sufficiently challenged.

With the help of the British taxpayer, the total collapse of the bank was avoided. It later cut back its operations and shifted its focus away from investment banking in favor of its retail business. However, RBS continued to suffer from the poor decisions that were made in the events described above. For ten consecutive years following the ABN Amro takeover, RBS was not able to report a single pound of profit.

Sources: *Brinded (2015); FSA (2011); telegraph.co.uk (2011a); Treanor (2017); Wilson et al. (2011).*

Discussion questions

- What were the main reasons for the failure of RBS?
- Which decision pitfalls do you recognize in the RBS case?
- How would you assess the quality of the group decision processes at RBS?
- What could the bank do to avoid similar poor decisions in the future?

Conclusion

As we have seen in this chapter, decision making in an organizational context is a complex task, both for individual managers and for teams. We can try to follow a rational decision process and consider all potential pitfalls. We can also use sophisticated analytics and decision support systems. However, in the face of uncertainty, there is no real substitute for managerial judgment, forming your own opinion about a decision after a careful evaluation of all the evidence. The quality of managerial judgment does not only depend on the decision maker's ability and the team's competence, but also on the available evidence. It is therefore crucial for managers to collect the right amount of information (this means sufficient information, not as much as possible); to distinguish clearly between facts and opinions; to look behind the data, questioning by whom and for what purpose it was produced; and to assess whether it has been distorted by emotions or personal and group interests.

In the story at the beginning of this chapter, several publishers declined J. K. Rowling's request to publish her first Harry Potter novel—probably one of the most regretted decisions in their professional lives, which cost their companies hundreds of millions of pounds in revenues. How could this collective misjudgment happen to experienced decision makers who presumably all comprehensively understood how their industry worked?

Probably, it was this very experience that turned into a liability. The publishers might have followed learned industry heuristics (mental shortcuts) in reaching their decision. The whole publishing industry—from publishers to bookstore chains—tends to think in categories. They ask: In which box (or bookshelf) does this new proposal fit? How well have books of this type sold before? Is it similar to previous books that turned into bestsellers? And here is the catch: it was not possible to put Harry Potter into any existing box. It became a new category on its own.

The publishers probably thought that if it was unlike any other book that had been successful, why should it sell? But that was exactly why it became an unprecedented success: Harry Potter was new, very different, and therefore exciting. It was a structural interruption, impossible to judge by putting it into pre-existing categories. If they had recognized the novelty of the text, the publishers could have involved trial readers—both children and adults—in their decision, or they could have felt the magic through reading the book themselves. (Judging from my own experience as a book publisher, I doubt that many of the publishers who declined the manuscript actually read it from cover to cover.)

Questioning your own decision-making heuristics can lead to greater effectiveness, especially when it comes to unprecedented decision issues. Making smarter decisions than others in your industry can become a veritable competitive advantage. "It is our choices, Harry, that show what we truly are, far more than our abilities,"[140] writes J. K. Rowling in *Harry Potter and the Chamber of Secrets*. Worldwide, around half a billion Harry Potter books have been sold to date. J. K. Rowling's publisher Bloomsbury definitely made a good decision.

✓ Review questions

1 What are the main steps of a rational decision-making process?
2 How should a problem be framed?
3 How can managers widen the options space to find better solutions to a problem?
4 What is a decision tree and how can it be used in managerial decision making?

5   What is the role of risk and uncertainty in decision making?
6   Which strategies can be used to resolve trade-off situations when conflicting objectives exist?
7   What are the differences between the three main thinking modes (categorical thinking, intuitive thinking, and rational-analytic thinking)?
8   What are the advantages and disadvantages of each of the three thinking modes in a managerial context?
9   How can data analytics and decision support systems help managers in their decision making?
10   What are the main decision-making pitfalls that managers should be aware of?
11   How can managers avoid these common pitfalls?
12   What are the advantages of group decision making over individual decision making?
13   What additional pitfalls can occur when decisions are made by a group?
14   What is "groupthink" and how can it be avoided?
15   How can a team leader optimize a group decision process?

⑦ Critical reflection questions

1   If following a fully rational decision-making process is probably a rare exception rather than the rule in managerial practice, does it really make sense for management students to consider the individual steps of such a process in more detail?
2   Many managers are convinced that experience is the best guide to making decisions. Do you agree?
3   Critically assess to what extent data analytics and decision support systems can contribute to more effective decision making.
4   Which external conditions or pressures to which managers are exposed in their role could contribute to making ineffective or even unethical decisions?
5   What is your usual approach to decision making? Would you change anything about this approach based on what you have learned in this chapter?

☛ Managerial implications

- To be effective and reach their organizations' goals, managers need to make the right decisions. In a dynamic and uncertain environment, it is often impossible to be 100 percent accurate. Nevertheless, following a structured approach to decision making can help managers to thoroughly think through their different options, thereby raising the chances of choosing the right path.
- A rational-analytic decision process would involve: clearly defining the problem and the manager's objectives, identifying a sufficent range of solutions, determining possible outcomes for all the options under differing circumstances and estimating their probability, considering risk preferences, assessing trade-offs and finally making a choice, followed by sensitivity and "no regrets" tests.
- Even though most managerial decisions do not follow all the steps in the process, being aware of the factors that could influence the outcome of a decision can help managers to make more informed choices.
- In addition to the rational-analytic approach, intuitive and categorical thinking play a major role in managerial decision making—each has its own merits and disadvantages. Therefore, managers need to consider carefully when to use the different thinking modes. Intermodal thinking, which integrates both intuitive and rational-analytic aspects, is recommended for more complex decisions with potentially serious consequences.
- Managers, as human beings, can fall into a range of different thinking traps. These can be avoided by taking a more open-minded approach to decision making, considering different viewpoints and acknowledging the potential flaws in their own hypotheses and decisions.

- Group decisions can profit from the diversity of experiences, ideas, knowledge, and problem-solving skills of the group members. Nevertheless, they have their own pitfalls, which can be avoided by following some of the strategies outlined in this chapter (e.g. encouraging constructive conflict, paying attention to procedural justice, and letting others express their ideas before hearing the leader's opinion).

Endnotes

1 *The Scotsman* (2003).
2 Horst Pirker, CEO of Styria Media Group AG (a leading Austrian media group) from 1999 to 2010; oral communication with the author.
3 Baron (2008), p. 6.
4 These questions are also raised—albeit in different wording—by Hammond et al. (1999).
5 Drucker (1974), p. 389.
6 Dörner (1989).
7 Hammond et al. (1999), pp. 19–23.
8 Kahneman and Lovallo (1993), p. 23.
9 Hammond et al. (1999), p. 31.
10 These suggestions are following Hammond et al. (1999), pp. 35–40
11 Hammond et al. (1999), p. 42.
12 Hammond et al. (1999), pp. 48–50.
13 Hammond et al. (1999), p. 50.
14 Murdoch (1997).
15 Poetz et al. (2014).
16 bbc.com (2011).
17 Baron (2008).
18 Sox et al. (2007).
19 Schonberg et al. (2011).
20 March and Shapira (1987).
21 Loewenstein et al. (2001).
22 March (1994), p. 3.
23 March and Shapira (1987).
24 Apgar (2006).
25 Schmidt and Larson (2010), p. 152.
26 The four strategies presented in the following are based on Payne et al. (1993), pp. 27–28.
27 Bazerman and Moore (2009).
28 Bell (1982).
29 Doyle (2003), p. 107.
30 Simon (1957).
31 Bargh and Chartrand (1999); Hogarth (2001); Pacini and Epstein (1999).
32 Stanovich and West (2000).
33 Macrae and Bodenhausen (2000), p. 96.
34 Kruschke (2005), p. 183.
35 Goldstone and Hendrickson (2010).
36 Bingham and Eisenhardt (2011).
37 Chan (2015).
38 cnet.com (2008).
39 Macrae and Bodenhausen (2000), p. 105
40 Raidl and Lubart (2000/2001), p. 219.
41 Dane and Pratt (2007).
42 Aristotle (2009), p. 107.
43 Hodgkinson et al. (2009).
44 Simon and Chase (1973).
45 Dane and Pratt (2007).

46 Khatri and Ng (2000), p. 58.
47 The three factors were proposed by Hodgkinson et al. (2009), p. 287.
48 Dane and Pratt (2007).
49 Lieberman (2000).
50 Epstein (1990).
51 Pelzmann (2007).
52 Pelzmann (2007).
53 Daft (2016).
54 Daft (2016).
55 Mintzberg and Westley (2001), p. 90.
56 Mintzberg and Westley (2001).
57 McAfee and Brynjolfsson (2012).
58 Hayashi (2014).
59 Petersen (2016).
60 Petersen (2016).
61 Sanders (2016), p. 36.
62 McAfee and Brynjolfsson (2012), p. 66.
63 Hayashi (2014).
64 Chai and Shih (2017).
65 Macrae and Bodenhausen (2000), p. 105.
66 Rosch (1999), p. 190.
67 Sherman et al. (1998).
68 Dane and Pratt (2007).
69 Quoted by Theodor Reik (1948), p. vii. Reik recalled this quote from a conversation with his mentor Sigmund Freud.
70 Khatri and Ng (2000).
71 Khatri and Ng (2000).
72 Dane and Pratt (2007).
73 Wegner (1994).
74 Simon (1987), p. 61.
75 Hodgkinson and Sadler-Smith (2003).
76 Djonlagic et al. (2009).
77 Walker and Stickgold (2010).
78 Varma (2017).
79 March (1994), p. 9.
80 Simon (1957)
81 March (1994), p. 10.
82 March (1994), p. 24.
83 Baron (2008), pp. 56–57.
84 Tversky and Kahneman (1973).
85 Bazerman and Moore (2009).
86 Tversky and Kahneman (1974).
87 March (1994).
88 March (1994).
89 March (1994).
90 March (1994).
91 Bacon (1869), pp. 79–82.
92 Wright et al. (2004).
93 March (1994), p. 183.

94 Mintzberg et al. (2009), p. 19.
95 Staw and Ross (1978).
96 Schkade and Kahneman (1998).
97 Schkade and Kahneman (1998), p. 345.
98 Elfenbein (2007).
99 Popper (1935).
100 Baron (2008).
101 March (1994), p. 263.
102 Bazerman and Moore (2009), p. 112.
103 Lord et al. (1984).
104 Mintzberg et al. (2009), p. 177.
105 Kahneman and Lovallo (1993).
106 Bazerman and Moore (2009), p. 195.
107 Baron (2008), p. 200.
108 Baron (2008), p. 62.
109 Kirby and Stewart (2007), p. 79.
110 Kirby and Stewart (2007), p. 79.
111 Kirby and Stewart (2007), p. 79.
112 Kirby and Stewart (2007), p. 79.
113 Powell et al. (2011), p. 1378.
114 Frisch (2011).
115 Maier (1967).
116 Jehn (1995).
117 Simons and Peterson (2000).
118 Eisenhardt (1997), p. 59.
119 McClelland (1987).
120 March (1994), p. 170.
121 Meyer (2017), p. 75.
122 Meyer (2017), p. 75.
123 Janis (1971).
124 Janis (1971).
125 Garvin and Roberto (2001).
126 The following six points are based on Garvin and Roberto (2001).
127 de Montaigne (2004), pp. 33–34.
128 Thibaut and Walker (1975).
129 Lind et al. (1997).
130 Garvin and Roberto (2001), p. 116.
131 The following suggestions are based on Kahneman et al. (2011)
132 Wilson et al. (2011).
133 FSA (2011), p. 22.
134 FSA (2011), p. 25.
135 FSA (2011), p. 7.
136 FSA (2011), p. 40.
137 Brinded (2015).
138 Wilson et al. (2011).
139 Wilson et al. (2011).
140 Rowling (1998), p. 333.

 Visit the companion website at macmillanihe.com/sternad-management to access multiple choice questions, useful weblinks and additional materials.

Pixabay/Gerd Altmann

MANAGING STRATEGY

Outline of chapter

This chapter will enable you to

- Develop your strategic thinking skills.
- Apply tools to analyze and assess opportunities and threats in the macro and industry environment as well as the strengths and weaknesses of an organization.
- Evaluate different opportunities for organizations to grow, cooperate, and create sustainable portfolios of businesses.
- Define and analyze the strategic position of an organization within its industry.
- Assess different tactics for dealing with competitive threats.
- Discuss the impact of digital technology on the strategy of organizations.

Introduction

A 2007 issue of *Forbes*, a leading American business magazine, ran the headline "Nokia: One Billion Customers—Can Anyone Catch the Cell Phone King?"[1] in celebration of the Finnish corporation's successful strategy. The corresponding story read: "If you judge a brand on influence or reach, Nokia may be the most successful brand in history."[2] Nokia prided itself on having the widest cell phone portfolio in the industry, and on being on the path from mere manufacturer to integrated service and Internet company.

Four years later, *Forbes* ran another article about Nokia, this time less enthusiastic, titled "Last call."[3] The company was facing rapidly declining revenues and market shares, reporting losses and thousands of layoffs, and had its bonds downgraded to junk status.[4] How could the seemingly unbeatable industry leader have lost ground and virtually crashed in such a short time?

Several reasons have been posited for Nokia's decline. Commentators criticized the corporation for being too complacent; slow to adapt to a new competitive situation when Apple's iPhone redefined the smartphone market; failing to innovate its products and reinvent its business; not comprehending that mobile devices were more than just telephones; and entering into the wrong alliances, eventually being squeezed between more successful competitors in both the premium and low-cost ends of the market.[5] In short, critics suggested that Nokia did not have the right strategy to allow the company to sustain its competitive advantage and thrive in a dynamic market environment.

The origins of the word **strategy** can be traced back to the Greek word for an army commander, στρατηγός (*strategos*), the person who directs troops in war and builds and maintains their capacity to fight during peace. While usually operating in a less martial environment, effective managers also need to fulfill both roles of the *strategos*, (a) providing **direction** for the members of their organizations and (b) developing the capacity or **potential** in the form of resources and capabilities that enable the organization to achieve its goals in the long term.

Effective managers achieve their goals. In order to do so, they must first set the right goals for their organization. The aim of this chapter is to introduce the **basic concepts of strategic management** to explore how managers can set the right goals and define a clear direction for the future development of their organizations. Specifically, we will discuss:

- what it means to **think and plan strategically** (*Section 7.1*);
- which tools can be used to **analyze** factors within and outside of an organization that are relevant to developing a sound strategy (*Section 7.2*);
- how to best define the **scope of an organization**, i.e. deciding where an organization aims to create value (*Section 7.3*);
- how to find a **sustainable strategic position**, thereby also answering the question of how the organization aims to create long-term value (*Section 7.4*).

In recent years, digital technologies have fundamentally changed the way in which value is created in many industries. Consequently, managers need to adapt the strategies of their organizations to the new realities of the digital world. We will therefore also explore how managers can develop **digital strategies** for their organizations (in *Section 7.4*).

Strategy:
A general direction for an organization in terms of how to create and offer value and develop the potential to successfully follow this direction in the face of competition, and under changing environmental circumstances.

Strategic management:
The process of defining major goals for the organization and setting initiatives for reaching these goals.

Strategic position:
A set of fundamental choices that determines where and how an organization creates and offers value and how the value creation and value offer model can be sustained in the face of competition.

7.1 Thinking strategically

GETTY

In brief

- Thinking strategically means thinking about the future of an organization, determining its direction and resource allocations in order to continuously create value for customers, shareholders, and other stakeholders.

- Deliberate strategies can be developed following a formal strategic planning process, including the analysis of internal and external factors that can influence an organization's future as well as defining the organization's scope and its positioning in specific markets.

- The strategy that is eventually realized is an outcome of social processes and individual managerial decisions, and therefore often differs from the original deliberate strategy.

- Mapping out a strategy is an essential activity for managers to enable their organizations to adapt to a changing environment and to provide the members of the organization with meaningful common goals.

What do we mean when we talk about **strategy**? In everyday language, strategy often refers to a series of actions taken to achieve a certain goal (e.g. What is the best strategy to convince my boss to raise my salary?). However, **tactics**, described in the *Merriam Webster* dictionary as "the art or skill of employing available means to accomplish an end,"[6] might be a more suitable term for such goal-oriented actions. Instead of just searching for the most appropriate means to reach an end, strategic thinking is primarily concerned with **defining the ends** themselves, as well as with **creating the prerequisites and means to achieve these ends** (rather than just deploying the available means). Having one or a few clearly defined strategic goals is imperative for every organization, because "if you are everywhere you are nowhere."[7]

Strategists combine outside and inside views. The **outside view** acknowledges that organizations constantly interact with an ever-changing environment—with the changing needs of suppliers and customers, the changing strategies of competitors, the changing requirements of capital providers, and the wider environment and society at large. The purpose of the **inside view** is to identify the resources and capabilities that enable an organization to create value. **Value** is a key term here. It refers to the purpose of the organization to create something that is *of value*, i.e. reaps more benefits than it costs, for a certain target group. If competitors are able to provide more—or at least the same—value more efficiently, the *raison d'être* of the organization will be at risk. Therefore, an organization's strategy cannot be seen as independent of its competitors' strategies.

Value:
What something (e.g. a business or an asset) is worth—in business often measured in monetary terms (i.e. what someone is willing to pay for it).

Taken together, **strategy** is about *setting direction to create and offer value and to develop the potential to successfully follow this direction in the face of competition, and under changing environmental circumstances.*

The **five main questions that a strategist needs to answer** are:

1   Where and for whom do we create value?
2   What is the value that we create?
3   How do we create that value?
4   How do we sustain our value creation model against the competition?
5   How do we adapt our value creation model to align with a changing environment?

Think about a large company based in your hometown or region. Imagine that you took over a top management position in this company. In your new managerial role, what steps would you take to find answers to the five key strategic questions (see the previous page) for the company?

The purpose of strategy

Fundamentally, **strategizing** is about:

- defining how an organization differentiates itself from others and setting goals related to **creating unique benefits and value** for a certain group of people;
- understanding and nurturing the factors that enable future performance, thereby **building the potential** to reach the long-term goals of an organization;
- **creating alternative options** for moving the organization forward (coordinated initiatives that enable an organization to survive and thrive under changing circumstances); and
- providing the members of the organization, as well as outside stakeholders, with a **compelling story** that allows them to focus their efforts on achieving meaningful goals.

Strategy is often likened to the game of chess, in which having the right strategy plays a crucial role (for example, a chessboard is often used as a visual symbol for strategy). Lessons about strategy that could be transferred from chess to an organizational context are presented in the box *What strategists can learn from a chess grandmaster*.

FROM A DIFFERENT ANGLE

What strategists can learn from a chess grandmaster

Chess is the epitome of a strategy game. In his book *How Life Imitates Chess*, Garry Kasparov, one of the greatest chess players of all time, summarized what business strategists can learn from chess:[8]

- *Think backwards:* Good chess strategists first set goals in the distant future, from which they work backwards in a chain of intermediate objectives. Working backwards means setting milestones that need to be achieved in order to reach the ultimate goal. Strategists can then identify tactical moves (or combinations of actions) which are required to reach the milestones. If the ultimate goal in chess is beating the opponent's king, for example, a chess player's intermediate objective is trading pieces in a way that will substantially weaken the protective barrier around the king. If the ultimate goal of an organization is to become the service quality leader in its industry, intermediate objectives could be set regarding the training of service staff or the introduction of

IT systems that support the optimization of service processes.

- *Question yourself:* One of Kasparov's main tenets is that you can only win if you know yourself well. Knowing yourself—your strengths as well as weaknesses—requires constantly questioning yourself. Kasparov refers to an example of a world championship game in 2000 in which he confronted his former student Viktor Kramnik. Kramnik managed to manoeuver the game into a situation in which he had a clear advantage over Kasparov. Instead of bringing the position back into calmer waters more suited to his own style, Kasparov took it as a challenge, and tried to beat Kramnik at his own game—and failed dramatically, losing the title of World Champion for the first time in 15 years. According to Kasparov, it is also important to know your own habits well. Predictability makes you most vulnerable to your opponents. If they can guess what combinations you will use, their counterstrategy will have much higher chances of success. Also managers as strategists need to know the strengths and weaknesses of their own organization well, especially in comparison to other players in the industry.

- *Think in options:* A chess player needs to consider countless moves to reach a certain aim. Kasparov's teacher, Michail Botwinnik, the first of seven Soviet chess world champions, taught Kasparov not to avoid complexity just on the basis of its complexity. In a strategically important decision in an organization, there are usually also various alternatives. If there is time, Kasparov recommends carefully examining other options, and gathering

as much information as needed to make a qualified decision between them.

- *Take initiative:* In Kasparov's experience, attacking players generally have an advantage. By taking the initiative, they control the game instead of being forced to constantly react to the opponent's moves. Wary strategists consider every advantage as a temporary and dynamic factor, which can quickly disappear without a new initiative. This is also an important reason why innovation is a key success factor for organizations that operate in a fast-changing environment.

Source: *Based on information in Kasparov (2007).*

The strategic planning process

Emergent strategies:
Strategies that result from a (previously unintended) pattern of decisions which together propel the organization in a certain direction.

Mission:
A short statement that describes the core purpose or *raison d'être* of the organization.

Vision:
A short statement that describes what the organization wants to become or would like to accomplish in the (distant) future.

Corporate level strategy:
Setting the general direction for a multi-business organization, especially deciding where (in which industries or markets) to compete, how to grow the organization, and how to cooperate with other organizations.

Strategies can either be deliberately formulated, or—as Henry Mintzberg famously observed—emerge from a stream of situational decisions which propel an organization in a certain direction (**"emergent strategies"**).[9] In most cases, the strategy that is eventually realized will be a combination of deliberate and emergent strategies.[10]

Deliberate **strategy formulation** (which—to emphasize the last point again—is not an absolute precondition for having a strategy) helps to structure the top management team's thinking and decision-making processes on issues that have wide-ranging consequences for an organization. An overview of a **systematic strategic planning process** is presented in Figure 7.1.

To begin with, managers must clarify the organization's main purpose—in particular its **mission** ("What are we here for?") and **vision** ("What do we want to become?"). After gaining an initial common understanding about what the organization is supposed to be and do, the strategy team will usually thoroughly **analyze the current situation**, externally (including developments in the wider or macro environment and the specific industry), as well as inside the organization. The external analysis should reveal the main opportunities and threats in the environment, while the internal analysis highlights the strengths and weaknesses of the organization. These four factors—strengths, weaknesses, opportunities, and threats—can then be combined using an integrated analysis tool such as a SWOT matrix or an I-O/O-I analysis (see Section 7.2).

The analysis can help to generate different **options for strategic positioning**. These options usually include choices about the arenas in which an organization wants to be actively engaged (**corporate level strategy**—"Where and for whom do we create value?"), its **value proposition** for the market ("What is the value that we create?"), and its value creation strategy ("How do we create that value?") (**business level strategy**).

The options for strategic positioning at both the corporate and business levels will then be evaluated against different criteria (e.g. whether the option is based on an organization's **core competencies**, whether the resources are available to implement it, whether it is acceptable for stakeholders) to select the most suitable direction. Finally, it is also advisable to undertake a feasibility check ("Are there enough resources available? Are there any insurmountable obstacles?") before eventually starting to implement the strategy (for more information on how to implement a strategy, see Chapter 8).

The individual steps of this process are not always followed in a linear way. Often, new insights gained during one step in the process will create a need to revisit prior steps. The process is therefore best thought of as an iterative one.

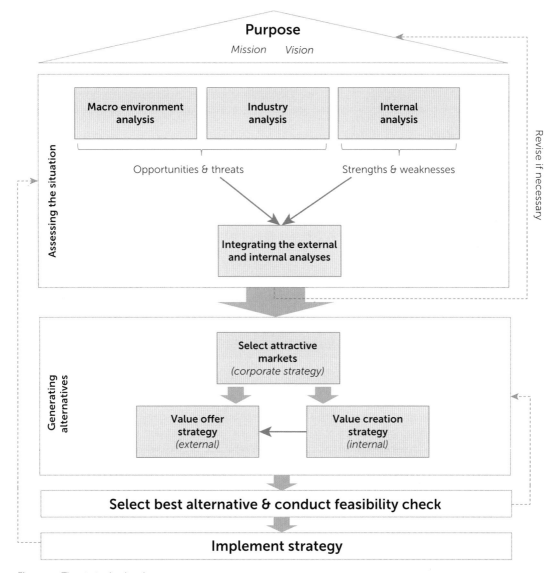

Figure 7.1 The strategic planning process

Business level strategy:
Setting direction on how to create value and how to compete in a certain product or service market.

Core competency:
Key organizational capabilities which can be used for creating value and achieving a sustainable competitive advantage in a variety of different markets.

Strategy development is not only a structured thinking process; it is also a **social process**. Strategies are conceived and implemented by people within an organization. They are also the outcome of a process of negotiation in which a dominant coalition of powerful actors determines the overall direction of an organization in a way that best suits their interests.[11] An organization's realized strategy, however, is dependent not only on the direction that is officially communicated in strategy documents, but also on the **resource allocation decisions** made by managers at all levels of the organization on a day-to-day basis.[12] "Once you realize that resource allocation decisions make your strategy, then you know you can't rely on a system to manage the resource allocation process," Bower and Gilbert argue. "No planning or capital budgeting procedure can substitute for the best leaders in the company making considered judgments about how to allocate resources."[13]

7.2 Assessing the situation

iStock.com/Sjale

In brief

- Effective strategies are based on a thorough evaluation of the current situation and main trends in the environment as well as in the organization itself.
- Relevant trends in the general environment can be analyzed using the PESTEL framework.
- Several tools can also be used to understand the structure, trends, and key success factors in the particular industry within which an organization operates.
- Taking an inside view, it is necessary to clarify (a) the organization's purpose, (b) its overall goals, (c) the value creation model, and (d) major capabilities and strengths.
- The results of the external and internal analyses can be combined either in a classic SWOT analysis or in an I-O/O-I analysis with the aim of matching organizational strengths with opportunities in the market.

Macro environment (general environment): External factors (outside of an organization's control) that can influence an organization's strategy, value creation process, or performance (including political, economic, socio-demographic, technological, environmental, and legal influences).

It is good practice for physicians to first make a diagnosis before deciding on the right therapy. Likewise, a good strategist will start with a thorough **assessment of the situation**, analyzing all the important external (environmental) and internal (organizational) factors that have a potential influence on the organization's value creation process.

In particular, strategic decision makers need to find out:

- which developments in the **(general) or macro environment** could present challenges and opportunities for the organization;
- how the organization's specific **(industry) or micro environment** is structured, and which trends have an impact on the individual players within the industry;
- the major (or even unique) **resource- and capabilities-based strengths**, as well as the significant **weaknesses** of the organization; and
- how strengths and capabilities can be harnessed to **explore and exploit opportunities** and create superior value under the current, as well as changing, external conditions.

We will now look at these four questions in more detail.

Taking a look outside

Micro environment (industry environment): Factors in the immediate surroundings of an organization that can influence an organization's strategy, value creation process, or performance (e.g. customers, suppliers, distribution partners, investors, or competitors).

"In order to give the true science of the flight of birds through the air you must first give the science of the winds,"[14] said Italian Renaissance artist and scientist Leonardo da Vinci. Organizations cannot be seen as independent of their environment. The environment is the source of all resources that an organization requires to create value, and is where the customers who are willing to pay for the organization's products or services are found. It is therefore essential for an organization to stay in tune with and adapt its strategy to its environment.[15]

The environment can be analyzed on two levels. The general (or macro) environment comprises broader societal influences on the organization (e.g. economic cycles, socio-demographic developments, or changes in legislation). The industry (or micro) environment includes all those outside factors and actors that directly influence an organization's value creation system (e.g. customers, suppliers, competitors, or investors).

PESTEL analysis:
A tool for systematically analyzing political, economic, socio-demographic, technological, environmental, and legal factors that can have an influence on an organization's strategy, value creation process, or performance.

A common tool for assessing the **macro environment** is the **PESTEL analysis**. PESTEL is an acronym that stands for **p**olitical, **e**conomic, **s**ocio-cultural, **t**echnological, (physical) **e**nvironmental, and **l**egal factors. The main aim of the PESTEL analysis is to identify developments within these six dimensions that represent current (or future) opportunities for or threats to the organization (see also the box *Zooming in on the PESTEL analysis*).

Zooming in on ▶ THE PESTEL ANALYSIS

The PESTEL analysis is a tool that can help you to better understand the environment in which your organization operates. Here are the main steps involved in a thorough PESTEL analysis.

1 Identify all external factors that have a potential influence on the organization or its industry, both on a global and a local (e.g. country or regional) level:
   (a) *Political factors* (What governmental and political actions could have an effect on the organization and its activities?);
   (b) *Economic factors* (How does the economic situation or future economic development affect your organization?);
   (c) *Social factors* (Which demographic developments or attitudes and values in the population could have an impact on your organization?);
   (d) *Technological factors* (Which existing or newly developed technologies could potentially affect your industry?);
   (e) *Environmental factors* (What ecological and environmental aspects could potentially affect your organization?);
   (f) *Legal factors* (What laws, legislative frameworks, regulations, or standards need to be considered by your organization now and in the future?).

2 Determine the most likely future development scenario for these factors (but also take possible alternative scenarios into account).

3 Assess whether the selected factors will create opportunities or threats for your organization, and, if yes, how.

Some examples of factors that can be included in a PESTEL analysis are presented in Table 7.1. The list is by no means complete; the relevant factors will vary from context to context.

Table 7.1 Examples of factors that can be included in a PESTEL analysis

PESTEL dimension	Typical factors to be analyzed
Political	• Stability of the political system • Political integration trends (e.g. free-trade zones, economic unions) • Relationships with other countries (trade barriers) • Major current and planned political initiatives • Economic and social policies • Political influence on the industry
Economic	• Key economic indicators (interest rates, unemployment rates, inflation, GDP growth rates, savings and investment rates) • Economic outlook • Currency exchange rates (current and projected) • Dependency of the organization's industry on economic cycles • Resource availability • Globalization trends
Socio-cultural	• Demographic developments • Lifestyle trends • Changes in consumer attitudes • Societal values (especially also work-related values) • Educational trends • Income distribution

PESTEL dimension	Typical factors to be analyzed
Technological	• Current technological level • New technological developments with an impact on the industry • Disruptive technologies • Research and development infrastructure and initiatives
Environmental	• Environmental issues with relevance for the industry • Ecological footprint • Energy use and renewable energy sources • Environmental regulations
Legal	• Legal certainty/rule of law • Intellectual property protection • Labor law • Consumer protection law • Competition/antitrust law • Taxation law

Born global:
A new business venture that from its launch pursues a strategy of operating across national borders and aims to globalize its business rapidly.

AROUND THE GLOBE

Different strategies for different institutional environments

An important part of the macro environment is the **institutional environment**, which can be said to encompass all formal and informal rules and laws that shape and impact organizations' behavior and success in that environment. This includes political and legal institutions (e.g. is there a functioning legal system?), economic institutions (e.g. are there functioning markets for goods and services?), and socio-cultural institutions (e.g. what informal norms and customs do organizations need to follow in order to operate successfully in a particular country?). The institutional environment can have a considerable impact on an organization's strategies and decisions. This is particularly relevant in emerging markets: relatively low- or middle-income countries which are characterized by high economic growth rates but also "institutional voids," the absence of certain regulations, intermediaries, or structures that allow organizations to enforce contracts.[16] Companies that want to do business in China, for example, have to consider that intellectual property rights are generally not very well protected, that there are considerable restrictions on foreign investors, and that it is "difficult to imagine a

successful business in China that hasn't had something to do with the government."[17] In Russia, in turn, businesses can be hampered by high levels of corruption and bureaucracy, as well as by economic sanctions that Western countries and Russia have imposed on each other following the conflict in Ukraine from 2014 onwards. When developing strategies for emerging markets, managers need to decide whether to adapt their organization's business model, try to change the institutional environment (if their organization is powerful enough—for example, through political lobbying or sponsoring campaigns for a certain cause), or stay away from markets in which the institutions required by their business model are lacking or do not work well. In any case, it is important to consider the peculiarities of the local institutional environment before determining the strategies for a foreign market, something which is particularly relevant for managers in multinational companies and **born globals** (start-ups that operate across national borders).

Source: *Based on information in Henisz and Delios (2002); Khanna et al. (2005).*

Understanding the industry

In addition to identifying general environmental developments, strategists need to clearly understand the **structure, trends, and key success factors of their industry**. First, there is the seemingly trivial—but sometimes tricky—question: "In which industry do we compete?"

We can **define an industry** as a group of organizations that provide the same kind of value to the same target markets. In a classic *Harvard Business Review* article called "Marketing myopia," Theodore Levitt argued that defining an industry too narrowly in a product-oriented (as opposed to customer value-oriented) way can lead to negative consequences.[18] He used the example of the declining railroads which defined their industry as the "railroad business." Levitt suggested that if they had understood that they were actually part of the "transportation business" (a customer value-oriented industry definition), they might have been able to react much faster to the threats from other players in this industry, such as airlines.

The following questions can help to **identify the industry** in which an organization is embedded:

1 Who are we creating value for?
2 What is the value that we create for our customers?
3 Who else does—or could—create the same value (with either the same or a similar offer or with a substitute product or service)?

While overly narrow industry definitions should generally be avoided, it is also possible to err on the overly broad side. Industry definitions in which customer groups, products and service offers, and geographic regions can no longer be clearly identified are of little help for further analyses and strategic moves.[19] Organizations can, of course, work in several industries (e.g. widely diversified multinational **conglomerates**). In this case, the different industries in which the organization operates need to be analyzed separately.

As a basis for further strategy development, managers need to identify some **basic features of their organization's playing field**, including:

- *size* (of overall market and of market segments—both in terms of turnover and units);
- *growth* (overall industry and segment growth);
- *competition* (number and size of competitors; key players; market share [per segment]; positioning and main strategic trajectories of competitors);
- *customers* (needs; structure; strategy [in the case of business customers]; behavior).

In many industries, secondary data will be available for most of these factors. However, desk research is usually not enough. Peter Drucker points out that "[w]hat the people in the business think they know about the customer and market is more likely to be wrong than right," because the only person who really knows what the customer wants is the customer.[20] Thus, it is necessary to understand customers' thoughts and behavior well, either by asking or observing them (or—even better—by a combination of both).

To gain a better understanding of the main trends in customer needs and behaviors, it also makes sense to integrate members of the organization who are in constant contact with the customers "at the frontline" in the strategic analysis process.

Tools for industry analysis

Several tools have been developed to systematically analyze industry structure and developments. Four of the most commonly used tools are **Porter's five forces** model, the **strategic group map**, the **industry life cycle analysis**, and the **value curve**. These tools are described in more detail on the following pages.

Porter's five forces:
A strategic tool developed by Harvard Professor Michael Porter for analyzing the competitive intensity in an industry. The "five forces" are the extent of rivalry within an industry, the bargaining power of suppliers, the bargaining power of buyers, the threat of new entrants, and the threat of substitutes.

Porter's five forces[21]

Harvard Professor Michael Porter originally devised the model of the five forces to analyze the competitive intensity and root causes of profitability in an industry. According to Porter, the three main forces along the industry value chain are:

- the **bargaining power of suppliers** and the **bargaining power of buyers** (determined, for example, by the costs of switching from one supplier to another, the degree of supplier/buyer concentration, the importance of the organization's demand or supply volume for the supplier/buyer, or the availability of substitutes); and
- the intensity of **competitive rivalry within the industry** (influenced, for example, by the degree of industry concentration, the degree of differentiation of offers, industry growth, exit barriers, or capacity utilization rates).

The other two forces are:

- the **threat of new entrants** (contingent on industry entry barriers); and

Substitutes:
Different products or service offers that create equivalent value for customers.

- the threat of **substitutes,** i.e. different products or services that create equivalent value for customers.

For example, a five forces analysis of the soft drinks industry could reveal that:

- the *bargaining power of suppliers* is low (because the main ingredients are water and sugar, and it is easy for soft drinks companies to find alternative suppliers for these commodities);
- the *bargaining power of buyers* is medium (because consumers can easily switch from one brand to another, but there is also quite a high degree of brand loyalty);
- the *rivalry among existing players in the industry* is high (because there are a few very strong competitors such as Coca-Cola and Pepsi, as well as additional competition from the low-priced private labels of retail chains);
- the *threat of new entrants* is medium (because it is easy to set up a new soft drinks firm on the one hand, but quite difficult to win market share and match the cost advantages of the large incumbents on the other); and
- the *threat of substitute products or services* is high (because other carbonated beverages and sparkling water are easily available).

A five forces analysis based on the thorough compilation of industry data can help to explain the power structures, profitability potential, and key trends within an industry. According to Porter, a rigorous analysis of the industry structure will also:

a. try to find out whether changes and trends are structural (i.e. permanent) or cyclical (i.e. temporary)—most industries have their own specific business cycles, and the analyses should therefore cover the whole cycle;
b. include quantitative analyses rather than just the description of qualitative factors; and
c. acknowledge the systemic nature of an industry and the interconnections between the individual players and forces within it.[22]

Strategic group map[23]

Organizations that follow similar strategies in strong direct competition with each other are considered to be part of one **strategic group**. Strategic groups usually offer similar product lines, have similar price levels and cost structures, and use similar technologies. There are **mobility barriers** that make it difficult to enter or leave these strategic groups (e.g. economies of scale or significant investments that are needed to match a certain offer).[24] Strategic group maps can be used to visualize competitive closeness. Competitors are placed on a matrix with two dimensions (e.g. pricing policy, quality level, service level, distribution channels, or degree of specialization) which are of high importance for the overall industry (see Figure 7.2 for an example). As a third dimension, a circle can be

Strategic group:
A group of organizations with a similar strategic position.

drawn around the company, and its size represents a company's turnover or market share. Organizations which are close to each other on the map can be identified as a strategic group.

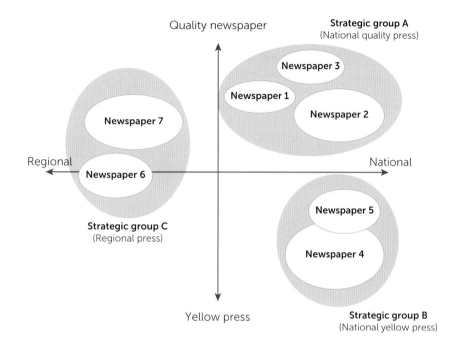

Figure 7.2 An example of a strategic group map in the newspaper industry

Industry life cycle

Industry life cycle:
The typical development of an industry through different stages (usually start-up/ introduction, growth, maturity, and decline).

Industries do not remain static; they evolve over time. The classic **industry life cycle** describes industry development over time as an S-curve with four phases: start-up, growth, maturity, and decline (see Figure 7.3). However, not all industries follow this evolutionary pattern. New technologies and new business models can lead to radical declines (e.g. in the US newspaper advertising industry after the rise of online media), or to a surprising revitalization (e.g. the increase in demand for postal services following the e-commerce boom). To make the right positioning and investment (or divestment) decisions, it is important to understand which phase an industry is in. When analyzing industry developments, one

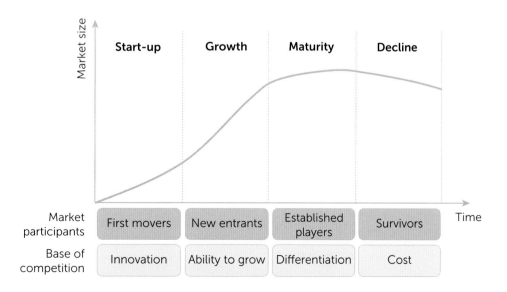

Figure 7.3 The industry life cycle S-curve

should also keep in mind that industry structures are by no means "like a law of nature," [25] as some managers might assume; they can change fast.

The value curve

Value curve:
A tool for visualizing value propositions (the benefits that a certain group of customers get from a product and/or service offer).

Kim and Mauborgne's concept of the **value curve** is built on the main "factors that the industry competes on and invests in"[26]—factors that represent the value that is created for customers and that usually also form the basis of customer decisions. The value curve, which is also known under the term *strategy canvas*, can be used to identify the main areas of competition in different strategic groups (as well as to identify potential areas for innovation—see also Chapter 10). The example in Figure 7.4 shows the value curve for three selected segments of the car industry. The curves in the example show that different strategic groups in the car industry compete on different factors. In addition to juxtaposing different industry segments, the value curve can also help in comparing the offers of individual competitors with those of one's own organization, thereby making differentiation (and potential for differentiation) visible.

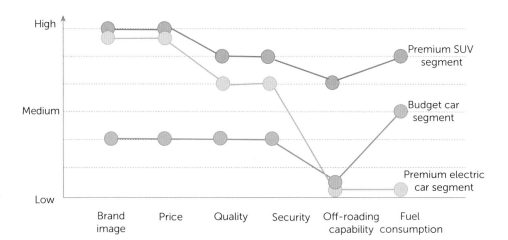

Figure 7.4 An example of a value curve for selected segments of the car industry

Mental model:
Simplified understanding of a cause–effect relationship that a person holds about a certain phenomenon.

Once the main factors and developments that drive and influence an industry are understood, they need to be connected with each other. It has been found that **mental models**—simplified interpretations of cause–effect relationships that managers hold about how the business environment works—influence the quality of decision making.[27] Managers do not necessarily need to know every detail about the entire business environment. In fact, in most cases, this is far from feasible. However, research results show that mental models about the **key principles** at work in a certain business environment improve decisions and subsequent performance outcomes.[28] For example, a manager of a car manufacturing company could form a mental model about what will most probably determine success in the industry in the future (e.g. offering electric vehicles with extended range capacity or developing cars that are able to drive autonomously). If this manager adjusts the strategy of the company accordingly, this will raise the chances of achieving a good strategic position for the company in the future—but only under the condition that the mental model adequately represents how the industry works in reality. Managers can attend industry trade shows and conferences, become involved in industry associations, or talk to customers, suppliers, and industry experts to better understand the key forces shaping the industry and form more accurate mental models about the main causal relationships that can lead to success or failure.

Looking inwards

In addition to understanding the macro environment and the structure and development of the industry, strategists also need to evaluate their own organization's situation. The four main questions to consider in an internal analysis are:

- *What are we here for?* Every organization has a fundamental purpose. The role of a **mission statement** is to make this purpose explicit. An example of a mission statement is Google's: "Our mission is to organize the world's information and make it universally accessible and useful."[29]

- *What do we want to become?* A **vision statement** describes the organization's desired state in the future. It provides the members of an organization with a clear picture of what the outcome of their efforts could be in the long run. For example, L'Oréal, the French world market leader in cosmetics, has set itself the following vision: "Our ambition for the coming years is to win over another one billion consumers around the world by creating the cosmetic products that meet the infinite diversity of their beauty needs and desires."[30] Both the mission and the vision statement function as basic guidelines for strategic decision making; each strategic move can be tested against whether or not it helps to fulfill the organization's mission and vision.

- *How do we create value?* The **business model** describes the underlying economic logic of value creation and includes a number of building blocks: (1) the *value proposition* (what does an organization offer to its customers), (2) the *target customers*, (3) the *way of interacting with customers* (distribution channel and customer relationship strategy), (4) the *revenue model* (a description of how the organization generates income from selling products or services), (5) the *cost structure*, (6) the *processes and activities* necessary to create value, (7) the *core competencies* needed, and (8) the relationships with partners in a *value creation network*.[31] An investigation of the individual factors of the business model and how they interrelate can lead to a better understanding of how the organization generates value.

- *What are our main strengths?* In the **resource-based view (RBV)** of the firm, value is generally created by combining **resources** (tangible and intangible assets that can create economic value) and **capabilities** (the skills used to combine resources in order to produce certain outputs).[32] To create value that is superior to what competitors offer, organizations must have a unique set of resources and capabilities that sets them apart from others. The **VRIO model** can be used to check whether particular resources have the potential to form the basis for sustainable advantage.[33] According to this model, strategically relevant resources or capabilities should be:

  a. **v**aluable for exploiting opportunities,
  b. **r**are among both existing and future competitors,
  c. **i**mperfectly imitable, and
  d. suitable for being exploited by a particular **o**rganization.

Prahalad and Hamel term VRIO capabilities that can be used for a variety of products and markets and clearly contribute to customer benefit **core competencies**.[34] As part of the internal strategic analysis, the major resources and capabilities that a company holds (e.g. employee skills, technological capabilities, intellectual property, process knowledge, access to markets, relationship of trust with customers, marketing capabilities, leadership abilities, or innovation power, to name just a few categories) are first identified and then evaluated using the VRIO framework (see Table 7.2 for an example). A thorough analysis also includes second-order or **dynamic capabilities**, which represent the organization's ability to learn and to create new or adapt existing resources and capabilities; or, in other words, the "competence to build new competence."[35]

Based on the internal analysis, a manager should understand for whom and how the organization creates value.

Business model:
A representation of the main business decisions and the logic behind how a business generates value (for both customers and for the organization).

Resource-based view (RBV):
A general theory of management that postulates that having access to and being able to make use of specific resources and capabilities is the key factor for achieving competitive advantage.

VRIO model:
A framework for analyzing whether an organization's resources and capabilities can be used as a basis for achieving competitive advantage. VRIO stands for resources or capabilities that are valuable, rare, imperfectly imitable, and suitable to be exploited by a particular organization.

Dynamic capabilities:
The skills and routines that allow an organization to learn and create new or adapt existing resources or capabilities.

Table 7.2 Example of a VRIO analysis

Special resources/capabilities that the firm has access to	Is it valuable?	Is it rare?	Is it difficult to imitate?	Is the firm organized to capture the value?	Result
Technological know-how (application programming)	YES	YES	NO	NO	*Not VRIO*
Financial resources for product development	YES	NO	NO	YES	*Not VRIO*
Innovation culture within the team	YES	YES	YES	YES	**VRIO**
State-of-the-art IT infrastructure	YES	NO	NO	YES	*Not VRIO*
Image as a quality leader in the industry	YES	YES	YES	YES	**VRIO**

Integrating the external and internal analyses

Having identified the main developments of the macro and industry environment as well as inside the organization, the findings of the two analyses need to be combined. One of the most popular methods of integrating the internal and external view is the **SWOT analysis**. In its very basic form—which is also the most frequently used—the **SWOT matrix** includes a list of an organization's strengths and weaknesses from the internal analysis, and a list of opportunities and threats from the external analysis. In a detailed study on the use of SWOT analyses in UK companies, Hill and Westbrook found that the SWOT lists produced in the various organizations were, in most cases, full of ambiguous words and phrases, and showed a lack of verification of statements or opinions. They were neither prioritized nor used in subsequent stages of the strategy process, which led Hill and Westbrook to conclude that "it's time for a product recall"[36] of the SWOT analysis. To avoid ending up with these long lists instead of strategic conclusions, every SWOT analysis should be complemented by a **"So-what" analysis**. In other words, managers should answer the question: "So what does this mean for the strategic decisions that we need to make in our organization?" They could ask, for example:

SWOT matrix:
A strategic tool that helps to identify the strengths and weaknesses of the organization as well as opportunities and threats in the environment.

- Which strengths are crucial for exploiting opportunities and how could we further develop these strengths? (S/O)
- How can we protect our existing strengths in light of imminent threats? (S/T)
- In which areas do we need to overcome our weaknesses in order to be able to exploit opportunities? (W/O)
- In which areas do we need to overcome our weaknesses in order to avoid threats leading to actual negative consequences for our business? (W/T)

I-O/O-I analysis (short for Inside-out/Outside-in analysis):
A tool that helps to link the results of the external and internal strategic analyses through finding out (a) which opportunities can be exploited with an organization's existing resources and capabilities, and (b) which resources and capabilities an organization should develop in order to be able to exploit major opportunities.

The **Inside-out/Outside-in (I-O/O-I) analysis**, presented in Figure 7.5, is an alternative, more structured tool for integrating the findings of the external and internal strategic analyses (see the box *Zooming in on the I-O/O-I analysis*). This tool focuses on strengths rather than weaknesses and on opportunities rather than threats, thereby following Peter Drucker's argument that the main purpose of an organization actually lies in making strengths productive.[37] Focusing on matching opportunities and strengths leads to a concentration of efforts rather than a dissipation of the organization's energies that could arise when all possible combinations of strengths, weaknesses, opportunities, and threats are considered as being equally important (as in a traditional SWOT analysis).

I-O

Inside →→→→ Out

VRIO resource/ capability	Competitive performance on resource/capability	Value/customer benefits created	Opportunity to be exploited
Know-how in flexible manufacturing	Very strong (++)	Price advantage for smaller order sizes	Higher demand for low-volume customized products
...	...	...	...

O-I

Outside →→→→ In

Opportunity	Resources/capabilities needed for exploiting the opportunity	Strength compared to competition	Potential initiatives to build resource/capability
High market growth in country A	Market access	Weaker (−)	Competition could be matched through cooperation with firm X
...	...	...	...

Figure 7.5 An example of an Inside-out/Outside-in (I-O/O-I) analysis

---

Zooming in on ▶ THE I-O/O-I ANALYSIS

The Inside-out/Outside-in (I-O/O-I) analysis is a tool that can help you to integrate the findings of the external and internal strategic analyses. It allows you to draw conclusions about where to focus strategic efforts for further development of the organization. Here is how the analytical tool works:

(a) *Inside-out*: The I-O part of the analysis answers the question: "Which opportunities can be exploited with our unique competencies?" For this purpose:

  1 make a list of the organization's main internal VRIO resources and capabilities;

  2 evaluate your organization's performance relative to the competition on each of the VRIO resources and capabilities;

  3 for each resource or capability, explore which distinct value and customer benefits it can help to create; and

  4 think about which opportunities the resource or capability could help to exploit.

(b) *Outside-in*: The O-I part of the analysis answers the question "Which resources and capabilities should (and can) be developed to exploit the main opportunities?" For this purpose:

  1 start with the opportunities identified in the environmental analysis;

  2 for each opportunity, list the resources and capabilities that are needed to exploit it;

  3 evaluate the relative strengths or weaknesses of your organization in relation to the required resources and capabilities compared to the competition; and

  4 derive possible initiatives for developing the requisite resources or capabilities.

As an outcome of the I-O/O-I analysis, you should know which opportunities your organization is best prepared to exploit and which strategic initiatives could help your organization to build the resources and capabilities needed to exploit the most promising opportunities.

The advantage of this type of analysis over a simple SWOT list is that I-O/O-I forces the strategist to systematically match internal strengths with external opportunities (and vice versa). Moreover, this tool makes the relative performance against competitors clear, and facilitates the formulation of concrete and actionable initiatives.

If you were responsible for developing a strategy for either the institution you are studying in or the organization you work for, which main opportunities (in the environment) on the one hand and VRIO resources and capabilities (of the organization) on the other hand could you identify? Can you conduct an I-O/O-I analysis that integrates the opportunities and resources/capabilities that you identified? Which initiatives would you suggest to the organization as a result of your analysis?

Red Bull: Taking wings in the energy drinks business

When Dietrich Mateschitz visited Thailand on a business trip as the international marketing director of a toothpaste maker in the early 1980s, he came across a new, innovative energy drink called *Krating Daeng* ("red gaur"), which allegedly helped to cure his jet lag. He entered into a partnership with T. C. Pharmaceuticals, the producer of the drink, adapted the formula to Western tastes and created a new energy drink company called Red Bull GmbH. Red Bull, with its main ingredients water, caffeine, b-group vitamins, sugars, and the amino acid taurine, was launched in Mateschitz's home country of Austria in 1987, and entered the US market via California in 1997 (the nationwide rollout was only completed in 2002).

Rather than aiming for comprehensive distribution coverage, the company first started in a few selected places in each area to target the "in-crowd." It set up its own distribution system to avoid being just one of many products in the established distribution channels. The "lifestyle beverage" brand soon gathered a following among young people, especially on the sports scene (through "sportsmen opinion-leaders,"[38] as Mateschitz called them) as well as in discos and clubs. The company employed unusual marketing strategies such as sponsoring and organizing extreme sports events like the *Red Bull Cliff Diving* competition and free mass sampling through student brand ambassadors and "consumer education teams" driving around in cars topped by oversized Red Bull cans.

Rumors about secret ingredients (some even talked about bull semen), drug-like stimulant effects and negative health impacts did not hurt Red Bull's success. On the contrary, it raised interest in the new product, especially among the young target group. Meanwhile, Red Bull tried to position itself as a performance-enhancing drink, using the slogan, it "gives you wings." It continued to avoid the classic mass marketing strategies; instead sponsoring countless extreme sports events (e.g. the Red Bull Air Race) and adventure sports athletes. Red Bull also bought its own Formula 1 racing team as well as several soccer teams (e.g. the New York Red Bulls in the US or RB Leipzig in Germany). It secured global news coverage as a result of the space diving project Red Bull Stratos in which Austrian skydiver Felix Baumgartner broke the sound barrier in a record-breaking jump from an altitude of approximately 39 kilometers (24 miles).

In 2018, Red Bull sold more than 6.7 billion cans in over 170 countries, resulting in a turnover of more than €5.5 billion. Red Bull's success has not gone unnoticed, however. The soft drinks giant Coca-Cola, followed by other brands, tried to launch its own energy drink brand KMX but did not succeed in threatening the new category leader. In 2014, Red Bull was the market leader in the US with a 43 percent market share, followed by two newcomers Monster (39 percent) and Rockstar (10 percent), which both copied Red Bull's affiliation with action sports. Brands owned by Coca-Cola and PepsiCo followed with a 3 percent market share each.

A market expert characterized Red Bull in the *New York Times* as "a classic category pioneer that's been circled by the sharks."[39] In 2015, Coca-Cola announced a strategic partnership with Monster. Coca-Cola transferred the ownership of its own energy drinks business to Monster, acquired an approximate 17 percent stake in the company, and opened its global distribution network to Red Bull's rival, which offered its energy drinks in 16-ounce cans at the same price as Red Bull's 8.4-ounce can.

Experts predicted a 40 percent growth of the global energy drinks market between 2015 and 2020. The entry of new functionally enhanced water, juice and tea drinks could threaten the position of the traditional energy drinks, especially among more health-conscious consumers.

Health concerns also led to sales restrictions and marketing bans for energy drinks in some countries.

For a long time, Red Bull relied on a very small product portfolio of energy drink varieties compared to its competitors. In 2017, however, Mateschitz launched a new product line, comprising "all natural" cola, ginger ale, tonic water, and bitter lemon drinks.

Sources: Corts and Freier (2003); Curtis (2006) Mitchell (2015); The Coca-Cola Company (2015); Red Bull (2019); Rodgers (2001); Starling (2016).

Discussion questions

- What main strategic choices did Red Bull make when entering the US market? How do these choices differ from the way that the traditional soft drinks industry works?
- How would you assess the attractiveness of the energy drink industry?
- Which reasons could explain why the incumbent giants in the soft drinks industry have not been able to match Red Bull's success?
- Why do you think Red Bull entered the all-natural drinks market with its *Organics by Red Bull* product line? How could Red Bull's existing resources and capabilities be used to exploit the opportunities in the market for healthier organic refreshments?

7.3 Choosing the arena: Where to create value?

Pixabay/Pexels

In brief

- Many organizations operate in more than one business area. In the field of corporate strategy, decisions are made about the overall scope and direction of a multi-business enterprise.

- Managers need to evaluate whether and how diversification into new businesses adds value, how to develop an optimal portfolio of business units that balances performance today with building potential for the future, and whether and how to grow.

- Following goals that are beyond the current abilities of the organization does not necessarily require internal growth. It is also possible to use a cooperative strategy approach to jointly reach outcomes that would not be achievable by one organization on its own.

Portfolio strategy: As part of corporate level strategy, portfolio strategy comprises high-level decisions about which business units an organization invests in.

Before thinking strategically about *how* to create value, it is necessary to define *where* an organization wants to create value. Choosing the arena in which an organization wants to play a role is the realm of **corporate strategy**. The main questions that need to be answered in this context are:

1 Which industries or market environments do we want to compete in?
2 How do we want to grow?
3 Should we cooperate with other organizations to reach our strategic goals?

We will take a closer look at each of these questions in the following sections about **portfolio strategy**, **growth strategy**, and **cooperative strategy**.

Strategic business unit (SBU): An independently managed part of an organization that offers products and services in one particular market.

Portfolio strategy

Many organizations are stretching beyond their original business and adding new **strategic business units (SBUs)** that generate value in different markets. An SBU—sometimes also

Mergers and acquisitions (M&A):
The area in strategic management that deals with combining different organizations into one organization (mergers) or purchasing other organizations or parts thereof (acquisitions).

referred to as a "division"—is an independently managed part of an organization that offers products and services in one particular market. New SBUs can either be added through **mergers and acquisitions**, but also through launching new products or services for new markets.

For example, the international energy company Royal Dutch Shell Group is not only active in the oil and gas business, but also developed a new SBU that is focused on renewable energies including, for example, wind and solar power generation. Another example is Johnson & Johnson, a corporation or "family of companies" that is well known for its consumer products like baby care or skin care. The consumer products division is only one of Johnson & Johnson's SBUs, however. The others are medical devices (e.g. surgical technology) and pharmaceutical products. **Diversification** is seen as a "key to longevity" for the over 130-year-old company.[40] According to Johnson & Johnson's Chief Financial Officer Joe Wolk, diversification "insulates us from the ebbs and flows of the market,"[41] especially when times are more challenging in one particular business.

General **reasons for diversification** into new product–market combinations include:[42]

Diversification:
In strategic management, diversification describes the process of entering into new markets with new products or services.

- spreading risks across several businesses;
- adding businesses in growth markets to businesses in stagnating or declining markets;
- using existing capabilities in new environments;
- trying to gain more market power; or
- using **economies of scope** effects (cost reduction from producing different products or services in combination).

Economies of scope:
Cost advantages that result from using one resource base for producing or selling two or more distinct products (leading to lower unit costs).

Diversification, however, is not an end in itself. It only creates value if the investment in new business areas yields more than it would have in the original business, and if the future value creation opportunities are higher in the diversified than in the focused configuration of the organization. This is not always the case, as the high failure rate of mergers and acquisitions demonstrates—it has been estimated that over 50 percent of all mergers and acquisitions fail.[43]

Piskorski proposed two tests that can be used to assess whether it makes sense to add an additional business to existing ones:[44]

1 The **"Better-Off Test"**: Is there a clear economic and/or competitive advantage in combining the businesses? An example of such an advantage are economies of scope, when jointly producing two goods costs less than producing them separately (e.g. due to the higher capacity utilization of one asset that can be used to produce other goods, or the joint use of research and development capabilities, manufacturing know-how, or management skills). Another example is cross-selling opportunities that arise from having a joint sales force.

2 The **"Ownership Test"**: Is there a clear advantage of both businesses being held by the same owners? As an alternative to owning an additional business, the economic and/or competitive advantage that can potentially be reaped from a combination of businesses could also be exploited through contractual relationships (as, for example, in the case of airline alliances or distribution partnerships). Forming one joint organization only makes sense when contractual arrangements are too risky or costly (i.e. when transaction costs are high), and when internal coordination costs (ownership costs) do not exceed the costs of setting up and enforcing a contract with external partners.

Cash cow:
One of the four categories of the BCG matrix that includes business units (or products and services) with a strong market position in a low-growth (mature) market. It is called "cash cow" because it ought to generate high amounts of cash that can be "milked" by the organization.

Diversification results in a **portfolio** of business units. One frequently used method to display a portfolio of businesses is the BCG (Boston Consulting Group) matrix (see Figure 7.6). This is used to evaluate business units on their competitive position (relative market share[45]) and industry attractiveness (growth rate). These positions are plotted on a matrix in which the size of the circle represents the current size (usually in terms of revenue) of the unit (see also the box *Zooming in on creating a BCG portfolio*).[46] The **BCG matrix** (also known as "growth/share matrix") classifies business units as: "dogs" (units without any further potential), **"cash cows"** (highly profitable units, usually at later stages of their life cycle), "stars" (profitable high-growth businesses), and "question marks" (usually new businesses with strong development needs). The growth/share portfolio approach has been criticized for its simplicity, for not taking into account VRIO-based resources and synergies between businesses, and for overemphasizing market share as a key success factor.[47] Nevertheless, it provides managers with an overview of the relative position of an organization's different businesses and can therefore form a basis for discussing which businesses to invest in or divest from.

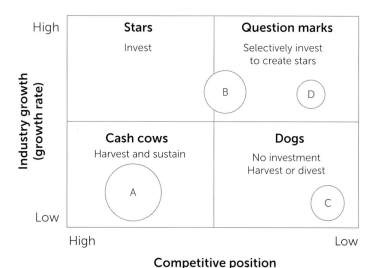

Figure 7.6 An example of a BCG portfolio

Source: Based on ideas from Hedley (1970), with permission of the Boston Consulting Group (BCG).

Zooming in on ▶ CREATING A BCG PORTFOLIO

Using the following six steps, you can create and analyze your own BCG portfolio matrix for an organization.

1 *Choose the unit of analysis.* Would you like to make a portfolio of business units, products, or individual brands?

2 *Identify the market for each unit.* To calculate a market share, you need to know what market you want to compete in (for example, the overall market for a certain product or just the premium segment).

3 *Calculate the relative market share of each unit.* Divide your own unit's market share (or revenues) by the market share (or revenues) of the third-largest competitor[48] in the relevant market to determine the unit's position along the x-axis.

4 *Assess the market growth rate.* Use industry reports or expert estimations to find out how strong market growth is (in percent per year) for the individual units of analysis. This determines the unit's position along the y-axis. The cut-off point for the center line can vary from one industry context to another.

5 *Determine the size of the circles.* After positioning the individual units in the matrix according to the outcome of your analysis under steps 3 and 4, make the circles bigger or smaller depending on the revenues of each unit in relation to the revenues of the other units on the matrix.

6 *Determine the best strategy for each unit.* On the upper section of the matrix, "stars" are candidates for further investment, while investment in "question marks" should be more carefully selected. Ideally, the organization should only invest in "question mark" units that have the potential to become stars. On the lower section of the matrix, "cash cows" should be harvested (trying to get the maximum profits out of them), but with a view to sustaining them without too much new investment. For "dogs," divestment (i.e. selling or shutting down these units) needs to be considered.

The portfolio approach was originally based on the assumption that new business units need to be financed by existing profitable ones. Easier access to external sources of financing, especially between the late 1980s and the beginning of the 21st century, led to a new paradigm: **value-based strategy**.[49] The focus of value-based strategy lies on maximizing **shareholder value**, which in a simplified form can be thought of as the net present value of all future cash flows that a business will be able to generate for its shareholders minus the value of the debt capital used to finance the business. Under this perspective, it is less important to create a balanced portfolio of business units in which "cash cows" are financing promising new businesses. The focus is on generating as much shareholder value as possible in all business units instead. This means that individual business units are assessed in the same way as shareholders would value a whole company on the stock market—mainly by their ability to create current and future cash flows and a high return on capital. If managers use a value-based strategy approach to build or reshape a portfolio of businesses, they can increase shareholder value. At the same time, they might fall into the trap of being exclusively oriented on short-term cash flow maximization without adequately taking care of making investments in new, future-oriented business areas. Such a myopic strategy can in the worst case lead to a decrease in the organization's potential to create value in the long term, and also to the neglect of non-financial results categories (see Chapter 9).

Shareholder value:
The total monetary value that shareholders obtain from their investment in a company (including dividend payments, gains from share price increases, or any other payouts).

Growth strategy

Similarly to living organisms, organizations develop over time. Many organizations pursue **quantitative growth strategies**, either through:

- trying to increase the market share of their existing businesses in existing markets (**market penetration**);
- developing new offers for existing markets (**product development**);
- entering new markets with existing products and services (**market development**); or
- entering new markets with new products or services, either horizontally at the same stage of the value chain or vertically into adjacent stages of the value chain (entering current suppliers' or direct customers' businesses) (**diversification**).[50]

Organic growth:
Expanding a business through using its own resources (rather than through mergers and acquisitions).

These four basic methods of growth (also known as **Ansoff's growth strategies**)[51] can be implemented organically (i.e. by developing the business out of the existing organization), through mergers and acquisitions, or by cooperating with third parties in the form of strategic alliances. While **organic growth** builds on existing resources and capabilities for new business creation, **mergers and acquisitions** offer a fast track way to gain market share or enter new markets. They do, however, also have a high risk of failure if the expected synergies cannot be generated or if combining different organizations and cultures causes friction. **Strategic alliances**, in turn, offer the possibility to benefit from the advantages of size and scope without having to grow the organization itself (see also the box *Joining forces to create a sustainable closed-loop solution for electric car batteries*).

Strategic alliance:
A partnership agreement under which two separate organizational entities join forces to reach a common goal.

Joining forces to create a sustainable closed-loop solution for electric car batteries

Before Marc Grynberg joined the management team of the Belgian company Umicore in 2008, its primary activities lay in the high-polluting smelting business. As a Group Controller, CFO, and CEO, he helped to transform Umicore into a global materials technology group that focused on green and clean technologies including, for example, emission control catalysts, materials for rechargeable batteries and photovoltaics, and recycling. After selling the loss-making smelters, Grynberg and his colleagues in the Umicore management team changed their strategy to the core principles of (a) creating new growth options based on existing competencies in material science, chemistry, and metallurgy; and (b) identifying new market opportunities in growing clean technology sectors. The company's growth strategy included both organic growth and selective acquisitions in areas where additional competencies were required. Organic growth was to come through high investment in research and development and the development of innovative business models such as a closed-loop solution for batteries in which the materials are recycled after the end of their useful life. In 2018, at a time when the global market for electrified vehicles was taking off, Grynberg decided to form a strategic alliance with carmaker BMW and battery cell manufacturer Northvolt. The aim of the alliance was to combine the three companies' core competencies of supplying materials and recycling (Umicore), battery cell

design and manufacturing (BMW), and innovative processes in high-volume battery cell production (Northvolt) to create a sustainable value chain for batteries from the development and raw materials supply through production and use to recycling. The alliance aimed to make electric mobility even more environmentally friendly (by reducing unrecyclable or difficult to recycle waste materials from batteries). "It is rewarding to see that Umicore's product technologies and recycling service are key enablers for this technology alliance,"[52] said Grynberg about the project through which the partners aimed to jointly advance the sustainable industrialization of battery cells in Europe.

→ Key takeaway

Strategic alliances can be an effective way to combine the competencies of different organizations in order to explore and exploit new strategic opportunities.

Sources: *Based on information in Balch (2013); Umicore (2018).*

Quantitative growth is not an end in itself. In some businesses, it is necessary to achieve a minimum size in order to survive (e.g. due to competitive cost pressures that require a certain level of economies of scale). However, it is also possible to stretch growth beyond the point of adding value. For example, in 1998, German automotive manufacturer Daimler-Benz acquired US carmaker Chrysler in an effort to grow its global business. The Daimler–Chrysler merger was later called a "marriage of dread" and a "gigantic flop."[53] The management underestimated the cultural differences that resulted in internal controversies instead of the hoped-for synergies. The German automotive manufacturer's growth adventure in the US ended with the sale of Chrysler in the years 2007 to 2009. It allegedly cost Daimler several dozen billions of euros.[54]

Qualitative growth:
A strategy that is oriented toward achieving a higher quality standard.

As an alternative to quantitative growth, organizations can follow a different path: **qualitative growth**. In a qualitative growth strategy, the emphasis lies in becoming better as opposed to bigger. Qualitative growth strategies include investing in product, service, and process quality, and also in the quality of relationships with customers, suppliers, employees, and the community. Superior value for customers is created through a clearly differentiated quality offer, personal service, or the sense that they are contributing to a valuable cause (as in the case of companies with a strong social or ecological commitment)—even if this comes with a higher price tag due to a lack of economies of scale. If higher quality levels meet with a quality-oriented and less price-sensitive clientele, qualitative growth will lead to higher margins and better business results.

One example of qualitative growth is the family-owned Italian coffee company illycaffè. (We often observe qualitative growth strategies in long-term-oriented family-owned firms.) The Illy family decided to reduce the range of different coffee blends that it offered from around twenty to only one, aiming to make it the best coffee in the world. "Our route to perfect quality is infinite,"[55] said illycaffè CEO Andrea Illy in an interview with the author of this book. Showing concern for the living and working conditions of coffee growers, illycaffè founded a corporate "university of coffee" as a knowledge hub to promote the constant education of partners from growers to baristas. The company also created an exceptional consumer experience that includes a strong focus on arts and design. illycaffè has thus positioned itself in the absolute premium segment of the coffee market. The company's dedication to providing the "perfect cup of coffee" allowed illycaffè to operate with higher price (and margin) levels than most of its competitors and paved the way for the company's success in global markets.

Any type of growth, whether quantitative or qualitative, needs investment. Growth redirects attention and cash from existing activities to future activities. Because investment in growth ties up resources, decisions about such investment should be carefully considered, taking the following questions on the **growth strategy analysis checklist** into account.

1   Is the intended growth strategy consistent with the organization's vision and mission?
2   How does the intended growth strategy add value for the overall organization?
3   Does the intended growth strategy strengthen the existing business (or are any negative effects to be expected)?
4   Does the intended growth strategy build on, and/or extend, the organization's VRIO resources and core competencies?
5   Are adequate resources (time, finances, people, capabilities) available to follow and sustain the intended growth strategy?
6   Is the intended growth strategy consistent with the interests of the organization's main stakeholders?

Cooperative strategy

When talking about strategy, we often use words that represent a competitive view of the world (e.g. *rivals, competitive advantage, attacking, or outperforming the competition*) and regard business as a zero-sum game (in which one firm's win means another's loss). However, strategy can also mean pursuing goals in a cooperative way with **strategic partners**. For example, Apple cooperates with MasterCard to give cardholders the opportunity to use Apple Pay as a mobile payment option.[56] Instead of competing with each other, the two companies decided to share their customer base and make use of their joint payment and mobile technology capabilities, thus creating more value for both sides. In another example, US retail giant Walmart and Japanese internet services company Rakuten announced a strategic alliance to launch an online grocery delivery service in Japan, utilizing and leveraging Walmart's experience in the grocery business and Rakuten's expertise in e-commerce and knowledge of the local market.[57]

Organizations can have different **reasons for following a cooperative strategy** (see Figure 7.7):[58]

- *Market seeking*: gaining access to new markets through a partner.
- *Resource seeking*: joining efforts with partners with complementary assets and capabilities.
- *Cost reduction*: using synergies or economies of scale and scope together with partners.
- *Risk reduction*: sharing investments and collaborating with partners who are more experienced in a certain field.

Despite the potential benefits of jointly using resources and capabilities without having to invest in them separately, **strategic alliances also carry risks**:[59]

- Alliance partners can act opportunistically and exploit the partnership. In extreme cases, new competitors can emerge from an alliance.
- Alliances can lead to a strong dependency on one partner, thus reducing the strategic options available.

Establishing trust between partners, as well as **building an effective control system** (e.g. splitting management control, putting each partner in charge of activities that are more closely connected with its respective organization-specific resources and competencies),[60] are major building blocks for successful partnerships.

There are some general **preconditions for a successful strategic partnership**. The partners need to (a) have complementary resources and skills, (b) commit themselves to

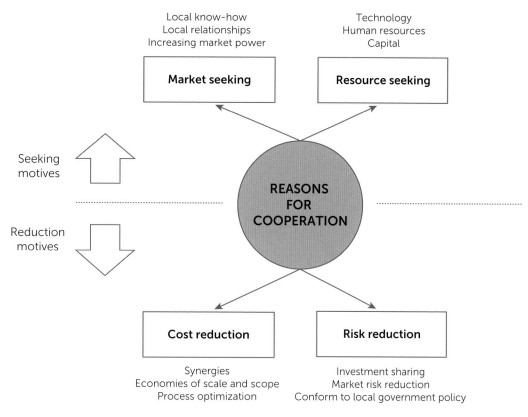

Figure 7.7 Reasons for following a cooperative strategy

Source: Sternad, D., Knappitsch, E. and Mundschütz, C. (2012) *Cross-Border Cooperation: European Institutional Framework and Strategies of SMEs* (Stuttgart: Franz Steiner Verlag), p. 41. Reprinted with permission.

contributing an adequate amount of resources to reach the joint goal, (c) have compatible, non-conflicting overall strategic plans, organizational cultures and working styles, and (d) offer added value for the other partners in at least one of the four dimensions presented in Figure 7.7.[61]

Further success factors for strategic alliances include an open exchange of mutual expectations, setting up a suitable governance structure (contract-based, relationship-based, or in the form of a joint venture) with clearly defined rights and responsibilities for each of the partners, creating a mechanism that determines how to deal with potential conflicts, establishing effective cooperation management systems, and developing a common cooperation culture. Although effective alliances are not easy to establish, they can have a profound effect. "If an enemy has alliances, the problem is grave and the enemy's position strong," said the ancient Chinese philosopher Sun Tzu, "if he has no alliances the problem is minor and the enemy's position weak."[62]

Which questions would you ask yourself before deciding to enter into a strategic partnership?

7.4 In search of a sustainable value creation model

Getty Images/Martin Poole

In brief

- When an organization has decided on *where* to compete, it can turn to the question of *how* to compete in that market environment.

- An integrated business strategy will include a capabilities-based internal strategic value creation model (with a focus on brand building, offering high product quality, excellent operations, innovation, or deal making), as well as a clear and distinct value offer for customers.

- To sustain a competitive advantage in creating customer value, organizations need to constantly reinvest in creating and sustaining unique resources and competencies, and combine them in a way that is difficult for others to reproduce.

- Digital technologies are opening new possibilities for value creation, but also have the potential for disrupting existing value creation models. Managers therefore need to think about mapping out a digital strategy for their organization.

Value proposition:
A statement that clearly describes the benefits that a certain group of customers get from the product and/or service offers of an organization.

Creating value means efficiently combining resources and capabilities to offer unique benefits to customers. To be relevant to customers (and therefore worth parting with their money), an organization's **value proposition** needs to differ from others, by providing products or services that others do not offer, making them available where others do not, offering better prices, or creating emotional value by building strong relationships with customers or a brand image that conveys a positive feeling in a way that others are not able to match.

Finding the right position for an organization is not sufficient, however. When others (which, in the realm of strategy, are usually called **competitors**) notice that someone is creating high value, they often want a share. They will try to copy the model and offer the same benefits to customers. Therefore, organizations also need to think about how to sustain their position in the face of actual or potential competition.

Finding the right position

Generic strategies:
A model (proposed by Michael Porter) of three basic strategies that can generally be used to achieve a competitive advantage (cost leadership, differentiation, focus).

Business-level strategy is about the positioning choices that an organization makes in one specific market arena. **Positioning** means finding one's distinct position relative to other organizations that are offering their products and services in the same market. For Porter, there are three **generic strategies** that can be used for positioning:[63]

- **Cost leadership**: producing a product or service at a lower cost than the competition (e.g. due to standardized mass production and economies of scale, a steeper learning curve, simple product design, a distinct technology or special process knowledge) and then being able to offer lower prices to customers.
- **Differentiation**: offering distinct benefits to customers (e.g. in terms of product quality or service) that cannot be matched by others. A sustainable differentiation strategy needs to be built on unique (VRIO) resources or capabilities (see Section 7.2).
- **Focus**: offering highly customized products or services in one or a few niche markets that are targeted toward fulfilling the needs of a specific, clearly defined customer group. A thorough understanding of the needs of the target group and good relationships with customers are key success factors in this type of strategic positioning.

Lacking a clear position or trying to be all things at once can lead to being "stuck in the middle" which leaves customers without any clearly distinguishable value proposition.[64] Although there are examples of successful **"hybrid" strategies** that simultaneously combine differentiation with cost leadership (the Swedish furniture retailer IKEA is often cited), empirical research has confirmed that there is generally a positive correlation between strategic purity and business performance, especially in developed markets because pure strategies (a) provide a clear direction for the organization, (b) avoid trade-offs and suboptimal compromises, and (c) do not open two flanks simultaneously to potential competitor attacks.[65]

Porter's generic strategies take an external view of positioning. Treacy and Wiersema's three **value disciplines** add an internal perspective on which organizations can focus:

1 **operational excellence** (being able to offer lower prices by streamlining operations);
2 **product leadership** (being able to offer the best product or service); or
3 **customer intimacy** (providing the best overall solutions by building strong customer relationships and an in-depth understanding of customer needs).[66]

In a similar vein, in their study of family businesses with an outstanding long-term performance track record, Miller and Le Breton-Miller identified five general **strategic foci** of successful businesses.[67]

- **Brand builders** are marketing experts that invest heavily in intensive promotion and are proficient at building emotional links with their customers (e.g. Estée Lauder is the US market leader in cosmetics with a portfolio of strong consumer brands).
- **Craftspeople** have a passion for quality and constantly aim to develop their skills to make the best possible products for their customers (e.g. Timken, the global industry leader in bearings, has quality as the cornerstone of its business).
- **Operators** create new and highly efficient forms of operations, enabling them to add value to their (usually price-sensitive) customers at low costs (IKEA is again an example, as it radically transformed the furniture industry through functional product design and a customer-self-collection logistics model).
- **Innovators** are constantly looking for new product and process solutions, and are quick to implement new ideas (e.g. the tire maker Michelin, the inventor of both the radial tire and the fuel-efficient tire).
- **Deal makers** are able to spot opportunities early and use their (political) connections and negotiation experience to exploit them (e.g. Bombardier, the world's leading regional jet manufacturer, which has made more than a dozen successful acquisitions in its major business areas of aerospace and rail transportation).

Understanding the basis of value creation is as important for a successful strategy as having an unambiguous position within the market. Value cannot be provided on the outside without the right value creation strategies within the organization. Conversely, the best product innovations and the most efficient operations are of no use without an adequate positioning in the market. Therefore, strategists always need to keep two questions in mind simultaneously:

1 What are the **distinct benefits** that we offer our customers? (value offer—external perspective)
2 What is the unique way in which we **produce value**? (value creation—internal perspective)

The combined answers to these questions form the basis of an **integrated strategic positioning**, which takes both the resource-based view and the market perspective into account. But even the best combinations of value creation and value offer strategies cannot lead to high performance if they are not deployed in an attractive market segment that provides enough potential for economic success. Figure 7.8 presents the complete model of integrated strategic positioning based on the three pillars of **value creation**, **value offer**, and an **attractive market segment**.

INTEGRATED STRATEGIC POSITIONING

In an attractive market segment

- Size
- Growth
- Competitive forces

EXTERNAL PERSPECTIVE

Value offer
A unique combination of customer benefits

INTERNAL PERSPECTIVE

Value creation
A unique way of combining resources and capabilities

Rational value
- Product
- Service
- Availability
- Price

Emotional value
- Brand
- Relationship

based on
- Marketing capabilities
- Quality products or services
- Operational excellence
- Innovation power
- Relationship building

Figure 7.8 Integrated strategic positioning

Sustaining a strategic position

In a rapidly changing environment, competitive advantages can be overturned. New market entrants, products and services, production technologies or innovative solutions for customer problems pose latent threats to established market players. In addition to finding the right position for their organization's offering, strategists also need to think about how this position can be sustained and how they can adapt their organization to changes in the environment (see also the box *Digital transformation strategy at Wolters Kluwer*).

Digital transformation strategy at Wolters Kluwer

When Nancy McKinstry became the first female and non-Dutch CEO of Wolters Kluwer in 2003, the company was a print-focused publishing house that operated primarily on the European market. While the Internet was about to revolutionize the way that people used information, Wolters Kluwer's revenues were decreasing. Just 15 percent of the overall turnover came from digital products. McKinstry recognized that she had to lead the company on a transformation path and find a strategic position that was also sustainable in the future. "I realized

that I had to make clear right away where I wanted to go,"[68] said McKinstry. She knew that in order to change something, you need a clear vision and direction for the business that gives "people the opportunity to get engaged around it."[69] She organized a lot of small meetings and held personal conversations across the organization to explain the company's new digital transformation strategy. While she wanted everyone to understand the new goals, she also gave managers and employees inside the company a lot of freedom to decide how to reach these goals, being convinced that you "shouldn't standardize the way of thinking or doing."[70] She decided to divest some of the traditional print businesses and acquire new digital and software services businesses. Every year, 8–10 percent of revenues were invested into new innovative products and services, almost three times as much as before. The competency base of the company was deliberately expanded from mainly editorial to combined editorial, technological, and software skills. Within 15 years, McKinstry transformed Wolters Kluwer into a market leader for digital information and analytics tools and services solutions for professional customers in different sectors (mainly healthcare and tax, legal, and accounting services)

in over 180 countries around the world. In 2018, close to 90 percent of revenues came from digital products and services.

→ Key takeaway

As competitive advantages are usually temporary, it is sometimes necessary to fundamentally transform organizations in order to create and maintain a sustainable strategic position. This is particularly important in business sectors that are undergoing dramatic changes due to the rise of new technologies.

Sources: *Based on information in Bryant (2009c); Itzenson (2013); wolterskluwer.com (2018).*

A competitive advantage is only sustainable when it is difficult for others to imitate. In addition to **protected patents or copyrights** and a **strong brand image**, there are two other main barriers to imitation:[71]

Tacit competencies: Competencies that are not easy to codify, thus making it difficult to transfer them from one context (or organization) to another.

- **Complex, specific, and tacit competencies**: Complexity stems from the interdependence of several connected elements; specificity relates to the attachment of competencies to specific processes or market environments, and tacit means that the competencies are not easy to codify, thus making it difficult to transfer them from one context to another. Generally, building a strategy on VRIO resources and competencies (as discussed in Section 7.2) will increase the chances of creating a lasting advantage. Distinct value offers for customers are usually also based on specific competencies (see Figure 7.9).
- **Causal ambiguity**: "While operational effectiveness is about achieving excellence in individual activities, or functions, strategy is about *combining* activities,"[72] says Michael Porter. If outsiders do not comprehend how competitive advantage is created (due to the complexity of the system that creates it), and if the cause–effect relationship between actions and superior performance remains unclear, it will be impossible to copy a "success strategy." "A competitor's failure to identify or understand how a focal firm uses a key competency," argues Adelaide Wilcox King, "severely limits that competitor's options for closing the gap with regards to that competency."[73] For example, a distinct organizational culture rooted in the organization's unique development and history can be very difficult to describe (even for insiders). Even if it were possible to describe the culture, it is even more difficult to transfer it, especially when the distinctness of the culture depends on a certain constellation of people.[74]

To provide value in …		… organizations need to perform in the area of …		… based on the following key competencies
Product features	⟶	Technology	⟶	Innovation
Service	⟶	People	⟶	HR management
Availability	⟶	Distribution	⟶	Logistics
Price	⟶	Cost base	⟶	Operational excellence
Brand	⟶	Branding	⟶	Marketing skills
Customer relationship	⟶	Trust	⟶	Relationship building

Figure 7.9 Examples of key competencies needed to create certain value offers

In many cases, real sustainable competitive advantage does not lie in one single factor, but in a combination of "hard" and "soft" components of an organization. In the famous **McKinsey 7-S Framework**, the hard factors *strategy*, *structure*, and *systems* are complemented by the soft factors *staff*, *style*, *skills*, and *superordinate goals* (the fundamental purpose as well as values and ideas upon which a business is built).[75] It is the combination of these factors that counts. "If there is no fit among activities, there is no distinctive strategy and little sustainability,"[76] says Michael Porter. The best strategy or structure cannot work without the right people (*staff*) with the right competencies (*skills*) and the right leadership culture (*style*), which motivates employees to reach the organization's *superordinate goals*.

The interconnected hard and soft circles in Figure 7.10 are another way of looking at the same general idea. Effective managers need to take both **"hard" factors** (strategy, structure, processes, systems, and infrastructure) and **"soft" factors** (people, culture, competencies, attitudes, and leadership) into account when making strategic decisions, and make sure that these factors align. For example, strategy is deeply intertwined with the people who craft and execute it. When studying US football teams, Federico Aime and his colleagues found that losing key employees who have knowledge of, as well as the skills to use, certain advanced routines (or processes) can shift competitive positions in favor of the hiring organization.[77]

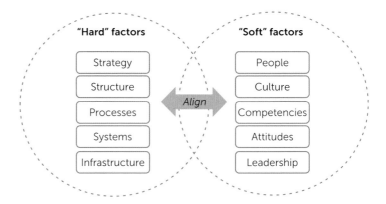

Figure 7.10 Aligning "hard" and "soft" factors of a business

Sustaining an advantage also requires **constant investment**—either by reinvesting in existing sources of competitive advantage, or investing in potential new sources of advantage. Thus, the organization can become a "moving target" for its competitors, which is much harder to attack than a static and predictable one.[78]

D'Aveni, Dagnino, and Smith doubt that sustainable competitive advantage can exist at all in dynamic contexts. Rather, they see this as being an **"age of temporary advantage,"** in which firms pursue a series of relatively short-lasting economic opportunities rather than sticking "with just one advantage over their lifetime."[79] The counterargument is that even in an environment in which advantages are temporary, certain sustainable advantages last, usually in the form of dynamic capabilities such as flexibility, innovation power, or the ability to explore and exploit new opportunities.

Suppose you have found a suitable integrated strategic positioning for your organization. Its products or services are well received by customers, however it is now threatened by the market entry of a competitor with a very similar positioning but a considerably lower price level. What would you do to sustain the leading market position of your own organization?

Dealing with low-cost competition

Even when organizations take every possible precaution to create sustainable competitive advantage, many will still face competitors that attack their positions head on. A particular challenge occurs when low-cost rivals enter the scene, offering the same—or at least similar—customer benefits at considerably lower prices. Kumar proposed five different **tactics to react to the entry of a low-cost competitor**.[80]

1 *Wait and watch*: if the competitor is not yet pursuing your own customers.
2 *Increase differentiation*: to avoid a head-on price war that would be detrimental to the whole industry in the long term.
3 *Learn to live with a smaller size* or merge the business with other competitors.
4 *Set up a separate low-cost business*: if there are synergies with the traditional business, an additional low-cost business might be able to outperform the rival.
5 *Transform into a solutions provider*: offer integrated and customized systems services that cannot be copied by means of simple mass production.

In any case, it makes sense for organizations to develop what we might call **"competitive empathy,"** the ability to see the world through the eyes of the competitors and to understand their motives, interests, and typical patterns of behavior. As Chinese military strategist Sun Tzu noted as far back as 2,500 years ago: "Know the enemy, know yourself; your victory will never be endangered."[81] Further advice from military strategy that organizations could potentially draw on can be found in the box *Strategy lessons from the US Marine Corps*.

FROM A DIFFERENT ANGLE

Strategy lessons from the US Marine Corps

General A. M. Gray wrote a short book called *Warfighting,* which became the doctrine of the US Marine Corps. It describes the military unit's approach to strategy. While written in a very different environment, it can still shed some light on how to think and act when competing forces collide in a business context. Here is some of General Gray's advice:

- In an uncertain environment, it is best to combine simple, flexible plans (including strategies for dealing with contingencies) with clear processes for standard situations and encourage self-initiative in all parts of the organization.[82]
- Decentralization helps to increase tempo, which, as General Gray writes, "is itself a weapon—often the most important."[83]
- The ability to adapt is crucial in a dynamic, uncertain environment. But as human systems are unable to

continuously change, periods of high activity need to alternate with periods which are more oriented toward gathering information and building potential for the future.[84]
- It is better to attack opponents on their flanks and where they least expect it than frontally where they focus their attention.[84]
- Strategists must put themselves in the enemy's shoes to anticipate how it might see its own weaknesses and the best strategy that the enemy might choose to attack (in order to prepare for such a move).[86]
- Keeping options open and leaving the enemy in doubt about which option will be chosen will help to appear "ambiguous and threatening."[87]
- Always prepare well because "failure in preparation leads to disaster on the battlefield."[88]

Source: Based on information in The US Marine Corps (1994).

The best way to compete—especially in the face of low-cost competition—is to create your own space in the market that is devoid of direct competitors. How is that possible? Kim and Mauborgne distinguish between two types of market environments: red oceans and blue oceans.[89] **Red oceans** are markets in which all companies operate and compete on similar bases—with similar product and service offerings provided through the same or similar distribution channels to the same customer groups. The consequence is "bloody" head-on competition that makes the market (or "ocean") red and unprofitable. For example, the traditional coffee market has been a strongly contested "red ocean," in which many coffee brands compete without much distinction.

Red ocean:
Crowded market space with strong competition.

Blue ocean:
New market space (devoid of competition) that is created by offering a set of customer benefits that no one else is offering.

Blue oceans, in contrast, are new, untapped and uncontested market spaces, which are created by companies that offer a combination of customer benefits that are clearly distinguished from all other offers in the market. When the Swiss Nestlé group introduced their innovative coffee capsule system Nespresso to the market, they created such a blue ocean. The easy-to-use capsules (which Nestlé also defended against the competition with a range of patents) became an instant hit on the market. The additional benefits for the consumers (choice of flavor, easy preparation, a lifestyle brand image conveyed by actor George Clooney) allowed Nestlé to escape the low-price competition and create a completely new market segment.

One way to reach the blue ocean, according to Kim and Mauborgne, is to first think about the main customer benefits in a certain industry (e.g. quality, price, service, availability, image, etc.) and then to try to create a new value curve (see Section 7.2 for a description of the tool) in which some of the benefits are strongly reduced, or even eliminated (thus saving costs), while other benefits are newly introduced or clearly raised above industry standards. (The latter is exemplified by Nestlé's creation of distinct customer value with Nespresso, the convenient ready-to-use capsule system.) This can result in a completely new type of offering that stands out from the field and will form the basis for creating a new blue ocean.

Digital strategy

Digital strategy:
A high-level plan for using digital information and communication technologies for improving business performance and creating competitive advantage.

As the Internet and digital technologies become increasingly pervasive in today's business environment and pose challenges to existing ways of doing business, managers also need to think about their organization's **digital strategy**. A digital strategy is much more than just an IT strategy. It is a systematic way of developing an organization and creating value through the integration of digital technologies. Managers need to think about how their organization can make use of **digital tools** (for example, mobile devices or certain software services that can be used over the Internet), **data collection and analysis** methods, and **digital platforms** such as social media or online marketplaces.[90]

Digital technologies can be used for:

a **Digitally enhanced customer engagement** (e.g. increasing customer loyalty by offering data-based customized services; staying in touch with customers using social media; offering new electronic sales and communication channels; using online marketplaces; integrating the offline and online customer experience).

Supply chain management:
Activities that are oriented toward optimizing the entire network of individuals and organizations that are involved in the process of creating and distributing a product or service (from the provider of source materials to the end consumer).

b **Digitally enhanced product/service development** (e.g. offering data as an additional service for customers; digitizing existing products or services; digitally enabled mass customization of products; creating new "smart" products that integrate digital elements into traditional products or services; digital prototyping and testing).

c **Digitally enhanced operations and supply chain management** (e.g. digital procurement; integration of systems with suppliers; digitization of processes; paperless supply chain; self-diagnosis and self-optimization of manufacturing systems; using digital communication and collaboration tools inside and outside the organization).[91]

The main foci of interest for developing a digital strategy are summarized in the "**House of Digital Strategy**" (see Figure 7.11). As with every house, it needs to be built on a strong foundation. In this case, the foundation is digital competence.

House of Digital Strategy:
A framework that includes the main foci of interest for developing a digital strategy.

Digital competence is the ability to spot trends in digital technology that might have a potentially disruptive or enhancing effect in your industry on the one hand, and the ability to integrate digital technology in the three main spheres of activity shown in Figure 7.11 on the other hand. Digital competence includes information technology literacy as well as the ability to adopt new and innovative ways of working. As digital technologies are rapidly evolving, allocating resources to digital initiatives and developing capabilities in the field of digital business is becoming a cornerstone of strategic management in the 21st century.

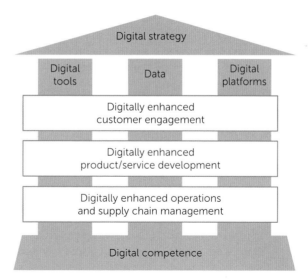

Figure 7.11 The "House of Digital Strategy"

Major trends in digital technology

There are a few recent trends in digital technology which could—and in many cases already do—have a particularly strong impact on the strategies of organizations in different sectors: the availability of huge amounts of data (**"big data"**) as a basis for analysis, prediction, and decision-making processes (see Section 6.2), **cloud computing**, **artificial intelligence**, **augmented reality**, **Internet of Things**, and the **blockchain**. Managers need to be aware of the potential of these new technologies for changing the way that business is conducted in their industry in order to be able to adapt their organization's digital strategy accordingly.

Cloud computing is a term for the use of computing services over the Internet (also referred to as the "cloud"). Examples of cloud-based services include software applications (e.g. office tools such as Microsoft Office 365 or Google Docs, but also specialized professional software such as sales management or customer relationship management systems), data storage and exchange (saving data in a remote database or exchanging data over Internet-based platforms such as Dropbox), data backup and recovery services, or computing power (e.g. large amounts of memory that engineers need for solving complex mathematical problems). A range of major technology companies are offering cloud services, including Amazon Web Services, Google Cloud, or Microsoft Azure.

Cloud computing has several **advantages**:[92]

- The use of computing services is not limited to a particular location because services can be accessed from anywhere with an Internet connection.
- Organizations can use computing resources without expensive investments in their own information technology (IT) infrastructure and without having to calculate capacity in their IT infrastructure.
- Organizations can become more agile because they can add new, or change existing, IT resources and applications very quickly.
- Economies of scale effects can lower prices as many people and organizations use the same cloud-based services.

Managers should, however, also bear in mind that using computing services over the Internet also bears potential **disadvantages**:[93]

- If there are problems with the Internet connection, access to cloud-based services can either slow down or be lost altogether.
- When sensitive data are stored, data security and privacy become an issue because using cloud services means that the data are stored in databases that are physically outside of

the boundaries of the organization. Because cloud-based data are generally accessible over the Internet, they are also potentially vulnerable to attacks by computer hackers (like the 2018 attack in which hackers stole personal information from up to 500 million Marriott guests by breaching the hotel chain's reservation system).[94]

- Organizations have less control over cloud-based infrastructure than their own local IT infrastructure.
- When cloud-based services are used, it might become more difficult to move data from one service provider to another.

Before using cloud-based tools, data storage services, or platforms, it always makes sense for managers to ask themselves what the desired benefits of the service are for the organization, and also what risks are involved and what they could do to mitigate these risks (e.g. hiring experts for cyber protection or offering data security training for employees).

Artificial intelligence (AI) refers to IT systems and machines in which human intelligence is simulated. These systems of machines work with algorithms that are able to process large amounts of data and learn from experience through constantly improving their ability to recognize patterns in the data. Joseph Sirosh, AI expert at Microsoft, sees the availability of enormous computing power in the cloud as "the ocean in which AI is born," vast amounts of data that are coming from sensors and all types of media (e.g. images, sounds, and videos) as "the oxygen that AI lives on," and the algorithms that allow machines to understand the data and make predictions as the "eyesight" of AI.[95] Artificial intelligence technologies can be used for automatizing business processes (e.g. automatically making sense of the contents of e-mails and updating customer files accordingly), detecting patterns and interpreting the meaning of large sets of data (e.g. making predictions about what customers might want to buy), using robots that learn how to better perform certain tasks, speech and image recognition, or interacting with employees or customers (e.g. with intelligent agents that are trained to automatically answer frequently asked questions).[96] There are risks related to the adoption of AI systems in organizations, however, including potentially misleading results in the case of errors or bias in the machine-learning algorithms or reputational risks when an AI system is biased, hacked, or used for purposes that are considered unethical.[97] There are also concerns that AI-based automation could lead to massive job losses.[98]

One example of the adoption of an AI system is the Swedish SEB Bank's use of an intelligent agent (also known as a "chatbot") named Aida—first internally for supporting employees with IT-related questions, later also externally for answering customer requests. Aida used a huge data pool to answer standard questions such as how to open an account. The chatbot was even able to analyze the tone of voice of the customer (e.g. whether someone was frustrated or in a positive mood), and to react accordingly. In the approximately 30 percent of cases that Aida was not able to solve a problem, the caller was referred to a "real" human agent. Directing simple questions to Aida also meant that the employees of the bank could focus on the more complex cases.[99] One of SEB's competitors, the Swedish online bank Nordnet, followed suit by employing a similar new "digital employee" called Amelia. However, it soon found out that customer response was "ok but not overwhelming,"[100] as Nordnet's CEO Peter Dahlgren put it. Amelia did not seem to be the right fit in that particular case, so she was fired.

Augmented reality (AR) is a term that is used for technologies that "augment" (or enhance) the physical world with related digital data (e.g. images, text, or sound). AR is currently primarily used with mobile devices such as smartphones or "smart glasses," specialized head-mounted displays that resemble spectacles. One widely known example is Pokémon GO, a game for smartphones in which digital characters are superimposed on the player's real-world surroundings. But AR is not just for computer games—it also has potential applications in an organizational context, for example:

- in research and development (where researchers could collaboratively improve product designs with 3-D models);
- in manufacturing and logistics (where up-to-date information about the status of certain machines or the location of different goods is made available);

- in marketing and sales (e.g. for three-dimensional presentations or virtual showrooms);
- in after-sales service (e.g. through connecting remote experts with customers); or
- for training purposes (e.g. by directly overlaying instructions on the object about which a person is trained).[101]

In one example, the Swiss industrial corporation ABB worked on an AR solution that allowed technicians wearing smart glasses to see what customers are looking at, thus being able to guide the customer through the repair process without the need to be physically present.[102]

Internet of Things (IoT) is a term that is used for the network of all physical objects, devices, or machines that are able to exchange data over the Internet. This goes far beyond the standard Internet clients such as smartphones, tablets, or PCs, and can include any object that transmits or receives data via the Internet, from domestic appliances and cars to wearable devices or robots that are used in manufacturing. There is high potential for the use of IoT technologies in enhancing the efficiency of supply chains and production processes. Sensors—which are a major precondition for many IoT applications—can be used, for example, for tracking (and with the collected data later optimizing) movement patterns in factories, monitoring machines to preemptively maintain them before major problems occur, measuring the consumption of energy or water, or locating certain items and assets along the supply chain and during a production process.[103]

There are also potential dangers associated with AR and IoT technologies, however. More connected devices, more sensors, more access points, and huge amounts of data also mean that there are more possibilities for both systems failures and security and data privacy breaches with all the accompanying negative effects on the reputation of an organization.

The **blockchain** is a technology in which records (also known as "blocks") are cryptographically secured and linked with each other. It can be thought of as a kind of "open, distributed ledger"[104] or a "peer-to-peer network"[105] in which transactions between different parties are permanently stored in a way that is non-manipulable, as the records are kept in many identical databases and transactions cannot be altered once they are recorded. Blockchains can also be used as a basis for self-executing (or "smart") contracts (e.g. automatically triggering payment when location-tracking software has reported that certain goods have been delivered at the agreed time and place).[106] As a transparent system for recording transactions, the blockchain technology (which is also the basis of virtual currencies such as bitcoin) can be used, for example, for tracking items through long and complex supply chains, for digital identity verification, or for building open, transparent trading platforms. The *New York Times* reported that US supermarket giant Walmart planned to use a blockchain to keep track of lettuce and spinach, thus being able to better locate potentially contaminated batches of the green vegetables.[107] Further examples of the use of blockchain technology in organizations include Eastman Kodak trying out a blockchain that supports photographers in recording ownership for their photos or IBM's efforts to support financial institutions with a blockchain-based payment solution that improves both the speed and security of cross-border payment transactions.[108]

As for all other digital technologies, using a blockchain is not without risks. The interfaces between a blockchain and the users (just think about weak passwords) or other digital applications are potentially vulnerable to hacker attacks.[109] Whenever they decide to adopt new digital technologies for their organizations, therefore, managers are always well advised to consult an IT security expert.

Managing the digital transformation

What do these trends in digital technologies mean for the manager's job as a strategist? First, it is important to **build digital competence** as the foundation of the "House of Digital Strategy" (see Figure 7.11). This means that managers need to understand which technologies could help the organization to create additional value or increase efficiency. In other words: How can technology help the organization to do business differently? At the same time, it is also important to understand what the limitations of the technologies are and what risks are potentially involved in using them (e.g. regarding data security and privacy).

To further construct the "House of Digital Strategy," managers can ask the following questions:

- Which digital tools, data sources, and digital platforms could be used to enhance customer experience or create a completely a new customer experience?
- Which digital tools, data sources, and digital platforms could be used to develop new, or reshape existing, products or services?
- Which digital tools, data sources, and digital platforms could be used to make production processes and the supply chain more efficient?

On a more general level, managers can also ask whether digital technologies have the potential to **profoundly disrupt the way that an industry works**, for example, through enabling completely new business models (as the peer-to-peer ridesharing platform Uber or online booking platforms have done in the taxi and travel agencies industries, respectively). One way of approaching this question is to think about how an industry would look if it were completely transferred to the digital domain.

The answers to the above questions could lead to a list of ideas for **digital transformation initiatives** that might include, for example, the introduction of new digital tools, using the services of digital platforms (or creating your own new platform), or using "big data" (see Chapter 6) and artificial intelligence to make more informed decisions. For the most promising of these initiatives, **pilot projects** can then be initiated. Such projects on a limited scale have the advantage of providing the opportunity to test a new technology, learn from the test run, and adapt it accordingly. In many cases, it will not suffice to just introduce a new technology, however. Managers also need to think about changing business processes and convincing employees, customers, and partners that it also makes sense for them to use the new systems. Once a new system has demonstrated that it can create additional value for the organization in a pilot project, the solution can be rolled out across the whole organization, a process that is often linked with massive training efforts and sometimes even with major changes in the organizational culture.[110]

Westfield Corporation: Integrating bricks and clicks

Together with his brother Peter, Steven Lowy is the Co-CEO of Westfield Corporation, an Australian shopping center giant. In 1959, their father Frank Lowy founded his first shopping center in the outskirts of Sydney. Decades of rapid expansion followed until, in 2014, Westfield separated its Australian and New Zealand businesses (now combined in the Scentre Group) from its other international businesses (now Westfield Corporation).

Westfield Corporation owns 35 shopping centers across the US and UK, together accounting for US$16 billion in retail sales in 2015. The two main pillars of Westfield's strategy are upgrading its shopping center portfolio and integrating digital technology to create better shopping experiences. To reach the first strategic goal, the corporation systematically disposes of less productive assets, refurbishes centers in prime locations (e.g. by adding entertainment, sports, or leisure facilities), and develops new centers in the world's leading cities (e.g.

the recently opened shopping center in New York City's World Trade Center or a newly developed center in Milan, Italy).

The role of shopping centers has significantly changed over the last few decades. They are no longer seen primarily as a place for purchasing goods. When consumers visit shopping malls, they are looking for experiences: they go there to socialize, eat and drink, watch out for new trends, or seek entertainment. Meanwhile, the centers' shopping function has been increasingly replaced by online stores and marketplaces. According to a National Retail Federation/Forrester study, 11.6 percent of US retail sales were made online in 2016, while 49 percent of all retail sales were somehow influenced by online touch points (NRF/Forrester, 2017). In a global PricewaterhouseCoopers (PwC) consumer survey, 68 percent of respondents said that they have engaged in what is called "showrooming"—visiting a physical store to browse products, but then buying them online. This trend is also supported by new technology. For example, online retailer Amazon has developed an augmented reality mobile phone app that allows consumers to identify products simply by aiming a mobile phone camera at them. The app can automatically suggest online purchasing opportunities for these products, often at significantly lower prices than in the physical store. However, 70 percent of the respondents in the PwC survey also said that they have previously browsed products online and then decided to buy them in-store (also known as "webrooming"). In recognition of this trend, online retailer Amazon opened its first physical bookstores in Westfield malls.

"We once saw technology as a threat to malls," said Steven Lowy in an interview with Inc.com, "but now we see it as an enhancement" (Carmody, 2016). In 2012, Westfield Labs was founded in San Francisco with the aim of bringing digital innovation to the shopping center corporation. The Labs developed a "searchable mall" guide with up-to-date stock information for all retailers in an Australian mall, an app that allowed visitors to browse the menu and make a booking in all 17 restaurants in a New York mall, a system that allowed visitors to reserve parking places in a London mall, and a system that could be used to broadcast digital storefronts to malls around the world. Geolocation technology (which helps to determine exactly where a consumer stands in a mall), scanning

technologies (e.g. for scanning number plates to direct visitors to their parking space), mobile payment solutions, big data analysis systems, or in-house Wi-Fi networks that allow the shopping center to send targeted messages to consumers are just some of the digital technologies that could be used to transform the physical shopping experience.

Building on the work of the Labs, Westfield Retail Solutions was established as a more permanent new technology unit of Westfield Corporation in 2016. Its goal is to provide consumers with integrated digital and physical shopping experiences based on digital products, data, and analytics. Steven Lowy is convinced that this can be achieved when shopping centers, retailers and brands share their consumer data to tailor the shopping experience to the customer. Different offers and experiences could be provided along the shopper's journey depending on whether the customer is, for example, a mother with young kids or a young, single sports addict. In Steven Lowy's opinion, "collaboration is the new competition" (McDonald, 2016). "Malls first started because no retailer could afford the real-estate, so we aggregated the cost across multiple retailers," he says, pointing out that the same model could also work in the digital realm (Carmody, 2016).

Sources: Carmody (2016); McDonald (2016); NRF/Forrester (2017); PricewaterhouseCoopers (2015); retaildesignworld.com (2015); Westfield Corporation (2017).

Discussion questions

- Which portfolio strategy has Westfield Corporation followed?
- How does Westfield Corporation position itself (in terms of target market segments, value offer, and value creation)?
- How would you evaluate the strategies that Westfield Corporation is using to deal with the threat posed by online commerce?
- What might be the advantages and disadvantages for shopping centers, retailers, and global brands of following a cooperative strategy in the digital space?

Conclusion

The story of the demise of the former global cell phone market dominator Nokia in the introduction to this chapter reminds us of the need to adapt strategy in the light of changing circumstances. Unlike most major competitors, Nokia turned down the offer to join the Open Handset Alliance, a consortium led by Internet giant Google, when it was developing open standards for mobile devices—most notably the Android operating system. Nokia was convinced that its approach—focusing fully on its proprietary Symbian operating system—was the right way. After all, the company strategy had been successful in the past, so why would it not work in the future, too? However, Android—supported by a wide range of mobile handset manufacturers, semiconductor companies, software firms, applications developers and telecommunication companies, rather than just a single firm—soon became the world market leader, leaving Nokia to plough a lonely furrow.

Stubbornly pursuing a single route forward can be risky. Nokia's competitor Samsung decided against putting all of its eggs in one basket and simultaneously offered phones running on three different operating systems—Android, Windows, and Bada (the company's homegrown system).[111] By keeping its options open, Samsung did not become dependent on the development of a single system. As Android prevailed, the South Korean company was able to grab the biggest share of the Android market, becoming the leader in the global smartphone market in the process.

The story of Nokia holds several strategy-related lessons:

1   **Do not rest on your laurels**. Even the most successful strategies should remain open to revision. What worked well in the past will not necessarily work well under new circumstances in the future. "The strategist's method is very simply to challenge the prevailing assumptions with a single question: Why? and to put the same question relentlessly to those responsible for the current way of doing things until they are sick of this,"[112] said Kenichi Ohmae, a Japanese strategy expert.
2   **Think in terms of options**. In a world of uncertainty, having more alternatives will increase the chances of success.
3   **Think beyond the boundaries of the organization**. Most organizations are embedded in an ecosystem, which includes a network of companies that create value together and share common interests.[113] Strategies therefore also need to address the development of the whole ecosystem, rather than just the individual organization.

It is not an easy task to strike the right balance between following a clear strategic direction and changing the direction when the circumstances demand it. Evolution, however, has shown that variation, recombination, cooperation, and adaptation are preconditions for survival in the long run. As the Roman mime writer Publilius Syrus wrote, "It is a bad plan that cannot be changed."[114]

✓ Review questions

1   What does "strategy" mean in an organizational context?
2   What are the key questions that a strategist needs to answer in relation to their organization?
3   What are the main steps of a strategic planning process?
4   Why do organizations need a strategy?
5   Which tools can be used to assess key developments in the general (or macro) and industry (or micro) environment in which an organization operates?
6   Which tools can be used to understand the strengths and weaknesses of an organization?
7   How can the results of internal and external strategic analyses be combined?
8   What is the difference between corporate strategy and business-level strategy?
9   What are the main questions that a corporate strategy should be able to answer?
10 How can managers assess whether a specific business unit fits into the portfolio of a corporation?
11 Which strategies can be used to grow an organization?
12 What are the main reasons for and risks of following a cooperative strategy?
13 What options do organizations have to position themselves in a particular market?
14 How can organizations sustain their strategic advantages when they are threatened by competitors with a similar and/or lower-priced offerings?
15 What are the main elements of a digital strategy for an organization?

? Critical reflection questions

1   Do you think that classical strategy work (i.e. following a systematic strategic planning process and a clear strategic direction) is outdated in the face of a fast-changing and more dynamic global business environment?

2   Vision and mission statements are often criticized for being superficial, interchangeable, and far from organizational realities. What is your opinion about the use of such "grand" statements?

3   Strategies are often oriented toward "beating" the competition (e.g. outperforming others or taking away their market share). Do you see competitive focus as the right one or do you see merit in taking a more cooperative approach?

4   Traditional strategic thinking postulates that companies can either be successful with a cost leadership strategy or with a differentiation or niche (focus) strategy. Recently, more hybrid models have emerged (e.g. cheap but chic design hotel chains or discount stores offering high-quality organic food). What enables these companies to survive and thrive with hybrid strategy models?

5   Digitalization is affecting almost all areas of society. Does that mean that every organization should have its own digital strategy?

☛ Managerial implications

- Managerial effectiveness is inextricably bound with setting and reaching the right goals, that is, having a strategy. Therefore, effective managers also need to be competent strategists for their organizations.

- Managers can develop strategies in a structured strategic planning process, in which the resources, capabilities, strengths and weaknesses of the organization are identified and juxtaposed with the opportunities and threats in the environment in order to find a sustainable strategic positioning for the organization.

- Strategic management goes far beyond strategic planning, however. In an "age of temporary advantage,"[115] managers must think strategically on an ongoing basis. This means keeping an eye on developments in the environment, constantly reviewing whether the organization is still able to generate unique benefits and value for its customers and other stakeholders, focusing on building potential for future performance, and creating alternative options for moving the organization forward.

- In a world that is increasingly affected by digital technologies, managers also need to think about defining digital strategies for their organizations.

- Effective strategies are, above all, also good stories. They provide the members of an organization with a direction and a sense of purpose. The effective manager-strategist is therefore also a good storyteller.

/ Endnotes

[1] *Forbes* cover page 11 December 2007 (Vol. 180, Issue 10),
[2] Upbin (2007), p. 48.
[3] Woyke (2011), p. 52.
[4] bbc.co.uk (2012).
[5] bloomberg.com (2010); wired.com (2012);
[6] Merriam Webster (2019).
[7] de Montaigne (2004), p. 69.
[8] Kasparov (2007).
[9] Mintzberg and Waters (1985).
[10] Mintzberg and Waters (1985).
[11] Thompson (1967).
[12] Bower and Gilbert (2007).
[13] Bower and Gilbert (2007), p. 79.
[14] da Vinci (2008), p. 84.
[15] Sternad (2011).
[16] Khanna et al. (2005), p. 63.
[17] Khanna et al. (2005), p. 73.
[18] Levitt (1960).
[19] Porter (2008b).

[20] Drucker (1993), p. 94.
[21] Porter (1980; 2008b).
[22] Porter (2008b).
[23] Porter (1980), p. 129.
[24] McGee and Thomas (1986).
[25] Drucker (1993), p. 106.
[26] Kim and Mauborgne (2005), p. 25.
[27] Gary and Wood (2011).
[28] Gary and Wood (2011).
[29] google.com (2019).
[30] L'Oréal (2019).
[31] Osterwalder et al. (2005). p. 18.
[32] Wernerfelt (1984); Danneels (2008).
[33] Barney (1991); Barney and Hesterly (2015).
[34] Prahalad and Hamel (1990).
[35] Danneels (2008), p. 519.
[36] Hill and Westbrook (1997).
[37] Drucker (1999a), p. 60.
[38] Curtis (2006).
[39] Curtis (2006).

[40] Shayon (2018).
[41] Shayon (2018).
[42] Johnson et al. (2017).
[43] Straub (2007), p. 3.
[44] Piskorski (2007).
[45] Market share relative to market share of the competitor with the third-ranked market share.
[46] Hedley (1970).
[47] Carpenter and Sanders (2009), p. 223.
[48] Reeves (2014), Exhibit 2, Footnote 3.
[49] Collins and Montgomery (1995).
[50] Ansoff (1965).
[51] Ansoff (1965).
[52] Umicore (2018).
[53] sueddeutsche.de (2010a).
[54] sueddeutsche.de (2010a).
[55] Sternad et al. (2016), p. 158.
[56] mastercard.com (2014).
[57] walmart.com (2018).

[58] Sternad et al. (2012).
[59] Lei and Slocum (1992).
[60] Choi and Beamish (2004).
[61] Shah and Swaminathan (2008).
[62] Sun Tzu (1963), p. 78.
[63] Porter (1980).
[64] Porter (1980).
[65] Shinkle et al. (2013); Thornhill and White (2007).
[66] Treacy and Wiersema (1997).
[67] The following section (including examples) is based on Miller and Le Breton-Miller (2005).
[68] Itzenson (2013).
[69] Bryant (2009c).
[70] wolterskluwer.com (2018).
[71] Reed and DeFillippi (1990).
[72] Porter (1996), p. 70.
[73] King (2007), p. 167.
[74] Bharadwaj et al. (1993).
[75] Waterman et al. (1980).
[76] Porter (2008a), p. 63.
[77] Aime et al. (2010).

[78] Porter (1985), p. 20.
[79] D'Aveni et al. (2010), p. 1371–1372.
[80] Kumar (2006).
[81] Sun Tzu (1963), p. 129.
[82] The United States Marine Corps (1994), p. 8.
[83] The United States Marine Corps (1994), p. 37.
[84] The United States Marine Corps (1994), p. 10.
[85] The United States Marine Corps (1994), p. 45.
[86] The United States Marine Corps (1994), p. 85.
[87] The United States Marine Corps (1994), p. 79.
[88] The United States Marine Corps (1994), p. 70.
[89] The ideas in this paragraph stem from Kim and Mauborgne (2005).
[90] Favoro (2016).
[91] Nylén and Holmström (2015); Ross et al. (2017).
[92] amazon.com (2019a).
[93] Larkin (2018).
[94] Perlroth et al. (2018).
[95] Sirosh (2018).
[96] Davenport and Ronanki (2018).

[97] Boillet (2018).
[98] Garimella (2018).
[99] The Aida story is based on Wilson and Daugherty (2018).
[100] Business Insider Nordic (2018).
[101] Porter and Heppelmann (2017).
[102] Morse (2017).
[103] IBM (2017a).
[104] Iansiti and Lakhani (2017), p. 120.
[105] Iansiti and Lakhani (2017), p. 121.
[106] Iansiti and Lakhani (2017).
[107] Corkery and Popper (2018).
[108] Corkery and Popper (2018); IBM (2017b).
[109] Orcutt (2018).
[110] Davenport and Ronanki (2018).
[111] wired.com (2012).
[112] Ohmae (1983), p. 57.
[113] Iansiti and Levien (2004).
[114] Publilius Syrus (2019) [The Latin original is "Malum est consilium, quod mutari not potest"].
[115] D'Aveni et al. (2010), p. 1371–1372.

Visit the companion website at macmillanihe.com/sternad-management **to access multiple choice questions, useful weblinks and additional materials.**

E+/wragg

THE EXECUTION CHALLENGE

Outline of chapter

This chapter will enable you to

- Identify the main steps that are necessary to implement a strategy.
- Recognize the main building blocks of organizational design and assess their suitability in different organizational contexts.
- Explain how managers can influence others through persuasion, building and maintaining reciprocal relationships, and shaping the culture of an organization.
- Plan an organizational change initiative.
- Examine different strategies for dealing with resistance to change.

Introduction

In August 2015, eleven years after its founding, the social media platform Facebook was used by more than a billion people on a single day for the first time.[1] How did Mark Zuckerberg, Facebook's founder and CEO, manage to create the world's largest social network and thereby also one of the most successful enterprises of the Internet age? "I think if we just do a good job executing, then that to me is by far the biggest variable in what we achieve,"[2] said Zuckerberg in an interview.

Strategy development cannot be strictly separated from strategy **execution**. As Roger Martin points out, employees at the frontline are not "choiceless doers."[3] They constantly make decisions about how to do things, and in doing so co-determine organizational outcomes. If they make sound choices, strategy execution will be successful; if not, it will be a failure. Using metaphors, Martin says that we should not see an organization as having a "brain" (those people who conceive a strategy) and a "body" (those who just execute on the lower levels of a hierarchy), but rather as a "white-water river" in which choices cascade from one level to the next, with all of them being important for the final outcome. "Strategy as a choice cascade" is how he describes it, with broader, more abstract choices being made by general management and a lot of day-to-day choices with a direct influence on customers being made by the employees "at the frontline." To be able to achieve an organization's strategic goals, these choices—the broader ones as well as the ones made on a daily basis—need to be consistent and aligned with each other.[4]

This also means that when managers make strategic choices, they need to find out whether the organization has the ability—or at least the potential—to implement these choices. As Hrebiniak put it, execution cannot be left to "worry about later."[5] It therefore also makes sense to give people who will presumably play a key role in execution a voice in the strategy development process. People who feel that they were adequately included in the decision-making process for determining a particular strategic path will also be more likely to act as a driving rather than a restraining force in the change endeavors that are required for implementing a strategy.

Managers of all kinds of organizations—not only those in the Internet business as in the case of Facebook—need to take care about both the "hardware" and "software" required for execution. Organizational structures, processes, and systems are the "**hardware**," the basic infrastructure for translating plans into action; but they are of no use without the "**software**"— people who are able, willing, and committed to implement the strategy.

In this chapter we will take a closer look at both, the "hardware" and "software" of execution, as well as at their interrelations:

- *Section 8.1* introduces the **implementation path**, five key steps that managers need to take in order to execute a strategy effectively, including identifying the critical tasks that need to be accomplished, matching those tasks with the right people, energizing people, and setting up adequate coordination and control mechanisms.
- Structures, systems, and processes, the key elements of **organizational design** are especially useful for the *coordination* and *control* steps of the implementation path. With these tools, managers can align the tasks and activities of all members of an organization toward achieving a common goal. The basics of organizational design are introduced in *Section 8.2*.
- Besides organizational design, there are other approaches to **exerting** influence on others and encouraging behaviors that support the implementation of organizational strategies. *Section 8.3* introduces the basic principles of persuasion and shows how managers can influence others through relationships and shaping organizational culture.
- The execution of strategies usually involves change. Effective execution therefore goes hand in hand with **effective change management**. In *Section 8.4*, we explore the main steps in an organizational transformation process and discuss how to address doubts and reservations that people may have about change initiatives.

Execution:
In a business context, execution refers to the decisions and actions that are taken to implement a strategy effectively.

Implementation path:
Five key activities that managers need to undertake in order to transform a strategy into actual organizational performance: identify critical tasks, match tasks and people, coordinate, energize, and control.

Organizational design:
The process by which managers create structures, processes, and systems that together help to coordinate the decisions and actions of the members of an organization in order to achieve a common goal.

Change management:
A systematic approach of initiating, coordinating, and controlling transition and transformation efforts in an organization.

8.1 The implementation path

Getty Images/E+

In brief

● To put a strategic plan into action, managers need to take a structured approach to implementation. The five-step implementation path presented in this section offers one such example.

● The first step of the implementation path is to identify the key tasks that need to be performed in order to reach the strategic goals.

● In step two, these tasks are allocated to suitable people.

● Step three is about setting up coordination mechanisms that enable the different team members to collaborate in an effective way.

● In step four, managers need to make sure that everyone stays motivated and committed to working toward achieving the set goals.

● Finally, setting up a control system can help to keep everyone on track.

To be able to implement a strategy, managers need to ensure that people with the right skills carry out the right tasks in a coordinated way, and that they have access to the resources needed for that purpose. It is not enough have a good plan. There also needs to be some sort of accountability, or, in Peter Drucker's words, "[t]he program must be converted into work for which someone is responsible."[6]

Individual responsibility for getting things done is necessary but on its own is insufficient for achieving the desired organizational outcomes. It is equally important to **coordinate individual contributions** toward reaching the common goal. Finally, managers need to make sure that people actually accomplish the tasks that were allocated to them, and that they also remain motivated to dedicate all the necessary effort to achieve the set goals.

Figure 8.1 shows the **implementation path** comprising the five main activities that managers need to undertake in order to transform a strategy into concrete performance:

1 **Identify critical tasks:** Recognizing the component tasks that need to be accomplished to make a strategy work.
2 **Match tasks and people:** Finding people with the right skills and attitudes to execute these necessary tasks.
3 **Coordinate efforts:** Making sure that everyone knows exactly what they are responsible for and where they need to set their priorities; setting up the structures, systems, and processes that ensure an efficient combination of individual efforts; providing everyone who is working on a certain project or initiative with the resources they require.
4 **Energize the team:** Influencing others to keep them motivated and oriented toward the organization's goals.
5 **Control the direction:** Ensuring that everyone is on the right track and taking corrective action if necessary.

The individual steps of the implementation path do not always follow this order. It is also possible that some of them actually run in parallel, which is symbolized by the overlaps of the circles in Figure 8.1. In any case, execution is not a one-time event but a process that includes a whole set of decisions and actions over time.[7] We will now take a closer look at the individual steps of the implementation path.

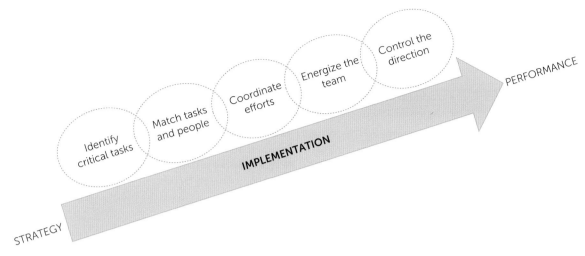

Figure 8.1 The implementation path

Implementation step 1: Identify critical tasks

To execute a strategy, managers first need to translate the broad vision into concrete, key component tasks that are necessary to move the organization from its current state to realizing its strategic goals. The emphasis lies on the word "key" here—prioritizing those initiatives that can be expected to contribute most significantly to reaching the organization's strategic goals.

Three questions can help to **identify the critical tasks**:

1   Does accomplishing this task contribute to creating value or to increasing the potential to create value?
2   What would happen if this task was not performed?
3   What else depends on accomplishing (or not accomplishing) this task?

Once the critical tasks are defined, they need to be assigned to the right people.

Implementation step 2: Match tasks and people

"Organizations don't execute unless the right people, individually and collectively, focus on the right details at the right time,"[8] wrote former CEO of American conglomerate Honeywell, Larry Bossidy, and his co-authors. But how do managers identify the "right people" to implement a certain task? On the one hand, the person needs the necessary skills (or at least the potential to develop the skills) to accomplish the task. This requires a good understanding of individual team members' strengths. On the other hand, as pointed out in Chapter 3, matching tasks and strengths is not enough to generate high performance. People also need to be motivated to execute a certain task, a large part of which involves having the right attitude. Without the right attitude, it is hard to make skills fully productive.

In order to be able to execute a task well, people also need **clear and focused goals and priorities**. Chances are that by simultaneously trying to follow 20 goals, we will not be able to reach any of them. Focusing on one or two really important issues will lead to a much higher probability of getting them resolved.

A study among more than 26,000 employees in various companies showed that in organizations which are strong in execution, there is a clear understanding of individual responsibility for decisions and actions.[9] The process of passing on both the authority and responsibility for making such decisions or carrying out such actions is called **delegation**.

For delegation to be effective, people need to know what is expected of them (see Chapter 3 for more information about effective delegation). There also needs to be a clear agreement

Delegation:
The transfer of both responsibility and authority for completing a task to another person.

about the timing and nature of follow-up reviews of the task. The main steps of the **delegation process** are:

1 Define the task to be accomplished (set goals in an unambiguous, specific, measurable, and timed way).
2 Clarify which authorities (decision rights) and resources are to be transferred.
3 Confirm understanding of and commitment to the task.
4 Agree on a feedback and review procedure to ensure accountability.

Accountable:
Being obliged to take responsibility for your actions and give defendable reasons for them.

Although tasks and responsibilities can be delegated, managers still remain **accountable** for the decisions and actions of their subordinates. Therefore, delegation does not mean abdication of responsibility, but a transition from being responsible for performing the task itself to making sure that the task is performed appropriately by others.

Implementation step 3: Coordinate efforts

Once broader tasks have been split up into smaller chucks and assigned to different people or organizational units, managers need to make sure that these different strands all work together to achieve the common goals. The role of structures, systems, and processes for the effective coordination of work is described in more detail in Section 8.2.

Budget:
An estimate of revenues and expenditures for a certain period of time (used for planning and performance control purposes).

To be able to effectively perform their tasks, people also need access to resources. Managers therefore need to make sure that adequate resources are available to those responsible for implementation. The main instrument for resource allocation in organizations is the **budget**. Budgeting is not usually an activity that gains much love in organizations because it takes time and effort. Budgets are usually set annually toward the end of the tax year for the following year. Many people from different departments are usually included in a budgeting process, which requires considerable coordination efforts. The budget is a tool for forecasting the revenues and expenditures of an organization, but also for controlling whether the actual income and expenses are in line with the expected figures.

By the time it is implemented—which could be more than a year after it was originally compiled—the budget is usually already outdated, and people often spend a whole year trying to come close to numbers that were conceived when today's new developments and circumstances were still far away in the future. What's more, managers love to play **"budgeting games"**—with superiors often demanding unrealistically high numbers and subordinates proposing unrealistically low ones, just to meet somewhere in the middle. To avoid such political games, Jack Welch, the successful long-term CEO of General Electric, advocates abandoning this "compromise exercise," as he calls it, and instead measuring performance only against the competition or in relation to last year's performance.[10] Such an approach is only feasible, however, under the precondition that the performance measures of competitors are available (in many cases they are not) and that the environmental conditions have not substantially changed from one year to another (which they often do).

Despite its limitations, a budget can be very useful as a coordination tool for allocating (financial) resources to different organizational units. It forces managers to discuss resource needs with the heads of different units, and provides a structured way of identifying and resolving conflicts in which different units or projects compete for limited resources.

Implementation step 4: Energize the team

Living organisms cannot survive without energy. This is also true for organizations as living social systems. They need a certain level of energy to sustain and further develop their activities. In order to implement a strategy, managers need to ensure that the people within the organization are motivated and willing to put all their efforts toward reaching the joint goals. In other words, they need to keep **energy levels** high.

Assume that you are taking over a new managerial role. During the first few weeks in your new job, you get the feeling that the energy level in your team is relatively low. Everyone seems to be quite content with working at a slow pace, no one seems to show any particular passion for working toward your unit's goals. What would you do to energize your team and increase their productivity?

Bruch and Ghoshal suggested that organizations can have four different **energy zones**:[11]

- the "aggression zone" (a high level of negative energy);
- the "passion zone" (a high level of positive energy);
- the "resignation zone" (a low level of negative energy);
- the "comfort zone" (a low level of positive energy).

According to Bruch and Ghoshal, managers can influence the energy level of their organization in two very different ways:

- First, they can try to exert influence on the members of the organization through highlighting opportunities and communicating a vision of how these opportunities could lead to a better future for the organization (a strategy directed toward reaching the "passion zone").[12] For example, Bill Gates, the founder of Microsoft, already at the end of the 1970s and beginning of the 1980s had the vision of "a computer on every desk and in every home"[13]—a goal that seemed to be incredibly bold at the time, but one that generated a lot of energy in the company for decades.
- The second approach is to make everyone aware of a significant external threat to the organization. This approach is directed toward reaching the "aggression zone." As an example, a manager could point out that the main competitors are winning more and more market share with their new products, thus threatening the existence of the company unless it focuses all its energy toward becoming more innovative.

In both cases, whether the focus is on a positive vision or an immediate threat, it is important to create a shared understanding within the organization of what must be done, but even more importantly, of *why* something must be done. According to former Stanford Professor James March, an expert in organizational theory, shared understanding is "the basis for conversations among human actors."[14] Likewise, conversations form the basis for the coordinated action that is fundamental to executing a strategy.

In addition to a compelling positive vision or a realistic external threat, people can also be energized in their day-to-day work through engaging interactions with others (especially when they feel that they are making positive contributions) and when they see visible signs of progress.[15] For managers, this means that they can also try to increase the energy level in their team through encouraging every team member to contribute to group discussions, acknowledging the value of these contributions, and giving regular feedback on their perception of individual team members' or the whole team's progress toward achieving individual or collective goals (see Section 3.1 on motivating people).

Implementation step 5: Control the direction

Control means more than just checking on people. It is about helping them to keep on track or get back on track if they become derailed—be it through constructive feedback, coaching, or providing them with extra resources that they require to get things done. Sometimes, tasks are just "forgotten"—due to the multiple demands of day-to-day work—without appropriate follow-up. "The failure to follow through is widespread in business, and a major cause of poor execution,"[16] says Larry Bossidy, from whom we heard at the start of the chapter. To ensure effective execution, therefore, managers need to set up review mechanisms that allow both them and their team to track progress toward the goals and the milestones on the way.[17] A review and feedback cycle that is too short could irritate employees, but the danger of one that is too long is that it reduces the opportunity to take corrective action.

Output control:
A type of control that measures the outcome of activities after they were performed.

There are three basic types of **managerial control system**:[18]

– **Output control**. Managers can use **key performance indicators (KPIs)** to measure the outcome of activities after they are performed. KPIs can be either financial figures (e.g. average cost of goods sold as a percentage of revenues or average revenue per transaction in a retail store) or operational measures (e.g. number of customers per day or visitor-to-customer conversion rate in a retail store). Output control systems can also be linked to reward systems to reinforce their effect (see Section 8.2).

Key performance indicator (KPI):
A measure of performance that allows the management to monitor to what extent a person or an organization achieves major goals.

– **Behavioral control**. Through direct personal contact (e.g. a regular weekly meeting in which team members report on the progress of their work), rules and procedures (e.g. travel guidelines or authorization requirements for certain expenses), or through machine assistance (e.g. time stamp clocks or computer logs of the activities of a call center agent), managers can try to monitor and thereby also directly influence the behavior of other people.

– **Cultural control**. Shared values and beliefs are a powerful force in shaping people's behaviors. A strong **organizational culture** (see Section 8.3) can therefore also function as a complement or even a substitute for formal control mechanisms.

Behavioral control:
A type of control that tries to directly monitor and influence the behavior of people.

Whatever the control mechanism, its effectiveness depends on the attitude that people have toward it. Control can have a positive motivational effect because it provides people with feedback, gives them the feeling of being seen, or is linked to rewards and recognition; but it can also lead to demotivation if it is seen as a nuisance, a threat, or a loss of autonomy.[19] As in all other steps of the implementation path, the way in which managers communicate can have a strong influence on the level of commitment shown by team members toward the execution of a certain strategy (see the box *CEO best practice: Communication as a key factor for effective strategy execution*).

Cultural control:
A type of control that tries to shape people's behavior through creating and maintaining a system of shared values and beliefs.

Managers can use digital tools to support their endeavors along the implementation path (in particular for coordinating efforts and controlling the direction). Examples include **project management** and **issue tracking software systems** which can help to allocate responsibilities and resources and track progress on certain tasks (see also Section 8.2).[20]

CEO BEST PRACTICE

Communication as a key factor for effective strategy execution

In 2005, Gregory ("Greg") Case was elected as president and CEO of the professional services firm Aon plc., a leading global player in the insurance brokerage and risk consulting industry. Case soon started work on creating a common vision for the company, which was centered around "either helping clients or helping colleagues help clients."[21] For Aon, helping clients first and foremost meant helping business customers to better manage their risk, thus supporting them in improving their financial and operating performance. Once the basic vision for the future of the company had been determined, Case travelled around the world to ask clients about their risk management-related needs and what Aon could do to better serve them. He was convinced that "[w]ithout talking to clients, you're not going to get the insight you need to be effective."[22] In order to

implement what the clients needed, he tried to make sure that the right people were working in the right places. "People allocation is as powerful as financial allocation,"[23] he once said. At the same time, he also communicated with as many Aon employees (whom he consistently refers to as "colleagues") as possible, both in formal meetings as well as in informal conversations, so that he could better understand what they needed in order to more effectively serve clients, and also to make sure that everyone understood and was aligned around what Aon wanted to accomplish as a firm. Being aware that "having the same conversation with the same 20 people is interesting but not very impactful,"[24] he tried to talk to people from all hierarchical layers. "It's really in that context that you go out and have a conversation, and it turns out people are excited about that,"[25] he commented, adding that he saw listening and engaging with his colleagues as the basis for the momentum that he was able to build in the firm. This momentum has been long-lasting. The London-based global services firm, with its 50,000 "colleagues" in 120 countries around the world, has continued to thrive under Case's leadership. In 2018, his contract as president and CEO of Aon was renewed until 2023.

→ **Key takeaway**

Communication is a key task for managers who want to implement a strategy. At all stages of the implementation path, managers need to stay in touch with people who are affected by the strategic initiatives, both inside and outside the organization.

Sources: Based on information in Charan et al. (2018); Cottrill (2008); Leaders Magazine (2013); Ralph (2018).

8.2 Designing the organization

E+/pixdeluxe

In brief

- In organizations that consist of more than just a few people, key parts of the implementation path (coordination and control, in particular) can only be adequately managed with the help of organizational structures, processes, and systems.

- Setting up these structures, processes, and systems and keeping them aligned with the strategic direction of the organization is the purpose of organizational design.

- Organizational structure divides the work within an organization and is also a coordination mechanism because it clarifies who reports to whom.

- Processes define the sequence of activities and workflows, both within and across different organizational units.

- Organizational systems are an institutionalized way of providing information and feedback, and of controlling whether certain standards are maintained.

- In combination, structure, processes, and systems provide the formal infrastructure for executing a strategy, ensuring that people within the organization know their roles, tasks, and responsibilities, and are provided with the necessary resources for working together efficiently and in a coordinated way.

Organizational culture:
Basic assumptions, values, beliefs, norms, and tendencies in behavioral patterns that are shared among the members of a certain organization.

Organizational structure:
The allocation of tasks, responsibilities, and hierarchical relationships within an organization.

To perform effectively through other people, managers can either exert personal influence or set up organizational structures and rules that provide clear guidelines for individuals on what they are responsible for, what they should (and should not) do, and how they relate to others in the organization. In very small organizations, managers can rely on personal interaction alone to get things done. As size and complexity increases, however, there is no substitute for more formalized tools for the distribution and coordination of tasks and activities.

Organizational design is the process by which managers create structures, processes, and systems that together help to coordinate the decisions and actions of the members of an organization in order to achieve a common goal. Some management theorists also include deliberate interventions to shape the organizational culture as part of organizational design (see Section 8.3 for more details on organizational culture).

The basic tasks of organizational design are quite straightforward:

1 Let everyone in the organization know what is expected of them, what they are responsible for, and who reports to whom (**organizational structure**).

Process management:
A systematic approach to identify and optimize the flow of activities that transform inputs into outputs.

Organizational systems:
Institutionalized practices that provide information and feedback, or are used to control and reward people in organizations.

2   Make sure that people who are working on different tasks and in different organizational units collaborate well in pursuit of a common goal (**coordination mechanisms**).

3   Optimize the flow of activities that transform inputs into outputs (**process management**).

4   Institutionalize practices that provide information and feedback, and are used to control and reward people in organizations (**organizational systems**).

Theorists have argued over the direction of influence between structure and strategy. Alfred Chandler famously postulated that "**structure follows strategy**," indicating that organizations should generally be designed in a way that optimally supports the implementation of the strategy of an organization.[26] Hall and Saias argued instead that structural decisions also limit an organization's strategic choices ("strategy follows structure").[27] Henry Mintzberg tried to reconcile the two perspectives suggesting a more symbiotic relationship in which structure follows strategy "as the left foot follows the right."[28] However, one element that is universally agreed upon is that creating a "**fit**" (in the sense of a good match) between strategy and organizational design is a necessary precondition for being able to achieve an organization's strategic goals (see Figure 8.2).

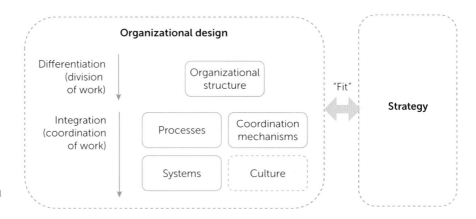

Figure 8.2 The main elements of organizational design

Finding the right structure

Turning to the first component of organizational design, organizational structure is "the **formal system of task and authority relationships** that control how people coordinate their actions and use resources to achieve organizational goals."[29] Structure is required for clarifying the division of work and allocation of tasks (who does what in the organization) as well as for coordination purposes (combining positions into subunits and determining who reports to whom).

Differentiation:
In an organization science context, differentiation describes the division of work within an organization into subunits.

Integration:
In an organization science context, integration describes the endeavor to combine the efforts of different subunits to enable them to work in a coordinated way toward a common goal.

There are several ways of dividing work into subunits (also called **differentiation**) and making sure that the various subsystems of the organization follow overall goals in a coordinated way (also called **integration**).[30]

The basic organizing principles for the **division of work** are (see also Figure 8.3):[31]

–   **The functional structure**: This creates subunits based on their primary function, such as purchasing, production, marketing, sales, or finance. The main advantage of this type of structure is that specialization and economies of scale effects (within the functions) can be used. As an example, Standards Australia, an organization which develops internationally aligned national technical standards, is organized into four units that comprise different functional areas: Operations (includes standards development, publishing, information technology, and project office teams), Corporate Services (includes support functions such as finance and human resources), Stakeholder Engagement (responsible for aligning activities with national and international stakeholders), and Strategy and Public Affairs (with a focus on business strategy, commercial partnerships, member relations, and public relations activities). The standards organization's management is convinced that the functional structure is conducive to "maximizing the skills of Standards Australia's

Functional structure:
An organizational arrangement that leads to the creation of subunits based on their primary function (e.g. purchasing, production marketing, sales, or finance).

people and contributors."[32] However, a functional organization can also lead to several interfaces (points where two organizational units need to interact in order to get a step ahead in a certain process) and coordination requirements, and bears the danger of becoming specialist-centric rather than being focused on the overall organizational goals.

- **The divisional structure**: This combines all the tasks related to certain product lines (product orientation), customer groups (market orientation), or regions (geographic orientation) in subunits. For example, the globally active logistics company DHL has four product-oriented divisions in the Indian market: DHL Express (parcels and documents delivery services for business customers), DHL eCommerce (shipping and fulfillment solutions for e-commerce customers), DHL Global Forwarding (international air, sea, and ground forwarding), and DHL Supply Chain (integrated warehousing and transport solutions).[33] The divisional structure allows for more flexible adjustments to the demands of a certain target group and changes in the market environment. It can also result in a more entrepreneurial stance being taken by divisional managers who have a holistic responsibility for all functions within their unit. On the downside, a divisional structure can lead to unhealthy rivalry between divisions and to the duplication of tasks (redundancies).

Divisional structure:
An organizational arrangement that combines all the tasks related to a certain product, customer group, or geographical region in distinct subunits.

- **The matrix structure**: It combines two (or more) organizing principles, e.g. functional and product orientation. This structure usually leads to more flexibility at the expense of more complexity, better information flow but also more conflicts, and more integrative solutions to problems but at a higher level of ambiguity. It is useful when more than one orientation is critical for implementing the organization's strategy, and when resources (e.g. expensive specialists) need to be shared between different units.[34] For a long time, the Procter & Gamble Company (P&G), a globally active consumer goods company, was regarded as a prime example of a well-functioning matrix structure that combined 16 global business units, six regions, and several business functions. In 2017, however, P&G announced that it would abandon the matrix in favor of a simpler divisional structure based on product categories.[35] P&G's management expected the new structure to be faster and more accountable than the old matrix structure that was internally called "the thicket" for its complexity and overlapping responsibilities.[36]

Matrix structure:
An organizational arrangement in which two organizing principles are combined, which means that employees have more than one superior (e.g. a functional manager and a country manager).

- **The network structure**: It is characterized by **outsourcing** parts of the tasks for implementing a strategy to other organizations and focusing on the coordination and control tasks of the value creation process. Such a structure reduces the internal resource requirements for achieving certain desired outcomes through allocating tasks to specialized organizations. Disadvantages include the need to manage multiple interfaces and high dependence on partner organizations that operate under different control mechanisms. As an example, the Coca-Cola Company owns the Coca-Cola brand, manufactures and sells concentrates and syrups as basic ingredients for soft drinks, and is specialized in consumer marketing. It works in a network of both company-owned and independent local bottling partners that are responsible for manufacturing and packaging the final soft drinks products and selling and distributing them through various sales channels.[37] With this network structure, Coca-Cola is able to combine specialization advantages and global synergies in the fields of manufacturing key ingredients and marketing with low transportation costs and a high degree of responsiveness to local market needs.

Network structure:
A flexible organizational arrangement in which a part of the tasks that an organization wants to accomplish are outsourced to other legally independent organizations while a coordinative role is retained.

The choice of structure also depends on the **main strategic focus of the organization**. If the focus lies on cost efficiency and reaching economies of scale (following a cost leadership strategy), functional structures are usually more appropriate.[38] Large car manufacturers, for example, for whom efficiency and economies of scale are key success factors, are often organized along the functions of new product development, procurement, production and logistics, sales and marketing, and corporate support services. If the organization follows a diversification strategy and places emphasis on providing the best possible solutions for specific target groups, a divisional structure may be the better choice.[39] In conglomerates, we often find divisional structures which combine businesses from completely different industries. Global strategies, in which a diverse set of products or services are offered in a range of different markets, lend themselves well to being implemented in a matrix structure.[40]

Outsourcing:
A business practice in which non-core tasks or activities of an organization are performed by another organization on a contract basis.

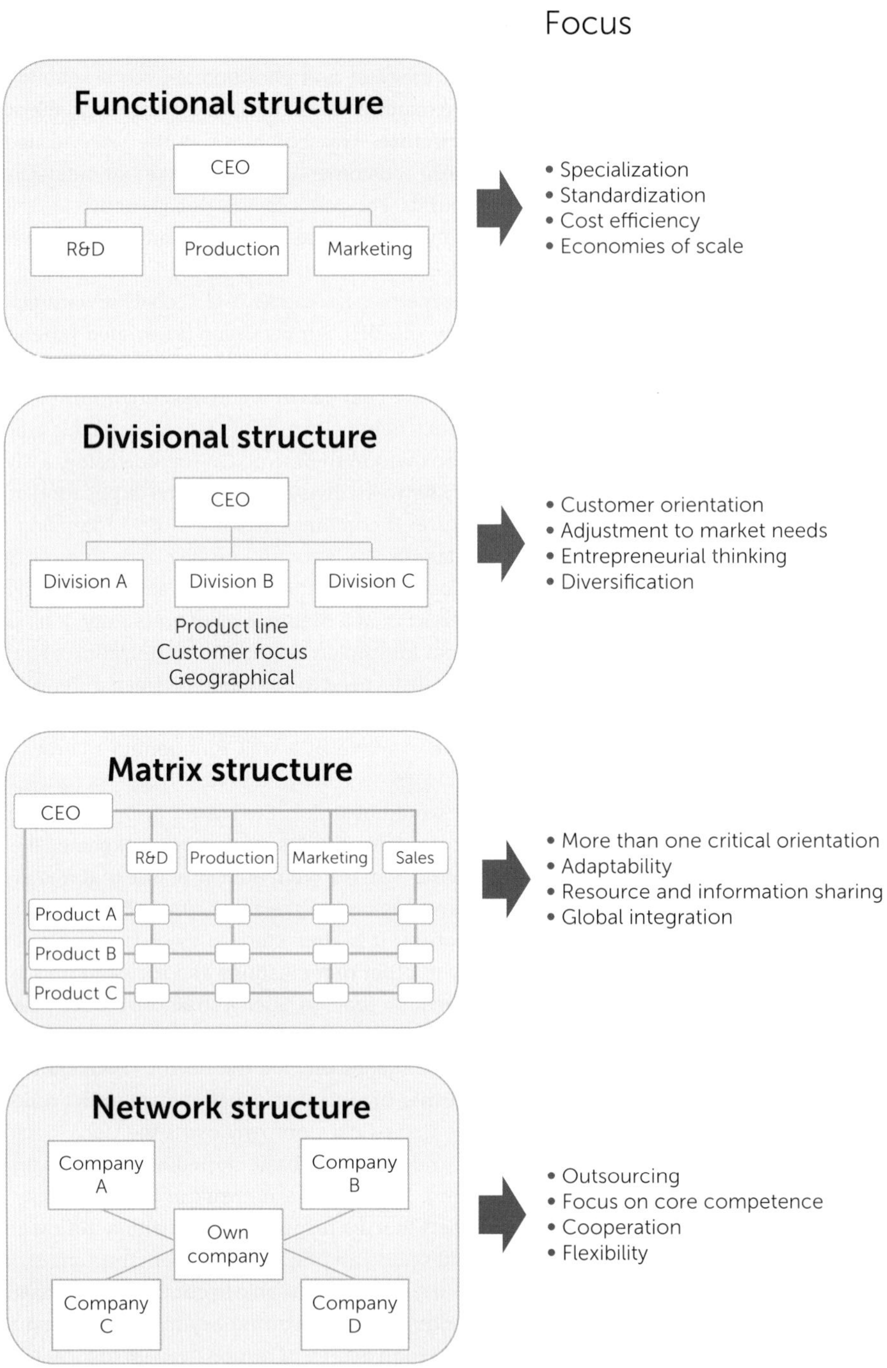

Focus

Functional structure

CEO

R&D | Production | Marketing

- Specialization
- Standardization
- Cost efficiency
- Economies of scale

Divisional structure

CEO

Division A | Division B | Division C

Product line
Customer focus
Geographical

- Customer orientation
- Adjustment to market needs
- Entrepreneurial thinking
- Diversification

Matrix structure

CEO

R&D | Production | Marketing | Sales

Product A
Product B
Product C

- More than one critical orientation
- Adaptability
- Resource and information sharing
- Global integration

Network structure

Company A | Company B

Own company

Company C | Company D

- Outsourcing
- Focus on core competence
- Cooperation
- Flexibility

Figure 8.3 Basic organizational structuring principles and their foci

In addition to the primary structure (e.g. functional or divisional) for the whole organization, organizations can also use a **secondary structural layer** to add an additional focus. The primary structure can be seen as the "base frame" that helps an organization to efficiently and effectively handle the routine tasks of its core business.[41] Many organizations are faced with more complex tasks or problems, however, such as large innovation projects or nonstandard customer wishes that require additional coordination across different organizational units. In such cases, it is possible to introduce a secondary structure that overlays the primary one. Examples include product or brand management structures (to coordinate all activities related to a certain product or product line), key account management structures (to coordinate all activities related to particular customers) or project structures (to coordinate collaborative undertakings that include people from different departments).[42] In a matrix structure, a secondary structural layer is permanently added to the primary structure. It is also possible, however, to use a non-permanent secondary structural layer, such as project structures which are set up for a limited period of time.

Dependent on the situation, organizations can also use all kinds of combinations of the different structuring principles.

Choosing the coordination mechanism

The division of tasks and their allocation to different organizational subunits also requires a process of **integration** to bundle individual efforts toward achieving common goals. Organizational units do not work in isolation but are usually interdependent. As shown in Figure 8.4, they may:

- use the same resource pool, for example, when one person (as a "human resource") works in different projects for different organizational units (**pooled interdependence**);
- use the outputs of one unit as inputs for another one, for example, on an assembly line or when the marketing department produces a brochure that is used by the sales department for informing customers about the benefits of a certain product or service (**sequential interdependence**);
- require inputs from each other, for example, when a chef in a restaurant needs information about the customer orders from a waiter, and the waiter, in turn, needs the food prepared by the chef to serve to the customers (**reciprocal interdependence**);
- need to combine skills and collaborate closely to accomplish a certain task, for example, in a complex innovation project in which people from different business functions (such as marketing, sales, and R&D) need to work in close consultation with one another (**team-oriented interdependence**).[43]

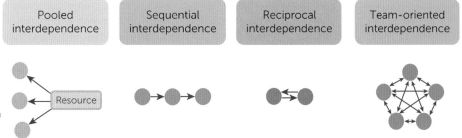

Figure 8.4 Basic types of interdependence

Sources: Inspired by concepts in Thompson (2007); Van de Ven and Ferry (1980).

Managers can use several tools to ensure that interdependent units collaborate effectively. The main **coordination tools** are:[44]

- **coordination through direction**: allocating responsibilities and managing conflicts through the hierarchical line;
- encouraging trust-building and **self-coordination** between the individual units;
- creating boundary-spanning **liaison roles** (coordinators) or **cross-unit committees**;
- **standardization** through rules, guidelines, and coordinated plans (see the box *Ancient rules, still valid today*);
- **incentive systems** that align the interests of individuals or organizational units with the interests of the overall organization;
- **intra-organizational markets** that align supply and demand between different organizational units.

The choice of the most suitable coordination tool is dependent on the type of interdependence. Hierarchical dispute handling (coordination through direction) could, for example, be the method of choice when conflicts over resources (pooled interdependence) emerge; though an alternative resolution method could be to use rules and aligned budgets (standardization).[45] Sequential interdependence can be coordinated with plans, schedules (standardization), or market mechanisms such as transfer pricing (intra-organizational markets), while reciprocal and team-oriented interdependence are usually better approached with face-to-face interaction (self-coordination) or by providing incentives for following common goals (incentive systems).[46]

Determining the right structure and coordination tools is not always straightforward because each tool has its advantages and disadvantages. It is almost impossible to find "the one" perfect organizational structure, especially under constantly changing environmental conditions. Generally, a structure needs to fulfill certain criteria to serve as an effective tool for implementing a strategy:

1 **Strategic alignment**: Is the structure congruent with the strategic priorities and the main focus of the organization (e.g. customer-centricity, global reach, efficiency, or innovation capacity)?
2 **Efficiency**: Does the structure minimize interfaces and coordination needs?
3 **Flexibility**: Is the structure flexible enough to allow the organization to adapt to a changing environment?

Holacracy:
A decentralized organizational approach that is based on the distribution of decision-making rights across the organization. The basic elements of a holacracy are autonomous, self-managing teams (called "circles") in which people fill well-defined roles and work according to a specific set of rules.

The challenges of a fast-changing environment also led to the proposal of new decentralized organizational forms. One example is **holacracy**, an organizational approach that was developed by Brian Robertson at Ternary Software in 2007. It has been widely discussed and adopted by a range of different organizations after Robertson published his book *Holacracy: The New Management System for a Rapidly Changing World* in 2015.[47] The basic components of holacracy are self-managing teams called "circles." Each circle has a concrete purpose and consists of a set of clearly defined roles. The roles are usually smaller than traditional jobs, which means that one person can fill different roles, also in different circles. The circles are embedded within larger "super-circles" (which again have a specific purpose within the organization), with the organization as a whole being the largest circle of all. Instead of having a strict chain of command, organizations that work according to the principles of holacracy are more oriented toward a wider distribution of power. "Super-circles" usually do not interfere in the internal organization and management of their "sub-circles" (although they do play a key role in defining their purpose). There are clear rules for decision-making processes in a holacracy, and power is shifted from individual persons to unambiguously defined processes and rules (for example, a written "constitution" of the organization).[48] Critics point out that the rules and "weighty democratic procedures" that are proposed by the advocates of holacracy could constitute a "bureaucratic distraction from the real work of adding value to customers"[49] and could lead to problems like "ambiguity and lack of clarity around progression, compensation, and responsibilities" and employees who complain about not getting any "definitive answers."[50]

FROM A DIFFERENT ANGLE

Ancient rules, still valid today

Human societies have long used a very basic coordination tool: *rules*—guidelines for conduct or action. One of the most famous rulebooks in history is the *Rule of Saint Benedict*, written by Benedict of Nursia, a Christian saint who founded several monastic communities in the 5th and 6th century AD. His "Rule" contains a prologue and 73 chapters with precepts (or authoritative orders) for his monks, including:

● values they should follow (e. g. "to reach the greatest height of humility");

● organizational regulations (e.g. rules for the election of the Abbot or for the assignment of specific tasks to different organizational functions in the monastic community, for example the *Cellarer*, who is responsible for the supply of food and drink and for the monastery's business);

● the process of admitting new monks;

● daily routines (e.g. how many psalms are to be said in the night office at specified times);

- clothing and footwear (e.g. "for a temperate climate a cowl and a tunic for each monk are sufficient"); and

- practical advice for daily life (e.g. "not to be a great eater" or "one hemina of wine a day is sufficient for each one").

The *Rule of Benedict* also gives advice to the Abbot on how to deal with violations of the rules (e.g. "But let the brother who is found guilty of a graver fault be excluded from both the table and the oratory"). The approximately 14,000 words (in the original Latin) of the "Rule" have served hundreds of autonomous, self-governing Benedictine communities all over the world for around 1,500 years. One of the reasons for its success might be the balance that Benedict found between general institutional guidelines and the reliance on responsible individuals. Rather than blindly setting up formal principles, Benedict emphasized values and what we would today call "organizational culture" ("How we do things around here") as a basis for building thriving communities.

Sources: Based on information in ben.edu (2019); stiftmelk.at (2019).

Managing processes

Many of the activities that people within an organization perform stray beyond the neat structural boundaries of individual organizational units. For example, in product development individuals in R&D collaborate with colleagues in the marketing and sales departments; in another example, processing a customer request for a new product design requires interaction between customer service, sales, product design, and production. When a hierarchical organizational structure is complemented with a **process-based organization**, the individual organizational functions and units can collaborate more efficiently in fulfilling their interdependent tasks.[51]

Process (or business process):
A clearly defined sequence of activities that are carried out to transform inputs into outputs.

A **process** is a **clearly defined sequence of activities** that are carried out to transform inputs into outputs. **Process management** means that one person (also known as the "process owner") has responsibility for setting up and optimizing a certain process. **Process optimization** means trying to reduce cost and cycle time (the period that it takes to complete the process), while at the same time maintaining or increasing quality (both in terms of process stability as well as outcomes) and—if necessary—flexibility.

As a first step in a process optimization project, managers need to identify the **critical processes** in their area of responsibility. Critical processes are usually characterized by:

a. high relevance for (internal or external) customers;
b. a high share of the total costs; and
c. high potential for improvement.[52]

Several **process management tools** (e.g. process flow charts or process cost analysis) can be used to analyze existing processes and identify areas for improvement; for example, through omitting unnecessary process steps, eliminating bottlenecks, reducing redundant work steps or holding times, or adding new activities that increase the efficiency of the overall process (see also the box *Zooming in on using process flow charts*).

Organizations can also use information technology to automatize processes, thereby being able to standardize and measure process execution. For example, **workflow management systems** are used to define and monitor a sequence of tasks and processes in which different people or organizational units are involved. **Enterprise resource planning (ERP) systems** like SAP collect and integrate data from different business functions such as procurement, inventory management, human resources management, distribution, or accounting. With data being entered in a standardized form, stored in one centralized location, and shared across functional silos, ERP systems can help to eliminate redundant processes and improve coordination between different business functions. These systems also provide real-time data that enable managers to better control the individual business processes as well as the business as a whole. There are also disadvantages to consider, however; for example, high costs for investing in and maintaining such systems, high dependency on the software vendor, or rigidity in terms of the need to conform to standard processes that are defined by the software (and again high costs for adapting the system to changing needs).

Zooming in on ▶ USING PROCESS FLOW CHARTS

A process flow chart graphically represents a process (e.g. an administrative process or a production process) and all its individual steps. A simple code with symbols of different shapes is used to describe the flow of the process (see Figure 8.5). You can draw your own process flow chart if you follow these six steps:

1 *Define the process*: What is the process about? Which title could you give to the process?

2 *Identify the starting and ending points of the process*: What is the trigger for the process? Where and when does it end?

3 *Identify the activities that need to be performed*: What are the main process steps? Which decisions need to be made? What kind of inputs—e.g. data or materials—are needed? What outputs are produced?

4 *Arrange the individual process steps in a sequence and draw arrows that link the process steps in the right sequence*: Which step needs to be concluded before the following step can start?

5 *Gather feedback from key people involved in or knowledgeable about the process*: Do they agree that the flow chart correctly represents the process? Would they suggest any changes?

6 *Revise the flow chart if necessary*.

The completed flow chart can be used as a starting point for identifying problems (e.g. any process steps that cause delays or do not add value at all) and assessing potential for improvement (e.g. steps that could be eliminated, steps that could be improved, or new steps that could be introduced to render the whole process more efficient).

A useful method of generating ideas for process improvement is **good practice sharing**, either between different units of an organization, or across organizational boundaries—a structured process of comparing performance metrics with other organizations or internal organizational units also known under the term "**benchmarking**." Trying to find out about successful measures implemented by others and learning from such examples allows managers to adopt specific practices that have already proved to be efficient. At the same time managers need to be aware that emulating others can help the organization to catch up, but will not be sufficient to overtake others, which usually requires a unique approach.

Benchmarking:
The practice of comparing the key metrics of your own organization with other (often best-in-class) organizations in order to identify opportunities for improvement.

Setting up organizational systems

Because a perfect fit between strategy and organizational structure is illusionary, Robert P. Kaplan and David P. Norton instead believe that organizations "should choose a structure that is reasonably compatible with their strategy and works without major conflicts, and look to the system to complete the alignment process."[53] **Organizational systems** are institutionalized practices of providing information and feedback, as well as for controlling and rewarding people. In fact, control systems are not limited to use in the domain of organizations. They are "fundamental to all life and human endeavor," said former MIT Professor Jay Wright Forrester. "Everything we do as individuals, as an industry, or as a society is done in a context of an information-feedback system."[54]

Control systems are a set of procedures that are designed to evaluate the behavior and performance of people, organizational processes, and the use of resources in order to support the management to achieve the organization's goals. Control systems monitor the activities of individual members of an organization or of organizational units to ensure that their efforts are focused in the right direction. The major question that control systems help to answer is: "Are we on the right track?"

Managers can exert control either personally (through observations or asking questions) or through setting up structured control systems. These systems can take several forms. They can either focus on outputs (e.g. whether financial and non-financial objectives are reached), behavior (what people actually do), or culture (the kind of behaviors that are

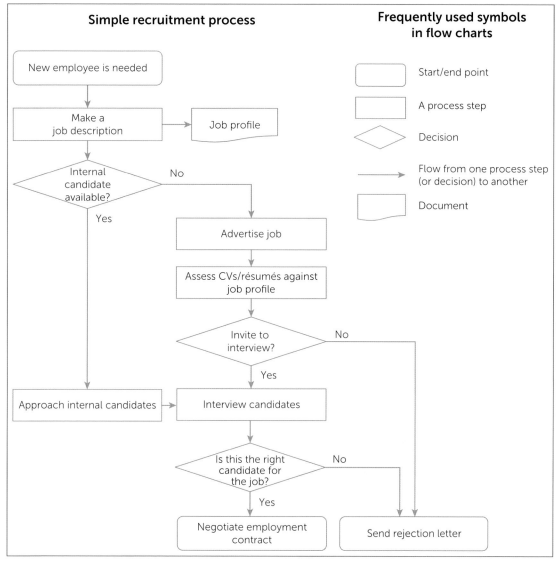

Figure 8.5 Example of a flow chart

Let us assume that you are nominated as the leader of a new project. Which systems could you set up at the very beginning of the project to ensure that everyone in your team will "do the right things" as well as "do things right" for achieving the joint project goals?

generally accepted and reinforced in the organization). Figure 8.6 provides an overview of the different control systems that can be used by managers.

Control systems are created to **influence the behavior** of people within organizations and to direct their attention toward following certain goals. If they are too rigidly designed, however, they can also have negative effects, such as a single-minded focus on what is controlled while neglecting other important aspects of one's organizational task, or demotivation due to a feeling of loss of autonomy.

For a control system to be effective, it needs clear **standards** and objectives against which actual performance can be compared. If deviations occur, it is possible to either implement interventions to bring behavior back in line with the existing standards and objectives, or—if necessary—to adapt the standards and objectives themselves. Because a control system should be designed to allow corrective action, it needs to be based on measures that are (a) predictive of the desired outcome (i.e. if the measure changes it will also have a clear effect

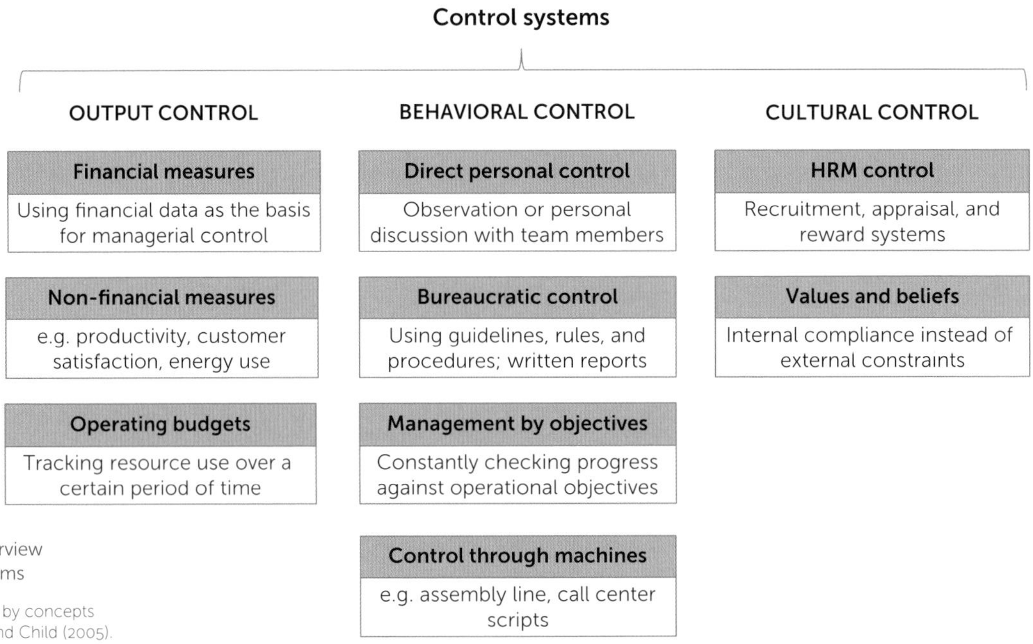

Control systems

OUTPUT CONTROL	BEHAVIORAL CONTROL	CULTURAL CONTROL
Financial measures Using financial data as the basis for managerial control	**Direct personal control** Observation or personal discussion with team members	**HRM control** Recruitment, appraisal, and reward systems
Non-financial measures e.g. productivity, customer satisfaction, energy use	**Bureaucratic control** Using guidelines, rules, and procedures; written reports	**Values and beliefs** Internal compliance instead of external constraints
Operating budgets Tracking resource use over a certain period of time	**Management by objectives** Constantly checking progress against operational objectives	
	Control through machines e.g. assembly line, call center scripts	

Figure 8.6 Overview of control systems

Sources: Inspired by concepts in Boddy (2017) and Child (2005).

on the outcome) and (b) within the power of influence by the responsible individual.[55] Instead of measuring the amount of safety incidents, for example, a control system could measure employees' compliance with the key safety standards, thus focusing on behavior that individuals can influence and that is likely to be predictive of the desired outcome.[56]

To be effective, control systems should also:

- **measure those activities which are most critical** for the performance of an organizational unit;
- be **well understood and accepted** by those who are controlled;
- ensure that what is controlled **corresponds with the responsibilities and competencies** of the person or unit that is under control;
- be **based on valid and reliable information**;
- deliver **feedback as "real time" as possible**; and
- be flexible and **under review themselves**.[57]

Several management books have proposed the use of **"scoreboards"** so that people know how they perform against their objectives. These may either take the form of simple graphs[58] or the more sophisticated form of Kaplan and Norton's **balanced scorecard**, a tool that translates a strategy into a limited set of traceable key financial and non-financial measures in four perspectives: the customer, financial, business process, and learning and growth perspectives.[59]

Balanced scorecard: A management tool (developed by Robert S. Kaplan and David P. Norton) for translating a strategy into a limited set of traceable key financial and non-financial indicators.

Performance measurement and control systems are often also tied to **reward systems**, which are usually introduced to attract and retain valuable employees and to encourage desired behavior, above-average efforts and performance ("going the extra mile"), and innovative contributions.[60] From an employee perspective, fair treatment (in comparison to others) and the feeling that particular efforts are also recognized (and maybe also rewarded) are important features of such systems.

Reward systems need to be very carefully designed because they can focus people on the wrong priorities. For managers, it is important to keep in mind that "**you always get what you measure**." If salespeople are paid solely on the level of sales revenues, for example, they will usually try to maximize sales regardless of margins and profitability or even at the expense of unhealthy discounting, which could turn out to be highly detrimental to the firm in the long term.

Performance measurement and reward systems are often criticized for being too strongly **focused on the short term**, inducing people to follow immediate (often quarterly or yearly) goals without adequate attention to building performance potential for the future (see also Chapter 1).[61]

To counteract this tendency, a Swiss bank introduced a bonus model in which managers only get one-third of the bonus they earned in the first year; the second and third parts of the bonus are paid out in the subsequent two years, but contingent on (and adjusted according to) the performance in these years.[62] Thus, the bank's managers are encouraged to put their focus on both performing well in the current period and building performance potential for the future.

Studio Moderna: Organizing a multi-country, multi-channel retailer

Studio Moderna is a leading multi-channel electronic retailer in Central and Eastern Europe (CEE). The company, which employs around 8,000 people, actually calls itself an "omnichannel" retailer because it uses digital response television (DRTV) and home-shopping channels, websites, catalogues and brochures, direct mail, wholesale, telemarketing, and over 400 retail stores to sell its products across 21 different countries in the CEE region.

Studio Moderna was founded by Livija Dolanc and Sandi Češko in 1992 with the purpose of selling an innovative back pain relief product in their home country Slovenia. During the following twelve years, the company entered almost all other countries in CEE. In addition to selling its own product, Studio Moderna set up a teleshopping retail business, a chain of retail stores and a wholesale business, in which the company offered a wide product portfolio including, for example, mattresses, footwear, vacuum cleaners, kitchenware, cosmetics, and health, beauty, and diet products. In 2004, Studio Moderna launched its first e-commerce website. In 2019, it operated more than 180 webstores and over 100 social media pages.

Unlike typical Western DRTV companies, the company did not follow an outsourcing strategy. Product sourcing, call center operations, or TV infomercial production were all done in-house to ensure quality standards and maintain full control over the value chain. Building on its own call center infrastructure, the company developed telemarketing as one of its strongest sales channels. The local call centers in the different CEE countries were originally used to process inbound calls when the company's products were advertised on TV. To develop an outbound call center business (in which unused call center capacity was sold to other companies), Češko decided to spin it off and form a separate company called Linea Directa.

Studio Moderna featured in a Harvard Business School case study.[63] The case described how the company used a matrix structure to organize its business. On the corporate level, in addition to the top management team, there were corporate channel managers (who were in charge of their particular sales channel across countries) and central

support services (e.g. TV infomercial production, logistics, media and analytics, e-ordering, IT, and finance). Country managers were responsible mainly for developing the different sales channels in their local market, buying and selling products according to local market demands, operating the local call center, and order fulfillment. Local sales channel or service function managers reported to two people: their corporate channel or service function manager and their local country manager. A central idea behind this structure was to allow decision makers to be close to local needs, but at the same time keep corporation-wide efficiency and development potentials intact. A side-effect of the matrix structure were conflicting interests between different parts of the organization, which led to many internal negotiations.

Studio Moderna also used intra-organizational markets as a coordination mechanism. Goods and services were directly exchanged between different units. A subsidiary in one country with high demands for a certain product could, for example, purchase the goods from another subsidiary with excess inventory. "We decrease top-down command, and increase multilateral control," said Češko, "we are a networked economy making efficient, rapid, local decisions."[64]

The company saw the use of IT systems as a key success factor. Consider the product information system. If enough country and functional managers voted for a particular new product on the company's internal product information site, it was adopted for a market test. Further systems were used for electronic ordering, media planning, real-time analytics of return on media investment, virtual warehousing, customer relationship management, call center operations, and accounting. An OLAP (online analytical processing—see Chapter 6) management information system allowed managers both in the centralized business functions as well as in the subsidiaries in the individual countries to monitor and analyze all relevant key performance indicators (KPIs).

KPIs like annual sales growth, margins, stock turnover, back orders, order mistakes, up-selling as a percentage of total revenues, or various cost measures were used to analyze the performance of the different organizational units. Managers could also earn significant bonuses based on meeting KPI target levels.

Building on the ongoing success of its innovative memory-foam mattresses in CEE markets, Studio Moderna decided to expand its business to other geographical regions. The US, Canada, the UK and Japan were targeted with mattresses and bedding goods. Meanwhile, Česko also launched a separate company, Vanema, to exploit the potential of the patented foam spring technology in the aircraft seating business.

Sources: *Eddy (2012); Isenberg (2009); octaspringtechnology.com (2017); Schackt (2009); studio-moderna.com (2017; 2019).*

💬 Discussion questions

● What are the main elements of Studio Moderna's organizational design?
● What are the potential advantages and disadvantages of the matrix structure that Studio Moderna is using?
● How does the company deal with the trade-off between adaptation to local needs and efficiencies that are gained through corporation-wide standardization?
● Which control systems does Studio Moderna use to ensure that its business is developing in the right direction in each of the 21 countries where the company operates?

8.3 Exerting influence

© Royalty-Free/Corbis

In brief

● Influence is based on power, comes in many different forms, and does not necessarily depend on having a formal position.

● In addition to setting up structures, processes, and systems, managers can also use "softer" approaches to induce people to work toward reaching the organization's goals.

● Managers can follow four principles of persuasion—understanding the audience, building credibility, presenting a solid case, and communicating well—to convince their team members and other potential supporters of the importance of a cause.

● Another influencing strategy is to identify people who carry a lot of informal power and bring them on your side through building strong relationships and coalitions.

● Finally, managers can also influence others through shaping the culture of the organization. Being a role model who lives and works according to the desired values and norms, using stories and symbols, aligning reward and recognition systems, and choosing the right people for key positions are some of the approaches that managers can follow to shape the culture of their organization.

Strategy implementation as a "**translation into collective action**,"[65] in the words of Mintzberg and Waters, needs to go beyond the introduction of a new formal organizational design. Strategies are executed by people. Organizational structure, processes, and systems as well as rules and guidelines can help people understand what is expected of them, but are not sufficient to guarantee the behavior that is needed to get things done. It is usually not enough to "force" people to do something just by way of hierarchical power. Most strategy implementation endeavors require a behavior change in people, such as improving customer service or increasing innovativeness and responsiveness.[66]

Managers therefore also need to focus on the **"soft" side of strategy implementation** (see Figure 8.7), on making sure they win the minds and hearts of their people in addition to setting up formal structures and systems. There are three major "soft" ways of exerting influence:

- influencing through **persuasion**;
- influencing through **relationships**;
- influencing through **culture**.

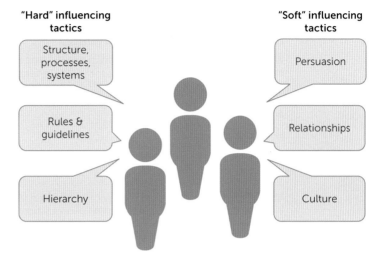

Figure 8.7 "Hard" and "soft" influencing tactics

Before we discuss the three "soft" influencing tactics in more detail, we also need to understand where the ability of managers to influence others actually comes from.

Power and organizational politics

Power:
The capacity (or ability) to exert influence on other people.

The potential or ability to influence the behavior of others is called **power**. In interviews with senior managers, INSEAD Professor Manfred Kets de Vries found that most thought that "effectiveness in an organizational setting will always require the recognition, acquisition, and use of power."[67] Without power it is difficult to be an effective leader.

So how do people attain power? In their classic categorization, John French and Bertram Raven identified five **bases of social power**:[68]

1   **Reward power**: The ability to reward others with something of value (e.g. to raise a salary).
2   **Coercive power**: The ability to punish others if they do not conform (e.g. to fire someone).
3   **Legitimate power**: Having a formal role and authority that is accepted by others (e.g. being the direct supervisor in the organizational hierarchy).
4   **Referent power**: Being perceived positively by others (e.g. being seen as a charismatic person).
5   **Expert power**: Being in a position of expertise based on your knowledge, skills and competencies (e.g. being the only person in the organization with crucial technological know-how).

All five of these types of power can be found in organizations. Although "being the boss"—legitimate power based on formal authority with the potential to reward or punish subordinates—is arguably the most visible form of power, it is not necessarily the most effective. Formal reporting relationships do not always mirror actual power relationships within an organization. **Informal leaders** (who are being followed, for example, due to their expertise or reputation among peers) often become more influential than their formal counterparts.

Informal leader:
A person who influences and leads other people in the organization without holding a formal authority position.

Organizations are inherently **political entities**. People within organizations try to build networks and make friends with key influencers, lobby, form coalitions, withhold or distort information, bargain, control agendas, and see conversations and meetings as opportunities to promote themselves and their interests.[69] In Kets de Vries' view, many executive boards "engage in ritual activities that center on political gamesmanship and posturing rather than substance."[70] For example, manager A could veto a very reasonable proposal that manager B made—just to prevent manager B from being seen as the initiator of a successful project and potentially be considered for promotion before manager A.

In such a political environment, influencing others involves understanding and sometimes playing "power games" as well as building and maintaining a network of influential people both within and outside the organization, people whose support can be harnessed to achieve your goals (see also Section 1.4).

Zooming in on ▶ PLAYING THE POWER GAME

Whether we like it or not, politics are a natural part of organizational life. Politics can even intrude on students' projects; for example, when several students would like to take over the role of the project leader or when team members disagree on which direction the project should take. Therefore, it is helpful to know how to play the power game.

Here is how it works:

1 *Actively work on your reputation*. Your reputation is what people in the organization say about you when you are not there. Think about how you want to be perceived, and then ensure that your actions send this message. For example, if you want to be seen as a very committed team player, try to contribute more than asked.
2 *Connect with the right people*. Who do people listen to in your organization? Who seems to have the most influence? Establish and maintain good relationships with influential people (for example, try to get a mentor high up in the organization's ranks), while at the same time keeping your distance from people who are considered underperformers or otherwise "suspect" by the more powerful people in the organization.
3 *Convey the impression that you are indispensable*. It is important that powerful people in the group or organization believe that you are essential to achieving the organization's goals. Make sure that others know about special skills that you have. Close network contacts with people outside the organization (e.g. with customers, professional associations, politically influential people, or the media) are particularly useful.
4 *Help others to reach their goals*. Doing other people a favor usually increases their attachment to you and gives you the opportunity to ask for a favor in return if you need future allies for a certain initiative.
5 *Try to be visible*. Make sure that your performance is noticed by the top people in the organization but be wary of bluntly showing off, which can have a negative impact on your reputation. Self-promotion is more effective when positive remarks come from colleagues or satisfied customers, and when you give professional progress reports to your boss and other influential people.

Sources: Inspired by Dwyer (2007); Robbins and Coulter (2018).

Influencing through persuasion

"Communication is critical to bringing dreams to life,"[71] write Nonaka and Takeuchi in their article "The wise leader." Persuasion is a special form of communication that aims to influence the attitudes or behavior of other people. It is an essential skill for managers in an environment in which there is growing skepticism toward a "command-and-control" approach.

Imagine that you have to convince a peer (who does not have a formal reporting relationship with you) to take over a time-intensive task. You know that your colleague is already completely overloaded with work, but you need to persuade them to take over this additional job as a strategic priority. What would you do to persuade your colleague to help you?

Effective persuasion is based on four different elements:[72]

1 **Understanding the audience**. To persuade others, it is important to understand what they value (i.e. what values they hold and what interests they have), and which kind of messages (both in terms of content and form of delivery) resonate with them. It is also

useful to understand their decision-making tendencies. Some people are more rational and numbers-focused, others tend to make decisions on the basis of relationships or emotions; some are very fond of their own ideas, others are more open to follow the opinion of the majority or of powerful individuals. If people are addressed in a way that is attuned to their own decision-making style, a proposal will have a higher chance of being considered.

2 **Building credibility**. To accept a manager's proposal, the listener must perceive the person who suggests it as competent and trustworthy and the idea as sound. Trust can be earned through keeping promises, telling both sides of a story, putting the interests of others first, and being consistent in your statements and actions. Competence and expertise can be shown, for example, with relevant personal experience, supporting data from trusted sources, or endorsements from authorities in the field. Building credibility is a long-term task that usually starts way before the actual proposal is made.

3 **Presenting a solid case**. Managers need a compelling argument to persuade others. Compelling means that the argument is not only logical and supported with facts (and experience), but also framed in a way that matches the interests of the audience, preempts and mitigates potential counterarguments, and presents a solution to a problem (see also the box *Zooming in on presenting a convincing proposal*).

4 **Communicating well**. Communication is a two-way process. To get their message across, managers need to choose a communication channel that the intended audience will most likely respond to, use clear language that the audience can follow and understand, and receive and interpret feedback signals from the audience. Feedback can also come "between the lines," in the way people say something about the proposal or through their body language. Managers can also use trusted informants to learn more about the moods, expectations, or maybe also fears of their audience in order to better address them in their communication endeavors.

Zooming in on ▶ PRESENTING A CONVINCING PROPOSAL

How can you put forward an idea in a way that convinces other people? G. Richard Shell and Mario Moussa in their book *The Art of Woo: Using Strategic Persuasion to Sell Your Ideas* suggest a simple framework for structuring your argument: the "PCAN" model (see Figure 8.8). We will use the example of a project leader who needs to convince other members of the project team that they will not be able to finish a project on time if they continue to work in such an uncoordinated way:

1 *Problem*: Describe the problem that your idea will solve. Ideally, present the problem in a way that is relevant for your audience.
  - You could highlight the negative effect that an unfinished project would have on all team members.

2 *Cause*: Explain what causes the problem.
  - You could point out to the team that they are working without a clear project plan and without a tool that helps you to track progress.

3 *Answer*: Propose your solution to the problem.
  - You might suggest the introduction of a simple planning and scheduling tool that allows the team to plan and track all tasks, responsibilities, and the project's progress.

4 *Net benefits*: Provide arguments for why your idea is the best possible answer, and compare it to alternatives.
  - You could point out that you will be able to spot potential problems with the progress of the project early with the help of the planning and scheduling tool, thus allowing the team to quickly take adaptive action. You could also present alternative tools for coordinating project work, and emphasize the advantages of the tool that you are suggesting over others.

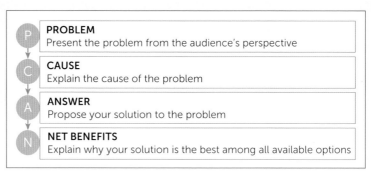

Figure 8.8 The "PCAN" model for presenting a convincing proposal

Source: Based on ideas in Shell and Moussa (2007).

Good arguments are definitely important for persuading others. Persuasion is much more than just arguments, however. It is a process in which creating a "common ground," showing the audience that a proposal will also improve *their* situation, is as important as establishing an **emotional connection** with them.[73] This includes showing your own emotional commitment to the idea (emotions can be contagious), and also trying to sense the emotional state of the audience and adjusting the contents and the tone of delivery of the message accordingly.[74]

Exerting influence through a motivational speech

In one of the most iconic moments of US sports, the 1980 American Olympic ice hockey team, consisting mainly of amateur players, defeated the hotly favored stars of the Soviet Union team (who had won the gold medal for four Olympic games in a row) in a medal-round game. After two of the three periods, the Soviet Union led 3–2. US coach Herb Brooks knew that he would have to focus all his team's remaining mental energy to hold the Soviets' pace. In an inspirational pre-game speech (that was later recreated for the sports docudrama *Miracle*), he said the famous words, "Great moments are born from great opportunity. And that's what you have here tonight, boys."[75] Although the Soviets dominated the game, the "Miracle on Ice," as it was later called, happened: the Americans scored two more goals in the last period and won the game 4–3. Coach Brooks' powerful words had played their part in energizing his players, persuading them that the unthinkable was indeed possible.

Source: Based on information in Shea (2001).

Influencing through relationships

Reciprocity:
The practice of two parties giving something to each other for mutual benefit.

As with all social systems, organizations are also systems of **social exchange** built on **reciprocity** (the expectation that people will respond positively to favors or benefits that they receive from others). Cohen and Bradford use the metaphor of "**currencies of exchange**" for resources that can be offered to others in exchange for their cooperation.[76] In order to exert influence, people need to be able to give something that others value (i.e. a "currency"). In organizations, there are **inspiration-related currencies** (e.g. a vision that provides meaning and identity), **task-related currencies** (e.g. new resources, challenges, information, or recognition), **relationship-related currencies** (e.g. emotional backing), and **personal-related currencies** (e.g. affirmation of personal values).[77] The value of a currency is determined by what other people want and need, by what really matters to *them*. Using the currencies of exchange (e.g. providing colleagues with confidential information that is highly valuable to them) and expecting certain reciprocal behavior (e.g. receiving confidential information from these colleagues when needed) is one possible social influencing strategy.

Another strategy is to **form coalitions** with powerful people in a network. If they can be convinced to support a certain idea or initiative, they can then become role models for others in the organization. In each organization, some people will be more influential than others. It goes without saying that formal decision makers can make or break the acceptance of a proposal. But there are usually other **centers of influence** (also known as **opinion leaders**) who carry a lot of informal power and can shape the attitudes and behavior of other people in the organization.[78] Identifying these centers of influence and convincing them to support your ideas is a powerful strategy for exerting influence in an organization.

A tool that can help managers understand the web of influence in and beyond an organization is the **influence map** (see the box *Zooming in on drawing an influence map*).[79] It includes all the people with a stake in a particular issue and their influence relationships. The people with the strongest influence are usually key players who need to be convinced in order to gather the necessary support for implementing a proposal.

Coalition:
An alliance between different people with the aim of achieving a common goal.

Influence map:
A tool for displaying who has more or less influence within a certain group of people.

Zooming in on ▶ DRAWING AN INFLUENCE MAP

An influence map is a tool that helps you to understand the key stakeholders in a particular unit or issue and their interrelationships (see Figure 8.9 for an example). With the following steps, you can draw your own influence map:

1 Define the unit or issue that you are interested in (e.g. a project team as an example of a unit, or everyone who is involved in the decision-making process for making a purchasing decision as an example of an issue).
2 Identify the key people in the unit or the key influencers on a particular issue.
3 Mark the formal decision maker (in Figure 8.9 denoted with an asterisk).
4 Draw arrows between people who influence each other. The bolder the arrows, the stronger the mutual influence.
5 Identify people with a central position in the web of influence (i.e. people with a lot of strong links to others).

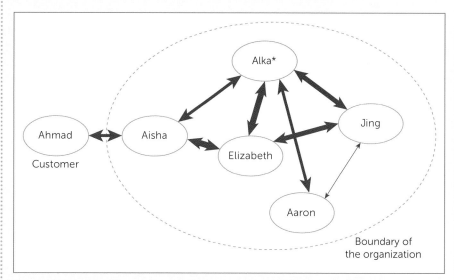

Figure 8.9 Example of an influence map

Influencing through culture

Because people are influenced by the culture in which they are socialized or immersed, shaping culture also means influencing people. Both national culture (see also Chapter 5 and the box

Around the globe: How to persuade people in different cultural contexts) and organizational culture can have an effect on how people think and act. Organizational culture is often referred to as "the way we do things around here." Edgar Schein more formally defines culture as a "pattern of shared assumptions that was learned by a group as it solved its problems of external adaptation and internal integration."[80] He also points out that there are **three layers of culture**:[81]

- **artifacts** (the visible products and symbols of a group, including organizational structures and processes);
- **espoused beliefs and values** (rules of behavior and ideas of what is right and what is not—sometimes also explicitly stated);
- **deeper, underlying assumptions** that people hold; for example, about human nature, the appropriateness of certain behavioral patterns, or the relationship between people. The basic underlying assumptions are usually implicit and unconscious, and therefore often difficult to define and describe. But they can have a strong impact on how people behave in organizations or in their subunits.

A strong organizational culture can bind people together and function as a kind of social control mechanism that helps to achieve persistently high performance levels.[82] It can, however, also become a main obstacle to change. With its multi-level and multi-faceted nature, shaping culture is a challenging endeavor, especially when it comes to underlying assumptions and values. But managers sometimes need to change a culture; for example, when it is evident that the existing culture has become an obstacle to realizing an intended strategy.

Some approaches that managers can follow to **shape the culture of their organization** are:

- **Being a role model**. What managers say is important, but what they do is even more important for shaping the culture of their organizations. What is on a manager's agenda, what a manager spends time on, and what gets followed up rather than forgotten sends out signals to the rest of the organization about priorities in a particular culture.[83]
- **Using symbolic actions and telling stories**. Managers can use symbols, language, and ceremonies to convey a consistent message to the members of the organization.[84] How things are referenced (e.g. using terms with either a positive or a negative connotation), what questions are asked, and what words are repeatedly used can help the members of the organization to recognize priorities. Stories can have a particularly strong impact on people. Managers can, for example, use stories about why the old culture was helpful previously but is no longer appropriate in the new environment, or about how new practices can achieve superior results.
- **Aligning reward and recognition systems**. Rewards and recognition can reinforce behavior that is in line with cultural expectations. When employees receive bonuses for achieving quarterly rather than annual results, they will not be very likely to contribute to a long-term-oriented organizational culture. It is therefore important to make sure that the official reward systems are in line with the desired culture. But positive feedback—for example, in the form of personal recognition or public acknowledgement of achievements—can also have a strong effect in this respect, because it increases the visibility of behavior that aligns with cultural expectations.
- **Putting the right people in the right places**. Managers can hire and promote people who are thinking and acting in congruence with the new norms and values. The recruitment and selection process is therefore an important tool for shaping culture. In addition to hiring the "right" kind of people, an intense period of socialization (e.g. with the help of training or mentoring) can also ensure that new recruits adopt the core values of the organization.

Cultural change is one of the most difficult parts of an organizational transformation process. It is therefore usually the last rather than the first step in a change process, as John Kotter points out: "Culture changes only after you have successfully altered people's actions, after the new behavior produces some group benefit for a period of time, and after people see the connection between the new actions and the performance improvement."[85] Culture change requires a lot of discussion, but even more consistent action and visible positive outcomes of the new approach.[86]

How to persuade people in different cultural contexts

Let us assume that you would like to persuade a co-worker over whom you do not have any formal authority to assist you with a task. Your choice of an appropriate persuasion strategy would, of course, depend on the situation and personal characteristics of your co-worker. But you might also take cultural factors into account. Researchers studied how receptive the employees of a multinational bank were to different influencing strategies in the bank's subsidiaries in different world regions:

- In North America, for example, the research team observed a "market-oriented" approach to the decision whether or not to support a colleague. "Will this person help me to achieve my own objectives" or "has this person done me a favor recently" are questions that a US colleague could have in mind before agreeing to help you out.

- In a more collectivistic society like China, the bank's employees were more inclined to take a "familial-oriented" approach, asking themselves

whether the person who requested a favor has ties with someone who plays an important role in their group or has power over them.

- Spanish employees, in turn, often used an "affiliate-oriented" approach to persuasion, asking themselves whether the person who was requesting a favor was either a friend or connected to a friend of theirs.

- In Germany, it might be particularly relevant for the colleague to know whether the request is consistent with the company's official rules and guidelines. Following a "legal-bureaucratic-oriented" approach, the German colleague could make his or her consent to a request contingent on the answer to the question: "Am I officially supposed to assist you?"[87]

Given the differences in the underlying cultural patterns of when and how people feel obliged to help others, it also makes sense to think about adapting your persuasion strategy accordingly.

Source: *Based on information in Morris et al. (2001).*

8.4 Making change happen

Getty Images/iStockphoto/Thinkstock/Cathy Keifer

In brief

- Implementing a new strategy usually also means initiating change in an organization. It is therefore important to understand the questions, reservations, and doubts that people usually have about change in order to be able to address them in an organizational transformation endeavor.

- John Kotter's change process model can be used as a general guideline for change initiatives. It starts with creating a sense of urgency, forming a guiding coalition and formulating a vision, and describes the main steps that are necessary to turn a vision into reality: communicate the vision, empower others, focus on short-term wins, consolidate improvements, and institutionalize new ways of working.

- As change usually does not come without opposition, it is important to explore various strategies for addressing resistance.

- Managers also need to be aware of what to avoid in change processes. Uncertainty, unfairness, and change without end are particularly detrimental to reaching a new equilibrium after a change initiative.

Organization chart:
A visual representation of the organizational structure (including the main positions or organizational subunits and the reporting relationships between them).

As social systems, organizations are by nature constantly in a state of flux. "Perfect balance in a business exists only on the **organization chart**," said Peter Drucker. "A living business is always in a state of imbalance, growing here and shrinking there, overdoing one thing and neglecting another."[88] Change can come in many forms, varying in scope (incremental versus radical change), origin (change that is initiated from the top down versus bottom up), timing (slow versus fast change), and magnitude of the rollout (organization-wide versus localized change).[89] Strategy execution efforts, in particular, usually require the initiation of major change initiatives in an organization. Some successful organizations even build their business model on their superior ability to adapt and change (see, for example, the box *Embracing change in the fashion business*).

But **managing change** is not an easy endeavor. Some estimates even suggest that more than two-thirds of all change efforts fail.[90] This is partly due to the systemic nature of organizations, in which one intervention can have multiple—and often also unwanted—consequences (see also the concept of the "double multiplicity" of management in Chapter 1). Moreover, effective organizational change is only possible when people within the organization change as well. Those who are affected by an organizational change often also need to go through personal transitions, and it takes time and effort to cope with such transitions.[91] People are sometimes reluctant to change, especially if they fear that the change will lead to disadvantages for them.

As a consequence, change management needs to go far beyond the mere adaptation of the organizational "hardware," the structures, processes, and systems. To increase the chances for a change effort to succeed, it is crucial to set a strong focus on the "soft" side too, on addressing the feelings and interests of the people who are involved in or affected by a change.

CEO BEST PRACTICE

Embracing change in the fashion business

With a tenure of well over 50 years, Leslie Wexner has been the longest serving CEO in the Fortune 500 list of the world's largest corporations. He developed the fashion company L Brands from a single store in a local shopping mall in Upper Arlington, Ohio, into a market-leading lingerie, beauty, and personal care retailer, including well-known brands such as Victoria's Secret and Bath & Body Works. In total, the group controls more than 3,000 stores. Its lingerie brands account for more than 40 percent of the US market.[92] Wexner is also widely recognized as a philanthropist who generously supports educational and research institutions as well as arts and community initiatives.

Constant change lies at the heart of Wexner's approach to doing business. He embraces the inherent logic of the fashion business and transfers it to the organization of his business operations. "If you don't want to be obsolete, you have to reinvent," he said in an interview with *Leaders* magazine. "If you have that as a habit, you stay nimble and able to change. A lot of businesses get set in their ways, and when they have to change, they can't."[93] Changing sometimes also means being willing to let something go. Wexner, for example, decided to sell very successful brands

such as Abercrombie & Fitch or The Limited in order to focus his corporation on a portfolio of brands with unrivalled market positions.

Wexner has been described as an "endlessly curious" person with a passion for speed.[94] He has set up a very agile organization that allows L Brands to develop, test, and produce products much faster than the competition.[95] "You've got to test things because you don't want to make big mistakes,"[96] is how he explains his approach. Instead of indulging in what he has already achieved, he continues to learn and change. "Being optimistic by nature and wanting to improve and change things is a youthful attribute, regardless of your actual age," he says, adding: "I still have those youthful attributes."[97]

→ Key takeaway

The ability to create an agile organization in which learning and change become second nature can be an important competitive advantage, especially in a fast-moving market environment.

Sources: Based on information in Alexander (2014); Born (2016); Leaders Magazine (2014).

Six questions about change

Organizations can only profoundly change when people are willing to change their attitudes and behaviors. When faced with change, people usually have two categories of questions about it (see Figure 8.10):

a   They want to **understand** what the change is about.
b   They **evaluate** the change and its effects from their own perspective.

Figure 8.10 Six key questions that people ask about change

If managers want people to **understand a change effort**, they need to address the following questions:

- **Why do we need to change?** People need a compelling reason for change. This can either be a major crisis or threat to the organization or a very promising opportunity that could not be realized without the change. Bruch and Vogel call the strategy of mobilizing a team through painting a vivid picture of a significant danger for the organization "slaying the dragon," and of creating enthusiasm for pursuing a unique opportunity "winning the princess"[98] (see also the "Energize the team" step in the implementation path presented in Section 8.1). In both cases, it is important to create a sense of urgency through a convincing story.

- **What will change?** People want to know about the nature of a change. This might sound self-evident, but it is not. Many change attempts fail because they focus on one half of the change contents only: the starting point. This could be costs that are too high (and need to be cut) or insufficient growth (that needs to be stimulated). Of equal importance, however, is the end point of the change effort. In other words, we need both a focal problem (e.g. the threat) and a goal.[99] Where does the change lead the organization? What is the vision for the future? To be motivated to change, people need goals with a promise, or at least a good chance that there will be a benefit if they contribute to the change.

- **How will the change be implemented?** When a change initiative is announced, people want to know what exactly they can expect to happen, in order to assess whether and how the change could affect their own interests. Change entails uncertainty, and uncertainty arouses fears. Clear planning and communication of implementation steps can reduce the uncertainties that are brought along with change. People want to know the details to be able to assess whether a change effort will actually succeed. If the key actions and milestones are seen as achievable, the overall change project—even if it seems huge at first sight—will become more realistic.

From the announcement of a change initiative people also start **evaluating**. In this context, it is important to provide answers to the following questions asked by people who are affected by the change:

- **What will I gain or lose?** People do not only evaluate a change initiative from the perspective of its impact on the organization, but primarily also on what it means for them personally. Will their tasks and positions change? Will they be threatened by layoff? What will they have to do differently in the future? They will very quickly assess whether they will be better or worse off, be it in terms of task and workload distribution, working conditions, status, power, remuneration, or job security. Managers should be aware of the "communication collision," in which they primarily talk about what change means for the business, thereby neglecting that what employees really want to know is what the change means *for them* (or the people in their organizational unit).[100]
- **Will I be able to cope with the change?** For many people, change arouses anxieties about whether they will be able to cope with the new operating environment. Anxieties can prevent people from fully focusing on their tasks. Managers therefore need to find ways to address the emotional needs of their team members.[101] It also means that managers must ensure that they treat those who are negatively affected by a change in a fair way.
- **How do others see the change?** Change is a social process. As social animals, human beings turn to those around them for signals about how to assess a change. Thus, the more opinion leaders support a change initiative, the higher the chances of its successful implementation. Furthermore, change is also a political process. A change will only be successfully executed if a sufficient number of powerful actors within an organization commit to it. Public commitments by influential people can therefore function as a powerful catalyst for change.

Suppose that you have to introduce new processes that would influence almost everyone's work. You estimate that approximately a quarter of your team would highly welcome the process reengineering, half of the team would be more or less neutral, but another quarter would probably have considerable reservations against the change initiative. Which steps would you take in order to ensure a smooth transition to the new processes?

A model of organizational transformation

As a result of studying both successful and failed change efforts, John Kotter developed a **process model for change** that can be used as a guideline for major organizational transformation initiatives. Kotter's model identifies eight phases through which change initiatives typically need to pass:[102]

1 **Create a sense of urgency**—make sure that people understand the imminent crisis, potential crisis, or opportunity.
2 **Form a guiding coalition**—ensure support and commitment to the change effort from a critical number of powerful actors and build a change team.
3 **Formulate a vision**—tell a compelling story about the (better) future of the organization.
4 **Communicate**—use all possible communication channels to ensure that the vision is understood and act as a role model for the new culture.
5 **Help others to act on the vision**—remove obstacles and alter systems and structures that block the implementation.
6 **Ensure short-term wins**—set initiatives that lead to quick positive results and reward those who contribute to the change.
7 **Consolidate improvements**—continue to set up new structures and policies and hire and promote people who fit the new culture and goals.
8 **Institutionalize the new way of working**—ensure that the next generation of leaders represents the new attitude and connect positive outcomes to the changes made.

Kotter's change management process addresses several of the questions that are typically asked by people who are affected by change efforts. Establishing a sense of urgency, for example, will answer the "Why do we need to change?" question; forming a guiding coalition will allow members of the organization to observe the attitudes of key actors toward the change ("How do others see the change?"); the vision will address the "What will change?" question (preferably in the form of a simple, albeit compelling story). Questions about the concrete implementation steps and personal consequences ("Will I gain or lose?"; "Will I be able to cope with the challenges?"), though not explicitly mentioned in Kotter's process, could (and should) be addressed in managerial communication efforts when conveying the vision, as well as throughout the change initiative.

Communication plays a key role in every major change effort in organizations.[103] It does not just entail informing other people about a change, but also means listening to the concerns of those who are affected by a change, including stakeholder groups within and outside of the organization. It is good practice for managers to think about the possible positive and negative implications of a change initiative on all the key stakeholders before making the final decision to go ahead, thereby also evaluating whether and to what extent resistance to change can be expected.

Dealing with resistance to change

A key issue for effective change management is how to address resistance to change.

In their **change formula** (based on an original idea attributed to David Gleicher), Kathleen Dannemiller and Robert Jacobs postulate that

$$D \times V \times F > R$$

meaning that change will be possible if the product of **d**issatisfaction with the current state (D), a compelling **v**ision of the future (V) and **f**irst concrete steps toward the vision (F) is greater than **r**esistance to change.[104] The first three variables are explicitly addressed in Kotter's change model. Being able to manage resistance, however, is also a major precondition for making change possible.

It is a natural tendency for people to favor stability over the uncertainty of change, and to follow their already established beliefs and practices rather than embrace novelty.[105] To deal effectively with resistance to change, managers first need to understand the various underlying **reasons for resistance**, including:[106]

- **Self-interest**: Fear of losing something that is of value because of the change.
- **Lack of understanding**: Not being fully aware of why change is needed, what exactly will change, and how this will affect the organization and the individuals working within it.
- **Lack of trust** in the person who initiated the change.
- **Different assessment** of the situation: Seeing more disadvantages (also for the organization) than the management does.
- **General low tolerance for change**: Motivated by the fear of not being able to perform well in a new environment.

Depending on the situation and the reasons for resistance, Kotter and Schlesinger propose a set of **strategies for handling resistance to change**:[107]

- **Education and communication**: Making sure that everyone fully understands the change initiative and its reasons and implications.
- **Participation and involvement**: Listening to people's opinions and trying to integrate their ideas into the change initiative.
- **Facilitation and support**: Providing both emotional and training support to help people to work well under the changed circumstances.
- **Negotiation and agreement**: Offering something of value (e.g. higher salaries) in return for compliance to the change.

- **Manipulation and co-optation**: Using information selectively or giving people (or a group of people) a key role in the change process.
- **Explicit or implicit coercion**: Forcing people to comply with a change, e.g. through threatening them with something that makes them worse off.

The process model in Figure 8.11 can support a manager in finding the right strategy for handling resistance to change under different circumstances.

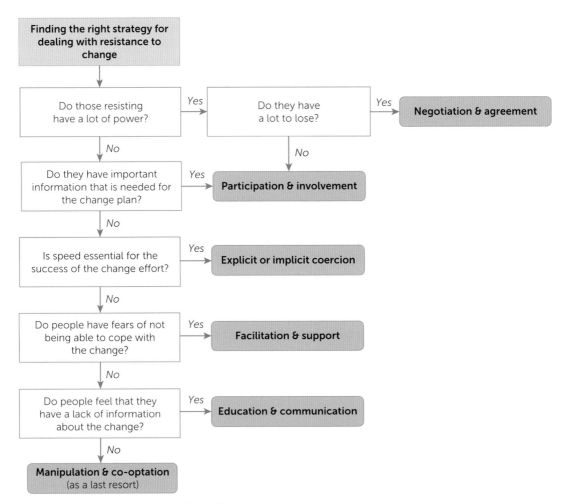

Figure 8.11 Choosing the right strategy for dealing with resistance to change

Source: Inspired by concepts in Kotter and Schlesinger (2008), p. 136.

Resistance to change, however, is not necessarily something negative that managers must "deal with" or "get rid of." The concerns that people voice about change initiatives can also provide valuable feedback that can help managers to recognize potential pitfalls in the change project.[108] As James March pointed out, "most novel ideas are bad ones—that is, they will subsequently be judged unsuccessful."[109] Sometimes, resistance can help to filter out the bad ideas.

Furthermore, open resistance also creates an opportunity for managers to address concerns. Giving a voice to people—making them feel heard—is an important step in itself toward more participation and engagement during a change effort.[110] Kets de Vries speaks of "resistance judo" when he points out that instead of directly attacking people's defenses against change, it is necessary to "move with the person; otherwise, he or she may dig in and become resistant to any further help."[111] Specifically, he recommends asking open questions and listening to people who are showing defensive behavior, thus at least giving them the chance to express their opinions and feelings.[112]

What to avoid in a change process

People's negative reaction toward change often does not stem from the fact that something is changed itself, but from the uncertainty that comes with it, from perceived unfairness in the way that change is managed, or from a general lack of stability in their work. Managers who are aware of these **three challenges** and try to address them appropriately can avoid or at least mitigate their negative effects:

- **Avoiding uncertainty**: When people do not know the exact details of a change process and its possible effects on themselves, uncertainty can generate more anxiety or fears than facts—even if the facts are negative ones.[113] Managers can reduce uncertainty through being as clear as possible about what individuals can expect from a change and making sure that they provide answers to the six key questions about change (see pp. 281-282). People can often deal with a bitter truth better than with an uncertain future.
- **Avoiding unfairness**: Negative emotions in change processes often stem from managerial actions that are perceived as a breach of agreements or of trust, or as injustice and unfairness (see also Chapter 3).[114] Managers need to take these issues seriously if they want to avoid negative emotions during a period of change.
- **Avoiding perpetual change**: Research has shown that organizations that rhythmically change with alternating periods of transition and stability on average perform better than those that are changing erratically or all of the time.[115] People have a need for both stability and development. Finding a balance between the two, letting neither stability nor transition periods last for too long, will avoid both inertia as well as change ad nauseam that people are unwilling to endure. As the American essayist and philosopher Ralph Waldo Emerson said, "[m]otion or change, and identity or rest, are the first and second secrets of nature: Motion and Rest. The whole code of her laws may be written on the thumbnail, or the signet of a ring."[116]

"Operation Crossover" at Comair Limited

CASE STUDY

The South African airline Comair was founded by three air force pilots in 1946. It mainly focused on charter services to remote places in Africa before entering the main domestic routes in 1992 after the government started to deregulate the airline industry. Comair became a franchise partner of British Airways in 1996, which also allowed the airline to use the renowned British Airways brand on its planes. In 2001, following US and European models, Comair launched kulula.com ("kulula" means "easily" in the Zulu language) as South Africa's first budget airline. This move did not go unchallenged, though, with competitors 1time and Mango (a subsidiary of flag carrier South African Airways) entering the market soon after. Comair also added other business units over time, launching catering services, a travel distribution network, airport lounges, and its own training center. In 2019, Comair operated 26 aircraft and employed around 2,000 people.

Even as the organization increased in both size and complexity, a family business-like culture and evolved systems remained intact for some years. After former financial director Erik Venter and former marketing director Gidon Novick took over as co-CEOs in 2006 (Novick left the company in 2011), however, it became more and more evident that the company needed a more structured and professional approach to managing its operations. Several dozen non-integrated IT systems, different measurement systems, data formats and control systems in the company's various units, as well as two different spheres of influence that emerged around the two co-CEOs, were increasingly problematic, causing challenges in a competitive environment that called for streamlined operations and tight cost control.

After a strategic review, the introduction of a new, integrated IT system was seen as a potential solution to overcome these challenges. As a precondition, all core processes needed to be reengineered across the company, which affected every individual member of the organization. In addition to structural changes, systems changes, and process changes, the transformation also required changes in attitudes and the corporate culture. Comair's top management team used the services of gothamCulture, an organizational development consulting firm, to plan and implement the transformation process.

The transformation project started with analyzing the culture and change readiness of the organization (e.g. with personal interviews and focus group discussions). Several problem areas were identified, such as an unclear vision and strategy, general skepticism regarding change (specifically skepticism toward implementing a new integrated IT system), a misaligned leadership team, a lack of communication and a lack of integration of activities across different organizational units. The positive elements of the prevailing culture were found to be a high level of creativity and a strong focus on both safety and customer service.

The detailed change program that was subsequently developed included the appointment of a change and communication manager and a change management team consisting of representatives from all parts of the organization, the reformulation of the company's vision, mission, and strategy, comprehensive transition and communication plans, the analysis of risks associated with the transition, the development of tactics for mitigating risks, and a review of the role of the leadership team.

Erik Venter spent considerable time personally communicating the reasons and details of the transition initiative, called "Operation Crossover," using the metaphor of a bridge that led from the family business-like way of doing things to a professionally run organization. Benefits for the organization and potential impacts for individuals received special attention in the communication efforts. A project intranet website and regular "push messages" kept employees up to date with the current implementation status of the project.

In addition, managers were equipped with a change management "toolkit" (including guidance on how to deal with the change and potential reservations to the change). Change agents were appointed to support the implementation efforts on the ground in all parts of the organization. Short surveys were used throughout the implementation process to get feedback about how the members of the organization responded to the change.

During an intensive 10-week training period, 1,172 staff members were trained on the new system. Peer coaches also provided additional support. After a few simulated airport "dry runs," the new system was introduced on one big cutover day. The transition was regarded as very successful both internally and by external partners. It also enabled Comair employees to develop new skills in managing complex projects.

Comair's management could not rest on its laurels, however. Significant price competition and pressure on margins, volatile fuel prices, and the first wage strike in the company's history in 2016 posed new challenges. Comair CEO Venter would probably need to continue to use what he saw as his key talent: persistence.

Sources: Comair (2017); comair.co.za (2017; 2019); gothamCulture (2017); Jaffit et al. (2015); Phathi (2016); successness.com (2015).

 Discussion questions

- What were the main reasons why Comair's top management initiated a change process?
- What would you consider as the main factors that contributed to the success of the "Operation Crossover" transition project?
- Why can the transition to a new IT system have widespread repercussions in an organization?
- How did Erik Venter and his team try to persuade the members of the organization of the need for change?

Conclusion

Top managers are often also called **executives**. Executives are paid for getting things done. They therefore need to understand how they can turn visions, ideas, and strategies into reality. This chapter provided an overview of the main concepts and methods that can help managers in this ongoing endeavor.

Being able to execute—to carry out your plans and implement strategies—lies at the heart of what managerial effectiveness is all about. The Roman Emperor Marcus Aurelius gave the advice to "[t]ake no enterprise in hand at haphazard, or without regard to the principles governing its proper execution"[117]—a message that is echoed in modern management thinking. In a study of 160 companies over a ten-year period, flawless execution was identified as one of the main drivers of superior business performance.[118] Another study, however, revealed that employees in a majority of companies judged their organizations as being weak in execution.[119]

To become effective, every strategy needs to be translated into concrete action—into single steps that people in the organization can take one after the other. One of the secrets of successful execution is therefore deciding upon **the right next steps**, those actions that can best bring an organization nearer to achieving its major goals. Returning to the example of Facebook, Mark Zuckerberg also gave some advice on how to identify the right next step: "I think a simple rule in business is," he says, "if you do the things that are easier first then you can actually make a lot of progress."[120]

The example of Facebook also shows, however, that being able to execute well is not sufficient on its own for achieving effectiveness. In 2018, Zuckerberg had to admit that Facebook had made a "big mistake" when the company allowed user data to be misused for political purposes: "[I]t's clear now that we didn't do enough to prevent these tools from being used for harm,"[121] he said, acknowledging that in addition to great execution skills, organizations and their managers also need to understand their ethical responsibility (see also Chapter 5). Execution is highly important—but effectiveness means that the *right things* are executed well.

✓ Review questions

1   What are the main steps that a manager needs to take in order to implement a strategy?
2   What is organizational design and what are the main tasks of a manager in designing an organization?
3   What does a manager need to consider when choosing between different organizational structuring principles?
4   Which coordination mechanisms can be used to combine and integrate individual efforts in an organization?
5   Why does an organization need process management?
6   What is the role of control systems in management?
7   Which tactics can managers use to exert influence on others?
8   How can managers effectively persuade others of certain ideas?
9   What is an influence map and what can it be used for?
10 How can managers shape the culture of their organization?
11 What are the main questions that people usually ask about change?
12 Which steps do successful change initatives typically pass through?
13 How can managers deal with resistance to change?
14 What should managers avoid during a change process?
15 Why do managers have to take care of both "hard" (organizational design) and "soft" (people, culture) issues in strategy implementation processes?

⑦ Critical reflection questions

1   What is more important, a good strategy or effective execution?
2   In some organizations, we can observe a strong tendency to formalize processes and introduce new guidelines, rules, and procedures in order to ensure that the behavior of the members of the organization is in line with what is expected of them by the management. What is your opinion about such a managerial tendency to build tight control systems?
3   Some people claim that hierarchical structures are outdated, and that organizations need more flexible, democratic structures in order to survive and thrive in a dynamic globalized business environment. Do you agree?
4   Do you see any disadvantages of a strong organizational culture?
5   Which approach to influencing people would you see as more effective for an organizational change endeavor—the use of "hard" influencing tactics (e.g. structural changes, changes in processes, or clear guidelines) or of "soft" influencing tactics (e.g. personal persuasion, relationships, or trying to shape the organizational culture).

☛ Managerial implications

- Strategies can only be effective if they are well implemented. Effective managers break down strategies into tasks for which individuals are responsible. They must also ensure that appropriate coordination mechanisms are in place in order to align the individual contributions with the organizational goals.
- Managers can use the elements of organizational design—organizational structure, processes, and systems—to provide a framework for coordinating actions within an organization. It is important that the individual "hard" elements of organizational design are well aligned with each other, as well as with the "soft" people- and culture-oriented facets of the organization.
- Effective managers get things done through other people. For that purpose, they need to exert influence on others. They can do so through the elements of organizational design, but also through persuasion, building reciprocal relationships, and shaping the culture of their organizations.
- Executing strategies is intrinsically linked to initiating and managing change processes in organization. Effective managers therefore also need to be effective change managers.
- The first step to becoming an effective change manager is understanding the needs and fears of the people who are potentially affected by a change. Having clear reasons for a change and a convincing vision about a (better) future state, being able to communicate the reasons, vision, and necessary change steps well, and effectively dealing with resistance to change are further major preconditions for a successful transition process.

✐ Endnotes

1 Facebook (2016).
2 Döpfner (2016).
3 Martin (2010).
4 Martin (2010).
5 Hrebiniak (2005), p. 9.
6 Drucker (2011), p. 204.
7 Hrebiniak (2005), p. 11.
8 Bossidy et al. (2002), p. 33.
9 Neilson et al. (2008).
10 Welch (n.d.).
11 Bruch and Ghoshal (2003).
12 Bruch and Ghoshal (2003).
13 Bae (2015).
14 March (2010), p. 70.
15 Cross et al. (2002).
16 Bossidy et al. (2002), p. 71.
17 Mintzberg et al. (2003), p. 90.
18 Boddy (2017); Child (2005).
19 Boddy (2017).
20 Kerzner (2018).
21 Leaders Magazine (2013), p. 75.
22 Cottrill (2008).
23 Charan et al. (2018), p. 19.
24 Cottrill (2008).
25 Cottrill (2008).
26 Chandler (1962).
27 Hall and Saias (1980).
28 Mintzberg (1990), p. 183.
29 Jones (2013), p. 30 (emphasis in bold added by the author).
30 Lawrence and Lorsch (1967).
31 Vahs (2012).
32 Standards Australia (2017).
33 DHL (2019).

34 Hatch (2018).
35 P&G (2017).
36 P&G (2017).
37 coca-colacompany.com (2019).
38 Hrebiniak (2005).
39 Hrebiniak (2005).
40 Hrebiniak (2005).
41 Vahs (2012).
42 Vahs (2012).
43 Picot et al. (2005); Thompson (2007).
44 Schreyögg (2008); Vahs (2012).
45 Hrebiniak (2005).
46 Hrebiniak (2005).
47 Robertson (2015).
48 Robertson (2015).
49 Denning (2014).
50 Bernstein et al. (2016), p. 40.
51 Kumar (2018).
52 Vahs (2012), p. 241.
53 Kaplan and Norton (2006), p. 4.
54 Forrester (1961), p. 15.
55 McChesney et al. (2012), p. 47.
56 McChesney et al. (2012), p. 59.
57 Hrebiniak (2005), p. 204; Mullins (2016).
58 McChesney (2012), p. 67.
59 Kaplan and Norton (2005).
60 Child (2005), pp. 140–141.
61 Sternad (2014).
62 The Economist (2008).
63 Isenberg (2009).
64 Isenberg (2009), p. 8.
65 Mintzberg and Waters (1985), p. 259.
66 McChesney et al. (2012), p. 4.
67 Kets de Vries (2009), p. 11.

68 French and Raven (1968).
69 Eisenhardt and Bourgeois (1988); Buchanan (2008).
70 Kets de Vries (2006), p. xv.
71 Nonaka and Takeuchi (2011), p. 65.
72 Harvard Business School Publishing (2013).
73 Conger (1998).
74 Conger (1998).
75 Shea (2001).
76 Cohen and Bradford (2017).
77 Cohen and Bradford (2017).
78 Harvard Business School Publishing (2013).
79 Watkins (2010).
80 Schein (2004), p. 17.
81 Schein (2004).
82 Sørensen (2002).
83 Tushman and O'Reilly III (2002).
84 Tushman and O'Reilly III (2002).
85 Kotter (1996), p. 156.
86 Kotter (1996).
87 Morris et al. (2001), p. 97.
88 Drucker (1993), p. 159.
89 Raffaelli (2016).
90 Higgs and Rowland (2005).
91 Hayes (2018).
92 Alexander (2014).
93 Leaders Magazine (2014), p. 272.
94 Born (2016).
95 Born (2016).
96 Born (2016).
97 Leaders Magazine (2014), p. 273.
98 Bruch and Vogel (2011).
99 Kets de Vries (2006), p. 220.
100 Quirke (1995), p. 118.

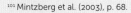

[101] Mintzberg et al. (2003), p. 68.
[102] Kotter (2007), p. 99.
[103] Lewis (2019).
[104] Dannemiller and Jacobs (1992).
[105] March (2010), p. 76.
[106] Kotter and Schlesinger (2008).
[107] Kotter and Schlesinger (2008).

[108] Ford and Ford (2009).
[109] March (2010), p. 75.
[110] Ford and Ford (2009).
[111] Kets de Vries (2006), p. 240.
[112] Kets de Vries (2006), p. 241.
[113] Bartunek et al. (2011).
[114] Bartunek et al. (2011).

[115] Klarner and Raisch (2013).
[116] Emerson (1860), p. 175.
[117] Marcus Aurelius (2004), p. 28.
[118] Nohria et al. (2003).
[119] Neilson et al. (2008).
[120] Zuckerberg (2011).
[121] Rushe (2018).

Visit the companion website at macmillanihe.com/sternad-management to access multiple choice questions, useful weblinks and additional materials.

PART

ENHANCING ORGANIZATIONAL SUCCESS

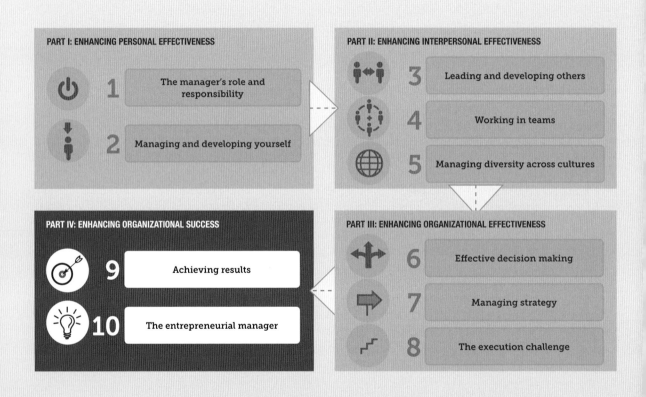

PART I: ENHANCING PERSONAL EFFECTIVENESS

1   The manager's role and responsibility

2   Managing and developing yourself

PART II: ENHANCING INTERPERSONAL EFFECTIVENESS

3   Leading and developing others

4   Working in teams

5   Managing diversity across cultures

PART IV: ENHANCING ORGANIZATIONAL SUCCESS

9   Achieving results

10   The entrepreneurial manager

PART III: ENHANCING ORGANIZATIONAL EFFECTIVENESS

6   Effective decision making

7   Managing strategy

8   The execution challenge

Effective managers achieve results through their organization and for their organization. But they are also able to build the right kind of organization in the first place—an organization that is successful in creating value for different stakeholder groups. Part IV is devoted to exploring what managers can do to enhance the performance of their existing organization (or organizational unit) in different results categories, and to how they can create "new" organizations—both in the sense of establishing completely new entrepreneurial ventures and in terms of rejuvenating established organizations.

In **Chapter 9,** *Achieving results,* we will see that the term "results" has many different facets in an organizational context. Profit and cash flow are two common ways of measuring financial results. But there are also forms of value creation that go far beyond short-term profitability and the optimization of cash inflows and outflows. Responsible managers also keep an eye on creating long-term economic value, and actively strive to improve the social and environmental performance of their organization. In this chapter, we discuss what managers can do to achieve positive outcomes in all these results categories—how they can improve profitability, how they can manage cash flows, how they can increase the long-term value of their organizations, and what they can do to ensure that their organization has a positive impact on both society and the environment (or at least avoid negative effects).

In **Chapter 10,** *The entrepreneurial manager,* we take a closer look at the manager's role as an entrepreneur. This role is not bound to founding and starting up new ventures. An entrepreneurial mind-set is also needed to adapt established organizations to a changing environment. The chapter begins with a discussion of what it means to think and act in an entrepreneurial way, and what managers can do to encourage creativity and innovativeness—two essential ingredients for successful entrepreneurship—on an organizational level. Entrepreneurial managers are able to effectively pursue entrepreneurial opportunities—they connect unmet needs with innovative solutions, thereby creating new value. In the second part of this chapter, we will examine how managers can recognize and assess opportunities, and what different options they have for transforming opportunities into value-creating activities.

iStock.com/Jirapong Manustrong

ACHIEVING RESULTS

Outline of chapter

This chapter will enable you to

- Distinguish between different categories of results as an outcome of managerial work.
- Analyze what managers can do to influence the different results categories.
- Identify opportunities for improving the profitability of an organization.
- Explain different tactics for improving the cash position of an organization.
- Recognize the main drivers of business value.
- Discuss the need for managers to consider non-financial results categories.

Introduction

Conventional wisdom has it that higher costs will reduce profitability and cost cutting will improve business results. But this is not necessarily the case. In 2015, Mark Bertolini, chairman and CEO of the managed healthcare giant Aetna, announced that the minimum wage in the company would be raised to US$16 per hour. This meant an average pay rise of 11 percent for 5,700 people, and, as a consequence, additional costs of more than US$10 million per year for the company.[1] Did this mean that business results suffered? Far from it! Aetna's net income rose by more than 17 percent in 2015 compared to the previous year, while the share price more than doubled in value between 2015 and 2018. This was thanks to another of the company's strategies that focused on creating trusted relationships with consumers and other stakeholders in the healthcare sector.[2] Bertolini is a good example of a long-term-oriented manager. Setting Aetna "on a course for the next 160 years"[3] was one of his main objectives when he took over as CEO. He aims for sustainable value creation rather than short-term profit maximization, understanding that business results do not necessarily equate with quarterly financial results.

We can identify four very different **categories of business results**: profit, cash flow, value creation, and impact on stakeholders. Each section of this chapter is devoted to one of these results categories.

- **Profit** is the financial result of a business during a certain period measured in terms of how much the revenue generated from business activities exceeds the expenses required to conduct these activities. Different tactics for improving the profitability of an organization are discussed in *Section 9.1*.
- **Cash flow** is the difference between cash inflows and cash outflows over a certain period. Because an organization that is running out of cash faces severe troubles (including a potential threat to its very existence), cash management is a key responsibility of managers who are in charge of an organization. Different methods for improving the cash position of an organization are presented in *Section 9.2*.
- **Value creation** is about increasing the potential of organizations to generate profits and cash in the future. Value is more than just a function of current financial results. It is also linked to future growth opportunities, risks, and the relative competitive position of the business. Approaches to valuation and risk management as a main driver of value creation are the focus of *Section 9.3*.
- Organizations not only create results for shareholders, but also for a range of other **stakeholder groups**. In addition to financial performance, organizations have a **social and environmental performance**. We will take a look at how managers can account for value creation—in its *real*, not solely financial meaning—for different stakeholder groups in *Section 9.4*.

As this short overview of what is covered in this chapter demonstrates, the term "results" has many meanings. It is not enough to just consider short-term financial indicators if we are aiming to assess the overall performance of a manager. A more encompassing perspective on managerial performance will include an evaluation of all the different results categories outlined above.

9.1 Improving profitability

Pikaboy/Nattanan Kanchanaprat

In brief

- Organizations must be profitable—at least over time—to ensure their long-term viability. Managers must be aware, however, that profit figures in an income statement are based on various assumptions and estimates, and must therefore be treated with care.

- Managers have a range of different options to influence the profitability of their organizations, on both the cost and revenue sides.

- When managers consider cost reductions, they should be aware of potential repercussions; for example, on employee motivation. Ideally, cost reductions are combined with positive, future-oriented initiatives.

- On the revenue side, various pricing strategies can help to improve the profitability of an organization.

Expenses:
Costs incurred in order to generate revenue in a certain period.

Income statement:
A summary statement of total revenue and expenses that led to the profit (or loss) of an organization over a certain timeframe (e.g. a month, quarter, or year).

Revenue:
The total income that an organization receives from its normal business activities (usually from selling goods and services) before expenses are deducted.

Gross profit margin:
A financial metric that describes what percentage of the money received as revenue is left after deducting the cost of goods sold. It can be calculated in two steps: (1) deduct cost of goods sold from revenue; and (2) divide the result by revenue and express the resulting proportion as a percentage.

Profit is the net income of an organization during a certain period of time, the financial gains that result from the difference between what is earned in that period and all the **expenses** that accrue from buying and producing products or services as well as maintaining a functioning organization. An **income statement** (also known as a **profit and loss account**) is a tool for providing a true and fair representation of the profitability of a business (at least this is what an income statement is supposed to do if it is prepared by managers and accountants who are following legal reporting standards).

INCOME STATEMENT (PROFIT AND LOSS ACCOUNT)

Revenue (turnover)
 −Cost of goods sold (COGS)

Gross profit
 −Selling, general, and administrative expenses (SGA)
 −Depreciation
 +/−Other income or expenses

Earnings before interest and taxes (EBIT)
 +/−Interests

Earnings before taxes (EBT)
 −Taxes

Net profit

Figure 9.1 The structure of an income statement

As we can see in Figure 9.1, income statements include a number of different definitions of profit:

- Gross profit—also known as **gross income**—is the total **revenue** minus cost of goods sold **(COGS)**, costs that are directly attributable to the production of goods or services (e.g. raw material or direct labor costs). The **gross profit margin** (gross profit divided by total revenue) can help to assess the production efficiency of a business.
- **Earnings before interest and taxes** (EBIT)—also known as operating profit—is the net income (revenue minus all costs that accumulate in an organization in order to produce its products and services and to maintain its existence) that is earned from all ongoing

EBT:
Short for *earnings before taxes*. It is an indicator of the pre-tax profitability of an organization. EBT is calculated as revenue minus all expenses (including interest on debt but excluding taxes) in a certain period.

business activities without taking the cost of capital (interest) and taxes into account. EBIT is an indicator of the profitability of the core business activities.

- **Earnings before taxes (EBT)** is calculated by deducting all expenses for both operating and financing the business (including interest on debt) from revenue. It is the amount of money that is retained within the organization during a certain period before taxes are paid to the government.
- **Net profit**—also known as **net income** or the **"bottom line"**—is the result of revenue minus all costs of doing business, including COGS, selling expenses, administrative expenses and overhead costs, **depreciation** of tangible assets and **amortization** of intangible assets, interests, taxes, and any other expenses, in a defined accounting period. Net profit increases (or decreases) **shareholders' equity** on the balance sheet.

Managers need to be careful about **interpreting profit figures**. They do not represent an "absolute truth," but are usually based on a number of assumptions and estimates; for example, regarding the portion of revenue or expenses allocated to a particular period (**accruals**), the allocation of costs in relation to tangible and intangible investments over the period during which they are used (**depreciation** and **amortization**), the timing of the recognition of revenue, or decisions about whether some items are considered **operating expenses (OPEX)** or **capital expenditure (CAPEX)**.[4] Because such types of accounting decisions involve judgments, managers should always remind themselves of the old saying that "profit is an opinion, but cash is a fact."

Depreciation:
The allocation of the decrease in value (or "write-off") of a tangible asset over its estimated useful life. The amount of depreciation that is allocated to a certain period is recorded as an expense on the income statement for that period.

Options for improving profitability

Many managers find themselves under pressure to improve the **profitability** of their organization. Pressure can come from outside (e.g. from the capital market) or from inside (usually in the form of a gradual transmission down the organizational hierarchy).

Amortization:
The allocation of the decrease in value of an intangible asset over its estimated useful life. The amount of amortization that is allocated to a certain period is recorded as an expense on the income statement for that period.

Shareholders' equity:
In a balance sheet, shareholders' equity is the difference between total assets and total liabilities. It represents the total amount that shareholders have invested in a company, either directly (in the form of capital stock) or indirectly through retained earnings.

Accruals:
Accounting entries for expenses or revenue that have already been incurred in a certain period without having been invoiced or paid yet.

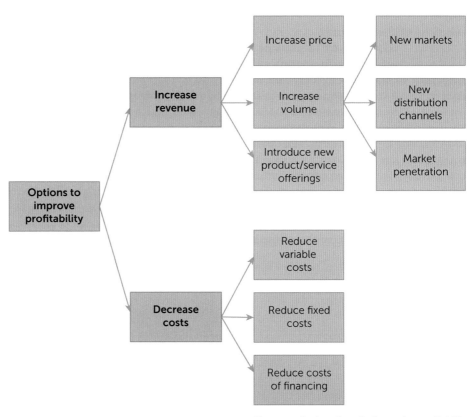

Figure 9.2 Basic options for improving profitability

Operating expenses (OPEX):
Ongoing costs that are incurred in running the day-to-day business operations. OPEX are exhausted within one taxable year.

Capital expenditure (CAPEX):
Money that an organization spends to acquire or add value to fixed assets that are used for creating future benefit beyond one taxable year.

Economies of scale:
Cost advantages that result from higher production or sales volumes (leading to lower unit costs).

Economies of scope:
Cost advantages that result from using one resource base for producing or selling two or more distinct products (leading to lower unit costs).

Variable costs:
Costs that vary depending on the changing volume of an activity or an output (e.g. the amount of units produced).

Fixed costs:
Costs that do not vary over a certain period of time, regardless of a change of volume of either an activity or output during that period.

Managers have a range of different options for improving the profitability of their organizational unit (see Figure 9.2). Essentially, they can either attempt to increase revenue or decrease costs. Because revenue results from multiplying price and volume sold, managers can try to **increase price levels** (as long as this does not disproportionately affect the volume sold) or **increase the profitable sales volume** by entering new markets, opening new distribution channels, or a stronger penetration of existing markets. Marketing and sales can play a key role in forming a strategy to increase volume (although we should not neglect to consider that such activities also incur costs).

Increasing volume can also lead to **economies of scale**, which are cost advantages that arise from higher production volumes—obtained, for example, by spreading fixed costs (costs that occur in an organization regardless of how many units are produced) over a larger number of produced units. Further examples of the effects of economies of scale are the availability of lower purchasing prices for higher quantities (one of the reasons why large supermarket chains have a cost advantage over smaller independent stores), specialization effects (productivity can be enhanced when the individual steps of a production process can be distributed between specialized functions and departments in larger organizations), or the ability of larger organizations to make more costly capital investments (e.g. in sophisticated technology) that can lead to greater efficiency and decrease unit costs.

Besides price increases and trying to increase the sales volume of existing products or services, another option to improve revenue is the **development of new product or service offers**—ideally drawing on existing resources and unused capacity.

In one example, a newspaper company improved its profitability by adding a Sunday edition to its existing Monday to Saturday offering. The existing infrastructure was used to produce the new edition, and much of the paper's content was provided by the existing editorial staff. The Sunday edition was only available to subscribers for an extra charge, so the company's profitability increased considerably with the introduction of the new product (as did overall readership numbers because the Sunday paper captured a new audience of weekend readers). This is an example of **economies of scope**, lower average costs per product when synergies are generated from the joint production of different, complementary products (in this case a weekday daily newspaper and a Sunday newspaper) in one organizational unit. As with all profitability-enhancing activities, managers also need to consider all the effects that their decisions have. In the newspaper example, the synergies could also come at a cost for the members of the editorial staff, who probably need to work overtime and feel more pressure because they have to write for seven instead of just for six newspaper issues per week.

The other basic strategy for profitability improvement is **cost reduction** (although we have already seen that revenue-oriented measures can also have an impact on costs through economies and scale and scope effects). There are various options for decreasing costs. Managers can try to (a) reduce **variable costs**, for example raw materials, energy usage, or directly attributable labor in the production process, or (b) decrease **fixed costs** such as rent, insurance, depreciation, or salaries of staff functions. In addition, they can also optimize the financing of their organization by reducing interest costs; for example, through finding the best ratio between debt financing and the amount of money that the organization receives from shareholders, asking the bank to reduce interest rates in exchange for offering properties or other assets to secure the loan, or refinancing debt with another bank that is offering a lower rate.

As straightforward as these options may sound, they are not always easy to implement. As discussed in Chapter 1, organizations are complex systems. Any intervention, whether with the purpose of increasing revenue or decreasing costs, can lead to multiple repercussions. In the worst-case scenario, they can even have adverse effects on profitability. Managers need to beware of **follow-up costs** (or "second-effect costs") that can arise as a result of cost-cutting measures—also elsewhere in the organization (e.g. liability claims when customer orders cannot be fulfilled in an out-of-stock situation following an initiative to reduce the cost of stock).[5] Keeping that in mind, however, ongoing cost management is a crucial task for a manager, as there is "a natural tendency for costs to grow in an organization"[6] (spending more money is always easier than spending less).

How to effectively reduce costs

There is no one best solution for lowering costs. In a *Harvard Business Review* article, Kevin Coyne and his colleagues go so far as to suggest that as a manager, you should "forget about a single idea that would radically change a cost structure of your organization or department ... Instead, you should plan to reach your goals with a combination of 10 or more actions."[7] This is also in line with the idea of the "double multiplicity" of management presented in Chapter 1—that managers need to acknowledge that organizations are complex cause-and-effect webs, and that it is therefore often more effective to initiate multiple actions (rather than just one) to achieve a desired effect.

There are usually plenty of **opportunities to reduce historically accumulated costs**. Here are some questions that can help explore these opportunities:[8]

Zero-based budgeting:
A method for preparing a budget that starts from scratch (or "from zero"). Under the zero-based budgeting approach, all expenses need to be justified for the new budgeting period without using prior years' budgets or actual figures as a basis.

- Can we eliminate waste and duplication?
- Are all activities that we currently conduct really necessary? Do they all add value for customers?
- Are there any potential synergies with other departments? Can we save money through a better coordination of activities or a joint use of resources?
- How would we organize a particular activity in the most cost-effective way if we had the chance to set it up again from scratch (**zero-based budgeting**)?
- Are there any new (digital) technologies that could improve efficiency?
- Can we learn from best practice elsewhere (benchmarking)?
- Can supplier contracts be renegotiated?
- Can we get more favorable offers from alternative suppliers?
- Can we simplify our products and services—or adjust our product portfolio?
- Could changes in any processes lead to cost savings?
- Could we save costs by shifting the timing of activities to other times of the day, week, or year?
- Could we save costs by outsourcing activities that are currently done in-house?
- Could we save costs by **insourcing** activities that are currently outsourced?
- Do we need to reduce human resources costs?

Insourcing:
A business practice in which non-core tasks or activities of an organization are performed internally instead of being outsourced to another organization (although this would be possible for these particular tasks or activities).

Managers actually often view the last option—rather simplistically in the form of layoffs—as their first option when they have to achieve a cost reduction target. This is not necessarily a good strategy, however, because employees are not only a "cost position," but one of the most valuable assets of an organization. With their tacit knowledge, they are often the main source of competitive advantage. There are alternatives to layoffs—from short-time working to postponing pay raises—and responsible managers will first consider all alternatives before cutting jobs.

When deciding on cost reduction initiatives, managers first need reliable data about the existing cost structure of their organizations. **Cost accounting** systems can help managers to make well-informed decisions. Managers should also be aware, however, that they could also potentially fall into the trap of being misled by some of the data that such systems provide (see the box *Beware of cost allocation*).

Cost accounting:
The process of recording, classifying, and analyzing all costs that are incurred in an organization's activities in order to establish a basis for controlling and managing costs.

Cost reduction as a leadership task

Reducing costs is not only a technical task but often affects people. Managers therefore need to convince members of their organization that cost measures are important and necessary. Convincing others to accept changes or do something differently is part of the leadership

FROM A DIFFERENT ANGLE

Beware of cost allocation

It is common practice in the cost accounting systems of many organizations to allocate **indirect costs** ("general" costs that are not assigned to one specific cost object) to certain products, organizational units, or activities for reporting purposes. For example, an organization might assign the total costs payable to a cleaning company to different departments. To do so, it will try to find a **cost allocation base**—a variable that can be used as a basis for dividing the costs between different units. In the case of the cleaning costs, the cost allocation base might be the room size of the departments, or alternatively the relative time spent on cleaning each department. This example shows that simply by changing the cost allocation base (e.g. from room size to time spent in a department), a particular department will most probably end up with different overall costs, although it did not actually generate more or less costs.

Making decisions on the basis of data that include cost allocations is dangerous, because the results are potentially misleading. Instead, it makes more sense to focus on those cost categories that can actually be influenced by the management of a certain organizational unit. This does not mean, of course, that indirect costs should be left unattended. But they should be addressed at the managerial level which has control over them, and not by the managers of the subordinate units to which these indirect costs are allocated by means of a more or less arbitrary cost allocation base.

Cost allocation on a product level might even lead to a product that is seemingly not profitable from a total cost perspective (including allocated indirect costs) being dropped, although the product might make a valuable **contribution** to covering the fixed costs (i.e. have a positive gross margin between the price and the variable costs) and therefore also to the profitability of an organization.[9] As long as there is free capacity, any revenue that is higher than the **marginal cost** of the additional activity can actually help to increase profits.

Indirect costs:
Costs that cannot be directly attributed to a specific cost object (e.g. a product, department, or project). Indirect costs are usually distributed between different cost objects by means of a cost allocation base.

Cost allocation base:
A variable that is used for allocating indirect costs to specific cost objects (e.g. products, projects, or departments).

Contribution:
In cost accounting, contribution is the difference between product-related revenue and product-related variable costs.

role that forms an integral part of the manager's job. Thus, we can also see cost reduction initiatives as a leadership task. In order to persuade others of the necessity for cost reduction measures, it is advisable to accompany them with **cultural interventions**. Here are some examples:[10]

- Managers need to create a **sense of urgency** and tell a convincing story about why cost reductions are imperative. This can be achieved, for example, through presenting benchmark results which clearly highlight that the organization is falling behind its competitors.
- Having a **"Dr. No,"** a powerful person in the top management team (or at least with its full support) who can withhold resources and help ensure that the whole organization spends less. This could, for example, be the chief financial officer (CFO) or another high-ranking executive who is involved as a key decision maker in the budgeting process.
- **Restricting or eliminating privileges** for top managers (such as travelling business class or buying expensive new company cars) can signal to all employees that the organization is really serious about cost reductions.
- Asking everyone in the organization to **"spend money like it was their own"**[11] is another way of focusing people on cost consciousness.

It is usually not enough to announce cost reduction initiatives once. The issue needs to be raised in regular face-to-face follow-up meetings with line managers or other employees in order to have a sustainable effect. Managers must, however, also be aware that cost cutting can have **negative motivational effects**. Therefore, ideally, cost reduction is not an isolated strategy, but embedded in a wider concept that also includes forward-looking initiatives to provide a positive perspective for the members of the organization. After all, cost reduction can improve an organization's profitability, but is usually not the main driver of value creation.

Responsible cost reduction at Starbucks

Howard Schultz developed Starbucks from a local coffee store in Seattle to a global market leader in coffee retailing. When he reentered the position of president and CEO after an eight-year hiatus in 2008, he faced big challenges, because the detrimental effects of excessive growth and strong competition had placed considerable pressure on the company's profitability. Schultz immediately announced a cost-cutting initiative. Not taking anything for granted, he began "turning over the rocks," trying to find anything "we didn't get right,"[12] as he said. With a highly self-critical approach, he scrutinized advertising investments, new product introductions, entry costs into new markets, and the whole supply chain. Waste was reduced, support structures resized, and unprofitable coffee shops were closed, leading to savings of hundreds of millions of dollars during the following months. Yet Schultz refused to compromise on quality. When someone made him aware that a 5 percent reduction in quality would potentially save the company a hundred million dollars, he simply said: "We would never do that."[13] He was convinced that the value of

Starbucks did not come from low costs but from "the pursuit of an unequivocal, absolute commitment to quality."[14] Because Starbucks is as much about creating a customer experience as it is preparing a good cup of coffee, the relationship between the customer and the barista is seen as a key success factor. Consequently, despite not being able to avoid layoffs, Schultz decided to reinvest in people and their training even in times of severe cost pressure. He wanted "to preserve and enhance the integrity of the only asset we have as a company," as he called it: "our values, our culture and guiding principles, and the reservoir of trust with our people."[15]

→ Key takeaway

When cost cutting is unavoidable, try to ensure that costs are reduced in a way that does not compromise the key assets of the organization and the quality of its products or services.

Sources: Based on information in Ignatius (2010); Webb (2011).

Marginal cost:
Additional costs that accrue when one additional unit of a good or service is produced.

Margin (also called profit margin):
The ratio of profit to total revenue in a certain period (usually expressed as a percentage).

Price elasticity of demand:
The degree to which demand changes as a response to a change in price (usually calculated as percentage change in demand quantity divided by percentage change in price).

In business, value is created when great products, services, and brands are offered to customers at a competitive price in combination with a general attitude of economy and processes that keep costs reasonably low (see also the box on *Responsible cost reduction at Starbucks*).

Pricing as a tool to improve profitability

Let us now turn from costs to the top line of the income statement—turnover, which also offers possibilities to improve profitability. In particular, managers can use **pricing strategies** to influence the revenue and gross profit **margin** of the business for which they are responsible.

Table 9.1 shows a simple example of how a 10 percent change in variable costs, fixed costs, sales volume, or price affects profit levels. As we can see from the example, price changes can have a particularly strong effect on profitability. Every cent or penny of the higher price goes directly into profits—of course this is only under the condition that the higher prices are also enforceable in the market and do not lead to lower sales volumes (i.e., when there is a low **price elasticity of demand**).

Managers need to take into account, however, that blindly raising prices can lead to negative effects on demand. For example, raising the price of a cup of coffee in a bar from €2 to €20 might result in a very nice margin for each cup sold but if no one is willing to buy coffee at such an exceptionally high price, the overall revenue and profitability of the bar will dramatically decrease. Therefore, an integrated way of finding the optimal price will also consider potential changes in demand. One method that includes demand-side consideration is the **contribution margin approach to pricing** (see the *Zooming in on the contribution margin approach to pricing* box).[16]

Table 9.1 The effect of a price increase on profitability

	Base scenario	−10% Variable costs	−10% Fixed costs	+10% Volume	+10% Price
Price per unit	5.00				5.50
Variable cost per unit	3.00	2.70			
Volume (units)	1,000			1,100	
Revenues	5,000.00	5,000.00	5,000.00	5,500.00	**5,500.00**
−Variable costs	3,000.00	2,700.00	3,000.00	3,300.00	**3,000.00**
Contribution	2,000.00	2,300.00	2,000.00	2,200.00	**2,500.00**
−Fixed costs	1,500.00	1,500.00	1,350.00	1,500.00	**1,500.00**
Profit	500.00	800.00	650.00	700.00	**1,000.00**
		↓	↓	↓	↓
Profit increase compared to base scenario		+60%	+30%	+40%	+100%

Zooming in on ▶ THE CONTRIBUTION MARGIN APPROACH TO PRICING

Kostis Indounas, a pricing expert from the University of Athens, proposed the following market-oriented (rather than cost-based) five-step process for finding the optimal price for a product or service:[17]

1 *Evaluate a price change with regard to the quantity required to make it profitable.* Decision makers first need to understand how much additional sales volume is required to achieve the same level of contribution (and profit) after a price reduction, or how much the sales volume could decrease before the contribution is negatively affected by a price increase (see Figure 9.3).

2 *Understand the value that customers attach to a product or service offer.* Taking a direct approach, customers can be asked about their perception of the value of a product or service. What they say is not always what they would really do, however. Taking an indirect approach, the price of the best alternative offered by competitors can be used as a reference, to which a certain sum is then added (or subtracted) for features that differentiate the two offers. For customers, relative price levels are important—that's how they usually evaluate price fairness.[18]

3 *Estimate how customers react to changes in price levels.* Customers have different zones of price indifference (in which there is no change of demand when the price changes) for different product or service offerings, mainly influenced by the costs that are incurred in the search for alternatives.[19] The inclination to switch to the competition following a price change can vary significantly, for example, between financial products (very low zone of price indifference) and branded consumer goods (high zone of price indifference).[20] Qualitative market research—for example, in the form of focus groups, or using different prices in test markets—can help to identify customer sensitivity to different price levels.

4 *Take the competition into account.* First, this means getting information about the price level of the competition. Industry experts or customers can be a source of price information if it is not publicly available (e.g. in the case of industrial goods). Second, it is also important to think about how the competition is likely to react to a price change and what repercussions this could have. An evaluation of competitors' reactions in the past can help to assess potential future competitive moves.

5 *Make a price change* if the expected total contribution (unit contribution multiplied by the estimated number of units sold) after the price change is higher than the current total contribution before the price change.

$$\text{Percentage change of sales} = \frac{-\text{Unit price change}}{\text{Unit contribution} + \text{Unit price change}} \times 100$$

EXAMPLE

Price per unit	$ 50
Variable costs per unit	$ 35
Unit contribution (price minus variable costs)	$ 15
Price change of −5%	−$ 2.5

$$\text{Percentage change in sales} = \frac{2.5}{15+(-2.5)} \times 100 = 20\%$$

➔ In this case, a price change of −5% requires additional sales of +20% to achieve the same level of contribution (and profit)

Figure 9.3 Calculating a change of sales volume that offsets a change in price

Source: Based on information in Indounas (2006).

Most organizations offer a range of different products and services at different price levels. It is important to find out which of these prices (usually those for the base products or services) has the function of an **anchor price**—the price that is most commonly used for price comparisons by customers.[21] This could, for example, again be the price of a cup of coffee in a bar. Changing an anchor price can potentially influence the general price perceptions of customers relative to the competition (what would you think of a bar that charges €20 for a cup of coffee?).

On a more strategic level, there are a range of different **pricing strategies** that managers can use to increase their organization's profitability:[22]

1 **Versioning**: offering different versions of a product or service at different price levels;
2 **Price bundling**: combining different products for one joint price;
3 **Price unbundling**: selling basics and extras separately; setting higher prices for ancillary products or services;
4 Setting **prices according to capacity utilization**, e.g. different prices for peak and off-peak times;
5 **Discriminating between customer groups**, e.g. setting different prices for different age groups, or for corporate clients and consumers;
6 **Communicating value to customers** to increase customers' perception of value and decrease their price sensitivity;
7 Offering a **fixed price at a future date** (e.g. discounts for pre-orders);
8 **Splitting the total price** into different price or discount components;
9 Increasing prices **in small, incremental steps**;
10 **Changing the general pricing logic**, e.g. from pay-per-use to prepaid subscription.

Some organizations have also started to use **pricing software tools** that allow managers to combine data from different sources (e.g. past pricing and customer demand data, competitors' prices, or data on discounts) in order to analyze which prices lead to the highest profit levels. Such software solutions can help to estimate the price elasticity of demand of different target segments, run pricing simulations, and find the optimal price level for certain products or services with the help of mathematical and statistical methods. A survey conducted by a globally active management consultancy firm found a strong correlation between the use of pricing software and the satisfaction that managers in the business-to-business segment expressed regarding the pricing decisions that were made in their organization.[23]

Whatever pricing strategy they use in their organizations, and regardless of whether pricing software tools are used or not, managers need to be aware that the price level must always be in line with the value perceptions of customers. When prices are higher than the perceived value, customers simply will not buy a product or service—and that would be the end of profitability.

WHAT WOULD YOU DO

Think of your favorite local restaurant. If you were the manager of this restaurant, which three actions do you think would be most effective in sustainably improving the restaurant's profitability level?

9.2 Managing cash flow

Pixabay/PublicDomainPictures

In brief

● Managing cash flow is an essential task for managers in charge of an organization. An organization that does not have enough cash and is not able to pay its bills puts its very existence at risk.

● The cash flow statement summarizes the cash inflows and cash outflows of an organization during a certain period. Cash flow can relate to operating activities (transforming inputs into outputs in the core business), investment activities, or financing activities.

● To deliberately influence cash flow from operating activities, managers need to understand the cash conversion cycle and its individual components: days payable outstanding, days sales outstanding, and days in inventory.

● Effective open receivables management and inventory management, in particular, can help to improve the cash position of an organization.

Cash:
In accounting terms, cash is used for money in hand (coins and banknotes that were issued by the government) and in bank accounts as well as payment tools such as checks or money orders. Sometimes the term cash also includes *cash equivalents*, highly liquid assets that can be quickly converted into cash (e.g. marketable securities).

Cash is often characterized as the "lifeblood of an organization." Without adequate liquidity—having enough cash to meet all immediate and short-term payment obligations (for example, to suppliers and employees)—an organization faces **insolvency**. Managing cash is therefore a vital task for managers to keep their organizations alive. In a financial context, cash includes the physical form of currency (banknotes and coins) in the cash register and also deposits held in bank and money market accounts. Inflows and outflows of cash during a certain accounting period are recorded in the **cash flow statement**, divided into **cash flow from operating activities**, **cash flow from investment activities**, and **cash flow from financing activities** (see Figure 9.4).

Insolvency:
The inability of an organization to meet its financial obligations when they become due.

Cash flow statement:
A summary statement of the cash transactions (sources and uses of cash) of an organization during a certain period.

Cash flow from operating activities:
A summary statement of the amount of cash that an organization generates and uses in its regular business activities.

Cash flow from investment activities:
A summary statement of the amount of cash that an organization receives or pays in selling and purchasing long-term assets.

Cash flow from financing activities:
A summary statement of the amount of cash that an organization receives or pays in its external financing activities, for example, raising new share capital (e.g. through issuing more stock) or repaying investors (e.g. in the form of dividends or repurchasing stock), issuing or paying off bonds, and increasing or repaying loans.

Cash conversion cycle:
A financial metric that measures the time that it takes for an organization to convert cash outflows for stocking up its inventory into cash inflows from sales to customers.

CASH FLOW STATEMENT

Cash receipts from customers
  −Cash paid to suppliers and employees
  −Cash paid for other operating expenses
  −Interest paid (or + interest received)
  −Income taxes paid

1. Net cash flow from operating activities

  −Purchases of property, plant, and equipment
  +Proceeds from sale of property, plant, and equipment

2. Net cash flow from investing activities

  +Proceeds from issue of share capital
  +Proceeds from long-term borrowings
  −Repayment of borrowings/payments of finance lease liabilities
  −Dividends paid

3. Net cash flow from financing activities

Cash at beginning of period
+/− 1./2./3.
Cash at end of period

Figure 9.4 Typical structure of a cash flow statement (direct method)

The cash conversion cycle

The cash position of an organization can be improved by selling assets, receiving new capital from shareowners or bank loans, or increasing the amount of cash that is generated from operating activities. For the latter, managers need to understand the **cash conversion cycle (CCC)**, which measures the average number of days between cash outflows for supplies provided and invoiced by external suppliers and cash inflows from goods and services that the organization sells (see Figure 9.5). During the CCC, cash is invested and "tied up" in purchasing supplies, the production process, holding inventory, and the sales process before new cash flows in from selling goods and services. The CCC consists of three parts: days in inventory, days payable outstanding, and days sales outstanding.

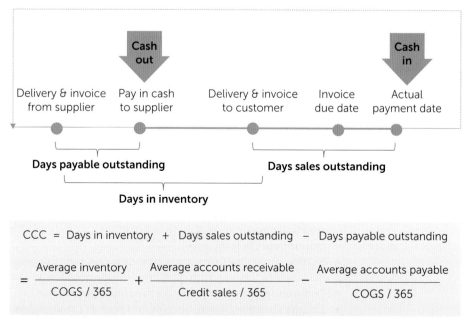

Figure 9.5 The cash conversion cycle (CCC)

Days in inventory refers to the average number of days between the date of delivery of the resources by the supplier and the date of delivery of the final goods to the customer. In the interim the resources are held as stock or used in the production process. For example, in a brewery, days in inventory will be the average time it takes between receiving hops, malt, and yeast from suppliers and delivery of the beer to customers. To calculate the days in inventory, the average value of inventory at the beginning and the end of an accounting period is divided by the average total cost of goods sold (COGS) per day.

The term **days payable outstanding** refers to the average number of days between the date of delivery of resource inputs from suppliers and the date the organization actually makes payment to suppliers. In business-to-business relationships, most payments are made on open account. This means that the buyer agrees to pay the invoice at a future date rather than at the time of delivery or invoicing. Our brewery could, for example, make an agreement with its hops, malt, and yeast suppliers that it will pay the invoices for these raw materials within a maximum of 30 days after delivery. In the (unlikely) case that no other resources would be needed for the beer production (just think about the beer bottles), the brewery would have 30 days payable outstanding if it always fully used the 30 days supplier credit. Days payable outstanding are calculated as the average amount of accounts payable (money that an organization owes to suppliers for goods and services that have already been delivered or used but have not been paid yet) at the beginning and the end of an accounting period divided by the average purchases per day. Average purchases per day are usually calculated as the cost of goods sold per year divided by 365 days.

Days sales outstanding is the average number of days between the delivery of goods to the organization's customers and receipt of payment from them. The brewery might have an arrangement with a customer (e.g. a supermarket chain) which allows the customer to pay for the beer within a period of 45 days after delivery. If the supermarket chain was the only customer of the brewery and if it always fully used the 45 days credit, the 45 days would also be the days sales outstanding of the brewery. Days sales outstanding are calculated as the average amount of accounts receivable (legally enforceable claims for payment of goods and services that have been delivered to or used by customers without having been paid yet) at the beginning and the end of an accounting period divided by the average credit sales per day.

Figure 9.5 provides formulas for calculating these financial ratios and the CCC. By multiplying the CCC (in days) with average sales per day, managers can estimate the **working capital** requirements for financing the operations of their organization, i.e. the funds that are needed to pay all short-term business-related obligations and bridge the gap between operative cash outflows and cash inflows.

So what can managers do to **improve the operating cash flow** of their organizations? They can either try to minimize expenses (through cost reductions, see Section 9.1) or introduce initiatives that "condense" the CCC, through decreasing days in inventory, decreasing days sales outstanding, or increasing days payable outstanding.

Working capital:
A financial measure (usually calculated as current assets minus current liabilities) that indicates whether an organization can cover its short-term obligations with its short-term assets (in accounting terms, short-term means less than 12 months).

Tactics to improve the cash position

The challenge in **inventory management** is to reduce the inventory as much as possible, but never beyond the point where there is not enough stock to continue the production and provision of goods or services to meet customer needs. **Tactics for inventory reduction** include:

- Shifting parts of the inventory to suppliers (e.g. closing an agreement with a supplier to hold immediately accessible inventory of the raw materials that you need directly at or close to your production site).
- Shifting parts of the inventory to customers (e.g. shipping goods to distributors who then hold them in their stocks immediately after the goods are produced).
- Upgrading forecasting systems for sales and inventory use.
- Selling excess inventory of discontinued product ranges or perishable goods at the end of their shelf life at a discount.

Cycle time:
The total time that it takes to complete one "cycle" of a process or operation (i.e. how long it takes from the start to the end of the process).

- Simplifying the product design (in order to reduce the number of parts that need to be kept in inventory).
- Standardizing the product or service offers (to limit variation).
- Optimizing processes (avoid machine downtimes or speed up **cycle time** in order to have fewer inventory needs).
- Implementing inventory management software systems that help managers to track inventory, make more accurate forecasts, and optimize order quantities and reorder points.

Demand variability:
A measurement for how strongly customer demand fluctuates over time (i.e. changes from one period to another).

- Actively trying to reduce **demand variability** (e.g. special offers for non-peak times) in order to reduce the need to hold buffer inventories (safety stock that is used to avoid out-of-stock situations in cases of sudden surges in demand).
- Implementing strategic management approaches oriented toward eliminating inventory and waste; for example, lean manufacturing (see the box *Eliminating waste*) or just-in-time concepts (which are focused on delivering raw materials and producing goods and services exactly at the time when they are needed).

FROM A DIFFERENT ANGLE

Eliminating waste

One strategic approach to reduce inventory is lean manufacturing, which has its roots in the unique production system of Japanese carmaker Toyota. Lean manufacturing is focused on reducing the "3 Mus," waste ("Muda" in Japanese), *overburden* ("Muri"), and *unevenness* ("Mura"). "Muda" includes, for example, unnecessary transportation and waiting times, defects, components that are not processed right away, finished products that are not sold and used, or any work that does not add value. "Muri" occurs when machines or people are overburdened beyond their natural limits to a point where they break down or start making mistakes, respectively. "Mura," unevenness, can result, for example, from fluctuations in customer demand, irregular production schedules, or any other variation during the operation of a process. It is better to work "steady and slow like the tortoise than fast and jerky like a rabbit"[24]—this is how lean management expert Jeffrey Liker explained the principle that continuous flow at a slower speed is usually more effective in terms of eliminating waste (and reducing

inventory) than a production process that is characterized by frequent fluctuations in the amount and speed of work.

The "3 Mus" are inextricably linked with each other. "Mura" in the form of fluctuations in demand and variation in workload can lead to "Muri," the overburden of machines or people, which again often results in different forms of waste, "Muda." Machines that break down or people who are exhausted by the pressure that is put on them, in turn, can also cause unevenness in production processes and waste, for example in the form of downtime or defects.

Managers who follow a lean manufacturing approach will try to fight all "3 Mus" at the same time; for example, through simplifying and standardizing the design of products and production processes, ensuring continuous flow through the processes, and trying to identify and eliminate the root causes of unevenness and overburden of machines and people.

Sources: Based on information in Eaton (2013); Liker (2004).

Open receivables:
Legally enforceable (but usually unsecured) claims for the payment of goods and services that an organization has already delivered, but which have not yet been paid by the customer.

The challenge of **decreasing days sales outstanding** lies in getting paid as quickly as possible by your customers without any negative effects on future business opportunities with them. The following tactics can be used to **reduce open receivables**, money that is owed by customers who have not yet paid for goods and services that they have already received or used:[25]

- Avoiding high-risk customers through a rigorous credit review of every new customer.
- Ongoing customer reviews to drop customers who are notorious defaulters.

- Adjusting payment terms, the conditions that are agreed upon between a buyer and a seller about when and how a payment will be made for the delivery of goods and services (e.g. reducing the payment period from 30 to 14 days).
- Offering early payment discounts to motivate customers to pay sooner (e.g. the offer to deduct 2 percent from the invoice sum when the invoice is paid within 7 days instead of the usual 30 days).
- Improving quality management procedures (because quality problems or late delivery can result in delayed payment).
- Establishing good relationships with customers (to get preferred treatment and payment).
- Using a factoring model in which open receivables are sold to a third party (usually a financial institution, also known as the "factor") at a discount in exchange for immediate cash payment.
- Tighter open receivables management, including a systematic collection policy that is also rigorously enforced, using capable people for the collection of open receivables, daily analysis of overdue customers, and constant follow-up ("making noise").

The challenge of **increasing days payable outstanding** is getting and using supplier credit for a longer period without negative impact on the organization's credit rating and relationships with suppliers. Managers can try to increase the time between receiving goods or services from suppliers and payment to them, for example, by paying at the latest point that the credit terms allow, renegotiating payment terms with suppliers, establishing good relationships with suppliers that allow them to get their support in times when the cash situation is more difficult, or purchasing on **consignment** if possible.[26]

In addition to operative measures for improving the CCC, managers can also take a strategic approach and think about whether a **change of business model** could fundamentally improve their organization's cash situation. For example, a video streaming platform could considerably improve its cash position by changing its business model from pay-per-use to a prepaid subscription offer, in which cash is received on a regular basis before users watch the videos.

Consignment:
A trust-based trading arrangement whereby party A hands over goods to another party B who is supposed to sell the goods. The goods remain in the legal ownership of party A until party B has actually sold them.

Think about your favorite local restaurant again. If you were the manager of this restaurant, which three actions would you take to condense the cash conversion cycle of the business?

Whether through short-term or more strategic measures, managing cash flow is an important managerial task. Any organization needs to pay its bills. And bills are not paid from profits but from cash, "because profits aren't real money. Cash is."[27] This is also the reason why it is important for managers to regularly monitor cash flow and to establish a reliable system for **cash flow forecasting**. Cash inflows and cash outflows are usually planned on a yearly basis as part of an integrated financial planning process. They include the cash demands of running the business, and also investments, tax payments, and cash requirements for business growth, as well as the sources of financing.

In a highly dynamic and uncertain environment, it can also make sense to analyze cash needs in different scenarios. Ideally, the resulting cash plan is aligned with both investors (owners) and lenders of capital. Making ongoing twice monthly (or at least monthly) cash projections for 30, 60, and 90 days, as well as for a year, is good practice.[28] Cash reports are often prepared by a controlling or finance department on a weekly basis, and are reviewed and discussed in top management meetings—often as the first item on the agenda, thus acknowledging the overarching importance of cash flow as the lifeblood of a business.[29]

ALDI: The "gigantic cash machine"

In the early 1960s, brothers Karl and Theo Albrecht reorganized their family business, a chain of retail stores in Germany, into two separate entities. Karl's company, ALDI Süd, would cover the southern part of the country, and Theo's company, ALDI Nord, the northern part. The two brothers introduced a new store concept to the market—the discount store (ALDI stands for "Albrecht Discount"). Their basic idea was to sell only a limited selection of groceries at very cheap prices directly from cartons wheeled on pallets into a no-frills storage and sales room.

The concept was an instant success, and all other outlets of the Albrechts' retail chains were quickly converted to the new discount model too. "The investments into a new store are already covered after half a month," wrote *Frankfurter Allgemeine Zeitung*, one of Germany's leading daily newspapers, calling ALDI a "gigantic cash machine."[30] A German business professor even speculated that ALDI had a negative cash conversion cycle, meaning that it received money from its customers before it had to pay its suppliers.[31] In 2019, the two ALDI companies operated several thousand retail stores in Germany and 18 other countries in Europe, America, Asia, and Australia.

In every market ALDI enters, it becomes a menace to incumbent grocery retailers. For example in the US, ALDI and its German rival Lidl have recently expanded their store network and market share aggressively. Consumers from all educational backgrounds and income levels are attracted by the low prices and no-nonsense shopping experience that allows them to buy essential goods in a fast and convenient way (the stores are relatively small and have an easy-to-understand standardized layout) without having to compromise on quality. ALDI actually puts a very strong emphasis on quality, with high quality standards for suppliers, standardized quality management processes, daily blind tastings, and extensive quality controls that considerably exceed both legal and industry standards. ALDI also has a generous returns policy when consumers are not entirely satisfied with their purchase.

Although concrete business figures remain a secret in the privately held ALDI group, industry experts estimate that ALDI's profit margin lies way above the industry average. But how is ALDI able to profitably offer high-quality goods at extremely low price levels? Commentators have highlighted the following reasons:

- ALDI is strongly devoted to keeping things as simple as possible. As an organization, ALDI has flat hierarchies, lean corporate functions (the most important are centralized purchasing and cash management), fast decision-making processes, and clear targets and competencies that everyone understands. Instead of having inflated corporate structures, ALDI is organized as a network of decentralized regional companies that are typically responsible for around 50–70 stores in a limited geographic area. Decentralization reduces complexity while increasing flexibility and local market knowledge.

- In an ALDI store, there are usually only around 1,000 to 1,500 items (weekly "must-haves") on offer. A typical German supermarket would offer 10,000–15,000 stock-keeping units, a Walmart store in the US 30,000–40,000. The limited product line allows ALDI to focus on merchandise that is sold in high turnover in smaller stores that have lower rent and electricity costs than traditional supermarkets. To avoid failure, new merchandise is first tested in a few stores before being rolled out across the store network.

- The vast majority of articles are sold under private labels (the retailer's in-house brands). The goods are purchased in high quantities to reap the advantages of economies of scale.

- ALDI does not have complex terms of purchase for its suppliers. The goods are exclusively delivered in cartons on pallets, and are then placed in the store in a logistically optimized way. There are no in-store promotions, coupons, loyalty cards, or other promotional deals.

- The core store staff in the stores is well trained and able to work in different functions (e.g. at the cash desk, in arranging fruits and vegetables, or in quality control). Because the pallets are wheeled in by forklifts, shelf-stocking tasks are minimized. Counter service departments do not exist.

- Frugality is a core value that permeates the organization. Legend has it that Karl Albrecht used both sides of each sheet of paper to avoid waste and would always turn out the light when daylight was getting brighter. Cost cutting did not affect wages, however. ALDI Süd's staff receives wages that are considerably above the industry average, because Karl Albrecht was convinced that "[w]ell paid people perform better."[32]

- All processes are standardized and constantly optimized to maximize productivity. For example, there are three to four bar codes on each product sold at ALDI to shorten scanning times at the cash desks. Merchandise is commissioned in central warehouses in exactly the same order as it is later placed in the store. Everything is pre-packaged and self-service.

Consumer preferences and the competitive situations change, however. Traditional retailers are luring customers with attractive new counters, high-quality regional and organic products, friendly staff, smaller packages for the increasing number of single households, and aggressive pricing of their own private label budget brands. In the US, market leader Walmart has slashed prices in an effort to compete head on with ALDI. Online retail giant Amazon. com also entered the bricks-and-mortar grocery business with the acquisition of the American supermarket chain Whole Foods and the launch of the checkout-less convenience store Amazon Go, while at the same time extending its online grocery delivery service.

In recent years, for the first time in decades, discounters have begun to lose market share in Germany. But ALDI has a track record of adapting to changing consumer needs. It

has reacted by further enhancing the attractiveness of weekly non-food special buys, online services and travel offers, an extensive organic food product line, an enhanced wine department, and automatized ovens to offer fresh bakery goods. Billions of euros are being invested in a store revamping initiative with the goal of making the stores brighter, more neatly arranged, and more appealing to consumers. The initiative also included the extension of fresh produce offers. An analyst on the BBC website commented that these are "features we would traditionally associate with a supermarket than a discounter," suggesting that "they are expanding growth by moving away from a pure discounter model."[33]

Sources: aldi-sued.de (2019); bbc.com (2017); Bose (2017); Brandes (2004); forbes.com (2015); Gnirke et al. (2016); Harris (2018); Koether (2012); Müller von Blumencron (2014); Sachon and Mitchell (2005).

💬 Discussion questions

- Why was ALDI called a "gigantic cash machine" in a German newspaper?
- What does ALDI do to achieve cost and price leadership?
- How would you evaluate the strategies that ALDI follows to react to changing consumer needs and industry trends from a profitability and cash management perspective?
- What could a company in a completely different industry (take a manufacturing firm in the business-to-business sector, for example) learn from the cost and cash management approaches of ALDI?

9.3 Increasing value

iStock.com/simonkr

In brief

- Although the balance sheet gives an overview of an organization's present asset base, it tells us little about the actual value of an organization.

- The value of an asset or a business as a whole is determined by its potential to generate profits and cash in the future, which is linked, in turn, not only to current profitability and cash flow levels, but also to future growth opportunities, the existence of a sustainable competitive advantage, and the level of risk to which the asset or business is exposed.

- Several valuation methods exist, but they only provide estimates. An "absolutely true" value of a business is difficult to determine.

- Although some organizations see risk management mainly as a means to avoid losses in value, it can also be used as a strategic tool for creating value.

Value:
What something (for example, a business or an asset) is worth—in business often measured in monetary terms (i.e. what someone is willing to pay for it).

Profits and positive cash flow are highly important for the survival of an organization. An organization's ultimate purpose, however, usually lies in **value creation**. According to the *Oxford Dictionary*, value is the "importance, worth, or usefulness of something."[34] It can refer to both the monetary or material worth of something, but also—in a more encompassing

"Real value":
A contribution to improving the material and immaterial quality of life of different stakeholder groups.

sense—to **"real value,"** everything that enables people to live a better life (see also Section 9.4).[35] Although there are certainly exceptions, businesses are often oriented primarily toward the creation of value in a monetary sense. In this context, the value of something (e.g. a company or an asset) is—in very simple terms—how much money someone is willing to pay for it.

The balance sheet (see Figure 9.6) is a summary of what an organization owns (**assets**) and owes (**liabilities**), as well as what shareholders have invested in the business (**shareholders' equity**), at a certain point in time. It is usually created according to national or international accounting standards and aims to provide a true and fair representation of the current assets base, as well as of the sources of financing of an organization. A balance sheet does not, however, provide comprehensive information about the actual value of an organization.

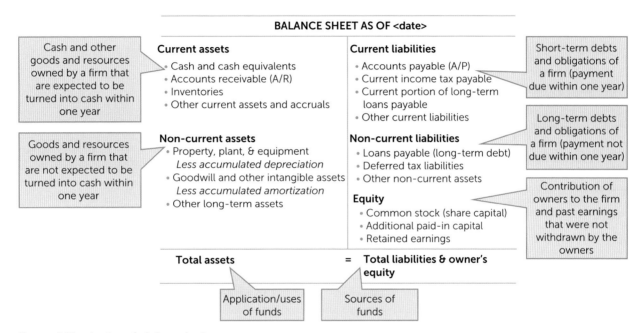

Figure 9.6 The structure of a balance sheet

Assets:
Resources of measurable economic value that are owned by an individual or organization.

The value of an asset or company is linked to its **potential to generate profits and cash**. The potential to generate profits and cash in the future, however, is not necessarily equivalent to yesterday's profits or cash flow. It is also dependent on **future growth opportunities** (growth means that more profits and cash can potentially be generated in the future), the existence of a **sustainable competitive advantage** (as a precondition for being able to sustain profitability and cash flow levels in the future), and the **risks** involved in the business (and, by implication, also the resilience of an organization in relation to these risks).

Out of the four main **drivers of business value** (see Figure 9.7), only profitability and cash flow can actually be seen in the balance sheet or any other financial statement. Competitive advantage, resilience, and growth potential can lie, for example, in having a good reputation with customers, a highly educated and motivated team, special know-how about the use of cutting-edge technology, or the unique spirit of an organizational culture—and it is anything but easy to measure such factors in an objective way.

Liabilities:
Obligations of an organization that are expected to lead to cash outflows in the future (e.g. amounts that a company owes to lenders and suppliers).

Valuation methods

As Figure 9.7 shows, it is not enough to solely consider financial figures when trying to determine the value of an organization. That said, different financial methods of estimating the value of a business have been developed. The most commonly used methods include:[36]

● **Market capitalization** of public companies: Multiplying the stock price by the number of shares outstanding.

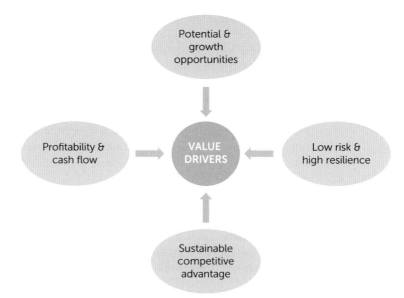

Figure 9.7 The drivers of
business value

Profit multiples:
A (relatively simplistic)
method of valuing a
business by means of
multiplying profit
figures by a factor that
reflects the ratio
between profits and the
market value of
comparable businesses.

- **Industry rules of thumb**: In some industries, there are more or less commonly agreed ideas of how much a business is worth in relation to certain financial indicators (e.g. a certain percentage of annual commissions for an insurance agency or a certain sum per guestroom for a hotel);
- **Market value approach**: Comparing the business with other businesses that were recently sold, for example, according to **profit multiples** or a **price-to-earnings ratio**.
- **Asset-based valuation**: Trying to determine the fair current market value of all assets that a company owns minus its total liabilities.
- **Discounted cash flow method**: Forecasting the cash flow that a business will most likely generate in the future, and then discounting the cash flow to its net present value (determining the value today using the estimated cost of capital as a **discount rate**).

**Price-to-earnings
ratio (P/E ratio):**
A financial ratio that is
calculated by dividing
the share price by the
earnings per share of a
company. It describes
how many times the
stock price is higher
than the earnings
(usually defined as net
income minus
dividends for preferred
stock) that are allocated
to each outstanding
share of common stock.

Managers need to be aware that all of these methods are based on estimates and assumptions. Determining the "absolute" value of a business is therefore an illusion. Using multiple methods and comparing their results can, however, at least help make better estimates.

Managers can try to **increase the value** of their organization by setting initiatives related to all four value drivers shown in Figure 9.7. They can, for example, optimize profitability (see Section 9.1) and the cash position (see Section 9.2), develop and implement strategies that enhance the competitive position, actively build potential, create growth opportunities for their organizations (see Chapter 7), and identify, avoid, or mitigate risks, thus improving their organizations' resilience.

Managing risks

Risks can come in many forms. To name just a few, machine breakdowns or supply shortages can bring production to a halt; debtors can default; goods can be damaged in transport; new technologies can render existing solutions irrelevant; new market entrants can create more value for customers; fluctuating exchange rates can result in losses for international businesses; and new laws can have a negative effect on business conditions.

Mitigating risks is one path to value creation. **Risk management** is a coordinated approach to identifying the most important threats to an organization, assessing their potential impact, and developing and implementing strategies to avoid or reduce negative impacts. Basic strategies for managing risks include:[37]

- **Risk assessment**: Trying to find out what would happen if certain events occurred; assessing the likely consequences and possible reactions.

Discounted cash flow method:
A method for analyzing the value of a company or an asset by means of calculating the present value of all anticipated future cash flows using the estimated cost of capital as a discount rate. It is based on the idea of the time value of money—that cash flows today are worth more than cash flows in the future (because today's cash flows can be invested to generate more returns in the future).

Discount rate:
In discounted cash flow analysis, the discount rate is the estimated cost of capital that is used to determine the net present value of future cash flows. A frequently used discount rate is the average rate of return that the shareholders and lenders expect to receive from the company.

- **Risk avoidance**: Trying not to engage in risky activities, for example not entering a new foreign market with high legal or political risks.
- **Risk reduction**: Taking precautionary measures to decrease the likelihood of an event with a negative impact, for example improving safety at work or regular maintenance of equipment.
- **Risk transfer**: Insuring against risks or trying to transfer the risk to suppliers, customers, distributors, or outsourcing partners.

An important way to reduce risks is **diversification**. Being dependent on just a few customers or suppliers, one particular market, or one key employee—to highlight just a few examples—can be dangerous because the loss of one partner or a downturn in one market would lead to a crisis situation for the whole organization. Not investing all efforts and resources into just one project (or person, product, business partner, or market) is therefore an important strategy to reduce risk and achieve a higher level of resilience.

The rise of the Internet as a ubiquitous communication medium has strongly increased one particular type of risk, **reputational risk**. An organization's reputation can be damaged not only by events that lead to negative publicity (for example, ethically questionable behavior—see also Chapter 5), but also by the management's reaction to these events. Thinking upfront about how to communicate in a crisis situation can therefore also be seen as a strategy for risk reduction. Reputational risks are also becoming more relevant as expectations about the social and environmental performance of organizations grow (see Section 9.4).

Zooming in on ▶ RISK ASSESSMENT

A widely used tool to analyze the risks that are involved in a project, business process, or organization is the risk assessment matrix. It provides a one-page overview of the main risks. Its basic function is to prioritize risks, usually according to two dimensions: probability that the risk will occur and severity of impact if it does happen. Here is how the risk assessment process usually works:[38]

1 *Identify all the risks that could have a negative impact*. It is important in this first phase to take a wider perspective in order to make sure that no important risk category is neglected. The PESTEL and Porter's five forces frameworks (see Chapter 7) can be used to examine political, economic, socio-demographic, technological, environmental, or legal risks in the macro environment as well as risks in the industry environment. Internal risks include, for example, the risk of financial losses, operational risks (e.g. machine breakdowns, damage of goods during transportation, or IT system failures), and compliance risks (e.g. the violation of data protection laws, accounting fraud, or other corrupt practices).

2 *Assess risks according to pre-defined assessment criteria*. The most widely used criteria are probability of impact (e.g. on a scale of "almost certain," "likely," "possible," "unlikely," and "rare"—with certain percentages attached for the chance of occurrence within a certain timeframe, e.g. >80 percent within the next three years for "almost certain") and severity of impact (e.g. on a scale of "extreme," "major," "moderate," "minor," and "incidental")—with a definition of the amount of financial losses or negative effects on staff motivation or reputation for each rating. The likelihood and impact of each risk can be analyzed with the help of internal and external data, expert opinions, interviews, surveys or workshops. Another criterion that can be used for risk assessment is speed of onset (i.e. the time that it takes for an organization to feel the negative effects after a certain event occurs).

3 *Prioritize risks with the help of the risk assessment matrix*. Each risk can be plotted on a risk assessment matrix (also known as "risk map" or "heat map") (see Figure 9.8). Risks with higher likelihood and greater impact are seen as the most critical.

4 *Manage the critical risks*. Appropriate response strategies should be developed for the critical risks that were identified in the risk assessment matrix. Are there possible actions that could be taken in order to avoid, reduce or transfer the risk, or do we need to accept the risk?

Risk assessment is not a one-time event, but an ongoing endeavor because risks are likely to change over time. It is also important to be aware that inputs and outputs of risk assessment matrices are often based on subjective interpretations. Thus, they need to be used with an adequate level of caution.[39]

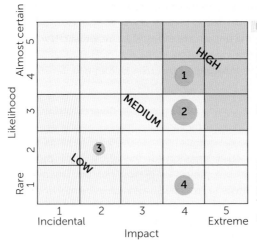

Figure 9.8 An example of a risk assessment map

Figure source: Adapted from Exhibit 7: Illustrative Heat Map, p.16 in Curtis, P. and Carey, M. (2012) *Thought Leadership in ERM: Risk Assessment in Practice* (Durham, NC: COSO), available at https://www.coso.org/Documents/COSO-ERM-Risk-Assessment-in-Practice-Thought-Paper-October-2012.pdf. Reprinted with permission from Committee of Sponsoring Organizations of the Treadway Commission. Copyright © 2012 COSO.

Box source: Inspired by Curtis and Carey (2012).

Think of your favorite local restaurant again. What would you see as the most important risks that could have a negative impact on the business? If you were the manager of this restaurant, how would you manage these risks?

9.4 Beyond financial results

In brief

- As sustainability and stakeholder-oriented concepts are becoming more important, so is the need for a more encompassing perspective on organizational results.

- In addition to financial outcomes, organizations also have their social and environmental performances to consider. Several methods have been developed to account for these results categories. The triple bottom line, for example, is a tool that managers can use to assess the effect of their organization on the "3Ps:" people, profit, and the planet.

- By being involved in the process of defining a purpose for their organizations, managers can also influence which results are considered important. Maximizing shareholder value is one, but not the only, purpose that an organization can follow.

- Organizations can also opt for a strategy of creating "real value" in the sense of striving to improve the quality of life for different stakeholder groups (e.g. customers, employees, or the community).

Profitability and positive cash flow are absolutely important for the **short-term economic viability** of an organization. Optimizing both is part of the performance responsibility of a manager. Value creation in financial terms (as described in Section 9.3), in turn, relates to a manager's **long-term potential-building responsibility** (see Chapter 1). All these results categories are oriented toward maintaining the economic health of the organization and expanding the wealth of its shareholders. They do not, however, explicitly address the societal side of managerial responsibility.

Non-financial results categories

With increasing doubts about the **shareholder value paradigm**, which asserts that maximizing the wealth of shareholders should be the highest (or even only) goal for businesses, **sustainability**, **shared value**, and stakeholder-oriented business concepts are gaining more and more support (although there are still regional differences here—see the box *Cross-cultural differences and perspectives on performance*). These approaches require new, broader ways of measuring organizational performance. Because it is commonly realized that "today's reality is that firms are under tremendous pressure to monitor and report on more than just their economic performance,"[40] over 90 percent of the world's largest 250 companies are now reporting on non-financial outcomes of their activities.[41]

There are several reasons for the increased use of systems to assess an organization's **social performance** (the impact of the organization on the communities in which it is embedded) and **environmental performance** (the natural resource use and environmental emissions that can be attributed to an organization) in addition to its **economic performance**:

- legislative pressure in an increasing number of countries;
- peer pressure as other companies in an industry start to account for the sustainability of their organizations;
- "greenwashing"—trying to show the organization in the best possible light to the public for marketing purposes without really being fully committed to sustainability;
- ethical reasons (a moral obligation felt by managers); and
- seeing a business case in sustainability (i.e. potential for cost reductions or an increase in sales).[42]

Many managers recognize that their organizations' sustainability-related behaviors and outcomes can become a competitive advantage that helps them to attract talent and convince customers that they are a more responsible—and thus preferable—choice than the competition.[43] In addition, collecting data and reporting on the **non-financial performance** of an organization can also be seen as a strategic tool to map potential future risks, enabling the organization to address them as early as possible.[44]

Methods of reporting on social and environmental performance

The social and environmental impacts of an organization can be reported in the following formats, for example:[45]

- **Tables of key social and environmental performance indicators** for a certain period.
- **Input-output analysis**, accounting for the material and energy inputs that are used by an organization and the emissions and waste that it produces within a certain timeframe.
- **Life cycle assessment**, an analysis of the environmental impacts of producing and using a product "from cradle to grave," i.e. from raw material extraction to disposal or recycling.
- Reports on the **distribution of the economic value added** that is created by an organization between different stakeholder groups (e.g. management, employees, shareholders, community, financial partners, local authorities, and state authorities).[46]

Shareholder value paradigm:
The idea that maximizing the wealth of shareholders is the ultimate purpose of a business, and that management should first and foremost consider shareholders' interests when making business decisions.

Sustainability:
In an organizational context, sustainability means trying to ensure that current economic, social, and environmental demands and requirements are met without compromising the organization's ability to meet such demands and requirements in the future too.

Shared value:
Proposed by Michael E. Porter and Mark R. Kramer in 2011, the concept of shared value describes strategies and practices that simultaneously create economic value for a business (through enhancing its competitiveness) and social value for the communities in which the business operates (through having a positive impact on societal conditions).

Cross-cultural differences and perspectives on performance

In setting goals for their organizations, managers can be influenced by both the cultural and institutional environment. In the US, for example, a team of researchers from different continents observed a relatively strong managerial focus on business growth, profitability in the current year, and increasing personal wealth. There, large businesses are typically run by executives on behalf of anonymous shareholders who are usually highly interested in maximizing short-term profits. In contrast, the long-term continuity of the business and family interests are stronger focuses for managers in the British Commonwealth countries, such as India, Jamaica, and the Bahamas, where family-owned companies form the backbone of the economy. In several Northern European countries, by comparison, responsibility toward employees and society ranks comparatively high on the agenda.

Recent studies have confirmed that European companies clearly outperform North American and Asian ones in **corporate social performance**. Possible explanations for this include different consumer demands and pressure for social responsibility, different regulatory environments (including reporting requirements for social and environmental performance), and generally a more stakeholder-oriented model of corporate governance in Europe. For example, in some European countries such as Germany, Austria, and the Netherlands, corporations have a two-tier board structure with an executive board and a non-executive supervisory board, which appoints the executive directors and reviews major business decisions. It is required by law that both shareholder and employee representatives are adequately represented in the supervisory board. Thus, employee interests are more in the spotlight than in the Anglo-American model in which the single-tier boards of directors are usually dominated by shareholder representatives. Cultural factors could play a role here, too. For example, research results indicate that companies tend to have better corporate social performance in cultures where people have a higher preference for non-materialistic values such as progress toward a more humane society and in societies where developing new ideas for the future is given more prominence than financial considerations.

Sources: Based on information in Arminen et al. (2018); Ho et al. (2012); Hofstede et al. (2002)

Corporate social performance:
Outcomes of pro-social behavior by organizations that are beneficial for society and the environment from the perspective of key stakeholder groups.

- **Narratives of sustainability-related actions** as well as social and environmental impacts. Social reports, for example, can summarize how an organization performs in relation to respecting human rights, complying with legal and moral standards, ensuring the welfare of its employees and the health and safety of its customers, maintaining fair relationships with suppliers, contributing to local communities, or limiting inequity—both inside the organization and along the whole value chain, i.e. also regarding impacts that are originated by the suppliers of inputs or by distribution partners.

Some organizations publish separate **sustainability reports** on a regular basis; others integrate information on their social and environmental performance in their annual reports. External verification of these reports and attestations by auditors are becoming more widespread.[47]

Triple bottom line:
A term used by John Elkington to point out that organizations do not only have one results category (the financial "bottom line"), but that three dimensions of organizational performance should be taken into account: financial, environmental, and social.

A common method for accounting for all three aspects of an organization's sustainability performance, the effect on people (social responsibility), the planet (environmental responsibility), and profits (economic responsibility), is the **triple bottom line (TBL)** approach.[48] The TBL adds environmental and social measures of performance to financial results, thereby challenging "the traditionally held assumption that *any* number alone—including net income—can meaningful[ly] capture the appropriate assessment of corporate performance."[49] Of the several versions of TBL, the **Global Reporting Initiative (GRI)** standard, developed in a multi-stakeholder dialogue, is one of the most widely used. It includes both a comprehensive set of indicators (see Table 9.2) and detailed implementation guidelines.

Table 9.2 The triple bottom line indicators of the Global Reporting Initiative

Category	Sub-category	Aspects
Economic		Economic Performance Market Presence Indirect Economic Impacts Procurement Practices Anti-corruption Anti-competitive Behavior
Environmental		Materials Energy Water Biodiversity Emissions Effluents and Waste Environmental Compliance Supplier Environmental Assessment
Social	Labor Practices and Decent Work	Employment Labor/Management Relations Occupational Health and Safety Training and Education Diversity and Equal Opportunities
	Human Rights	Non-discrimination Freedom of Association and Collective Bargaining Child Labor Forced or Compulsory Labor Security Practices Right of Indigenous Peoples Human Rights Assessment
	Society	Local Communities Supplier Social Assessment Public Policy
	Product Responsibility	Customer Health and Safety Marketing and Labeling Customer Privacy Socio-economic Compliance

Source: Based on information in GRI (2016), p. 3.

For smaller organizations, all-encompassing reporting guidelines like those proposed by the GRI are often too resource intensive to implement. These organizations can still follow a TBL approach, however, by identifying and tracking a reduced set of key performance indicators in the areas of economic, social, and environmental responsibility. In addition to ensuring transparency of the organizational performance toward stakeholders, a main function of sustainability accounting is to provide relevant information for managerial decision making—i.e. to assist managers in reaching organizational goals.[50]

If you were the manager of your favorite restaurant, which key performance indicators would you use to track the social and environmental impact of your business?

The ultimate purpose of the organization

Although initiatives like the GRI have increased the availability of instruments and standards for measuring non-financial organizational results, they often fail to provide guidance about how these results should be prioritized.[51] Despite a historically widespread belief that maximizing shareholder wealth is the top priority or "ultimate yardstick" for business success, Cornell Law School Professor Lynn Stout argues that shareholders are just one party with a contract which gives them limited legal claims toward an organization. However, there is no legal obligation for managers to put the interests of shareholders over the interest of other stakeholder groups such as employees or the local community.[52] It thus lies within the responsibility of top managers to set the priority goals for their organizations, regardless of whether they are monetary or non-monetary goals.

Managers can, of course, choose to make maximizing shareholder value their first priority. However, recognizing "that there is other 'value' than that of money—the value of life, the value of society, the value of quality,"[53] they can also justifiably choose to follow a different strategy of focusing on the creation of what can be referred to as "real value," a contribution to improving people's lives.[54] This is possible not only in public institutions or non-profit organizations, but also in the private sector. Strategic goals and reporting tools can be adjusted to inform managers about progress toward reaching the desired levels of environmental and social outcomes as well as financial results. It also requires active leadership to guide the members of an organization toward a shared commitment to the creation of both, financial and "real" value.

Improving social and environmental performance

Tracking non-financial indicators under a triple bottom line approach can help managers to get a better picture of the social and environmental performance of an organization, just as financial and cost accounting forms the basis for understanding an organization's economic performance. Financial accounting alone does not improve performance, however. Likewise, tracking social and environmental indicators does not automatically improve the social and environmental performance of an organization. In order to do so, managers need to first set priorities about what needs to be improved and then initiate concrete actions that can lead to the desired performance improvements.

CEO BEST PRACTICE

The triple bottom line at Novo Nordisk

According to the 2015 edition of *Harvard Business Review*'s ranking of top executives, Lars R. Sørensen, who heads up the Danish pharmaceutical company Novo Nordisk, was the world's "best-performing CEO." Sørensen is not presumptuous, though, attributing his success as a business leader less to his own strategic genius than to "luck," because his company has focused on providing drugs to treat increasingly widespread illnesses such as diabetes. Novo Nordisk is also known for its socially responsible actions, including the creation and continuous support of a non-profit organization which aims to prevent and treat diabetes in poorer world regions (the *World Diabetes Foundation*).

Novo Nordisk follows a triple bottom line approach to measuring and reporting its results. Sørensen is convinced that social and environmental issues are strongly connected to the long-term viability and value of the business. "If we keep polluting, stricter regulations will be imposed, and energy consumption will become more costly," he said in an interview with *Harvard Business Review*, pointing out that the same logic also applies on the social side. "If we don't treat employees well, if we don't behave as good corporate citizens in our local communities, and if we don't provide inexpensive products for poorer countries, governments will impose regulations on us that will end up being very costly."[55] Rather than just focusing on money making, he tries to engage his team with a higher purpose: "There is nothing more motivating for people than to go to work and save people's lives,"[56] he said, referring to the millions of people who would suffer without the medicine provided by Novo Nordisk.

Interestingly enough, while he may be the "best-performing CEO in the world," Sørensen was also one of the least well paid on the top 100 CEOs list.

→ **Key takeaway**

Having a higher purpose as an organization and doing business in a socially and environmentally responsible way can have a strong positive connection with financial value creation—especially in the long term.

Source: Based on information in Ignatius and McGinn (2015).

Three criteria can be used to **set priorities for social and environmental issues**:[57]

1 What could have significant (positive or negative) impacts on the organization's economic, social, and environmental performance?
2 What is highly important from the perspective of key stakeholders?
3 Where do we have a high potential for improvement?

The process of trying to improve the **social or environmental performance** of an organization could, for example, follow the model described in Figure 9.9.

After the priority issue has been identified (i.e. the manager has a clear understanding of what needs to be improved), it is important to set clear goals about the desired level of performance on specific social or environmental results criteria. For example, if energy use is the priority issue, specific goals could be set to reduce the amount of fuel or electricity consumption within a certain timeframe. In the next step, managers need to identify the processes that affect the social or environmental performance in the results criteria that are the focus of the improvement initiative. Energy use could, for example, depend on the design of the production process, the energy efficiency of the machines, or on logistics processes (e.g. longer transport routes lead to higher energy consumption). It is then possible to think about concrete action steps that could be implemented to change the processes in a way that improves social or environmental results. For example, shipments could be consolidated to reduce the amount of transport, or older machines could be replaced with energy-efficient new ones. The actual results are then monitored and evaluated against the desired level of performance. Did the change in the production and logistics processes, for example, really accomplish the desired reduction in energy use? If necessary, further corrective actions can

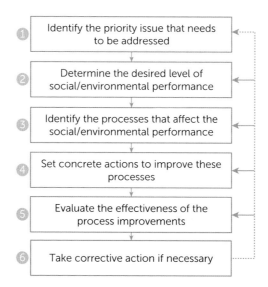

Figure 9.9 A process for improving the social or environmental performance of an organization

Source: Inspired by concepts in Hubbard (2009).

be taken (e.g. further reducing energy use through organizing joint transport in cooperation with other organizations).

Launching and implementing initiatives to improve the social and environmental performance of an organization is also a **change management process**. The people who are managing, contributing to, and affected by the processes that need to be adapted during such initiatives ideally support the change, or at least should not oppose it. Thus, improving the social and environmental performance of an organization is not only a technical task, but also a leadership challenge similar to other strategy execution efforts (see also Chapter 8).

Brunello Cucinelli: Gracious growth of value

Brunello Cucinelli, an Italian fashion entrepreneur, was born into a peasant family in a small village near Perugia, Umbria in the 1950s. When he was a boy, his father abandoned the family farm to earn a wage as a factory worker. Observing how his father felt humiliated and treated like "a slave"[58] in the factory made a deep impression on the boy, who would later become an advocate of a more humane form of capitalism with high respect for human dignity.

In the late 1970s, Cucinelli had the business idea of selling dyed cashmere in the "absolute luxury" segment of the fashion market. His high-quality "sporty-chic" fashion items were well received on both the Italian and international markets. High-quality raw materials sourced through fair and long-lasting supplier relationships, outstanding design, 100 percent Italian craftsmanship in collaboration with over 300 artisanal workshops, and an exclusive retail network form the main pillars of the company's business model. The garments are sold in over 120 Brunello Cucinelli-branded boutiques in upscale high street locations and exclusive multi-brand stores and luxury department stores around the world. Exclusivity has its price, however. For example, men can buy a handwoven cardigan for around €3,000, women a down jacket for over €5,000.

Despite the extremely high prices and fierce competition in the absolute luxury segment, the company's products are selling well around the world. Cucinelli is convinced that "[t]here will always be someone wanting to ... purchase these special handcrafted products."[59] In the financial year 2017, Brunello Cucinelli reported revenue of over €505 million (compared to €281 million in 2012 and €415 million in 2015). In terms of total revenue, 16.8 percent came from Italy, 30.0 percent from the rest of Europe, 35.5 percent from North America, 8.5 percent from Greater China, and 9.2 percent from the rest of the world. Greater China had the highest revenue growth rate in 2017, with +36.2 percent compared to the previous year. The company's operating profit (EBIT) was €64.7 million (up 14.3 percent from the previous year).[60]

Cucinelli, however, realized "that economic value is nothing without the human component and that the former cannot survive without the latter."[61] After a few years in business, he moved the business to Solomeo, a small hamlet in rural Umbria that would become the showcase for his philosophy of "human capitalism." He used 20 percent of the company's profits (and later of his dividends) for "investing in humanity,"[62] as he called it, started to renovate the castle and other parts of the village, and established a theater, an amphitheater, a library, and a school of arts and crafts where people could learn skills such as tailoring or gardening.

Cucinelli's workers, who are generally paid approximately 20 percent more than the industry average, arrive at work at 8 a.m., work in light-filled rooms with a view across the Umbrian hills and enjoy a 90-minute lunch break with a subsidized meal (three courses for €3) in a dining hall in a medieval castle (of course, there is also good Italian wine available). The employees are generally not allowed to work or even send e-mails beyond 5:30 p.m. because Cucinelli is convinced that people need to rest: "If I make you overwork, I have stolen your soul,"[63] he said in an interview with *Bloomberg*.

Consultants have reportedly proposed that the company should expand its production more aggressively and shift some of the manufacturing operations to low-cost countries in order to increase profit margins. But Cucinelli fundamentally disagrees. He wants healthy (or "gracious") growth for his company, but not to the disadvantage of his employees or anyone else.

In an effort to increase the financial soundness of his company, in April 2012 Cucinelli decided to list it on the Milan stock exchange, while still remaining the majority shareholder. The initial price per share was €7.75. It increased by almost 50 percent on the first day of trading. After some ups and downs, it reached an all-time-high of €40.80 in August 2018. Despite such high valuation, the company acknowledged that there were also potential risks involved in its business; for example, in the supply and purchasing prices of high-quality cashmere, the availability of adequately skilled craftspeople, or in changing lifestyles as well as new trends and consumer tastes in the fashion market.[64]

Since taking his company public, Cucinelli has remained strongly devoted to placing the human being at the center, striving to "combine the ethics of profit with the in-born value of quality in all its forms: dignity of work, beauty of life, value of craftsmanship, promotion of creativity and exclusivity, harmony with the surrounding environment and the ability to keep pace with the times."[65] In Cucinelli's newest endeavor, called the "Project for Beauty," old factory sites are being pulled down to make way for three huge parks in the valley below Solomeo. With this initiative, Cucinelli wants to preserve "the territory in all its beauty" and leave behind "lovely, harmonious places for those who will come after us."[66]

Sources: Bloomberg (2015); Brunello Cucinelli (2017; 2018); brunellocucinelli.com (2017a; 2017b); Davis (2015); Ford (2012); Koh (2015); Sanderson (2016).

Discussion questions

- What would you see as the main drivers of business value at Brunello Cucinelli?
- What kind of value is Brunello Cucinelli creating beyond financial value?
- Where do you see potential trade-offs between creating financial value and "real value" (improving the quality of life of various stakeholder groups) at Brunello Cucinelli?
- In what way could the creation of "real value" be conducive toward increasing the financial value of the company?

Conclusion

As we have seen in this chapter, managerial results are by no means one-dimensional. Outcomes of managerial work cannot be reduced to a single figure. No doubt, profit and cash flow are important to keep a company alive and thriving, but they are not necessarily an end in themselves. Value creation—both in a financial as well as in a broader, societal sense—goes far beyond a single-minded focus on short-term profit maximization. However, focusing on long-term value creation without keeping an eye on the short-term profit and cash situation can potentially lead to disaster (or, in business terms, to bankruptcy). Thus, it remains a constant challenge for managers to find the right balance between the different results categories.

There are always trade-offs to be made, not only between short-term financial results optimization and long-term value creation or between maximizing monetary outcomes and having a positive impact on society and the environment. Even short-term liquidity and profitability goals can conflict; for example, when holding more cash means that an organization cannot invest money in activities that potentially increase profitability. Managers must therefore always keep an eye on all four major results categories—profit, cash flow, financial value creation, and societal value creation—in order to be able to meet their responsibilities both for the performance of the organization and for building the potential for future performance.

Keeping an eye on all results categories and striking a balance between them does not necessarily mean that all areas of results need to be treated as equally important. As in other trade-off situations, managers can—and must—set priorities. Sometimes, results-related priorities can change for a limited period of time. In crisis times, for example, cash management often takes precedence. Without a clear understanding of the general organizational priorities in terms of results and outcomes, however, it is hard to make the right managerial choices to effectively accomplish the organizational purpose.

Aetna's CEO Mark Bertolini, whom we met in the Introduction to this chapter, clearly makes long-term value creation the focus of his managerial work. He thinks that in management education "we're focusing [too much] on the short term, on a set of metrics that are not really relevant [and] don't really create value in the long run."[67] There is much more to management than just spreadsheets and financial results. According to Bertolini, "in the end, it's not the numbers. It's actually your ability to see the world in a very different way ... then you can start moving the numbers to help support that, and then build a followership and make the tough decisions necessary to make it happen."[68]

✓ Review questions

1   What are the main categories of business results and how are they related?
2   What do we mean when we talk about "profit" and "profitability" in an organizational context?
3   Which general options do managers have to increase the profitability of their organization?
4   Which specific approaches can managers follow to reduce costs in the organization or organizational unit for which they are responsible?
5   Why is cost reduction seen as a leadership task?
6   How can pricing be used as a tool to improve profitability?
7   What is the cash conversion cycle and why is it important for managers?
8   What can managers do to "condense" the cash conversion cycle?
9   Why should managers pay attention to cash flow planning and forecasting?
10   What is the function of a balance sheet and why might the balance sheet fail to provide sufficient information about the actual value of an organization?
11   What are the main drivers of business value?
12   Which methods can be used to determine the value of a business?
13   What can managers do to assess and manage risks?
14   Which approaches can be used to evaluate the social and environmental performance of an organization?
15   How can managers improve the social and environmental performance of their organization?

⑦ Critical reflection questions

1   Investors on the stock exchange often seem to "celebrate" announcements of rigorous cost-cutting initiatives, especially if they are also combined with layoffs. What is your opinion about this?
2   Some organizations try to improve their cash position by paying their bills as late as possible while demanding fast payment from their own debtors. What do you think about such business practices?
3   In this chapter, we briefly discussed different valuation methods. Which method would you see as the most accurate to determine the "true" value of a business?
4   More and more organizations have started to measure and manage their environmental and social performance in addition to their economic performance. In your opinion, is this shift in attention justified or does it distract managers from following and reaching the economic (or financial) goals of their organizations?
5   "Maximizing profits is the ultimate purpose of private sector enterprises." How would you judge this statement?

☛ Managerial implications

- Effective managers achieve results. They ensure that their organization remains liquid and profitable over time, and are oriented toward creating value—both in a financial and a "real" sense (i.e. improving the lives of others). A manager's overall effectiveness will ideally be judged by means of a holistic evaluation of these different results categories rather than solely on the basis of short-term profitability measures.
- Managers have different options for improving the profitability of their organizations, including various pricing strategies, increasing profitable sales volume, introducing new product and service offerings to the market, and reducing costs. Cost cutting is often

associated with layoffs, although a broad range of alternatives exist. Cost reduction is also a leadership task because it affects people and their motivational levels. Ideally, it is not a stand-alone activity, but will be complemented by positive initiatives that pave the way to a better future for the organization.

- Managing cash flow is an essential task for managers because organizations that do not generate enough cash to pay their bills will cease to exist. Thorough cash planning and forecasting as well as thinking about the cash flow implications of managerial decisions form the basis of good cash management. Cash flow from operating activities can be improved by optimizing inventory management, using supplier credit, and trying to reduce the time that elapses before open receivables are paid.

- For managers who aim to increase the value of their organization, it is not enough to focus on cash flow and profitability. Indeed, short-term cash and profit maximization can be detrimental to the value of a business because it might distract attention and funds from creating potential for the future and from developing a sustainable competitive advantage, or could expose the organization to higher risks. Value-oriented managers take all four drivers of value creation into account, and will strive for a balance between optimizing profitability and cash flow, developing potential and growth opportunities for the future, ensuring that the organization has a sustainable competitive advantage, and controlling risks.

- Responsible managers look beyond financial results. They understand that businesses are more than pure cash generation machines, and that organizations also have social and environmental responsibilities. Thus, they see their organizations—and themselves—as accountable not only for the economic, but also for the social and environmental impact of their activities, and establish and use appropriate reporting systems to monitor these non-financial results categories, too.

Endnotes

1 Katzenbach et al. (2015).
2 Net income according to the Aetna 2015 Financial Annual Report (http://investor.aetna.com/phoenix.zhtml?c=110617&p=irol-reportsAnnual, accessed 22 November 2016); share price comparison between 5 Jan 2015 (US$ 88.14) and 5 January 2018 (US$ 183.70) according to www.nyse.com/quote/XNYS:AET (accessed 29 October 2018).
3 Katzenbach et al. (2015).
4 Berman and Knight (2013).
5 Sack (2008), p. 2.
6 Marshall (2010), p. 2.
7 Coyne et al. (2010), p. 75.
8 See also Altman et al. (2002); Coyne et al. (2010).
9 Sack (2008), p. 3.
10 These examples are based on Marshall (2010).
11 Marshall (2010), p. 3; written in capital letters in the original.
12 Webb (2011).
13 Ignatius (2010), p. 111.
14 Ignatius (2010), p. 111.
15 Ignatius (2010), p. 110.
16 Indounas (2006).
17 This approach is based on Indounas (2006).

18 Kohli and Suri (2011).
19 Kohli and Suri (2011), p. 568.
20 Baker et al. (2010).
21 Kohli and Suri (2011).
22 Kohli and Suri (2011); Potter (2000).
23 Kermisch and Burns (2018).
24 Liker (2004), p. 116.
25 Jassy et al. (1998).
26 Jassy et al. (1998).
27 Berman and Knight (2013), p. 128.
28 Jassy et al. (1998).
29 Jassy et al. (1998).
30 Müller von Blumencron (2014).
31 Koether (2012), p. 212.
32 Müller von Blumencron (2014).
33 bbc.com (2017).
34 oxforddictionaries.com (2019).
35 Sternad et al. (2016).
36 Berman and Knight (2013); Reinbergs (2001).
37 Roggi (2016).
38 This is a shortened version of the process proposed by Curtis and Carey (2012).
39 Cox (2008).
40 Hubbard (2009), p. 178.
41 KPMG (2015).
42 Schaltegger and Burritt (2010).

43 Hart (1995).
44 Kiron and Kruschwitz (2015).
45 Lamberton (2005).
46 Perrini and Tencati (2006).
47 Kolk (2008).
48 Elkington (1997).
49 Pava (2007), p. 107.
50 Lamberton (2005).
51 Lamberton (2005).
52 Stout (2013).
53 Gray (2006), p. 809.
54 Sternad et al. (2016).
55 Ignatius and McGinn (2015), p. 62.
56 Ignatius and McGinn (2015), p. 63.
57 GRI (2013); Sternad and Mödritscher (2018).
58 Davis (2015), p. 69.
59 Davis (2015), p. 68.
60 Brunello Cucinelli (2018).
61 brunellocucinelli.com (2017b).
62 Ford (2012), p. 35.
63 Bloomberg (2015).
64 Brunello Cucinelli (2018).
65 Brunello Cucinelli (2017).
66 Davis (2015), p. 66.
67 Bertolini (2016).
68 Bertolini (2016).

Visit the companion website at macmillanihe.com/sternad-management to access multiple choice questions, useful weblinks and additional materials.

iStock.com/paad

THE ENTREPRENEURIAL MANAGER

Outline of chapter

This chapter will enable you to

- Describe what managers do in their entrepreneurial role.

- Discuss the role of creativity, innovation, and corporate entrepreneurship in advancing organizations.

- Devise strategies for encouraging creativity and innovativeness in an organization.

- Recognize and assess entrepreneurial opportunities.

- Develop a business plan for an entrepreneurial venture.

- Contrast a planned approach and a more experimental ("lean") approach to pursuing entrepreneurial opportunities.

Introduction

In the mid-1960s, when Phil Knight was taking an entrepreneurship class at Stanford University, he came up with the idea of importing Japanese-made running shoes into the United States. Together with his former track and field coach Bill Bowerman, Knight co-founded a company called Blue Ribbon Sports to turn his business idea into reality. In its early years, the new venture faced several obstacles, including late or mismatched shipments from Japan, a tight financial situation, and a breach of the exclusive distribution agreement by the manufacturing partner.[1]

While Knight was managing these challenges, Bowerman experimented with different materials and was always full of ideas for enhancing the running experience. On one occasion, while eating waffles for breakfast, he realized that the distinct pattern of the waffles might also be used to improve the traction of running shoes. He put some rubber into the waffle iron, which ruined the iron, but at the same time produced a first prototype that was a big step toward revolutionizing the athletic shoe industry.[2] Sixteen years after it was founded by Knight and Bowerman, the company—which had been renamed Nike—overtook German rival Adidas as the market leader in the US.

The foundation and rise of Nike is a classic entrepreneurial story. It features ingenious people who had the **ability to recognize and pursue opportunities**, a lot of **creativity and an innovative spirit**, and the **persistence to follow a vision despite the various challenges and obstacles** that needed to be overcome along the way.

Managers can learn a lot from successful **entrepreneurs**, because thinking and acting in an entrepreneurial way is also a core element of the managerial role. Whether they start up their own company, act as owner-managers, or work for established organizations, effective managers are not simply passive administrators, but actively shape the future of their organizations. They need to adapt and prepare their organizations for a changing environment and must be able to recognize, assess, and exploit opportunities for developing the business. Entrepreneurial managers create value through establishing new organizations and rejuvenating established ones.

In this chapter, we will look more closely at how managers can become effective in their entrepreneurial role:

- First, in *Section 10.1*, we will delve inside **the entrepreneurial mind**. How do entrepreneurs and entrepreneurial managers typically think and act? How do they approach problems and challenges? And what does it mean for managers to act as **intrapreneurs** in the context of larger, established organizations?
- We will then explore the nature of **creativity and innovation** as key building blocks of successful entrepreneurship in *Section 10.2*. After gaining a better understanding of the sources of creativity and the phases of the innovation process, we will be able to identify what managers can do to positively (or negatively) influence creativity and innovativeness in organizations.
- Effective entrepreneurial managers are able to recognize and exploit the **entrepreneurial opportunities** that arise when unmet needs are matched with innovative value-creating solutions which address them. In *Section 10.3*, we will discuss different strategies for identifying and assessing opportunities.
- Finally, in *Section 10.4*, we will juxtapose two different **approaches to pursuing entrepreneurial opportunities**: a more structured approach that is based on detailed planning on the one hand, and a "lean," more experimental and hypothesis-driven approach in which "learning by doing" plays an important role on the other hand.

Entrepreneur:
An individual who discovers, evaluates, and exploits opportunities for creating or developing a business.

Intrapreneur:
An employee who exhibits entrepreneurial behavior (i.e. discovers, evaluates, and exploits opportunities for creating or developing a business) within a larger organization.

Entrepreneurship:
The process of engaging in innovative activities which are oriented toward creating and exploiting new business opportunities.

You don't need to destroy waffle irons to become an effective entrepreneurial manager, but it is crucial to act as the root of the word **entrepreneurship** suggests: the Old French *"entreprendre"* means "to begin something" or "to undertake." Being an entrepreneurial manager therefore means not only having good ideas, but actually taking action and making a commitment to change. In the following sections, we will take a closer look at what managers can do to meet the entrepreneurial challenge.

10.1 Entrepreneurial thinking

Getty Images/Cultura RF/Monty Rakusen

In brief

- It is part of the managerial role to both encourage and personally engage in entrepreneurial activities that are oriented toward identifying, creating, and pursuing opportunities for new value creation.

- Entrepreneurial managers tend to be people-oriented, risk-conscious, creative, and resilient. They have a bias for action and usually follow a "learning by doing" approach.

- Design thinking—a user-centered, experimental problem-solving approach that is often used by creative designers—can help managers to find innovative solutions to entrepreneurial challenges.

- Entrepreneurial behavior is not singularly bound to new ventures, but is also important for the continuous self-renewal of established organizations (in the form of corporate entrepreneurship).

As we discussed in Chapter 1, managers are expected to fulfill a particular set of roles. In Henry Mintzberg's classification, being an **entrepreneur** is one of these ten major functions.[3] In everyday language, the term "entrepreneur" is often used to describe a person who establishes a new organization. But it can also be used in a wider sense to describe an individual who discovers, evaluates, and exploits opportunities for value creation.[4] As management expert Peter Drucker pointed out, **entrepreneurship** is not unique to newly launched ventures, but also occurs in established organizations, since the term "entrepreneurship" "refers not to an enterprise's size or age, but to a certain kind of activity."[5] According to Drucker, "the practice of systematic innovation" lies at the heart of this.[6] Entrepreneurs engage in what economist Schumpeter called "**creative destruction**."[7] They develop and implement new, innovative products, services, and processes that "destroy" the business models of incumbent firms and lead to new forms of value creation.

"As *entrepreneur*," highlighted Mintzberg, "the manager seeks to improve his [or her] unit, to adapt it to changing conditions in the environment."[8] We are currently living in an age that is characterized by rapidly **changing environmental conditions**, fueled by major technological advances—especially in the field of information and communication technology—and also by an acceleration of social change and the pace of life in general.[9] Such an "age of change" can become an "age of opportunity,"[10] especially for those who are creative enough to find innovative solutions to these new challenges and who are able to turn their ideas into reality.

Entrepreneurial manager:
A manager who is engaged in entrepreneurial activities (i.e. in recognizing, creating, and pursuing opportunities for value creation), regardless of whether these activities are performed in new ventures or established organizations.

A glimpse into the entrepreneurial manager's mind

Managers who are acting in an entrepreneurial role (also referred to as "**entrepreneurial managers**") have a certain way of thinking and behaving, regardless of whether they are working for their own business (as owner-managers) or for others (as **intrapreneurs,** a topic defined and discussed on pp. 327–328). Paul Burns, who has written several market-leading textbooks on entrepreneurship, identified the following **key behavioral characteristics of entrepreneurial managers**:[11]

- *Entrepreneurial managers are people-oriented*. They tend to be effective networkers and are good at establishing productive and lasting relationships with customers, suppliers, staff, and other partners. Personal relationships are often more important for

Innovation:
The development and actual implementation of new ideas for products and services, practices, or organizational procedures that create value for customers and the organization, respectively.

Empowerment:
The leadership practice of giving a person or a group of people more autonomy so that they can set their own priorities, make decisions, and solve problems independently.

Design thinking:
A systematic approach to solving complex problems that is based on methods that designers use in the design process.

them than formal structures, and they are also aware that too much structure and hierarchy can have detrimental effects on flexibility, which is necessary for pursuing opportunities as they arise.

- **Entrepreneurial managers are risk-conscious.** Entering new terrain (which is a key characteristic of entrepreneurship) is inherently risky. This does not mean that entrepreneurial managers are blind risk-takers, though. On the contrary, often they only take measured risks and strive to minimize these and their resource use whenever possible. Many entrepreneurial ventures are characterized by an incremental approach in which resources are gradually committed to a project as it becomes more established, in order to keep both capital investment and fixed costs at a minimum.
- **Entrepreneurial managers follow a "learning by doing" approach.** Instead of engaging in extensive planning, they have a bias for action and try things out. Although they usually have certain strategic goals in mind, entrepreneurial managers are flexible enough to change their strategies along the way, respond to new opportunities, and are open to learning from experimentation, customer feedback, and market testing.
- **Entrepreneurial managers focus on creativity and innovation.** While traditional management in larger organizations typically focuses on efficiency and control, entrepreneurial management is more oriented toward **empowerment** and creating the conditions in which people feel free to follow creative approaches to problem solving and to try out innovative ways of generating value.

Recognizing and pursuing opportunities lies at the core of entrepreneurship (see Section 10.3). Therefore, managers with an entrepreneurial mind always remain open and alert to spotting opportunities that emerge from changes and developments in the environment. Alternatively, they may create new customer needs and change the environment themselves. Recognizing opportunities is just the first step, however. Entrepreneurial managers are also able to take advantage of these opportunities when they arise—for example, through **designing appropriate solutions** for a particular customer problem (see the box *What can we learn from designers?*) and securing the resources that are needed for the implementation of these solutions.

FROM A DIFFERENT ANGLE

What can we learn from designers?

Design thinking is an approach to solving complex problems that is based on methods that designers use to create new products or services. One of the key proponents of design thinking in a business context is David M. Kelley, founder of both the global design and innovation company IDEO and Stanford University's Hasso Plattner Institute of Design, also known as "d. school." The core idea of design thinking is to put user needs in the center of the design process, with an interdisciplinary team exploring what users really want, followed by the rapid development of prototypes which are then tested in iterative cycles directly with the target group. A problem-solving process that follows a design thinking approach usually includes the following steps (see also Figure 10.1):

1 *Learn about the problem you are trying to solve (or the opportunity you are trying to exploit)*—for

example, through talking with experts in the field and other knowledgeable people.

2 *Understand the users*—not only through talking with them, but even more importantly through observing them—and then reframe the problem if necessary.

3 *Develop ideas for solving the problem*—ideally in a small but diverse team.

4 *Visualize the most promising ideas*—for example, in the form of physical models, prototypes, or videos that show how the solution could work. The idea behind this is that if you show people a solution, they will better understand and "feel" how it works than if you just tell them about it.

5 *Test the ideas and revise them*—show the prototype to the target group, and then revise and improve the prototype based on user feedback.

The process is an iterative one, in which it might be necessary to cycle back to former phases, even multiple times. Effective design thinking is not only based on following a certain process, however—it also has a cultural aspect, which Kelley calls "the hard part."

Managers need to create "an environment where a diverse group of people can work together" and build on each other's ideas.[12]

Sources: Based on information in Meinel and Leifer (2011); Rose (2013).

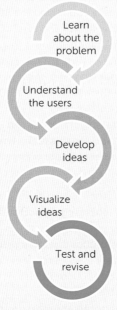

Figure 10.1 The design thinking process

Sources: Inspired by concepts in Meinel and Leifer (2011); Rose (2013).

Entrepreneurial managers need **resilience**—the ability to recover quickly from difficult situations and setbacks (see Chapter 2)—because setbacks are a normal by-product of engaging in innovative activities. When they fail, people with an entrepreneurial mind are able to deal with the failure emotionally, and then move on to new challenges.[13]

Although entrepreneurial managers by definition pursue opportunities for value creation, this does not mean that making a profit is necessarily the most important motivation for engaging in entrepreneurial activities. The survival of the business, creating meaningful work, personal development, or handing over a thriving organization to the next generation (in the case of family firms) can be equally important motives for entrepreneurs, as can be the drive to create "real value" in terms of improving the material and immaterial quality of life of different stakeholder groups (see also Chapter 9).[14] **Social enterprises**, for example, are organizations in which the entrepreneurial energy is directed toward fulfilling a social mission—having a positive impact on people and the environment—while making a profit. Whether in commercial or social enterprises, entrepreneurial managers share some characteristics which are summarized in Figure 10.2.

Let us assume that you are planning a dinner for university or work colleagues to celebrate the success of a project (as we all know, a good meal offers real value). How would you use the design thinking approach to optimize the experience for your colleagues?

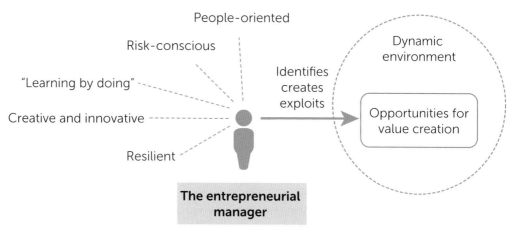

Figure 10.2 The
entrepreneurial
manager

Corporate entrepreneurship

**Corporate
entrepreneurship:**
Entrepreneurial
activities in larger,
established
organizations.

The term **corporate entrepreneurship** (also known as **intrapreneurship**) refers to entrepreneurial activities—for example, creating a new product or service or initiating significant
changes in the value creation system—within an existing organization. In a dynamic business environment where many start-up companies engage in the "creative destruction" of
established industry structures—for instance through recognizing and exploiting the opportunities that new technologies open—entrepreneurial behavior is also critical for the survival
and prosperity of larger, established organizations. An organization that fails to innovate is
not far from failing altogether. Corporate entrepreneurship can help to **rejuvenate an organization** and ensure its continued survival even when massive waves of technological and
social change are flooding an industry.

There are some **tensions**, however, between how established organizations typically
work and what entrepreneurial ventures require (see Table 10.1).

Table 10.1 Different requirements of established organizations and entrepreneurial ventures

Established organizations	Entrepreneurial ventures
Are designed to maximize efficiency	Are designed to innovate
Use standardized systems and procedures based on operational experience	Deviate from the standard way of doing things
Aim to reduce the risk of failure	Are inherently risky endeavors
Exercise tight control of all activities based on hard data	Are often less structured in the beginning, require a more experimental approach, and progress into unknown spaces for which no hard data are available
Emphasize rigor and discipline	Can be severely hampered by rigid control mechanisms and established systems (e.g. for budgeting or human resource management)
Have the tendency to integrate their activities and find a common way of doing things	Tend to strive for the development of an independent identity (which means that the culture of entrepreneurial units can clash with the existing organization)

Sources: Inspired by concepts in Chakravorti (2010); Garvin and Levesque (2006).

Due to these tensions, corporate entrepreneurship can be seen as a **balancing act** in which disciplined planning is combined with the ability to seize opportunities as they arise. People who are experienced in the existing business collaborate with fresh entrepreneurial minds, and strategic guidance is offered without tying a new venture too tightly to excessive rules and rigorous control systems.[15]

So what can managers actually do to **foster corporate entrepreneurship**? Research results suggest the following strategies:[16]

1 Ensure **top management commitment to promoting entrepreneurial behavior**, champion innovative ideas and approaches, and provide resources for entrepreneurial activities.

2 Provide an **adequate degree of autonomy** for internal entrepreneurial ventures, free them from excessive formal control mechanisms, and have a higher degree of failure tolerance than in the normal day-to-day business.

3 Make sure that **reward systems** are reinforcing rather than inhibiting entrepreneurial behavior. Instead of rewarding managers primarily on profitability increases, for example, bonuses might be tied to the percentage of sales that come from new products (an approach for which the technology company 3M became famous).

4 Ensure that people have **enough time** for innovative entrepreneurial activities. When people are working under constant pressure and with heavily overloaded schedules, they are unlikely to find time to engage in future-oriented entrepreneurial activities.

5 Enhance the **open flow of information** between organizational units and across the traditional divisions of the organization.

6 Establish **clear structures and processes for supporting innovation activities** (see also Section 10.2).

Creating the conditions under which corporate entrepreneurship can thrive not only paves the way for the ongoing self-renewal of established organizations, but enables them to keep up with trends and create new opportunities for growth. Organizations with an entrepreneurial spirit can also generate excitement among stakeholders and are often better able to attract, develop, and retain talent.[17]

CEO BEST PRACTICE

Corporate entrepreneurship at Air Liquide

Benoît Potier is chairman and CEO of Air Liquide, a French multinational company that specializes in the supply of industrial gases (most notably oxygen, nitrogen, and hydrogen) and provides services to various sectors, including the healthcare, chemical, and electronics industries. The company, which was founded in 1902, had a turnover of over €20 billion in 2017 and a workforce of 65,000. Although this is a large and long-established organization, Potier has been able to uphold an entrepreneurial spirit, thanks to his customer-centric approach and strong focus on innovation and creativity. In addition to making massive investments in research and development in the group's own research centers, Potier established Air Liquide's innovation laboratory, i-LAB, as a

"place for reflection and experimentation."[18] In the i-LAB, new growth opportunities are explored through a user-centric approach and in collaboration with different parts of the Air Liquide group. At the same time, Air Liquide also set up ALIAD, the group's venture capital investment subsidiary. It invests in innovative technology start-ups and provides them with privileged business agreements with the Air Liquide group. Examples include an Australian start-up that developed hydrogen storage technology, a Belgian company that offers clean solutions for producing gas from biomass, and a French venture that specializes in nanotechnology for gas analysis. Potier puts a strong emphasis on long-term value creation, which he thinks can be achieved through a shared vision and clear strategy, in addition to "good management [that] must be combined with an entrepreneurial spirit in the workplace ..., motivated teams that are connected to markets and capable of innovating for customers," and "the collective ability to anticipate the future and project ourselves into it."[19] As a visual sign of the group's strong focus on innovation, the slogan "Creative oxygen" is now used as a signature for the Air Liquide brand.

→ Key takeaway

It is possible for large, established companies to maintain an entrepreneurial spirit—especially if this spirit is fueled by a strong commitment to innovation from top management and structures that are explicitly designed for fostering entrepreneurial behavior.

Sources: Based on information in Air Liquide (2015); airliquide.com (2019a; 2019b).

10.2 Creativity and innovation

Getty Images/skynesher

In brief

- In a dynamic business environment, creativity and innovation can be major sources of competitive advantage.

- Creative solutions are often developed at interfaces, when people with a diverse set of knowledge, backgrounds, and expertise share ideas. In addition to creative-thinking skills, expertise and motivation also play an important role in the idea generation process.

- Idea generation is just one step in the overall innovation process because innovation means that novel ideas are not only conceived, but actually implemented in a way that creates value.

- Managers cannot force others to be creative or to innovate. What they can do, however, is to provide the structural and cultural conditions for creativity and innovativeness to thrive. Committing resources and devoting leadership attention to innovative activities are further important driving forces for encouraging creativity and innovativeness in organizations.

Creativity and innovation are core ingredients of successful entrepreneurship, whether in new ventures or established organizations. **Creativity** is the process of generating ideas for new, useful ways of doing things. **Innovation** is the combination of idea generation and the actual implementation of these ideas in new products and services, practices, or organizational procedures that, in turn, create value for customers and the organization. Thus, creativity is often seen as the first step in the innovation process, but effective innovation cannot happen until creative ideas are actually applied to create value.

Both creativity and innovation are important sources of competitive advantage.[20] They can help to create better offers for customers, and also to make organizations more efficient. In many industries—especially in dynamic contexts like the high-tech sector—companies can quickly lose their competitiveness if they fail to innovate. Kodak's failure to embrace the opportunities that digital photography presented is an often-cited case in point. Although it was a Kodak engineer who invented the first digital camera in the 1970s, Kodak's management was unable to see the market potential of the new technology and decided to continue to fully focus the business on film and photographic chemicals instead.[21] When they finally realized that digital photography would conquer the world, it was already too late. The company had to file for bankruptcy protection in 2012.

Effective managers understand the power that lies in creativity and innovation, and actively strive to provide the right conditions to enhance their organizations' creative potential and innovativeness.

The nature of creativity

What makes individuals, teams, and organizations creative? What enables them to generate novel ideas for solving problems and new approaches to seize opportunities? Harvard Business School Professor Teresa Amabile has conducted extensive research to find answers to these questions. As one of the most salient outcomes of her research, she proposed a **componential model of creativity**, in which she identified three components which together form the basic source of creativity in an organizational context:

1 creative-thinking skills;
2 expertise; and
3 motivation.[22]

A person with **creative-thinking skills** is imaginative and able to approach a problem in novel ways. However, these skills involve not only the ability to see a problem from a new perspective or to make uncommon associations, but also the willingness to deviate from standard thinking patterns in a particular organization or industry.[23] Of course, being creative is not just the responsibility of the individual, since creative-thinking skills can also exist on a team level, for example, in the form of certain norms that ensure productive team interactions or creativity techniques that a team is able to use effectively. One such tool for generating novel solutions in a team is brainstorming (see the box *Zooming in on brainstorming*).

Zooming in on ▶ BRAINSTORMING

Brainstorming is a widely used creativity technique for generating novel ideas and solutions for specific problems. The basic idea behind brainstorming is to facilitate a freewheeling group discussion in which a large number of ideas are produced, combined, and improved. Experts offer the following advice to make brainstorming sessions effective:

1 Include people with different expertise and from diverse backgrounds.
2 Defer judgment—do not allow ideas to be criticized during the brainstorming session.
3 Visualize all contributions (e.g. write them down on a flipchart or whiteboard).
4 Allow group members to challenge the definition and interpretation of the proposed problem to ensure that the real issue is tackled.
5 Combine group and solitary brainstorming (e.g. in the form of *brainwriting*, in which each group member writes down ideas for solving a certain problem and then passes these ideas on to the next person as an inspiration for further ideas) to avoid inadvertently overlooking good ideas from shyer participants.
6 Use electronic software that allows the instant pooling of multiple ideas while also ensuring anonymity, thus overcoming the social conformity tendencies that can often be found in traditional group brainstorming settings.

The next time you undertake a group project, try putting some of these tips into practice. Did you come up with creative ideas and solutions for your project?

Sources: Based on information in Brown and Paulus (2002); Saunders (1999).

Novelty—a core quality of creative solutions—usually arises from "connecting the dots," combining formerly disconnected pieces of information in a new way.[24] Naturally, to be able to connect the dots, we must first understand them, meaning that we need to have access to relevant knowledge. This is when **expertise** comes in, everything that an individual or team knows and is able to do in a certain domain. In the same way that good intuitive thinking is usually based on extensive domain-relevant experience (see Chapter 6), creativity relies on a wide domain-relevant knowledge base. A study that was conducted among Chinese entrepreneurs, for example, showed clear links between prior knowledge and entrepreneurial creativity.[25] The authors of the study found that creative entrepreneurs and managers typically try to learn as much as they can about their field. They tend to read a lot, continuously monitor what is going on in and around their industry environment, and remain alert to spotting new opportunities; in short, "they were creative because they did their background work."[26]

When more complex problems need to be solved, the most useful ideas are often developed when boundaries are crossed and knowledge from different domains is combined. For that purpose, creative people use information that they receive from their **network**— including people they see only occasionally, the **weak ties**.[27] Creative solutions frequently emerge at **interfaces**, when people from different domains share and combine ideas that were formerly unconnected. New ideas are more likely to be generated when people with different backgrounds meet. In one example, engineers from the aviation division of the industrial conglomerate General Electric (GE) developed a method for the continuous transmission of information about the blade speed and engine heat of aircraft engines. When their colleagues from GE's medical systems business learned more about this innovation, it helped them to develop a new self-monitoring system for heart pacemakers.[28]

In addition to creative-thinking skills and expertise, which Amabile refers to as the "raw material" of creativity, she also identifies motivation as an important third factor for actually sparking creativity.[29] In her earlier research, she emphasized **intrinsic motivation**—the internal desire or passion to create something new—as a key driving force behind finding creative solutions to problems. The basic idea is that the more interested you are in solving a specific problem, the higher the chances that you will actually be able to find an appropriate solution. In addition to strong evidence for the salient role of the inner emotional and motivational state, it was later found that **extrinsic motivators** (e.g. reward and recognition) can further support creativity, especially if they are aligned with intrinsic motivations and are not perceived as a control mechanism.[30]

Based on more recent research findings, the original componential model of creativity has been extended to include the idea that creativity in an organizational context is usually not a one-off event, but iterates through cycles in which people periodically reengage with a problem to find the best possible solution.[31] Even if no solution is in sight yet, a feeling of progress can fuel the motivation needed to continue the search for the optimal answer to a problem. This is called the "**progress principle**," and is especially valid in cases where people believe that they are making advances in meaningful work—work that is of importance for themselves, but especially also for others.[32] One example of the power of the progress principle is the artificial intelligence (AI) enterprise Deepmind. This is the company behind AlphaGo, the first computer program to beat the world's best player in Go (a game that is far more complex than chess). Pushing the boundaries of AI and making considerable progress toward being able to use it "to make the world a better place" through applying AI for tackling societal challenges (e.g. climate change or improving healthcare) keeps the Deepmind team on track despite their acknowledgement that "there are still many hurdles ahead."[33]

The componential model of creativity is shown (in a simplified form) in Figure 10.3. In this graphical representation, we can see that **influences in the work environment** can play an important role, especially in fostering or inhibiting creative-thinking skills and motivation. Managers can, for example, encourage or discourage creative thinking, the proposal of novel, out-of-the-box solutions, or challenges to the status quo. How superiors and colleagues respond to failures (which are a natural by-product of creativity) can make a difference, as can freeing up time to explore innovative ideas outside the demands of day-to-day work. In contrast, excessive bureaucracy and control mechanisms can hold people back from being creative. In summarizing her ample experience of studying how managers and organizations influence creativity, Teresa Amabile concluded that "there can be no doubt: creativity gets killed much more often than it gets supported."[34]

Weak ties:
People you know personally, but do not have a strong relationship with (e.g. acquaintances or former colleagues).

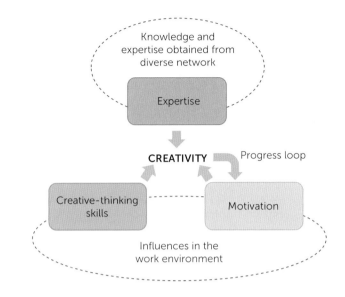

Figure 10.3 Key components of creativity

Source: Reprinted by permission of *Harvard Business Review*. Adapted from 'The Three Components of Creativity' in 'How To Kill Creativity' by Teresa M. Amabile, September–October 1998. Copyright ©1998 by Harvard Business Publishing; all rights reserved. Additional ideas incorporated from Amabile and Pratt (2016).

The innovation process

As mentioned earlier, creativity is an important ingredient for innovation, but innovation goes far beyond creativity, in that it also includes the implementation and exploitation of an idea in order to create value. There are many different **types of innovation** in an organizational context: product innovation, service innovation, brand innovation, and customer experience innovation can all enhance the value offers of an organization, while process innovation, business model innovation, and innovation along the value chain (e.g. a reorganization of the supply chain or of distribution channels) can change the way in which an organization creates value.[35] Start-up companies usually focus on product and service innovation, while process innovations are more common in the later stages of an organization's life cycle.[36]

Regardless of the type of innovation, the preconditions for innovation on an organizational level are similar to the key components of creativity on an individual or team level. We have already seen that individuals and teams need expertise to think creatively; in a similar way, organizations need **resources** (including knowledge, skills, infrastructure, and financial means) to support creative work. And just as individuals and teams require creative-thinking skills, organizations need **innovation management skills**. Finally, just as for individuals, **motivation** is crucial at an organizational level; for example, in the form of high-level leadership support for innovation.[37] In addition to the above, organizations also need adequate **structures and procedures** that support, or at least do not impede, innovativeness (such as a simple and non-bureaucratic system for proposing and implementing new ideas).[38]

Innovation management: Managerial practices that are oriented toward fostering innovativeness and initiating, designing, and managing innovation processes in organizations.

Innovation in organizations can be seen as a social process in which different people interact in order to create new value offers or accomplish changes in the value creation system.[39] Figure 10.4 summarizes the main steps in this **innovation process**, which will be discussed in more detail in the following pages.

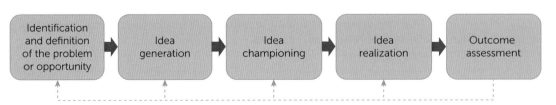

Figure 10.4 The innovation process

Sources: Inspired by concepts in Amabile and Pratt (2016); Kanter (1988); Perry-Smith and Mannucci (2017).

Step 1: Identify and define the problem or opportunity

The innovation process usually starts with the **identification and definition of a problem or an opportunity**. Without a problem to be solved or an opportunity to be seized, there is no need for innovation. Identifying the core problem and understanding the issues behind it is one of the most important parts of the innovation process, since a solution to the wrong problem is usually not particularly useful. It is good practice for innovators to spend time and energy on clearly defining what they actually want to achieve.[40] Only once the problem has been adequately defined and clear innovation goals have been set can **idea generation** start—the phase in the innovation process in which creativity is most needed.

Step 2: Generate ideas

Open innovation:
The idea (popularized by Henry Chesbrough) that organizations should combine internal and external ideas to find new solutions for creating value, and also think about offering their innovations to the market with the help of other organizations.

Ideas often come from contact with people from outside an individual's own field or from "direct personal confrontations with problem sources,"[41] for example, direct customer and user contact. In Peter Drucker's words, "would-be innovators must also go out and look, ask, and listen."[42] For complex problems in particular, the idea generation phase can require many resources. For example, market research or training activities might be needed to acquire the required expertise for systematically identifying and evaluating the solutions with the highest potential. In this phase, innovators can profit from "more relationships, more sources of information, more angles on the problem, [and] more ways to pull in human and material resources."[43]

One way to "pull in" more resources is **open innovation**, a concept that has been popularized by the work of Henry Chesbrough.[44] Chesbrough postulated that organizations should go beyond the confines of their institution in the innovation process, combining internal and external ideas to create value. They should also consider using outside support when offering their innovations to the market, such as through licensing agreements or spin-offs. Likewise, customers can be included in the idea generation and product development process, for example, through **crowdsourcing** (collecting ideas over the Internet). Suppliers, competitors, universities, or industry experts can be further sources of external help in the innovation process (see the box *Creating beauty at AmorePacific*).[45] The basic idea behind open innovation is to use the brain power of "smart people" from outside the organization for the benefit of the organization.

Crowdsourcing:
Obtaining certain resources (e.g. ideas, services, or content) from a large group of people (usually via the Internet).

CEO BEST PRACTICE

Creating beauty at AmorePacific

The roots of the South Korean cosmetics giant AmorePacific date back to the 1930s, when Suh Kyung-bae's grandmother Yoon Dokjeong began to produce hand-pressed camellia oils for beauty-conscious Korean women. In the 1990s, Suh took over the leadership of the company from his father and developed it into a global player that made it onto *Forbes* magazine's list of the 30 most innovative companies in the world. "The innovation DNA embedded in our corporate culture has made it possible for us to achieve sustainable growth," Suh commented in an interview with *The Korea Times*, pointing out that the company has constantly pursued the goal of becoming "a leading beauty creator."[46]

Suh is convinced that "[s]ociety cannot achieve growth without the development of science and technology."[47] He was the driving force behind setting up and expanding AmorePacific research centers around the world, where 500 researchers and chemists work on creating new solutions for beauty customers with a strong focus on natural ingredients. Under Suh's leadership, the company has followed an open research and innovation strategy, inviting academic institutions, research institutes, laboratories, and industry players of all sizes and from all world regions to join their innovation network. Through this, AmorePacific hopes to come up with new ideas which have the potential to disrupt the beauty industry, tapping into a "wealth of culturally and geographically relevant sources."[48] One such innovation was the development of a new cushion technology that combines skincare, sun protection, and liquid foundation into one formula. After passing through 3,600 tests, the new technology was enthusiastically accepted by the market, and was later also licensed to other industry players such as the French cosmetics behemoth Christian Dior.

Innovation ("We always look for new ways") is one of the company's core values, with the others being integrity, openness, challenge ("We constantly push ourselves beyond our limits") and proximity ("We understand our customers and stay next to them").[49] Suh is himself strongly committed to these values. "I visit our stores, both domestic and international, and listen to the voices of our clients and partners as much as possible,"[50] he comments to explain what proximity means for him. He also tries to

stay in touch with experts from different fields, including, for example, scholars, artists, and photographers, in order to get new insights because—in Suh's own words—"they often see the world from different points of view."[51]

On every occasion, Suh highlights the important role of innovation in the company's success, noting: "We tried to change the industry paradigm by introducing innovative products and services".[52] This strategy has helped him to become South Korea's second-richest citizen.

→ Key takeaway

Innovation can be a key source of competitive advantage. Being open to collaboration with others and keeping in touch with customers can enhance the effectiveness of the innovation process.

Sources: Based on information in AmorePacific (2018); Cornell (2013); Chung (2015); Hyo-sik (2012); Spencer (2017).

Of course, people who are engaged in creative work need more than just additional ideas from outside the organization. They also need **encouragement and emotional support** during the idea generation phase, as well as **constructive feedback** that helps them to enhance their ideas. Negative criticism, on the other hand, can have the opposite effect, discouraging people from pursuing promising ideas.[53]

Step 3: Champion the idea

When introducing new innovations into an organization, it is not sufficient to have a novel and potentially useful idea. The idea also needs to receive support from key players in the organization to have a chance of being implemented. **Idea championing** is therefore a crucial activity in the innovation process. In this phase, an idea is actively promoted and "sold," ideally in coalition with powerful backers.[54] The key goal is to achieve enough support—particularly in terms of resource commitment—to be able to realize the idea. The influencing strategies described in Chapter 8 can help in this endeavor.

Step 4: Implement the idea

If the innovation receives enough support, it can be implemented. In the **idea realization** phase, concepts are turned into reality.[55] Prototypes of a new product are developed, new services are introduced, or processes are adapted. It is important in this phase to create a shared understanding of what needs to be achieved and either align the new ideas with existing organizational structures or change the structures if necessary.[56] As in any implementation and change effort, this phase can include power struggles because the interests of different stakeholder groups could be affected. As Rosabeth Moss Kanter observed, "[i]nnovations always involve competition with alternative courses of action."[57] Thus, idea realization can also be seen as a change management effort (see Chapter 8).

Step 5: Assess the outcomes

In the last phase, the **outcomes** of the idea realization are assessed. Was the innovation a success or a failure, or did it at least help in making progress toward solving a particular problem? This assessment is usually made in a social process with powerful players in the organization judging the usefulness of the innovation. Further decisions will then be made about either continuing with the implementation across the organization or cycling back to an earlier phase of the innovation process.[58]

Cycling back and forth is a normal feature of the innovation process. Solutions to complex problems are rarely found straight away. Experimenting with different approaches, trying and trying again, being persistent even in the case of repeated failure, and showing discipline and perseverance are as important as having a good idea in the first place. The Wright brothers, for example, allegedly went through hundreds of unsuccessful trials before their glider eventually took off and they made it into the history books: first with a 622.5 foot (190 meter) record flight with a glider in 1902 and with humankind's first successful controlled and sustained motor flight in 1903.[59] "Above all," says Drucker, "innovation is work rather than genius"[60] (but this does not mean that entrepreneurial managers can't learn something from geniuses—see the *From a different angle* box).

FROM A DIFFERENT ANGLE

One of the greatest innovators of all time

By all standards, Leonardo da Vinci (1452–1519) was an exceptional individual. For many historians, he is the epitome of a "universal genius" because he made highly innovative contributions to many fields, including painting, sculpting, mathematics, botany, anatomy, architecture, and engineering. Can 21st-century managers learn something about innovation from this highly innovative Renaissance man? Perhaps they can, if we consider the following:

1 *Be well prepared*: Before da Vinci started to paint people, he spent considerable time examining human anatomy, as well as theoretical work in the arts—for example exploring perspective.

2 *Think across the boundaries of disciplines*: The best innovators are able to combine ideas from different domains and disciplines. Because da Vinci was not only a painter, but also a scientist, a builder, and a writer of fables, he was able to make more connections between different disciplines than others.

3 *Take an experimental approach*: Many successful innovators take an iterative approach and experiment with prototypes from the early stages of a project.[61] Da Vinci made numerous sketches before he started work on his most famous paintings. "First I shall test by experiment before I proceed further,"[62] wrote da Vinci in one of his notebooks. Detailed analyses of his painting style also revealed that he often made corrections in order to come closer to a perfect result.

4 *Be persistent*: To complete such grandiose works as da Vinci's famous *Last Supper*, that allegedly took him years to paint, you need to be extremely disciplined. As Harvard Business School's Stefan Thomke and Jason Randal wrote, "[p]ersistence is the key to success in virtually all aspects of life, and that's especially true in innovation."[63]

5 *Be ready to question yourself*: da Vinci was aware that innovators must first be willing and able to change their own views and mental state before they can change something on the outside. He was convinced that "[t]he greatest deception men suffer is from their own opinion."[64]

Fostering creativity and innovation in organizations

Innovativeness:
An organization's capacity to innovate.

What can managers do to foster the creativity and **innovativeness** (the capacity to innovate) of their teams and organizations? As a first step, they need to realize that creativity cannot be dictated. Just ordering people to "be creative" will not help. What managers can do, instead, is to provide the **conditions under which creativity and innovation can thrive**. Conditions related to structure, culture, the availability of resources, and leadership can either act as "driving forces" or as "restraining forces" (see Figure 10.5).[65] We will now discuss each of these factors in more detail.

Let us assume that you work for an advertising agency. You have just been promoted as the new manager of a department that is responsible for coming up with creative advertising solutions for the agency's clients. What would you do to foster creativity and innovativeness in your department?

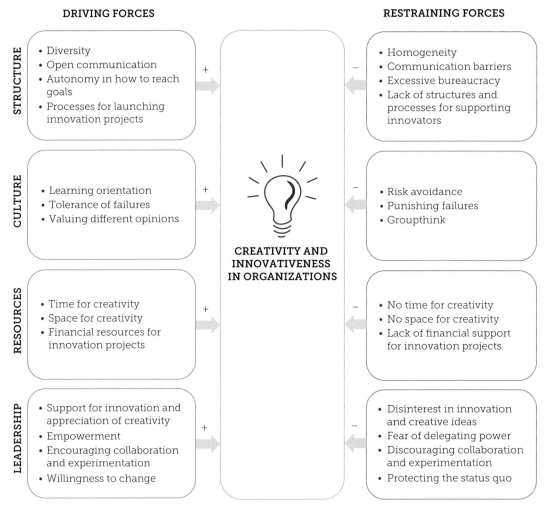

DRIVING FORCES

RESTRAINING FORCES

STRUCTURE
- Diversity
- Open communication
- Autonomy in how to reach goals
- Processes for launching innovation projects

+ / −

- Homogeneity
- Communication barriers
- Excessive bureaucracy
- Lack of structures and processes for supporting innovators

CULTURE
- Learning orientation
- Tolerance of failures
- Valuing different opinions

+ / −

- Risk avoidance
- Punishing failures
- Groupthink

CREATIVITY AND INNOVATIVENESS IN ORGANIZATIONS

RESOURCES
- Time for creativity
- Space for creativity
- Financial resources for innovation projects

+ / −

- No time for creativity
- No space for creativity
- Lack of financial support for innovation projects

LEADERSHIP
- Support for innovation and appreciation of creativity
- Empowerment
- Encouraging collaboration and experimentation
- Willingness to change

+ / −

- Disinterest in innovation and creative ideas
- Fear of delegating power
- Discouraging collaboration and experimentation
- Protecting the status quo

Figure 10.5 Driving and restraining forces of creativity and innovativeness in organizations

Structure

As we discussed earlier, innovation usually occurs when people with different experiences, functions, knowledge, and backgrounds meet and share ideas. Managers can actively try to build diverse teams (e.g. including younger and older people, more analytical and more creative minds, people from different hierarchical levels, and from different locations and cultural backgrounds, newcomers and experienced employees, people from within and outside the organization, and technology-savvy people as well as those who are good at understanding others) to foster the generation of novel ideas.[66] Likewise, it is also important to tear down communication barriers. People need to be able to exchange ideas freely across units and organizational boundaries. "When you build fences, you breed sheep,"[67] said a country manager of technology company 3M, a corporation that is often mentioned as a role model for innovativeness. Excessive bureaucracy can also be detrimental to innovation. If every idea needs approval from several hierarchical levels, many good ideas will either get lost on the way, or—even worse—people will stop voicing ideas altogether. Agreeing on goals, but leaving more freedom and autonomy to employees in how they reach them, can lead to more innovative solutions than strict rules and standards.[68] That is not to say that structures are not needed at all for innovation. Clear procedures for launching, funding, and implementing innovation projects can provide a guiding structure for those members of the organization who want to turn ideas into reality.

Culture

Innovation-friendly structures alone are not enough to make people in an organization more creative or more innovative. An organizational culture that allows and fosters innovation is just as important. When risk avoidance prevails, failures are punished, and only mainstream opinions receive support (refer back to the description of groupthink in Chapter 6), people tend to avoid voicing creative ideas. An innovative culture, in contrast, is characterized by a learning orientation and leaders who understand that setbacks are a normal side-effect of the endeavor to make progress. The famous inventor and vacuum cleaner tycoon James Dyson, for example, thinks that managers need to create a culture which allows creative people to have the courage to take risks: "They should have no fear of doing something that's not 'normal' or 'sensible' and worry I'll clip them round the ear and say 'don't be so bloody stupid'."[69] Tolerance for taking calculated risks and for "intelligent failure" (failure from which an organization can learn) can foster innovativeness. Understanding this, Procter & Gamble's feminine care division even offered a "Fail Forward" award to recognize intelligent failures.[70]

As the *Around the globe* box shows, not only organizational culture but also national culture can have an influence on individuals' attitudes towards risk taking.

AROUND THE GLOBE

Entrepreneurial thinking

A study among entrepreneurs in the US and Germany revealed interesting cross-cultural differences in entrepreneurial thinking. US entrepreneurs tend to be strongly driven by achievement needs and income-earning potential. "There really has to be the passion to be the very best that you can" and "I wanted to make more money, because I didn't want to just exist. I wanted to live"[71] are typical statements of American entrepreneurs. For Germans, self-fulfillment and seeking personal growth are often more salient motives for engaging in entrepreneurial activities. One German respondent, for example, pointed out that as an entrepreneur, "you do what you might have always been dreaming about."[72]

In addition to differences in why people engage in entrepreneurial activities, there are also country-specific differences in how many people actually decide to become an entrepreneur. Both in absolute numbers and as a percentage of the population, there are far fewer entrepreneurs in Germany than in the US. Whereas only 5.3 percent of the German population between the ages of 18 and 64 were either nascent entrepreneurs or owner-managers of a new business in 2017, the figure for the US was 13.6 percent in the same year.[73]

This might also have cultural roots. The US is typically seen as a country that "was founded and settled by innovators and risk-takers."[74] Having the

opportunity to become successful and prosperous through entrepreneurial endeavors is often seen as an important element of the "American Dream." It is usually perfectly fine to try, fail, and try again in the US, whereas failure in an entrepreneurial venture might lead to an irreversible loss of social status in Germany. Thus, engaging in entrepreneurial activities has a much higher degree of perceived personal risk. The different approaches to risk taking are also exemplified in two contrasting proverbs "A bold attempt is half success" (US) and "When the donkey gets overconfident he goes out on the ice and breaks a leg" (Germany).[75]

Another reason for the difference in entrepreneurial proclivity could lie in the high percentage of immigrants in the US, who were found to be much more inclined to engage in entrepreneurial activities than native-born US citizens. Although immigrants are often forced into self-employment due to discrimination in the labor market, a study has also confirmed the positive effect of immigrants' cross-cultural experiences on their level of creativity and their ability to identify new business opportunities. Living in different cultures can help people to transfer ideas and solutions from one cultural context to another country's customer needs and problems.

Sources: Based on information in Vandor and Franke (2016); Weber and Szkudlarek (2013).

Resource availability

To be creative and pursue innovation projects, people need sufficient time and space for reflecting on problems, finding ideas in collaboration with others, and for experimenting.[76] Constant time pressure and ever-increasing efficiency demands can be very detrimental in this respect. People who succumb to the pressures of day-to-day work and do not even find time to breathe will not be able to come up with innovative solutions for their organization. Some managers therefore deliberately provide their team members with more time and space for innovation. For example, companies like 3M or Google have allowed their employees to spend 15–20 percent of their time on "pet" projects in which they are personally interested. In another example, the German semiconductor company Infineon Technologies set up dozens of cross-functional innovation teams in which people from different locations are provided with "free space"—time to think creatively about issues that are very relevant to the future of the organization.[77] But space is also needed in a literal sense—for example, in the form of lounges or other communal areas where people from different parts of an organization can meet and exchange ideas. Finally, many innovation projects require financial resources. In most cases, innovation is not free, but it is an investment in the future of the organization.

Leadership

If they want their teams and organizations to be creative and innovative, managers must actively promote creativity and innovation.[78] They can put innovation high on the agenda; they can encourage collaboration (e.g. through actively supporting activities that are related to forming networks within and beyond the boundaries of the organization); they can try to ensure that their team members can work on challenging tasks that match their passions and skills; and they can be an "appreciative audience," showing their team members that they care about their creative ideas and innovative approaches.[79] Researchers have found that certain leadership behaviors are more conducive to engaging people in creative processes that, in turn, advance their organizations. For example, empowering leadership that invites participation in decision making, recognizes and points out the meaning and significance of employees' contributions, shows trust, and removes bureaucratic obstacles and constraints is more likely to foster engagement in creative activities.[80] Joaquim Vilà, Professor of Strategic Management at IESE Business School, has observed that senior managers in highly innovative companies pursue clear goals that make sense to people in the organization, encourage experimentation and new ways of thinking, persistently support innovative initiatives, even when they are met with resistance or an absence of short-term results, and are willing to accept negative feedback and adapt their own ideas and strategies, too.[81]

Regarding the setting and revising of goals, there seems to be a paradox. Although the purpose of creativity and innovation is to come up with new ideas and solutions, and to change the status quo for the better, changing innovation goals too frequently can actually have a negative effect. As Amabile noticed, innovation goals should ideally "remain stable for a meaningful period of time" because it is quite difficult or even impossible "to work creatively toward a target if it keeps moving."[82]

Pocket Sun: A shining entrepreneurial star

CASE STUDY

Pocket (Yiqing) Sun never expected to become an entrepreneur. She was very interested in music, reading, and writing songs and poetry when, at the age of 18, she decided to leave her Chinese hometown to attend college in Virginia (USA). She often felt lonely during her college years because she was neither used to group projects nor to making presentations. As a foreign student in the US, she had to learn how to "think on your feet,"[83] as she said in an interview with the *Straits Times*. After an internship with a public relations firm in Chicago, a sales job at Louis Vuitton (which she found very interesting in terms of learning about purchase behavior and customer psychology), and a short-term marketing job at Motorola, she decided to pursue a master's degree in Entrepreneurship and Innovation at the University of Southern California (USC)—a decision that would change her life.

During her studies, she realized that running her own business might be the right path for her, as she became fascinated by people who were able to create "something out of nothing."[84] But when she attended entrepreneurship events, she also noticed that female entrepreneurs were underrepresented, both on stage and in the audience. She decided to do something about it and founded SoGal, a community that promotes more diversity in entrepreneurship. From its humble beginnings as a student project at USC, SoGal has quickly developed into a global network with thousands of members. It brings young entrepreneurially minded women together and hosts networking events all around the world, thus contributing to "disrupt[ing] the boys' club."[85]

During the SoGal events, Sun realized that accessing funding was one of the major challenges that female entrepreneurs faced. For example, less than 3 percent of all venture capital (VC) funding was received by female CEOs in the years 2015 and 2016. Sun recognized this problem, and also saw it as an opportunity. She attended a one-week investment training program at Stanford University, where she met venture capitalists from all over the world. Through that program, she also met Elizabeth Galbut, who became her business partner in SoGal Ventures, a Singapore-based company that the founders call "the world's first female-led millennial venture capital firm."[86] Sun sees the relationship with her co-founder as particularly important because having a business partner whom she trusts gives her comfort. The partnership allows them to combine their complementary capabilities and to offer encouragement and support to each other.

Encouragement was indeed necessary, as the business was set up through "a lot of trial and error,"[87] as Sun later described it. However, convinced that "there's nothing you can't learn,"[88] she made connections with partners,

sponsors, and the media—and managed to get more and more attention despite her young age (she founded the firm long before she turned 25). This was testimony to her relentless energy and effective self-marketing; she considers her name "Pocket," inspired by her Chinese nickname meaning "little pocket," to be "very good branding."[89]

The two founders looked at how other firms in the venture capital industry work and then tried to find their own voice, focusing their firm on start-up companies with either female entrepreneurs or otherwise diverse founding teams, or product and service offers for a primarily female customer base. As a young Chinese woman, Sun does not conform to the stereotyped idea of a venture capitalist. Sun sees this difference as one of her biggest assets, however, as it provides her with the ability to connect to a "different set of people," and offer a "different kind of value."[90] With each new investment, Sun and her business partner learned and progressively built credibility. Within two years, they had invested in more than 30 start-up companies, and reportedly had millions of dollars under the management of their first fund.

When Sun makes decisions about investing in early-stage start-up companies, she does not have many numbers to hand, but rather looks for a compelling vision for the long term—whether the start-up has an exciting product which already shows signs of early success in the market (at least as a prototype), and whether she can find certain qualities among the founders, particularly the "ability to build rapport …, courage and perseverance to execute in any situation."[91]

Sun herself is a poster child for an entrepreneur with these abilities. Seeing herself as both "a daring visionary and a relentless executor," she is convinced that her "growth mindset," as she calls it, will help her to overcome all challenges: "If there's something I can't do now, I will figure it out later, or I will find someone to help me figure it out. I don't think there are any deadlocks. There are always things you can do about it."[92]

Sources: *Bassett (2017); Dublish (2017); Kim Hoh (2016); lapost.us (2016); Lim (2016); SoGal (2018); sogalventures.com (2018); Tan (2016); Toh (2017).*

Discussion questions

- How would you characterize Pocket Sun's entrepreneurial mind-set?
- Would you say that Sun is a "born" or "made" entrepreneur—are natural talents for entrepreneurship more important to her success, or life experiences that helped to shape her?
- In your opinion, is Sun taking the optimal approach to assessing investment opportunities in early-stage start-up companies? Would you do something differently if you were to make such decisions?
- What could an established organization that aims to become more innovative learn from Sun's entrepreneurial approach?

10.3 Entrepreneurial opportunities

Peter Burnett

In brief

- Entrepreneurial opportunities arise when unmet needs are matched with potentially value-creating solutions for meeting these needs.

- To recognize these opportunities, the entrepreneurial manager needs the ability to combine knowledge relating both to customer needs and to the potential solutions that address these needs, and to be alert to spotting situations that open up new possibilities for value creation.

- Effective entrepreneurial managers tend to actively search for opportunities. They often find sources of inspiration in customer needs, knowledge-based innovations, changes in market and industry structures, and changing societal trends.

- To find out whether an entrepreneurial opportunity is worth following, managers need to assess its potential impact, whether it fits with the strategic goals of the organization, whether their organization has the requisite abilities to pursue the opportunity, and whether the pursuit of the opportunity is defensible in the face of competition.

Entrepreneurial opportunities:
Previously unexploited ways of creating economic value through matching innovative solutions with unmet market needs.

As we have discussed in Chapter 1, managers are responsible for the short-term performance of their organizational unit, but at the same time also for building potential and laying the ground for performance in the medium and long term. Thus, they need to find the right balance between **exploitation**—getting the most out of what already exists in the organization—and **exploration**, searching for new opportunities for creating value in the future.

Entrepreneurial opportunities, previously unexploited ways of creating economic value, are the pivot of entrepreneurship.[93] They are in the focus of attention of managers who think and act strategically, and who strive to ensure that their organization continues to create and offer value also under changing environmental circumstances (see Chapter 7). Opportunities arise when unmet market needs are matched with ideas for value-creating solutions to meet these needs. Entrepreneurship Professors Shane and Venkataraman defined entrepreneurial opportunities as "those situations in which goods, services, raw materials, and organizing methods can be introduced and sold at greater than their cost of production."[94] An entrepreneurial opportunity is therefore more than just a **business idea**, a concept for a new product or service that could potentially add value; a business idea can only become an entrepreneurial opportunity if there are customers who are receptive to the idea, or—in other words—if enough people are willing to pay enough for the value that it provides.

Business idea:
A concept for generating economic value, for example, through offering a product or service that matches an unmet market need.

Entrepreneurial managers are able to recognize, assess, and pursue potentially profitable opportunities for value creation, either for their existing organizations or through building new ventures. We will now turn to the first stages in this process, **opportunity recognition** and **opportunity assessment**.

Opportunity recognition

Where do entrepreneurial managers get their ideas from? Research results indicate that three factors are particularly important for the recognition of entrepreneurial opportunities (see also Figure 10.6):

1 alertness to opportunities;
2 knowledge and expertise in a specific domain; and
3 actively searching for opportunities.[95]

Creativity of managers and employees
Research & development
Interaction with customers
Market research
Outside expertise
Networking

Knowledge about customer needs

Value

Knowledge about the potential solutions to customer needs

Entrepreneurial alertness

Active search

The identification of entrepreneurial opportunities

Figure 10.6 Identifying entrepreneurial opportunities

Alertness means being open and mentally prepared to spot opportunities. It is the propensity to be attentive to potential connections between unmet customer needs and the means to solve them. Alertness alone is not enough, however. Opportunities can only be discovered if you have sufficient **prior knowledge**, gained through previous business and life experience.[96] To recognize opportunities in a particular market, for example, you first need to understand it; an entrepreneurial manager with prior knowledge about customer needs is better equipped to recognize opportunities for serving these needs than someone who has never been in touch with the customer group.[97] Similarly, once you have identified a customer need, you can only solve the problem if you have the requisite knowledge to do so. Imagine there is a physiotherapist who has a personal interest in computer programming. If this person comes across new digital imaging technology, they might have an idea for a new tool that allows physiotherapists to more effectively document their diagnosis and therapy results in graphical form. This represents a business opportunity that others without domain-relevant knowledge in both physiotherapy *and* computer programming would probably never be able to recognize.

There is also evidence that successful entrepreneurs do more than passively wait for a business idea to strike them as a "flash of inspiration." Many successful founders of new ventures actually engage in an **active search for opportunities**, meaning that they deliberately look for ways to create new business ideas in a specific field that they are already knowledgeable about.[98] As the philosopher, statesman, and scientist Francis Bacon once said, "[a] wise man will make more opportunity than he finds."[99] Thus, entrepreneurial managers will also see the active search for opportunities as an important part of their monitoring and sensemaking task, which we identified as one of the key building blocks for achieving managerial effectiveness in Chapter 1.

Strategies for actively searching for opportunities include:[100]

- *Exploring customer needs*: Listening to customers is one of the best ways to get new business ideas. After all, business ideas are of no value at all if they do not offer value to customers. Where do customers see weaknesses in current product or service offers? What would they like to have but cannot get at the moment? Internally, anyone who has direct contact with customers can be a useful source of information, for instance, sales-people and service staff. Externally, adopting open innovation approaches (discussed in Section 10.2) and gathering information directly from outside sources, such as customers and suppliers, is a helpful strategy. One example of this is the "Lego Ideas" Internet platform, on which fans of the popular plastic construction toys can propose and discuss ideas for new Lego sets, and vote for their favorite suggestions. You might also make use of customer (or supplier) surveys or focus groups. Information on "lead users"—the early adopters of new technologies, products, services or processes—can be especially helpful for spotting new business opportunities. A final strategy when exploring customer needs is to observe their behavior—retail data, web analytics, and even studying your target customers as they go about their daily life (ethnographic observation) can all be helpful in this endeavor. The automaker Ford, for example, used a team of social scientists to study what people think and feel when they drive their new sports car. The information that they gained from their observations—that sensing the car's vibrations, hearing the engine, and having the feeling that a car "looked fast" were much more important than objective horsepower data when judging the "power" of a sports car—was then used by Ford as an input for redesigning the new Mustang sports car model.[101]

- **Exploiting new knowledge**: Knowledge-based innovations often take time to turn into concrete business opportunities, because new knowledge first needs to be translated into reliable technology and then applied in marketable products, services, or processes. Knowledge-based business opportunities can be created through extensive research and development efforts. Interestingly, it is not always the original researchers who benefit commercially from these developments. For example, Skype was neither the inventor of video telephony over the Internet nor the first software application that enabled video calls using that medium. Through its innovative business model, however, in which it offered some of its services for free (most notably audio and video calls within its network), Skype was able to become a successful "born global" firm (a firm that exploits the business opportunities that a new technology opens up in multiple international markets right after it was founded). New knowledge does not have to be *absolutely* new in order to form the basis of an entrepreneurial opportunity; it might just be new to a certain market or used in a novel way. Entrepreneurial managers sometimes transfer successful business models from one market to another by exploiting information asymmetries, a situation where one party has access to infor-mation that others do not. For instance, a company might discover a popular product or service in one geographical region which does not yet exist in their own market. They can then use this information to improve their own offering and get ahead of their competitors.

- **Exploiting changes in market and industry structures**: New opportunities can arise when markets are either rapidly growing or rapidly shrinking, or when the traditional ways of doing business are changing. The deregulation of formerly heavily regulated markets is one example where changes to the business landscape have provided oppor-tunities for new entrants to the market. For example, in some countries private parcel service companies have been able to take away business from formerly state-owned postal services. Participating in industry tradeshows, conferences and association meet-ings, talking with suppliers, distributors and industry experts, and following the news in relevant trade magazines and websites can help you to identify emerging trends in an industry.

- **Tracking societal trends**: Demographic trends can have an impact on business opportu-nities. For example, societies with an aging population have an increasing demand for products and services that are targeted at the needs of the elderly, including, for example, healthcare and leisure offers. Similarly, when people move from rural areas to growing metropolitan cities, new infrastructure needs to be created (e.g. in transport, energy supplies, water, and sanitation systems). But changes in societal perceptions, mood, and values—in how certain groups of people see the world—can also have an effect on businesses.[102] Take veganism as an example. As more and more people decide to become vegan, demand for vegan food, vegan restaurants, and vegan cookbooks soars.

For all these strategies, **social networks** can play an important role. One contact in your network—whether a friend, colleague, market researcher, or industry expert—might know something you don't about an unmet customer need. Another contact may have particular expertise in a technological field which could offer a solution to that need. If you are able to connect these two pieces of information, and perhaps bring these people together, you could open up an entrepreneurial opportunity. This also means that if you associate with people from a variety of very different fields, the chances are higher that you will spot opportunities that others overlook.[103]

Sometimes, opportunities can be found by going against mainstream thought. Entrepreneurial managers should be willing to "disregard the limitations of commonly accepted definitions of material inputs, practices, and definitions and standards, insisting instead on trying out solutions, observing, and dealing with the results."[104] Trying something out can mean offering new products or services for which customers have not yet realized their need. Steve Jobs' creation of the iPhone, for example, created a new customer need rather than responding to an existing one.[105] A structured way of challenging current assumptions in an industry is Kim and Mauborgne's concept of **value innovation** (see also Chapter 7).[106] This approach aims to simultaneously create a value offer that is clearly differentiated from other offers in the industry, while also reducing costs. The basic idea behind value innovation is that it is not necessary to outperform the competition in every aspect, but only in those which are particularly important for the customer (see *Zooming in on value innovation*).

Value innovation:
A systematic approach to achieve both differentiation and cost reduction through creating unique product and service offers that outperform the competition in some (important) aspects, while deliberately reducing the performance on other (less important) aspects.

Zooming in on ▶ VALUE INNOVATION

Value innovation is a concept that can help to identify new, unique configurations of product or service offers. It was developed by W. Chan Kim and Renée Mauborgne and based on their research on "how innovative companies break free from the pack by staking out fundamentally new market space."[107] In a nutshell, this is what you need to do:

1 Identify the main elements of a product or service offer in a particular industry.
2 Determine which of the product or service elements are most valued by customers.
3 Assess how incumbents in the industry typically perform on the different elements of the product or service offer (on a relative scale of low to high). If there are different strategic groups of incumbents, it can also make sense to map the typical performance profile of each strategic group separately.
4 Think about the elements of the product or service offer which could be completely eliminated or considerably reduced below the current industry standard without losing the majority of customers.
5 Think about the elements of the product or service offer which could be considerably enhanced above the current industry standard and which would create additional value for customers.
6 Think about any new elements which could be added to the product or service offer that are not yet provided by existing industry players, but which could potentially create additional value for customers.
7 Juxtapose a typical current value offer and your new value offer on a value curve (see the example in Figure 10.7).
8 Assess whether the new value offer could form the basis for a viable business opportunity.

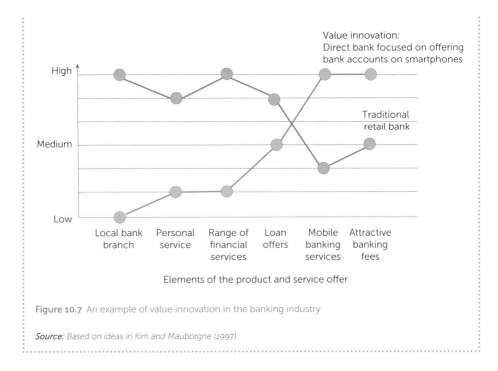

Figure 10.7 An example of value innovation in the banking industry

Source: Based on ideas in Kim and Mauborgne (1997).

Regardless of whether entrepreneurial managers use a systematic approach to identify entrepreneurial opportunities like value innovation or just come across a new business idea, it is unusual to get all the details right straight away. Often, entrepreneurial opportunities develop over time, with some important aspects being recognized from the outset, and others only being clarified in iterative steps, when the opportunity is explored in more depth.[108]

Opportunity assessment

Not every entrepreneurial opportunity that is spotted is worth pursuing. Managers need to stay focused on those opportunities that are in line with their organization's strategy (see Chapter 7), and that could help them to achieve the desired results for their organizations (see Chapter 9). Therefore, entrepreneurial managers should not only be able to recognize, but also to **assess opportunities**.

Identify one difficulty or annoyance that you face in your day-to-day life. Can you come up with a business idea to address this problem? What would you do to assess whether your idea could become a viable business opportunity?

Before resources and energy are committed to making a very detailed assessment of an opportunity, for example in the form of a sophisticated business model or a business plan (see Section 10.4), it usually makes sense to undertake a brief **preliminary opportunity assessment** using the following four questions (see also Figure 10.8):

- *Does the business idea really create value for both customers and the organization?* This question scrutinizes the potential impact of the idea—the "realness" of the opportunity.[109] Will enough people be willing to pay for the new value offer? To qualify as a worthwhile opportunity, a business idea should:

  a   provide a unique and safe solution to an unsolved problem or unmet need in a certain target group;

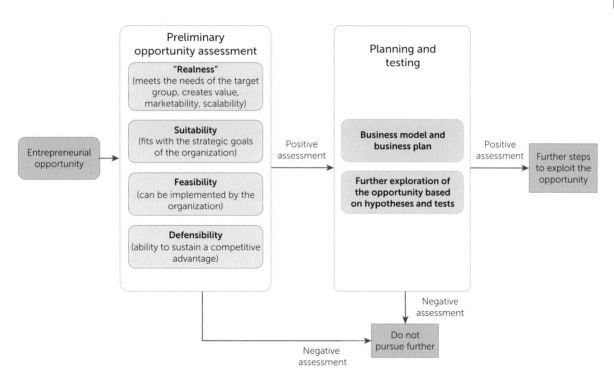

Figure 10.8 The opportunity assessment process

b   be so attractive that people in the target group will be willing to pay considerably more than it would cost the organization to produce (i.e. there must be a viable economic model behind the opportunity);

c   be marketable (How easy would it be to sell the new product or service? Are adequate **distribution channels** available and accessible?); and

d   be scalable (i.e. offer the potential to grow and become a sizeable business); one precondition for scalability is the existence of ongoing demand among a target group of adequate size.

Discussions with (prospective) customers and market research can help to assess the "realness" of the opportunity.

- *Which organization is best suited to implementing the idea?* This question is about the suitability or strategic fit of the business opportunity (see Chapter 7). Is the opportunity in line with the strategic goals of the organization? Does it make sense to follow this particular opportunity rather than other strategic options that the organization has? Or would it be better to implement the idea in another organization? If that is the case, would it make sense to collaborate with others to implement the idea, or would it be better to pursue the opportunity in an independent new venture?

- *Is the organization able to implement the idea?* This question is about feasibility— evaluating whether the organization has the technical, managerial, and business competencies to pursue the business idea.[110] Does the organization also have the necessary resources (e.g. financial resources, production facilities, time, and contacts) or, if not, will it be able to obtain them? Is the right team on board for making the business idea work? Or is it possible to extend the team with people with the right competencies? It is also important to check not only that the organization is able to create new products, services, or processes, but also that it is able to successfully promote and sell the innovations to the target group.

- *Is the opportunity sustainable in a competitive business environment?* Good business opportunities rarely remain unnoticed by the competition for long, especially once a company has started working on them. If the organization does not have a sustainable competitive advantage (see also Chapter 7), it might not be wise to follow an opportunity

Distribution channel:
The network of all people and organizations that are involved in delivering a product (or service) from the producer to the customers and final consumer.

that other, more powerful players could imitate. We just need to look at the fate of Netscape, a company that created a very attractive Internet browser, but then lost considerable market share after the software giant Microsoft embedded its own browser in its operating system.[111] Of course, since then, Microsoft's Internet Explorer has lost out to new competitors too. Therefore, it is important to ask whether the organization is able to protect its intellectual property, for example, in the form of copyrights, patents, or trademarks, or if it will be possible to offer something that is truly unique and difficult to copy or replicate by others?

If the preliminary assessment of the opportunity is positive—i.e. if the idea seems to have real market potential, is in line with the strategic goals of the organization, can be implemented by the organization, and is defensible against potential competitors—entrepreneurial managers can enter the next phase of the opportunity assessment process: the planning and testing stage.

10.4 Approaches to pursuing entrepreneurial opportunities

Pixabay/rawpixel

In brief

- There are two basic approaches to pursuing entrepreneurial opportunities:

    (a) a "traditional," structured approach in which a detailed business plan is first developed and then implemented, and

    (b) a "lean" approach in which a basic, unrefined version of the product or service is brought to market and tested in an iterative way.

- A business plan is a detailed document that describes how a business opportunity will be pursued. It usually includes information about the opportunity, a strategy for exploiting the opportunity, a marketing plan, an operations plan, and a financial plan, as well as information about the entrepreneurial team.

- The "lean start-up" is a more experimental approach, which is based on assumptions (or hypotheses) about which product and service offers, distribution and marketing strategies, and business activities would be most effective. The original business model is then continuously revised based on direct feedback from the market.

- Regardless of the approach taken, the manager's entrepreneurial role goes far beyond conceiving conceptual ideas and business models. In order to turn opportunities into value, managers need to bring other people along and manage the day-to-day challenges that breaking new ground always involves.

Business plan:
A document that describes in quite a detailed way how a business opportunity will be pursued. It usually includes a description of the opportunity, a strategy for exploiting the opportunity, information about the entrepreneurial team, a marketing plan, an operations plan, and financial forecasts.

There are **two basic ways in which managers can pursue entrepreneurial opportunities** which seem to have potential following the preliminary assessment (discussed in Section 10.3). The "traditional" approach is to first write a detailed **business plan**, then secure the necessary resources, and finally implement the plan. This is often demanded of managers by investors (in the case of new ventures) or senior managers (when new business projects are launched within larger organizations). But as heavyweight boxing champion Mike Tyson pointed out, "[e]verybody has plans until they get hit for the first time."[112] Most plans are already outdated by the time they face the reality of the market—especially in highly dynamic environments. For that reason, **hypothesis-driven entrepreneurship** (also known as the "**lean start-up**" approach) is becoming increasingly popular. The idea behind this approach is to develop a broad vision about how the entrepreneurial opportunity could be exploited, translate this vision into a **business model** and hypotheses about what might work, and then test a basic, unrefined version of the product or service in the market. Using customer feedback, you can then revise the business model and your original hypotheses in an iterative process.[113]

There is no clear-cut answer to the question of which of the two approaches is more effective. While some commentators point out that the majority of successful business ventures did not have a detailed business plan when they were launched, there are also research results that report on a higher likelihood of success for those entrepreneurs who write a business plan.[114] In the following paragraphs, we will discuss both approaches in more detail.

Writing a business plan

A **business plan** is a document that describes in quite a detailed way how a business opportunity will be pursued, either in a new venture or within an existing organization. In Chapter 1, we discussed that managerial effectiveness is about achieving a certain goal or desired outcome, but also about setting the right goals in the first place. The business plan is a tool that can help managers to become effective in exploiting an entrepreneurial opportunity. It usually includes the business goals and strategy, as well as a kind of "roadmap" of how these goals could be reached.

The structure of a typical business plan is presented in Table 10.2. Business plans vary in the details. Not all of them will include answers to every question in Table 10.2. In essence, however, they provide information about a business opportunity, the people who will pursue the opportunity, the context (i.e. "the bigger picture"—all factors that could have an impact on the success or failure of the business venture), and the concrete steps that the entrepreneurial team is planning to take in order to exploit the opportunity, as well as predictions for financial outcomes.

Lean start-up (or hypothesis-driven entrepreneurship): An approach to pursuing entrepreneurial opportunities that is based on setting up hypotheses about how an opportunity could be exploited, testing these hypotheses directly in the market, and then adjusting the business model accordingly.

Business model: A representation of the main business decisions and the logic behind how a business generates value (for both customers and the organization).

Table 10.2 Typical structure of a business plan

Business plan section	Possible contents
Executive summary	• Provide a short and concise overview of the key points (max. two pages)
The opportunity	• Describe the problem that the business idea aims to solve (or the need that it aims to satisfy or create) • Describe the product and service offer and how it will help to solve the problem or satisfy a need (the value proposition) • Explain what makes the product or service distinct • Describe the target market and distinct segments within this target market and estimate their size and growth potential • Describe the main factors that could positively or negatively influence the size of the opportunity • Explain why it is the right moment to pursue the opportunity
Strategy	• What are the strategic goals? • Who are the competitors? • What are the sources of competitive advantage? • How can competitive advantage be sustained? • What is the growth strategy for the business venture? • What are the risks involved in the business venture? • Are there any regulations that need to be considered? • What are the key success factors upon which the prosperity of the business depends? • Is intellectual property protection necessary and, if so, how will it be implemented?

Business plan section	Possible contents
Marketing plan	• Who is the target group? • What are the specific requirements of different target customer segments? • Based on what factors do members of the target group (or of different segments thereof) make their purchase decisions? • How will the value offer be positioned in the market? • How will the products or services be distributed? • Which pricing strategy will be followed? • Which promotion and sales activities will be used to reach the target audience? • How much will it cost to acquire and retain customers?
Operations plan	• What are the core processes that need to be set up to operate the business? • What needs to be done in-house and what could be outsourced? • How will the operations be organized? • Which supplier relationships are needed? How will they be organized?
Financial plan	• Include a cash plan (monthly cash inflow and cash outflow forecasts) for the first three to five years • Include monthly income statement forecasts for the first three to five years • Include plan balance sheets for the first three to five years (per quarter and/or per year) • Include a capital expenditure plan for the first three to five years • Include a plan for how the business venture should be funded • Calculate the break-even point, the point (either in time or in terms of number of units sold) when total revenue equals the total costs that have accumulated until this point (i.e. when loss-making ends and profit-making starts) • Include a sensitivity analysis (a test of the robustness of a financial model through calculating different scenarios of what would happen if certain assumptions were changed) and/or a realistic/best/worst case analysis
Management team and organization	• Who are the people who will implement the business plan? • Which qualifications, competencies, and network connections do they bring to the venture? • Who will do what? (include an organization chart) • What is the intended ownership structure? • How will investors be able to cash out on their investment? • Include CVs/résumés for the members of the future management team

What is the **purpose of a business plan**? First, a business plan is often needed because investors or creditors (or top managers in the case of entrepreneurial activities within an existing organization) demand a plan on which they can base their investment decisions. The business plan helps to build the credibility of entrepreneurial managers and their team, and reassures investors and other key stakeholders that the team has thoroughly considered all the important aspects of the business that they plan to launch. But there are also other reasons for investing time into drafting a business plan:[115]

- Working on a business plan forces the entrepreneurial team to think through and discuss all issues that affect future business success.
- Planning helps the entrepreneurial team to better see the connections between the individual elements of the business, and to identify any weak links.
- The business plan can be shared with trusted people outside of the entrepreneurial team as a basis for obtaining additional feedback and advice.
- The financial part of the business plan can be used as a budget, at least for some time after the launch of the project.

When a business plan is developed, it is important to **focus on the needs of the recipients** of the plan. Business plans should help the entrepreneurial team, investors, creditors, or senior managers to make their decisions, so the plan needs to include everything that the decision makers need to know for making well-informed decisions.[116] Actually, a business plan can also be seen as a "selling tool" which entrepreneurial managers can use to convince people to invest in an entrepreneurial venture.

The **financial plan** is a key element of the business plan. It is usually based on a sales plan (including prices and estimated sales volumes) and an estimation of the resource needs (including the cost of employing people, other expenses, capital expenditures, and financing costs) at different stages of the business venture. A detailed cash plan is particularly important because a business that runs out of cash can quickly cease to exist (see Chapter 9). The financial section of a business plan often also includes a sensitivity (or "what if") analysis, or an evaluation of how the figures could vary in a best case, worst case, and most likely scenario. As the assumptions vary, so do the financial outcomes (taking into account that the figures in a business plan are based on assumptions).

Business plans are, of course, not cast in stone. They should tell a compelling and coherent story about how a business idea could be turned into reality. At the same time, they should be open for **revision and reassessment** if certain assumptions or environmental conditions change. A business plan can be a starting point for an entrepreneurial venture, but it should not be confused with the venture itself.

The "lean start-up" approach

Even if considerable time is spent on planning, new ventures rarely proceed according to the original plan. For example, it is easy to put on paper that if only 0.05 percent of the Chinese population buy the new product, sales will skyrocket (0.05 percent of 1.4 billion means 700,000 people, by the way). But it is often a lot more difficult to convince even 100 real (in this case, Chinese) customers to spend their money on a new product or service. The numbers on paper can differ considerably from what entrepreneurs experience in the "real world." That is why the value of exact planning—despite the merits pointed out before—is increasingly challenged. The **"lean start-up"** approach is a new paradigm that favors experimentation over strict planning when it comes to either setting up new businesses or exploiting new business opportunities in established organizations. "Lean" in this context means saving resources and time, and shortening product and business development cycles, through working with hypotheses that are constantly revised based on feedback from the market. This is different, however, from a completely improvised approach in which entrepreneurs work without a clear sense of direction and without structured hypotheses testing.

The basis of a lean start-up (or a lean business development project in an established organization) is not an extensive business plan, but a summary of the main ideas, or hypotheses, in a business model. The **business model** is a roadmap for your venture, describing major business decisions and the logic behind how the business generates value. One of the most popular approaches for designing and explaining a business model is the **business model canvas,** proposed by Swiss business theorist Alexander Osterwalder and Belgian computer scientist Yves Pigneur. It consists of the following nine elements:[117]

1 **Customer segments**: For whom will we create value? What are the target groups for our value offer? (In some cases, like a marketplace or platform business model, it is possible that the business has very different target groups—for example, an online marketplace like Amazon has both retailers who want to sell something and consumers who buy on the marketplace as target groups).

Value proposition:
A statement that clearly describes the benefits that a certain group of customers get from the product and/or service offers of an organization.

2 **Value proposition**: What is the value that we offer to the target group? Which benefits will customers get from us and why would they buy from us rather than from our competitors?

3 **Revenue streams**: Where does the money come from? What are customers willing to pay for (e.g. purchase of tangible products or services, subscription fees, leasing fees, advertising, licensing fees, or brokerage fees)? Is the business based on one or more revenue streams? One example of a business sector with several revenue streams are newspapers which generate revenues from both subscribers and advertising customers.

4 **Channels**: How can we reach customers with our product or service offers? If there are different distribution and marketing channels (e.g. retail stores, a webshop, and direct selling), how will they be integrated?

5 **Customer relationships**: What kind of relationships do our customers expect with our organization (e.g. in terms of service, assistance, or community building)? How are we going to set up and maintain these relationships?

6 **Key activities**: Which activities are required to deliver the value offer for customers? Which additional activities are needed to keep the business running?

7 **Key resources**: What are the key physical, human, intellectual, and financial resources that are required to create the value offer? What capabilities are needed?

8 **Key partners**: Which partners (e.g. suppliers, alliance partners, outsourcing partners) are needed in order to make the business work?

9 **Cost structure**: What are the fixed and variable costs for producing and marketing the value offer and for keeping the business running?

Minimum viable product:

A simplified version of a product that is just good enough to deliver value for customers. It is usually used to test and refine product ideas.

The hypotheses in the business model—for example, regarding the right target customer segments, suitable product and service designs, best distribution channels, or most effective promotional activities—are then tested as quickly as possible by going out to the market. **Minimum viable products**—basic, unrefined versions of products or services which offer sufficient value to satisfy early users, but which have not yet been fully developed—can be used as a basis for getting feedback from customers, suppliers, and partners. Like all other parts of the business concept, they remain a work in progress and are continuously improved or redesigned in iterative cycles until a **product-market fit** is reached.[118] At that point, the organization can start to scale the new business. The whole process is similar to what is called agile development in the software industry, where software solutions are developed in a pragmatic and flexible manner, in collaboration between cross-functional teams and customers.[119]

You can also use this process to **test your hypotheses** by comparing different product or service ideas, or ways of working, to find out which offers the most value. In an A/B test, for instance, customers are divided into two groups with similar characteristics (a treatment group and a control group) and exposed to products or marketing methods that differ in at least one way. The outcomes for both groups (e.g. in terms of sales or usage numbers) are then compared to find out whether the modification had a positive or negative impact on the results.

There are some concerns about the lean start-up approach, however. For example, good ideas launched as minimum viable products might be stolen by others or that these "unfinished" products could have negative reputational effects for the organization. Whether entrepreneurial managers take a planned or a more "lean" approach to exploiting an opportunity will depend on a range of different factors; for example, the requirements of stakeholders, the dynamics of the market environment, or the risks involved in a project. In any case, a good business concept will not be enough. To become effective in managing entrepreneurial ventures, managers must also be able to tell a compelling story, convince people to adopt new ideas, and show resilience as they overcome the day-to-day challenges and obstacles involved in the implementation (see Chapter 8).

Yemeksepeti: Revolutionizing the food delivery business in Turkey and beyond

CASE STUDY

In 2015, Nevzat Aydın, co-founder and CEO of the Turkish food ordering company Yemeksepeti (the Turkish term for "food basket"), made news when he sold the former start-up for US$589 million to Delivery Hero, the global market leader in the food delivery business. It was not only the spectacular business success of the 15-year old venture with its continuing double-digit revenue growth rates that attracted high media attention, but also the fact that Aydın shared $27 million of the proceeds of the company's sale with 114 employees who had worked for Yemeksepeti for more than two years. On average, each of the employees received around 150 times their monthly salary. "Yemeksepeti's success story did not happen overnight and many people participated in this journey with their hard work and talent,"[120] commented Aydın in an interview with *CNN Money*.

Together with three of his former classmates, Aydın had established the company in Istanbul with an initial investment of US$80,000. Although the Internet penetration rate in

Turkey was only about 4 percent at the time, Aydın noticed that there was high growth potential for Internet-based businesses. After considering the advantages and disadvantages of four general business models—betting, auctions, matchmaking, and food delivery—he decided to launch a food ordering platform on which local restaurants could advertise their menus (including pictures of the food) and provide information on their delivery area, delivery times, and working hours. Consumers could then choose their location, favorite food type, and restaurant online, with their orders being forwarded to the restaurants which maintained responsibility for delivery and payment collection. Yemeksepeti, who acted as a broker between the consumers and the restaurants, received a commission for each order that was processed through its website. Consumers did not have to pay any additional fees. Direct online payment was later added to the system, as well as a mobile application that accounted for almost two-thirds of all orders by the end of 2016. Further revenue streams came from monthly fees that the restaurants paid for being listed on the Yemeksepeti portal, exclusive partnership deals (e.g. with a mobile phone company or a soft drinks brand), and online advertising offers.

Convincing restaurants and consumers of the benefits of online ordering was not an easy task at the beginning. Restaurants were reluctant to share their revenues with an intermediary and consumers had reservations about secure payment, food quality, or actually receiving what they paid for. To manage this, Yemeksepeti set up a call center that dealt with all concerns and questions. The call center became known as "one of the fastest service units in Turkey"[121] and would, for example, reassure users that their orders had been received, allow them to cancel, or inform consumers when ordered food was temporarily unavailable.

After a few well-known international restaurant chains enlisted on the platform, more and more restaurants began to trust the online food ordering marketplace. "Yemeksepeti only" deals were offered to increase the attractiveness for users, and there were reports that member restaurants could achieve increases in order volume of around 10—50 percent through using the platform.[122]

Consumers' trust was further strengthened by an online rating system where they could comment on food and service quality, as well as on the delivery speed of individual restaurants. Thanks to effective restaurant selection and performance management procedures, the fault rates of restaurants could be kept at a very low level.

From its humble beginnings as a small, local operation (the company made no profit for the first few years and the founders did not even receive a salary), the start-up developed into Turkey's leading online food delivery portal with operations in dozens of Turkish cities, several million active users, and more than 100,000 orders processed per day. The company also launched or acquired similar food delivery websites in several other countries in the Middle East and South East Europe.

In addition to expanding within Turkey and overseas, the company also added further revenue streams, such as the "Joker," a customer acquisition tool for restaurants. Based on a consumer's order history, Yemeksepeti would offer a 40 percent discount deal, valid for just 15 minutes, if the consumer tried a different restaurant that they had never ordered from before. With the "Joker" offer, consumers could get cheaper food and the restaurant won new customers, while Yemeksepeti kept a part of the discount in addition to the regular commission fee. Aydın also experimented with new food-related Internet portals, for example Yemek.com, a content platform with recipes and cooking videos.

The company collected a lot of user data, including personal data, addresses, food preferences, and ordering and eating habits. "Once I realized the power of data," said Aydın, "I was tempted to open a pizza chain,"[123] as there was probably no one in Turkey who better understood what, when, and where people like to eat. Yemeksepeti used this data, for example, for helping restaurants to make effective promotions for specific target segments in order to increase order frequency and amounts.

Despite its very strong market position, however, Yemeksepeti still faced challenges. Other big online players were launching their own food ordering services (for example, Uber Eats, the online meal ordering and delivery platform from US ridesharing multinational Uber). There were also negative news reports about Yemeksepeti being fined for preventing restaurants from working with competitors based on a contract clause that discouraged restaurants from offering lower prices on any other online platform.[124] Yet in the face of these challenges, Yemeksepeti remained competitive with approximately 27,000 affiliated restaurants and 11 million users in 2018— testament to Aydın's entrepreneurial drive, resilience, strategic thinking, and creativity.

Sources: Ablak (2016); Delivery Hero (2018); Ercu (2015); Henry (2015); Hurriyet (2018); Kerr et al. (2017); Kottasova (2015).

💬 Discussion questions

- Which factors contributed to Nevzat Aydın's successful recognition and exploitation of the opportunity that online food ordering offered?
- Would you say that Aydın took a "planned" or "lean" approach to developing Yemeksepeti into a market leader in the Turkish food delivery business?
- How would you describe the main elements of Yemeksepeti's business model?
- Does Yemeksepeti's business model offer a sustainable competitive advantage or is it easily replicable?

Conclusion

In a dynamic business environment, managers cannot confine themselves simply to supervising the existing business. Instead of being passive bystanders, they need to actively align their organizations to the changing circumstances. Regardless of whether they are responsible for a project team, a department, or an organization as a whole, managers who are able to think and act in an entrepreneurial way will be better prepared for success in a dynamic environment. They can, for example, use the design thinking process for finding creative solutions to complex problems, spot and assess opportunities for value creation within and outside the organization, initiate and implement innovation processes that enable them to put new ideas into practice, and create business plans or "lean" business models that help them to receive support from those with the power to allocate resources for new projects. The application of entrepreneurial methods and approaches is not limited to new ventures. Managers can also use them to improve processes and create value in established organizations.

In the Introduction to this chapter, we travelled back in time to discover the origins of Nike in the 1960s. The company has since developed into a global sports apparel powerhouse with more than US$30 billion in revenues. Does that mean that Nike is now less entrepreneurial than half a century ago? Mark Parker, who joined Nike as a designer in the late 1970s and has since become the company's CEO, said in an interview with *AnOther* magazine in 2016 that he sees more potential for change and meaningful innovation today than a few decades ago. He spoke about "lifting up rocks to find new solutions to problems, ... looking in places that maybe many people aren't looking," and being "a sponge"—"finding inspiration in anything, from the texture of that table, or the colour of the sunset, to the chromatic effect of the surface of a beetle's shell."[125] Recognizing opportunities for improving the company's products and creating innovative solutions for customers still lies in Nike's DNA. Its countless recent innovations include: manufacturing methods that produce less waste through using recycled threads, better cushioning solutions for athletic shoes, and adaptive lacing technology that electronically adjusts to the contours of each individual foot.

Phil Knight, Nike's co-founder and former CEO, said that what he particularly likes about his successor Parker is that "he's noted for being able to admit a mistake when he makes one."[126] Acknowledging that the "perfect manager" does not exist, he values the open and honest culture that Parker upholds in the company. In Nike, said Knight, "you don't get in trouble for making mistakes. You get in trouble for covering up mistakes."[127] Mistakes and failures inevitably happen when you try out new things. But not trying at all is the worst thing that an entrepreneurial manager can do.

The example provided by these two CEOs at Nike underlines what we have discussed in this chapter. Effective entrepreneurial managers—regardless of whether they create new ventures or work for established organizations—are customer-centered and open-minded, able to identify, actively create, and exploit opportunities for value creation, and committed to creating a culture that encourages creativity and innovation instead of punishing failures. Above all, they have a clear desire to learn, rather than an "I-know-it-all" attitude. Instead of being content to stand still, they always see room for improvement and growth for themselves and their organization.

In a recent interview with the podcast series *HBR IdeaCast*, Phil Knight remembered that his co-founder Bill Bowerman used to say that Nike's shoes were "the worst shoes in the world except for everybody else's," adding that he thought that today, "he'd still think the same, yes."[128]

✓ Review questions

1   What should managers do to fulfill their entrepreneurial role?
2   How would you characterize an "entrepreneurial manager"?

3   How can the design thinking approach help managers to solve complex problems?

4   What is corporate entrepreneurship and how can it be fostered by managers?

5   What tensions exist between the typical working patterns of established organizations and the requirements of new entrepreneurial ventures?

6   Why are creativity and innovativeness important for organizations?

7   What factors influence the creativity of individuals?

8   What is innovation?

9   What are the main steps of the innovation process?

10   What can managers do to foster creativity and innovativeness in their organization?

11   How can entrepreneurial managers find new opportunities for value creation?

12   Which questions could a manager ask to assess whether an entrepreneurial opportunity is worth pursuing?

13   What is a business model?

14   Why might we need a business plan and what elements does it usually include?

15   How does the "lean start-up" approach differ from the "traditional" approach to planning and implementing new ventures?

⑦ Critical reflection questions

1   Why do managers also need to be innovators and entrepreneurs? Isn't it enough to perform well in the "traditional" managerial role?

2   What do you see as more important for an organization, stability or constant innovation?

3   Reflecting on what you have read in this chapter, can creativity and innovation really be managed?

4   What is your opinion on open innovation? What are the advantages and disadvantages of including outsiders in an organization's innovation process?

5   Are comprehensive business plans outdated in an increasingly fast-changing business environment?

☞ Managerial implications

● Effective managers are aware of their entrepreneurial role—their responsibility for actively adapting their organization to a changing environment to ensure the organization's long-term survival and prosperity. Identifying, creating, and pursuing new opportunities for value creation lie at the heart of the entrepreneurial role.

● Entrepreneurship is not restricted to start-up companies. Entrepreneurial managers can be found in organizations of any age and size. They are not defined by the organizational context in which they work, but by their open mind-set, their drive to find new ways of solving problems and satisfying customer needs, and their ability to implement innovative ideas that create value for customers and the organization.

● Entrepreneurial managers foster creativity and innovativeness in their organizations through:
   — their own commitment to innovation;
   — ensuring an open communication flow within and across organizational boundaries;
   — supporting a learning-oriented culture in which different opinions are valued;
   — the provision of sufficient time, space, and financial resources for engaging in innovation;
   — establishing clear processes which support innovation; and
   — empowering people to take novel approaches to problem solving, instead of exerting excessive control.

● Effective entrepreneurial managers are alert to new business opportunities and are able to match customer needs with potential solutions which satisfy them in a way that creates value. But they do not simply wait for business ideas to present themselves. Instead, they actively search for opportunities and are able to assess whether they are real, suitable for the organization, feasible to implement, and defensible in the face of competition.

- Some managers prefer to think through an opportunity in considerable detail and write a business plan before they start to implement their idea. Others take a more hands-on approach, establish hypotheses, and then quickly test them in the market. Both approaches have their merits and disadvantages, so we cannot say that one is always better than the other. Regardless of the approach, however, entrepreneurial managers must have the courage to try out something new, and be open to revising their own assumptions and adapting their ideas when faced with the reality of the market.

Endnotes

[1]Wassermann and Anderson (2012).
[2]McGinn and Knight (2017).
[3]Mintzberg (1975).
[4]Shane and Venkataraman (2000).
[5]Drucker (1985), p. 67.
[6]Drucker (1985), p. 72.
[7]Schumpeter (2010).
[8]Mintzberg (1975), p. 56.
[9]Rosa (2013).
[10]Burns (2016).
[11]Burns (2016), pp. 6–8.
[12]Rose (2013), p. 29.
[13]Duening (2010).
[14]Dalborg et al. (2012).
[15]Garvin and Levesque (2006).
[16]Kuratko et al. (2014).
[17]Chakravorti (2010).
[18]airliquide.com (2019b).
[19]Air Liquide (2015), p. 4.
[20]Anderson et al. (2014).
[21]Mui (2012).
[22]Amabile (1998).
[23]Amabile and Pratt (2016).
[24]Ko and Butler (2007).
[25]Ko and Butler (2006).
[26]Ko and Butler (2007), p. 368.
[27]Ko and Butler (2007).
[28]Miller et al. (2007).
[29]Amabile (1998).
[30]Amabile and Pratt (2016).
[31]Amabile and Pratt (2016).
[32]Amabile and Pratt (2016).
[33]deepmind.com (2019).
[34]Amabile (1998), p. 77.
[35]Tuff (2011).
[36]Kanter (1988).
[37]Amabile and Pratt (2016).
[38]Amabile and Pratt (2016).
[39]Perry-Smith and Mannucci (2017).
[40]Thomke and Randal (2012).
[41]Kanter (1988), p. 97.
[42]Drucker (1985), p. 72.
[43]Kanter (1988), p. 101.
[44]Chesbrough (2006).
[45]West and Bogers (2014).

[46]Hyo-sik (2012).
[47]Jeong-Dong (2016).
[48]AmorePacific (2018).
[49]AmorePacific (2018).
[50]Cornell (2013).
[51]Cornell (2013).
[52]Hyo-sik (2012).
[53]Perry-Smith and Mannucci (2017).
[54]Kanter (1998); Perry-Smith and Mannucci (2017).
[55]Kanter (1998); Perry-Smith and Mannucci (2017).
[56]Perry-Smith and Mannucci (2017).
[57]Kanter (1988), p. 94.
[58]Amabile and Pratt (2016).
[59]time.com (2003).
[60]Drucker (1985), p. 72.
[61]Thomke and Randal (2012).
[62]da Vinci (2008), p. 8.
[63]Thomke and Randal (2012), p. 10.
[64]da Vinci (2008), p. 266.
[65]Amabile and Pratt (2016).
[66]Skarzynski and Gibson (2008).
[67]The quote is attributed to Horst Höller, former country manager of 3M in Austria, cited in Stern and Jaberg (2010), p. 70, translated by the author.
[68]Amabile and Pratt (2016).
[69]Wallis (2007).
[70]Birchall (2008).
[71]Weber and Szkudlarek (2013), pp. 45 and 49.
[72]Weber and Skudlarek (2013), p. 47.
[73]Global Entrepreneurship Monitor (2019).
[74]Weber and Skudlarek (2013), p. 43.
[75]Weber et al. (1998), p. 175.
[76]Skarzynski and Gibson (2008).
[77]Sternad et al. (2012).
[78]Zhang and Bartol (2010).
[79]Amabile and Khaire (2008).
[80]Zhang and Bartol (2010).
[81]Vilà (2011).
[82]Amabile (1998), p. 82.
[83]Kim Hoh (2016).
[84]Tan (2016).
[85]SoGal (2018).

[86]sogalventures.com (2018).
[87]Dublish (2017).
[88]Dublish (2017).
[89]Kim Hoh (2016).
[90]Lim (2016).
[91]lapost.us (2016).
[92]Lim (2016).
[93]Baron (2006); Shane and Venkataraman (2000).
[94]Shane and Venkataraman (2000), p. 220.
[95]Baron (2006).
[96]Baron (2006).
[97]Shane (2000).
[98]Patel and Fiet (2009).
[99]Bacon (1985), p. 214.
[100]Drucker (2015); Harvard Business School Press (2009).
[101]Cayla et al. (2013).
[102]Drucker (2015).
[103]George et al. (2016).
[104]Baker and Nelson (2005), p. 334.
[105]Suddaby et al. (2015).
[106]Kim and Mauborgne (1997).
[107]Kim and Mauborgne (1997), p. 172.
[108]Baron (2006).
[109]Stevenson and Spence (2009).
[110]Harvard Business School Publishing (2009).
[111]Stevenson and Spence (2009).
[112]LA Times (1987).
[113]Eisenmann et al. (2013).
[114]Greene and Hopp (2017); Tjan (2012).
[115]Harvard Business School Press (2005).
[116]Harvard Business School Press (2005).
[117]Osterwalder and Pigneur (2010).
[118]Eisenmann et al. (2013).
[119]Blank (2013).
[120]Kottasova (2015).
[121]De Mey (2011).
[122]De Mey (2011).
[123]Kerr et al. (2017), p. 6.
[124]Ablak (2016).
[125]Skidmore (2016).
[126]McGinn and Knight (2017).
[127]McGinn and Knight (2017).
[128]McGinn and Knight (2017).

 Visit the companion website at macmillanihe.com/sternad-management to access multiple choice questions, useful weblinks and additional materials.

APPENDIX: A very brief history of effective management

Outline of appendix

Introduction
Ideas about management in pre-industrial societies
Bureaucratic and scientific management
The first general theory of management
The human relations movement
Behavioral theories of management
Quantitative approaches and the quality management movement
Systems theory and the contingency approach
The top management view and strategic management
"New leadership" approaches
Management in the 21st century
Conclusion

This appendix will enable you to

- Identify the major schools of thought in the history of management and describe their key ideas and concepts.
- Review how different perspectives on effective management evolved over time.
- Examine how changes in the historical context affect what people perceive as effective management.
- Compare different approaches to management and their relative merits and drawbacks.
- Recognize how concepts of managerial effectiveness from the past still influence managerial practice today.
- Reflect on how and why the perception of effective management is changing over time.

Introduction

The great German poet and dramatist Johann Wolfgang von Goethe famously wrote that those who fail to learn from the last 3,000 years of history would stay "void of experience, in the dark, and live from day to day."[1] Because we would not want managers (and students of management) to stay void of experience, it might be worth taking a quick look back into history to learn more about what has been considered as effective management over the last few decades, centuries, or even 3,000 years.

Acquiring a good understanding of the history of the field can help us to develop a more nuanced view about what managerial effectiveness meant (and still means) in different environments, thus reminding us that our own **modern view on managerial effectiveness is inevitably context-bound**. As the nature of work changes, so does the nature of management. Nevertheless, many of today's management problems have occurred before, and smart people have already tried to find—and have found—solutions for these problems. Thus, going back in time to explore how people thought about managerial issues in the past can potentially help us to avoid mistakes in the future. It can also provide a fuller picture of what effective management means in different environments, and thereby enhance our ability to **develop new perspectives on effective management** today and in the future.

But can we really find examples of literature on effective management that are 3,000 years old? To use the famous words of former US President Barack Obama: "Yes, we can!" Perhaps these old manuscripts were not yet known as "management textbooks," but as we will see, people certainly thought and wrote about management and leadership issues a few thousand years ago.

Ideas about management in pre-industrial societies

Management has existed ever since people first started to cooperate in order to achieve common goals—which is to say probably for as long as human beings have existed. As soon as people began to write, they used **administrative records**. Examples include the first written records from Mesopotamia as far back as the fourth millennium BC, but also documents from ancient Egypt and China.[2] These administrative records were used to cope with the managerial demands posed by the development of more complex political and organizational structures in these ancient city-societies.[3]

We can find evidence for structured thinking about issues related to effective management dating back hundreds or even thousands of years in different world regions. For example, the book *The Art of War*, which is over 2,500 years old and generally accredited to the Chinese general and philosopher **Sun Tzu**, includes an extensive account of military strategies that continue to influence the strategic thinking of managers in modern organizations.[4] Also in China, **Han Fei Tsu**, who lived around 280–233 BC, influenced the emperors of the Qin dynasty with his treatise on management, in which he emphasized, for example, the importance of managing through setting standards, the observation of subordinates' strengths and motives, and the need to clearly describe the responsibilities of different organizational units.[5] In 14th-century North Africa, **Ibn-Khaldun** referred to leadership-related issues in his writings about the development of societies. For example, he pointed out the importance of being generous, kind, and protective of your subordinates, as well as of establishing what is called *asabiya* in Arabic (which could be translated as "a sense of solidarity" or "group feeling") among your followers as a precondition for effective leadership.[6]

We can identify a whole genre of **instruction literature** that deals with principles of effective management, leadership and administration, for example, in ancient Egypt, Greece, or Rome, as well as Europe in the Middle Ages and in Renaissance times.[7] Examples include:

* the *Instruction of Ptah-hotep* (written around 4,500 years ago by **Ptah-hotep**, a vizier, or highest official, of the Egyptian king Issis) with its advice on how to behave as a leader (e.g. "If you are a man of authority, be patient when you are listening to the words of a petitioner"[8]);
* the Greek philosopher **Plato** who wrote in *The Republic* (around 380 BC) that "the art of the ruler ..., whether in a state or in private life, could only regard the good of his flock or subjects;"[9]
* the Roman orator and statesman **Cicero** who in his treatise *On Obligations* (44 BC) considered self-management issues, such as focusing on priorities: "we should assess the importance of a project we seek to achieve, to ensure that neither more nor less attention and labour is expended than the case justifies;"[10]
* **Saint Benedict of Nursia**, whose management and leadership principles were laid down in the 6th century in his famous *Rule* and are still applied in Benedictine monastic communities all over the world (see also Chapter 8);[11]
* **Niccolò Machiavelli**'s *The Prince* (first published in 1513), a standard text for all those who want to gain power and stay in power, which includes strategies that are allegedly still used by unscrupulous managers. For example, those who follow Machiavelli's questionable advice that "since it is difficult to be both together, it is much safer to be feared than to be loved."[12]

Instruction literature was typically written in a way that addressed a specific person (for example, a king, prince, or abbot) and included examples of how wise leaders and administrators govern. It could be seen as a "forerunner of the twentieth century management science."[13]

In the 17th century, to reap the economic advantage of their expansive colonial policies, European states granted exclusive intercontinental trading rights to a select few companies, which led to the establishment of huge **pre-industrial multinational corporations**. These organizational behemoths virtually ruled the overseas territories in which they were active, and even had the right to wage wars (a right that they often used to the detriment of the local population). They usually worked with strictly hierarchical management systems.[14] Take, for example, the London-based **East India Company**, which was primarily active in organizing trade between Europe and India as well as other parts of Maritime East and Southeast Asia. The East India Company had elected executive directors who oversaw committees that handled different business functions such as communication with overseas subsidiaries, managing accounts, managing relations with financial markets, or warehousing and shipping, supported by "a small army of clerks" that were known as "writers."[15] Also in the **Vereenigde Oostindische Compagnie** (the Dutch East India Company), we already observe a separation between owner-ship and management as well as an early kind of shareholder value-orientation—features that are typically attributed to modern corporations.[16]

The Hudson's Bay Company: An example of effective management in the 17th century

The Hudson's Bay Company (HBC) was founded in 1670 in London to organize the fur trade from the shores of Hudson's Bay and James Bay in Canada. The company established trading posts that were typically more than ten travel days apart. These posts were run by managers, who were called "chief factors," and their staff, including assistant managers, laborers, tradesmen, and seamen. Not unlike modern top managers, the chief factors received three- to five-year contracts and reported to the HBC's Executive Committee in London, although they rarely met in person. The company used very structured management practices to organize its widely dispersed operations. Recruiting agents were employed to find new staff who then received detailed face-to-face instructions about their tasks and responsibilities. Strict documentation and communication norms (for example, structured annual letters that were sent to and from each trading post) ensured that both the Central Committee in London and the local managers in the trading posts were fully informed about the company's expectations and business results, and could control the development of what we would today call "key performance indicators." These norms and rules for communication between posts also helped them to collaborate in a coordinated way. Within this framework, local managers were given a high degree of autonomy. Knowing that "it is impossible at this distance to give such Orders as shall answer every occurrence and be strictly observed in all points ...," as was written in an instruction letter from the HBC's Executive Committee in London to one of its managers across the Atlantic, "we ... must leave much to your prudent conduct, having always in your eye the true interest & advantage of the Company."[17] The combination of clear structures and processes on the one hand and a high degree of trust and local discretion on the other has allowed the HBC to operate successfully for centuries, and it could be considered to be an early example of a "virtual" organization (in the sense that it is geographically widely dispersed). The company still exists and today is one of Canada's leading retail groups.

Source: Based on information in O'Leary et al. (2002).

To summarize, principles of effective management were already being discussed and applied long before the 20th century. What emerges is a pattern that we will continue to observe in the later development stages of management thought: theorists were either more focused on the **"human side" of management**—the principles of effective interactions between leaders and followers (as, for example, in much of the instruction literature)—or on the more **"mechanistic" precepts** of how to effectively manage an organization by means of devising and implementing strategies, structures, processes, and systems (such as in the administrative systems that were set up in the colonial trade corporations in the 17th and 18th centuries). Figure A1 provides an overview of people-centered and mechanistic approaches to management and leadership thought over time.

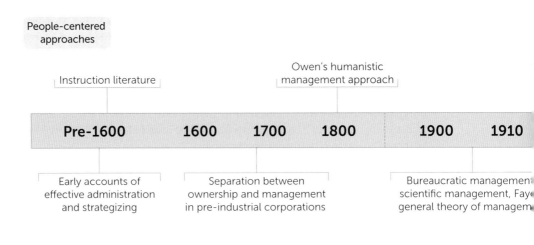

Figure A1 An overview of the main streams of management thought from ancient times to the 21st century

Bureaucratic and scientific management

As the Industrial Age came into full bloom from the 18th century onwards, power-driven machines enabled the concentration of production in large factories. By the turn of the 19th to the 20th century, US business tycoons such as John D. Rockefeller (in the oil business), Andrew Carnegie (steel), J. P. Morgan (banking) and Cornelius Vanderbilt (transportation) had created corporate giants with several thousand employees. In the early 20th century, **Henry Ford** fostered mass production with the development of the assembly line manufacturing system. He systematically lowered production costs, while also trying to pay fair wages to his workers.

It was soon recognized that such huge organizations could no longer be led solely by intuition. The German sociologist **Max Weber** (1864–1920), for example, pointed out the need for establishing more **bureaucratic organizations**. This might sound like a relatively quirky demand to our 21st-century ears because we tend to associate the word "bureaucracy" with red tape and working to the rulebook, which might bring organizations to a standstill. Weber, however, saw bureaucracy as an ideal form of a rationally managed organization. He was convinced that it was able to outperform other types of organization in which arbitrariness and the unpredictable caprices of individual bosses prevailed. He advocated the division of labor, the establishment of clear managerial hierarchies, formal selection of all employees based on their qualifications, and an impersonal application of rules.[18] He envisioned bureaucracy as a highly efficient form of organization in which qualifications (and merit) count more than personal loyalties and political maneuvering.

Another advocate of creating rationally optimized organizations was **Frederick Winslow Taylor**, who spearheaded the **scientific management** movement with his work *The Principles of Scientific Management* (1911). Taylor can be seen as one of the first management consultants in a modern sense. Very much in keeping with his education as a mechanical engineer and maybe also influenced by a rigidly controlled childhood,[19] he saw organizations as big machines which could—and should—be optimized in terms of efficiency in order to maximize entrepreneurs' profits. However, at the same time they should also provide benefit for workers because he was convinced that the main purpose of work lies in receiving wages. In his four main principles, he advocated the use of scientific methods (in the sense of measuring and testing how to best organize work) for managing an organization. In particular, he proposed to:

1   scientifically study and design each element of work instead of using approximate, intuitive, rule-of-thumb methods;
2   scientifically select, train, and develop workers;

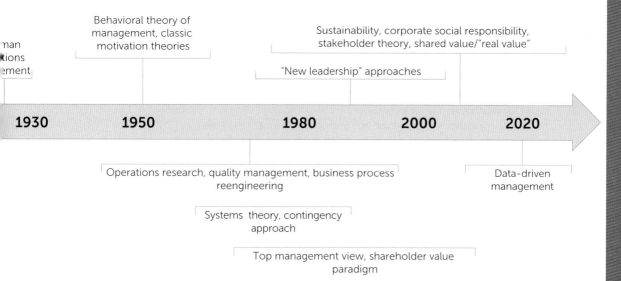

3   make sure that work is performed in accordance with scientifically developed standards; and

4   divide work and responsibilities between managers (who are responsible for planning, deci-
    sion making, and control) and workers (who are responsible for executing the actual work)
    and ensure what he called "cooperation" between the two groups—which in this case was
    another way of saying that workers had to do what the managers told them in return for
    their wages.[20]

What Taylorism meant in practice was that managers began using a stopwatch to measure
how much time a worker would need for the performance of a certain task and think about how
certain elements of the work could be optimized in order to avoid excess (or "wasted") motion
and achieve a higher output in a given period of time. **Frank and Lillian Gilbreth** perfected this
time and motion study method with the use of a motion picture camera. They also examined
factors that could decrease fatigue, thus pioneering what we today call **ergonomics**, the study of
optimizing the way that people interact with their working environments.[21] Another pioneer of
scientific management was **Henry L. Gantt**, who is today best known for his invention of the
Gantt chart, which illustrates the progress that has been made in a project and can help to spot
and manage overlapping demands. But Gantt was also one of the first management thinkers
who pointed out the social responsibility of business.[22]

The proponents of scientific management advocated a "fair day's wage for a fair day's work,"[23]
which basically meant that workers should be compensated according to certain standard
benchmarks rather than being at the mercy of their individual boss. The Taylorist system led to
improvements in efficiency and maybe also to more fairness, but was not free of negative side-
effects such as strikes, absenteeism, or sabotage when people felt exploited and exhausted
because they were unable to cope with the demands of the merciless stopwatch-based system.[24]

The first general theory of management

While Taylor and his fellow campaigners for scientific management tried to introduce their
machine-like management system in North America, a French mining engineer called **Henri
Fayol** created the first general theory of management on the other side of the Atlantic Ocean.
Fayol clearly had a more widely encompassing view of management than the narrow focus on
enhancing efficiency in scientific management. Actually, he was credited with being the first
person to structure the management process into **planning, organizing, commanding, coordinating, and controlling**, a structure that is still widely used in management education more
than a century later.

In his work *Administration industrielle et générale* (1916), Fayol proposed his famous **14 principles of (effective) management**:[25]

1 *Division of work*: With the aim of reaping advantages from work specialization such as being able to match tasks to the strengths of individual workers, increased productivity through learning effects when the same operation is continuously repeated, or saving time as people need less training when they perform fewer tasks.

2 *Authority and responsibility*: The right to give orders to subordinates, but on the understanding that you still accept responsibility for the final results.

3 *Discipline*: Obedience and respect of agreements.

4 *Unity of command*: Every subordinate should receive orders from only one boss.

5 *Unity of direction*: Each organizational unit should only have one head and one plan.

6 *Subordination of individual interest to general interest*: The organization's interests must take precedence over individual or group interests.

7 *Remuneration*: Depends on many factors, but should always be fair and motivating.

8 *Centralization*: Is not "good" or "bad" in itself, but managers should strive for the optimum degree of centralization versus decentralization.

9 *Scalar chain:* There should be a clear line of authority, so that it is always clear who reports to whom. Fayol also acknowledged, however, that some degree of structured lateral communication is needed in organizations.

10 *Order:* Every single thing should have its (fixed) place in an organization, and so should every person.

11 *Equity:* Managers should ensure that people are treated with "a combination of kindliness and justice."[26]

12 *Stability of tenure of personnel:* To ensure that all tasks are performed by well-trained people.

13 *Initiative:* Giving people the "freedom to propose and execute"[27] in order to move the business forward.

14 *Esprit de corps:* Gaining strength from unity, and trying to avoid too much conflict between the members of an organization.

Like scientific management, Fayol's principles were later criticized for being suitable only for relatively simple and stable organizations (which rarely exist in today's dynamic business environment) as well as failing to cover the relationship between organizations and their environment.[28] Nevertheless, Fayol made a first move toward acknowledging that managers are more than just efficiency-enhancing operators of organizational machines. His principles 11 to 14, in particular, indicate that he understood that organizations cannot become successful without people who are both able and motivated to perform well in their jobs.

The human relations movement

During the 1920s and 1930s, the tide clearly turned from a mechanistic view of management to a consideration of the human factor. One important trigger was the **Hawthorne studies**, which began in the 1920s in the Hawthorne plant of the Western Electric Company in Illinois, USA. The original aim of the studies was to observe the impact of physical working conditions (for example, different levels of lighting) on worker productivity. A team of psychologists led by **Elton Mayo** found that when the researchers changed the level of lighting and altered other physical conditions, productivity improved regardless of the direction of these changes. After some time, they concluded that the fact that attention was being paid to the workers by the researchers and management, as well as the workers feeling involved in changing their own working conditions, actually had a stronger effect on employee morale than any of the specific changes to physical conditions (the *"Hawthorne effect"*). The Hawthorne researchers received some criticism regarding their methods and conclusions, but they prompted a sea change in thinking about effective management: Suddenly, everyone was interested in the human side of organizations.

This is what we read in most textbooks about the emergence of the human relations movement. Actually, there had been much earlier attempts on the part of benevolent entrepreneurs and managers to care for the welfare of their workers. One salient example is the Welsh textile manufacturer and social reformer **Robert Owen**, who became the manager of the New Lanark cotton-spinning mill in Scotland in the year 1800, and subsequently not only tried to create good relationships with his workers, but also initiated a range of activities to improve their working and living conditions. For example, he introduced the eight-hour workday for his workers, provided them with meals in the factory, and set up stores where they could buy necessities at very low prices.[29] Owen's humanistic management approach was not only beneficial for the workers, but also helped to ensure good business results.[30]

Despite earlier precursors, the Hawthorne studies can still be credited with bringing the human factor of management to a wider spotlight.

There were other individuals advocating a similar approach. For example, **Mary Parker Follett** (1868–1933) wrote about power, the importance of harmonious human relations in organizations, group processes, and conflict management.[31] She also pointed out the value of constructive conflict for effective decision making.[32] **Chester I. Barnard** (1886–1961)—a business executive himself—saw organizations as cooperative systems and stressed the importance of effective communication as well as keeping individual goals and organizational goals in balance.[33] He also acknowledged the benefits of the informal organization in promoting information sharing and cohesiveness.[34]

The human relations movement directed managerial attention to psychological factors such as work motivation, interpersonal relationships, or group dynamics.[35] It also paved the way for the development of personnel management (later called human resource management) as a business function and for the rise of the classic behavioral theories of management.

Behavioral theories of management

Since 1947, when the American economist and later Nobel laureate **Herbert A. Simon** (1916–2001) published his magnum opus *Administrative Behavior*, it has become evident that people in organizations (and managers, in particular) are not the fully rational beings that earlier scientific theories of management wanted to make us believe.[36] Simon also reminded us that "the behavior of individuals is the tool with which [an] organization achieves its purposes."[37]

The behavior of individuals was also the focus of the **classic motivation theories** which were developed by American psychologists in the 1940s and 1950s:

- **Abraham Maslow** suggested a hierarchy of needs that range from low-level physiological and safety needs to higher-level belongingness, esteem, and self-actualization needs. He posited that people will only be motivated by higher-level needs when the needs on the lower levels have been adequately satisfied.[38]
- **Frederick Herzberg** proposed his "two factor" theory of work motivation, in which he distinguished between *hygiene factors* (that can demotivate when they are not present, but will not lead to higher motivation levels), such as working conditions or salary, and *growth factors* or *motivators* (that will usually not lower motivation in their absence, but can help to increase motivation when present), such as recognition, interest or challenging tasks.[39]
- **David McClelland** distinguished between three major motives that drive people's behavior: the need for achievement, the need for affiliation, and the need for power.[40]

Managers can have two fundamentally different perspectives on what drives motivation and—in a wider sense—human behavior in general. These perspectives were succinctly summarized by **Douglas McGrego**r under the terms **Theory X** and **Theory Y** (see Table A1).[41] Theory X is the belief that workers generally have a low level of ambition for work beyond following their self-interest, and that they will only perform well in an organizational context when they are controlled and receive rewards or punishments for their actions. In contrast, managers who follow Theory Y assume that people are generally self-motivated and like to take on responsibility for interesting tasks even if they do not receive direct rewards. Both theories seem to have their supporters among today's managers, some of whom think that every aspect of organizational life needs to be regulated and controlled, and others who believe in empowerment, self-organization, and the delegation of responsibilities and authority to members of their team.

Table A1 The basic assumptions of Theory X and Theory Y

Theory X	Theory Y
• People have the tendency to work as little as possible.	• People are inherently self-motivated and like to do interesting work.
• People generally do not like to take responsibility and prefer to be led by others.	• Most people are willing to take responsibility and are ready to contribute to the goals of an organization if they find meaning in its purpose.
• Most people are self-centered and will only focus their efforts on reaching the goals of the organization when they are controlled, rewarded, or punished.	• "Management by control" and coercion do not encourage people as much as giving them interesting tasks and meaningful work.
• It is the manager's task to direct and control the actions of the employees.	• It is the manager's task to create growth opportunities, remove obstacles, and help employees to develop their full potential.

Source: Inspired by concepts in McGregor (1960).

William Ouchi later complemented McGregor's categorization with **Theory Z**, a term which he used to describe management practices that he considered were typical of Japanese companies. Theory Z-style management is characterized, for example, by a high degree of employee participation in decision-making processes, long-term employment commitments from the company side, a strong focus on training and developing employees, and personal concern by the management for the welfare of employees.[42] Cooperation and harmonious working relationships are values that are held in high esteem in Theory Z-oriented organizations.

The behavioral perspective on organizations also fueled the **organizational development movement**, which has focused on improving organizational performance through effectively managing people-centered change processes. The importance of **organizational culture** for building high-performance organizations was also recognized, as was the role that **different national cultures** play in determining how people think and act in an organizational context (for example, in the works of **Geert Hofstede** or **Edward T. Hall**) (see Chapter 5).[43]

Managers also began to see the benefits of being close to their team members, for example, in facilitating information flow, creating a common sense of purpose and a coherent organizational culture, enhancing employee motivation, and identifying potentials for the continuous improvement of the organization. The term **"management by wandering around"** for managers who frequently leave their office to chat with employees across the organization was often associated with Hewlett-Packard's top managers in the 1970s. As so often in the history of management and leadership, however, we can find earlier examples. George Simpson, a manager of the Hudson's Bay Company in the 1820s, for example, used a strategy that was later called "management by canoeing around"—he frequently visited trading posts in the Canadian wilderness to reinforce key organizational values across the company.[44]

Behavioral theories of management were criticized for being somewhat simplistic, since they were unable to account for all of the complexities of individual behavior.[45] Nevertheless, it was clear by this point that effective management is more than just planning, organizing, commanding, coordinating, and controlling—that it is also about understanding the needs and behavior of employees. Those who wanted to be effective managers needed to become effective leaders of people.

Quantitative approaches and the quality management movement

After World War II—as a by-product of the use of mathematical and statistical methods for military purposes during the war—quantitative methods were increasingly applied in a business context.[46]

The terms **management science** and **operations research** referred to the application of a range of different analytical methods for problem solving and decision making. Mathematical models and statistical analyses were, for example, used for scheduling projects as well as for optimizing production layouts and schedules, capacity utilization, supply chains, routes in transport networks, workflows, or securities transactions—to name just a few fields of application. These methods helped to make manufacturing and service processes more efficient, reduce costs, and speed up the process of getting products to the customers.[47] The rise of computer technology further intensified the use of quantitative analysis techniques as a basis for managerial decision making and enhancing the efficiency of business operations.

Statistical methods were also used for **quality control**, especially after "quality gurus" such as **W. Edward Deming** or **Joseph M. Juran** successfully helped Japanese companies to implement process-oriented quality improvement methods from the 1950s on. Competitors from other parts of the world were shocked by the resulting competitive advantage of Japanese manufacturers. In the US, for example, the 1980 NBC documentary *If Japan Can Do It, Why Can't We?*, featuring W. Edward Deming, sparked high levels of managerial interest in quality management techniques.[48] In the following years, **quality management** systems and standards, **total quality management (TQM)** principles (with the aim of focusing the whole organization on delivering high quality for customers), **continuous improvement** (with the aim of enhancing the quality of products, services, and processes in a never-ending sequence of incremental improvement steps), and **lean management** (which combines the idea of continuous improvement with the aim of minimizing or eliminating waste in all forms) methods became omnipresent, especially in larger manufacturing companies.

The Toyota Production System: An example of a lean, quality-oriented management approach in the 20th century

The Japanese carmaker Toyota has long been regarded as a role model in terms of quality and efficiency for the automotive industry and for manufacturing companies in general. Toyota's success is generally accredited to the Toyota Production System (TPS), a manufacturing philosophy which aims to:

a   eliminate waste of all kinds (e.g. materials, labor, energy, or any other resources);

b   produce and provide everything that is needed "just-in-time" (i.e. exactly at the point and at the time when it is needed);

c   achieve "*jidoka*," which could be roughly translated as "automation with a human touch." The basic idea behind *jidoka* is that whenever a quality problem occurs, the production process automatically stops and the problem is corrected at that point. Only products that 100 percent comply with the strict quality standards proceed along the production process.

In the TPS, all activities are rigidly specified. Every step of the production process is clearly and unambiguously defined. Everyone knows who their internal or external customers are, and what exactly they need to do in order to meet their customers' requirements. Exactness and avoiding anything superfluous lies at the heart of the concept. Variations in any parts of the system are ideally detected right away in order to quickly eliminate their sources. This does not mean, however, that the system is inflexible. Every person in the company—whether worker or manager—has a responsibility to continuously reflect ("*hansei*") and improve ("*kaizen*") the system. Thus, the TPS does not remain static, but is continuously developing in order to reach even higher levels of quality and efficiency.

Sources: Based on information in Liker (2004); Toyota (2019).

In 1990, **Michael Hammer** wrote his *Harvard Business Review* article "Reengineering work: Don't automate, obliterate," in which he argued that controlling and optimizing processes is not enough. Instead, he argued that businesses should fundamentally rethink (or **"reengineer"**) their workflows and business processes in order to ensure that they were fully focused on satisfying customer needs in the most efficient way.[49]

Management science, quality management systems, and business process reengineering provided managers with a new toolkit for creating more efficient organizations. These approaches were, however, also critizised for being a "resurrection of Taylorism," for decreasing employee motivation due to the introduction of a whole range of new control mechanisms, and for totally neglecting all aspects of an organization that cannot be translated into numbers.[50]

Systems theory and the contingency approach

A new perspective on the role of management began with the application of the concepts of **systems theory** in an organizational context. Under this perspective, an organization was seen as an **open system**, a set of interrelated parts or elements that together achieve a common purpose while interacting with the environment (in contrast to a closed system that has no links with the external environment).[51] The organization as an open system takes inputs from the environment (e.g. material resources, information, or human resources) and transforms them into outputs (e.g. products and services, but also waste). A further major element of systems thinking is the notion of **feedback**—information about both outputs and the internal state of the system that can be used to realign the system and its individual parts in order to "stay on track" when the system deviates from its prescribed course (see also Figure A2).[52]

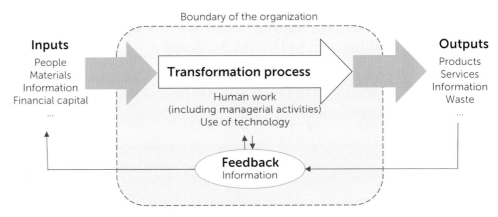

Figure A2 Model of an organization from a systems perspective

Source: Inspired by concepts in Robbins and Coulter (2018); Boddy (2017); Daft (2010).

Thinking in systems means not only focusing on optimizing one particular element or part of an organization, but always keeping in mind the (ever-changing) interaction among different units and the repercussions that decisions in one part of the organization can have on other parts of the organization (see also the concept of the "double multiplicity of management" in Chapter 1). In other words, managers were now required to think **holistically**, having the whole organization and all its many links with the environment in mind rather than just dealing with particular aspects.

In complex systems that operate in dynamic environments, it is difficult to find two situations in which all factors are exactly the same. Thus, instead of postulating universal, "one-size-fits-all" principles of effective management, the proponents of the **contingency approach** tried to explore what works best under certain circumstances. They were mainly concerned about finding the right "fit" between the management system and the internal and external environment.[53] The contingency approach (also known under the term **situational approach**) reminded managers that what is effective and what is not often depends on the situation, i.e. on contextual factors that should be taken into account, for example, when making decisions or using a certain leadership style. A highly participative leadership style could, for example, work well when expert organizations such as universities or management consulting firms decide on their future strategies, but may not be as highly recommended for an army platoon that is operating under fire.

Of course, this does not mean that the advent of the contingency approach replaced attitudes of "right" and "wrong" in management with "it all depends." The contingency approach was a good reminder, however, for managers that methods and actions that work in one setting may not necessarily be effective in a different context.[54]

The top management view and strategic management

Speaking of managerial effectiveness, it is about time we mention **Peter Drucker** (1909–2005) in our brief history of management thought. Born in Vienna (Austria), he has been widely credited with being one of the most influential management thinkers of the 20th century. In his seminal book *The Practice of Management* (first published in 1954), he saw the manager as "the dynamic, life-giving element in every business."[55] To his mind, managing was creative action. Thus, he turned attention to **the role of top management** in shaping organizations and determining the success of a business. In later decades, top managers stepped even more into the spotlight, when the media started to portray some chief executive officers (CEOs) like rock stars.

Drucker also popularized the concept of **management by objectives**, of trying to improve the performance of an organization by means of objectives upon which the managers and their subordinates agree.[56] As the strategic goals of the organization are broken down into clear and measurable departmental and individual objectives, each part of the organization should adequately contribute to the success of the whole. Drucker also distinguished between tactical and strategic decisions, and posited that "the important decisions, the decisions that really matter, are strategic."[57]

Scores of management scholars and practitioners soon agreed that it was difficult if not outright impossible for managers to become effective without having strategic goals and setting the right strategic initiatives to reach these goals. At the beginning of the 1960s, **Alfred Chandler** defined **strategy** as "the determination of the basic long-term goals and objectives of an enterprise, and the adoption of courses of action and the allocation of resources for carrying out these goals"[58] and pointed out that it was necessary to align the structure of an organization with its strategy. In particular, he promoted the "M" or "multidivisional" form of organization, in which the corporate headquarters oversees several business units (also called "divisions") that are relatively autonomously operating in different markets. Chandler's claim that "structure follows strategy" was later amended by **Henry Mintzberg** with "as the left foot follows the right," meaning that both are important for creating an effective organization, without one having precedence over the other.[59]

The Russian American applied mathematician **H. Igor Ansoff** argued in his 1965 book *Corporate Strategy* that in order to be effective, managers needed to approach strategic planning in a rational and systematic way.[60] Ideally, they would also use the analytic tools that he proposed: for example, the famous 2×2 "Ansoff Matrix" that can help managers to determine different growth strategies for their enterprises (market penetration, market development, product development, and diversification). Since then all kinds of 2×2 matrices have taken root with managers, management scholars, and management consultants (you will also find some in this book!).

The renewed interest in strategy—remember, Sun Tzu wrote about strategy over 2,500 years ago—also meant that managers were now strongly focused on monitoring activities outside the organization and trying to outsmart the competition. Outstanding contributions in this field were made by Harvard Professor **Michael E. Porter** with his book *Competitive Strategy* (1980), in which he advocated the idea that organizations that want to be successful in the market need to follow one of three generic strategies (cost leadership, differentiation, or focus on a niche market), and by INSEAD Professors **W. Chan Kim and Renée Mauborgne** with their global bestseller *Blue Ocean Strategy* (2005).[61] Kim and Mauborgne's basic argument was that companies should not compete with others head on in "red oceans" (highly competitive market spaces with a lot of "sharks"), but rather step into uncontested market space ("blue oceans") through creating new business models and unique value offers for customers.

Strategic management concepts have been used by managers to think about the long-term objectives of their organizations and about initiatives that could help them to achieve these objectives in a structured way. A systematic analysis of how the organization relates to its environment has enabled managers to make insightful decisions about the further developmental pathway of their organizations—despite certain doubts that have been raised about whether developing long-term strategies is still relevant in the highly dynamic business environment of the 21st century.[62]

"New leadership" approaches

The best strategies cannot be successfully implemented without people who are committed to making them work. Managers—people who are responsible for the performance and development of a group, an organizational unit, or an organization as a whole—also need to recognize that they have a leadership role in which they need to convince others to follow them in order to achieve certain goals.

This was recognized by **James MacGregor Burns**, the biographer of the former US President Franklin D. Roosevelt, for example. In 1978, Burns published his seminal book *Leadership*, in which he distinguished between transactional and transformational leadership.[63] **Transactional leadership** is fundamentally about exchange; for example, an employee gets a higher salary in return for putting in more effort. **Transformational leadership**, which Burns regards as more effective, is about understanding what followers need, about engaging and inspiring followers through trying to satisfy their higher needs, and about creating a stimulating relationship between the leader and the followers.[64] A very important factor in transformational leadership is *individualized consideration*, that is, treating everyone as an individual, caring for the employees' needs, empowering them, and helping them to achieve new levels of performance through personal coaching and guidance.[65] According to research results, transformational leadership can have a positive impact on employees' job performance.[66] It is strongly values based, and in Burns' view, the ideal transformational leader strives to reach a higher level of morality and contributes to the welfare of the team, the organization, and society as a whole.[67] This, of course, also meant that the expectations that managers (in their role as leaders) needed to meet rose dramatically.

At approximately the same time as Burns (well, actually one year earlier), Robert Greenleaf introduced the concept of **servant leadership**.[68] The basic idea of this leadership philosophy is that the main role of a leader is to serve—both the organization and its purpose and in particular also the people within the organization, their well-being and growth. Servant leaders understand that they are stewards of their organization.[69] Moreover, Greenleaf also turned the organizational hierarchy upside down. Instead of being the boss who issues commands, the effective servant leaders put the needs of others first, delegate power, and focus their energy on developing others and the organization.[70]

The "new leadership" approaches are not 100 percent consistent in terms of how they view the role of an effective leader. Whereas the ideal transformational leader is supposed to quasi single-handedly change an organization, his or her followers, and as a consequence even the world for the better, servant leaders are a bit more humble as they just see themselves as catalysts for enabling the development and growth of others. What both leadership philosophies have in common, however, is that they turn the attention of managers toward the needs of others, pointing out that without satisfying the needs of followers, they will not succeed in becoming effective leaders.

Management in the 21st century

Many of the earlier perspectives on effective management continue to influence how managers perceive their role in the 21st century. In the meanwhile, the new challenges of a dynamically changing global business environment add to the complexity of the managerial role.

In a **dynamically changing environment**, organizations need to become more flexible or "agile." Entrepreneurial thinking, creativity, and innovation management have begun to take the center stage of managerial attention (see also Chapter 10). Management scholars and managers started thinking about how to create more **agile organizations** that usually include self-organizing, cross-functional teams which are able to adapt quickly to changing demands. The basic assumption is that while detailed plans and rigid structures can work relatively well in predictable environments, it is much better to work in small, dedicated teams and in short, iterative cycles (also called "sprints") to solve business challenges in what management consultants call the "VUCA world." VUCA stands for volatility, uncertainty, complexity, and ambiguity, and is used to describe unpredictable environments that are subject to rapid changes.[71]

ING Netherlands: An example of an agile organization in the 21st century

ING is a global banking group that operates in a rapidly changing industry environment. Traditional face-to-face interactions with bank customers are increasingly being replaced by Internet platforms and mobile apps, and financial technology start-ups have emerged as serious challengers to the traditional banking services providers. ING's managers recognized that they needed to make their organization more agile in order to remain competitive in such a dynamic environment. Thus, they decided to restructure ING's Dutch retail groups around what they called *tribes*, *squads*, and *chapters*. Tribes consist of up to 150 people. They are organizational units that are clearly focused on certain business domains, for example, the mortgage business or private banking. Tribe leaders are responsible for setting priorities, budgeting, and ensuring that information and knowledge is shared within and across the tribes. Each tribe, in turn, consists of several squads—self-organizing, cross-functional teams of less than ten people. The squads address specific customer needs (e.g. creating a new product or service or improving the user experience of a mobile app) and stay together just as long as needed before they are disbanded in order to allow the creation of new teams that address new challenges. Each squad has a product owner who coordinates the squad's activities without being the formal leader. The squads are also supported by an "agile coach" who helps them with iterative problem solving. In order to share knowledge and best practices within certain business functions or disciplines (e.g. marketing people or IT engineers), the structure of each tribe is complemented by chapters. Chapter leads are responsible for the professional development and performance review of employees in the particular business function or discipline. Although some aspects of the new, agile organizational setup are challenging (e.g. the risk that squads deviate from following overall business goals), there are reports about positive effects of the new structures on customer satisfaction, employee satisfaction, and the time that it takes to get new products and services out to the market.

Source: Based on information in Barton et al. (2018).

One area that has undergone a particularly rapid development over the past few years is **digital technology**. Business intelligence systems have increased the capacity of managers to make sense of extremely high volumes of data (also known by the term **"big data"**) about what is going on within and outside of the organization.[72] Thus, management is generally becoming more **data driven**. Advanced communication technologies like videoconferencing have enabled the creation of virtual teams that are independent of physical locations. And digital technology is also used to streamline supply chains and optimize manufacturing systems, especially as the digital and the physical world are merged in the **"Internet of Things"** (IoT). These technological advancements create new opportunities for managing organizations in a more efficient way, and also new challenges for managers as complex IT systems further increase the degree of overall complexity of organizations.

In a **globalized business environment**, managers need to work across borders and consider different cultures, languages, and institutional environments. They also need to manage diversity and lead global virtual teams with the help of modern information and communication technology (see Chapter 5). At the same time, it is increasingly recognized that US-centered or, more generally, "Western" management approaches that have traditionally dominated management scholarship are not necessarily the most effective, especially when they are applied in different cultural environments. Integrating principles of the African philosophical concept of *ubuntu* (a Bantu dialect expression for "humanness") into organizational practices has, for example, been seen as a potential route for creating more sustainable organizations. Ubuntu can be defined as "a pervasive spirit of caring and community, harmony and hospitality, respect, and responsiveness—that individuals or groups display for each other,"[73] and could be regarded as an alternative to an individualistic, profit-maximizing perspective on management. Also, practices that are attributed to Indian business leaders (e.g. having a strong obligation toward employees, trying to encourage improvisation and enhance adaptability, or focusing the organization on fulfilling a broad mission that includes not only business but also social goals) were proposed as a potential role model for avoiding "some of the apparent rapaciousness and excesses of the American model."[74]

Excesses like well-publicized accounting frauds, shareholders celebrating the announcement of thousands of layoffs, or businesses that extensively harm the environment have also led to the general public taking a more critical stance toward the role that managers play in society. The **shareholder value** paradigm that sees businesses as a mere means to increase the wealth of stockowners is no longer palatable. Consumers and the general public tend to expect that managers build **sustainable organizations** that are behaving in a responsible way toward society and the environment. **Stakeholder theory** and **corporate social responsibility** have come to the center of managerial attention, and it is also increasingly recognized that managers can reorient their businesses from pure profit maximization to the creation of **"shared value"** or **"real value"** for different stakeholder groups (see Chapter 9).[75] Proponents of the **humanistic management** movement, in particular, argue that it is time to shift managerial attention from a "what-you-cannot-measure-you-cannot-manage" attitude to a stronger focus on what really matters for human beings, including well-being, human dignity, a healthy environment, and quality of life.[76]

Conclusion

Although we have covered the history of ideas on effective management and leadership in a more or less chronological way, we need to be careful not to mistake chronology with progress. The typical storyline goes like this: First came the "bad guys" like Frederick Winslow Taylor and other proponents of scientific management who saw people as nothing more than replaceable components of a machine and a mere means to an end; then came the "good guys" like Elton Mayo and his fellow "human relations" campaigners; and finally, management evolved toward more holistic, enlightened, responsible, sustainable, long-term oriented, and people-centered forms of "new leadership."

The story sounds nice and convincing, but it does not stand the test of reality. As we have seen, even thousands of years ago, we had both mechanistic and people-centered approaches to management, as we have today—in the whole spectrum between primarily data-driven and stakeholder value-driven management and responsible, sustainability-oriented servant leaders. There are still countless managerial control advocates who follow Theory X (which posits that people generally have a tendency to avoid work wherever possible), as well as countless humanistically oriented managers who follow Theory Y (the belief that people are self-motivated and like to do interesting work).

Management histories are always stories. They can make us think, inspire us, and maybe even help us discover things that we would or would not want to repeat. But in the end, managers have to create their own stories, find their own best way of performing through—and together with—other people. Those who learn from history and understand the responsibility that comes with the managerial role in their own particular organizational and environmental context have a higher chance of also becoming *effective managers*.

✓ Review questions

1   Why does it make sense to study the history of management?
2   How did management thought differ before and after the Industrial Revolution?
3   What were the main schools of management thought in the 20th century?
4   What are bureaucracies and what are their main advantages and disadvantages?
5   How would you describe the core principles of scientific management?
6   What did Henri Fayol contribute to our understanding of effective management?
7   Why have the Hawthorne studies commonly been regarded as a crucial turning point in management history?
8   How did classic motivation theories change the perception of what is regarded as effective management?
9   How do managers who adhere to either Theory X or Theory Y differ in their general approach to managing people and organizations?
10 How did the quantitative approaches and the quality movement change the nature of the managerial role?
11 What does "thinking in systems" mean in an organizational context?
12 How can the concepts of strategic management contribute to enhancing managerial effectiveness?
13 What is "new" about the "new leadership" approaches?
14 Which environmental factors change the nature of management in the 21st century?
15 Would you see the historical development of management thought as a linear progress toward a higher level of managerial effectiveness?

? Critical reflection questions

1   Take a look at Henri Fayol's 14 principles of effective management again. Which of those principles would you see as still being valid today? Which ones are probably outdated? Why?
2   Select two people-oriented and two mechanistic approaches from the historical overview of the development of management theories. What are the main limitations that you can see in these approaches or theories?
3   Does studying management history really help us to become more effective managers today and tomorrow when we are living and working in a rapidly changing environment?
4   Think about an organization with which you are familiar (maybe an organization that you are working for or the university you are studying at). Critically evalute the assumptions that managers in this organization presumably hold about the nature of effective management. To which schools of thought in the history of management do these assumptions relate?
5   In your opinion, what could be the effects of the rapid technological developments in the 21st century on the relative importance of mechanistic and people-centered approaches to management?

☛ Managerial implications

• What is considered effective management is contingent on the context. In a relatively stable and predictable environment, for example, planning and control have more relevance than in a complex and fast-changing environment, which requires a much higher degree of agility and innovation. This also means that managers need to understand the demands in their particular context, and adapt their managerial approach accordingly.
• More than 100 years after Henri Fayol structured the management process into planning, organizing, commanding, coordinating, and controlling, we must recognize that manage-ment is much more than just performing these mechanistic tasks. It is the manager's job to

achieve something together with other people. This means that effective managers need to be able to understand the needs and behavior of others, shape the culture of their organizations, and develop, motivate, and empower people in order to reach their goals together as a team.

- How managers approach their job also depends on their basic assumptions about human nature. Followers of McGregor's Theory X (which posits that people generally have a tendency to avoid work wherever possible) typically rely on formal control mechanisms. In contrast, those who follow Theory Y (the belief that people are self-motivated and like to do interesting work) will put a lot more emphasis on providing their team members with challenging tasks and giving them adequate reponsibility, autonomy, and support to enable them to accomplish these.

- New challenges require new managerial approaches. In a world that is characterized by digitization, globalization, and social acceleration, managers cannot solely rely on old formulae for success. Instead, there is one imperative for 21st century managers: never stop learning!

 # Endnotes

[1]Goethe (1914).
[2]Cooper (2004).
[3]Cooper (2004).
[4]Sun Tzu (1963).
[5]Chang (1976).
[6]Sidani (2008).
[7]Rutgers (1999).
[8]Tower Hollis (2009), p. 102.
[9]Plato (1888), p. 23.
[10]Cicero (2001), pp. 47–48.
[11]stiftmelk.at (2019).
[12]Machiavelli (2005), p. 58.
[13]Rutgers (1999), p. 19.
[14]Robins (2012), p. 26.
[15]Robins (2012), p. 26.
[16]Gelderblom et al. (2013).
[17]Rich (1948), p. 10.
[18]Wren and Bedeian (2009).
[19]Grey (2009).
[20]Taylor (2003), p. 36.

[21]Gilbreth and Gilbreth (1916).
[22]Gantt (1919).
[23]Grey (2009), p. 39.
[24]Grey (2009).
[25]Fayol (1949).
[26]Fayol (1949), p. 38.
[27]Fayol (1949), p. 39.
[28]Pindur et al. (1995).
[29]Robertson (1971).
[30]Robertson (1971).
[31]Graham (1995).
[32]Barnard (1938).
[33]Barnard (1938).
[34]Barnard (1938).
[35]Pindur et al. (1995).
[36]Simon (1947), p. 108.
[37]Simon (1947), p. 108.
[38]Maslow (1943).
[39]Herzberg (1959).
[40]McClelland (1961).

[41]McGregor (1960).
[42]Ouchi (1981).
[43]Hall (1976); Hofstede (1984).
[44]O'Leary et al. (2002).
[45]Pindur et al. (1995).
[46]Pindur et al. (1995).
[47]Slaaty (1988).
[48]Ross (1999).
[49]Hammer (1990).
[50]Boje and Winsor (1993).
[51]Kast and Rosenzweig (1972).
[52]Kast and Rosenzweig (1972).
[53]Luthans (1973).
[54]Pindur et al. (1995).
[55]Drucker (2007), p. 3.
[56]Drucker (2007), p. 105.
[57]Drucker (2007), p. 305.
[58]Chandler (1962), p. 13.
[59]Mintzberg (1990), p. 183.
[60]Ansoff (1965).

[61]Kim and Mauborgne (2005); Porter (1980).
[62]Farjoun (2007).
[63]Burns (1978).
[64]Burns (1978).
[65]Bass (1990), p. 22.
[66]Ng (2017).
[67]Burns (1978).
[68]Greenleaf (2002).
[69]Eva et al (2019).
[70]Greenleaf (2002).
[71]Bennett and Lemoine (2014); Rigby et al. (2016).
[72]McAfee and Brynjolfsson (2012).
[73]Mangaliso (2001), p. 24.
[74]Cappelli et al. (2010), p. 191.
[75]Carroll (1979); Freeman (1984); Porter and Kramer (2006); Sternad et al. (2016).
[76]Pirson (2017a; 2017b).

Visit the companion website at macmillanihe.com/sternad-management to access multiple choice questions, useful weblinks and additional materials.

GLOSSARY

A

ABCDE monitoring chart: A tool that allows managers to get an overview of key factors that can influence the sustainable performance of an organization.

Accountable: Being obliged to take responsibility for your actions and give defendable reasons for them.

Accruals: Accounting entries for expenses or revenue that have already been incurred in a certain period without having been invoiced or paid yet.

Affective conflict: A conflict that arises from incompatibilities in interpersonal relationships.

Agency dilemma: In agency theory, the agency dilemma (also known as the "principal-agent problem") describes a situation in which the "agent" (who makes decisions and works on behalf of the "principal") is motivated to follow their own best interest which might come into conflict with the principal's best interest.

Agency theory: An approach from economic theory that explains how to best organize the relationship between one person or entity (the "agent") who makes decisions and does work on behalf of another person or entity (the "principal").

Agenda setting: The activity of defining priority issues for the organization.

Agile: An approach to organizing that is based on using self-managed multi-disciplinary teams to tackle tasks in short iterative cycles and in close interaction with customers.

Ambidexterity: An organization's ability to balance exploration (preparing for future opportunities and challenges) and exploitation (efficiently managing its current activities).

Amortization: The allocation of the decrease in value of an intangible asset over its estimated useful life. The amount of amortization that is allocated to a certain period is recorded as an expense on the income statement for that period.

Assets: Resources of measurable economic value that are owned by an individual or organization.

Availability heuristic: A mental shortcut in which more salient and immediate examples more easily come to mind, thus potentially biasing our decision-making process.

B

Balanced scorecard: A management tool (developed by Robert S. Kaplan and David P. Norton) for translating a strategy into a limited set of traceable key financial and non-financial indicators.

BATNA: An acronym for "best alternative to a negotiated agreement"—the most favorable alternative option for a particular negotiation party in case agreement cannot be reached in a negotiation.

Behavioral control: A type of control that tries to directly monitor and influence the behavior of people.

Benchmarking: The practice of comparing the key metrics of your own organization with other (often best-in-class) organizations in order to identify opportunities for improvement.

Big data: Extremely large sets of both structured and unstructured real-time (or near real-time) data that are integrated from different sources in order to be analyzed with the help of computer technology.

Black swan events: An unpredictable event that has a high impact. The term was used by Nassim Nicholas Taleb based on the Latin poet Juvenal's reference to a "bird as rare as the black swan."

Blue ocean: New market space (devoid of competition) that is created by offering a set of customer benefits that no one else is offering.

Born global: A new business venture that from its launch pursues a strategy of operating across national borders and aims to globalize its business rapidly.

Bounded rationality: The idea that decision makers work under certain constraints including, in particular, limited information, the limited information-processing capacity of the human brain, and the limited time that is available for decision making.

Budget: An estimate of revenues and expenditures for a certain period of time (used for planning and performance control purposes).

Business idea: A concept for generating economic value, for example, through offering a product or service that matches an unmet market need.

Business intelligence: A strategic approach that uses technology to collect, integrate, and analyze large amounts of data for the purpose of supporting decision making in organizations.

Business level strategy: Setting direction on how to create value and how to compete in a certain product or service market.

Business model: A representation of the main business decisions and the logic behind how a business generates value (for both customers and the organization).

Business plan: A document that describes in quite a detailed way how a business opportunity will be pursued. It usually includes a description of the opportunity, a strategy for exploiting the opportunity, information about the entrepreneurial team, a marketing plan, an operations plan, and financial forecasts.

C

Capital expenditure (CAPEX): Money that an organization spends to acquire or add value to fixed assets that are used for creating future benefit beyond one taxable year.

Cash: In accounting terms, cash is used for money in hand (coins and banknotes that were issued by the government) and in bank accounts as well as payment tools such as checks or money orders. Sometimes the term cash also includes *cash equivalents*, highly liquid assets that can be quickly converted into cash (e.g. marketable securities).

Cash conversion cycle: A financial metric that measures the time that it takes for an organization to convert cash outflows for stocking up its inventory into cash inflows from sales to customers.

Cash cow: One of the four categories of the BCG matrix that includes business units (or products and services) with a strong market position in a low-growth (mature) market. It is called "cash cow" because it ought to generate high amounts of cash that can be "milked" by the organization.

Cash flow from financing activities: A summary statement of the amount of cash that an organization receives or pays in its external financing activities, for example, raising new share capital (e.g. through issuing more stock) or repaying investors (e.g. in the form of dividends or repurchasing stock), issuing or paying off bonds, and increasing or repaying loans.

Cash flow from investment activities: A summary statement of the amount of cash that an organization receives or pays in selling and purchasing long-term assets.

Cash flow from operating activities: A summary statement of the amount of cash that an organization generates and uses in its regular business activities.

Cash flow statement: A summary statement of the cash transactions (sources and uses of cash) of an organization during a certain period. It is usually divided in three parts: cash flow from operating activities, cash flow from investment activities, and cash flow from financing activities.

Categorical thinking: A fast thinking mode (a sub-category of System 1 thinking) in which we quickly react to stimuli through the use of heuristics and simplified categorizations.

Causality: A cause–effect relationship between different variables.

Cause and effect web: Multiple causal relations (and interrelations) between different factors and elements in a complex system.

Change management: A systematic approach of initiating, coordinating, and controlling transition and transformation efforts in an organization.

Coach: A person who helps another person to reach their potential, usually through discussing work-related issues and providing guidance and advice.

Coaching: A development process in which one person helps another person to reach their potential, usually through discussing work-related issues and providing guidance and advice (often through asking questions that help the other person to thoroughly reflect on an issue).

Co-acting group: A group that is working toward achieving a common goal without much personal communication and interaction.

Coalition: An alliance between different people with the aim of achieving a common goal.

Cognitive restructuring: The process of identifying and disputing negative and irrational thoughts and beliefs.

Collaborative software: Digital tools that are specifically designed to help teams accomplish their common tasks.

Conflict: A serious disagreement based on diverging interests, different points of view, or other incompatibilities.

Conflict management: The practice of finding solutions that maximize positive outcomes and minimize negative outcomes in conflict situations.

Consignment: A trust-based trading arrangement whereby party A hands over goods to another party B who is supposed to sell the goods. The goods remain in the legal ownership of party A until party B has actually sold them.

Contribution: In cost accounting, contribution is the difference between product-related revenue and product-related variable costs.

Core competency: Key organizational capabilities which can be used for creating value and achieving a sustainable competitive advantage in a variety of different markets.

Corporate entrepreneurship: Entrepreneurial activities in larger, established organizations.

Corporate level strategy: Setting the general direction for a multi-business organization, especially deciding where (in which industries or markets) to compete, how to grow the organization, and how to cooperate with other organizations.

Corporate social performance: Outcomes of pro-social behavior by organizations that are beneficial for society and the environment from the perspective of key stakeholder groups.

Corporate social responsibility (CSR): A management concept that orients businesses toward making positive impacts on society and the natural environment.

Correlation: A measure that indicates the extent to which two or more variables are statistically related to each other. When variables correlate, they occur or fluctuate together. This does not automatically imply that they are also causally connected.

Cost accounting: The process of recording, classifying, and analyzing all costs that are incurred in an organization's activities in order to establish a basis for controlling and managing costs.

Cost allocation base: A variable that is used for allocating indirect costs to specific cost objects (e.g. products, projects, or departments).

Co-variation: Two or more variables are changing at the same time (in correlation with each other).

Critical uncertainties: Those external events beyond the decision maker's influence that have the highest possible impact on the variation of the outcome of decisions.

Crowdsourcing: Obtaining certain resources (e.g. ideas, services, or content) from a large group of people (usually via the Internet).

Cultural control: A type of control that tries to shape people's behavior through creating and maintaining a system of shared values and beliefs.

Cultural dimensions: A generalized framework of relatively enduring sets of values and norms that are used to describe differences and commonalities between different cultures.

Cultural intelligence: The ability to interact effectively with people from different cultural backgrounds.

Culture: Basic assumptions, values, beliefs, norms, and tendencies in behavioral patterns that are shared among the members of a certain group or community.

Cycle time: The total time that it takes to complete one "cycle" of a process or operation (i.e. how long it takes from the start to the end of the process).

D

Data warehouse: A large, central database that is used as a repository of data generated by all parts of an organization for analytical or reporting purposes.

Decision tree: A tool for visualizing the options, critical uncertainties and their probabilities, and potential outcomes of decisions.

Delegation: The transfer of both responsibility and authority for completing a task to another person.

Deliberate practice: A learning process in which the learners try to enhance their performance through repeating activities with a conscious focus on improving certain aspects of these activities and reflecting on feedback that they receive on how they performed the activities.

Demand variability: A measurement for how strongly customer demand fluctuates over time (i.e. changes from one period to another).

Depreciation: The allocation of the decrease in value (or "write-off") of a tangible asset over its estimated useful life. The amount of depreciation that is allocated to a certain period is recorded as an expense on the income statement for that period.

Design thinking: A systematic approach to solving complex problems that is based on methods that designers use in the design process.

Development cycle: A four-step process (Challenge—Act—Feedback—Reflect & Correct) that describes how people can effectively develop skills and competencies.

Differentiation: In an organization science context, differentiation describes the division of work within an organization into subunits.

Digital strategy: A high-level plan for using digital information and communication technologies for improving business performance and creating competitive advantage.

Discounted cash flow method: A method for analyzing the value of a company or an asset by means of calculating the present value of all anticipated future cash flows using the estimated cost of capital as a discount rate. It is based on the idea of the time value of money—that cash flows today are worth more than cash flows in the future (because today's cash flows can be invested to generate more returns in the future).

Discount rate: In discounted cash flow analysis, the discount rate is the estimated cost of capital that is used to determine the net present value of future cash flows. A frequently used discount rate is the average rate of return that the shareholders and lenders expect to receive from the company.

Distribution channel: The network of all people and organizations that are involved in delivering a product (or service) from the producer to the customers and final consumer.

Distributive justice: Perceived fairness in the distribution of goods, benefits, and duties.

Distributive negotiation: A competitive negotiation in which all parties try to gain the larger share of a fixed amount of resources.

Diversification: In strategic management, diversification describes the process of entering into new markets with new products or services.

Diversity: Variation among people in visible and invisible characteristics (including, for example, age, gender, ethnicity, social class, religion, sexual orientation, values, personality, or physical ability).

Diversity climate: The extent to which members of an organization share the opinion that fostering diversity and inclusion should be valued and supported in the organization.

Diversity manager: A person who has the task of developing and implementing policies and practices that foster diversity and inclusion in an organization.

Diversity policies: A system of goals and principles that are used as a guideline for fostering diversity in an organization.

Diversity practices: A set of practices that are used to foster diversity in an organization.

Divisional structure: An organizational arrangement that combines all the tasks related to a certain product, customer group, or geographical region in distinct subunits.

"Double multiplicity" of management: The phenomenon that in organizations that are complex open systems with many interrelated elements, one decision can lead to multiple consequences and multiple actions are often needed to reach one goal.

Dynamic capabilities: The skills and routines that allow an organization to learn and create new or adapt existing resources or capabilities.

E

EBT: Short for *earnings before taxes*. It is an indicator of the pre-tax profitability of an organization. EBT is calculated as revenue minus all expenses (including interest on debt but excluding taxes) in a certain period.

Economies of scale: Cost advantages that result from higher production or sales volumes (leading to lower unit costs).

Economies of scope: Cost advantages that result from using one resource base for producing or selling two or more distinct products (leading to lower unit costs).

Effectiveness: The degree to which desired results or effects are reached.

Efficacy: The power or capacity to produce a certain effect.

Efficiency: The state of doing something in the most economical way.

Emergent strategies: Strategies that result from a (previously unintended) pattern of decisions which together propel the organization in a certain direction.

Empowerment: The leadership practice of giving a person or a group of people more autonomy so that they can set their own priorities, make decisions, and solve problems independently.

Entrepreneur: An individual who discovers, evaluates, and exploits opportunities for creating or developing a business.

Entrepreneurial manager: A manager who is engaged in entrepreneurial activities (i.e. in recognizing, creating, and pursuing opportunities for value creation), regardless of whether these activities are performed in new ventures or established organizations.

Entrepreneurial opportunities: Previously unexploited ways of creating economic value through matching innovative solutions with unmet market needs.

Entrepreneurship: The process of engaging in innovative activities which are oriented toward creating and exploiting new business opportunities.

Environment: The sum of the external factors and forces that can influence the performance and development of an organization.

Ethical ethnocentrism: The general belief that the ethical standards and values of one's own group or society are the "right" ones.

Ethical intelligence: The intellectual ability to make decisions based on principles of morality.

Ethical relativism: The general belief that the ethical standards and values of one society are just different, but not necessarily better or worse than those of another society.

Ethical standards: Principles of what is considered morally right behavior in a certain group or culture.

Ethical universalism: The general belief that there are moral values and a universal ethic that apply to everyone in the world, regardless of their cultural background or any other diversity-related characteristic.

Execution: In a business context, execution refers to the decisions and actions that are taken to implement a strategy effectively.

Expectancy theory: A theory of human motivation that suggests that people are motivated to put in more effort when they expect that their effort leads to higher performance that, in turn, can lead to positive outcomes that they value.

Expected value: In probability analysis, the expected value is computed by multiplying the value of each possible outcome with the probability that this particular outcome will occur, and then adding together all the resulting values.

Expenses: Costs that are incurred in order to generate revenue in a certain period. There are accounting rules about what qualifies as an expense. In addition to cash expenses there are also non-cash expenses related to the depletion of assets (e.g. depreciation or amortization) or incurrence of liabilities.

Exploitation: Organizational activities that are oriented toward efficiently exploiting existing competencies.

Exploration: Organizational activities that are oriented toward ensuring the future viability of an organization (e.g. through exploring new opportunities, building new competencies, learning, or innovating).

F

Feedback: Information that is given to an individual or a group of people about their prior behavior with the aim to either adjust or reinforce the behavior.

First-level effectiveness: The state of achieving a certain goal or desired outcome.

Fixed costs: Costs that do not vary over a certain period of time, regardless of a change of volume of either an activity or output during that period.

Framing: Setting a problem within a particular context that can determine the set of potential options to address the problem.

"F-R-E-P" model: A model for structuring a termination meeting in four phases: facts (coming straight to the point), reasons (inform the person about the reasons for terminating the employment contract), empathy (accept and understand emotional reactions), and perspective (provide information about future steps).

Functional structure: An organizational arrangement that leads to the creation of subunits based on their primary function (e.g. purchasing, production marketing, sales, or finance).

G

Generic strategies: A model (proposed by Michael Porter) of three basic strategies that can generally be used to achieve a competitive advantage (cost leadership, differentiation, focus).

Global virtual teams: Geographically dispersed teams composed of team members from different countries who are interacting primarily with the help of modern communication technology.

Goal-setting theory: A theory of human motivation that suggests that people are motivated when they (a) have specific, challenging, and accepted goals; and (b) regularly receive feedback on whether they are getting closer to reaching these goals.

Governance structures: Systems and processes by which organizations are directed and controlled in a way that ensures accountability.

Gross profit margin: A financial metric that describes what percentage of the money received as revenue is left after deducting the cost of goods sold. It can be calculated in two steps: (1) deduct cost of goods sold from revenue; and (2) divide the result by revenue and express the resulting proportion as a percentage.

Group norms: Standards for what is considered "normal" or "correct" behavior in a certain group.

Groupthink: A term introduced by social psychologist Irving Janis to explain the phenomenon of forced conformity and consent in groups in which diverging opinions are suppressed.

H

Helicopter view: The ability to see a problem in its overall context, while still being able to attend to details if necessary.

Heuristics: Simple rules or "mental shortcuts" by which decisions are made on the basis of learning from prior experience in similar situations.

High-context culture: A culture in which the context of how a message is delivered (e.g. body language, the tone of voice, facial expressions, or what is not said) provides important additional clues about what the sender really wants to convey.

Holacracy: A decentralized organizational approach that is based on the distribution of decision-making rights across the organization. The basic elements of a holacracy are autonomous, self-managing teams (called "circles") in which people fill well-defined roles and work according to a specific set of rules.

House of Digital Strategy: A framework that includes the main foci of interest for developing a digital strategy.

I

Implementation path: Five key activities that managers need to undertake in order to transform a strategy into actual organizational performance: identify critical tasks, match tasks and people, coordinate, energize, and control.

Inclusion: The act of creating an environment in which differences are valued and no one feels marginalized or excluded.

Inclusivity: The practice of including people from all diversity-related backgrounds without marginalizing or discriminating against any group of people.

Income statement: A summary statement of total revenue and expenses that led to the profit (or loss) of an organization over a certain timeframe (e.g. a month, quarter, or year).

Indirect costs: Costs that cannot be directly attributed to a specific cost object (e.g. a product, department, or project). Indirect costs are usually distributed between different cost objects by means of a cost allocation base.

Industry life cycle: The typical development of an industry through different stages (usually start-up/introduction, growth, maturity, and decline).

Influence: Having an effect on the opinion, beliefs, or behavior of other people.

Influence map: A tool for displaying who has more or less influence within a certain group of people.

Informal leader: A person who influences and leads other people in the organization without holding a formal authority position.

Informational justice: Perceived fairness in receiving adequate information about organizational decisions and processes.

Innovation: The development and actual implementation of new ideas for products and services, practices, or organizational procedures that create value for customers and the organization, respectively.

Innovation management: Managerial practices that are oriented toward fostering innovativeness and initiating, designing, and managing innovation processes in organizations.

Innovativeness: An organization's capacity to innovate.

Insolvency: The inability of an organization to meet its financial obligations when they become due.

Insourcing: A business practice in which non-core tasks or activities of an organization are performed internally instead of being outsourced to another organization (although this would be possible for these particular tasks or activities).

Integration: In an organization science context, integration describes the endeavor to combine the efforts of different subunits to enable them to work in a coordinated way toward a common goal.

Integrative negotiation: A joint problem-solving approach in which the negotiation partners try to find a "win–win" solution that creates value for all parties.

Interactional justice: Perceived fairness and respect in the way that people treat one another in an organization.

Intermodal thinking: Using a combination of different thinking modes to come to a conclusion; for example, first listening to our intuition and then consciously using a rational-analytic approach to make a decision.

Internal customer: A person or organizational unit that uses goods or services supplied by another person or unit within the same organization as inputs to their work.

Interpersonal conflict: A conflict that arises from personal differences (e.g. in values, attitudes, or personality) between two or more individuals.

Intrapreneur: An employee who exhibits entrepreneurial behavior (i.e. discovers, evaluates, and exploits opportunities for creating or developing a business) within a larger organization.

Intrinsic motivation: The drive to do something because performing the activity is in itself rewarding for an individual (including in the absence of any external rewards or control).

Intuition: A fast thinking mode (a sub-category of System 1 thinking) in which we quickly react to stimuli through the use of an experience-based holistic pattern-recognition process that leads to an emotional response.

I-O/O-I analysis (short for Inside-out/Outside-in analysis): A tool that helps to link the results of the external and internal strategic analyses through finding out (a) which opportunities can be exploited with an organization's existing resources and capabilities, and (b) which resources and capabilities an organization should develop in order to be able to exploit major opportunities.

J

Job profile: A description of the tasks, responsibilities, and required qualifications and skills for a particular position in an organization.

K

Key performance indicator (KPI): A measure of performance that allows the management to monitor to what extent a person or an organization achieves major goals.

L

Layoff: A term that was originally used for temporary suspension of employment, but is now more often used for the termination of an employment contract by the employer.

Leader: A person who is able to convince others to follow them (in thought and action) in order to achieve certain goals.

Leadership: A process of social influence in which one person is able to convince other individuals or groups of people to accomplish certain tasks or achieve certain goals.

Lean start-up (or hypothesis-driven entrepreneurship): An approach to pursuing entrepreneurial opportunities that is based on setting up hypotheses about how an opportunity could be exploited, testing these hypotheses directly in the market, and then adjusting the business model accordingly.

Liabilities: Obligations of an organization that are expected to lead to cash outflows in the future (e.g. amounts that a company owes to lenders and suppliers).

Line management: Management functions with subordinates who are directly involved in the core business activities of an organization.

Liquidity: The ability of an organization to meet all immediate and short-term payment obligations.

Low-context culture: A culture in which the information that is transmitted in oral or written form usually does not carry implicit meanings (i.e. people mean exactly what they say).

M

Macro environment (general environment): External factors (outside of an organization's control) that can influence an organization's strategy, value creation process, or performance (including political, economic, socio-demographic, technological, environmental, and legal influences).

Manager: A person who is responsible for the performance and development of a group, an organizational unit, or an organization as a whole.

Margin (also called profit margin): The ratio of profit to total revenue in a certain period (usually expressed as a percentage).

Marginal cost: Additional costs that accrue when one additional unit of a good or service is produced.

Matrix structure: An organizational arrangement in which two organizing principles are combined, which means that employees have more than one superior (e.g. a functional manager and a country manager).

Mental model: Simplified understanding of a cause–effect relationship that a person holds about a certain phenomenon.

Mentoring: A relationship in which a more experienced person (the mentor) offers personal and career guidance to a less experienced person (the mentee).

Mergers and acquisitions (M&A): The area in strategic management that deals with combining different organizations into one organization (mergers) or purchasing other organizations or parts thereof (acquisitions).

Micro environment (industry environment): Factors in the immediate surroundings of an organization that can influence an organization's strategy, value creation process, or performance (e.g. customers, suppliers, distribution partners, investors, or competitors).

Minimum viable product: A simplified version of a product that is just good enough to deliver value for customers. It is usually used to test and refine product ideas.

Mission: A short statement that describes the core purpose or *raison d'être* of the organization.

Monitoring: The activity of identifying and obtaining relevant information to understand what is going on both within and outside the organization.

Moral dilemma: A decision situation in which moral principles come into conflict.

Motivation: The inner drive to do something and to follow certain goals.

N

Natural employee turnover: The "normal" percentage of employees who leave an organization without being forced to leave within a certain timeframe.

Negotiation: A process in which two or more parties try to reach a mutually acceptable solution for an issue in which they have diverging interests or goals.

Negotiator's dilemma: The problem that disclosing information to a negotiation partner could help to maximize gains for all sides, but at the same time also put the party who discloses the information in a worse position for claiming value.

Network: A group of people with whom managers connect for the purpose of exchanging information and services.

Network structure: A flexible organizational arrangement in which a part of the tasks that an organization wants to accomplish are outsourced to other legally independent organizations while a coordinative role is retained.

"No regrets" test: As a final stage in a decision-making process, the outcome of the decision is assessed for potential negative consequences together with a judgment by the decision makers of whether they would be willing to cope with these consequences.

O

OLAP: Online analytical processing: Computer-based tools that allow an ad-hoc analysis of large amounts of multidimensional data.

Open innovation: The idea (popularized by Henry Chesbrough) that organizations should combine internal and external ideas to find new solutions for creating value, and also think about offering their innovations to the market with the help of other organizations.

Open receivables: Legally enforceable (but usually unsecured) claims for the payment of goods and services that an organization has already delivered, but which have not yet been paid by the customer.

Operating expenses (OPEX): Ongoing costs that are incurred in running the day-to-day business operations. OPEX are exhausted within one taxable year.

Operations: An organization's activities that are oriented toward transforming inputs (resources and competencies) into outputs (goods and services that create value for customers).

Organic growth: Expanding a business through using its own resources (rather than through mergers and acquisitions).

Organizational culture: Basic assumptions, values, beliefs, norms, and tendencies in behavioral patterns that are shared among the members of a certain organization.

Organizational design: The process by which managers create structures, processes, and systems that together help to coordinate the decisions and actions of the members of an organization in order to achieve a common goal.

Organizational justice: Employees' perceptions of how fairly they are treated within an organization.

Organizational structure: The allocation of tasks, responsibilities, and hierarchical relationships within an organization.

Organizational systems: Institutionalized practices that provide information and feedback, or are used to control and reward people in organizations.

Organization chart: A visual representation of the organizational structure (including the main positions or organizational subunits and the reporting relationships between them).

Output control: A type of control that measures the outcome of activities after they were performed.

Outsourcing: A business practice in which non-core tasks or activities of an organization are performed by another organization on a contract basis.

P

Performance potential: The capacity to perform in the future.

Performance review (or appraisal interview): A formal discussion (usually conducted annually) between a manager and an employee about their performance and development.

Personal productivity: A measurement for the ratio between the output that a person achieves and the efforts (e.g. in terms of working time) that are needed to achieve this output.

PESTEL analysis: A tool for systematically analyzing political, economic, socio-demographic, technological, environmental, and legal factors that can have an influence on an organization's strategy, value creation process, or performance.

Porter's five forces: A strategic tool developed by Harvard Professor Michael Porter for analyzing the competitive intensity in an industry. The "five forces" are the extent of rivalry within an industry, the bargaining power of suppliers, the bargaining power of buyers, the threat of new entrants, and the threat of substitutes.

Portfolio strategy: As part of corporate level strategy, portfolio strategy comprises high-level decisions about which business units an organization invests in.

Potential: Latent abilities that a person or organization could be capable of developing in the future.

Power: The capacity (or ability) to exert influence on other people.

Price elasticity of demand: The degree to which demand changes as a response to a change in price (usually calculated as percentage change in demand quantity divided by percentage change in price).

Price-to-earnings ratio (P/E ratio): A financial ratio that is calculated by dividing the share price by the earnings per share of a company. It describes how many times the stock price is higher than the earnings (usually defined as net income minus dividends for preferred stock) that are allocated to each outstanding share of common stock.

Primary stakeholders: Stakeholder groups that are in frequent direct contact with an organization and that are crucial for its continuing existence (e.g. customers, suppliers, employees, or shareholders).

Priorities management: The systematic process of first classifying issues and tasks into more or less important ones and then allocating more time to the important ones.

Procedural justice: Perceived fairness in the process of reaching and implementing a decision.

Process (or business process): A clearly defined sequence of activities that are carried out to transform inputs into outputs.

Process management: A systematic approach to identify and optimize the flow of activities that transform inputs into outputs.

Productivity: A measure of efficiency commonly defined as the ratio of outputs to inputs.

Profit multiples: A (relatively simplistic) method of valuing a business by means of multiplying profit figures by a factor that reflects the ratio between profits and the market value of comparable businesses.

Q

Qualitative growth: A strategy that is oriented toward achieving a higher quality standard.

Quantification trap: Focusing on quantifiable objectives and neglecting qualitative factors that are not easy to capture in numbers.

Quick wins: Visible improvements that can be achieved quite quickly and easily.

R

"Real value": A contribution to improving the material and immaterial quality of life of different stakeholder groups.

Reciprocity: The practice of two parties giving something to each other for mutual benefit.

Red ocean: Crowded market space with strong competition.

Resilience: The ability to adapt to or bounce back from adverse situations.

Resource-based view (RBV): A general theory of management that postulates that having access to and being able to make use of specific resources and capabilities is the key factor for achieving competitive advantage.

Résumé (or curriculum vitae (CV)): A written summary of a person's education, work experience, and skills.

Revenue: The total income that an organization receives from its normal business activities (usually from selling goods and services) before expenses are deducted.

Reverse delegation: A situation in which subordinates delegate tasks to their managers.

Risk: In a managerial context, risk is mostly seen as the potential of losing something that is of value. Sometimes, the term risk is used in a wider sense that can include the potential of gaining something.

Risk intelligence: The ability to assess risks based on experience.

Risk preferences: The tendency to either be willing to take risks or to try to avoid risks.

S

Secondary stakeholders: Stakeholder groups who are not very often in direct contact with an organization, but still have an interest in or are affected by its actions.

Second-level effectiveness: The ability to set the right goals.

Self-managing teams: Teams that are operating autonomously without being under the constant supervision of a formally appointed manager.

Sensemaking: The process of giving meaning to and trying to understand the potential impact of the events and developments that are going on both within and outside the organization.

Sensitivity analysis: A test of the robustness of a decision through calculating different scenarios of what would happen if the probabilities of critical uncertainties or the outcome values of different options change.

Shared value: Proposed by Michael E. Porter and Mark R. Kramer in 2011, the concept of shared value describes strategies and practices that simultaneously create economic value for a business (through enhancing its competitiveness) and social value for the communities in which the business operates (through having a positive impact on societal conditions).

Shareholders' equity: In a balance sheet, shareholders' equity is the difference between total assets and total liabilities. It represents the total amount that shareholders have invested in a company, either directly (in the form of capital stock) or indirectly through retained earnings.

Shareholder value: The total monetary value that shareholders obtain from their investment in a company (including dividend payments, gains from share price increases, or any other payouts).

Shareholder value paradigm: The idea that maximizing the wealth of shareholders is the ultimate purpose of a business, and that management should first and foremost consider shareholders' interests when making business decisions.

Short-time work: An agreement between the organization and its employees that everyone works less hours for less pay in order to avoid layoffs.

Social contract perspective: The idea that there is an implicit "contract" in which both society and businesses have certain obligations toward each other (e.g. society providing businesses with a functioning legal system, the right to own resources, infrastructure, an educated workforce, and businesses providing jobs, taking care of workers' interests, or doing no harm to the environment).

Socialization: The process of acquiring attitudes, behaviors, and values by means of learning from what others do or deem acceptable in a certain group or society.

Social loafing: The tendency of certain group members to "free ride"—to put in less effort in a group situation (because they expect others to do the work).

Staff function: Organizational functions that support line managers (e.g. with analysis, advice, or other forms of assistance) in performing effectively in their role, but do not directly work on the main purpose of the organization.

Stakeholders: All the parties that have an interest in an organization or are affected by the actions of an organization.

Stewardship theory: A theory that suggests that managers are intrinsically motivated to act in the best interest of the entity for which they are responsible.

Strategic alliance: A partnership agreement under which two separate organizational entities join forces to reach a common goal.

Strategic business unit (SBU): An independently managed part of an organization that offers products and services in one particular market.

Strategic group: A group of organizations with a similar strategic position.

Strategic management: The process of defining major goals for the organization and setting initiatives for reaching these goals.

Strategic position: A set of fundamental choices that determines where and how an organization creates and offers value and how the value creation and value offer model can be sustained in the face of competition.

Strategy: A general direction for an organization in terms of how to create and offer value and develop the potential to successfully follow this direction in the face of competition, and

under changing environmental circumstances.

Stress: Physical and mental tension resulting from excessive pressure or other demanding circumstances.

Substantive conflict: A conflict that arises from task- or content-related disagreements.

Substitutes: Different products or service offers that create equivalent value for customers.

Supply chain management: Activities that are oriented toward optimizing the entire network of individuals and organizations that are involved in the process of creating and distributing a product or service (from the provider of source materials to the end consumer).

Sustainability: The ability to meet current needs while at the same time retaining the capacity for meeting future needs. In an organizational context, sustainability means trying to ensure that current economic, social, and environmental demands and requirements are met without compromising the organization's ability to meet such demands and requirements in the future too.

SWOT matrix: A strategic tool that helps to identify the strengths and weaknesses of the organization as well as opportunities and threats in the environment.

System 1 thinking: A fast thinking mode in which our brain uses the automatic information-processing system.

System 2 thinking: A slow thinking mode in which our brain uses the rational information-processing system.

T

Tacit competencies: Competencies that are not easy to codify, thus making it difficult to transfer them from one context (or organization) to another.

Team role: A certain set of behaviors that a person usually shows in a team setting.

Theme-centered interaction (TCI): A method for working in groups developed by the psychotherapist Ruth Cohn. Part of TCI is the four factor model in which team leaders should keep the needs of individuals ("I"), the needs of the group as a whole ("WE"), the focus on the task ("IT"), and the consideration of outside influences and requirements ("GLOBE") in a dynamic balance.

Thinking modes: General ways in which our mind can approach the thinking task.

Time management: The systematic process of allocating time to different activities.

Trade-off: A situation in which it is not possible to attain all objectives at the

same time. In a trade-off situation, we need to give up something that we value in order to get something else that we value.

Triple bottom line: A term used by John Elkington to point out that organizations do not only have one results category (the financial "bottom line"), but that three dimensions of organizational performance should be taken into account: financial, environmental, and social.

V

Value: What something (for example, a business or an asset) is worth—in business often measured in monetary terms (i.e. what someone is willing to pay for it).

Value curve: A tool for visualizing value propositions (the benefits that a certain group of customers get from a product and/or service offer).

Value innovation: A systematic approach to achieve both differentiation and cost reduction through creating unique product and service offers that outperform the competition in some (important) aspects, while deliberately reducing the performance on other (less important) aspects.

Value proposition: A statement that clearly describes the benefits that a certain group of customers get from the product and/or service offers of an organization.

Values: Lasting beliefs of a person or group about what is right or wrong, good or bad, or desirable or undesirable.

Variable costs: Costs that vary depending on the changing volume of an activity or an output (e.g. the amount of units produced).

Virtual meeting: A meeting in which people do not meet in person, but remain in different physical locations and connect with each other with the help of technological means (e.g. videoconferencing software).

Vision: A short statement that describes what the organization wants to become or would like to accomplish in the (distant) future.

VRIO model: A framework for analyzing whether an organization's resources and capabilities can be used as a basis for achieving competitive advantage. VRIO stands for resources or capabilities that are **v**aluable, **r**are, **i**mperfectly imitable, and suitable to be exploited by a particular **o**rganization.

W

Weak ties: People you know personally, but do not have a strong relationship with (e.g. acquaintances or former colleagues).

Weighted scoring model: A tool that allows decision makers to choose between different options by means of evaluating their relative performance on meeting the weighted objectives that the decision makers want to achieve in a decision situation.

Working capital: A financial measure (usually calculated as current assets minus current liabilities) that indicates whether an organization can cover its short-term obligations with its short-term assets (in accounting terms, short-term means less than 12 months).

Z

Zero-based budgeting: A method for preparing a budget that starts from scratch (or "from zero"). Under the zero-based budgeting approach, all expenses need to be justified for the new budgeting period without using prior years' budgets or actual figures as a basis.

REFERENCES

Ablak, E. (2016) 'Yemeksepeti.com is fined, will others follow?', available at www.hurriyetdailynews.com/opinion/ersu-ablak/yemeksepeticom-is-fined-will-others-follow--101302, published 7 July 2016, accessed 31 January 2019.

Ackoff, R. (1979) 'The future of operational reseach is past', *Journal of the Operational Research Society*, 30(2): 93–104.

Adams, J. S. (1965) 'Inequity in social exchange', in Berkowitz L. (ed.), *Advances in Experimental Social Psychology, Vol. 2* (pp. 267–299) (New York, NY: Academic Press).

Ahuja, M. K. and Galvin, J. E. (2003) 'Socialization in virtual groups', *Journal of Management*, 29(2): 161–185.

Aime, F., Johnson, S., Ridge, J. W. and Hill, A. D. (2010) 'The routine may be stable but the advantage is not: Competitive implications of key employee mobility', *Strategic Management Journal*, 31(1): 75–87.

Air Liquide (2015) *2014 Annual* Report (Paris: L'Air Liquide S.A.).

airliquide.com (2019a) 'Group', available at www.airliquide.com/group, accessed 29 January 2019.

airliquide.com (2019b) 'i-Lab Air Liquide, available at https://ilab.airliquide.com/home/, accessed 29 January 2019.

Akechi, H., Senju, A., Uibo, H., Kikuchi, Y., Hasegawa, T. and Hietanen, J. K. (2013) 'Attention to eye contact in the West and East: Autonomic responses and evaluative ratings' , *PLoS One*, 8(3), available at https://doi.org/10.1371/journal.pone.0059312, published 13 March 2013, accessed 23 January 2019.

aldi-sued.de (2019) 'Über ALDI SÜD', available at https://unternehmen.aldi-sued.de/de/ueber-aldi-sued/unser-unternehmen/, accessed 21 January 2019.

Alexander, D. (2014) 'Victoria's other secret: The low-key billionaire behind the lingerie giant', at www.forbes.com/sites/danalexander/2014/09/30/victorias-other-secret-the-low-key-billionaire-behind-the-lingerie-giant/#58511b1512be, published 30 September 2014, accessed 3 January 2019.

Allen, D. (2001) *Getting Things Done: The Art of Stress-Free Productivity* (New York, NY: Penguin Books).

Allen, D. and Schwartz, T. (2011) 'Being more productive', *Harvard Business Review*, 89(5): 83–87.

Altman, V., Kaplan, M. and Corbett, A. (2002) 'Turn cost cutting into a core competency', *Harvard Management Update*, December.

Amabile, T. M. (1998) 'How to kill creativity', *Harvard Business Review*, 76(5): 76–87.

Amabile, T. M. and Khaire, M. (2008) 'Creativity and the role of the leader', *Harvard Business Review*, 86(10): 100–109.

Amabile, T. M. and Kramer, S. J. (2007) 'Inner work life', *Harvard Business Review*, 85(5): 72–83.

Amabile, T. M. and Kramer, S. J. (2011) 'The power of small wins', *Harvard Business Review*, 89(5): 70–80.

Amabile, T. M. and Kramer, S. J. (2012) 'How leaders kill meaning at work', *McKinsey Quarterly* (January): 124–134.

Amabile, T. M. and Pratt, M. G. (2016) 'The dynamic componental model of creativity and innovation in organizations: Making progress, making meaning', *Research in Organizational Behavior*, 36: 157–183.

amazon.com (2019a) 'What is cloud computing', available at https://aws.amazon.com/what-is-cloud-computing/, accessed 28 January 2019.

amazon.com (2019b) 'Why sell on Amazon?', available at https://services.amazon.com/selling/benefits.html, accessed 5 February 2019.

AmorePacific (2018) 'Our values', available at www.apgroup.com/int/en/our-values.html, accessed 5 January 2018.

Amos, E. A. and Weathington, B. L. (2008) 'An analysis of the relation between employee-organization value congruence and employee attitudes', *The Journal of Psychology*, 142(6): 615–632.

Anderson, N. H. (1974) 'Cognitive algebra: Integration theory applied to social attribution', in Berkowitz, L. (ed.), *Advances in Experimental Social Psychology*, 7 (pp. 1–101) (New York, NY: Academic Press).

Anderson, N., Potočnik, K. and Zhou, J. (2014) 'Innovation and creativity in organizations: A state-of-the-science review, prospective commentary, and guiding framework', *Journal of Management*, 40(5): 1297–1333.

Ansoff, H. I. (1965) *Corporate Strategy: An Analytic Approach to Business Policy for Growth and Expansion* (New York, NY: McGraw-Hill).

Apgar, D. (2006) *Risk Intelligence: Learning How to Manage What We Don't Know* (Boston, MA: Harvard Business School Publishing).

Ardichvili, A., Page, V. and Wentling, T. (2003) 'Motivation and barriers to participation in virtual knowledge-sharing communities of practice', *Journal of Knowledge Management*, 7(1): 64–77.

Aristotle (2009) *The Nicomachean Ethics* (Oxford/New York: Oxford University Press).

Aritzeta, A., Swailes, S. and Senior, B. (2007) 'Belbin's team role model: Development, validity and applications for team building', *Journal of Management Studies*, 44(1): 96–118.

Arminen, H., Puumalainen, K., Pätäri, S. and Fellnhofer, K. (2018) 'Corporate social performance: Inter-industry and international differences', *Journal of Cleaner Production*, 177: 426–437.

Arnkoff, D. B. (1986) 'A comparison of the coping and restructuring components of cognitive restruc-turing', *Cognitive Therapy and Research*, 10(2): 147–158.

Athanasopoulou, A. and Dopson, S. E. (2018) 'A system-atic review of executive coaching outcomes: Is it the journey or the destination that matters the most?', *Leadership Quarterly*, 29(1): 70–88.

Aytemiz Seymen, O. (2006) 'The cultural diversity phenomenon in organisations and different approaches for effective cultural diversity management: A literary review', *Cross Cultural Management: An International Journal*, 13(4): 296–315.

Bacon, F. (1869) *The Works of Francis Bacon*, Vol. VIII, edited by Spedding, J., Ellis, R. L., and Heath, D. D. (New York and Cambridge: Hurd and Houghton/ Riverside Press).

Bacon, F. (1985) *The Essays* (London: Penguin Books).

Badaracco Jr., J. L. and Webb, A. P. (1995) 'Business ethics: A view from the trenches', *California Management Review*, 37(2): 8–28.

Bae, H. (2015). 'Bill Gates' 40th anniverary email: Goal was "a computer on every desk"', available at http://money.cnn.com/2015/04/05/technology/bill-gates-email-microsoft-40-anniversary/index.html, published 6 April 2015, accessed 3 January 2019.

Baker, T. and Nelson, R. E. (2005) 'Creating something from nothing: Resource construction through entrepreneurial bricolage', *Administrative Science Quarterly*, 50(3): 329–366.

Baker, W. L., Marn, M. V. and Zawada, C. (2010) *The Price Advantage*, 2nd edn (New York, NY: Wiley).

Balch, O. (2013) 'The smelting company that became an urban mining pioneer', available at www.theguardian.com/sustainable-business/blog/umicore-smelting-company-clean-tech, published 19 August 2013, accessed 28 January 2019.

Bandiera, O., Guiso, L., Prat, A. and Sadun, R. (2011) 'What do CEOs do?', *Harvard Business School Working Paper* 11-081 (Cambridge, MA: Harvard Business School): 1–24.

Bandiera, O., Hansen, S., Prat, A. and Sadun, R. (2017) 'CEO behavior and firm performance', *Harvard Business School Working Paper* 17-083 (Cambridge, MA: Harvard Business School): 1–24.

Bandura, A. (1977) 'Self-efficacy: Toward a unifying theory of behavioral change', *Psychological Review*, 84(2): 191–215.

Bandura, A. and Locke, E. A. (2003) 'Negative self-efficacy and goal effects revisited', *Journal of Applied Psychology*, 88(1): 87–99.

Bargh, J. A. and Chartrand, T. L. (1999) 'The unbearable automaticity of being', *American Psychologist*, 54(7): 462–479.

Barley, S. R. and Kunda, G. (1992) 'Design and devotion: Surges of rational and normative ideologies of control in management discourse', *Administrative Science Quarterly*, 37(3): 363–399.

Barley, S. R., Meyerson, D. E. and Grodal, S. (2011) 'E-mail as a source and symbol of stress', *Organization Science*, 22(4): 887–906.

Barnard, C. I. (1938) *The Functions of the Executive* (Cambridge, MA: Harvard University Press).

Barney J. (1991) 'Firm resources and sustained competi-tive advantage', *Journal of Management*, 17(1): 99–120.

Barney, J. B. and Hesterly, W. S. (2015) *Strategic Manage-ment and Competitive Advantage*, 5th global edn (Harlow: Pearson).

Baron, J. (2008) *Thinking and Deciding*, 4th edn (New York, NY: Cambridge University Press).

Baron, R. A. (2006) 'Opportunity recognition as pattern recognition: How entrepreneurs "connect the dots" to identify new business opportunities', *The Academy of Management Perspectives*, 20(1): 104–119.

Bartels, L. K., Nadler, J. T., Kufahl, K. and Pyatt, J. (2013) 'Fifty years after the Civil Rights Act: Diversity-management practices in the field', *Industrial and Organizational Psychology*, 6(4): 450–457.

Bartlett, C. A., Dessain, V. and Sjöman, A. (2006) 'IKEA's global sourcing challenge', Harvard Business School case nr. 9-906-414.

Barton, D., Carey, D. and Charman, R. (2018) 'One bank's agile team experiment', *Harvard Business Review*, 96(2): 59–61.

Bartunek, J. M., Balogun, J. and Do, B. (2011) 'Considering planned change anew: Stretching large group interventions strategically, emotionally, and meaningfully', *Academy of Management Annals*, 5(1): 1–52.

Basar, S. (2017) 'Barclays' aim: agility', available at www.marketsmedia.com/barclays-aims-agile/, published 5 February 2017, accessed 18 December 2018.

Bass, B. M. (1990) 'From transactional to transformational leadership: Learning to share the vision', *Organizational Dynamics*, 18: 19–31.

Bassett, K. (2016) 'I built my business by ripping up the rulebook', available at www.managementtoday.co.uk/i-built-business-ripping-rulebook/women-in-business/article/1417855, published 6 December 2016, accessed 11 December 2018.

Bassett, K. (2017) 'Pocket Sun, SoGal Ventures: "I don't look anything like a typical VC', available at www.managementtoday.co.uk/pocket-sun-sogal-ventures-i-dont-look-anything-typical-vc/women-in-business/article/1439994, published 25 July 2017, accessed 31 January 2019.

Bazerman, M. H. and Moore, D. A. (2009) *Judgement in Managerial Decision Making*, 7th edn (Hoboken, NJ: Wiley).

BBC News (2005) '"Infomania" worse than marijuana', available at http://news.bbc.co.uk/2/hi/uk_news/4471607.stm, published 22 April 2005, accessed 8 January 2019.

bbc.co.uk (2012) 'Moody's agency downgrades Nokia bonds to "junk" status', available at www.bbc.co.uk/news/business-18460636, published 15 June 2012, accessed 28 January 2019.

bbc.com (2011) 'How Unilever, Coke and the Mini car got it so wrong', available at www.bbc.com/news/business-13285504, published 8 May 2011, accessed 6 February 2019.

bbc.com (2015) 'Barclays sacks boss Antony Jenkins in row over strategy', available at www.bbc.com/news/business-33438914, published 8 July 2015, accessed 18 December 2018.

bbc.com (2017) 'Aldi reports record sales but profits drop amid price war', available at www.bbc.com/news/business-41384179, published 25 September 2017, accessed 2 May 2019.

Belbin, R. M. (1993) *Team Roles at Work* (Oxford: Butterworth-Heinemann).

Belbin, R. M. (2004) *Management Teams: Why They Succeed or Fail*, 2nd edn (Oxford: Butterworth-Heinemann).

Bell, D. E. (1982) 'Regret in decision making under uncertainty', *Operations Research*, 30(5): 961–981.

ben.edu (2019) 'The Rule of St. Benedict', available at www.ben.edu/center-for-mission-and-identity/resources/rule-of-st-benedict.cfm, accessed 3 January 2019.

Bennett, N. and Lemoine, J. (2014) 'What VUCA really means for you', *Harvard Business Review*, 92 (1/2): 27.

Bentham, J. (1839) *The Works of Jeremy Bentham, Part VII* (Edinburgh: William Tait).

Berezin, R. (2013) 'The neuroscience of communication', available at www.psychologytoday.com/blog/the-theater-the-brain/201312/the-neuroscience-communication, published 19 December 2013, accessed 11 December 2018.

Bergiel, B. J., Bergiel, E. B. and Balsmeier, P. W. (2008) 'Nature of virtual teams: A summary of their advantages and disadvantages', *Management Research News*, 31(2): 99–110.

Berman, K. and Knight, J. (with Case, J.) (2013) *Financial Intelligence: A Manager's Guide to Knowing What the Numbers Really Mean*, rev. edn (Boston, MA: Harvard Business Review Press).

Bernstein, E., Bunch, J., Canner, N. and Lee, M. (2016) 'Beyond the holacracy hype', *Harvard Business Review*, 94(7), 38–49.

Berry, G. R. (2011) 'Enhancing effectiveness on virtual teams: Understanding why traditional team skills are insufficient', *Journal of Business Communication*, 48(2): 186–206.

Berry, P. (2014) 'Communication tips for global virtual teams', available at https://hbr.org/2014/10/communication-tips-for-global-virtual-teams, published 30 October 2014, accessed 25 January 2019.

Bertolini, M. (2016) 'Aetna CEO Mark Bertolini on leadership, yoga and fair wages', http://knowledge.wharton.upenn.edu/article/aetna-ceo-on-leadership-yoga-and-fair-wages/. Published 22 June 2016, accessed 21 January 2019.

Bertrand, N. (2014) 'How Amazon's ugly fight with a publisher actually started', available at www.businessinsider.com/how-did-the-amazon-feud-with-hachette-start-2014-10?IR=T, published 7 October 2014, accessed 31 July 2017.

Bharadwaj, S. G., Varadarajan, P. R. and Fahy, J. (1993) 'Sustainable competitive advantage in service industries: A conceptual model and research propositions', *Journal of Marketing*, 57(4): 83–99.

Bhargava (2016) 'Jugnoo accuses Ola of unethical practices', available at www.thehindu.com/business/Industry/Jugnoo-accuses-Ola-of-%E2%80%98unethical-practices%E2%80%99/article14171374.ece, published 23 March 2016, accessed 10 January 2019.

Bigoness, W. J. and Blakely, G. L. (1996) 'A cross-national study of managerial values', *Journal of International Business Studies*, 27(4): 739–748.

Bingham, C. B. and Eisenhardt, K. M. (2011) 'Rational heuristics: The ́simple rules ́ that strategists learn from process experience', *Strategic Management Journal,* 32(13): 1437–1464.

Birchall, J. (2008) 'Tales of brand revolution from P&G', available at www.ft.com/content/febfe328-064b-11dd-802c-0000779fd2ac, published 9 April 2008, accessed 4 January 2018.

Birkner, C. (2016) 'Meet the woman who could turn Jet. com into the digital era's ultimate challenger brand', available at www.adweek.com/brand-marketing/meet-woman-who-could-turn-jetcom-digital-eras-ultimate-challenger-brand-174030/, published 16 October 2016, accessed 10 January 2019.

biv.com (2014) 'Laurie Schultz', available at www.biv.com/article/2014/2/laurie-schultz/, published 23 February 2014, accessed 27 December 2018.

biv.com (2016) 'Peer to peer: Re-evaluate finances, software and strategy', available at www.biv.com/article/2016/5/peer-peer-re-evaluate-finances-software-and-strate/, published 17 May 2016, accessed 1 August 2017.

Blaggan, I. (2017) 'I am Samar Singla, Founder & CEO of Jugnoo, and this is how I work', www.lifehacker.co.in/productivity/i-am-samar-singla-ceo-of-jugnoo-and-this-is-how-i-work/articleshow/60924631.cms, published 4 October 2017, accessed 8 November 2017.

Blank, S. (2013) 'Why the lean start-up changes everything', *Harvard Business Review*, 91(5): 63–72.

Bloomberg (2015) 'Brunello Cucinelli insists on balance at his business', available at www.businessoffashion.com/articles/news-analysis/italian-fashion-brunello-cucinelli, published 5 November 2015, accessed 21 January 2019.

bloomberg.com (2010) 'Nokia's downfall holds three lessons for Europe: Matthew Lynn', available at www.bloomberg.com/news/articles/2010-09-13/nokia-s-decline-holds-three-lessons-for-europe-commentary-by-matthew-lynn, published 14 September 2010, accessed 28 January 2019.

Blumberg, M. and Pringle, C. D. (1982) 'The missing opportunity in organizational research: Some implications for a theory of work performance', *Academy of Management Review*, 7(4): 560–569.

Boddy, D. (2017) *Management: An Introduction*, 7th edn (Harlow, UK: Pearson).

Boillet, J. (2018) 'AI: A risk and a way to manage risks', available at www.ey.com/en_gl/assurance/why-ai-is-both-a-risk-and-a-way-to-manage-risk, published 1 April 2018, accessed 29 January 2019.

Boje, D. M. and Winsor, R. D. (1993) 'The resurrection of Taylorism: Total quality management's hidden agenda', *Journal of Organizational Change Management*, 6(4): 57–70.

Born, B. (2016) 'Leslie Wexner on building an empire', available at http://wwd.com/business-news/human-resources/leslie-wexner-l-brands-10445521/, published 17 September 2016, accessed 3 January 2019.

Bose, N. (2017) 'Exclusive: Aldi raises stakes in U.S. price war with Wal-Mart', available at www.reuters.com/article/us-aldi-walmart-pricing-exclusive-idUSK-BN1870EN, published 11 May 2017, accessed 21 January 2019.

Bossidy, L., Charan, R. and Burck, C. (2002) *Execution: The Discipline of Getting Things Done* (London: Random House Business Books).

Bouton, K. (2015) 'Recruiting for cultural fit', available at https://hbr.org/2015/07/recruiting-for-cultural-fit, published 17 July 2015, accessed 16 September 2016.

Bower, J. L. and Gilbert, C. G. (2007) 'How managers' everyday decisions create or destroy your company's strategy', *Harvard Business Review*, 85(2): 72–79.

Brandes, D. (2004) 'Das Geheimnis des Aldi-Erfolgs', available at www.manager-magazin.de/unternehmen/karriere/a-291316.html, published 23 March 2004, accessed 21 January 2019.

Brett, J. M., Behfar K. and Kern, M. C. (2006) 'Managing multicultural teams', *Harvard Business Review*, 84(11): 84–91.

Brinded, L. (2015) 'The sorry history of the near-destruction of investment banking at RBS', available at www.businessinsider.com/why-rbs-failed-as-an-investment-bank-2015-3?IR=T, published 6 March 2015, accessed 5 February 2019.

Brown, V. R. and Paulus, P. B. (2002) 'Making group brainstorming more effective: Recommendations from an associative memory perspective', *Current Directions in Psychological Science*, 11(6): 208–212.

Bruch, H. and Ghoshal, S. (2003) 'Unleashing organizational energy', *MIT Sloan Management Review*, 45(1): 45–51.

Bruch, H. and Vogel, B. (2011) *Fully Charged: How Great Leaders Boost Their Organization's Energy and Ignite High Performance* (Boston, MA: Harvard Business School Publishing).

Brundtland, G. H. (1987) *Our Common Future: The World Commission on Environment and Development* (Oxford: Oxford University Press).

Brunello Cucinelli (2017) *Brunello Cucinelli 2016 Annual Report* (Solomeo: Brunello Cucinelli).

Brunello Cucinelli (2018) *Brunello Cucinelli 2017 Annual Report* (Solomeo: Brunello Cucinelli).

brunellocucinelli.com (2017a) *Brunello Cucinelli Corporate Website*, available at http://www.brunellocucinelli.com/en, accessed 4 December 2017.

brunellocucinelli.com (2017b) 'Investor relations', available at http://investor.brunellocucinelli.com/en, accessed 4 December 2017.

Bruton, S. V. (2004) 'Teaching the Golden Rule', *Journal of Business Ethics*, 49(2): 179–187.

Bryant, A. (2009a) 'He wants subjects, verbs and objects', www.nytimes.com/2009/04/26/business/26corner.html, published 25 April 2009, accessed 27 December 2018.

Bryant, A. (2009b) 'He was promotable, after all', *The New York Times*, 2 May, available at www.nytimes.com/2009/05/03/business/03corner.html?_r=0. Published 2 May 2009, accessed 10 January 2019.

Bryant, A. (2009c) 'Managing globally, and locally', available at www.nytimes.com/2009/12/13/business/13corner.html, published 12 December 2009, accessed 28 January 2019.

Bryant, A. (2013) 'Laurie Schultz of ACL goes looking for the leaders', available at http://www.nytimes.com/2013/08/30/business/laurie-schultz-of-acl-goes-looking-for-the-leaders.html, published 29 August 2013, accessed 1 August 2017.

Bryman, A. (1992) *Charisma and Leadership in Organizations* (London: Sage).

Buchanan, D. A. (2008) 'You stab my back, I'll stab yours: Management experience and perceptions of organization political behaviour', *British Journal of Management,* 19(1): 49–64.

Burnison, G. (2011) 'How Pepsi's Indra Nooyi learned to be a CEO', available at www.fastcompany.com/1750645/how-pepsis-indra-nooyi-learned-be-ceo, published 29 April 2011, accessed 8 January 2019.

Burns, J. M. (1978) *Leadership* (New York, NY: Harper & Row).

Burns, P. (2016) *Entrepreneurship and Small Business: Start-up, Growth and Maturity*, 4th edn (London: Red Globe Press).

Burns, T. (1957) 'Management in action', *Operational Research Quarterly*, 8(2): 45–60.

Burton, B. K. and Goldsby, M. (2005) 'The Golden Rule and business ethics: An examination', *Journal of Business Ethics*, 56(4): 371–383.

Business Insider Nordic (2018) 'A bank just fired its world-famous AI assistant', Amelia, available at https://static2.businessinsider.com/a-bank-just-fired-its-world-famous-ai-assistant-amelia-2018-7, published 10 July 2018, accessed 28 January 2019.

Business Week (2002) 'How East meets West at Canon', available at www.businessweek.com/stories/2002-09-12/how-east-meets-west-at-canon, published 12 September 2002, accessed 8 January 2019.

businesstimes.com.sg (2016) 'The billionaire retail rebel (amended)', available at www.fastretailing.com/eng/about/business/, published 2 July 2016, accessed 23 February 2019.

Byza, O. A., Dörr, S. L., Schuh, S. C. and Maier, G. W. (2017) 'When leaders and followers match: The impact of objective value congruence, value extremity, and empowerment on employee commitment and job satisfaction', *Journal of Business Ethics*, published online before print, DOI https://doi.org/10.1007/s10551-017-3748-3.

Cai, D. A., Wilson, S. R. and Drake, L. E. (2000) 'Culture in the context of intercultural negotiation', *Human Communication Research*, 26(4): 591–617.

Campbell, J. P., McCloy, R. A., Oppler, S. H. and Sager, C. E. (1993) 'A theory of performance', in Schmitt, E., Borman, W. C., and Associates (eds), *Personnel Selection in Organizations* (pp. 35–70) (San Francisco, CA: Jossey Bass).

Cappelli, P., Singh, H., Singh, J. and Useem, M. (2010) *The India Way: How India's Top Business Leaders are Revolutionizing Management* (Boston, MA: Harvard Business Press).

Cardona, P. and Miller, P. (2000) 'Leadership in work teams', *IESE Business School Technical Note* nr. FHN-325-E0-400-027 (January).

Carmody, B. (2016) 'The future of retail: Bridging digital with the physical', available at www.inc.com/bill-carmody/the-future-of-retail-bridging-digital-with-the-physical.html, published 17 May 2016, accessed 5 July 2017.

Caro, F. and Martínez de Albéniz, V. (2013) 'Optimizing operations decisions the Zara way', IESE insight, available at www.ieseinsight.com/doc.aspx?id=1491&idioma=2&utm_source=Web&utm_medium=Portal&utm_campaign=NotiIESE_Zara_eng&_ga=2.49994405.2039507893.1500906577-1637759911.1474292540, accessed 5 February 2019.

Carpenter, M. A. and Sanders, W. G. (2009) *Strategic Management: A Dynamic Perspective*, 2nd edn (Upper Saddle River, NJ: Pearson/Prentice Hall).

Carroll, A. B. (1979) 'A three-dimensional conceptual model of corporate performance', *Academy of Management Review*, 4(4): 497–505.

Carroll, A. B. (1991) 'The pyramid of corporate social responsibility: Toward the moral management or organizational stakeholders', *Business Horizons*, 34(4): 39–48.

Carroll, A. B. (1999) 'Corporate social responsibility: Evolution of a definitional construct', *Business and Society*, 38(3): 267–295.

Carroll, A. B. and Shabana, K. M. (2010) 'The business case for corporate social responsibility: A review of concepts, research, and practice', *International Journal of Management Reviews*, 12(1): 85–105.

Caulkin, S. (2003) 'Who's in charge here', *The Guardian*, 27 April.

Cayla, J., Beers, R. and Arnould, E. (2013) 'Stories that deliver business insights', available at https://sloanreview.mit.edu/article/stories-that-deliver-business-insights/, published 19 December 2013, accessed 31 January 2019.

census.gov (2015) 'Detailed languages spoken at home and ability to speak English for the population 5 years and over: 2009-2013', available at www.census.gov/data/tables/2013/demo/2009-2013-lang-tables.html, published October 2015, accessed 25 January 2019.

Chai, S. and Shih, W. (2017) 'Why big data isn't enough', *MIT Sloan Management Review*, 58(2): 57–61.

Chakravorti, B. (2010) 'A note on corporate entrepreneurship: Challenge or opportunity', *Harvard Business School Background Note* nr. 9-810-145. (Boston, MA: Harvard Business School).

Chan, J. (2015) '3 proven startup strategies for success', available at https://foundr.com/3-proven-startup-strategies-for-success/, published 10 August 2015, accessed 5 February 2019.

Chandler, A. D. Jr. (1962) *Strategy and Structure: Chapters in the History of the American Industrial Enterprise* (Cambridge, MA: MIT Press).

Chang, Y. N. (1976) 'Early Chinese management thought', *California Management Review*, 19(2): 71–76.

Charan, R., Barton, D. and Carey, D. (2018) *Talent Wins: The New Playbook for Putting People First* (Boston, MA: Harvard Business Review Press).

Chesbrough, H. W. (2006) *Open Innovation: The New Imperative for Creating and Profiting from Technology* (Boston, MA: Harvard Business School Press).

Child, J. (2005) *Organization: Contemporary Principles and Practice* (Malden, MA: Blackwell/Wiley).

Choi, C.-B. and Beamish, P. W. (2004) 'Split management control and international joint venture performance', *Journal of International Business Studies*, 35(3): 201–215.

Christensen, C. M. (2010) 'How will you measure your life?', *Harvard Business Review*, 88(7/8): 46–51.

Chung, G. (2015) 'How South Korea's AmorePacific became one of the world's most innovative companies', available at www.forbes.com/sites/gracechung/2015/08/19/how-south-koreas-amorepacific-became-one-of-the-worlds-most-innovative-companies/#57888bb52b2b, published 19 August 2015, accessed 31 January 2019.

Cicero, M. T. (2001) *On Obligations* (Oxford: Oxford University Press).

Clapp-Smith, R., Hammond, M. M., Lester, G. V. and Palanski, M. (2018) 'Promoting identity development in leadership education: A multidomain approach to developing the whole leader', *Journal of Management Education*, published online before print, DOI: 1052562918813190.

Clawson, J. G. (2012) 'Energy management exercise', University of Virginia Darden School of Business note nr. UVA-OB-0716 (Charlottesville, VA: Darden Business Publishing).

Clegg, A. (2017) 'How to bring cross-cultural teams together', available at www.ft.com/content/01503bd8-fd00-11e6-8d8e-a5e3738f9ae4, published 30 March 2017, accessed 6 September 2017.

Clement, R. W. (2006) 'Just how unethical is American business?', *Business Horizons*, 49(4): 313–327.

cnet.com (2008) 'The greatest defunct Web sites and dotcom disasters', available at https://web.archive.org/web/20080607211851/http://crave.cnet.co.uk/0,39029477,49296926-8,00.htm, published 5 June 2008, accessed 5 February 2019.

coachmag.co.uk (2016) 'Women at their best: Jenny Biggam', available at www.coachmag.co.uk/people/5287/women-at-their-best-jenny-biggam, published 18 April 2016, accessed 11 December 2018.

Coca-Cola Company, The (2015) 'The Coca-Cola Company and Monster Beverage Corporation close on previously announced strategic partnership', at www.coca-colacompany.com/press-center/press-releases/the-coca-cola-company-and-monster-beverage-corporation-close-on-previously-announced-strategic-partnership, published 12 June 2015, accessed 28 January 2019.

coca-colacompany.com (2019) 'The Coca-Cola system', available at www.coca-colacompany.com/our-company/the-coca-cola-system, accessed 2 January 2019.

Cockburn, H. (2015) 'No job titles, as much holiday as staff like – meet Jenny Biggam of media agency the7stars', available at www.londonlovesbusiness.com/entrepreneurs/famous-entrepreneurs/no-job-titles-as-much-holiday-as-staff-like-meet-jenny-biggam-of-media-agency-the7stars/11105.article, published 30 September 2015, accessed 11 December 2018.

Cohen, A. and Bradford, D. (2017) *Influence Without Authority*, 3rd edn (Hoboken, NJ: John Wiley & Sons).

Cohn, R. C. (1975) *Von der Psychoanalyse zur themenzentrierten Interaktion* (Stuttgart: Klett-Cotta).

Collins, D. and Montgomery, C. (1995) 'Corporate strategy: A conceptual framework', Harvard Business School note no. 9-391-284 (Boston, MA: Harvard Business School Publishing).

Colquitt, J. A., Conlon, D. E., Wesson, M. J., Porter, C. O. and Ng, K. Y. (2001) 'Justice at the millennium: A meta-analysis of 25 years of organizational justice research', *Journal of Applied Psychology*, 86(3): 425–445.

Comair (2017) *2016 Integrated Annual Report* (Kempton Park, South Africa: Comair Limited).

comair.co.za (2017) 'The Comair story', available at www.comair.co.za/about-us/the-comair-story, accessed 10 July 2017.

comair.co.za (2019) 'Fleet', available at www.comair.co.za/about-us/fleet, accessed 7 January 2019.

Confucius (2007) *The Analects of Confucius*, translated by Burton Watson (New York, NY: Columbia University Press).

Conger, J. A. (1998) 'The necessary art of persuasion', *Harvard Business Review*, 76(3): 84–97.

Continental (2015) *Continental AG Annual Report 2014*, available at https://www.continental-corporation.com/resource/blob/10960/88183aef3b16e96591becc398e0ed5b0/annual-report-2014-data.pdf, accessed 1 May 2019.

Cooper, J. S. (2004) 'Babylonian beginnings: The origin and cuneiform writing system in comparative perspective', in Houston, S. D. (ed.), *The First Writing: Script Invention as History and Process* (pp. 71–99) (Cambridge: Cambridge University Press).

Corkery, M. and Popper, N. (2018) 'From farm to block-chain: Walmart tracks its lettuce', available at www.nytimes.com/2018/09/24/business/walmart-block-chain-lettuce.html, published 24 September 2018, accessed 28 January 2019.

Cornell (2013) 'Bringing beauty to the world, inside and out', available at www.johnson.cornell.edu/About/Notable-Alumni/Profiles-in-Leadership/Profile-in-Leadership-Article/ArticleId/36438/Bringing-Beauty-to-the-World-Inside-and-Out, published 1 June 2013, accessed 30 January 2019.

Corts, K. S. and Freier, D. (2003) 'Judo in action', Harvard Business School case nr. 9-707.454 (Boston, MA: Harvard Business School Publishing).

Cottrill, M. (2008) 'How Aon CEO Gregory Case achieved clarity of focus to achieve a turnaround', available at www.sbnonline.com/article/clarity-of-focus-how-gregory-case-engaged-employees-and-clients-to-fine-tune-the-vision-at-aon-corp/?all=1, published 27 May 2008, accessed 23 February 2019.

Coutu, D. L. (2002) 'How resilience works', *Harvard Business Review*, 80(5): 46–51.

Coutu, D. (2009) 'Why teams don't work (Interview with J. R. Hackman) ', *Harvard Business Review*, 87(5): 98–105.

Cox Jr., A. (2008) 'What's wrong with risk matrices?', *Risk Analysis*, 28(2): 497–512.

Coyne, K. P., Coyne, S. T. and Coyne, Sr., E. J. (2010) 'When you've got to cut costs now', *Harvard Business Review*, 88(5): 74–82.

Craumer, M. (2001) 'The effective meeting: A checklist for success', *Harvard Management Communication Letter,* 4(3) (March): 1–3.

Cross, R., Baker, W. and Parker, A. (2003) 'What creates energy in organizations', *MIT Sloan Management Review*, 44(4): 51–56.

Crowne, K. A. (2008) 'What leads to cultural intelligence?', *Business Horizons*, 51(5): 391–399.

Curtis, B. (2006) 'Herr Mateschitz wants to juice you up', *The New York Times*, 29 October.

Curtis, P. and Carey, M. (2012) *Thought Leadership in ERM: Risk Assessment in Practice* (Durham, NC: COSO).

D'Aveni, R. A., Dagnino, G. B. and Smith, K. G. (2010) 'The age of temporary advantage', *Strategic Management Journal*, 31(13): 1371–1385.

Da Vinci, L. (2008) *Notebooks* (New York, NY: Oxford University Press).

Daft, R. L. (2010) *Management*, 9th edn (Mason, OH: South-Western Cengage Learning).

Daft, R. L. (2016) *Management*, 12th edn (Boston, MA: South-Western Cengage Learning).

dailyindian.com (2016) '"Nobody remembers your failures once you succeed"', available at www.dailyindian.com/2016/12/22/nobody-remembers-your-failuers-once-you-succeed/, published 22 December 2016, accessed 10 January 2019.

Dalborg, C., von Friedrichs, Y. and Wincent, J. (2012) 'Beyond the numbers: qualitative growth in women's businesses', *International Journal of Gender and Entrepreneurship*, 4(3): 289–315.

Dane, E. and Pratt, M. G. (2007) 'Exploring intuition and its role in managerial decision-making', *Academy of Management Review,* 32(1): 33–54.

Danneels, E. (2008) 'Organizational antecedents of second-order capabilities', *Strategic Management Journal,* 29(4): 519–543.

Dannemiller, K. D. and Jacobs, R. W. (1992) 'Changing the way organizations change: A revolution of common sense', *Journal of Applied Behavioral Science*, 28(4): 480–498.

Denning, S. (2014) 'Making sense of Zappos and holacracy', available at www.forbes.com/sites/stevedenning/2014/01/15/making-sense-of-zappos-and-holacracy/#131360bc3207, published 15 January 2014, accessed 2 January 2019.

Davenport, T. H. and Ronanki, R. (2018) 'Artificial intelligence for the real world', *Harvard Business Review*, 96(1): 108–116.

Davis, J. (2015) 'The natty professor', *Esquire*, spring/summer 2015 UK edition: 65–69.

Davis, J. H., Schoorman, F. D. and Donaldson, L. (1997) 'Toward a stewardship theory of management', *Academy of Management Review*, 22(1): 20–47.

De Geus, A. (1997) *The Living Company: Habits for Survival in a Turbulent Business Environment* (Boston, MA: Harvard Business School Press).

De Mey (2011) 'What is a strong e-commerce business model: Yemek Sepeti (Turkey) as a leading example', www.boardofinnovation.com/blog/2011/09/17/a-strong-e-commerce-business-model-yemek-sepetiu-turkey/, published 17 September 2011, accessed 31 January 2019.

De Montaigne, M. (2004) *On Friendship* (London: Penguin Books).

De Saint-Exupéry, A. (1968) *Wind, Sand and Stars* (New York, NY: Harcourt Brace Jovanovich).

Deal, T. and Kennedy, A. (2000) *Corporate Cultures: The Rites and Rituals of Corporate Life* (Cambridge, MA: Basic Books).

Dean, D. and Webb, C. (2011) 'Recovering from information overload', *McKinsey Quarterly*, 1, 80–88.

Dean, S. (2017) 'Akzo Nobel boss Ton Büchner steps down as CEO for health reasons', available at www.telegraph.co.uk/business/2017/07/19/akzo-nobel-boss-ton-buchner-steps-ceo-health-reasons/, published 19 July 2017, accessed 10 January 2019.

Deckers, L. (2018) *Motivation: Biological, Psychological, and Environmental*, 5th edn (New York, NY: Routledge).

deepmind.com (2019) 'Solve intelligence. Use it to make the world a better place', available at https://deepmind.com/about/, accessed 30 January 2019.

Delivery Hero (2018) 'About', available at www.delivery-hero.com/about/, accessed 19 January 2018.

Della Cava, M. (2017) 'Microsoft's Satya Nadella is counting on culture shock to drive growth', available at https://eu.usatoday.com/story/tech/news/2017/02/20/microsofts-satya-nadella-counting-culture-shock-drive-growth/98011388/, publsihed 20 February 2017, accessed 12 December 2018.

delta.com (2016) 'Leader bio: Richard Anderson, Executive Chairman of the Board', available at http://news.delta.com/leader-bio-richard-anderson-executive-chairman-board, published 9 March 2016, accessed 3 November 2016.

Den Hartog, D. N. and Koopman, P. (2001) 'Leadership in organizations', in: Anderson, N., Ones, D. S., Sinangil, H. K. and Viswesvaran, C., *Handbook of Industrial, Work & Organizational Psychology, Vol. 2 Organizational Psychology* (pp. 166–187) (London: Sage).

Denning, S. (2018) *The Age of Agile* (New York, NY: AMACOM).

DHL (2019) 'Our divisions', available at www.logistics.dhl/in-en/home/our-divisions.html, accessed 2 January 2019.

Dias, D. (2016) 'Five tips for building the perfect startup team from Envato founder Cyan Ta'eed', available at www.smartcompany.com.au/startupsmart/advice/five-ways-australias-coolest-tech-company-excels-at-people-management/, published 24 August 2016, accessed 8 January 2019.

Djonlagic, I., Rosenfeld, A., Shohamy, D., Myers, C., Gluck, M. and Stickgold, R. (2009) 'Sleep enhances category learning', *Learning & Memory,* 16(12): 751–755.

Dobbin, F. and Kalev, A. (2016) 'Why diversity programs fail: And what works better', *Harvard Business Review*, 94(7/8): 52–60.

Doktor, R. H. (1990) 'Asian and American CEOs: A comparative study', *Organizational Dynamics,* 18 (3): 46–56.

Donaldson, T. (1982) *Corporations and Morality* (Englewood Cliffs, NJ: Prentice-Hall).

Donaldson, T. (1996) 'Values in tension: Ethics away from home', *Harvard Business Review*, 74(5): 48–62.

Döpfner, M. (2016) 'Mark Zuckerberg talks about the future of Facebook, virtual reality and artificial intelligence', available at www.businessinsider.com/mark-zuckerberg-interview-with-axel-springer-ceo-mathias-doepfner-2016-2?IR=T, published 28 February 2016, accessed 3 January 2019.

Dörner, D. (1989) *Die Logik des Mißlingens: Strategisches Denken in komplexen Situationen* (Reinbek bei Hamburg: Rowohlt).

Douglas, N. (2017) 'I'm Jet.com President Liza Landsman, and this is how I work', available at https://lifehacker.com/im-jet-com-president-liza-landsman-and-this-is-how-i-w-1818580728, published 20 September 2017, accessed 10 January 2019.

Dowsett, S. (2018) 'Zara looks to technology to keep up with faster fashion', available at www.reuters.com/article/us-inditex-technology-focus/zara-looks-to-technology-to-keep-up-with-faster-fashion-idUSKBN1JB0HG, published 15 June 2018, accessed 5 February 2019.

Doyle, A. C. (2003) *The Complete Sherlock Holmes*, Vol. II. (New York, NY: Barnes & Noble Classics).

Drew, C. (2012) 'Lockheed's incoming chief forced out over ethics violation', available at www.nytimes.com/2012/11/10/business/lockheed-citing-ethics-violation-says-incoming-chief-has-quit.html?mcubz=1, published 9 November 2012, accessed 25 January 2019.

Drucker, P. F. (1967) *The Effective Executive* (New York, NY: Harper & Row).

Drucker, P. F. (1974) *Management: Tasks, Responsibilities, Practices* (New York, NY: Harper & Row).

Drucker, P. F. (1985) 'The discipline of innovation', *Harvard Business Review*, 63(3): 67–72.

Drucker, P. F. (1993) *Managing for Results: Economic Tasks and Risk-taking Decisions* (New York, NY: HarperBusiness).

Drucker, P. F. (1999a) *The Effective Executive* (Amsterdam: Elsevier/Butterworth-Heinemann).

Drucker, P. F. (1999b) 'Managing oneself', *Harvard Business Review*, 77(2): 64–74.

Drucker, P. F. (2007) *The Practice of Management*, Classic Drucker Collection edition (Amsterdam: Elsevier).

Drucker, P. F. (2011) *Managing for Results: Economic Tasks and Risk-Taking Decisions* (New York, NY: Routledge).

Drucker, P. (2015) *Innovation and Entrepreneurship: Practices and Principles* (London and New York: Routledge).

Duarte, D. L. and Snyder, N. T. (2006) *Mastering Virtual Teams: Strategies, Tools, and Techniques That Succeed*, 3rd edn (San Francisco, CA: Jossey-Bass).

Dublish, P. (2017) 'Singapore dispatch: Pocket Sun is knocking down doors', available at https://thestoryexchange.org/singapore-dispatch-pocket-sun-problem-conversation/, published 6 March 2017, accessed 31 January 2019.

Duening, T. N. (2010) 'Five minds for the entrepreneurial future: Cognitive skills as the intellectual foundation for next generation entrepreneurship curricula', *The Journal of Entrepreneurship*, 19(1): 1–22.

Dunn, L. E. (2017) 'Women in business Q&A: Liza Landsman, President, Jet.com', available at www.huffingtonpost.com/entry/women-in-business-qa-liza-landsman-president-jetcom_us_59632963e4b0cf3c8e8d5a02, published 10 July 2017, accessed 10 January 2019.

Dutton, J. E. (2003) *Energize Your Workplace: How to Build and Sustain High-Quality Relations at Work* (San Francisco, CA: Jossey-Bass).

Dwyer, K. (2007) 'How to win at office politics', available at www.cbsnews.com/news/how-to-win-at-office-politics/, published 2 July 2007, accessed 3 January 2019.

Earley, P. C. and Mosakowski, E. (2004) 'Cultural intelligence', *Harvard Business Review*, 82(10): 139–146.

Eaton, M. (2013) *The Lean Practitioner's Handbook* (London: Kogan Page).

Economist, The (2008) 'Payback: Bankers' pay is a complex subject that arouses simple emotions', *The Economist*, 20 November.

economist.com (2014) 'Frozen conflict', available at www.economist.com/news/business-and-finance/21632802-deal-between-two-firms-unlikely-end-dispute-over-prices-and-profits-e-books-frozen, published 14 November 2014, accessed 11 December 2018.

Eddy, K. (2012) 'Studio Moderna: Slovenia's multi-channel retailer, going global', available at http://blogs.ft.com/beyond-brics/2012/09/20/slovenias-multi-channel-retailer-going-global/?mhq5j=e1, published 20 September 2012, accessed 11 July 2017.

Ehrlinger, J., Johnson, K., Banner, M., Dunning, D. and Kruger, J. (2008) 'Why the unskilled are unaware: Further explorations of (absent) self-insight among the incompetent', *Organizational Behavior and Human Decision Processes*, 105(1): 98–121.

Eigsti, I.-M., Zayas, V., Mischel, W., Shoda, Y., Ayduk, O., Dadlani, M. B., Davidson, M. C., Aber, J. L. and Casey, B. J. (2006) 'Predicting cognitive control from preschool to late adolescence and young adulthood', *Psychological Science*, 17(6): 478–484.

Eisenberger, R., Stinglhamer, F., Vandenberghe, C., Sucharski, I. L. and Rhoades, L. (2002) 'Perceived supervisor support: Contributions to perceived organizational support and employee retention', *Journal of Applied Psychology*, 87(3): 565–573.

Eisenhardt, K. M. (1989) 'Agency theory: An assessment and review', *The Academy of Management Review*, 14(1): 57–74.

Eisenhardt, K. M. (1997) 'Conflict and strategic choice: How top management teams disagree', *California Management Review*, 39(2): 42–62.

Eisenhardt, K. M. and Bourgeois, III, L. J. (1988) 'Politics of strategic decision making in high-velocity environments; Toward a midrange theory', *Academy of Management Journal*, 31(4): 737–770.

Eisenmann, T., Ries, E. and Dillard, S. (2013) 'Hypothesis-driven entrepreneurship', *Harvard Business School Background Note* nr. 9-812-095 (Boston, MA: Harvard Business School).

Elberse, A. (2013) 'Ferguson's formula', *Harvard Business Review*, 91(10): 116–125.

Elfenbein, H. A. (2007) 'Emotions in organizations: A review and theoretical integration', *Academy of Management Annals,* 1(1): 315–386.

Elkington, J. (1997) *Cannibals with Forks: The Triple Bottom Line of 21st Century Business* (Oxford: Capstone).

Ellis, A. (1994) *Reason and Emotion in Psychotherapy* (Secaucus, NJ: Birch Lane Press).

Ellis-Petersen, H. (2014) 'Amazon and publisher Hachette end dispute over book sales', available at www.theguardian.com/books/2014/nov/13/amazon-hachette-end-dispute-ebooks, published 13 November 2014, accessed 11 December 2018.

Emerson, R. W. (1860) *Essays: Second Series* (Boston: Ticknor and Fields).

Epictetus (2019) *The Enchiridion*, translated by Elizabeth Carter, available at http://classics.mit.edu/Epictetus/epicench.html, date accessed 10 January 2019.

Epstein, S. (1990) 'Cognitive-experiental self-theory', in Pervin, L. (ed.), *Handbook of Personality: Theory and Research* (pp. 165–192) (New York, NY: Guilford Press).

Ercu (2015) 'Yemeksepeti: Operational excellence in online food ordering', available at https://rctom.hbs.org/submission/yemeksepeti-operational-excellence-in-online-food-ordering/, published 7 December 2015, accessed 31 January 2019.

Ericsson, K. A. (2018) 'The differential influence of experience, practice, and deliberate practice on the development of superior individual performance of experts', in Ericsson, K. A., Hoffmann, R. R., Kozbelt, A. and Williams, A. M. (eds), *The Cambridge Handbook of Expertise and Expert Performance,* 2nd edn (pp. 745–769) (New York, NY: Cambridge University Press).

Ericsson, K. A., Krampe, R. T. and Tesch-Römer, C. (1993) 'The role of deliberate practice in the acquisition of expert performance', *Psychological Review,* 100(3): 363–406.

Ertel, D. and Gordon, M. (2007) 'Best practices: Negotiating—what's the point of the deal, really?', *Ivey Business Journal,* September/October., available at http://iveybusinessjournal.com/publication/best-practices-negotiating-whats-the-point-of-the-deal-really/, accessed 11 December 2018.

Eva, N., Robin, M., Sendjaya, S., van Dierendonck, D. and Liden, R. C. (2019) 'Servant leadership: A systematic review and call for future research', *The Leadership Quarterly,* 30(1): 111–132.

Evans, S. and Tourish, D. (2017) 'Agency theory and performance appraisal: How bad theory damages learning and contributes to bad management practice', *Management Learning,* 48(3): 271–291.

Facebook (2016) 'Our history', available at http://newsroom.fb.com/company-info/, accessed 1 December 2016.

Falk, C. F., Dunn, E. W. and Norenzayan, A. (2010) 'Cultural variation in the importance of expected enjoyment for decision making', *Social Cognition,* 28(5): 609–629.

Falk, E. and Scholz, C. (2018) 'Persuasion, influence, and value: Perspectives from communication and social neuroscience', *Annual Review of Psychology,* 69(1): 329–356.

Farjoun, M. (2007). 'The end of strategy?', *Strategic Organization,* 5(3): 197–210.

fastretailing.com (2019) 'Our business', available at www.fastretailing.com/eng/about/business/, accessed 23 February 2019.

Faulkner, W. and Stein, J. (1956) 'William Faulkner, The Art of Fiction No. 12', interview by Jean Stein, *The Paris Review,* Spring 1956, no. 12, available at www.theparisreview.org/interviews/4954/the-art-of-fiction-no-12-william-faulkner, accessed 10 January 2019.

Favoro, K. (2016) 'Don't draft a digital strategy just because everyone else is', available at https://hbr.org/2016/03/dont-draft-a-digital-strategy-just-because-everyone-else-is, published 16 March 2016, accessed 28 January 2019.

Fayol, H. (1917) *Administration industrielle et générale* (Paris: H. Dunod et E. Pinat).

Fayol, H. (1949) *General and Industrial Management* (Oxford: Oxford University Press).

Feldman, D. C. and Lankau, M. J. (2005) 'Executive coaching: A review and agenda for future research', *Journal of Management,* 31(6): 829–848.

Feloni, R. (2015) 'Pepsi CEO Indra Nooyi explains how an unusual daily ritual her mom made her practice as a child changed her life', www.businessinsider.com/pepsico-indra-nooyi-life-changing-habit-2015-9?IR=T, published 9 September 2015, accessed 8 January 2019.

Fernández-Aráoz, C., Groysberg, B. and Nohria, N. (2009) 'The definitive guide to recruiting in good times and bad', *Harvard Business Review,* 87(5): 74–84.

Ferrazzi, K. (2014) 'Managing yourself: Getting virtual teams right', *Harvard Business Review,* 92(12): 120–123.

Ferrazzi, K. (2015) 'How to run a great virtual meeting', available at https://hbr.org/2015/03/how-to-run-a-great-virtual-meeting, published 27 March 2015, accessed 11 December 2018.

Fisher, L. M. (2005) 'Ricardo Semler won't take control', *Strategy and Business,* 41, available at www.strategy-business.com/article/05408?gko=3291c, published 29 November 2005, accessed 27 December 2018.

Fisher, R., Ury, W. and Patton, B. (2011) *Getting to Yes: Negotiating Agreement Without Giving In,* updated, revised edition. (New York, NY: Penguin Books).

Forbes Insights (2018) *The Elusive Agile Enterprise: How the Right Leadership Mindset, Workforce and Culture Can Transform Your Organization* (Jersey City, NJ: Forbes Insights in association with ScrumAlliance).

forbes.com (2015) 'ALDI is a growing menace to America's grocery retailers', available at www.forbes.com/sites/thehartmangroup/2015/04/14/aldi-is-a-growing-menace-to-americas-grocery-retailers/#30aa9748f077, published 14 April 2015, accessed 21 January 2019.

ForbesCustom (2018) 'Japan: Looks to the future', available at www.forbes.com/custom/2018/02/21/japan-looks-to-the-future/, published 22 February 2018, accessed 17 April 2019.

Ford, E. (2012) 'Benign king of cashmere prepares to tackle the corporate hamster wheel', *The Times,* 10 April 2012, p. 35.

Ford, J. D. and Ford, L. W. (2009) 'Decoding resistance to change', *Harvard Business Review*, 87(4): 99–103.

Forrester, J. W. (1961) *Industrial Dynamics* (Cambridge, MA: The MIT Press).

Forsyth, D. R. (2019) *Group Dynamics,* 7th edn (Boston, MA: Cengage Learning).

Frankl, V. E. (2006) *Man's Search for Meaning* (Boston, MA: Beacon Press).

Franklin, B. (2008) *Autobiography and Other Writings* (New York, NY: Bantam Classic).

Freeman, R. (1984) *Strategic Management: A Stakeholder Approach* (Boston, MA: Pitman).

Freeman, R. E., Harrison, J. S. and Wicks, A. C. (2007) *Managing for Stakeholders: Survival, Reputation, and Success* (New Haven, CT: Yale University Press).

Freeman, R. E., Harrison, J. S., Wicks, A. C., Parmar, B. L. and De Colle, S. (2010) *Stakeholder Theory: The State of the Art* (Cambridge: Cambridge University Press).

French, J. P. R. Jr. and Raven, B. (1968) 'The bases of social power', in Cartwright, D. and Zander, A. F. (eds), *Group Dynamics: Research and Theory*, 3rd edn (pp. 259–269) (New York, NY: Harper & Row).

Friedersdorf, C. (2014) 'Why PepsiCo CEO Indra K. Nooyi can't have it all', available at www.theatlantic.com/business/archive/2014/07/why-pepsico-ceo-indra-k-nooyi-cant-have-it-all/373750/, published 1 July 2014, accessed 9 October 2017.

Friedman, M. (1962) *Capitalism and Freedom* (Chicago, IL: University of Chicago Press).

Frisch, B. (2011) 'Who really makes the big decisions in your company?', *Harvard Business Review,* 89(12): 104–111.

Fritz, C., Lam, C. F. and Spreitzer, G. M. (2011) 'It's the little things that matter: An examination of knowledge workers' energy management', *Academy of Management Perspectives*, 25(3): 28–39.

Frost, D. and Kalman, D. (2016) *Inclusive Talent Management: How Business Can Thrive in an Age of Diversity* (London: Kogan Page).

FSA (2011) *The Failure of the Royal Bank of Scotland: Financial Services Authority Board Report* (London: Financial Services Authority).

ft.com (2012) 'Executive sick list reflects demands', available at www.ft.com/content/d97a4c10-027d-11e2-9e53-00144feabdc0, published 21 September 2012, accessed 8 January 2013.

Furnham, A. and Treglown, L. (2018) *Disenchantment: Managing Motivation and Demotivation at Work* (London: Bloomsbury).

Galbraith, J. K. (1969) *Ambassador's Journal: A Personal Account of the Kennedy Years* (Boston, MA: Houghton Mifflin).

gallup.com (2016) 'Gallup's leadership research', available at http://strengths.gallup.com/110251/gallups-leadership-research.aspx, accessed 16 September 2016.

Gantt, H. (1919) *Organizing for Work* (New York, NY: Harcourt, Brace & Howe).

Gao, Y. (2017) 'Business leaders' personal values, organisational culture and market orientation', *Journal of Strategic Marketing*, 25(1): 49–64.

Gardenswartz, L. and Rowe, A. (2010) *Managing Diversity: A Complete Desk Reference & Planning Guide,* 3rd edn (Alexandria, VA: The Society for Human Resource Management).

Garimella, K. (2018) 'Job loss from AI? There's more to fear!', available at www.forbes.com/sites/cognitive-world/2018/08/07/job-loss-from-ai-theres-more-to-fear/#759d372923eb, published 7 August 2018, accessed 29 January 2019.

Garvin, D. A. and Levesque, L. C. (2006) 'Meeting the challenge of corporate entrepreneurship', *Harvard Business Review*, 84(10): 102–112.

Garvin, D. A. and Margolis, J. D. (2015) 'The art of giving and receiving advice', *Harvard Business Review*, 93(1/2): 60–71.

Garvin, D. A. and Roberto, M. A. (2001) 'What you don't know about making decisions', *Harvard Business Review,* 79(8): 108–116.

Gary, M. S. and Wood, R. E. (2011) 'Mental models, decision rules, and performance heterogeneity', *Strategic Management Journal*, 32(6): 569–594.

Gates, B. (2013) 'Bill Gates: Teachers need real feedback (TED talk)', available at www.ted.com/talks/bill_gates_teachers_need_real_feedback, published May 2013, accessed 27 December 2018.

Gelderblom, O., De Jong, A. and Jonker, J. (2013) 'The formative years of the modern corporation: the Dutch East India Company VOC, 1602–1623', *The Journal of Economic History*, 73(4): 1050–1076.

Gentile, M. (1995)) 'Ways of thinking about and across difference', *Harvard Business School Background Note* nr. 9-395-117 (Boston, MA: Harvard Business School Publishing).

genuineguildan.com (2017a) 'Message from the President and CEO', available at www.genuinegildan.com/en/company/message-management/, accessed 30 August 2017.

genuineguildan.com (2017b) 'Company overview', available at www.genuinegildan.com/en/company/company-overview/, accessed 30 August 2017.

George, J. M. (2000) 'Emotions and leadership: The role of emotional intelligence', *Human Relations*, 53(8): 1027–1055.

George, N. M., Parida, V., Lahti, T. and Wincent, J. (2016) 'A systematic literature review of entrepreneurial opportunity recognition: Insights on influencing factors', *International Entrepreneurship and Management Journal*, 12(2): 309–350.

Ghoshal, S. and Bruch, H. (2003) 'Going beyond motivation to the power of volition', *MIT Sloan Management Review*, 44(3): 51–57.

Gilbreth, F. B. and Gilbreth, L. M. (1916) *Fatigue Study: The Elimination of Humanity's Greatest Unnecessary Waste* (New York, NY: Sturgis & Walton).

Gildan (2016) *Gildan Activewear Inc. Diversity and Inclusion Policy* (Montréal: Gildan Activewear Inc.).

gildancorp.com (2017) 'Diversity and inclusion', available at www.gildancorp.com/diversity-and-inclusion, accessed 30 August 2017.

gildancorp.com (2019) 'Our company', available at www.gildancorp.com/company-landing-page, accessed 28 January 2019.

Gilligan, C. (1977) 'In a different voice: Women's conceptions of self and of morality', *Harvard Educational Review*, 47(4): 481–517.

Gilson, L. L., Maynard, M. T., Jones Young, N. C., Vartiainen, M. and Hakonen, M. (2015) 'Virtual teams research: 10 years, 10 themes, and 10 opportunities', *Journal of Management*, 41(5): 1313–1337.

Global Entrepreneurship Monitor (2019) 'Entrepreneurial behaviour and attitudes', available at www.gemconsortium.org/data, accessed 30 January 2019.

Globe Project (2019) 'Overview', available at https://globeproject.com/studies, accessed 23 January 2019.

Gnirke, K., Hengst, B. and Kollenbroich, B. (2016) 'Billig, aber edel', available at www.spiegel.de/wirtschaft/unternehmen/aldi-billig-aber-edel-das-neue-konzept-im-check-a-1092074.html, published 15 May 2016, accessed 21 January 2019.

Goethe, J. W. v. (1914) *West-Eastern Divan*, translated by Edward Dowden (London: J. M. Dent & Sons).

goldmansachs.com (2018) 'Bob Iger: Leading the Walt Disney Company into the future', available at www.goldmansachs.com/insights/talks-at-gs/bob-iger.html, published 23 March 2018, accessed 10 January 2019.

Goldstone, R. L. and Hendrickson, A. T. (2010) 'Categorical perception', *Wiley Interdisciplinary Reviews: Cognitive Science*, 1(1): 69–78.

google.com (2019) 'About Google', available at www.google.com/intl/en/about/, accessed 28 January 2019.

gothamCulture (2017) 'Comair: Organizational change management', available at https://gothamculture.com/clients/case-studies/comair-organizational-change-management/, accessed 10 July 2017.

Govindarajan, V. and Gupta, A. K. (2001) 'Building an effective global business team', *MIT Sloan Management Review*, 42(4): 63–71.

Graham, L. O. (1997) *Proversity: Getting Past Face Values and Finding the Soul of People* (New York, NY: Wiley & Sons).

Graham, P. (ed.) (1995) *Mary Parker Follett: Prophet of Management* (Washington, DC: Beard Books).

Graham, P. (ed.) (2003) *Mary Parker Follett Prophet of Management: A Celebration of Writings from the 1920s* (Washington, DC: Beard Books).

Grant, A. M. (2008) 'The significance of task significance: Job performance effects, relational mechanisms, and boundary conditions', *Journal of Applied Psychology*, 93(1): 108–124.

Grant, A. M. (2012) 'Leading with meaning: Beneficiary contact, prosocial impact, and the performance effect of transformational leadership', *Academy of Management Journal*, 55(2): 458–476.

Gratton, L. and Erickson, T. J. (2007) 'Eight ways to build collaborative teams', *Harvard Business Review*, 85(11): 100–109.

Gray, R. (2006) 'Social, environmental and sustainability reporting and organisational value creation? Whose value? Whose creation?', *Accounting, Auditing & Accountability Journal*, 19(6): 793–819.

Greenberg, P. S., Greenberg, R. H. and Antonucci, Y. L. (2007) 'Creating and sustaining trust in virtual teams', *Business Horizons*, 50(4): 325–333.

Greene, F. J. and Hopp, C. (2017) 'Research: Writing a business plan makes your startup more likely to succeed', available at https://hbr.org/2017/07/research-writing-a-business-plan-makes-your-startup-more-likely-to-succeed, published 14 July 2017, accessed 31 January 2019.

Greenfield, P. (2017) 'Yellow Pages to stop printing from January 2019', available at www.theguardian.com/media/2017/sep/01/yellow-pages-to-stop-printing-from-january-2019, published 1 September 2017, accessed 8 January 2019.

Greenleaf, R. K. (2002) *Servant Leadership: A Journey Into the Nature of Legitimate Power and Greatness*. 25th Anniverary Edition (Mahwah, NJ: Paulist Press).

Grey, C. (2009) *A Very Short, Fairly Interesting, and Reasonably Cheap Book About Studying Organizations*, 2nd edn (Thousand Oaks, CA: Sage).

GRI (2013) *G4 Sustainability Reporting Guidelines* (Amsterdam: Global Reporting Initiative).

GRI (2016) *Consolidated Set of GRI Sustainability Reporting Standards* (Amsterdam: Global Reporting Initiative).

Habermas, J. (1999) *Moral Consciousness and Communicative Action*, translated by Lenhard, C. and Weber Nicholsen, S., 6th printing (Cambridge, MA: The MIT Press).

Hackman, J. R. (2011) *Collaborative Intelligence: Using Teams to Solve Hard Problems* (San Francisco, CA: Berrett-Koehler).

haier.net (2011) 'Haier and Sanyo sign final agreement', available at www.haier.net/en/about_haier/news/201110/t20111028_83307.html, published 18 October 2011, accessed 25 January 2019.

haier.net (2017) 'About Haier', available at www.haier.net/en/about_haier/, accessed 6 September 2017.

Hales, C. (1986) 'What do managers do? A critical review of the evidence', *Journal of Management Studies*, 23(1): 88–115.

Hall, D. J. and Saias, M. A. (1980) 'Strategy follows structure!', *Strategic Management Journal*, 1(2): 149–163.

Hall, E. T. (1976) *Beyond Culture* (Garden City, NY: Anchor Press).

Hambrick, D. C. and D'Aveni, R. A. (1988) 'Large corporate failures as downward spirals', *Administrative Science Quarterly*, 33(1): 1–23.

Hammer, M. (1990) 'Reengineering work: Don't automate, obliterate', *Harvard Business Review*, 68(4): 104–112.

Hammond, J. S., Keeney, R. L. and Raiffa, H. (1999) *Smart Choices: A Practical Guide for Making Better Decisions* (Boston, MA: Harvard Business School Press).

Hansen, S. (2012) 'How Zara grew into the world's largest fashion retailer', available at www.nytimes.com/2012/11/11/magazine/how-zara-grew-into-the-worlds-largest-fashion-retailer.html, published 9 November 2012, accessed 5 February 2019.

Haraty, M., McGrenere, J. and Tang, C. (2016) 'How personal task management differs across individuals', *International Journal of Human-Computer Studies*, 88: 13–37.

Harris, M. (2018) 'Amazon Go: Convenience and concern at new checkout-free corner shop', available at www.theguardian.com/us-news/2018/jan/22/amazon-go-convenience-store-corner-shop, published 22 January 2018, accessed 21 January 2019.

Harris, P. R. and Moran, R. T. (1991) *Managing Cultural Differences*, 3rd edn (Houston, TX: Gulf Publishing Company).

Hart, S. (1995) 'A natural-resource-based view of the firm', *Academy of Management Review*, 20(4): 986–1014.

Harvard Business School Press (2005) *Entrepreneur's Toolkit: Tools and Techniques to Launch and Grow Your Business* (Boston, MA: Harvard Business Press).

Harvard Business School Press (2009) *The Innovator's Toolkit: 10 Practical Strategies to Help You Develop and Implement Innovation* (Boston, MA: Harvard Business Press).

Harvard Business School Publishing (2002) *Harvard Business Essentials: Hiring and Keeping the Best People* (Boston, MA: Harvard Business School Publishing).

Harvard Business School Publishing (2003) *Harvard Business Essentials: Negotiation* (Boston, MA: Harvard Business School Press).

Harvard Business School Publishing (2005) *Harvard Business Essentials: Time Management: Increase Your Personal Productivity and Effectiveness* (Boston, MA: Harvard Business School Publishing).

Harvard Business School Publishing (2013) *Power, Influence, and Persuasion: Sell Your Ideas and Make Things Happen* (Boston, MA: Harvard Business School Publishing).

Hatch, M. J. (2018) *Organization Theory: Modern, Symbolic, and Postmodern Perspectives*, 4th edn (Oxford: Oxford University Press).

Hayashi, A. M. (2014) 'Thriving in a big data world', *MIT Sloan Management Review*, 55(2): 35–39.

Hayes, J. (2018) *The Theory and Practice of Change Management*, 5th edn (London: Red Globe Press).

Hedley, B. (1970) 'The product portfolio', www.bcg.com/publications/1970/strategy-the-product-portfolio.aspx, published 1 January 1970, accessed 28 January 2019.

Henisz, W. J. and Delios, A. (2002) 'Learning about the institutional environment', in Ingram, P. and Silverman, B. S. (eds), *The New Institutionalism in Strategic Management*, pp. 339–392 (New York, NY: JAI Press).

Henningsen, D. D., Henningsen, M. L. M. and Russell, G. A. (2017) 'Do groupthink symptoms reflect a single social influence process? ', *Groupwork*, 27(1): 28–48.

Henry, Z. (2015) 'This is the GrubHub of Turkey,' available at https://www.inc.com/zoe-henry/this-is-the-grubhub-of-turkey.html, published 26 May 2015, accessed 7 May 2019.

Hermann, A. and Rammal, H. G. (2010) 'The grounding of the "flying bank"', *Management Decision*, 48(7): 1048–1062.

Herzberg, F. (1959) *The Motivation to Work* (New York, NY: John Wiley and Sons).

Higgs, M. and Rowland, D. (2005) 'All changes great and small: Exploring approaches to change and its leadership', *Journal of Change Management,* 5(2): 121–151.

Hill, L. (1994) 'Managing your team', Harvard Business School Class Discussion Note (Boston, MA: Harvard Business School).

Hill, L. and Lineback K. (2011) *Being the Boss: The 3 Imperatives for Becoming a Great Leader* (Boston. MA: Harvard Business School Publishing).

Hill, N. S. and Bartol, K. M. (2018) 'Five ways to improve communication in virtual teams', *MIT Sloan Management Review*, 60(1): 18–20.

Hill, T. and Westbrook, R. (1997). 'SWOT analysis: It's time for a product recall', *Long Range Planning,* 30(1): 46–52.

Hindustan Unilever (2019) 'Enhancing livelihoods', available at www.hul.co.in/sustainable-living/india-sustainability-initiatives/enhancing-livelihoods.html, accessed 14 January 2019.

Hine, L. (2014) 'Jenny Biggam – founder of the7stars', at www.femalefounderfridays.com/theinterviews/2014/12/15/jenny-biggam-founder-of-the7stars, published 19 December 2014, accessed 11 December 2018.

Ho, F. N., Wang, H. M. D. and Vitell, S. J. (2012), 'A global analysis of corporate social performance: The effects of cultural and geographic environments', *Journal of Business Ethics*, 107(4): 423–433.

Hodgkinson, G. P. and Sadler-Smith, E. (2003) 'Complex or unitary? A critique and empirical re-assessment of the Allinson-Hayes cognitive style index', *Journal of Occupational & Organizational Psychology,* 76(2): 243–268.

Hodgkinson, G. P., Sadler-Smith, E., Burke, L. A., Claxton, G. and Sparrow, P. R. (2009) 'Intuition in organizations: Implications for strategic management', *Long Range Planning,* 42(3): 277–297.

Hofstede, G. (1984) *Culture's Consequences*, abridged edition (Newbury Park, CA: Sage Publications).

Hofstede, G. (2011) 'Dimensionalizing cultures: The Hofstede model in context', *Online Readings in Psychology and Culture*, 2(1), 1–26.

Hofstede, G. and Bond, M. H. (1988), 'The Confucius connection: From cultural roots to economic growth', *Organizational Dynamics*, 16(1): 5–21.

Hofstede, G., Van Deusen, C. A., Mueller, C. B. and Charles, T. A. (2002) 'What goals do business leaders pursue? A study in fifteen countries', *Journal of International Business Studies*, 33(4): 785–803.

Hogarth, R. M. (2001) *Educating Intuition* (Chicago, IL: University of Chicago Press).

Holmberg, I. and Tyrstrup, M. (2010) 'Well then – what now? An everyday approach to managerial leadership', *Leadership*, 6(4): 353–372.

Hooker, J. (2009) 'Corruption from a cross-cultural perspective', *Cross Cultural Management: An International Journal*, 16(3): 251–267.

Hooker, J. N. (2012) 'Cultural differences in business communication', in Paulston, C. B., Kiesling, S. F. and Rangel, E. S. (eds), *The Handbook of Intercultural Discourse and Communication* (Chichester: Wiley-Blackwell): 389–407.

House, R. J. (1996) 'Path-goal theory of leadership: Lessons, legacy, and a reformulated theory', *The Leadership Quarterly*, 7(3): 323–352.

House, R. J., Hanges, P. J., Javidan, M., Dorfman, P. W. and Gupta, V. (eds) (2004) *Culture, Leadership, and Organizations: The GLOBE Study of 62 Societies* (Thousand Oaks/London/New Delhi: Sage).

Hrebiniak, L. G. (2005) *Making Strategy Work: Leading Effective Execution and Change* (Upper Saddle River, NJ: Pearson Education/Prentice Hall).

Hubbard, G. (2009) 'Measuring organizational performance: Beyond the triple bottom line', *Business Strategy and the Environment*, 19: 177–191.

Humphrey, S. E. (2014) 'Team microdynamics: Toward an organizing approach to teamwork', *The Academy of Management Annals*, 8(1): 443–503.

Hurriyet (2018) 'Burgers, döner, lahmacun: Most popular food orders of 2018 in Turkey', available at www.hurriyetdailynews.com/burgers-doner-lahmacun-most-popular-food-orders-of-2018-in-turkey-140026, published 26 December 2018, accessed 31 January 2019.

Hyo-sik, L. (2012) '"Innovation DNA" behind Amore's ascent', available at www.koreatimes.co.kr/www/nation/2017/11/178_120387.html, published 19 September 2012, accessed 31 January 2019.

Iansiti, M. and Lakhani, K. R. (2017) 'The truth about blockchain', *Harvard Business Review*, 95(1): 118–127.

Iansiti, M. and Levien, R. (2004) 'Strategy as ecology', *Harvard Business Review*, 82(3): 68–78.

IBM (2017a) 'The top 5 industrial IoT use cases', available at www.ibm.com/blogs/internet-of-things/top-5-industrial-iot-use-cases/, published 19 April 2017, accessed 28 January 2019.

IBM (2017b) 'IBM announces major blockchain solution to speed global payments', available at www-03.ibm.com/press/us/en/pressrelease/53290.wss, published 16 October 2017, accessed 28 January 2019.

iese.com (2013) 'Haier: Will it clean up or be a washout', at www.ieseinsight.com/review/CaseForum.aspx?seccion=13&cas_id=16, published 21 February 2013, accessed 6 September 2017.

Iglesias, O., Markovic, S., Singh, J. J. and Sierra, V. (2019) 'Do customer perceptions of corporate services brand ethicality improve brand equity? Considering the roles of brand heritage, brand image, and recognition benefits', *Journal of Business Ethics*, 154(2), 441–459.

Ignatius, A. (2010) '"We had to own the mistakes"', *Harvard Business Review*, 88(7–8): 108–115.

Ignatius, A. (2011) 'Technology, tradition & the mouse', *Harvard Business Review*, 89(7/8): 112–117.

Ignatius, A. (2015) 'How Indra Nooyi turned design thinking into strategy', *Harvard Business Review*, 93(9): 80–85.

Ignatius, A. and McGinn, D. (2015) '"Consultants will tell you this strategy won't work, but it ensures our reputation"', *Harvard Business Review*, 93(11): 60–63.

IKEA (2007) 'The IKEA way of preventing child labor', available at www.ikea.com/ms/nl_BE/about_ikea/pdf/IWAY_preventing_child_labour.pdf, published 10 January 2007, accessed 25 January 2019.

IKEA (2016) 'IWAY standard', available at www.ikea.com/ms/nl_BE/pdf/reports-downloads/ikea-code-of-conduct-the-iway-standard.pdf , published 29 April 2016, accessed 25 January 2019.

independent.co.uk (2012) 'Akzo Nobel chief on leave with "temporary fatigue"', available at www.independent.co.uk/hei-fi/business/akzo-nobel-chief-on-leave-with-temporary-fatigue-8156232.html, published 12 September 2012, accessed 10 January 2019.

Inditex (2015) 'Innovation in customer services', available at http://static.inditex.com/annual_report_2015/en/our-priorities/innovation-in-customer-services.php, accessed 5 February 2019.

Inditex (2017) 'Our story', available at www.inditex.com/about-us/our-story, accessed 25 July 2017.

Indounas, K. (2006) 'Making effective pricing decisions', *Business Horizons*, 49: 415–424.

ipa.co.uk (2018) 'the7stars', available at https://ipa.co.uk/membership/our-members/agency-members/the7stars, accessed 6 December 2018.

Isenberg, D. (2009) 'Studio Moderna—A venture in Eastern Europe', Harvard Business School case nr. 9-808-110 (Boston, MA: Harvard Business School Publishing).

Itami, H. and Roehl, T. W. (1987) *Mobilizing Invisible Assets* (Boston, MA: Harvard University Press).

Itzenson, J. (2013) 'Above and beyond: Nancy McKinstry '84, CEO Wolters Kluwer', available at https://www8.gsb.columbia.edu/media/newsn/2541/MBAMEC.com, published 26 November 2013, accessed 28 January 2019.

Jaffit, M., Maphalala, J. and Scheepers, C. (2015) 'Technology driven transformation at Comair Limited', Ivey Publishing case nr. W15070.

Janis, I. L. (1971) 'Groupthink', *Psychology Today,* 5(6): 43–46; 74–76.

Janssen, J. (2013) 'A day in the life of the CEO, Collis Ta'eed', available at https://envato.com/blog/day-life-ceo-collis-taeed/, published 27 November 2013, accessed 8 January 2018.

Jarvenpaa, S. L. and Leidner, D. E. (1998) 'Communication and trust in global virtual teams', *Organization Science*, 10(6): 791–815.

Jassy, A. R., Katz, L. E., Kelly, K. and Kochar, B. (1998) *Cash Management Practices in Small Companies (Background note)* (Boston, MA: Harvard Business School).

Jehn, K. A. (1995) 'A multimethod examination of the benfits and detriments of intragroup conflict', *Administrative Science Quarterly,* 40(2): 256–282.

Jehn, K. A., Northcraft, G. B. and Neale, M. A. (1999) 'Why differences make a difference: A field study of diversity, conflict and performance in work-groups', *Administrative Science Quarterly*, 44(4): 741–763.

Jeong-Dong, C. (2016) 'AmorePacific chairman to fund science research', available at http://koreajoongang-daily.joins.com/news/article/article.aspx?aid=3023356, published 2 September 2016, accessed 30 January 2019.

Jiang, J., Dai, B., Peng, D., Zhu, C., Liu, L., and Lu, C. (2012) 'Neural synchronization during face-to-face communication', *Journal of Neuroscience, 32*(45): 16064–16069.

Jimenez, A., Boehe, D. M., Taras, V. and Caprar, D. V. (2017) 'Working across boundaries: Current and future perspectives on global virtual teams', *Journal of International Management*, 23(4): 341–349.

Johnson, B. and Dobni, D. (2016) 'Is managerial work in the public and private sectors really "different"? A comparative study of managerial work activities', *International Journal of Public Administration*, 39(6): 459–469.

Johnson, G., Whittington, R., Scholes, K., Angwin, D. and Regnér, P. (2017) *Exploring Strategy: Text and Cases,* 11th edn (Harlow: Pearson).

Johnson, S. K. (2017) 'What 11 CEOs have learned about championing diversity', available at https://hbr.org/2017/08/what-11-ceos-have-learned-about-championing-diversity, published 17 August 2017 (updated 29 August 2017), accessed 22 January 2019.

Jones, G. R. (2013) *Organizational Theory, Design, and Change*, 7th edn (Harlow: Pearson).

Jones, R. J., Woods, S. A. and Guillaume, Y. R. (2016) 'The effectiveness of workplace coaching: A meta-analysis of learning and performance outcomes from coaching', *Journal of Occupational and Organizational Psychology*, 89(2): 249–277.

Jones, S. and Donnelly, G. (2017) 'Only 1 in 5 new board appointees at Fortune 500 companies are not white', available at http://fortune.com/2017/06/19/one-in-5-fortune-500-board-appointees-last-year-was-from-an-underrepresented-group/, published 20 June 2017, accessed 25 January 2019.

Jonsen, K., Maznevski, M. L. and Schneider, S. C. (2011) 'Diversity and its not so diverse literature: An international perspective', *International Journal of Cross Cultural Management*, 11(1): 35–62.

Jordan, M. (1994) *I Can't Accept Not Trying: Michael Jordan on the Pursuit of Excellence* (San Francisco, CA: HarperSanFrancisco).

Kabir, A. (2018) 'Companies need to be more human to be more successful: Leena Nair', available at https://en.prothomalo.com/opinion/news/178942/Companies-need-to-be-more-human-to-be-more, published 2 July 2018, accessed 14 January 2019.

Kahneman, D. and Lovallo, D. (1993) 'Timid choices and bold forecasts: A cognitive perspective on risk and risk taking', *Management Science,* 39(1): 17–31.

Kahneman, D., Lovallo, D. and Sibony, O. (2011) 'Before you make that big decision', *Harvard Business Review,* 89(6): 50–60.

Kant, I. (1788) *The Critique of Practical Reasoning,* translated by Thomas Kingsmill Abbott, available at www.gutenberg.org/cache/epub/5683/pg5683-images.html, published 15 July 2013, accessed 25 January 2019.

Kanter, R. M. (1988) 'When a thousand flowers bloom: Structural, collective, and social conditions for innovation in organization', *Research in Organizational Behavior*, 10: 169–211.

Kanter, R. M. (2011) 'The cure for horrible bosses', *Harvard Business Review,* 89(10): 42.

Kaplan, R. (2007) 'What to ask the person in the mirror', *Harvard Business Review*, 85(1): 86–95.

Kaplan, R. (2008) 'Reaching your potential', *Harvard Business Review*, 8 (7/8): 45–49.

Kaplan, R. S. and Norton, D. P. (2005) 'The balanced scorecard—measures that drive performance', *Harvard Business Review*, 83(7/8): 172–180.

Kaplan, R. S. and Norton, D. P. (2006) 'Why system, not structure, is the way toward strategic alignment: A historical perspective', *Harvard Business Publishing Newsletters*, Article Nr., B0607A, 15 July.

Kara, S. (2014) *Tainted Carpets: Slavery and Child Labor in India's Hand-Made Carpet Sector* (Boston, MA: Harvard University FXB Center for Health and Human Rights).

Karam, E. P., Hu, J., Davison, R. B., Juravich, M., Nahrgang, J. D., Humphrey, S. E. and Scott DeRue, D. (2019) 'Illuminating the "face" of justice: A meta-analytic examination of leadership and organizational justice', *Journal of Management Studies*, 56(1): 134–171.

Kasparov, G. (2007) *How Life Imitates Chess: Making the Right Moves, From The Board to the Boardroom* (New York, NY: Bloomsbury).

Kast, F. E. and Rosenzweig, J. E. (1972) 'General systems theory: Applications for organization and management', *Academy of Management Journal*, 15(4): 447–465.

Katzenbach, J. R. and Smith, D. K. (1993) 'The discipline of teams', *Harvard Business Review*, 71(2): 111–120.

Katzenbach, J., Anderson, G. and Kleiner, A. (2015) 'Mark Bertolini's preventive disruption', available at http://www.strategy-business.com/article/00324?gko=1c407, published 13 April 2015, accessed 21 January 2019.

KC, D. S., Staats, B. R., Kouchaki, M. and Gino, F. (2017) 'Task selection and workload: A focus on completing easy tasks hurts long-term performance', *Harvard Business School Working Paper*, No. 17-112, June 2017.

Kellerman, B. (2012) *The End of Leadership* (New York, NY: Harper Business).

Kellogg, C. (2014) 'Amazon and Hachette: The dispute in 13 easy steps', available at www.latimes.com/books/jacketcopy/la-et-jc-amazon-and-hachette-explained-20140602-story.html, published 3 June 2014, accessed 31 July 2017.

Kennedy, J. (1987) *Getting Behind the Resume: Interviewing Today's Candidates* (Paramus, NJ: Prentice Hall).

Kermisch, R. and Burns, D. (2018) 'Is pricing killing your profits', available at www.bain.com/insights/is-pricing-killing-your-profits/, published 13 June 2018, accessed 21 January 2019.

Kerr, W. R., Yucaoglu, G., and Kuzucu, E, (2017) 'Yemeksepeti: Growing and expanding the business model through data', Harvard Business School case nr. 9-817-095 (Boston, MA: Harvard Business School).

Kerzner, H. (2018) *Project Management: Best Practices*, 4th edn (Hoboken, NJ: Wiley).

Kets de Vries, M. F. R. (2006) *The Leader on the Couch: A Clinical Approach to Changing People and Organizations* (San Francisco, CA: Jossey-Bass).

Kets de Vries, M. F. R. (2009) 'The many colors of success: What do executives want out of life', *INSEAD Faculty & Research Working Paper Series* (Fontainbleau: INSEAD), 1–25.

Kets de Vries, M. F. R. (2011) 'Changing reflective leaders & authentizotic organizations', in Schein, E. et al., *Creating the Future*, IEDC Bled School of Management Book of the Year (pp. 6–12) (Bled, Slovenia: IEDC Poslovna šola).

Khanna, T., Palepu, K. G. and Sinha, J. (2005) 'Strategies that fit emerging markets', *Harvard Business Review*, 83(6): 63–76.

Khatri, N. and Ng, H. A. (2000) 'The role of intuition in strategic decision making', *Human Relations,* 53(1): 57–86.

Kidder, D. L., Lankau, M. J., Chrobot-Mason, D., Mollica, K. A. and Friedman, R. A. (2004) 'Backlash toward diversity initiatives: Examining the impact of diversity program justification, personal and group outcomes', *International Journal of Conflict Management*: 15(1), 77–102.

Kim, T. Y. and Leung, K. (2007) 'Forming and reacting to overall fairness: A cross-cultural comparison', *Organizational Behavior and Human Decision Processes*, 104(1): 83–95.

Kim, W. C. and Mauborgne, R. (1997) 'Value innovation: The strategic logic of high growth', *Harvard Business Review*, 75(1): 103–112.

Kim, W. C. and Mauborgne, R. (2005) *Blue Ocean Strategy: How to Create Uncontested Market Space and Make the Competition Irrelevant* (Boston, MA: Harvard Business School Press).

Kim Hoh, W. (2016) 'Little Pocket's big dream for women entrepreneurs', available at www.straitstimes.com/business/little-pockets-big-dream-for-women-entrepreneurs, published 31 July 2016, accessed 31 January 2019.

King, A. W. (2007) 'Disentangling interfirm and intra-firm causal ambiguity: A conceptual model of causal ambiguity and sustainable competitive advantage', *Academy of Management Review*, 32(1): 156–178.

Kirby, J. and Stewart, T. A. (2007) 'The institutional yes', *Harvard Business Review*, 85(10): 74–82.

Kiron, D. and Kruschwitz, N. (2015) 'Sustainability reporting as a tool for better risk management', *MIT Sloan Management Review*, 56(4): 34–40.

Klarner, P. and Raisch, S. (2013) 'Move to the beat—Rhythms of change and firm performance', *Academy of Management Journal*, 56(1): 160–184.

Ko, S. and Butler, J. E. (2006) 'Prior knowledge, bisociative mode of thinking and entrepreneurial opportunity identification', *International Journal of Entrepreneurship and Small Business*, 3(1): 3–16.

Ko, S. and Butler, J. E. (2007) 'Creativity: A key link to entrepreneurial behavior', *Business Horizons*, 50(5): 365–372.

Koether, R. (2012) *Distributionslogistik: Effiziente Absicherung der Lieferfähigkeit* (Wiesbaden: Springer Gabler).

Koh, W. (2015) 'The humanist capitalist: Brunello Cucinelli', *The Rake*, March: 84–93.

Kohli, C. and Suri, R. (2011) 'The price is right? Guidelines for pricing to enhance profitability', *Business Horizons*, 54: 563–573.

Kolbjørnsrud, V., Amico, R. and Thomas, R. J. (2016) 'The promise of artificial intelligence: Redefining management in the workforce of the future', available at www.accenture.com/_acnmedia/PDF-19/AI_in_Management_Report.pdf, accessed 9 January 2019.

Kolk, A. (2008) 'Sustainability, accountability and corporate governance: exploring multinationals' reporting practices', *Business Strategy and the Environment*, 17(1): 1–15.

Kottasova, I. (2015) 'CEO shares $27 million with staff after selling his firm', available at http://money.cnn.com/2015/07/28/news/companies/turkish-ceo-staff-bonus-millions/index.html, published 29 July 2015, accessed 31 January 2019.

Kotter, J. P. (1982) 'What effective general managers really do', *Harvard Business Review,* 60(6): 156–168.

Kotter, J. P. (1996) *Leading Change* (Boston, MA: Harvard Business Review Press).

Kotter, J. P. (2007) 'Leading change: Why transformation efforts fail', *Harvard Business Review,* 85(1): 96–103.

Kotter, J. P. and Schlesinger, L. A. (2008) 'Choosing strategies for change', *Harvard Business Review*, 86(7/8): 130–139.

KPMG (2015) 'Currents of change: The KPMG survey on corporate responsibility reporting 2015', available at https://assets.kpmg.com/content/dam/kpmg/pdf/2016/02/kpmg-international-survey-of-corporate-responsibility-reporting-2015.pdf, published November 2015, date accessed 21 January 2019.

Krattenmaker, T. (2008) 'Make every meeting matter', *Harvard Management Update*, available at https://hbr.org/2008/02/make-every-meeting-matter.html, published 27 February 2008, accessed 11 December 2018.

Kruschke, J. K. (2005) 'Category learning', in Lamberts, K. and Goldstone, R. L. (eds), *The Handbook of Cognition* (pp. 183–201) (London: Sage).

Kübler-Ross, E. (2014) *On Death & Dying: What the Dying have to Teach Doctors, Nurses, Clergy & Their Own Families*, trade paperback edition of the original work from 1969 (New York, NY: Scribner).

Kulik, C. T. (2014) 'Working below and above the line: The research–practice gap in diversity management', *Human Resource Management Journal*, 24(2): 129–144.

Kumar, A. (2018) *Business Process Management* (New York, NY: Routledge).

Kumar, N. (2006) 'Strategies to fight low-cost rivals', *Harvard Business Review*, 84(12): 104–112.

Kuratko, D. F., Hornsby, J. S. and Covin, J. G. (2014) 'Diagnosing a firm's internal environment for corporate entrepreneurship', *Business Horizons*, 57(1): 37–47.

Kurtessis, J. N., Eisenberger, R., Ford, M. T., Buffardi, L. C., Stewart, K. A. and Adis, C. S. (2017) 'Perceived organizational support: A meta-analytic evaluation of organizational support theory', *Journal of Management*, 43(6): 1854–1884.

Kusyk, S. (2010) 'Learning to navigate the rough sea of ethics', *IESEinsight*, issue 5: 31–37.

LA Times (1987) 'James has a notion where blame belongs', available at http://articles.latimes.com/1987-08-28/sports/sp-2763_1_blame-belongs, published 28 August 1987, accessed 24 January 2018.

Lamberton, G. (2005) 'Sustainability accounting—a brief history and conceptual framework', *Accounting Forum*, 29(1): 7–26.

Lamparter, D. (2013) 'Elmar Degenhart: Auffallend unauffällig', available at www.zeit.de/2013/27/ elmar-degenhart, published 27 June 2013, accessed 12 December 2018.

lapost.us (2016) 'Pocket Sun: Rising & shining', available at http://lapost.us/?p=342, published 12 July 2016, accessed 31 January 2019.

Larkin, A. (2018) 'Disadvantages of cloud computing', available at https://cloudacademy.com/blog/ disadvantages-of-cloud-computing/, published 26 June 2018, accessed 28 January 2019.

Latham, G. P. (2018) 'The effect of priming goals on organizational-related behavior', in Oettingen, G., Sevincer, A. T. and Gollwitzer, P. M., *The Psychology of Thinking About the Future* (pp. 392–404) (New York and London: The Guilford Press).

latimes.com (1997) 'IKEA investigates child labor allegations', available at http://articles.latimes. com/1997/oct/24/business/fi-46077, published 24 October 1997, accessed 12 September 2017.

Laud, R., Arevalo, J. and Johnson, M. (2016) 'The changing nature of managerial skills, mindsets and roles: Advancing theory and relevancy for contemporary managers', *Journal of Management & Organization*, 22(4): 435–456.

Lawrence, P. R. and Lorsch, J. W. (1967) 'Differentiation and integration in complex organizations', *Administrative Science Quarterly*, 12(1): 1–47.

Lax, D. A. and Sebenius, J. K. (1986) *The Manager as Negotiator* (New York, NY: Free Press).

Leaders Magazine (2013) 'Risk and people: An interview with Greg Case, President and Chief Executive Officer, Aon plc.', *Leaders Magazine*, 36(4): 75.

Leaders Magazine (2014) 'Brand builder: An interview with Leslie H. Wexner, Chairman, and Chief Executive Officer, L Brand, Inc. ', *Leaders Magazine*, 37(4): 272–273.

Lee, C. Y. (2012) 'Korean culture and its influence on business practice in South Korea', *Journal of International Management Studies*, 7(2): 184–191.

Lei, D. and Slocum, J. W. (1992) 'Global strategic alliances: Payoffs and pitfalls', *Organizational Dynamics,* 19(3): 44–62.

Lepsinger, R. (2018) 'Five highly effective virtual communication skills', available at www.onpointconsulting llc.com/blog/five-highly-effective-virtual-communication-skills, published 8 May 2018, accessed 24 January 2019.

Levin, M. (2017) '9 ways to reinforce and live your company's core values every day', available at www. inc.com/marissa-levin/9-ways-to-reinforce-and-live-your-companys-core-values-every-day.html, published 31 May 2017, accessed 8 March 2019.

Levinthal, D. and March, J. G. (1993) 'The myopia of learning', *Strategic Management Journal,* 14 (Special Winter Issue): 95–112.

Levitt, T. (1960) 'Marketing myopia', *Harvard Business Review*, 38(4): 45–56.

Lewis, L. (2019) *Organizational Change: Creating Change Through Strategic Communication*, 2nd edn (Hoboken, NJ: Wiley).

Lewis, R. D. (2006) *When Cultures Collide: Leading Across Cultures*, 3rd edn (Boston, MA: Nicholas Brealey Publishing).

Lieberman, M. D. (2000) 'Intuition: A social cognitive neuroscience approach', *Psychological Bulletin,* 126(1): 109–137.

Liker, J. K. (2004) *The Toyota Way: 14 Management Principles from the World's Greatest Manufacturer* (New York, NY: McGraw-Hill).

Lim, X. (2016) 'Pocket Sun: The sky's the limit', available at www.hnworth.com/article/2016/09/30/pocket-sun-sogal-ventures/, published 30 September 2016, accessed 31 January 2019.

Lind, E. A., Tyler, T. R. and Huo, Y. R. (1997) 'Procedural context and culture: Variation in the antecedents of procedural justice judgements', *Journal of Personality and Social Psychology*, 73, (4): 767–780.

Linders, B. (2016) 'Benefits of agile transformation at Barclays', available at www.infoq.com/ news/2016/09/benefits-agile-barclays, published 8 September 2016, accessed 18 December 2018.

Lindsey, A., King, E., Membere, A. and Cheung, H. K. (2017) 'Two types of diversity training that really work', available at https://hbr.org/2017/07/two-types-of-diversity-training-that-really-work, published 28 July 2017, accessed 25 January 2019.

Locke, E. A. and Latham, G. P. (1990) *A Theory of Goal-Setting and Task Performance* (Englewood Cliffs, NJ: Prentice Hall).

Lockheed Martin (2015) 'Our commitment to compliance with anti-corruption laws', available at www. lockheedmartin.com/us/who-we-are/ethics/1209-hewson.html, published 9 December 2015, accessed 20 September 2017.

Lockheed Martin (2016) 'Setting the standard: Code of ethics and business conduct', available at www. lockheedmartin.com/content/dam/lockheed/data/ corporate/documents/ethics/code-of-conduct.pdf, published February 2016, accessed 20 September 2017.

Lockheed Martin (2017) 'Ethics', available at www. lockheedmartin.com/us/who-we-are/ethics.html, accessed 20 September 2017.

Loewenstein, G. F., Weber, E. U., Hsee, C. K. and Welch, N. (2001) 'Risk as feelings', *Psychological Bulletin,* 127(2): 267–286.

London Business School (2018) 'Barclays: Agility is key to better business outcomes', video available at www.youtube.com/watch?v=R7RxXrChoAQ, published 27 March 2018, accessed 18 December 2018.

Lord, C. G., Lepper, M. R. and Preston, E. (1984) 'Consider the opposite: A corrective strategy for social judgement', *Journal of Personality and Social Psychology*, 47(6): 1231–1243.

L'Oréal (2019) 'Our ambition', available at www.loreal.com/group/who-we-are/our-ambition, accessed 28 January 2019.

Luce, E. (2004) 'IKEA's grown up plan to tackle child labour', available at www.ft.com/content/b08b6b0e-066e-11d9-b95e-00000e2511c8, published 14 September 2004, accessed 12 September 2017.

Luecke, R. A. (2004) *Manager's Toolkit: The 13 Skills Managers Need to Succeed* (Boston, MA: Harvard Business School Press).

Luthans, F. (1973) 'The contingency theory of management: A path out of the jungle', *Business Horizons*, 16(3): 67–72.

Luthans, F. (1987) 'Successful vs. effective real managers', *Academy of Management Executive*, 2(2): 127–132.

Luthans, F. (2011) *Organizational Behavior: An Evidence-Based Approach*. 12th edn (New York, NY: McGraw Hill/Irwin).

Maak, T. and Pless, N. M. (2006) 'Responsible leadership in a stakeholder society – a relational perspective', *Journal of Business Ethics*, 66(1): 99–115.

Maaravi, Y. and Levy, A. (2017) 'When your anchor sinks your boat: Information asymmetry in distributive negotiations and the disadvantage of making the first offer', *Judgement and Decision Making*, 12(5): 420–429.

McAfee, A. and Brynjolfsson, E. (2012) 'Big data: The management revolution', *Harvard Business Review*, 90(10): 60–68.

McChesney, C., Covey, S. and Huling, J. (2012) *The 4 Disciplines of Execution: Achieving Your Wildly Important Goals* (New York, NY: Free Press).

McClelland, D. C. (1961) *The Achieving Society* (Princeton, NJ: Van Nostrand).

McClelland, D. C. (1987) *Human Motivation* (New York, NY: Cambridge University Press).

McCorquodale, S. (2009) 'Winning over shoppers with sound ethics', available at www.retail-week.com/home/winning-over-shoppers-with-sound-ethics/5007356.article, published 23 October 2009, accessed 12 September 2017.

McDonald, C. (2016) 'NRF 2016: Shopping centres will become "platforms for experiences", says Westfield co-CEO', available at www.computerweekly.com/news/4500271576/NRF-2016-shopping-centres-will-become-platforms-for-experiences-says-West-field-co-CEO, published 22 January 2016, accessed 5 July 2017.

McGee, J. and Thomas, H. (1986) 'Strategic groups: Theory, research and taxonomy', *Strategic Management Journal*, 7(2): 141–160.

McGinn, D. and Knight, P. (2017) 'Nike's co-founder on innovation, culture, and succession', available at https://hbr.org/ideacast/2017/07/nikes-co-founder-on-innovation-culture-and-succession, published 13 July 2017, accessed 31 January 2019.

McGregor, D. (1960) *The Human Side of Enterprise* (New York, NY: McGraw-Hill).

McKay, P. F., Avery, D. R. and Morris, M. A. (2008) 'Mean racial-ethnic differences in employee sales performance: The moderating role of diversity climate', *Personnel Psychology*, 61(2): 349–374.

McLuhan, M. (1964) *Understanding Media: The Extensions of Man* (New York, NY: McGraw Hill).

Machiavelli, N. (2005) *The Prince*, trans. and ed. by Peter Bondanella (Oxford: Oxford University Press).

Macrae, C. N. and Bodenhausen, G. V. (2000) 'Social cognition: Thinking categorically about others', *Annual Review of Psychology*, 51: 93–120.

Maddux, J. E. (2009) 'Self-efficacy: The power of believing you can', in Lopez, S. J. & Snyder, C. R. (eds), *Oxford Handbook of Positive Psychology*, 2nd edn (pp. 335–344) (Oxford: Oxford University Press).

Magpili, N. C. and Pazos, P. (2018) 'Self-managing team performance: A systematic review of multilevel input factors', *Small Group Research*, 49(1): 3–33.

Mahieu, C. (2001) 'Management development in Royal Dutch/Shell', *Journal of Management Development*, 20(2): 121–130.

Maier, N. R. F. (1955) *Psychology in Industry*, 2nd edn (Boston, MA: Houghton Mifflin).

Maier, N. R. F. (1967) 'Assets and liabilities in group problem solving: The need for an integrative function', *Psychological Review*, 74(4): 239–249.

Makarius, E. E. and Larson, B. Z. (2017) 'Changing the perspective of virtual work: Building virtual intelligence at the individual level', *Academy of Management Perspectives*, 31(2): 159–178.

Malhotra, A., Majchrzak, A. and Rosen, B. (2007) 'Leading virtual teams', *The Academy of Management Perspectives*, 21(1): 60–70.

Malhotra, D. (2010) 'Hamilton Real Estate (TN)', *Harvard Business School Teaching Note* 910-037, February.

Malhotra, D. and Bazerman, M. H. (2007) 'Investigative negotiation', *Harvard Business Review*, 85(9): 72–78.

Malik, F. (2004) *Führen, Leisten, Leben: Wirksames Management für eine neue Zeit*, 14th edn (Stuttgart: Deutsche Verlags-Anstalt).

Malkoc, S. A. and Tonietto, G. N. (2019) 'Activity versus outcome maximization in time management', *Current Opinion in Psychology*, 26, 49–53.

Maltarich, M. A., Kukenberger, M., Reilly, G. and Mathieu, J. (2018) 'Conflict in teams: Modeling early and late conflict states and the interactive effects of conflict processes', *Group & Organization Management*, 43(1): 6–37.

Management Today (2006) 'The MT interview: Graham Mackay (interview by Andrew Davidson) ', available at www.managementtoday.co.uk/news/535825/MT-Interview-Graham-Mackay/?DCMP=ILC-SEARCH, published 16 January 2006, accessed 8 January 2019.

manager-magazin.com (2016) 'Conti erhöht Prognose – Degenhart, der Unangreifbare', available at www.manager-magazin.de/unternehmen/autoindustrie/continental-hauptversammlung-elmar-degenhart-bester-dax-chef-a-1089946.html, published 29 April 2016, accessed 12 December 2018.

Mangaliso, M. P. (2001) 'Building competitive advantage from Ubuntu: Management lessons from South Africa', *Academy of Management Perspectives*, 15(3): 23–33.

March, J. G. (1994) *A Primer on Decision Making: How Decisions Happen* (New York, NY: The Free Press).

March, J. G. (2010) *The Ambiguities of Experience* (Ithaca, NY and London: Cornell University Press).

March, J. G. and Shapira, Z. (1987) 'Managerial perspectives on risk and risk taking', *Management Science*, 33(11): 1404–1418.

Marcus Aurelius (2004) *Meditations* (London: Penguin Books).

Marsalis, W. and Nooyi, I. (2014) 'Jazz legend Wynton Marsalis and PepsiCo Chairman and CEO Indra K. Nooyi swing in harmony', available at https://wyntonmarsalis.org/news/entry/wynton-marsalis-indra-k.-nooyi-the-dialogues-connecting-leaders-specials-eg, published 14 April 2014, accessed 8 January 2019.

Marshall, P. A. (2010) *A Note on Cost Reduction in Financially Troubled Organizations (Note for class discussion)* (Boston, MA: Harvard Business School).

Martin, J. S. and Chaney, L. H. (2012) *Global Business Etiquette: A Guide to International Communication and Customs* (Santa Barbara, CA: Praeger).

Martin, R. L. (2010) 'The execution trap', *Harvard Business Review*, 88(7/8): 64–71.

Maslach, C. and Leiter, M. P. (2008) 'Early predictors of job burnout and engagement', *Journal of Applied Psychology*, 93(3): 498–512.

Maslow, A. H. (1943) 'A theory of human motivation', *Psychological Review*, 50(4): 370–396.

Mason, M. F., Wiley, E. A. and Ames, D. R. (2018) 'From belief to deceit: How expectancies about others' ethics shape deception in negotiations', *Journal of Experimental Social Psychology*, 76: 239–248.

Masten, A. S., Cutuli, J. J., Herbers, J. E. and Reed, M.-G. J. (2009) 'Resilience in development', in Lopez, S. J. and Snyder, C. R. (eds), *Oxford Handbook of Positive Psychology* (pp. 117–131) (Oxford: Oxford University Press).

mastercard.com (2014) 'MasterCard works with Apple to integrate Apple Pay', available at https://newsroom.mastercard.com/press-releases/mastercard-works-apple-integrate-apple-pay/, published 9 September 2014, accessed 28 January 2019.

Maurer, R. and Meyer, E. (2015) 'Cultural differences at work: A Q&A with Erin Meyer', available at www.shrm.org/hr-today/news/hr-magazine/pages/0315-meyer-cultural-differences.aspx, published 1 March 2015, accessed 27 December 2018.

Meinel, C. and Leifer, L. (2011) 'Design thinking research', in Plattner, H., Meinel, C. and Leifer, L., *Design Thinking: Understand–Improve–Apply* (pp. xiii–xxi) (Heidelberg: Springer).

Melchers, K. (2014) 'Jenny Biggam of the7stars on client relationships, programmatic advertising and what excites her about the pitch process', available at www.creativebrief.com/blog/2014/07/18/jenny-biggam-of-the7stars-on-client-relation-ships-programmatic-advertising-and-what-excites-her-about-the-pitch-process/, published 18 July 2014, accessed 1 August 2017.

Mercer, D., Paludi, M. I., Mills, J. H. and Mills, A. J. (2015) 'Intersectionality at the intersection', in Bendl, R., Bleijenbergh, I., Henttonen, E. and Mills, A. J. (eds), *The Oxford Handbook of Diversity in Organizations* (pp. 435–453) (Oxford: Oxford University Press).

Merriam Webster (2019) 'Tactics', at www.merriam-webster.com/dictionary/tactics, accessed 28 January 2019.

Meyer, E. (2015) 'Getting to Sí, Ja, Oui, Hai, and Da', *Harvard Business Review*, 93(12): 74–80.

Meyer, E. (2017) 'Being the boss in Brussels, Boston, and Beijing', *Harvard Business Review*, 95(4): 70–77.

Meyrowitz, C. (2014) 'The CEO of TJX on how to train first-class buyers', *Harvard Business Review*, 92(5): 45–48.

Michailova, S. and Worm, V. (2003) 'Personal networking in Russia and China: blat and guanxi', *European Management Journal*, 21(4): 509–519.

Miller, D. and Le Breton-Miller, I. (2005) *Managing For the Long Run: Lessons in Competitive Advantage from Great Family Businesses* (Boston, MA: Harvard Business School Publishing).

Miller, D. J., Fern, M. J. and Cardinal, L. B. (2007) 'The use of knowledge for technological innovation within diversified firms', *Academy of Management Journal*, 50(2): 307–325.

Mintzberg, H. (1973) *The Nature of Managerial Work* (New York, NY: Harper & Row).

Mintzberg, H. (1975) 'The manager's job: Folklore and fact', *Harvard Business Review*, 53(4), 49–61.

Mintzberg, H. (1990) 'The design school: Reconsidering the basic premises of strategic management', *Strategic Management Journal*, 11(3): 171–195.

Mintzberg, H. (2011) *Managing* (San Francisco, CA: Berrett-Koehler).

Mintzberg, H. and Waters, J. A. (1985) 'Of strategies, deliberate and emergent', *Strategic Management Journal*, 6(3): 257–272.

Mintzberg, H. and Westley, F. (2001) 'It's not what you think', *MIT Sloan Management Review,* 42(3): 89–93.

Mintzberg, H., Ahlstrand, B. and Lampel, J. (2009) *Strategy Safari: Your Complete Guide Through the Wilds of Strategic Management*, 2nd edn (Harlow: Financial Times Prentice Hall).

Mintzberg, H., Lampel, J., Quinn, J. B. and Ghoshal, S. (2003) *The Strategy Process: Concepts Contexts Cases*, 2nd European edn (Harlow: Pearson Education).

Miscenko, D., Guenter, H. and Day, D. V. (2017) 'Am I a leader? Examining leader identity development over time', *The Leadership Quarterly*, 28(5): 605–620.

Mischel, W., Ebbesen, E. B. and Raskoff Zeiss, A. (1972) 'Cognitive and attentional mechanisms in delay of gratification', *Journal of Personality and Social Psychology*, 21(2): 204–218.

Mitchell, D. (2015) 'These are the top 5 energy drinks', at http://time.com/3854658/these-are-the-top-5-energy-drinks/, published 11 May 2015, accessed 28 January 2019.

Mitleton-Kelly, E. (2003) 'Ten principles of complexity and enabling infrastructures', in Mitleton-Kelly, E. (ed.), *Complex Systems and Evolutionary Perspectives on Organisations: The Application of Complexity Theory to Organisations* (pp. 23–50) (Oxford: Pergamon/Elsevier).

Molinsky, A. (2012) 'How to network across cultures', available at https://hbr.org/2012/01/how-to-network-across-cultures, published 17 January 2012, accessed 8 January 2019.

Möller, F. (2012) *Proverbes Français: Französische Sprichwörter* (Munich, Germany: Deutscher Taschenbuch Verlag).

Molloy (2017) 'Simplifiers interview: Liza Landsman, President and Sumaiya Balbale, VP of Marketing at Jet.com', available at www.siegelgale.com/simpli-fiers-interview-president-jet-com-liza-landsman-vp-marketing-jet-com-sumaiya-balbale/, published 5 March 2017, accessed 10 January 2019.

Mone, E. M.and London, M. (2018) *Employee Engagement Through Effective Performance Management: A Practical Guide for Managers,* 2nd edn (New York, NY: Routledge).

Moran, R. T., Remington Abramson, N. and Moran, S. V. (2011) *Managing Cultural Differences*, 9th edn (London and New York: Routledge).

Mornell, P. (2003) *45 Effective Ways for Hiring Smart! : How to Predict Winners & Losers in the Incredibly Expensive People-Reading Game* (Berkeley, CA/ Toronto: Ten Speed Press).

Morris, M. W., Podolny, J. M. and Ariel, S. (2001) 'Cultural norms and obligations: Cross-national differences in patterns of interpersonal norms and felt obligation toward co-workers', in Wosinska, R. B., Cialdini, B. W., Barrett, D. W. and Reykowski, J. (eds) *The Practice of Social Influence in Multiple Cultures* (pp. 97–124) (Mahwah, NJ: Lawrence Erlbaum Associates).

Morse, G. (2017) 'One company's experience with AR', *Harvard Business Review*, 95(6): 60–61.

Mui, C. (2012)) 'How Kodak failed', available at www.forbes.com/sites/chunkamui/2012/01/18/how-kodak-failed/#22f1ca8f6f27, published 18 January 2012, accessed 30 January 2019.

Müller von Blumencron, M. (2014) 'Karl Albrecht: "Ich habe Glück gehabt"', available at www.faz.net/aktuell/wirtschaft/menschen-wirtschaft/ein-besuch-bei-aldi-gruender-karl-albrecht-13057122.html, published 21 July 2014, accessed 21 January 2019.

Mullins, L. J. (2016) *Management & Organisational Behaviour*, 11th edn (Harlow: Pearson).

Murdoch, A. (1997) 'USA: Lateral benchmarking or ... what Formula One taught an airline', available at www.managementtoday.co.uk/usa-lateral-benchmarking-formula-one-taught-airline/article/410740, published 1 November 1997, accessed 5 February 2019.

Nadella, S., Shaw, G. and Nichols, J. (2017) *Hit Refresh: The Quest to Rediscover Microsoft's Soul and Imagine a Better Future for Everyone* (London: William Collins).

Nair, L. (2016) 'Why you need to innovate your diversity model', available at www.linkedin.com/pulse/why-you-need-innovate-your-diversity-model-leena-nair/, published 8 March 2016, accessed 14 January 2019.

Nair, L. (2018) 'Why diversity is personal for me', available at www.linkedin.com/pulse/why-diversity-personal-me-leena-nair/, published 31 May 2018, accessed 14 January 2019.

Nair, L. (2019) 'Leena Nair LinkedIn profile', available at www.linkedin.com/in/nairleena/?originalSubdomain=uk, accessed 14 January 2019.

Nash, L. and Stevenson, H. (2004) 'Success that lasts', *Harvard Business Review*, 82(2): 102–109.

Neilson, G., Martin, K. L. and Powers, E. (2008) 'The secrets to successful strategy execution', *Harvard Business Review,* 86(6): 60–70.

Ng, T. W. (2017) 'Transformational leadership and performance outcomes: Analyses of multiple mediation pathways', *The Leadership Quarterly*, 28(3): 385–417.

Nicholson, N. (2003) 'How to motivate your problem people', *Harvard Business Review*, 81(1): 56–65.

Noel, A. (1989) 'Strategic core and magnificent obsessions: Discovering strategy formulation through daily activities of CEOs', *Strategic Management Journal*, 10(1): 33–39.

Nohria, N., Joyce, W. and Roberson, B. (2003) 'What really works', *Harvard Business Review*, 81(7): 42–52.

Nonaka, I. and Takeuchi, H. (2011) 'The wise leader', *Harvard Business Review*, 89 (5): 57–67.

NRF/Forrester (2017) *The State of Retailing Online 2017: Key Metrics, Business Objectives and Mobile* (Washington, DC: National Retail Federation/ Forrester Research).

Nydegger, R. and Nydegger, L. (2010) 'Challenges in managing virtual teams', *Journal of Business & Economics Research (JBER)*, 8(3): 69–82.

Nylén, D. and Holmström, J. (2015) 'Digital innovation strategy: A framework for diagnosing and improving digital product and service innovation', *Business Horizons,* 58(1): 57–67.

octaspringtechnology.com (2017) 'About us', available at http://www.octaspringtechnology.com/about-us-3/, accessed 11 July 2017.

O'Donnell, J. (2011) 'Behind the bargains at T.J. Maxx, Marshalls', available at http://usatoday30.usatoday.com/money/industries/retail/story/2011-10-25/tjx-ceo-carol-meyrowitz/50916340/1, published 25 October 2011, accessed 27 December 2018.

O'Gorman, C., Bourke, S. and Murray, J. A. (2005) 'The nature of managerial work in small growth-oriented businesses', *Small Business Economics*, 25(1): 1–16.

Ohmae, K. (1983) *The Mind of the Strategist: The Art of Japanese Business* (New York, NY: Penguin).

O'Leary, M., Orlikowski, W. and Yates, J. (2002) 'Distributed work over the centuries: Trust and control in the Hudson's Bay Company, 1670–1826', in Hinds, P. and Kiesler, S. (eds), *Distributed Work* (pp. 27–54) (Cambridge, MA: The MIT Press).

Oncken Jr., W. and Wass, D. L. (1974) 'Management time: Who's got the monkey', *Harvard Business Review*, 52(6): 75–80.

O'Neill, T. A. and Salas, E. (2018) 'Creating high performance teamwork in organizations', *Human Resource Management Review*, 28(4): 325–331.

O'Neill, T. A., McLarnon, M. J., Hoffart, G. C., Woodley, H. J. and Allen, N. J. (2018) 'The structure and function of team conflict state profiles', *Journal of Management*, 44(2): 811–836.

Orcutt, M. (2018) 'How secure is blockchain really?', *MIT Technology Review*, available at www.technologyreview.com/s/610836/how-secure-is-blockchain-really/, published 25 April 2018, accessed 29 January 2019.

Osterwalder, A. and Pigneur, Y. (2010) *Business Model Generation: A Handbook for Visionaries, Game Changers, and Challengers* (Hoboken, NJ: John Wiley & Sons, Inc.).

Osterwalder, A., Pigneur, Y. and Tucci, C. L. (2005) 'Clarifying business models: Origins, present and future of the concept', *Communications of the Association for Information Science (CAIS)*, 16: 1–25.

Ouchi, W. (1981) *Theory Z: How American Businesses Can Meet The Japanese Challenge* (New York, NY: Avon).

Overby, S. (2017) 'Ride sharing goes hyperlocal with Jugnoo', available at www.digitalistmag.com/iot/2017/05/10/ride-sharing-goes-hyperlocal-with-jugnoo-04960458, published 10 May 2017, accessed 9 November 2017.

Oxford Dictionaries (2017) 'Time', available at http://oxforddictionaries.com/definition/english/time, accessed 10 January 2019.

oxforddictionaries.com (2019) 'Value', available at www.oxforddictionaries.com/definition/english/value, accessed 21 January 2019.

P&G (2017) 'P&G is executing a strategy that works', available at www.pginvestor.com/interactive/newlookandfeel/4004124/Strategy_Slides.pdf, published September 2017, accessed 2 January 2019.

Pacini, R. and Epstein, S. (1999) 'The relation of rational and experiential information processing styles to personality, basic beliefs, and the ratio-bias problem', *Journal of Personality and Social Psychology,* 76(6): 972–987.

Paine, L. S. (2010) 'The China rules', *Harvard Business Review*, 88(6): 103–108.

Parker, G. (1990) *Team Players and Teamwork: The New Competitive Business Strategy* (San Francisco, CA and Oxford: Jossey-Bass).

Pascal, B. (2007) *Blaise Pascal: Thoughts, Letters, and Minor Works* (New York, NY: Cosimo).

Patel, P. C. and Fiet, J. O. (2009) 'Systematic search and its relationship to firm founding', *Entrepreneurship Theory and Practice*, 33(2): 501–526.

Pausanias (1918) *Description of Greece* (Cambridge, MA: Harvard University Press).

Pava, M. L. (2007) 'A response to "getting to the bottom of 'triple bottom line'", *Business Ethics Quarterly*, 17(1): 105–110.

Payne, J. W., Bettman, J. R. and Johnson, E. J. (1993) *The Adaptive Decision Maker* (Cambridge: Cambridge University Press).

Pell, S. (2016) 'Strategy, context and clarity: Collis Ta'eed, CEO at Envato', available at http://managementdisrupted.com/collis-taeed-strategy-context-and-clarity/, published 9 August 2016, accessed 8 January 2019.

Pelzmann, L. (2007) 'Qualifizierte Intuition', in Neumann, R. and Graf, G. (eds), *Management-Konzepte im Praxistest* (pp. 693–703) (Wien: Linde International).

Pentland, A. (2012) 'The new science of building great teams', *Harvard Business Review*, 90(4): 60–69.

Perlroth, N., Tsang, A. and Satariano, A. (2018) 'Marriott hacking exposes data of up to 500 million guests', available at www.nytimes.com/2018/11/30/business/marriott-data-breach.html, published 30 November 2018, accessed 28 January 2019.

Perrini, F. and Tencati, A. (2006) 'Sustainability and stakeholder management: the need for new corporate performance evaluation and reporting systems', *Business Strategy and the Environment*, 15(5): 296–308.

Perry-Smith, J. E. and Mannucci, P. V. (2017) 'From creativity to innovation: The social network drivers of the four phases of the idea journey', *Academy of Management Review*, 42(1), 53–79.

Petersen, R. (2016) '37 big data case studies', available at www.businessesgrow.com/2016/12/06/big-data-case-studies/, published 6 December 2016, accessed 5 February 2019.

Phathi, D. (2016) 'We are not happy with Comair at all', available at www.iol.co.za/business-report/companies/we-are-not-happy-with-comair-at-all-2009073, published 13 April 2016, accessed 10 July 2017.

Phoel, C. M. (2009) 'Feedback that works', available at https://hbr.org/2009/04/feedback-that-works, published 27 April 2009, accessed 30 April 2019.

Picot, A., Dietl, H. and Franck, E. (2005) *Organisation: Eine ökonomische Perspektive*, 4th edn (Stuttgart: Schäffer Poeschel).

Pierson, D. and Lien, D. (2017) 'Diversity training was supposed to reduce bias at Google. In case of fired engineer, it backfired', available at www.latimes.com/business/technology/la-fi-tn-james-damore-google-20170809-story.html, published 9 August 2017, accessed 22 January 2019.

Pindur, W., Rogers, S. E. and Suk Kim, P. (1995) 'The history of management: A global perspective', *Journal of Management History*, 1(1): 59–77.

Pirson, M. (2017a) *Humanistic Management: Protecting Dignity and Promoting Well-Being* (Cambridge: Cambridge University Press).

Pirson, M. (2017b) 'What is humanistic management?', available at http://humanisticmanagement.international/what-is-humanistic-management/, publsihed 12 June 2017, accessed 15 January 2019.

Piskorski, M. J. (2007) 'Choosing corporate and global scope', *Harvard Business School note* Nr. 9-707-496 (Boston, MA: Harvard Business School Publishing).

Pistrui, J. and Dimov, D. (2018) 'The role of a manager has to change in 5 key ways', available at https://hbr.org/2018/10/the-role-of-a-manager-has-to-change-in-5-key-ways, published 26 October 2018, accessed 8 January 2019.

Plato (1888) *The Republic of Plato*, translated by B. Jowett, 3rd edn (Oxford: Clarendon Press).

Ployhart, R. E. (2008) 'The measurement and analysis of motivation', in Kanfer, R., Chen, G. and Pritchard R. D. (eds), *Work Motivation: Past, Present, and Future* (pp. 17–61) (New York, NY: Routledge).

Podolny, J. M. (2011) 'A conversation with James G. March on learning about leadership', *Academy of Management Learning and Education*, 10(3): 502–506.

Poetz, M., Franke, N. and Schreier, M. (2014) 'Sometimes the best ideas come from outside your industry', available at https://hbr.org/2014/11/sometimes-the-best-ideas-come-from-outside-your-industry/, published 21 November 2014, accessed 6 February 2019.

Popper, K. (1935) *Logik der Forschung* (Wien: Julius Springer).

Porter, M. E. (1980) *Competitive Strategy* (New York, NY: Free Press).

Porter, M. E. (1985) *Competitive Advantage: Creating and Sustaining Superior Performance* (New York, NY: Free Press).

Porter, M. E. (1996) 'What is strategy? ', *Harvard Business Review*, 74(6): 61–78.

Porter, M. E. (2008a) *On Competition*, updated and expanded edition (Boston, MA: Harvard Business School Publishing).

Porter, M. E. (2008b) 'The five competitive forces that shape strategy', *Harvard Business Review*, 86(1): 78–93.

Porter, M. E. and Heppelmann, J. E. (2017) 'Why every organization needs an augmented reality strategy', *Harvard Business Review*, 95(6): 46–57.

Porter, M. E. and Kramer, M. R. (2006) 'The link between competitive advantage and corporate social responsibility', *Harvard Business Review*, 84(12): 78–92.

Porter, M. and Nohria, N. (2018) 'How CEOs manage time', *Harvard Business Review*, 96(4): 42–51.

Potter, D. V. (2000) 'Discovering hidden pricing power', *Business Horizons*, 43(6): 41–48.

Powell, T. C., Lovallo, D. and Fox, C. R. (2011) 'Behavioral strategy', *Strategic Management Journal,* 32(13): 1369–1386.

Pozen, R. C. (2011) 'Extreme productivity', *Harvard Business Review,* 89 5): 127–131.

Prahalad, C. K. and Hamel, G. (1990) 'The core competence of the corporation', *Harvard Business Review,* 68(3): 79–91.

premierleague.com (2019) 'Manager profile Alex Ferguson', available at www.premierleague.com/managers/344/Alex-Ferguson/overview, accessed 8 January 2019.

PricewaterhouseCoopers (2015) 'Total retail 2015: Retailers in the age of disruption', available at www.pwc.com/gx/en/retail-consumer/retail-consumer-publications/global-multi-channel-consumer-survey/assets/pdf/total-retail-2015.pdf, published February 2015, accessed 5 July 2017.

Publilius Syrus (2019) 'Sententiae', available at www.thelatinlibrary.com/syrus.html, accessed 28 January 2019.

Quirke, B. (1995) *Communicating Change* (Maidenhead: McGraw-Hill).

Raffaelli, R. (2016) 'Leading and managing change', *Harvard Business School Background Note* no. 9-415-040 (Boston, MA: Harvard Business School Publishing).

Rahim, M. A. (2002) 'Toward a theory of managing organizational conflict', *The International Journal of Conflict Management,* 13(3): 206–235.

Rahim, M. A. and Magner, N. R. (1995) 'Confirmatory factor analysis of the styles of handling interpersonal conflict: First-order factor model and its invariance across groups', *Journal of Applied Psychology,* 80(1): 122–132.

Raidl, M. H. and Lubart, T. I. (2000/2001) 'An empirical study of intuition and creativity', *Imagination, Cognition and Personality,* 20(3): 217–230.

Ralph, O. (2018) 'Aon chief warns that insurance industry is losing its relevance', available at www.ft.com/content/ce59de0c-47de-11e8-8ee8-cae73aab7ccb, published 25 April 2018, accessed 24 February 2019.

Rath, T. and Conchie, B. (2008) *Strengths Based Leadership: Great Leaders, Teams, and Why People Follow* (New York, NY: Gallup Press).

Ravlin, E. C. and Meglino, B. M. (1989) 'The transitivity of work values: Hierarchical preference of socially desirable stimuli', *Organizational Behavior and Human Decision Processes,* 44(2): 494–508.

Red Bull (2019) 'The company behind the can', available at https://energydrink.redbull.com/company, accessed 28 January 2019.

Reed, R. and DeFillippi, R. (1990) 'Causal ambiguity, barriers to imitation, and sustainable competitive advantage', *Academy of Management Review,* 15(1): 88–102.

Reeves, M., Moose, S., and Venema, T. (2014) 'BCG Classics Revisited: The Growth Share Matrix', available at www.bcg.com/en-us/publications/2014/growth-share-matrix-bcg-classics-revisited.aspx, published 4 June 2014, accessed 27 August 2019.

Reik, T. (1948) *Listening With the Third Ear: The Inner Experience of a Psychoanalyst* (New York, NY: Farrar, Straus and Co.).

Reinbergs, I. A. (2001) *Note on Valuing Private Businesses* (Note for class discussion) (Boston, MA: Harvard Business School).

Renkema, M., Bondarouk, T. and Bos-Nehles, A. (2018) 'Transformation to self-managing teams: lessons learned: A look at current trends and data', *Strategic HR Review,* 17(2): 81–84.

retaildesignworld.com (2015). 'The digital future of shopping centres according to Westfield Labs CEO Kevin McKenzie', available at https://retaildesign-world.com/interviews/5538b478b7cf7-the-digital-future-according-to-westfield-labs/, published 23 April 2015, accessed 2 May 2019.

Rich, E. E. (ed.) (1948) *Copy-Book of Letters Outward &c., Begins 29th May, 1680 Ends 5 July, 1687* (Toronto: Champlain Society).

Richard, O. C., Barnett, T., Dwyer, S. and Chadwick, K. (2004) 'Cultural diversity in management, firm performance, and the moderating role of entrepreneurial orientation dimensions', *Academy of Management Journal,* 47(2): 255–266.

Riegel, J. W. (1935) 'Some basic managerial responsibilities', *Harvard Business Review,* 13(3): 286–308.

Rigby, D. K., Sutherland, J. and Takeuchi, H. (2016) 'Embracing agile', *Harvard Business Review,* 94(5): 40–50.

Robbins, S. P. and Coulter, M. (2018) *Management,* 14th global edn (Harlow, UK: Pearson).

Roberts, M. J. (1993) 'Note on the hiring and selection process', *Harvard Business Review Case Study Note* (Boston, MA: Harvard Business School).

Robertson, A. J. (1971) 'Robert Owen, cotton spinner: New Lanark', in Pollard, S. and Salt, J. (eds), *Robert Owen: Prophet of the Poor* (pp. 145–166) (Lewisburg: Bucknell University Press).

Robertson, B. J. (2015) *Holacracy: The New Management System for a Rapidly Changing World* (New York, NY: Henry Holt and Company).

Robins, N. (2012) *The Corporation That Changed the World: How the East India Company Shaped the Modern Multinational,* 2nd edn (London: Pluto Press).

Robinson, G. and Dechant, K. (1997) 'Building a business case for diversity', *The Academy of Management Executive,* 11(3): 21–31.

Rodgers, A. L. (2001) 'It's a (red) bull market after all', at www.fastcompany.com/64658/its-red-bull-market-after-all, published 30 September 2001, accessed 28 January 2019.

Roggi, O. (2016) *Risk, Value and Default* (Singapore: World Scientific Publishing).

Roither, M. (2014) 'Kommunikation in Management und Leadership', available at www.wdf.at/assets/uploads/WdF_Studie_Kommunikation_2014_Vollauswertung.pdf, accessed 11 December 2018.

Rokeach, M. (1973) *The Nature of Human Values* (New York, NY: The Free Press).

Rokeach, M. (1979) *Understanding Human Values* (New York, NY: The Free Press).

Rosa, H. (2013) *Social Acceleration: A New Theory of Modernity* (New York, NY: Columbia University Press).

Rosch, E. (1999) 'Principles of categorization', in Margolis, E. and Laurence, S. (eds), *Concepts: Core Readings* (pp. 189–206) (Cambridge, MA: MIT Press).

Rose, C. (2013) 'Design thinking: Ready for prime-time', *Rotman Management* (Fall 2013): 29–32.

Rose, J. M. (2007) 'Corporate directors and social responsibility: Ethics versus shareholder value', *Journal of Business Ethics*, 73(3): 319–331.

Ross, J. E. (1999) *Total Quality Management: Text, Cases and Readings*, 3rd edn (Boca Raton, FL: St. Lucie Press).

Ross, J. W., Beath, C. M. and Sebastian, I. M. (2017). 'How to develop a great digital strategy', *MIT Sloan Management Review*, 58(2): 7–9.

Roux, T. (2017) 'What will the manager 3.0 look like in tomorrow's companies', available at https://atelier.bnpparibas/en/life-work/article/manager-3-0-to-morrow-s-companies, published 19 July 2017, accessed 9 January 2019.

Rowley, I., Tashiro, H., and Lee, L. (2005) 'Canon: Combat-ready', *Business Week*, Issue 3949, 5 September: 48–49.

Rowling, J. K. (1998) *Harry Potter and the Chamber of Secrets* (London: Bloomsbury).

Rushe, D. (2018) 'Zuckerberg will defend Facebook as "positive force in the world" in testimony', available at www.theguardian.com/us-news/2018/apr/09/mark-zuckerberg-facebook-testimony-congress, published 9 April 2018, accessed 3 January 2019.

Rutgers, M. R. (1999) 'Be rational! But what does it mean? A history of the idea of rationality and its relation to management thought', *Journal of Management History*, 5(1): 17–35.

RW3 (2016) 'Trends in global virtual teams', http://cdn.culturewizard.com/PDF/Trends_in_VT_Report_4-17-2016.pdf, published 17 April 2016, accessed 25 January 2019.

Sachon, M. and Mitchell, J. (2005) 'ALDI: A German retailing icon', IESE Business School case nr. P-1071-E0-606-009.

Sack, R. (2008) *Key Cost Management Principles Every Executive Must Know (Technical note)* (Charlottesville, VA: Darden Business Publishing).

Safian, R. (2014) '"It's got to be a passion, it's gotta be your calling": Indra Nooyi', available at www.fastcompany.com/3036581/its-got-to-be-a-passion-its-gotta-be-your-callingindra-nooyi, published 14 October 2014, accessed 9 January 2019.

Salacuse, J. W. (1999) 'Intercultural negotiation in international business', *Group Decision and Negotiation*, 8(3): 217–236.

Sánchez-Runde, C., Lee, Y. and Reiche, S. (2012) 'Hailing a new era: Haier in Japan (A)', IESE Business School case nr. IES340.

Sánchez-Runde, C., Lee, Y. and Reiche, S. (2013) 'How Haier handled foreign traditions', available at www.ft.com/content/71fb8438-98b8-11e2-867f-00144fe-abdc0, published 1 April 2013, accessed 6 September 2017.

Sanders, N. R. (2016) 'How to use big data to drive your supply chain', *California Management Review*, 58(3): 26–48.

Sanderson, R. (2016) 'Brunello Cucinelli, philosopher and cashmere capitalist', available at www.ft.com/content/06ccc99a-031f-11e6-99cb-83242733f755, published 22 May 2016, accessed 4 December 2017.

Saunders, R. (1999) 'Better brainstorming', *Harvard Management Communication Newsletter* nr. C9911C, November 1999.

Schackt, E. (2009) 'Studio Moderna', at www.dmslo.si/media/dms-smk-2009-schackt.pdf, accessed 3 January 2019.

Schaltegger, S. and Burrit, R. (2010) 'Sustainability accounting for companies: Catchphrase or decision support for business leaders?', *Journal of World Business*, 45(4): 375–384.

Schein, E. H. (1993) 'On dialogue, culture, and organizational learning', *Organizational Dynamics*, 22(2): 40–51.

Schein, E. H. (2004) *Organizational Culture and Leadership: A Dynamic View*, 3rd edn (San Francisco, CA: Jossey-Bass).

Schkade, D. and Kahneman, D. (1998) 'Does living in California make people happy? A focusing illusion in judgments of life satisfaction', *Psychological Science*, 9(5): 340–346.

Schmidt, E. E. and Larson, C. (2010) 'Googlopolis', *Foreign Policy*, 181(Sept–Oct): 152.

Schonberg, T., Fox, C. R. and Poldrack, R. A. (2011) 'Mind the gap: Bridging economic and naturalistic risk-taking with cognitive neuroscience', *Trends in Cognitive Sciences*, 15(1): 11–19.

Schramm, W. L. (1954) *The Process and Effects of Mass Communication* (San Champaign, IL: University of Illinois Press).

Schreyögg, G. (2008) *Organisation*, 5th edn (Wiesbaden: Gabler).

Schultz, L. (2016) 'Lessons from HBO's Silicon Valley', available at www.theglobeandmail.com/report-on-business/small-business/sb-growth/lessons-from-hbos-silicon-valley/article31230969/, published 30 August 2016, accessed 27 December 2018.

Schultz, L. (2018) 'CEOs need to be invested in their employees' careers', available at www.theglobeandmail.com/business/commentary/article-ceos-need-to-be-invested-in-their-employees-careers/, published 29 July 2018, accessed 27 December 2018.

Schumpeter, J. (2010) *Capitalism, Socialism and Democracy* (Abingdon: Routledge) [first published in the UK in 1943].

Schwartz, S. H. (1992) 'Universals in the content and structure of values: Theoretial advances and empirical tests in 20 countries', *Advances in Experimental Social Psychology*, 25: 1–65.

Schwartz, S. H. (1999) 'A theory of cultural values and some implications for work', *Applied Psychology*, 48(1): 23–47.

Semco Partners (2017) 'Company history', available at www.semco.com.br/en/about-us/, accessed 5 July 2017.

semcostyle.org (2018) 'About Semco Style Institute', available at https://semcostyle.org/about, accessed 27 December 2018.

Semler, R. (1989) 'Managing without managers', *Harvard Business Review*, 67(5): 76–84.

Semler, R. (2004) *The Seven-Day Weekend: Changing the Way Work Works* (New York, NY: Portfolio).

Semler, R. (2018) 'Ricardo Semler – rebel with a cause', available at www.moneymarketing.co.za/ricardo-semler-rebel-with-a-cause/, published 12 July 2018, accessed 27 December 2018.

Sensen, O. (2011) *Kant on Human Dignity* (Berlin: Walter de Gruyter).

Shachaf, P. (2008) 'Cultural diversity and information and communication technology impacts on global virtual teams: An exploratory study', *Information & Management*, 45(2): 131–142.

Shah, R. H. and Swaminathan, V. (2008) 'Factors influencing partner selection in strategic alliances: The moderating role of alliance context', *Strategic Management Journal,* 29(5): 471–494.

Shane, S. (2000) 'Prior knowledge and the discovery of entrepreneurial opportunities', *Organization Science*, 11(4): 448–469.

Shane, S. and Venkataraman, S. (2000) 'The promise of entrepreneurship as a field of research', *Academy of Management Review*, 25(1): 217–226.

Shayon, S. (2018) 'Diversification key to Johnson & Johnson's longevity', www.brandchannel.com/2018/09/15/diversification-key-to-johnson-johnson-longevity/, published 15 September 2018, accessed 28 January 2019.

Shea, K. (2001) 'Spotlight pinnacle', available at www.hhof.com/htmlSpotlight/spot_pinnacleb200601.shtml, published 20 June 2001, accessed 3 January 2019.

Shell, G. R. and Moussa, M. (2007) *The Art of Woo: Using Strategic Persuasion to Sell Your Ideas* (New York, NY: Portfolio).

Sherman, J. W., Lee, A. Y., Bessenoff, G. R. and Frost, L. A. (1998) 'Stereotype efficiency reconsidered: Encoding flexibility under cognitive load', *Journal of Personality and Social Psychology*, 75(3): 589–606.

Shinkle, G. A., Kriauciunas, A. P. and Hundley, G. (2013) 'Why pure strategies may be wrong for transition economy firms', *Strategic Management Journal*, 34(10): 1244–1254.

Shockley-Zalabak, P. S. (2015) *Fundamentals of Organizational Communication*, 9th edn (Upper Saddle River, NJ: Pearson).

Shoda, Y., Mischel, W. and Peake, P. K. (1990) 'Predicting adolescent cognitive and self-regulatory competencies from preschool delay of gratification: Identifying diagnostic conditions', *Developmental Psychology*, 26(6), 978–986.

Sidani, Y. M. (2008) 'Ibn Khaldun of North Africa: An AD 1377 theory of leadership', *Journal of Management History*, 14(1): 73–86.

Simon, H. A. (1947) *Administrative Behavior* (New York, NY: Macmillan).

Simon, H. A. (1957) 'A behavioral model of rational choice', in Simon, H. A. (ed.), *Models of Man, Social and Rational: Mathematical Essays on Rational Human Behavior in a Social Setting.* (New York, NY: Wiley).

Simon, H. A. (1987) 'Making management decisions: The role of intuition and emotion', *Academy of Management Perspectives*, 1(1): 57–64.

Simon, H. A. and Chase, W. G. (1973) 'Skills in chess', *American Scientist*, 61(4): 394–403.

Simons, T. L. and Peterson, R. S. (2000) 'Task conflict and relationship conflict in top management teams', *Journal of Applied Psychology*, 85(1): 102–111.

Sirosh, J. (2018) 'How AI and location intelligence can drive business growth', available at www.esri.com/about/newsroom/podcast/ai-and-location-will-drive-tomorrows-digital-transformations/, published 30 May 2018, accessed 28 January 2019.

Skarzynski, P. and Gibson, R. (2008) *Innovation to the Core: A Blueprint for Transforming the Way Your Company Innovates* (Boston, MA: Harvard Business Press).

Skidmore, M. 'Nike's Mark Parker on imagination, innovation and art', available at http://www.anothermag.com/fashion-beauty/9171/nikes-mark-parker-on-imagination-innovation-and-art, published 12 October 2016, accessed 7 May 2019.

Slaaty, T. L. (1988) *Mathematical Methods of Operations Research* (Mineola, NY: Dover Publications).

Slater, P. E. (1992) *A Dream Deferred: America's Discontent and the Search for a New Democratic Ideal* (Boston, MA: Beacon Press).

Slater, S. F., Weigand, R. A. and Zwirlein, T. J. (2008) 'The business case for commitment to diversity', *Business Horizons*, 51(3): 201–209.

Slawson, N. (2017) 'Dove apologises for ad showing black woman turning into white one', available at www.theguardian.com/world/2017/oct/08/dove-apologises-for-ad-showing-black-woman-turning-into-white-one, published 8 October 2017, accessed 7 March 2019.

Snyder, B. (2016) 'Pepsi CEO: Break with the past, and don't play too nice', available at www.gsb.stanford.edu/insights/pepsi-ceo-break-past-dont-play-too-nice, published 31 May 2016, accessed 9 October 2017.

SoGal (2018) 'SOGAL', www.iamsogal.com/global-team, accessed 17 January 2018.

sogalventures.com (2018) 'Sogal Ventures', available at www.sogalventures.com/, accessed 17 January 2018.

Sonnentag, S. and Frese, M. (2001) 'Performance concepts and performance theory', in Sonnentag, S. (ed.), *Psychological Measurement of Individual Performance* (pp. 3–26) (Chichester: John Wiley & Sons).

Sørensen, J. B. (2002) 'The strength of corporate culture and the reliability of firm performance', *Administrative Science Quarterly*, 47(1): 70–91.

Souza (2017) 'Jet's Liza Landsman, Sam's Club's Tracey Brown share insights, like not working with "jerks"', available at https://talkbusiness.net/2017/06/jets-liza-landsman-sams-club-tracey-brown-share-insights-like-not-working-with-jerks/, published June 2017, accessed 10 January 2019.

Sox, H. C., Blatt, M. A., Higgins, M. C. and Marton, K. E. (2007) *Medical Decision Making* (Philadelphia, PA: American College of Physicians).

Spector, P. E. (1986) 'Perceived control by employees: A meta-analysis of studies concerning autonomy and participation at work', *Human Relations*, 39(11): 1005–1016.

Spencer, N. (2017) 'AmorePacific advances research and innovation efforts in Singapore', available at www.cosmeticsdesign-asia.com/Article/2017/01/24/AmorePacific-opens-research-and-innovation-laboratory-in-Singapore, published 24 January 2017, accessed 31 January 2019.

spiegel.de (2012) 'Daimler löscht auf Wunsch Mails seiner Mitarbeiter', available at www.spiegel.de/netzwelt/web/daimler-loescht-e-mails-im-urlaub-a-868960.html, published 23 November 2012, accessed 10 January 2019.

spiegel.de (2012) 'Diego Maradona ignoriert Rauswurf', available at www.spiegel.de/sport/fussball/diego-maradona-ignoriert-entlassung-bei-al-wasl-in-dubai-a-843939.html, published 11 July 2012, accessed 8 January 2019.

Spielmann, J. (2017) 'What is TCI?', in Schneider-Landolf, M., Spielmann, J. and Zitterbarth, W. (eds), *Handbook of Theme-Centered Interaction (TCI)* (pp. 14–16) (Göttingen: Vandenhoeck & Ruprecht).

Spinnarke, S. (2015) 'Elmar Degenhart: Führungskompetenz ist alles', available at www.produktion.de/veranstaltungen/fabrik-des-jahres/continental-chef-elmar-degenhart-beantwortet-standort-fragen-399.html, published 8 April 2015, accessed 14 October 2016.

Stahl, G. K., Maznevski, M. L., Voigt, A. and Jonsen, K. (2010) 'Unraveling the effects of cultural diversity in teams: A meta-analysis of research on multicultural work groups', *Journal of International Business Studies*, 41(4): 690–709.

Standards Australia (2017) 'Changes to functional structure and executive responsibilities', available at www.standards.org.au/news/changes-to-functional-structure-and-executive-responsibilities, published 16 January 2017, accessed 2 January 2019.

Stanford University (2007) 'Robert Joss: "Leadership is not about you"', available at www.gsb.stanford.edu/news/research/joss_you.html, published 1 August 2007, accessed 27 December 2018.

Stanovich, K. E. and West, R. F. (2000) 'Individual differences in reasoning: Implications for the rationality debate', *Behavioral and Brain Sciences*, 23(5): 645–726.

Starling, S. (2016) 'The world's unquenchable thirst for energy drinks', at www.beveragedaily.com/Markets/The-world-s-unquenchable-thirst-for-energy-drinks, published 13 June 2016, accessed 28 January 2019.

startuptalky.com (2018) 'Jugnoo – story, founder, business model, funding, team, news', available at https://startuptalky.com/jugnoo-indian-startup-success-story/, published 5 October 2018, accessed 10 January 2019.

Staw, B. M. and Ross, J. (1978) 'Commitment to a policy decision: A multi-theoretical perspective', *Administrative Science Quarterly*, 23(1): 40–64.

Stephens, J. P. and Lyddy, C. J. (2016) 'Operationalizing heedful interrelating: How attending, responding, and feeling comprise coordinating and predict performance in self-managing teams', *Frontiers in Psychology*, 7, Article 362.

Stern, T. and Jaberg, H. (2010) Erfolgreiches *Innovations-management: Erfolgsfaktoren—Grundmuster—Fallbeispiele*, 4th edn (Wiesbaden, Germany: Gabler Verlag).

Sternad, D. (2011) *Strategic Adaptation: Cross-Cultural Differences in Company Responses to an Economic Crisis* (Vienna, Austria: Springer).

Sternad, D. (2013a) 'Managerial long-term responsibility in family-controlled firms', *Management*, 8(2): 93–117.

Sternad, D. (2013b) 'Towards an eclectic framework of external factors influencing work motivation', *SBS Journal of Applied Business Research*, 2(1): 7–19.

Sternad, D. (2014) 'Guiding managerial behavior toward the long term: The role of performance measurement and compensation systems', in Davila, A., Epstein, M. J. and Manzoni, J.-F. (eds), *Performance Measurement and Management Control: Behavioral Implications and Human Actions* (pp. 235–255) (Bingley: Emerald).

Sternad, D. (2015) 'A challenge-feedback learning approach to teaching international business', *Journal of Teaching in International Business*, 26(4): 241–257.

Sternad, D. and Kennelly, J. J. (2017) 'The sustainable executive: Antecedents of managerial long-term orientation', *Journal of Global Responsibility*, 8(2): 179–195.

Sternad, D. and Mödritscher, G. (2018) *Qualitatives Wachstum: Der Weg zu nachhaltigem Unternehmenserfolg* (Wiesbaden: Springer Gabler).

Sternad, D., Kennelly, J. J. and Bradley, F. (2016) *Digging Deeper: How Purpose-Driven Enterprises Create Real Value* (Saltaire: Greenleaf Publishing).

Sternad, D., Knappitsch, E. and Mundschütz, C. (2012) *Cross-Border Cooperation: European Institutional Framework and Strategies of SMEs* (Stuttgart: Franz Steiner Verlag).

Sternad, D., Brodel, D., Kandolf, T., Wriessnegger, C. and Wellenzohn, G. (2012) 'The innovation challenge at Infineon Technologies Austria AG', available on the website of the *Academy of Management* under http://aom.org/Multi-Media/Teaching-Resources/The-Innovation-Challenge-at-Infineon-Technologies-Austria-AG(1).aspx, accessed 31 January 2019.

Stevenson, H. H. and Spence, S. M. (2009) 'Identifying and exploiting the right entrepreneurial opportunity ... for you', *Harvard Business School Background Note* nr. 9-808-043 (Boston, MA: Harvard Business School).

Stewart, G. L. and Barrick, M. R. (2000) 'Team structure and performance: Assessing the mediating role of intrateam process and the moderating role of task type', *Academy of Management Journal*, 43(2): 135–148.

Stewart, G. L., Courtright, S. H. and Barrick, M. R. (2012) 'Peer-based control in self-managing teams: Linking rational and normative influence with individual and group performance', *Journal of Applied Psychology*, 97(2): 435–447.

Stewart, R. (1967) *Managers and Their Jobs* (London: Macmillan).

Stewart, R. (1983) 'Managerial behaviour: How research has changed the traditional picture', in Earl, M. J. (ed.), *Perspectives on Management: A Multidisciplinary Analysis* (pp. 82–98) (Oxford: Oxford University Press).

stiftmelk.at (2019) 'Regula', available at www.stiftmelk.at/regula/regula.htm, accessed 3 January 2019.

Stone, F. (2017) 'The conversation: ACL Services boss Laurie Schultz knows fraud when she sees it', available at www.bcbusiness.ca/ACL-Services-Boss-Laurie-Schultz-knows-fraud-when-she-sees-it, published 7 February 2017, accessed 27 December 2018.

Stout, L. A. (2013) 'The shareholder value myth', *The European Financial Review*, available at www.europeanfinancialreview.com/?p=883, published 30 April 2013, accessed 8 January 2019.

Straub, T. (2007) *Reasons for Frequent Failure in Mergers and Acquisitions: A Comprehensive Analysis* (Wiesbaden: Deutscher Universitäts-Verlag).

Streitfeld, D. (2014) 'Amazon and Hachette resolve dispute', available at www.nytimes.com/2014/11/14/technology/amazon-hachette-ebook-dispute.html, published 13 November 2014, accessed 11 December 2018.

studio-moderna.com (2017) 'Connecting with people for a quarter of the century' available at www.studio-moderna.com/history-and-milestones, accessed 11 July 2017.

studio-moderna.com (2019) 'Welcome to Studio Moderna' available at www.studio-moderna.com, accessed 3 January 2019.

successness.com (2015) Erik Venter, CEO of Comair, available at https://successness.com/2015/03/erik-venter-ceo-comair/, accessed 6 May 2019.

Suddaby, R., Bruton, G. D. and Si, S. X. (2015) 'Entrepreneurship through a qualitative lens: Insights on the construction and/or discovery of entrepreneurial opportunity', *Journal of Business Venturing*, 30(1): 1–10.

sueddeutsche.de (2010a) 'Hochzeit des Grauens', available at www.sueddeutsche.de/wirtschaft/daimler-und-chrysler-hochzeit-des-grauens-1.464777, published 17 May 2010, accessed 28 January 2019.

sueddeutsche.de (2010b) 'Wir lernen nur durch Scheitern', interview with Reinhold Messner, available at www.sueddeutsche.de/leben/reinhold-messner-wir-lernen-nur-durch-scheitern-1.335957, published 17 May 2010, accessed 10 January 2019.

Sun Tzu (1963) *The Art of War*, translated by Samuel B. Griffith (Oxford: Oxford University Press).

Ta'eed, C. (2016) 'How I started as a web designer and built a 250 person company', available at www.vandelaydesign.com/envato-web-designer-built-250-person-company/, published 31 May 2016, accessed 8 January 2019.

Takeuchi, H. (2012) 'Fast Retailing Group', Harvard Business School case nr. 9-711-496 (Boston, MA: Harvard Business School).

Tan, P. (2016) 'Women of our time: 4 visionaries making a difference in our society', available at www.harpersbazaar.com.sg/tag/pocket-sun/, published 23 August 2016, accessed 17 January 2018.

Taylor, F. W. (2003) *Scientific Management* (Abingdon: Routledge).

telegraph.co.uk (2011a) 'RBS timeline: How it all went wrong', available at www.telegraph.co.uk/finance/newsbysector/banksandfinance/8363453/RBS-time-line-how-it-all-went-wrong.html, published 12 December 2011, accessed 5 February 2019.

telegraph.co.uk (2011b) 'Staff to be banned from sending emails', available at www.telegraph.co.uk/technology/news/8921033/Staff-to-be-banned-from-sending-emails.html, published 28 November 2011, accessed 10 January 2019.

Tengblad, S. (2006) 'Is there a "new managerial work"? A comparison with Henry Mintzberg's classic study 30 years later', *Journal of Management Studies*, 43(7): 1437–1461.

Tengblad, S. (2017) 'Management practice—and the doing of management', in Wilkinson, A., Lounsbury, M. and Armstrong, S. J. (eds), *The Oxford Handbook of Management* (pp. 325–342) (Oxford: Oxford University Press).

Tenzer, H. and Pudelko, M. (2016) 'Media choice in multilingual virtual teams', *Journal of International Business Studies*, 47(4): 427–452.

Texas Instruments (2019) 'The TI ethics quick test', available at www.ti.com/corp/docs/company/citizen/ethics/quicktest.shtml, accessed 25 January 2019.

The Scotsman (2003) 'The JK Rowling story', *The Scotsman*, 16 June 2003. www.scotsman.com/lifestyle/books/book-reviews/the_jk_rowling_story_1_652114, accessed 5 February 2019.

the7stars.co.uk (2017) 'Star facts', available at www.the7stars.co.uk/who-we-are/, accessed 1 August 2017.

theconversation.com (2017) 'Four cultural clashes that are holding East Asian employees back', available at http://theconversation.com/four-cultural-clashes-that-are-holding-east-asian-employees-back-72661, published 5 March 2017, accessed 21 December 2018.

Theorell, T. and Karasek, R. A. (1996) 'Current issues to the psychosocial job strain and cardiovascular disease research', *Journal of Occupational Health Psychology*, 1(1): 9–26.

Thibaut, J. and Walker, L. (1975) *Procedural Justice: A Psychological Analysis* (Hillsdale, NJ: Erlbaum).

Thiel, C. E., Griffith, J. A., Hardy III, J. H., Peterson, D. R. and Connelly, S. (2018) 'Let's look at this another way: How supervisors can help subordinates manage the threat of relationship conflict', *Journal of Leadership & Organizational Studies*, published online before print, doi:1548051817750545.

Thomas, A. and Bhattacharya, A. (2016) 'How Samar Singla pulled off a jugaad with autorickshaw aggregator startup Jugnoo', available at https://economictimes.indiatimes.com/small-biz/startups/how-samar-singla-pulled-off-a-jugaad-with-autorickshaw-aggregator-startup-jugnoo/articleshow/54518687.cms, published 26 September 2016, accessed 10 January 2019.

Thomas, D. C. and Inkson, K. (2009) *Cultural Intelligence: Living and Working Globally,* 2nd edn (San Francisco, CA: Berrett-Koehler Publishers).

Thomas, L. and Reagan, C. (2018) 'Watch out, retailers. This is just how big Amazon is becoming', available at www.cnbc.com/2018/07/12/amazon-to-take-almost-50-percent-of-us-e-commerce-market-by-years-end.html, published 13 July 2018, accessed 5 February 2019.

Thomke, S. and Randal, J. (2012) 'Innovation magic', *Harvard Business School Background Note* nr. 9-612-099 (Boston, MA: Harvard Business School).

Thompson, J. D. (1967) *Organizations in Action: Social Science Bases of Administrative Theory* (New York, NY: McGraw-Hill).

Thompson, J. D. (2007) *Organizations in Action: Social Science Bases of Administrative Theory,* 5th printing of the 2003 edition (New Brunswick, NJ: Transaction Publishers).

Thornhill, S. and White, R. E. (2007) 'Strategic purity: A multi-industry evaluation of pure vs. hybrid business strategies', *Strategic Management Journal,* 28(5): 553–561.

time.com (2003) 'Wilbur and Orville Wright', available at http://content.time.com/time/specials/packages/article/0,28804,1981290_1981362_1981628,00.html, published 12 September 2003, accessed 31 January 2019.

Tjan, A. K. (2012) 'Great businesses don't start with a plan', available at https://hbr.org/2012/05/great-businesses-dont-start-wi, published 16 May 2012, accessed 31 January 2019.

Toh, M. (2017) 'The VC who didn't dare to call herself a VC', available at http://fortune.com/2017/05/04/sogal-ventures-vc-female-founders/, published 4 May 2017, accessed 31 January 2019.

Tower Hollis, S. (2009) 'Egyptian literature', in Ehrlich, C. S. (ed.), *From an Antique Land: An Introduction to Ancient Near Eastern Literature* (pp. 77–136) (Lanham, Maryland: Rowman & Littlefield).

Toyota (2019) 'Toyota production system', available at www.toyota-global.com/company/vision_philosophy/toyota_production_system/, accessed 14 January 2019.

Transparency International (2019) 'Corruption Perception Index 2018 shows anti-corruption efforts stalled in most countries', available at www.transparency.org/news/pressrelease/corruption_perceptions_index_2018, published 29 January 2019, accessed 7 March 2019.

Treacy, M. and Wiersema, F. (1997) *The Discipline of Market Leaders: Choose Your Customers, Narrow Your Focus, Dominate Your Market* (New York, NY: Basic Books).

Treanor, J. (2017) 'The RBS crisis: A timeline of events', available at www.theguardian.com/business/2017/may/21/royal-bank-of-scotland-a-timeline-of-events, published 22 May 2017, accessed 5 February 2019.

trend (2005) 'Mann des Jahres: Interview mit Herbert Stepic', *trend*, issue 12/2005.

Trevino, L. K. and Brown, M. E. (2004) 'Managing to be ethical: Debunking five business ethics myths', *Academy of Management Perspectives*, 18(2): 69–81.

Triandis, H. C. (2006) 'Cultural intelligence in organizations', *Group & Organization Management*, 31(1): 20–26.

Trompenaars, F. and Hampden-Turner, C. (2012) *Riding the Waves of Culture*, 3rd edn (New York, NY: McGraw-Hill).

Tsui, A. S., Egan, T. D. and O'Reilly III, C. A. (1992) 'Being different: Relational demography and organizational attachment', *Administrative Science Quarterly*, 37(4): 549–579.

Tuckman, B. W. (1965) 'Developmental sequence in small groups', *Psychological Bulletin*, 63(6): 384–399.

Tuckman, B. W. and Jensen, M. A. C. (1977) 'Stages of small-group development revisited', *Group & Organization Studies*, 2(4): 419–427.

Tuff, G. (2011) 'How hot is your next innovation', *Harvard Business Review*, 89(5): 40–41.

Tushman, M. L. and O'Reilly III, C. A. (2002) *Winning Through Innovation: A Practical Guide to Leading Organizational Change and Renewal* (Boston, MA: Harvard Business School Press).

Tversky, A. and Kahneman, D. (1973) 'Availability: A heuristic for judging frequency and probability', *Cognitive Psychology*, 5(2): 207–232.

Tversky, A. and Kahneman, D. (1974) 'Judgement under uncertainty: Heuristics and biases', *Science*, 185(4157): 1124–1131.

Tversky, A. and Kahneman, D. (1981) 'The framing of decisions and the psychology of choice', *Science*, 211(4481): 453–458.

Tyler, T. R. (1994) 'Psychological models of the justice motive: Antecedents of distributive and procedural justice', *Journal of Personality and Social Psychology*, 67(5): 850–863.

Umicore (2018) 'BMW Group, Northvolt and Umicore join forces to develop sustainable life cycle loop for batteries', available at www.umicore.com/en/media/press/bmw-group-northvolt-and-umicore-join-forces-to-develop-sustainable-life-cycle-loop-for-batteries, published 15 October 2018, accessed 28 January 2019.

UNICEF India (2017) 'Child labor in India', available at http://unicef.in/Whatwedo/21/Child-Labour, accessed 12 September 2017.

Unilever (2018) 'Unilever charts 2008–2017', available at www.unilever.com/Images/unilever-charts-2017_tcm244-516457_en.pdf, accessed 19 January 2019.

Unilever (2019) 'Advancing diversity and inclusion', available at www.unilever.com/sustainable-living/enhancing-livelihoods/opportunities-for-women/advancing-diversity-and-inclusion/, accessed 19 January 2019.

United Nations (1948) *Universal Declaration of Human Rights*, United Nations General Assembly Resolution 217A (Paris: United Nations).

United Nations (2011) *Guiding Principles on Business and Human Rights* (New York and Geneva: United Nations).

United Nations (2019) 'The ten principles of the UN Global Compact', available at https://www.unglobalcompact.org/what-is-gc/mission/principles, accessed 25 January 2019.

Upbin, B. (2007) 'The next billion', *Forbes*, 180(10): 48–56.

Urbany, J. E., Reynolds, T. J. and Phillips, J. M. (2008) 'How to make values count in everyday decisions', *MIT Sloan Management Review*, 49(4): 75–80.

US Marine Corps, The (1994) *Warfighting: The US Marine Corps Book of Strategy* (New York, NY: Currency Doubleday).

Vahs, D. (2012) *Organisation*, 8th edn (Stuttgart: Schäffer-Poeschel).

Van de Ven, A. H. and Ferry, D. L. (1980) *Measuring and Assessing Organizations* (New York, NY: John Wiley and Sons).

Van Loon, N., Kjeldsen, A. M., Andersen, L. B., Vandena-beele, W. and Leisink, P. (2018) 'Only when the societal impact potential is high? A panel study of the relationship between public service motivation and perceived performance', *Review of Public Personnel Administration*, 38(2): 139–166.

Van Loon, R. and van Dijk, G. (2015) 'Dialogical leadership: Dialogue as condition zero', *Journal of Leadership, Accountability and Ethics*, 12(3): 62–75.

Vandor, P. and Franke, N. (2016). 'Why are immigrants more entrepreneurial?', available at https://hbr.org/2016/10/why-are-immigrants-more-entrepre-neurial, published 27 October 2016, accessed 31 January 2019.

Varma, A. (2017) 'Zara's secret to success lies in big data and an agile supply chain', available at www.straitstimes.com/lifestyle/fashion/zaras-secret-to-success-lies-in-big-data-and-an-agile-supply-chain, published 25 May 2017, accessed 5 February 2019.

Vauhini, V. (2015) 'The push against performance reviews', available at www.newyorker.com/busi-ness/currency/the-push-against-performance-reviews, published 24 July 2015, accessed 27 December 2018.

Velasquez, M. G. (2014) *Business Ethics: Concepts and Cases*, 7th edn (Harlow: Pearson).

Verschoor, C. C. (1998) 'A study of the link between a corporation's financial performance and its commitment to ethics', *Journal of Business Ethics*, 17(13): 1509–1516.

Vilà, J. (2011) 'Innovative culture: Values, principles and practices of senior executives in highly innovative companies', *IESE Business School Technical Note* nr. SMN-681-E (Barcelona, Spain: IESE).

Vroom, V. H. (1964) *Work and Motivation* (New York, NY: Wiley).

Vuilleumier, P. (2005) 'How brains beware: Neural mechanisms of emotional attention', *Trends in Cognitive Sciences, 9*(12), 585–594.

Wajcman, J. and Dodd, N. (eds) (2016) *The Sociology of Speed: Digital, Organizational, and Social Tempo-ralities* (Oxford: Oxford University Press).

Walker, M. P. and Stickgold, R. (2010) 'Overnight alchemy: Sleep-dependent memory evolution', *Nature Reviews Neuroscience, 11*(3): 218–219.

Wallis, I. (2007) 'James Dyson: Dyson', available at https://startups.co.uk/james-dyson-dyson/, published 3 October 2007, accessed 31 January 2019.

walmart.com (2018) 'Walmart and Rakuten announce new strategic alliance', available at https://news.walmart.com/2018/01/26/walmart-and-rakuten-announce-new-strategic-alliance, published 25 January 2018, accessed 28 January 2019.

Ware, J. and Barnes, L. B. (1985) 'Managing interpersonal conflict', *Harvard Business School Class Discussion Note* (Boston, MA: Harvard Business School).

Wasserman, N. and Anderson, K. (2012) 'Knight the king: The founding of Nike', *Harvard Business School case* nr. 9-810-077 (Boston, MA: Harvard Business School).

Waterman, R. H., Peters, T. J. and Phillips, J. R. (1980) 'Structure is not organization', *Business Horizons*, 23(3): 14–26.

Watkins, M. D. (2000) 'The power to persuade. Class discussion note' (Boston, MA: Harvard Business School).

Watkins, M. D. and Rosen, S. (2001) 'Rethinking "prepara-tion" in negotiations', *Harvard Business School Class Discussion Note* (Boston, MA: Harvard Business School).

Webb, A. (2011) 'Starbucks' quest for healthy growth: An interview with Howard Schultz', available at www.mckinsey.com/global-themes/employment-and-growth/starbucks-quest-for-healthy-growth-an-interview-with-howard-schultz, published March 2011, accessed 21 January 2019.

Weber, E. U., Hsee, C. and Sokolowska, J. (1998) 'What folklore tells us about risk and risk taking: Cross-cultural comparisons of American, German, and Chinese proverbs', *Organizational Behavior and Human Decision Processes*, 75(2): 170–186.

Weber, H. F. and Szkudlarek, B. (2013) 'In search of the meaning of entrepreneurship', *International Journal of Economics and Management Engineering*, 7(1): 242–251.

Wech, B. A., Mossholder, K. W., Steel, R. P. and Bennett, N. (1998) 'Does work group cohesiveness affect individuals' performance and organizational commitment? A cross-level examination', *Small Group Research*, 29(4): 472–494.

Wegner, D. M. (1994) 'Ironic processes of mental control', *Psychological Review,* 101(1): 34–52.

Weick, K. E. (1995) *Sensemaking in Organizations* (Thousand Oaks, CA: Sage).

Weinberger, M. (2017) 'How Microsoft CEO Satya Nadella explains the "not universally loved" changes he made to a luxury executive retreat', available at https://nordic.businessinsider.com/microsoft-satya-nadella-company-culture-2017-9/, published 27 September 2017, accessed 12 December 2018.

Welch, J. (n.d.) 'A conversation with Jack Welch. Video of a discussion with Jack Welch at MIT', available at http://video.mit.edu/watch/a-conversation-with-jack-welch-9939/, accessed 14 November 2016.

Wentling, R. M. (2004) 'Factors that assist and barriers that hinder the success of diversity initiatives in multinational corporations', *Human Resource Development International*, 7(2): 165–180.

Werhane, P. H. (1999) *Moral Imagination and Management Decision Making* (New York, NY: Oxford University Press).

Wernerfelt B. (1984) 'A resource-based view of the firm', *Strategic Management Journal,* 5(2): 171–180.

West, J. and Bogers, M. (2014) 'Leveraging external sources of innovation: A review of research on open innovation', *Journal of Product Innovation Management*, 31(4): 814–831.

Westfield Corporation (2017) *Westfield Shareholder Review 2017* (Sydney, Australia: Westfield Corporation).

Whetten, D. A. & Cameron, K. A. (2011) *Developing Management Skills*, 8th edn (Upper Saddle River, NJ: Pearson).

Wicks, A. C. (2009) 'An introduction to ethics', *Darden Business Publishing Technical Note* nr. UV1040.

Williams, K. Y. and O'Reilly, C. A. III (1998) 'Demography and diversity in organizations: A review of 40 years of research', in Staw, B. M. and Cummings, L. L., *Research in Organizational Behavior* (pp. 77–140) (Greenwich, CT: JAI Press).

Williams, S. L. (2011) 'Engaging values in international business practice', *Business Horizons*, 54(4): 315–324.

Wilson, H. J. and Daugherty, P. R. (2018) 'Collaborative intelligence: Humans and AI are joining forces', *Harvard Business Review*, 96(4): 114–123.

Wilson, H., Aldrick, P. and Ahmad, K. (2011) 'Royal Bank of Scotland investigation: The full story of how the "world's biggest bank" went bust', available at www.telegraph.co.uk/finance/newsbysector/banksandfinance/8496654/Royal-Bank-of-Scotland-investigation-the-full-story-of-how-the-worlds-biggest-bank-went-bust.html, published 5 March 2011, accessed 5 February 2019.

wired.com (2012) www.wired.com/gadgetlab/2012/04/5-reasons-why-nokia-lost-its-handset-sales-lead-and-got-downgraded-to-junk/, published 27 April 2012, accessed 28 January 2019.

wolterskluwer.com (2018) 'Nancy McKinstry, CEO Wolters Kluwer: "Create freedom: Don't standardize the way of thinking and doing"', available at https://wolterskluwer.com/company/newsroom/news/2018/05/nancy-mckinstry-ceo-wolters-kluwer-%E2%80%9Ccreate-freedom.-don%E2%80%99t-standardize-the-way-of-thinking-or-doing.%E2%80%9D.html, published 4 May 2018, accessed 28 January 2019.

Woods, J. (2016) 'How ACL creates culture in an office-less work environment', available at https://techvibes.com/2016/02/25/how-acl-creates-culture-in-an-office-less-work-environment-2016-02-24, published 25 February 2016, accessed 27 December 2018.

worldvaluessurvey.org (2019a) 'Welcome to the World Values Survey', available at www.worldvaluessurvey.org/wvs.jsp, accessed 23 January 2019.

worldvaluessurvey.org (2019b) 'Findings and insights', available at www.worldvaluessurvey.org/wvs.jsp, accessed 23 January 2019.

Worstall, T. (2014) 'The real story behind the Amazon v Hachette fight', available at www.forbes.com/sites/timworstall/2014/05/24/the-real-story-behind-the-amazon-v-hachette-fight/#161c65f73c3c, published 24 May 2014, accessed 31 July 2017.

Worthington, I., Ram, M., Boyal, H. and Shah, M. (2008) 'Researching the drivers of socially responsible purchasing: a cross-national study of supplier diversity initiatives', *Journal of Business Ethics*, 79(3): 319–331.

Woyke, E. (2011) 'Last call', *Forbes,* 188(10): 52–56.

Wrapp, H. E. (1967) 'Good managers don't make policy decisions', *Harvard Business Review*, 45(5): 91–99.

Wren, D. A. and Bedeian, A. G. (2009) *The Evolution of Management Thought*, 6th edn (Hoboken, NJ: John Wiley & Sons).

Wright, G., Van der Heijden, K., Bradfield, R., Burt, G. and Cairns, G. (2004) 'The psychology of why organizations can be slow to adapt and change', *Journal of General Management,* 29(4): 21–36.

Wrosch, C., Scheier, M. F., Miller, G. E., Schulz, R. and Carver, C. S. (2003) 'Adaptive self-regulation of unattainable goals: Goal disengagement, goal reengagement, and subjective well-being', *Personality & Social Psychology Bulletin*, 29(12): 1494–1508.

wsj.com (2012) 'Akzo Nobel's deal paints pretty picture', available at http://online.wsj.com/article/SB10001424127887323981504578179343390630024.html, published 14 December 2012, accessed 8 January 2013.

Yeomans, W. N. (1998) *7 Survival Skills for a Reengineered World* (New York, NY: Plume).

Zhang, X. and Bartol, K. M. (2010) 'Linking empowering leadership and employee creativity: The influence of psychological empowerment, intrinsic motivation, and creative process engagement', *Academy of Management Journal*, 53(1): 107–128.

Zofi, Y. (2012) 'Why cross-cultural communication is critical to virtual teams and how to overcome the intercultural disconnect', *People and Strategy*, 35(1): 7–8.

Zuckerberg, M. (2011) 'Mark Zuckerberg and Sheryl Sandberg interview on Charlie Rose', available at www.youtube.com/watch?v=eqxNtEc4rzc , accessed 3 January 2019.

INDEX OF ORGANIZATIONS

INDEX OF PEOPLE

SUBJECT INDEX